The Eighteenth Century

A CURRENT BIBLIOGRAPHY

Endpapers:
Library of Zacharias Konrad von Uffenbach

Title page illustration:
"The Critic" by Karl Stilp (1704-26)

The Eighteenth Century

A CURRENT BIBLIOGRAPHY

n.s.17—for 1991

GENERAL EDITOR

Jim Springer Borck

AMS PRESS, INC.
NEW YORK
1998

The Eighteenth Century

A CURRENT BIBLIOGRAPHY

General Editor

Jim Springer Borck, *Louisiana State University*

Assistant General Editors

Robert G. Dryden, *Louisiana State University*
Christina M. Valley, *Louisiana State University*

Bibliographic Studies

James E. May, *Pennsylvania State University*
Henry L. Snyder, *ESTC*
Laura Snyder, *The Huntington Library*

Comparative Literature

John Burke, *University of Alabama*

English and American Literature

Helen M. Barber, *New Mexico State University*
Jerry C. Beasley, *University of Delaware*
Patricia Craddock, *The University of Florida*
Dana Nelson, *The University of Kentucky*
H.-J. Müllenbrock, *Georg-August Universität zu Göttingen*
Alan T. McKenzie, *Purdue University*
Alexander Pettit, *The University of North Texas*
Cedric D. Reverand II, *University of Wyoming*
Leland E. Warren, *Kansas State University*

International Standard Book Number
Series: 0-404-62200-3
n.s.17: 0-404-62222-4

Copyright © 1998 by AMS Press, Inc.

ISSN: 0161-0996

MANUFACTURED IN THE UNITED STATES OF AMERICA

Fine Arts

Paul Yoder, *The University of Arkansas*

French Literature

Adrienne Hytier, *Vassar College*

German Literature

John Pizer, *Louisiana State University*

History

Raymong Birn, *The University of Oregon*
David B. Jordan, *The University of Illinois*
Jean Rivière, *Université Paris IX*

History of Science

Robert A. Hatch, *University of Florida*

Intellectual History

Kevin Cope, *Louisiana State University*
Moti Feingold, *Boston University*
Bertram E. Schwarzbach, *Paris, France*

Italian Literature

Alexander Sokalski, *University of Saskatchewan*

Music

Gloria Eive, *San Leandro, California*
Susan Snook-Luther, *The University of Wyoming*

Philosophy and Religoin

Henry L. Fulton, *The University of Central Michigan*

Spanish Literature

Carmen Chavez Tesser, *The University of Georgia*

Contents

The bibliography lists significant books, articles, and reviews
published during 1991 together with some from preceding years.

FOREWORD

Compiling, editing, and producing the Bibliography remains a very large and time-consuming task, and the editors and contributors for this volume have once again earned the eighteenth-century scholarly community's thanks for their work. Despite this being a period of time when support for scholarly inquiry and bibliographic review continues to diminish, editors and contributors alike continue to donate their unique talents to our annual survey. Very special thanks are due to the Assistant Bibliographers for this volume, Robert G. Dryden and Christina M. Vallery. In particular, as the Bibliography's senior graduate assistant whose primary responsibility this volume was, Christina Vallery gave very large amounts of time and skill to the project, hours in number much beyond those assigned to her. I deeply appreciate her careful, detailed service. Two other other graduate students in eighteenth-century studies at LSU, Steve Price and Steve Raynie, voluntarily spent manifold hours in the General Editor's office with copy editing and data entry chores. The undergraduate assistants—Tai Anderson, Dewonna Arnold, Misty Millen, Dana Leigh Talbert, and Jonel Thaller—have provided superb service during the five years this volume was in the editorial offices, and to them I also extend my grateful thanks, especially to Jonel Thaller. Here too I'd like to thank Jerry Beasley's graduate assistant, Chris Johnson (The University of Delaware), David Jordan's graduate assistant, John Abbot (The University of Illinois), Cedric Reverand's graduate assistant, Victor Jones (The University of Wyoming), and Patricia Craddock's graduate assistant, Sandra F. Plympton (The University of Florida).

Special acknowledgments are also due the four editors for the disciplines who patiently read and reread portions of this volume in page proof: Jerry C. Beasley, Adrienne Hytier, James E. May, and Cedric D. Reverand. I continue to be indebted for the on-going technical support given to the Bibliography by Neal Stoltzfus from LSU's Department of Mathematics; any computer wizardry I may exhibit in editorial compilation and production is actually his, donated freely for the past twenty years. I here also acknowledge the administrative services of both the Department of English and the College of Arts and Sciences's staff, especially Jennifer Anne Gore, Susan Kohler, Clint Reid, and the resource assistance provided by Blackwell's International, LSU's Middleton Library, and LSU's Hill Memorial Library, the editorial division of AMS Press, and several specific individuals at LSU and at other campuses: Caroline Becker, Kevin L. Cope, John I. Fischer, Daniel M. Fogel, John R. Peters, Karl A. Roider, Jr., and Peter Shillingsburg. Deserving special note are the two decades of generous institutional support which Louisiana State University has given the Bibliography, support patiently administered by the Associate Dean of the College of Arts and Sciences, Craig M. Cordes.

In my post as the General Editor, and as a former student of his, and as is the Bibliography's practice, in the Foreword I'd like to acknowledge the assistance tendered to me and to the Bibliography by Howard D. Weinbrot, especially that which he gave the Bibliography in its early years in the late 60s and early 70s during its change to an interdisciplinary, international review, and later to me in the very early years during the 1980s when I was reshaping—among other matters—the production sequences. Always enthusiastic to me about the tasks concurrent with being the General Editor, an enthusiasm and energy found in his own scholarship and teachings, and likewise exhibited whenever he has been elected to administrative offices in ASECS, Howard has prompted, prodded, and encouraged me unfailingly for the past 30 years. Passionate about his and his colleagues' scholarship, rigorous in his demands for historical accuracy and precise detail, he has remained a gentle, compassionate person. By this dedication I am able to express my appreciation for a person who in his person and teachings had a great influence on this Bibliography.

—Jim Springer Borck, General Editor

Printing and Bibliographic Studies

ABHA: Annual Bibliography of the History of the Printed Book and Libraries. Vol. 20. Compiled and edited by the Department of Special Collections at the Koninklijke Bibliotheek at The Hague, with an international team of contributors. Dordrecht: Kluwer, 1991. Pp. xii + 432; indices.

Adams, Gillian (ed.). "The Year's Work in Children's Literature Studies: 1987." *Children's Literature Association Quarterly*, 14 (1989), 8–96; [for 1988] 15 (1990), 58–107; [for 1989] 16 (1991), 101–227, with index [added to the format in 1991].

The bibliography contains general sections on history and illustration but is principally a list by author, noting studies on Blake, Bunyan, Defoe, Swift, and others.

Adams, J. R. R. "Belfast Almanacs and Directories of Joseph Smyth." *Linen Hall Review*, 8 (1991), 14–15.

Adams, J. R. R. *The Printed Word and the Common Man: Popular Culture in Ulster, 1700–1900.* Belfast: Institute of Irish Studies, Queen's U. of Belfast, 1987. Pp. viii + 218; bibliography; illustrations.

Rev. (with two other books) by S. J. Connolly in *Victorian Studies*, 34 (1991), 401–03.

Agueda Méndez, María. "The Mexican Inquisition vs. the Spirit of Independence." *Dieciocho*, 14 (1991), 92–101.

A survey of the 2000 texts in the Archivo General de la Nación (Mexico City) reveals that most suppression by the Holy Office involved religious transgression, not political, but that political suppression occurred as well, particularly during crises in 1702, 1761, and 1810. Agueda Méndez writes as the general coordinator for a projected catalogue of the literary texts in the Archives.

Aguilar Piñal, Francisco (comp.). *Bibliografía de autores españoles del siglo XVIII.* Vol. 6: *N-Q.* Madrid: Consejo Superior de Investigaciones Cientificas, 1991. Pp. 688.

The five earlier volumes were published 1981–1989.

Aguilar Piñal, Francisco. "Ilustración y periodismo." *Estudios de historia social*, 52–53 (1990), 9–16.

Aguilar Piñal, Francisco. "Ilustración y periodismo." *Insula*, 45 (1990), 31–32.

Ahrens, Rüdiger. "The Political Pamphlet: 1660–1714. Pre- and Post-Revolutionary Aspects." *Anglia*, 109 (1991), 21–43.

Albert-Samuel, Collette (gen. ed.), Rene Cuenot, I. Frolova, M. Nortier, and Claire Vernon (eds.). *Bibliographie annuelle de l'histoire de France: Année 1990*. Paris: CNRS, 1991. Pp. C + 1160.

Includes headings for bibliographies, dictionaries and for libraries.

Albina, Larissa L., and Anthony L. Strugnell. "Recherches nouvelles sur l'identification des volumes de la bibliothèque de Diderot." *Recherches sur Diderot et sur l'Encyclopédie*, 9 (1990), 41–54.

Alblas, Jacques B. "Richard Allestree's *The Whole Duty of Man* (1658) in Holland: The Denominational and Generic Transformations of an Anglican Classic." *Nederlands archief voor kerkgeschiedenis*, 71 (1991), 92–104; illustrations.

Alexander, John K. *The Selling of the Constitutional Convention: A History of News Coverage*. Madison, WI: Madison House, 1990. Pp. ix + 246.

Almuiña Fernández, Celso. "Negocio e ideología en la España de la segunda mitad del XVIII: la Compañia de Impresores y Mercaderes de libros en Madrid." *Revista de investigaciones históricas*, 9 (1989), 71–96.

Altholz, Josef L. *The Religious Press in England, 1760–1900*. (Contributions to the Study of Religion, 22.) Westport, CT: Greenwood Press, 1989. Pp. xii + 215; bibliography; indices.

Ammon, Harry. *James Monroe: A Bibliography*. (Meckler's Bibliographies of the Presidents of the United States, 5.) Westport, CT: Meckler, 1991. Pp. xxxi + 125.

Rev. (favorably) by David A. Carson in the *Virginia Magazine of History and Biography*, 99 (1991), 536; (favorably and with another work) by C. V. Stanley in *Choice*, 28 (1991), 1753.

Anderson, Gillian B., with editorial assistance from Neil Ratliff (comp.). *Music in New York During the American Revolution: An Inventory of Musical References in Rivington's* New York Gazette. (MLA Index and Bibliography Series, 24.) Bloomington, IN: Music Library Association, 1987. Pp. xxix + 135.

Rev. by Karl Kroeger in *Notes: Quarterly Journal of the Music Library Association*, 47 (1990), 384–85.

Anderson, Patricia J. *The Printed Image and the Transformation of Popular Culture, 1790–1860*. New York: Oxford U. Press; Oxford: Clarendon Press, 1991. Pp. x + 211; bibliography; illustrations.

Andries, Lise. *La Bibliothèque bleue au dix-huitième siècle: Une tradition éditoriale*. (Studies on Voltaire and the Eighteenth Century, 270.) Oxford: The Voltaire Foundation at the Taylor Institution, 1989. Pp. vii + 211; bibliography; illustrations. Cf. *ECCB*, n.s. 15, I:1–2.

Rev. by P. France in *French Studies*, 45 (1991), 324–35; by Anne Sauvy in *Bulletin du bibliophile*, (1991), 465–66.

Anfält, Tomas. "Consumer of Enlightenment: Charles De Geer—Savant and Book Collector in Eighteenth-Century Sweden." *The Book Collector*, 40 (1991), 197–210; 4 plates.

Ankarcrona, Anita. *Bud på böcker: Bokauktioner i Stockholm (1782-1801)* (Bids for Books: Book Auctions in Stockholm, 1782–1801; dissertation). Stockholm: A. Ankarcrona, 1989. Pp. xii + 308; bibliography; summary in English.

Rev. by P. Hogg in *Library*, 13 (1991), 77.

Anselment, Raymond A. "Fracastoro's *Syphilis*: Nahum Tate and the Realms of Apollo." *Bulletin of the John Rylands University Library of Manchester*, 73 (Spring 1991), 105–18.

On Tate's 1686 translation *Syphillis: or, a Poetical History of the French Disease*, printed repeatedly in the Dryden-Tonson *Poetical Miscellanies*.

Arbena, Joseph L. (comp.). *An Annotated Bibliography of Latin American Sport: Pre-Conquest to the Present*. Westport, CT: Greenwood Press, 1989. Pp. xiii + 324; indices.

Rev. (favorably) by Evelio Echevarria in *Revista Inter-Americana de Bibliografia*, 40 (1990), 218–19; (favorably) by Dennis J. Phillips in *American Reference Books Annual*, 22 (1991), 320–21.

Armstrong, Katherine A. "The Balkie Library at Tankerness House Museum, Kirkwall, Orkney." *Library Review*, 40 (1991), 37–44.

Arndt, Karl John Richard, and Reimer C. Eck (eds.). *The First Century of German Language Printing in the United States of America. Bibliography Based on the Studies of Oswald Seidensticker and Wilbur H. Oda*. Compiled by Gerd-J. Bötte and Werner Tannhof using a preliminary compilation by Annelies Müller Vol. 1: *1728–1807*; Vol. 2: *1808–1830*. (Publications of the Pennsylvania German Society, 21–22.) . Göttingen: Niedersächsische Staats- und Universitätsbibliothek Göttingen, 1989. Pp. xxix + 1245; bibliography [1: xxv-xxiv]; illustrations. Cf. *ECCB*, n.s. 16, I:2; 15, I:2–3.

Rev. (favorably) by Bernhard Fabian and Marie-Luise Spieckermann in *Zeitschrift für Bibliothekswesen und Bibliographie*, 38 (1991), 36–39; (favorably) by Charles H. Glatfelter in *Pennsylvania History*, 58 (1991), 345–46; G. Nattrass in *The Book Collector*, 40 (1991), 116–19; by M. S. Wokeck in *Pennsylvania Magazine of History and Biography*, 115 (1991), 126–28.

Arner, Robert D. *Dobson's* Encyclopaedia: *The Publisher, Text, and Publication of America's First* Britannica, *1789–1803*. Philadelphia, PA: U. of Pennsylvania Press, 1991. Pp. xviii + 295; appendices; bibliography; illustrations.

Arnold, Günter. "Ideale und reale Bedingungen für Editionen und die geplante Fortführung der Herder-Briefausgabe." Pp. 53–61 of *Edition als Wissenschaft: Festschrift für Hans Zeller*. Edited by Gunter Martens and Winfried Woesler. (Beihefte zu Editio, 2.) Tübingen: Niemeyer, 1991.

Artier, Jacqueline. "Aux origines de la bibliothèque de la Sorbonne: la création de la bibliothèque de l'Université de Paris, 1689–1770." *Mélanges de la bibliothèque de la Sorbonne*, 11 (1991), 33–58.

Atkins, Peter J. *The Directories of London, 1677–1977*. London and New York: Mansell, 1990. Pp. 732; illustrations. Cf. *ECCB*, n.s. 16, I:3.

Rev. (favorably) by Susan Ebershoff-Coles in *American Reference Books Annual*, 22 (1991), 52; by A. Winchester in the *Journal of the Society of Archivists*, 12 (1991), 68–69.

Aubrey, Bryan (comp.). *English Romantic Poetry: An Annotated Bibliography*. (Magill Bibliographies.) Englewood Cliffs, NJ, and Pasadena, CA: Salem Press, 1991. Pp. ix + 296; bibliography.

Rev. (favorably) by S. R. Moore in *Choice*, 29 (1991), 52.

Backscheider, Paula R. "Recent Studies in the Restoration and Eighteenth Century." *Studies in English Literature 1500–1900*, 30 (1991), 569–614.

Baker, William. "Recent Work in Bibliography." *Analytical and Enumerative Bibliography*, 5 (1991), 126–55.

The annotations to entries contain good summaries and analyses.

Balayé, Simone. *La Bibliothèque Nationale des origines à 1800*. Preface by Andre Miquel. (Histoire des idées et critique littéraire, 262.) Geneva: Droz, 1988. Pp. x + 546; illustrations; 62 plates. Cf. *ECCB*, n.s. 16, I:3; 15, I:3; 14, I:1.

Rev. (favorably) by Michel Delon in *Revue d'histoire littéraire de la France*, 91 (1991), 106–108.

Balsamo, Luigi. *Bibliography: History of a Tradition*. Translated by William A. Pettas. Berkeley, CA: Bernard M. Rosenthal, 1990. Pp. iv + 209. Cf. *ECCB*, n.s. 16, I:3.

Rev. (favorably) by D. W. Krummel in *Library Quarterly*, 61 (1991), 227–28; by Raymond Josué Seckel in *Bulletin du bibliophile* (1991), 452–55.

Bandry, Anne. "The Publication of the Spurious Volumes of *Tristram Shandy*." *The Shandean*, 3 (1991), 126–137; illustrations.

Focused on a third volume published in September 1760 and a ninth, in February 1766.

Barbe, Leo. "La bibliothèque d'un médecin gascon au milieu du XVIIIe siècle." *Bulletin de la Société archéologique historique littéraire et scientifique du Gers*, (1991), 200–13.

Barber, Giles. *Daphnis and Chloe: The Markets and Metamorphoses of an Unknown Bestseller*. (Panizzi Lectures, 1988.) London: The British Library, 1989. Pp. x + 86; illustrations.

Rev. (favorably) by Alain-Marie Bassy in *Library*, 13 (1991), 173–76; by Véronique Gély-Ghédira in *Bulletin du bibliophile*, (1991), 223–26; by Robin Healey in *Notes and Queries*, 236 (1991), 208–09; by Christopher Smith in *Journal of European Studies*, 21 (1991), 75–76; in *Quaerendo*, 21 (1991), 150.

Barnhill, Georgia Brady (ed.). *Prints of New England*. Worcester, MA: American Antiquarian Society, 1991. Pp. viii + 164; bibliography; illustrations.

Rev. (favorably) by Elton W. Hall in the *New England Quarterly*, 64 (1991), 516–20.

Includes a checklist of prints in an exposition and several essays on the eighteenth century, as Wendy Reaves' on American portrait prints and Stefanie Winkelbauer on William Bentley.

Barr, C. B. L., and W. G. Day. "Sterne and the York Minster Library." *The Shandean*, 2 (1990), 8–21.

Barr, Ehrhard, and Walter K. Stewart. "North American Goethe Dissertations: 1988 Supplement." *Goethe Yearbook*, 5 (1990), 293–303.

Barrero Pérez, Oscar. "La Recuperación de un periódico del siglo XVIII *El Corresponsal del ecologista*." *Estudios de historia social*, 52–53 (1990), 61–64.

Barrio Moya, Jose Luis. "La Libreria del obispo José González Díaz de Villalobos." *Hispania sacra*, 43 (1991), 329–41.

Barron, Janet, and David Nokes. *An Annotated Critical Bibliography of Augustan Poetry*. Hemel Hempstead, Hertfordshire, UK: Harvester Wheatsheaf; New York: St. Martin's Press, 1989. Pp. xiii + 158. Cf. *ECCB*, n.s. 16, I:31; 15, I:9–10.

Rev. (severely) by James K. Bracken in *American Reference Books Annual*, 22 (1991), 493; (unfavorably and with other books) by Stephen Copley in *British Journal for Eighteenth-Century Studies*, 14 (1991), 231–32; (with reservations and with another annotated bibliography) by Donald C. Mell in *The Scriblerian*, 23 (1990/91), 286-89.

Bates, Catherine. "Pope's Influence on Shakespeare?" *Shakespeare Quarterly*, 42 (1991), 57–59.

Batschelet, Margaret W. *Early American Scientific and Technical Literature: An Annotated Bibliography of Books, Pamphlets, and Broadsides*. London and Metuchen, NJ: Scarecrow Press, 1990. Pp. xii + 136; indices. Cf. *ECCB*, n.s. 16, I:4.

Rev. (summary) by James C. Bradford in *Journal of the Early Republic*, 10 (1990), 629; (with reservations) by Susan Davis Herring in *American Reference Books Annual*, 22 (1991), 591; (favorably) by Marion S. Muskiewicz in *RQ: Reference Quarterly*, 30 (1991), 414–15; in rev. article ("Best Bibliographies in History") by Hope Yelich in *RQ: Reference Quarterly*, 31 (1991), 31.

Beavan, Iain. "The Book Trade in Aberdeen and Area 1700–1830." Pp. 54–75 of *Studies in the Provincial Book Trade of England, Scotland, and Wales before 1900: Papers Presented to the British Book Trade Index, Seventh Annual Seminar, Aberystwyth, 11–3 July 1989*. Edited by David A. Stoker. Aberystwyth, UK: Department of Information and Library Studies, U. College of Wales, 1990.

Beckmann, Friedhelm. *Französische Privatbibliotheken Untersuchungen zu Lieratur-Systematik und Buchbesitz im 18. Jahrhundert*. (Archive für Geschichte des Buchwesens, 31.) Frankfurt: Buchhändler-Vereinigung, 1988. Pp. 260.

Rev. by Henri Duranton in *Francia*, 18 (1991), 259–60; (favorably) by Françoise Weil in *Revue d'histoire de littéraire de la France*, 91 (1991), 98–99.

Becq, Annie, and André Magnan. "Sur le frontispièce de l'*Encyclopédie*." Pp. 363–70 of *L'Encyclopédisme: Actes du colloque de Caen, 12–16 janvier 1987.* Edited by Annie Becq. Paris: Aux Amateurs de Livres, 1991.

Bednarska-Ruszajowa, Krystyna. *Od Homera do Jana Jakuba Rousseau: w Kregu lektur profesorów Krakowskich okresu Oswiecenia.* (Rozprawy Habilitacyjne, U. Jagiellonski, 210.) Cracow: Nakl. U. Jagiellonskiego, 1991. Pp. 235; bibliography; summary in German.

On publications and readers of eighteenth-century Cracow.

Beers, Henry Putney (comp.). *French and Spanish Records of Louisiana: A Bibliographical Guide to Archive and Manuscript Sources.* Baton Rouge, LA: Louisiana State U. Press, 1989. Pp. 371.

Rev. by Jack Bales in *American Reference Books Annual*, 21 (1990), 194.

Begheyn, Paul J., and Els F. M. Peters. *Gheprint te Nymeghen: Nijmeegse drukkers, uitgevers en boekverkopers, 1479–1794.* (Catalogi van het kunstbezit van de Gemeente Nijmegen, 6.) Nijmegen: Nijmeegs Museum "Commanderie van Sint-Jan": Gemeentearchief Nijmegen, 1990. Pp. 188; bibliography; illustrations.

Rev. in *Literatuur*, 8 (1991), 340–41; by P. G. Hoftijzer in *De Zeventiende Eeuw*, 7 (1991), 189–90.

Belcher, Françoise. *Les Ventes Publiques de livres en France 1630–1750: Répertoire des catalogues conservés à la Bibliothèque Nationale.* Oxford: The Voltaire Foundation at the Taylor Institution, 1991. Pp. 156.

Bell, Maureen, George Parfitt, and Simon Shepherd (eds.). *A Biographical Dictionary of English Women Writers, 1580–1720.* Boston, MA: G.K. Hall; London and New York: Harvester Wheatsheaf, 1990. Pp. xxvi + 298.

Rev. (favorably) by N. Knipe in *Choice*, 28 (1991), 749; (favorably) by James Rettig in *Wilson Library Bulletin*, 65 (1990), 147; by Lynn F. Williams in *American Reference Books Annual*, 22 (1991), 477.
    Bibliographical research drawn from Wing STC, checked against the British Library catalogue and *National Union Catalogue*; also includes posthumous publications after 1720, as diaries and letters.

Bellettini, Pierangelo. "Gli anni ravennati della stamperia Dandi (1694–1698)." *Studi Secenteschi*, 32 (1991), 269–314; illustrations.

Benedetto, Robert, assisted by Betty K. Walker (comp.). *Guide to the Manuscript Collections of the Presbyterian Church, U.S.* (Bibliographies and Indexes in Religious Studies, 17.) Westport, CT: Greenwood Press, 1990. Pp. xvi + 571; bibliography.

Benedict, Barbara M. " 'Service to the Public': William Creech and the Sentiment for Sale." *Eighteenth-Century Life*, 15 (1991), 119–46; appendix with table of contents of Creech's *Edinburgh Fugitive Pieces*, 1791.

Benhamou, Paul. "La Lecture des oeuvres de l'Abbé Prévost à Paris et en province dans la seconde moitié du XVIIIᵉ siècle." *Cahiers Prévost d'Exiles*, 6 (1989), 151–66.

Benhamou, Paul. "The Reading Trade in Pre-Revolutionary France." *Documentatieblad Werkgroep achttiende eeuw*, 23 (1991), 143–50.

Benson, Charles. "Research Resources in Trinity College, Dublin." *The East-Central Intelligencer*, 5 (January, 1991), 20–22.

Benton, Rita, with Jeanne Halley. *Pleyel as Music Publisher: A Documentary Sourcebook of Early 19th-Century Music*. (Annotated Reference Tools in Music, 3.) Stuyvesant, NY: Pendragon Press, 1990. Pp. xxviii + 398.

Rev. (favorably) by Renee J. LaPerriere in *American Reference Books Annual*, 22 (1991), 505.
Halley has completed the labors of the deceased Benton to provide an index of compositions by Ignace Pleyel (1757–1831), organized by composer, providing titles, opus numbers, and publication dates.

Berger, Sidney E. "The Exhibition Catalogue Awards for 1991." *Rare Books and Manuscript Librarianship*, 6 (1991), 119–26.

Berry, John Charles. "British Serial Production: Author, Audience, Text." Diss. U. of Rochester, 1989. *Dissertation Abstracts International*, A50, (December 1989), 1660–61. Pp. 250.

Discusses Samuel Richardson and Laurence Sterne (*Tristram Shandy*) while examining how publication in a periodical series affects the literary form and meaning.

The Best and Fynest Lawers and Other Rare Books: a Facsimile of the Earliest List of Books in the Advocates' Library, Edinburgh. Introduced by Maureen Townley. Edinburgh, Scotland: Edinburgh Bibliographical Society, 1990. Pp. 163; photographic facsimiles.

Facsimile reproduction of 1683 Latin manuscript catalogue of Advocates Library, now in National Library of Scotland (H.35.d.1[5]).

Bicknell, Peter. *The Picturesque Scenery of the Lake District, 1752–1855: A Bibliographical Study*. Winchester, Hampshire: St. Paul's Bibliographies (distributed in North America through Detroit, MI: Omnigraphics), 1990. Pp. x + 198; appendices, chronological list; 196 facsimile illustrations of title-pages; 12 plates. Cf. *ECCB*, n.s. 16, I:4–5.

Rev. (favorably) by Janet Adams Smith in *The Book Collector*, 40 (1991), 263–65.

Björkman, Margareta. "Circulating Libraries in Late Eighteenth-Century Stockholm." *Documentatieblad Werkgroep achttiende eeuw*, 23 (1991), 191–99.

Black, Jeremy. "The Beinecke Collection of Late Eighteenth-Century English Provincial Newspapers." *Yale University Library Gazette*, 65 (1991), 159–82.

Black, Jeremy. "The Development of the Provincial Newspaper." *British Journal of Eighteenth-Century Studies*, 14 (1991), 159–70.

Blain, Virginia, Patricia Clements, and Isobel Grundy. *The Feminist Companion to Literature in English: Women Writers from the Middle Ages to the Present.* London: B. J. Batsford; New Haven, CT: Yale U. Press, 1990. Pp. xvi + 1231; bibliography.

Rev. (favorably) in the *Antioch Review*, 49 (1991), 306–07; (favorably) by N. Knipe in *Choice*, 28 (1991), 912.

Bléchet, François. "De la Bibliothèque du Roi à la Bibliothèque nationale: permanence et ruptures." *Mélanges de la bibliothèque de la Sorbonne*, 10 (n.d. [c. 1990]), 139–51.

Bléchet, François. *Les ventes publiques de livres en France, 1630–1750. Répertoire des catalogues conservés à la Bibliothèque Nationale.* Preface by Emmanuel Le Roy Ladurie. Oxford: Voltaire Foundation at the Taylor Institution; Paris: Universitas, 1991. Pp. 156; bibliography; illustrations; indices.

Rev. by Louis Desgraves in *Revue française d'histoire du livre*, 72–73 (1991), 313.

Bléchet, Françoise, and H. Bots. "La Librairie hollandaise et ses rapports avec la Bibliothèque du Roi." *Documentatieblad Werkgroep achttiende eeuw*, 23 (1991), 103–41.

Blom, F. J. M. "The Publications of Charles Leslie." *Edinburgh Bibliographical Society Transactions*, 6 (sessions for 1987-89, c. 1990), 10–36; checklist.

Blonska, Maria. "Druki Cyrylickie XV–XVIII Wieku w Panstwie Polsko-Litewskim: Tematyka, aktualnosc historyczna, osiagniecia, zwiazek z kultura polska." Pp. 61–76 of *Prace Badawcze i bibliograficzne nad Zbiorami Rzadkich i Cennych Ksiazek i dokumentów.* Edited by Paulina Buchwald-Pelcowa, et al.(Prace Dzialu Zbiorow Specjalnych Biblioteki Narodowey, 2.) Warsaw: Biblioteka Narodowa, 1991. Bibliography; summary in English.

Blum, Lothar. "Prolegomena zu einer Historisch-Kritischen Ausgabe der 'Kinder- under Hausmärchen' der Brüder Grimm, Mit textgenet: Betrachtung des 'Konigs Drosselbart.'" *Editio*, 3 (1989), 177–92.

Bockelkamp, Marianne. "Wasserzeichen in neueren Handschriften: Ihre Erfassung und Auswertung." *Editio*, 4 (1990), 21–43; abstract (in French); bibliography of watermark studies; illustration.

Bödeker, Hans-Erich. "Livres pour et contre la Révolution française: La clientèle du librairie de Münster Theissing entre 1790 et 1800." *Leipziger Jahrbuch zu Buchgeschichte*, 1 (1991), 139–53.

Bold, Alan Norman. *A Burns Companion.* New York: St. Martin's Press, 1991. Pp. xiv + 447; bibliography; illustrations; indices; map; 20 plates.

Rev. (favorably) by H. M. Barber in *Choice*, 28 (1991), 1611–12.

Previously issued with identical contents in the series Macmillan Literary Companions (Basingstoke: Macmillan, 1990).

Böning, Holger, and Reinhart Siegert (eds.). *Volksaufklärung. Biobibliographisches Handbuch zur Popularisierung aufklärerischen Denkens im deutschen Sprachraum von den Anfängen bis 1850.* Vol. 1: *Die Genese der Volksaufklärung und ihre Entwicklung bis 1780.* Stuttgart and Bad Cannstatt: Frommann-Holzboog, 1990. Pp. liv + 932; illustrations.

Rev. by Michael Hughes in *British Journal for Eighteenth-Century Studies*, 14 (1991), 240–41.

Bonnant, Georges. "La librairie genevoise en Grand-Bretagne jusqu'à la fin du XVIIIᵉ siècle." *Geneva*, 38 (1990), 131–53; illustrations.

Boos, Florence, assisted by Lynn Miller (comps.). *Bibliography of Women and Literature.* Vol. I: *Articles and Books (1974–1978) by and about Women from 600 to 1975;* Vol. II: *Supplement: Articles and Books (1979–1981) by and about Women from 600 to 1975.* London and New York: Holmes & Meier, 1989. Pp. xii + 439; [*vii*] + 342; indices.

Rev. (with reservations) by Isobel Grundy in *Review of English Studies*, 42 (1991), 235–36.

Booth, Alan. "Irish Exiles, Revolution, and Writing in England in the 1790s." Pp. 64–81 of *Irish Writing: Exile and Subversion.* Edited by Paul Hyland and Neil Sammells. New York: St. Martin's, 1991.

On the publications of the United Irishmen in the 1790s, especially *The Declaration.*

Bosch Carrera, María Dolors. "Costumbres y opinión en el periodismo del siglo XVIII." *Dissertation Abstracts International.* 1990 Fall; 51(3): Item 1480C.

Boucé, Paul-Gabriel. "Fielding et Smollett: travaux récents, 1985–90." *Études anglaises*, 44 (1991), 151–68.

Boy, Michel, and Thierry Remuzon. *Le Livre de raison du maître-papetier Louis Richard, 1720–1771: Texte et commentaire.* (Chroniques historiques d'Ambert et de son arrondissement, 17.) Avignon: Editions régionale Lavarois-Forez, 1991. Pp. 81; bibliography.

Boydell, Brian. *A Dublin Musical Calendar (1700–1760).* Dublin: Irish Academic Press, 1988. Pp. 320; illustrations; indices. Cf. *ECCB*, n.s. 15, IV:140.

Rev. (with another book) by Graydon Beeks in *Notes: Quarterly Journal of Music Library Association*, 47 (1990), 372–74; (favorably) by David Wyn Jones in *British Journal of Eighteenth-Century Studies*, 13 (1990), 282–83; by Rosamond McGuinness in *Music and Letters*, 71 (1990), 94–96.

Braches, Ernst. "The First Years of the Fagel Collection in Trinity College, Dublin." Pp. 189–96 of *Across the Narrow Seas: Studies in the History and Bibliography of Britain and the Low Countries: Presented to Ann E. C. Simoni.* Edited by Susan Roach. Foreward by Mirjam M. Foot. Bibliography by Dennis E. Rhodes. London: British Library, 1991.

Brack, O M, Jr. "Samuel Johnson Edits for the Booksellers: Sir Thomas Browne's *Christian Morals* (1756) and *The English Works of Roger Ascham* (1761)." Pp. 13–39 in *Essays in Honor of William B. Todd.* Compiled by Warner Barnes and Larry Carver. Austin, TX: Harry Ransom Humanities Research Center, 1991. Pp. 215; illustrations.

This festschrift for Professor Todd was also issued as nos. 3–4 of *The Library Chronicle of the University of Texas*, 21 (1991). The volume includes I. R. Willison's "Remarks on the History of the Book in Britain as a Field of Study Within the Humanities, With a Synopsis and Select List of Current Literature" (95–146) and a bibliography of William B. Todd's scholarship (187–213).

Bracken, James K. *Reference Works in British and American Literature*. 2 vols. Englewood, CO: Libraries Unlimited, 1990–91. Pp. xii + 252; indices; xxiv + 310.

Vol. 1 (1990) is the more valuable, covering handbooks, dictionaries, indices, and general and specific bibliographies; Vol. 2 provides sources for individual authors listed alphabetically.

Bridson, Gavin D. R., and James J. White. *Plant, Animal, and Anatomical Illustration in Art and Science: A Bibliographical Guide from the 16th Century to the Present Day*. Detroit, MI: Omnigraphics; Winchester, Hampshire: St. Paul's Bibliographies in association with the Hunt Institute for Botanical Documentation, 1990. Pp. xxxviii + 450; illustrations; 4 plates;

Rev. by R. Desmond in *TLS*, (January 4, 1991), 22; by W. Schupbach in *The British Journal for the History of Science*, 24 (1991), 488–89.

Briffaut, Pierre. "Une vente de matérial d'imprimerie cambrésienne en 1752 [by Nicholas Joseph Doulliez]." *Mémoires de la Société d'emulation de Cambrai*, 101 (1991), 81–89.

Britton, Allen Perdue, and Irving Lowens (comps.); completed by Richard Crawford. *American Sacred Music Imprints (1698–1810): A Bibliography*. Preface by Richard Crawford. Worcester, MA: American Antiquarian Society, 1989; reissued, Charlottesville, VA: U. Press of Virginia, 1990. Pp. xvi + 798; appendices; bibliographies; indices.

Rev. (favorably) by David Hunter in *The Papers of the Bibliographical Society of America*, 85 (1991), 435–38; (favorably) by Dorothy E. Jones in *American Reference Books Annual*, 22 (1991), 521; by L. Smith in *Choice*, 28 (1991), 1286; (favorably) by Karl Kroeger in *Notes: Quarterly Journal of the Music Library Association*, 48 (1991), 54–58.
A bibliography of 454 items, with a chronology, lists of composers and publishers, and a geographical directory of engravers, printers, and publishers.

Brogan, Martha L. *Research Guide to Libraries and Archives in the Low Countries*. (Bibliographies and Indexes in Library and Information Science, 5.) Westport, CT: Greenwood Press, 1991. Pp. xi + 547; indices.

The first part of this easily used tool is a "field guide" for researchers, treating such finding aids as national bibliographies, union lists, and directories; the second part, a "Guide to Libraries and Archives" proper, surveys those resources in Belgium, then Netherlands, then Luxembourg. An appendix even lists public and religious holidays. There are three indices: author/title (to Part 1); institutions (Part 2); and subjects (Parts 1–2).

Brouwer, Han. "Lezen in de Provincie: Zwolle in de late Achttiende en Negentiende Eeuw." Pp. 127–34 of *Balans en Perspectief van de Nederlanse Cultuurgeschiedenis: De productie, distributie, en consumptie van cultuur*. Edited by J. J. Kloek and W. W. Mijnhardt. Amersterdam: Rodopi, 1991.

Brouwer, Han. "Wordt er te Zwolle Veel Gelezen? Leescultuur in de late 18de en 19de Eeuw." *Spiegel Historiael*, 26 (1991), 143–48; illustrations.

Brown, Iain Gordon. *Building for Books: The Architectural Evolution of the Advocates' Library, 1689–1925.* Aberdeen, Scotland: Aberdeen U. Press in association with the National Library of Scotland, 1989. Pp. xx + 273; illustrations; maps; plans; portraits. Cf. *ECCB*, n.s. 16, I:7.

Rev. (favorably) by Thomas A. Markus in *Scottish Historical Review*, 70 (1991), 89–90; by P. S. Morrish in *Library History*, 8 (1990), 153–55; (favorably; with another book) by F. W. Ratcliffe in *Library*, 13 (1991), 176–182; by E. M. Rodger in *Journal of the Society of Archivists*, 11 (1990), 61–62; (with another book) by Priscilla Schlicke in *The Scottish Literary Journal*, 34 (1991), 24–27; (with another book) by Harry Gordon Slade in *TLS*, (March 2, 1991), 232.

Brüggermann, Theodor. "Galanterie und Weltschmerz in 'Frizchens Lieder' (1781) von Chr[ristian]. A. Overbeck." *Philobiblon*, 34 (1990), 300–08; 2 plates.

Bülow, Michael. *Buchmarkt und Autoreneigentum. Die Entstehung des Urhebergedankens im 18. Jahrhundert.* (Buchwissenschaftliche Beiträge aus dem Deutschen Bucharchiv München, 30.) Wiesbaden: Harrassowitz, 1990. Pp. 99; bibliography.

Butrón Prida, Gonzalo. "La Prensa en Cádiz durante la etapa ilustrada (1763–1808)." *Estudios de historia social*, 52–53 (1990), 73–80.

Cabeza Sánchez-Albornoz, María Cruz. "Catálog de obras del siglo XVIII existentes en la Biblioteca de la Facultad de Filosofía de la Universidad de Valencia." *Saitabi*, 41 (1991), 13–46.

Cadell, Patrick, and Ann Matheson (eds.). *For the Encouragement of Learning: Scotland's National Library 1689–1989.* Edinburgh, Scotland: HMSO, 1989. Pp. xii + 316; illustrations. Cf. *ECCB*, n.s. 16, I:8; 15, I:3.

Rev. by I. Campbell in *University of Edinburgh Journal*, 34 (1990), 205–06; (favorably and with another book) by F. W. Ratcliffe in *Library*, 13 (1991), 176–182; by G. Riddell in *Library Association Record*, 92 (1990), 229; (favorably and with another book) by Priscilla Schlicke in *The Scottish Literary Journal*, 34 (1991), 24–27; (with another book) by Harry Gordon Slade in *TLS*, (March 2, 1991), 232; by David H. Stam in *Albion*, 23 (1991), 370–71.

Cagle, William R. *A Matter of Taste: A Bibliographical Catalogue of the Gernon Collection of Books on Food and Drink.* New York: Garland Publishers, 1990. Pp. xxiv + 980; indices; plates.

Rev. by Paul Grinke in *The Book Collector*, 40 (1991), 437–38.

Cahn, Michael. *Der Druck des Wissens: Geschichte und Medium der wissenschaftlichen Publikation.* Wiesbaden: Reichert, 1991. Pp. 76.

A catalogue of a July 1991 exhibition at the Prussian State Library on "The Printing of Knowledge," with a broad theoretical essay, with applications, by Michael Cahn on the relationship of developments in communications technology (and so printing history) with the growth and nature of scientific knowledge; contains a bibliography of works in Dutch, English, French, German, and Italian.

Caillet, Maurice. "La bibliothèque du collège des Irlandais et son fonds de livres anciens." *Mélanges de la bibliothèque de la Sorbonne*, 11 (1991), 151–63.

Camara Aroca, Mercedes (ed.). *Impresos anteriores a 1801 en la Biblioteca de la Facultad de Veterinaria de Cordóba*. (U. of Cordóba Monografias, 180.) Cordóba: U. of Cordóba, 1990. Pp. 144; bibliography; facsimiles; illustrations.

Candido, Joseph. "The First Folio and Nicholas Rowe's 1714 *King John*." *Notes and Queries*, 236 (1991), 506–08.

Cardinale, Susan, and Hilda L. Smith (comps.). *Women and the Literature of the Seventeenth Century: An Annotated Bibliography Based on Wing's* Short-Title Catalogue. (Bibliographies and Indexes in Women's Studies, 10.) Westport, CT: Greenwood Press, 1990. Pp. xxi + 333; indices. Cf. *ECCB*, n.s. 16, V:325.

Rev. (favorably) by Philip R. Rider in *American Reference Books Annual*, 22 (1991), 476–77.
Part 1 covers publications by women only; Part 2 covers works for and about women mostly written by men. Most entries are from Wing's *STC*, with titles abridged, but some entries from other sources and so indicated (these largely from the British Library's catalogue, the *National Union Catalogue*, and OCLC.

Castellani, Carlo. "La réception en Italie et en Europe du *Saggio di Osservazioni microscopiche* de Spallanzani (1765)." *Dix-huitième siècle*, 23 (1991), 85–96.

Catalogue de cent un livres anciens rares ou précieux de la Bibliothèque de la Sorbonne. Dont l'exposition commencera le lundi 23 septembre 1991 et continuera les jours suivants en la chapelle de la Sorbonne. Introduction by Claude Jolly. Paris: U. of the Sorbonne, 1991. Pp. 155; illustrations.

Catalog of Dictionaries, Word Books, and Philological Texts, 1440–1900: Inventory of the Cordell Collection, Indiana State University. Complied by David E. Vancil. Bloomington, IN: Indiana U. Press, 1991.

The scope of the Cordell Collection is dictionaries that trace the development of English and, more generally, examples of the Western tradition of lexicography, and this catalog contains an inventory of the 5,046 pre-1901 imprints (including facimilies) held as of 1991. Items are listed in alphabetical order by author; and there are indices by date of publication, by language focus, and by subject. Each entry includes year of imprint, truncated title, truncated imprint, OCLC number (where one exists), and whether or not the work is of special emphasis. By looking at the text while consulting the indices readers will be able to scan for items printed during the eighteenth century or get some clues of the interest in England in foreign languages. The OCLC number will be very useful for those who have access to that database because many items in it include full title and imprint, a description, and subject headings, along with holding libraries, but the omission of information both from Robin Alston's comprehesive *A Bibliography of the English Language from the Invention of Printing to the Year 1800* and the *English Short Title Catalogue* is lamentable. Consultation with the *English STC*, which long has made an effort to distinguish between editions, would have enabled this catalog to distinguish for English imprints (and imprints in English published elsewhere than English-speaking countries).—Charles Egleston.

Cavanagh, John. *British Theatre: A Bibliography, 1901–1985*. Mottisfort, Hampshire, U.K.: Motley Press, 1989. Pp. 510.

Ceccarelli, Maria Grazia. *Vocis et animarum pinacothecae: cataloghi di biblioteche private dei secoli XVII-XVIII nei fondi dell'Angelica*. Rome: Ministero per i Beni Culturali e Ambientali; Biblioteca Angelica, 1990. Pp. xxii + 326; bibliography; illustrations.

Rev. by Bert van Selm in *De Zeventiende Eeuw*, 7 (1991), 68–69.

Censer, Jack R., and Jeremy D. Popkin (eds.). *Press and Politics in Pre-Revolutionary France*. Berkeley, CA, and London: U. of California Press, 1987. Pp. xiii + 252; illustrations. Cf. *ECCB*, n.s. 13, I:3.

Rev. (favorably) by Raymond Birn in *Journal of Modern History*, 62 (1990), 157–58; by Elizabeth L. Eisenstein in *American Historical Review*, 94 (1989), 456–57; by Alan Forrest in *Historian: A Journal of History*, 51 (1989), 328–29; by Norman Hampson in *English Historical Review*, 106 (1991), 207–08; by Julian Swann in *History: The Journal of the Historical Association*, 74 (1989), 136–37.

Chaison, Joanne D. "Indices for American Periodicals." *The East-Central Intelligencer*, 5 (January, 1991), 22–23.

On the use of Nelson F. Adkins' *Index to Early American Periodicals to 1850* (1964) and the computer-generated indices of *American Periodicals of the 1700's* and *American Periodicals, 1800–1850* prepared by Computer Indexed Systems. Reprinted from *The Book: Newsletter of the Program of the Book in American Culture*, published by the American Antiquarian Society (March 1990).

Chan, Mary, and Jamie C. Kassler. *Roger North: Materials for a Chronology of his Writings. Checklist No. 1*. (North Papers, 4.) Kensington, NSW, Australia: School of English, U. of New South Wales, 1989. Pp. v + 189; bibliography; indices.

Rev. (favorably) by Jeremy Black in *British Journal for Eighteenth-Century Studies*, 14 (1991), 216; by Penelope Gouk in *Music and Letters*, 70 (1989), 96.
    Contains a close physical examination of manuscripts to sort them and their chronology out. Some bibliographical information on North is also available in Chan and Kassler's edition of North's *Musical Grammarian (1728)* (Cambridge and New York: Cambridge U. Press, 1990); pp. xvii + 305; bibliography; musical examples; portrait.

Chapin, Chester. "The Poems of Abel Evans (1679–1737). *Notes and Queries*, 236 (1991), 178–81.

Evans did not write *Pre-Existence* (1714) but did write "On Blenheim House at Woodstock," often attributed to others.

Chartier, Roger. *The Cultural Uses of Print in Early Modern France*. Translated by Lydia G. Cochrane. Princeton, NJ: Princeton U. Press, 1987. Pp. xi + 354; illustrations. Cf. *ECCB*, n.s. 14, I:2; 13, I:3.

Rev. (favorably) by Giles Barber in *English Historical Review*, 106 (1991), 463–64; by Jack R. Censer in *American Historical Review*, 94 (1989), 1396–97; by David Nicholls in *History: The Journal of the Historical Association*, 74 (1989), 522–23; (favorably) by Jeremy D. Popkin in *Libraries and Culture*, 26 (1991), 515–16.

Chartier, Roger (ed.). *The Culture of Print: Power and Uses of Print in Early Modern Europe.* Princeton, NJ: Princeton U. Press, 1989. Pp. viii + 351; illustrations; 16 plates.

Rev. by John A. Hall in *British Journal of Sociology*, 42 (1991), 301–02; by Jeremy D. Popkin in *Libraries and Culture*, 26 (1991), 615–16.

English-language version of *Les Usages de l'imprime (XVe-XIXe siècle)*, 1987 (cited below).

Chartier, Roger (ed.). *Les Usages de l'imprime (XVe-XIXe siècle)*. Paris: Fayard, 1987. Pp. 446; bibliography; illustrations; 24 plates. Cf. *ECCB*, n.s. 13, I:3.

Rev. by Raymond Birn in *Journal of Modern History*, 61 (1989), 346–47; by Harry C. Payne in *American Historical Review*, 93 (1988), 679–80.

French-language first-edition of *The Culture of Print: Power and Uses of Print in Early Modern Europe*, 1989 [cited above].

Chartier, Roger. *Lesewelten: Buch und Lekture in der frühen Neuzeit.* Translated from the French by Brita Schleinitz und Ruthard Stäblein. (Historische Studien, 1.) Frankfurt am Main: Campus Verlag; Paris: Editions de la Maison des Sciences de l'Homme, 1990. Pp. 191; bibliography.

Rev. by Klaus Rek in *Leipziger Jahrbuch zur Buchgeschichte*, 1 (1991), 323–24.

The review's heading has the variant title *Lesenwelten: Literatur und Lektüre in der frühen Neuzeit*, but otherwise it matches the information above.

Chartier, Roger. "Text, Printing, Readings." Pp. 154–175 of *The New Cultural History*. Edited by Lynn Hunt. Berkeley, CA: U. of California Press, 1989.

Chayes, Irene H. "Words in Pictures. Testing the Boundary: Inscriptions by William Blake." *Word and Image*, 7 (1991), 85–97; illustrations.

Chédozeau, Bernard. *La Bible et la liturgie en français: L'Eglise tridentine et les traductions bibliques et liturgigues (1600–1789).* Paris: Editions du Cerf, 1990. Pp. 298.

Chédozeau, Bernard. "La Faculté de théologie de Paris au XVIIe siècle: un lieu privilégié des conflits entre gallicans et ultramontains (1600–1720)." *Mélanges de la bibliothèque de la Sorbonne*, 10 (n.d. [c. 1990]), 39–102.

Chevrier, Hervé. "Catalogue des imprimés provenant des archives de la Société des sciences historiques et naturelles de l'Yonne (1521–1800); deuxième partie: 1788–1800." *Bulletin de la Société des sciences historiques et naturelles de l'Yonne*, 122 (1990), 193–204.

Chiarmonte, Paula (ed.). *Women Artists in the United States: A Selective Bibliography and Resource Guide on the Fine and Decorative Arts, 1750–1986.* (A Reference Publication in Art History.) Boston, MA: G. K. Hall, 1990. Pp. xvii + 997. Cf. *ECCB*, n.s. 16, I:9.

Rev. (favorably) by Linda Keir Simons in *American Reference Books Annual*, 22 (1991), 369.

Childress, Boyd. "Charles Cist, Philadelphia Printer." *The Papers of the Bibliographical Society of America*, 85 (1991), 72–81; 2 plates.

Cist (1738–1785), for a time in a partnership with Melchior Steiner (1775–1781), printed in both English and German.

Chisick, Harvey, with Ouzi Elyada and Ilana Zinguer (eds.). *The Press in the French Revolution: Papers Presented for the Conference "Presse d'élite, presse populaire et propagande pendant la Révolution française," held at the University of Haifa, 16–18 May 1988.* (Studies on Voltaire and the Eighteenth Century, 287.) Oxford: The Voltaire Foundation at the Taylor Institution, 1991. Pp. viii + 423; bibliography; illustrations; 8 plates.

The section "Beginnings of the Revolution and its Impact on the Press" contains Denis Richet's "Les canaux de la propagation des idées contestataires avant la presse révolutionnaire" (19–24); Jean Sgard's "'On dit'" [on various journals of the 1780s] (25–32); Jacques Wagner's "Peuple et pouvoir dans le *Journal encyclopédique* à la veille de la Révolution française" (33–57); Raymond Birn's "The Pamphlet Press and the Estates-General of 1789" (59–69); and Pierre Rétat's "Pamphlet numéroté et journal en 1789" (71–82); the section on "Old Regime Journals Confront the Revolution" includes three essays particularly relevant to the history of the press: Jeremy D. Popkin's "The Élite Press in the French Revolution: The *Gazette de Leyde* and the *Gazette universelle*" (85–98); Harvey Chisick's "The Disappearance of a Great Enlightenment Periodical: the *Année littéraire*, 1789–1790" (119–30); and Jeremy Black's "The Challenge of the Revolution and the British Press" (131–41); and the section on "Journalists and Politics" includes Elizabeth L. Eisenstein's "The Tribune of the People: A New Species of Demagogue" (145–59); W. J. Murray's "Journalism as a Career Choice in 1789" (161–88; 4 tables classifying journalists); and Jack R. Censer's "Robespierre the Journalist" (189–96). In the last three sections ("Journalism and Politics: The Elitist Press," "Language and Revolution," and "Images and Their Uses"), only Jean-Paul Betaud's "L'Ami du roi de l'abbé Royou" (221–27) and Ouzi Elyada's "Les récrits de complot dans la presse populaire parisienne (1790–1791)" (281–92) need be noted for providing detailed information on the history of printing and the periodical press.

Chomarat, Michel, with the assistance of Jean-Paul Laroche. *Bibliographie Nostradamus, XVIe–XVIIe–XVIIIe siècles.* (Bibliotheca Bibliographica Aureliana, 123.) Baden-Baden: V. Koerner, 1989. Pp. 256; 133 illustrations.

Claridge, Henry, and Janet Goodwyn. "American Literature to 1900." *Year's Work in English Studies*, 72 (1991), 422–53.

Clark, Charles E. "Boston and the Nurturing of Newspapers: Dimensions of the Cradle, 1690–1741." *New England Quarterly*, 64 (1991), 243–71.

Clegg, Michael Barren (ed.). *Bibliography of Genealogy and Local History Periodicals with a Union List of Major U.S. Collections.* Fort Wayne, IN: Allen County Public Library Foundation, 1990. Pp. viii + 528.

Rev. (favorably) by Carol Willsey Bell in *American Reference Books Annual*, 22 (1991), 164; (mixed) by V. L. Close in *Choice*, 28 (1990), 450.

Cloonan, Michèle Valerie. *Early Bindings in Paper: A Brief History of European Hand-Made Paper-Covered Books, with a Multilingual Glossary.* Boston: G. K. Hall; Poole (Dorset): Mansell, 1991. Pp. xi + 146; bibliography; glossary of German, French, and Italian terms; illustrations; 8 plates.

Rev. (briefly) in *TLS*, (July 19, 1991), 25.

Cloonan Michèle Valerie (ed.). *Early Eighteenth-Century English Works on Bookbinding*. New York: Garland Publishers, 1990. Pp. xiv + various paginations of reprints [1–104; 137–42; 147–68; 283–95; 377–99]; illustrations.

Cloonan's introduction precedes parts of four books treating bookbinding: John Bagford's *Of Booke Binding Ancient Modourne* (c. 1710), Godfrey Smith's *The Laboratory or School of Arts* (excerpts from both 4th [1755] and 7th [1810] editions), Robert Dossie's *The Handmaid to the Arts* (1758), and John Baxter's *The Sister Arts* (1809).

Coates, Alan. "The Old Library of Trinity College, Oxford." *The Bodleian Library Record*, 13 (1991), 466–78.

Cohen, Norman S. *The American Presidents: An Annotated Bibliography*. Englewood Cliffs, NJ, and Pasadena, CA: Salem Press, 1989. Pp. viii + 202.

Rev. (favorably) by John P. Stierman in *American Reference Books Annual*, 22 (1991), 192.

Colla, Angela. "Tipografi, editori e librai." Pp. 109–62 of *Storia di Vincenza*. Vol. 3, part 2: *L'eta della repubblica veneta (1404–1797)*. Vincenza: Neri Pozza, 1990.

Conejo, Didier. "Chamfort en Italie: note bibliographique." *Studies on Voltaire and the Eighteenth Century*, 284 (1991), 343–62; bibliography of Italian editions.

Conlon, Pierre M. *Le Siècle des lumières. Bibliographie chronologique*. Vol. 6: *1748–1752*. (Histoire des idées et critique littéraire, 266.) Geneva: Droz, 1988. Pp. xxiii + 560. Cf. *ECCB*, n.s. 16, I:10; 14, I:6–7.

Rev. by Paule Jansen in *Revue d'histoire littéraire de la France*, 91 (1991), 97–98; by Franco Piva in *Studi francesi*, 34 (1990), 139–140.

Conlon, Pierre M. *Bibliographie chronologique*. Vol. 7: *1753–56*. (Histoire des idées et critique littéraire, 282.) Geneva: Droz, 1990. Pp. xxvii + 559. Cf. *ECCB*, n.s. 16, I:10.

Rev. (briefly) by Roland Desné in *Dix-huitième siècle*, 23 (1991), 451; (briefly and favorably) by Haydn Mason in *French Studies*, 45 (1991), 321.

Conlon, Pierre M. *Le Siècle des lumières. Bibliographie chronologique*. Vol. 8: *1757–1760*. (Histoire des idées et critique littéraire, 299.) Geneva: Droz, 1991. Pp. xxix + 586.

Another volume of Pierre Conlon's ambitious recension of French Enlightenment publications is now available. The 4988 entries gleaned from a growing network of 266 mostly public collections in Europe and North America and some 80 'secondary' sources, whether from the period or later, confirm a rising tide of francophone titles concurrent with an increasingly cosmopolitan print culture in 'developed' countries. (In previous reviews I have noted annual averages of French language publications of 976 at mid-century and 1172 in the mid-1750s.)

As Conlon notes in a brief preface, the late '50s are marked by a number of socio-political and cultural events, all of which announce a growing influence of the *Lumières*. The attempted assassination of Louis XV by Damiens unleashed several dozen tracts and poems deploring the outrage. Yet monarchical respect did not reduce remonstrances from the provincial *Parlements* to reduce royal taxation. As the yet-to-be-named Seven Years' War accumulated military defeats for France at home and abroad (Voltaire's exasperated '*quelques arpents de neige*' at the loss of North American lands), religious orthodoxy, proposes Conlon, was quietly challenged by increasing, but by no means officially recognized, pluralism.

The interruption of the *Encyclopédie* in 1757 and counter-attacks by *Anti-philosophes* (Palissot and cohorts) was tempered by the appearance of Helvétius' *De l'esprit*. A sharp rise in the availability of translated literatures–Italian (an anonymous 'drama' *Le monde renversé ou les hommes soumis à la domination des femmes*, Algarotti, Passoni, Goldini), German (Gessner, Abel, Haller, Klopstock), and above all English (Addison, Hume, Smollett, Johnson)–prompted Fougeret de Montbron's *Préservatif contre l'anglomanie*, a nationalist protectionism against overconsumption of foreign culture, not dissimilar from contemporary concerns about 'guest-workers' and imported products. Conlon also notes the appearance of innovative genres, such as Diderot's dramas and Voltaire's *Pierre le grand*, both of which had a lesser initial impact than *Candide*'s felicitous mixture of content and form.

In other reviews (see *ECCB*, n.s. 16, I:10), I have noted several shortcomings of presentation in the Conlon *Bibliographie*, lacunae probably inevitably given the limited human and material resources available to the industrious bibliographer. May I mention, then, a few not included in Conlon's 1759 list: the anonymous *Ami des femmes ou la philosophie du sexe,* Gay's *Fables* translated by Madame Keralio, and Los Rios' *Le joujou de nouvelle façon.*

Since there are no indices, not to mention systematic lists of reeditions, a CD-ROM version of the Conlon *Bibliographie* would be of great assistance in sorting out shifts in keyword frequencies and publication histories. As we await such enhancements, we can only wish Conlon well as he presses onward with his daunting and immensely useful project.—Richard L. Frautschi.

Connor, Paul, and Jill Roberts. *Pennsylvania German Fraktur and Printed Broadsides. A Guide to the Collection in the Library of Congress*. Introduction by Don Yoder. Washington, D.C.: Library of Congress, 1989. Pp. 48; illustrations.

Cop, Margaret (comp.). *Babel Unraveled: An Annotated World Bibliography of Dictionary Bibliographies, 1658–1988*. Tübingen: Niemeyer, 1990. Pp. lxxii + 195. Cf. *ECCB*, n.s. 16, I:10.

Rev. (with other books) by Klaus Schreiber in *Zeitschrift für Bibliothekswesen und Bibliographie*, 38 (1991), 283–86.

Copley, Stephen, and Alan Bower. "The Eighteenth Century." *Year's Work in English Studies*, 69 (1988), 336–80; 70 (1989), 351–400; 71 (1990), 358–95; 72 (1991), 246–68.

Coppa, Frank J., and William Roberts (comps.). *Modern Italian History: An Annotated Bibliography*. (Bibliographies and Indexes in World History, 18.) Westport, CT: Greenwood Press, 1990. Pp. ix + 226.

Rev. by J. C. Jurgens in *American Reference Books Annual*, 22 (1991), 213.

Cosgrove, Peter. "Undermining the Text: Edward Gibbon, Alexander Pope, and the Anti-Authenticating Footnote." Pp. 130–51 of *Annotation and Its Texts*. Edited by Stephen A. Barney. New York and Oxford: Oxford U. Press, 1991.

Among papers presented at the University of California, Irvine in April 1988. Contrasts the use of footnotes in Pope's *Dunciad Variorum* with those in Edward Gibbon's *Decline and Fall of the Roman Empire* to consider how the objectivity of footnotes has been questioned.

Coutts, Brian E., Ronald H. Fritze and Louis A. Vyhnanek (eds.). *Reference Sources in History: An Introductory Guide*. Santa Barbara, CA: ABC-CLIO, 1990. Pp. xvii + 319.

Rev. (favorably) by Charles C. Hay in *Library Journal*, 116 (April 15, 1991), 84; (with reservations) by L. Kincaid in *Choice*, 28 (1991), 1758.

Cowie, Leonard W. *Lord Nelson, 1758–1805: A Bibliography*. (Meckler's Bibliographies of British Statesmen, 7.) Westport, CT: Meckler, 1990. Pp. vii + 191; indices. Cf. *ECCB*, n.s.16, I:11.

Rev. (favorably) by Ronald H. Fritze in *American Reference Books Annual*, 22 (1991), 209; by R. Nash in *Choice*, 28 (1991), 1092; 1094.

Cowley, Jean (comp.). *A Descriptive Catalogue of Books Printed in England, Scotland, and Wales, 1483–1700*. Johannesburg: U. of Witwatersrand Library, 1989. Pp. iv + 76; illustrations.

Cox, Richard J. "Library History and Library Archives in the United States." *Libraries and Culture*, 26 (1991), 569–593.

Crompton, Virginia, and Janet Todd. "Rebellious Antidote: A New Attribution to Aphra Behn." *Notes and Queries*, 236 (1991), 175–77.

Reprints a 1685 broadside dialogue poem, *Rebellions Antidote*, attributing the poem's lines advocating tea and signed "A.B." to Behn.

Crosina, Maria Luisa. *La comunità ebraica di Riva del Garda (sec. XV–XVIII)*, [bound with] *La tipografia di Jacob Marcaria (1557–1563)* by Giuliano Tamani. With other contributions by Francesca Odorizzi, Nikolaus Vielmetti, and Federica Fanizza. Edited by Federica Fanizza and P. Christé. Trento: Provincia Autonoma di Trento, Servizio Beni Culturali; Riva del Garda: Comune di Riva del Garda, Biblioteca Civica, 1991. Pp. 265; illustrations.

Croutti, Luigi, and Maria X. Wells (eds.). *Libraries and Librarianship in Italy*. Special issue of *Libraries and Culture*, 25 (1990), 303–481.

Relevant to our period are "The Network of Libraries in the Old Italian States" by Enzo Bottasco (334–344); "The Endowed Municipal Public Libraries" by Ennio Sandal (358–71); "The Two National Centrol Libraries of Florence and Rome" by Franca Arduini (383–405); and "Bibliographical Studies in Italy since 1945" by Enzo Esposito and Giovanni Solimine (433–45). Aside from the first article, translated by Sandra da Conturbia, these articles are translated by Rino Pizzi and Prentiss Moore.

Culot, Paul (comp.). *Quatre siècles de reliure en Belgique, 1500–1900*. Preface by Michel Wittock. Brussels: Eric Speeckaert, 1989. Pp. 315; illustrations.

Rev. (favorably) by Jean Toulet in *Bulletin du bibliophile*, (1989), 459.

Daniel, Chantal, and Tanguy Daniel. "Le répertoire et la bibliothèque du théâtre de Brest à la fin de l'Ancien Régime." Pp. 589–614 of *Charpiana: mélanges offerts par ses amis à Jacques Charpy*. Rennes: Fédération des sociétés savantes de Bretagne, 1991.

Darnton, Robert. *Édition et sédition: L'univers de la littérature clandestine au XVIIIe siècle.* (NRF essais.) Paris: Gallimard, 1991. Pp. [4] + vii + 281; illustrations.

Rev. (with reservations) by Jeremy D. Popkin in *Eighteenth-Century Studies*, 25 (1991), 99–103.

Darnton, Robert. *The Kiss of Lamourette: Reflections in Cultural History.* New York: W. W. Norton, 1990. Pp. xxi + 393; illustrations.

Rev. by Thomas J. Schaeper in *Library Journal*, 114 (Nov. 15, 1989), 94.
A collection of previously published essays, such as "The Printed Word," "What Is the History of Books?" and "First Steps toward a History of Reading."

Darnton, Robert, and Daniel Roche (eds.). *Revolution in Print: The Press in France, 1775–1800.* Berkeley, CA: U. of California Press in collaboration with the New York Public Library, 1989. Pp. xv + 351; bibliography; illustrations; 8 plates. Cf. *ECCB*, n.s. 15, I:5.

Rev. in *Virginia Quarterly Review*, 65 (1989), 117–18; (mixed) by Jack R. Censer in *Journal of Modern History*, 63 (1991), 390-91; in rev. article ("More Than Words: The Printing Press and the French Revolution") by Joan B. Landes in *Eighteenth-Century Studies*, 25 (1991), 85–98.

Darnton, Robert. "Die Verbotenen Bestseller im vorrevolutionären Frankreich." *Leipziger Jahrbuch zu Buchgeschichte*, 1 (1991), 53–116.

Darricau, Raymond. "La publication des *Inédits* de Montesquieu par la Société des Bibliophiles de Guyenne (1889–1914)." *Revue française d'histoire du livre*, 70–71 (1991), 31–56.

David, Jean-Claude. "De Voltaire à Marmontel: Quelques autographes du dix-huitième siècle réunis par Jacques Charavay (1809–1867)." *Studies on Voltaire and the Eighteenth Century*, 278 (1990), 215–43.

Davidson, Cathy N. (ed.). *Reading in America: Literature and Social History.* Baltimore, MD, and London: Johns Hopkins U. Press, 1989. Pp. viii + 307. Cf. *ECCB*, n.s. 16, I:11.

Rev. by P. Miles in *Analytical and Enumerative Bibliography*, 5 (1991), 37–40; (with another book) by Wayne A. Wiegand in *Libraries and Culture*, 26 (1991), 550–53.

Davies, Simon. "*Northern Star*: The United Irish Newspaper." *Studies on Voltaire and the Eighteenth Century*, 264 (1989), 665–69.

Davis, Gwenn, and Beverly A. Joyce (comps.). *Poetry by Women to 1900: A Bibliography of American and British Writers.* (Bibliographies of Writings by American and British Women to 1900, 2.) Buffalo, NY, and Toronto: U. of Toronto Press; London: Mansell, 1991. Pp. xxv + 340.

A bibliography of printed books, providing publication information and indicating source; most books were located through the British Library's catalogue and the *National Union Catalogue* with some entries supplemented by the OCLC.

Dawson, Robert L. "Books Printed in France: The English Connection." *Studies on Voltaire and the Eighteenth Century*, 292 (1991), 139–68.

Dawson, Robert L. "Prose Fiction: The Editions Dilemma." Pp. 217–35 in *Dilemmes du roman: Essays in Honor of Georges May*. (Stanford French and Italian Studies, 65.) Edited by Catherine LaFarge. Saratoga, CA: ANMA Libri, 1989; bibliography of French prose fiction.

Dawson, Robert L. "Theatre and Research in the Arsenal: The Rondel 'Inventaire.'" *Studies on Voltaire and the Eighteenth Century*, 260 (1989), 465–512.

An introduction to the recently filmed shelf-list for the Arsenal's collection, using the "Inventaire" as a guide.

Decker, Uwe. "*Die Deutsche Encyclopädie* (1778–1807)." *Das achtzehnte-Jahrhundert*, 14 (1990), 147–51.

De Grazia, Margreta. *Shakespeare Verbatim: The Reproduction of Authenticity and the 1790 Apparatus*. New York: Oxford U. Press; Oxford: Clarendon Press, 1991. Pp. xi + 244; illustrations; 8 plates.

Rev. (with another work) by Marcus Walsh in *Essays in Criticism*, 42 (1992), 243–51.
   Considers the standards of authenticity preceding and within late eighteenth-century editions of Shakespeare.

De Gregorio, Mario. "'Le bindolerie pazzine': L'*Editio princeps* delle *Tragedie* alfieriane e la tipografia Pazzini Carli." *Studi Settecenteschi*, 9 (1987), 59–92.

Deluna, D. N. "Cotton Mather Published Abroad." *Early American Literature*, 26 (1991), 145–72; appendices; 4 illustrations.

Mather published 14 works in London between 1689 and 1702. He was inattentive to the London publishing world, misunderstanding it and its importance and, therefore, missing opportunities.

De Montluzin, Emily Lorraine. "Attributions of Authorship in the *Gentleman's Magazine*, 1731–77: A Supplement to Kuist." *Studies in Bibliography*, 44 (1991), 271–302.

A chronological listing followed by a synopsis by contributor.

Denecke, Ludwig, and Irmgard Teitge (comps.). *Die Bibliothek der Brüder Grimm. Annotiertes Verzeichnis des festgestellten Bestandes*. Edited by Friedhilde Krause. Stuttgart: Hirzel, 1989. Pp. 652; illustrations.

Rev. by Hartmut Broszinski in *Zeitschrift für Bibliothekswesen und Bibliographie*, 38 (1991), 156–60.

Descargues, Madeleine. "Ignatius Sancho's Letters." *The Shandean*, 3 (1991), 145–66; descriptive bibliography of eight editions 1782–1802; folding plate; illustration.

Desgraves, Louis. "Naissance de la 'science' des bibliothèques." *Revue française d'histoire du livre*, 70–71 (1991), 3–30; illustrations.

Desgraves, Louis (comp.). *Répertoire bibliographique des livres imprimés en France au XVIIIᵉ siècle*. Vol. 1: *Agen, Albi, Angoulême, Auch, Bayonne, Bergerac, Cahors, Castres, Condom, Dax, Fontenay-le-Comte, Limoges, Luçon*. (Bibliotheca Bibliographica Aureliana, 112.) Baden-Baden and Bouxwiller: V. Koerner, 1988. Pp. 203; tables of printers and publishers precede each section on a city.

The Bibliotheca Bibliographica Aureliana catalogues are arranged alphabetically by author or, for anonymous works, by titles; basic format information is offered and at least one but often several locations are listed. Each bibliographer has evidently made some individual decisions about how to index the bibliographical catalogue and what analytical tables to offer.

Desgraves, Louis (comp.). *Répertoire bibliographique des livres imprimés en France au XVIIIe siècle*. Vol. 2: *Montauban, Périgueux, Rochefort-sur-Mer, Rodez, Saintes, Saint-Jean-d'Angély, Sarlat, Tarbes, Tulle, Villefranche-de-Rouergue*. (Bibliotheca Bibliographica Aureliana, 115.) Baden-Baden and Bouxwiller: V. Koerner, 1988. Pp. 135; tables of printers and publishers precede each section on a city.

Desgraves, Louis (comp.). *Répertoire bibliographique des livres imprimés en France au XVIIe siècle*. Vol. 4: *Bordeaux*. (Bibliotheca Bibliographica Aureliana, 110.) Baden-Baden and Bouxwiller: V. Koerner, 1988. Pp. 427; indices.

Rev. (with another volume in the series by Marie-Anne Merland) by Albert Labarre in *Bulletin du bibliophile* (1989), 184–86.

Desgraves, Louis (comp.). *Répertoire bibliographique des livres imprimés en France au XVIIIe siècle*. Vol. 4: *Bordeaux: Première partie 1701–1760*. (Bibliotheca Bibliographica Aureliana, 130.) Baden-Baden and Bouxwiller: V. Koerner, 1991. Pp. 309; table of printers and publishers.

Détis, Elisabeth. *"The Life and Strange Surprising Adventures of Robinson Crusoe, of York, Mariner:* A Selective Critical Bibliography." *Bulletin de la société d'études anglo-américaines*, 33 (1991), 7–33.

De Voogd, Peter Jan "Henry William Bunbury, Illustrator of *Tristram Shandy*." *The Shandean*, 3 (1991), 138–43; illustrations; plates (1 folding).

De Voogd, Peter Jan "Recent Trends in Eighteenth-Century Studies." *Dutch Quarterly Review of Anglo-American Letters*, 21 (1991), 71–81.

Review essay of recent studies and editions.

Dewitte, A. "Oriëntatie van de Lectuur te Brugge 1780: een veilingscataloog van Joseph de Busscher." *Biekorf*, 91 (1991), 360–62.

Didier, Béatrice, and Jacques Neefs (general eds.). *La fin de l'Ancien Régime: Sade, Rétif, Beaumarchais, Laclos*. (Manuscrits modernes: Manuscrits de la Révolution, 1.) Paris: Diffusion, CID; Saint-Denis: Presses Universitaires de Vincennes, 1991. Pp. 207; illustrations.

Diederichs, Rainer, and Hermann Schneider (eds.). *Bibliothekstaschenbuch schweiz — Guide des bibliothèques suisses*. Aarau, Switzerland, and Frankfurt am Main: Sauerländer, 1988. Pp. 158.

A directory organized by city; the index has such headings as "Voltaire" and "Theology."

Diehl, Katharine Smith. *Printers and Printing in the East Indies to 1850; 1: Batavia, 1600–1850*. New Rochelle, NY: Cararzas, 1991. Pp. 445; bibliography; indices.

Rev. by R. McKitterick in *TLS*, (October 4, 1991), 36.

Dion, Marie-Pierre. "L'histoire des bibliothèques nobiliaires françaises au siècle des Lumières." *Mélanges de la bibliothèque de la Sorbonne*, 10 (c. 1990), 123–38.

Dillon Bussi, A., A. M. Figliolia Manzini, M. D. Melani, I. G. Rao, L. Bigliazzi, and A. R. Fantoni (eds.). *Incunaboli ed edizioni rare. La collezione di Angelo Maria D'Elci: Catalogo*. Florence: Biblioteca Medicea Laurenziana, 1989. Pp. 256; illustrations.

Rev. by C. B. in *La Bibliofilia*, 92 (1990), 229–30.

Dix, Robin. "Akenside's *An Ode to the Right Honourable The Earl of Huntingdon* (1748): The Ordering of Editions." *The Book Collector*, 40 (1991), 433–34.

Dodsley, Robert. *The Correspondence of Robert Dodsley, 1733–1764*. (Cambridge Studies in Publishing and Printing History.) Edited by James E. Tierney. Cambridge and New York: Cambridge U. Press, 1988. Pp. xxxvii + 599; portrait. Cf. *ECCB*, n.s. 16, I:13; 15, I:5.

Rev. by Carla H. Hay in *Literary and Culture*, 26 (1991), 620–21; (favorably) by William S. Peterson in *The Papers of the Bibliographical Society of America*, 85 (1991), 89–90; by Betty Rizzo in *The Age of Johnson*,4 (1991), 387–403; by Serge Soupel in *Études anglaises*, 44 (1991), 221–22; by John Stephens in *British Journal for Eighteenth-Century Studies*, 14 (1991), 230–31; (favorably) by Simon Varey in *The Book Collector*, 40 (1991), 265–66.

Domergue, Lucienne. "La Prensa periódica y la censura en la segunda mitad del siglo XVIII." *Estudios de historia social*, 52–53 (1990), 141–50.

Domingos, Manuela D. "Colporteurs ou Livreiros? Acerca do comercio livreiro em Lisboa, 1727–1754." *Revista da Biblioteca Nacional*, (1991), 109–42.

Dondertman, Anne. "Anthony, 'Lilius,' and the *Nova-Scotia Calendar*." *Papers of the Bibliographical Society of Canada*, 29 (1991), 32–50; 3 illustrations.

Donnachie, Ian, and George Hewitt. *A Companion to Scottish History from the Reformation to the Present*. London: Batsford; New York: Facts on File, 1989. Pp. 245; genealogical tables; illustrations; maps; 18 plates.

Rev. by Christine E. King in *American Reference Books Annual*, 21 (1991), 213; (favorably yet with reservations) by K. L. Strohmeyer in *Choice* , 28 (1990), 74.

Donnelly, Judy. "January Hath 31 Days: Early Canadian Almanacs as Primary Research Materials." *Papers of the Bibliographical Society of Canada*, 29 (1991), 7–31; 8 plates.

Dooley, Brendan. "L'unificazione del mercato editoriale: I libri contabili del giornalista Apostolo Zeno." *Società e Storia*, 14 (1991), 579–620.

Dörrbecker, D. W. "Blake and his Circle: An Annotated Checklist of Recent Publications." *Blake: An Illustrated Quarterly*, 23 (1989/90), 120–65; 25 (1991), 4–59.

See also "Corrigenda to Previous Checklists, 1986–1988" in Vol. 23 (1989/90), 165.

Dotoli, Giovanni. *Letteratura per il popolo in Francia (1600–1750).* Preface by Marc Soriano. Fasano: Schena editore, 1991. Pp. 407; 96 illustrations.

Doyle, A. I. "John Cosin (1595–1672) as a Library Maker." *The Book Collector*, 40 (1991), 335–57; plates.

On the Episcopal Library founded by Cosin in 1669 while Bishop of Durham, later becoming part of Durham U. Library. See also David Pearson below on collections at Durham.

Duggan, Margaret M. *English Literature and Backgrounds, 1660–1700: A Selective Critical Guide.* (Garland Reference Library in the Humanities, 711.) 2 vols. New York: Garland, 1990. Pp. xxv + 1160; indices. Cf. *ECCB*, n.s. 16, I:13.

Rev. (with reservations) by James Edgar Stephenson in *American Reference Books Annual*, 22 (1991), 475–76.

Dünnhaupt, Gerhard. *Personalbibliographien zu den Drucken des Barock. Zweite, verbesserte und wesentlich vermehrte Auflage des 'Bibliographischen Handbuches der Barockliteratur.'* Part 1: *Abele bis Bohse* ["1990" but published 1991]. Part 2: *Breckling bis Francisci* ["1990" but published 1991]. Part 3: *Franck bis Kircher* [1991]. Part 4: *Klaj bis Postel* [1991]. Part 5: *Praetorius bis Spee* [1991]. (Hiersemanns Bibliographische Handbücher, 9, parts 1-5.) Stuttgart: Hiersemann, 1990-1991. Pp. xxxviii + 1–758; [*vi*] 759–1550; [*vi*] 1551–2350; [*vi*] 2351–3144; [*vi*] 3145–3937.

A monumental work listing the publications of seventeenth-century writers, some of whom also wrote in the eighteenth century.

Durner, Manfred. "Das Projekt eines *Wissenschafts-historischen Berichts* im Rahmen der historisch-kritischen Schelling-Ausgabe." *Editio*, 5 (1991), 158–62; abstract in English.

Duyfhuizen, Bernard. " 'That Which I Dare Not Name': Aphra Behn's 'The Willing Mistress'." *English Literary History*, 58 (1991), 63–82.

A good textual history provides the basis for critical remarks.

Edwards, Paul, and David Dabydeen (eds.) *Black Writers in Britain (1760–1890).* Edinburgh, Scotland: Edinburgh U. Press, 1991. Pp. xv + 239; bibliography.

Contains extracts and an unannotated select bibliography of texts and critical studies.

Egert, Ilonka. "Die *Berlinische Monatsschrift* (1783–1796) in der deutschen Spätaufklärung." *Zeitschrift für Geschichtswissenschaft*, 39 (1991), 130–52.

Egressi, Erna. "A Komáromi Mindenes Gyüjtemény (1789–1792) nyelvhasználata." *Limes*, 2 (1990), 20–33.

Ehresmann, Donald L. *Fine Arts: A Bibliographic Guide to Basic Reference Works, Histories, and Handbooks*. 3rd ed. Englewood, CO: Libraries Unlimited, 1990. Pp. xvii + 373.

Rev. (favorably) by Frank J. Anderson in *American Reference Books Annual*, 22 (1991), 402.

The Eighteenth Century Short Title Catalogue [CD-ROM Version, with Users Manual]. London: The British Library, 1991.

Eisen, Cliff. *New Mozart Documents: A Supplement to O. E. Deutsch's Documentary Biography*. Stanford, CA: Stanford U. Press, 1991. Pp. xvii + 192; bibliography; illustrations; musical examples; 8 plates.

Elyada, Ouzi. *Presse populaire et feuilles volantes de la Révolution à Paris, 1789–1792. Inventaire méthodique et critique*. Preface by Michel Vovelle. Paris: Société des études robespierristes, 1991. Pp. xii + 288; bibliography; illustrations.

Endrei, Walter. "Batthyany Tódor müszaki könyvtára" [The Technical Library of Tódor Batthyany]. *Magyar Könyvszemle*, 107 (1991), 141–45.

Enyedi, Sándor. "Bécsi levelek Aranka Györgyhöz." *Magyar Könyvszemle*, 107 (1991), 132–40.

Erdman, David V., with the assistance of Brian J. Dendle, Robert R. Mollenauer, Augustus Pallotta, and James S. Patty (eds.). *The Romantic Movement: A Selective and Critical Bibliography for 1989*. West Cornwall, CT: Locust Hill Press, 1990. Pp. xxxii + 526.

With divisions for English, French, German, Italian, and Spanish.

Erdman, David V., with the assistance of Brian J. Dendle, Robert R. Mollenauer, Augustus Pallotta, and James S. Patty (eds.). *The Romantic Movement: A Selective and Critical Bibliography for 1990*. West Cornwall, CT: Locust Hill Press, 1991. Pp. xxxii + 473.

Esposito, Enzo. *Libro e biblioteca. Manuale di bibliografia e biblioteconomia*. Ravenna: A. Longo, 1991. Pp. 296.

Essick, Robert N. "Blake in the Marketplace, 1988." *Blake: An Illustrated Quarterly*, 23 (1989), 4-19; illustrations.

Essick, Robert N. "Blake in the Marketplace, 1989, Including a Report on the Recently Discovered Blake-Varley Sketchbook." *Blake: An Illustrated Quarterly*, 24 (1990), 220–37; illustrations.

Essick, Robert N. "Blake in the Marketplace, 1990." *Blake: An Illustrated Quarterly*, 24 (1990/91), 116–40.

Essick, Robert N. *William Blake's Commercial Book Illustrations: A Catalogue and Study of the Plates Engraved by Blake after Designs by Other Artists*. New York: Oxford U. Press; Oxford: Clarendon Press, 1991. Pp. xiii + 138; illustrations; 150 plates.

Estermann, Monika, and Michael Knoche (eds.). *Von Göschen bis Rowohlt: Beiträge zur Geschichte des deutschen Verlagswesens: Festschrift für Heinz Sarkowski zum 65. Geburtstag.* (Beiträge zum Buch- und Bibliothekswesen, 30.) Wiesbaden: Harrassowitz, 1990. Pp. viii + 393; illustrations.

Fahy, Conor. "A Printers' Manual from Bodoni's Parma: The 'Istruzioni pratiche' of Zefirino Campanini (1789)." *Library*, 13 (1991), 97–114.

Fairman, Elizabeth R. *Pleasures and Pastimes* [Exhibition Catalogue]. New Haven, CT: Yale Center for British Art, 1990. Pp. 38; plates.

Feather, John (comp.). *An Index to Selected Bibliographical Journals (1971–1985).* (Oxford Bibliographical Society Occasional Publication, 23.) Oxford: Oxford Bibliographical Society, 1991. Pp. 134.

Rev. by William S. Peterson in *The Papers of the Bibliographical Society of America*, 85 (1991), 88.

Fehér, Katalin. "A *Mindenes Gyüjtemény* és a felvilágosodás Kori pedagógia Kérdései" (*Mindenes Gyujtemy* and the Educational Problems in the Age of the Enlightenment). *Magyar Könyvszemle*, 106 (1990), 134–37.

Fetherling, Douglas. *The Rise of the Canadian Newspaper.* Oxford and Toronto: Oxford U. Press, 1990. Pp. x + 130; illustrations.

Felice, Domenico. *Pour l'histoire de la fortune de Montesquieu en Italie (1789–1945).* Bologne: Thema Editore, 1990. Pp. 147.

Rev. by Roger Barny in *Dix-huitième siècle*, 23 (1991), 458.

Ferguson, Stephen. "The 1753 *Carte chronographique* of Jacques Barbea-Dubourg." *Princeton University Library Chronicle*, 51 (1991), 190–230.

An appendix contains Diderot's article on DuBourg's *Carte chronographique*.

Ferrieu, Xavier. "L'Imprimerie à Rennes au 17e siècle et au début du 18e siècle." Pp. 283–307 of *La Bretagne au 17e siècle. Actes du colloque de la Société d'étude du 17e siècle (Rennes, 1–4 octobre 1986).* Vannes: Conseil général du Morbihan, 1991.

Field, Clive D. "Anti-Methodist Publications in the Eighteenth Century: A Revised Bibliography." *Bulletin of the John Rylands University Library of Manchester*, 73 (Summer 1991), 105–18; indices.

Fielding, Henry. *The Covent-Garden Journal and A Plan of the Universal Register-Office.* Edited by Bertrand A. Goldgar. (The Wesleyan Edition of the Works of Henry Fielding.) Middletown, CT: Wesleyan U. Press; Oxford: Clarendon Press, 1988. Pp. lxiv + 517. Cf. *ECCB*, n.s. 15, VI:328–29; 14, VI:318.

Rev. by Michael Harris in *Publishing History*, 30 (1991), 93–97.

Fierro, Alfred (ed.). *Bibliographie critique des mémoires sur la Révolution écrits ou traduits en français.* Preface by Jean Tulard. Paris: Service des travaux historiques de la ville de Paris, 1988 [1989]. Pp. 482.

Rev. (with other books) by Klaus Schreiber in *Zeitschrift für Bibliothekswesen und Bibliographie*, 38 (1991), 174–76.
Bibliography of personal narratives from 1789–1799.

Fierro, Alfred (ed.). *Bibliographie de la Révolution française: 1940–1988.* (Bibliographiques historiques.) 2 vols. Paris: Références, 1989 [1990].

Fitch, Donald. *Blake Set to Music: A Bibliography of Musical Settings of the Poems and Prose of William Blake.* (U. of California Publications, Catalogs and Bibliographies, 5.) Berkeley, CA: U. of California Press, 1990. Pp. xxix + 281; illustrations.

Rev. (favorably) by William S. Brockman in *American Reference Books Annual*, 22 (1991), 505–06.

Fitzmaurice, James. "Margaret Cavendish on Her Own Writing: Evidence from Revision and Handmade Correction." *The Papers of the Bibliographical Society of America*, 85 (1991), 297–308; 2 plates.

Fix, Ulla. "Schriftstellar über Sprache: Sprach- und Kommunikationskultur oder: Mit dem Pfunde Wuchern." *Sprachpflege und Sprachkultur*, 39 (1990), 5–8.

Flouret, Jean (comp.). *Répertoire bibliographique des livres imprimés en France au XVIIIe siècle.* Vol. 3: *La Rochelle.* (Bibliotheca Bibliographica Aureliana, 119.) Baden-Baden and Bouxwiller: V. Koerner, 1988. Pp. 263; indices; table with printers and publishers.

Fogel, Michèle. *Les Cérémonies de l'information dans la France du XVIe au XVIIIe siècles.* Paris: Fayard, 1989. Pp. 498; illustrations.

Forster, Antonia. *Index to Book Reviews in England, 1749–1774.* Carbondale, IL: Southern Illinois U. Press, 1990. Pp. xii + 307 Cf. *ECCB*, n.s. 16, I:15.

Rev. (favorably) by Paula Backscheider in *Studies in English Literature 1500–1900*, 31 (1991), 578–79; (favorably) by Helen M. Barber in *American Reference Books Annual*, 22 (1991), 480; (favorably) by James K. Bracken in *Choice*, 28 (1991), 1096; (favorably) by James E. May in *The East-Central Intelligencer*, 5 (September, 1991), 17–19.

Foxon, David. *Pope and the Early Eighteenth-Century Book Trade. The Lyell Lectures in Bibliography 1975–1976.* Revised and edited by James McLaverty. Oxford: Clarendon Press, 1991. Pp. xvii + 270; illustrations; index; tables.

Rev. (favorably) by Mervyn Jannetta in *Library*, 13 (1991), 371–74; (favorably) by Pat Rogers in *TLS*, (April 26, 1991), 5–6.
Foxon's last Lyell lecture, treating other authors, has been excluded but is available at libraries holding a deposit copy of the original, as the Beinecke and the Bodleian libraries.

Franklin, Colin. *Shakespeare Domesticated: The Eighteenth-Century Editions.* Aldershot, UK: Scolar Press; Brookfield, VT: Gower, 1991. Pp. xiv + 246; illustrations; 16 plates.

Frasca, Ralph. "From Apprentice to Journeyman to Partner: Benjamin Franklin's Workers and the Growth of the Early American Printing Trade." *Pennsylvania Magazine of History and Biography*, 114 (1990), 229–48.

Freeman, Arthur. "Swift Reconsidered." *The Book Collector*, 40 (1991), 51–56.

A rejoinder to F. P. Lock's article in the same issue, conceding some inappropriate books listed in manuscript on a sale catalogue for Swift's library might not have been Swift's but insisting that the bulk of the books were Swift's; cf. Lock's article below and other articles by Freeman and by David Woolley in *ECCB*, n.s. 16, I:15–16, 47.

Friedman, Muriel Sanderow. "Selective Bibliography I. 1988–1990." *Restoration and Eighteenth-Century Theatre Research*, 6 (1991), 35–53.

Rev. (noting omissions and errors) in *The Scriblerian*, 24 (1991), 42.

Furbank, P. N. "Diderot and the *Histoire de Madame de Montbrillant*." *British Journal for Eighteenth-Century Studies*, 13 (1990), 157–61.

Galiani, Celestino. *Carteggio (1714–1729)*. Edited by Franco Palladino and Luisa Simonutti. Florence: Olschki, 1989. Pp. 301; illustrations.

Rev. by Franco Arato in *Giornale storico della letteratura*, 167 (1990), 448–49.

Garcia, Garrosa, María Jesús, and Germán Vega Garcia-Luengos. "Las traducciones del teatro francés (1700–1835): Más impresos españoles." *Cuadernos de estudios del Siglo XVIII*, 1 (1991), 85–104.

Gargurevich, Juan. *Historia de la prensa peruana, 1594–1990*. Lima: La Voz, 1991. Pp. 286; bibliography.

Garnier, Nicole, in collaboration with Marie Christine Bourjol-Couteron. *L'Imagerie populaire française*. Vol. 1: *Gravures en taille-douce et en taille d'épargne*. Paris: Réunion des Musées nationaux, 1990. Pp. 481; bibliography; illustrations; plates.

Rev. by Giles Barber in *The Book Collector*, 40 (1991), 438–440.

Gelbart, Nina Rattner. *Feminine and Opposition Journalism in Old Regime France*: Le Journal des Dames. Berkeley, CA, and London: U. of California Press, 1987. Pp. xviii + 353; bibliography; 6 facsimiles. Cf. *ECCB*, n.s. 15, V:208; 14, V:215.

Rev. by Patricia Clancy in *Revue d'histoire littéraire de la France*, 90 (1990), 255–56.

Gelderblom, Arie-Jan. "The Publisher of Hobbes's Dutch *Leviathan* [1667]." Pp. 163–66 of *Across the Narrow Seas: Studies in the History and Bibliography of Britain and the Low Countries: Presented to Anna E. C. Simoni*. London: British Library, 1991.

Gilbreath, James, and Douglas L. Wilson (eds.). *Thomas Jefferson's Library: A Catalog with the Entries in His Own Order*. Washington, DC: Library of Congress, 1989. Pp. vii + 149; illustrations; 2 plates.

Rev. by S. K. Jordan in *Library Quarterly*, 61 (1991), 99–100.

Gillies, W. "Gaelic Songs of the 'Forty-five'." *Scottish Studies*, 30 (1991), 19–58.

Gilmore, William J. *Reading Becomes a Necessity of Life: Material and Cultural Life in Rural New England, 1780–1835*. Knoxville, TN: U. of Tennessee Press, 1989. Pp. xxvii + 538; bibliography; illustrations. Cf. *ECCB*, n.s. 16, I: 16.

Rev. (with another book) by Wayne A. Wiegand in *Libraries and Culture*, 26 (1991), 550–53; (favorably) in rev. article ("New Questions and New Approaches in the Study of the 'History of the Book'") by David A. Rawson in *Eighteenth-Century Life*, 15 (1991), 103–12.

Ginzburg, Carlo. *Ecstasies: Deciphering the Witches' Sabbath*. Translated (from Italian) by Raymond Rosenthal. New York: Pantheon, 1991. Pp. 339; bibliography; illustrations.

First American translation of *Storia notturna: Una decifrazione del sabba* (Torino: G. Einaudi, c. 1989); Rosenthal's translation was published with the variant title *Ecstasies: The Witches' Sabbath in History* (London: Hutchinson Radius, 1990), with identical pagination.

Giudicelli, Marie-Anne. "Le *Journal de Louis XVI et de son peuple* ou le défenseur de l'autel, du trône et de la patrie: publication d'un contre révolutionnaire anonyme 1790–1792." *Annales historiques de la Révolution française*, 285 (1991), 299–324.

Glen, Duncan. *The Poetry of the Scots: An Introduction and Bibliographical Guide to Poetry in Gaelic, Scots, Latin, and English*. Edinburgh, Scotland: Edinburgh U. Press, 1991. Pp. xxi + 149; bibliography.

With a chapter devoted to eighteenth-century poets.

Goffin, André-Marie. "L'Inventaire d'une imprimerie-librairie namuroise en 1795: la séparation Stapleaux-Legros." *Archives et bibliothèques de Belgique*, 60 (1989), 97–108.

Górska, Barbara, and Wieslaw Tyszkowski. *Katalog starych druków Biblioteki Zakladu Narodowego im. Ossolinskich: polonica wieku XVII*. Vol. 1: A-C. Wroclaw: Ossolineum, 1991. Pp. 398; bibliography.

Gough, Hugh. *The Newspaper Press in the French Revolution*. Chicago, IL: Dorsey Press; London: Routledge, 1988. Pp. 264; bibliography. Cf. *ECCB*, n.s. 15, I:6.

Rev. by Jeremy Black in the *English Historical Review*, 106 (1991), 1023; by Matthias Middell in *Leipziger Jahrbuch zu Buchgeschichte*, 1 (1991), 335–37.

Goulemot, Jean Marie. *Ces Livres qu'on ne lit que d'une main. Lecture et lecteurs de livres pornographiques du XVIIIe siècle*. (Collection de la Pensee.) Aix-en-Provence: Alinéa, 1991. Pp. 173; bibliography; illustrations.

Rev. (in French) by Marie-France Silver in *Eighteenth-Century Fiction*, 4 (1992), 179–80.

Graf, Martina. "Johann Joachim Eschenburgs 'Grundriß einer Anleitung zur Bücherkunde' (1792). Ein frühes Dokument einer buchwissenschaftlichen Vorlesung an einer höheren Bildungsanstalt." *Gutenberg-Jahrbuch*, 65 (1990), 360–79.

Graham, T. W. "A List of Articles on Scottish History Published during the Year 1989"; and "A List of Articles on Scottish History Published during the Year 1990." *The Scottish Historical Review*, 69 (1990), 185–96; 70 (1991), 172–80.

With period subdivisions. This list is regularly followed by a six- or seven-page "List of Essays on Scottish History in Books Published during the Year," apparently compiled in part by A. Grant, to whom readers are to send contributions. That list of essays in books published during 1990 is in Vol. 70 on pp 81–87.

Grappin, Pierre, and Jean Moes. *Sçavantes délices: Périodiques souabes au siècle des Lumières*. Paris: Didier-Erudition, 1989. Pp. 346.

Rev. by Michel Espagne in *Dix-huitième siècle*, 23 (1991), 454–55.

Grave, Floyd K., and Margaret G. Grave. *Franz Joseph Haydn: A Guide to Research*. (Garland Composer Resource Manuals, 31.) New York: Garland Publishers, 1990. Pp. xi + 451; indices. Cf. *ECCB*, n.s. 16, IV:210.

Rev. (favorably) by A. Peter Brown in *Music and Letters*, 72 (1991), 595–97; (favorably) by Robert Skinner in *American Reference Books Annual*, 22 (1991), 513–14; (favorably) by R. L. Wick in *Choice*, 28 (1991), 789.

Gravesteijn, Cora, and John J. McCusker. *The Beginnings of Commercial and Financial Journalism: The Commodity Price Currents, Exchange Rate Currents, and Money Currents of Early Modern Europe*. (Nederlandsch Economisch-Historisch Archief, ser. 3, no. 11.) Amsterdam: NEHA, 1991. Pp. 515; bibliography [primary, 451-59; secondary, 460-501]; illustrations.

Greco, Luigi. "Un libraire italien à Paris: Gian Claudio Molini (1724–1812)." *Mélanges de la bibliothèque de la Sorbonne*, 10 [c. 1990], 103–129; illustrations.

Greenwood, Val D. *The Researcher's Guide to American Genealogy*. 2nd ed. Baltimore, MD: Genealogical Publishing, 1990. Pp. xiv + 609; bibliography; illustrations.

Rev. by David V. Loertscher in *American Reference Books Annual*, 22 (1991), 166; by Judith P. Reid in *Library Journal*, 115 (April 1, 1990), 106.

Grimshaw, Polly Swift. *Images of the Other: A Guide to Microform Manuscripts on Indian-White Relations*. Champaign, IL: U. of Illinois Press, 1991. Pp. xxi + 174.

Rev. (favorably) by Donna Seaman in *American Literature*, 22 (1991), 1054.
Lists English-language documents in 65 collections.

Grmek, Mirko D. "La Réception du *De Sedibus* de Morgagni en France au 18e siècle." *Dix-huitième siècle*, 23 (1991), 59–74.

Grote, Dagmar, Jochen Hoock, and Wolfgang Starke. "Handbücher und Traktate für den Gebrauch des Kaufmanns, 1470–1820." *Tijdschrift voor Geschiedenis*, 103 (1990), 280.

Groves, David. "Blake, *The Grave*, and Edinburgh Literary Society." *Blake: An Illustrated Quarterly*, 24 (1990), 251–52.

Gruys, J. A., and C. de Wolf. *"Thesaurus 1473–1800*: Addenda and Corrigenda." *Dokumentaal*, 20 (1991), 79–83.

Gruys, J. A., and C. de Wolf. *Thesaurus 1473–1800: Nederlandse boekdrukkers en boekverkopers. Mit plaatsen en jaren van werkzaamheid* [Dutch Printers and Bookseller. With place and year of their activity]. (Bibliotheca bibliographica Neerlandica, 28.) Nieuwkoop: B. de Graff, 1989. Pp. xxiii + 293; indices. Cf. *ECCB*, n.s. 16, I:17.

Rev. (unsigned) in *Quaerendo*, 21 (1991), 76–77; B. Dongelmans in *Tijdschrift voor Nederlandse taal- en letterkunde*, 107 (1991), 145–50.
This is a revision, extended to 1800 of Gruys and C. de Wolf's *Thesaurus: Typographi & bibliopolae Neerlandici usque ad annum MDCC* (Nieuwkoop: B. De Graaf, 1980, listing dates, places, and parentage of book trade members.

Guedes, Fernando. *O Livro e a leitura em Portugal: Subsídios para a sua história, séculos XVIII e XIX*. Rpt. 1987. Lisbon: Verbo, 1991. Pp. 308; bibliography; illustrations; 6 plates.

Guentner, Wendelin. "Interartistic Dialogues: The Illustrated French Travel Narrative." *Rivista di letterature moderne e comparate*, 43 (1990), 129–149; illustrations.

Guide to Microforms in Print: Incorporating International Microforms in Print. 2 vols. [1: author, title; 2: subject]. Munich: Saur, 1990. Pp. xxxiv + 695; xl + 1080.

Rev. (with *Microform Market-Place* [1991]) by I. Großmann in *Zeitschrift für Bibliothekswesen und Bibliographie*, 38 (1991), 170–72.

Hagen, Waltraud. "Textfehler oder Sachirrtum: Textkritische Entscheidungen im Verhältnis zu Textverständnis und Autorisation." *Editio*, 5 (1991), 76–81; abstract in English.

Four examples from Schiller's *History of the Thirty Years War* demonstrate difficulties when textual errors result in spelling of different but actual place names.

Hale, John K. "Paradise Purified: Dr. Bentley's Marginalia for his 1732 Edition of *Paradise Lost*." *Transactions of the Cambridge Bibliographical Society*, 10 (1991), 58–74; illustrations.

Hall, Charles J. (comp.). *An Eighteenth-Century Musical Chronicle: Events 1750–1799*. Westport, CT: Greenwood, 1990. Pp. 177. Cf. *ECCB*, n.s. 16, I:17.

Rev. by Allie Wise Goudy in *American Reference Books Annual*, 22 (1991), 508; by George R. Hill in *Notes: Quarterly Journal of the Music Library Association*, 48 (1991), 84–85.

Handler, Jerome S. *Supplement to 'A Guide to Source Material for the Study of Barbados History, 1627–1834.'* Providence, RI: John Carter Brown Library and The Barbados Museum and Historical Society, 1991. Pp. xxii + 89; illustrations; maps; 4 plates.

Hanley, William. "Voltaire, Newton, and the Law." *Library*, 13 (1991), 48–65.

Hardin, James, and Christoph E. Schweitzer (eds.). *German Writers from the Enlightenment to Sturm und Drang, 1720–64*. (Dictionary of Literary Biography, 97.) Detroit: Gale, 1990. Pp. x + 399; bibliography; illustrations.

Rev. (favorably) by J. H. Spohrer in *Choice*, 28 (1991), 913.

Hardin, James, and Christoph E. Schweitzer (eds.). *German Writers in the Age of Goethe*: Sturm und Drang *to Classicism*. (Dictionary of Literary Biography, 94.) Detroit: Gale, 1990. Pp. xiii + 413; bibliography; illustrations.

Hardin, James, and Christoph E. Schweitzer (eds.). *German Writers in the Age of Goethe, 1789–1832*. (Dictionary of Literary Biography, 90.) Detroit: Gale, 1990. Pp. xi + 435; illustrations.

Rev. by Valerie R. Hotchkiss in *American Reference Books Annual*, 22 (1991), 497.

Harmon, Maurice. "Anglo-Irish Literature: A Survey of General Works (1)." *Études Irlandaises*, 26 (1991), 19–26.

Harris, Eileen, assisted by Nicholas Savage. *British Architectural Books and Writers, 1556–1785*. Cambridge and New York: Cambridge U. Press, 1990. Pp. 571; illustrations. Cf. *ECCB*, n.s. 16, I:18.

Rev. (favorably) by F. Blum in *Choice*, 28 (1991), 756; by I. G. Brown in the *Journal of the Society of Archivists*, 12 (1991), 153–54; (favorably) by Rand Carter in *Eighteenth-Century Studies*, 26 (1992/93), 330–34; (favorably) by David Watkin in *TLS*, (Dec. 28, 1990–Jan. 3, 1991), 1396.

Harris, Michael, and Robin Myers (eds.). *Pioneers in Bibliography*. Winchester, Hampshire, U.K.: St. Paul's Bibliographies (distributed through New Castle, DE: Oak Knoll), 1988. Pp. 117.

Rev. by David Hunter in *Libraries and Culture*, 25 (1990), 609–10.

Harris, Michael, and Robin Myers (eds.). *Property of a Gentleman: The Formation, Organisation, and Dispersal of the Private Library (1620–1920)*. Winchester, Hampshire, U.K.: St. Paul's Bibliographies (distributed through New Castle, DE: Oak Knoll), 1991. Pp. xii + 164; illustrations; index.

Eight papers from the twelfth annual conference on book trade history at Birkbeck College. Those with special focus on the eighteenth century are Frank Herrmann's "The Emergence of the Book Auctioneer as a Professional" (pp. 1–14), on early practitioners like Thomas Ballard (active 1706–1734); Esther Potter's "To Paul's Churchyard to Treat with a Bookbinder" (pp. 25–41), on bookbinding options for book owners; Brian North Lee's "Gentlemen and their Book-Plates" (pp. 42–76; illustrations); David Stoker's "The Ill-Gotten Library of 'Honest Tom' Martin" (pp. 91–111), which the Norfolk lawyer built up in the 1750s and sold off in the 1760s; and Robin Myers' "William Herbert [1718–1795]: His Library and His Friends" (pp. 133–158), discussing such topics as the scope of Herbert's library, his auction purchases, his bookplates, annotations, arrangement, and dispersal, concluding with a good bibliography of printed and manuscript sources on Herbert (pp. 156–58).

Harvey, A. D. *Lord Grenville, 1759–1834: A Bibliography*. (Meckler's Bibliographies of British Statesmen, 2.) Westport, CT: Meckler, 1990. Pp. vi + 94; plate. Cf. *ECCB*, n.s. 16, I:18.

Rev. (favorably) by William B. Robison in *American Reference Books Annual*, 22 (1991), 30.

Harvey, A. D. "The Public Record Office in London as a Source for English Literary Studies." *Études anglaises*, 43 (1990), 303–16.

Stresses that the PRO holds literary texts in addition to biographical documents.

Hausmann, Franz Joseph (ed.). *Hausmanns Wörterbucher: Ein internationales Handbuch zur Lexikographie / Dictionaries / Dictionnaires*. (Handbücher zur Sprach- und Kommunikationswissenschaft, 5.) 2 vols. Berlin: Walter de Gruyter, 1989–1990. Pp. lii + 1056; xxiii, 1057 + 2337 [i.e. Vol. 2 paginated i-xxiii, 1057-2337].

Rev. (with other books) by Klaus Schreiber in *Zeitschrift für Bibliothekswesen und Bibliographie*, 38 (1991), 283–86.

Hawley, Judith. "'Hints and Documents' (1): A Bibliography of *Tristram Shandy*." *The Shandean*, 3 (1991), 9–36; checklist.

Heaney, Michael. "Recent Periodicals." *Library*, 13 (1991), 86–95.

Cites many articles on eighteenth-century bibliography, by title or at least topic, printed in Eastern Europe and the USSR.

Hebert, Catherine. "French Publications in Philadelphia in the Age of the French Revolution: A Bibliographical Essay." *Pennsylvania History*, 58 (1991), 35–61.

Hebig, Christel. "Winckelmann als Bibliothekar in Nothnitz bei Dresden." *Biblos*, 40 (1991), 51–66.

Heintze, James R. *American Music before 1865 in Print and on Records: A Biblio-Discography*. (I. S. A. M. Monographs, 30.) Rev. ed. Brooklyn, NY: Brooklyn Institute for Studies in American Music, Conservatory of Music, Brooklyn College of the City U. of New York, 1990. Pp. xii + 248.

Rev. (favorably) by John Druesedow in *Notes: Quarterly Journal of the Music Library Association*, 47 (1991), 770.

Heintze, James R. *Early American Music: A Research and Information Guide*. (Music Research and Information Guides, 13.) New York: Garland, 1990. Pp. xii + 511. Cf. *ECCB*, n.s. 16, I:19.

Rev. (with reservations) by William S. Brockman in *American Reference Books Annual*, 22 (1991), 506; (favorably) by Karl Kroeger in *RQ: Reference Quarterly*, 30 (1990), 289–90; (favorably) by Larry Lipkis in *Library Journal*, 115 (May 15, 1990), 70; 72; (favorably) by L. Smith in *Choice*, 28 (1991), 1290.

Hench, John B. (ed.). *Three Hundred Years of the American Newspaper*. Worcester, MA: American Antiquarian Society, 1991. Pp. 100; illustrations.

Reprinted from *Proceedings of the American Antiquarian Society*, 100 (1990), 363–463; several of the six articles providing a history of the American newspaper concern the eighteenth century.

Hennings, Herzeleide, and Eckart Hennings (comps.). *Bibliographie Friedrich der Grosse 1786–1986. Das Schrifttum des deutschen Sprachraums und der Übersetzungen aus Fremdsprachen.* Berlin: Walter de Gruyter, 1988. Pp. xix + 511.

Rev. by Dominique Bourel in *Dix-huitième siècle*, 23 (1991), 453.

Herdemann, Frank. *Montesquieu in Deutschland im 18. und beginnenden 19. Jahrhundert.* Hildesheim: Olms, 1990. Pp. 313.

Rev. by Dominique Bourel in *Dix-huitième siècle*, 23 (1991), 458–59.

Hesse, Carla. *Publishing and Cultural Politics in Revolutionary Paris, 1789–1810.* (Studies on the History of Society and Culture, 12.) Berkeley, CA: U. of California Press, 1991. Pp. xvi +296; bibliography; illustrations; maps.

Hill, F. J. "The Shelving and Classification of Printed Books." Pp. 1–74 of *The Library of the British Museum: Retrospective Essays on the Department of Printed Books.* Edited by P. R. Harris. London: British Library, 1991. Pp. xiii + 305; appendices; illustrations.

A revision of a 1954 thesis that has long been a staff tool for understanding the original cataloguing system of British Library books; with a good account of the formation of the British Library and the organization of its earliest collections.

Hillyard, Brian. "William Ged and the Invention of Stereotype: Another Postscript." *Library*, 13 (1991), 156–57.

Hillyard, Brian, and David Fate Norton. "The David Hume Bookplate: A Cautionary Note." *The Book Collector*, 40 (1991), 539–44; illustration.

Hillyer, Richard. "Some Current Publications." *Restoration*, 15 (1991), 111–37.

Hines, W. D. *English Legal History: A Bibliography and Guide to the Literature.* (Garland Reference Library of the Humanities, 1011.) New York: Garland Publishing, 1990. Pp. 201.

Rev. by R. Fritze in *Choice*, 28 (1991), 1098; (favorably) by Nigel Tappin in *American Reference Books Annual*, 22 (1991), 225.

Hinrichs, Wiard, and Ulrich Joost (comps.). *Lichtenbergs Bücherwelt. Ein Bücherfreund und Benutzer der Göttinger Bibliothek: Katalog der Ausstellung im Foyer der Niedersächsischen Staats- und Universitätsbibliothek anläßlich der Jahrestagung der Lichtenberg-Gesellschaft 1989.* (Lichtenberg-Studien, 3.) Göttingen: Wallstein, 1989. Pp. 109; illustrations.

Rev. in *Philobiblon*, 34 (1990), 73; in *Das achtzehnte Jahrhundert*, 14 (1990), 302.

Hoare, Peter. "The Librarians of Glasgow University over 350 Years: 1641–1991." *Library Review*, 40 (1991), 27–43.

Hoftijzer, P. G. "Business and Pleasure: A Leiden Bookseller in England in 1772 [Johannes Luchtmans, 1726–1809]." Pp. 178–87 [1 plate] of *Across the Narrow Seas: Studies in the History and Bibliography of Britain and the Low Countries: Presented to Anna E. C. Simoni*. London: British Library, 1991.

Hoftijzer, P. G. *Engelse boekverkopers bij de beurs; de geschiedenis van de Amstedamse boekhandels Bruyning en Swart, 1637–1724*. Amsterdam and Maarsen: APA Holland U. Press, 1987. Pp. xxi + 398; bibliography; illustrations; 14 plates. Cf. *ECCB*, n.s. 16, I:20.

Rev. (favorably) by Theo Bogels in *English Studies*, 71 (1990), 171–72; by Kees Gnirrep in *Quaerendo*, 21 (1991), 315–20.

Höpker-Herberg, Elisabeth. "*Paradise Lost* und [Klopstock's] *Messias*." Pp. 44-52 of *Edition als Wissenschaft: Festschrift für Hans Zeller*. Edited by Gunter Martens and Winfried Woesler. (Beihefte zu Editio, 2.) Tübingen: Niemeyer, 1991. Pp. 149; illustrations.

Horowitz, Lois. *A Bibliography of Military Name Lists from Pre-1675 to 1900: A Guide to Genealogical Research*. London and Metuchen, NJ: Scarecrow Press, 1990. Pp. xxxvii + 1080.

Rev. (with reservations but favorably) by Donald E. Collins in *American Reference Books Annual*, 22 (1991), 164–65; by James Rettig in *Wilson Library Bulletin*, 65 (1990), 147; by Sandy Whiteley in *Booklist*, 87 (January 15, 1991), 1082.

Houston, R. A. *Literacy in Early Modern Europe: Culture and Education (1500–1800)*. New York: Longman, 1988. Pp. ix + 266; bibliography.

Rev. by L. W. B. Brockliss in *British Journal for Eighteenth-Century Studies*, 14 (1991), 79–80; J. A. Sharpe in *History: The Journal of the Historical Association*, 75 (1990), 483–84.

Houston, R. A. *Scottish Literacy and the Scottish Identity: Illiteracy and Society in Scotland and Northern England, 1600–1800*. Cambridge and New York: Cambridge U. Press, 1985. Pp. x + 325.

Rev. by Harvey J. Graff in *American Historical Review*, 92 (1987), 674–75; (favorably) in rev. article ("New Questions and New Approaches in the Study of the 'History of the Book'") by David A. Rawson in *ECLife*, 15 (1991), 103–12.

Hudi, József. "A Veszprém Megyei Sajtó Kezdetei (1788–1847)." *Limes*, 2 (1990), 77–90; illustrations.

Hughes, Gillian H. (ed.). *Hogg's Verse and Drama: A Chronological Listing*. Stirling: James Hogg Society, 1990. Pp. 40.

Rev. by Robin MacLachlan in *The Scottish Literary Journal*, Supplement 33 (1990), 111–14.

Humphrey, Carol Sue. *'This popular engine': New England Newspapers during the American Revolution, 1775–1789*. Newark, DE: Delaware U. Press (distributed through Cranbury, NJ: Associated University Presses), 1991. Pp. 204; illustrations.

Huneke, Friedrich. *Die* Lippischen Intelligenzblätter *(Lemgo 1767–1799): Lectüre und gesellschaftliche Erfahrung*. (Forum Lemgo, 4.) Forward by Neithard Bulst. Bielefeld: Forum Lemgo, 1989. Pp. 240; appendices; illustrations.

Hunter, David. "The Publishing of Opera and Song Books in England, 1703–1726." *Notes: Quarterly Journal of the Music Library Association*, 47 (1991), 647–85.

Rev. by François Moureau in *Dix-huitième siècle*, 23 (1991), 455.

Hutchison, Ross. *Locke in France (1688–1734)*. (Studies on Voltaire and the Eighteenth Century, 290.) Oxford: The Voltaire Foundation at the Taylor Institution, 1991. Pp. ix + 251; bibliography.

Iamartino, Giovanni. "The Lexicographer as a Biassed Witness: Social, Political, and Religious Criticism in Baretti's English-Italian Dictionary." *Aevum*, 64 (1990), 435–44.

IASAIL Bibliographical Committee [1988–1989, Maureen Murphy, Chair; 1990–91, William T. O'Malley, chair]. "IASAIL Bibliography Bulletin for 1988." *Irish University Review*, 19 (1989), 314–67; [for 1989] 20 (1990), 321–74; [for 1990] 21 (1991), 307–66.

Impressions Rèvolutionnaires de la Bibliothèque municipale de Pau: Fonds Casenave. Pau: Ville de Pau, 1989. Pp. 276; indices.

Index of English Literary Manuscripts. Vol. III: *1700–1800*. Pt. II: *John Gay-Ambrose Phillips*. Compiled by Margaret N. Smith. London: Mansell (distributed through Rutherford, NJ: Publishers Distribution Center), 1989. Pp. xix + 325; 14 plates.

Rev. (favorably) by Philip R. Rider in *American Reference Books Annual*, 22 (1991), 1189.

Infelise, Mario. *L'Editoria veneziana nel '700*. (Saggi di storia, 6.) Milan: Franco Angeli, 1989. Pp. 421.

Rev. (unsigned) in *La Bibliofilia*, 93 (1991), 209–10.
A second edition by the same publisher and with identical pagination appears in 1991.

Ioppolo, Grace. *Revising Shakespeare*. Cambridge, MA: Harvard U. Press, 1991. Pp. x + 247; bibliography; facsimiles; illustrations.

Rev. by Margaret K. Powell in *Library Journal*, 116 (Nov. 1, 1991), 98.

"Irish Literature in English: The Year's Work." *Études Irlandaises*, 26 (1991), 170–207.

Isaac, Peter (ed.). *Bewick and After: Wood-Engraving in the Northeast*. Newcastle-upon-Tyne: Allenholme Press for the History of the Book Trade in the North, 1990. Pp. [xii] + 144; illustrations.

Rev. (favorably with another book edited by Isaac) by R. J. Goulden in *Library*, 13 (1991), 374–78.
A gathered reprinting of essays on wood-engraving in the northeast, containing Margaret Gill's "The Beilby and Bewick Workshop" and Susan Doncaster's "Some Notes on Bewick's Trade Blocks."

Isaac, Peter (ed.). *Six Centuries of the Provincial Book Trade in Britain*. Forward by J. Michael Smethurst. Winchester, Hampshire, UK: St. Paul's Bibliographies, 1990. Pp. xii + 212; illustrations.

Nearly all of these papers–presented at the Eighth Seminar on the British Book Trade, Durham, July 1990–concern the eighteenth-century: F. W. Ratcliffe's "The Contribution of Book-Trade Studies to Scholarship" (1–11); David Pearson's "Cambridge Bindings in Cosin's Library, Durham" (41–60, with two pages of plates and an appended checklist with shelf numbers of bindings from the workshop of Daniel Boyse); Jeremy Black's " 'Calculated upon a Very Extensive and Useful Plan': The English Provincial Press in the Eighteenth Century" (61–72); Ian Maxted's "Mobility and Innovation in the Book Trades: Some Devon Examples" (73–85); P. J. Wallis's "Cross-Regional Connexions" (87–100 [a report of studies using subscription lists and other evidence to qualify the usual assumption that books overwhelmingly moved from London to the provinces]); Eiluned Rees's "The Welsh Printing House from 1718 to 1818" (101–24); Wesley McCann's "Patrick Neill and the Origins of Belfast Printing" (125–38); Vincent Kinane and Charles Benson's "Some Late 18th- and Early 19th-Century Dublin Printers' Account Books: The Graisberry Ledgers" (139–50; with Vincent Kinane's discussion of "Daniel Graisberry's Ledger 1777–1785" on 139–43, and Charles Benson's of "Graisberry and Campbell's Account Books [one a print house ledger of 1797–1806; one a cash book for 1799]" on 143–48); Michael Perkin's "Hampshire Notices of Printing Presses, 1799–1867" (151–64, with a checklist of those notices on 160–63); Adam McNaughtan's "A Century of Saltmarket Literature, 1790–1890" (165–80, with checklist of histories published c. 1840 on 178–80); Brian Hillyard's "Working toward a History of Scottish Book Collecting" (181–86); and J. C. Day and W. M. Watson's "History of the Book Trade in the North: The First Twenty-Five Years" (187–97, with a checklist of publications by the HBTN Project on 193–97).

Isaac, Peter. *William Davison's New Specimen of Cast-Metal Ornaments and Wood-Types: Introduced with an Account of His Activities as Pharmacist and Printer in Alnwick (1780–1858)*. London: Printing History Society, 1990. Pp. 39; illustrations.

Israel, Jonathan I. "Propaganda in the Making of the Glorious Revolution." Pp. 167–77 of *Across the Narrow Seas: Studies in the History and Bibliography of Britain and the Low Countries: Presented to Anna E. C. Simoni*. Edited by S. Roach. London: British Library, 1991. Illustrations.

On the simultaneous English and Dutch publication of William III's declaration of kingship.

Jackson, Mary V. *Engines of Instruction, Mischief, and Magic: Children's Literature in England from its Beginnings to 1839*. Lincoln, NE: U. of Nebraska Press, 1989. Pp. xiv + 318; illustrations.

Rev. by Karen Harris in *School Library Journal*, 36 (1990), 30–31; (favorably) by Betsy Hearne in *The Library Quarterly*, 60 (1990), 360–61; (mixed) by Peter Hunt in *British Journal for Eighteenth-Century Studies*, 14 (1991), 205; (mixed) by Andrea Immel in *The Book Collector*, 40 (1991), 267–68; (favorably) by Barbara Scotto in *Wilson Library Bulletin*, 64 (1990), 158; by C. John Sommerville in *Albion*, 23 (1991), 314–15.

Jager, Patrick, and Marie-Françoise Luna. "L'Iconographie gravée de l'écrivain sous la Révolution." Pp. 315–26 of *L'Écrivain devant la Révolution: 1780–1800, actes du colloque franco-italien de Grenoble, 24–26 septembre 1987*. Edited by Jean Sgard. Grenoble: U. Stendhal, 1990.

Jain, Nalini. "Johnson's *Irene: The First Draft*." *British Journal for Eighteenth-Century Studies*, 13 (1990), 163–68.

Jannsen, Frans A. "Ploos van Amstel's Description of Type Founding [1767–68]." *Quaerendo*, 20 (1990), 96–110.

Janosik, Robert J. *The American Constitution: An Annotated Bibliography*. (Magill Bibliographies.) Englewood Cliffs, NJ, and Pasadena, CA: Salem Press, 1991. Pp. xi + 254.

Rev. (favorably) by R. V. Labaree in *Choice*, 29 (1991), 575.

Janssens-Knorsch, Uta. "Commerce or Culture? The Fate of the First Circulating Library in the Netherlands." *Documentatieblad Werkgroep achttiende eeuw*, 23 (1991), 151–73; illustrations.

Jaugin, Elisabeth. "Les *Mélanges tirés d'une grande bibliothèque*: une collection du XVIIIᵉ siècle injustement méconnue?" *Bulletin du bibliophile* (1991), 380–403; abstract in English; 1 plate.

Jeannin, Pierre. "Les manuels de pratique commerciale imprimés pour les marchands français (XVIᵉ–XVIIIᵉ siècle)." Pp. 35–57 [5 maps] of *Le Négoce international, XIIIᵉ–XXᵉ siècle*. Edited by François M. Crouzet. Paris: Economica, 1989.

Jestin, Loftus. *The Answer to the Lyre: Richard Bentley's Illustrations for Thomas Grey's Poems*. Philadelphia, PA: U. of Pennsylvania Press, 1990. Pp. ix + 355; 48 facsimiles; illustrations; 118 plates.

Rev. (favorably) by Alan T. McKenzie in *The Scriblerian*, 23 (1990/91), 290–91.

Jimack, Peter. "Some Eighteenth-Century Imitations of Rousseau's *Emile*." *Studies on Voltaire and the Eighteenth Century*, 284 (1991), 83–105.

Johns, Adrian. "History, Science, and the History of the Book: The Making of Natural Philosophy in Early Modern England." *Publishing History*, 30 (1991), 5–30.

Johnstone, H. Diack, and Roger Fiske (eds.). *The Eighteenth Century*. (Blackwell History of Music in Britain, 4.) Oxford and Cambridge, MA: Blackwell Reference, 1991. Pp. 534; bibliography.

Rev. (favorably) by W. Metcalfe in *Choice*, 29 (1991), 114, noting an important 47-page bibliography aiding researchers in eighteenth-century English music.

Jolly, Claude. "La Bibliothèque de la Sorbonne de 1762 à 1987." *Mélanges de la bibliothèque de la Sorbonne*, 10 (n.d. [c. 1990]), 152–77.

Jolly, Claude. "Le Fonds imprimé de la bibliothèque des lycées de Paris au début du XIXᵉ siècle." *Mélanges de la bibliothèque de la Sorbonne*, 11 (1991), 59–79.

Jolly, Claude. [Introduction to] "Nouveau supplément au catalogue des manuscrits de la Bibliothèque de la Sorbonne." *Mélanges de la bibliothèque de la Sorbonne*, 11 (1991), 183–86.

Jolly, David C. (comp.). *Maps in British Periodicals*. Part I: *Major Monthlies before 1800*.
  Brookline, MA: David C. Jolly, 1990. Pp. 256; frontispiece; indices.

Rev. by Ronald H. Fritze in *American Reference Books Annual*, 22 (1991), 179.

Joost, Ulrich. "Überlegungen zu einer Historisch-kritischen, kommentierten Gesamtausgabe der
  Werke von Georg Christoph Lichtenberg." *Editio*, 4 (1990), 133–147; abstract in English.

Joost, noting a critical edition of Lichtenberg's works is long overdue, reviews earlier editions and other sources and
proposes a new edition requiring 12,000 pages in 16 volumes and some of the organizational effort needed to
complete it.

Joyce, William L. (ed.). *Archives Accessions Annual* (1988). Westport, CT: Meckler, 1990. Pp.
  129.

Rev. (with serious reservations) by Richard Cox in *American Reference Books Annual*, 22 (1991), 13.

Kaltwasser, Franz George. "Sammlung deutscher Drucke 1450–1945: Ein kooperatives
  Erwerbungsprogramm." *Zeitschrift für Bibliothekswesen und Bibliographie*, 37 (1991),
  115–28.

Kamber, Peter. "Enlightenment, Revolution, and the Libraries in Lucerne, 1787–1812." *Libraries
  and Culture*, 26 (1991), 199–218.

With a study of literacy noting close to 40% of Lucerne was illiterate and only 25% were fluent at reading and
writing.

Kamuf, Peggy. *Signature Pieces: On the Institution of Authorship*. Ithaca, NY: Cornell U.
  Press, 1988. Pp. xi + 237; bibliography.

Rev. by James F. Jones, Jr. in *Eighteenth-Century Studies*, 24 (1991), 373–75; by Stephen Adam Schwartz in
Modern Language Notes, 104 (1989), 936–39.

Kantha, Sachi Sri (comp.). *Prostitutes in Medical Literature: An Annotated Bibliography*.
  (Bibliographies and Indexes in Medical Studies, 6.) Westport, CT: Greenwood Press, 1991.
  Pp. xi + 245; indices.

Rev. by N. Kupferberg in *Choice*, 29 (1991), 575.

Keeling, Denis F. (ed.). *British Library History: Bibliography (1985–1988)*. Comp. by Audrey
  H. Brodie, et al. [others in the Library History Group of the Library Association].
  Winchester, Hampshire, U.K.: St. Paul's Bibliographies (Distributed in North America by
  New Castle, DE: Oak Knoll Press), 1991. Pp. x + 181.

With 698 entries in a sixth issue to a series begun in 1962.

Killen, John. *A History of the Linen Hall Library, 1788–1988*. Belfast: Linen Hall Library,
  1990. Pp. x + 261; illustrations.

Rev. (favorably) by Peter F. McNally in *Libraries and Culture*, 28 (1993), 349–51.

Kinane, Vincent. "*Les Liaisons dangereuses*: An Unrecorded Dublin Edition of 1784 and Its Counterfeit 'Geneva' Issue." *Eighteenth-Century Ireland*, 6 (1991), 159–60.

Kirkpatrick, D. L. (gen. ed.). *Reference Guide to English Literature*. 3 vols. 2nd ed. Chicago and London: St. James Press, 1991. Pp. xl + 677; xx + 679–1442; xviii + 1443–2143.

Rev. by Robert E. Brown in *Library Journal*, 116 (Nov. 15, 1991), 75–76.

Begins with a 150-page overview of periods and traditions, with Pat Rodgers on "Restoration and Eighteenth-Century Prose and Poetry" (46–57) and Arthur Scouten on "Restoration and Eighteenth-Century Drama" (58–66); then devotes most of Vol. 1 and Vol. 2 to an alphabetical survey of authors and Vol. 3 to another of individual works and topics, as Dryden's *Absolom and Achitophel* and Edward Young's *Night Thoughts*. These short articles are signed by contributors. All three volumes repeat an alphabetized list and a chronological list of writers survey.

Kirsop, Wallace. "Vers une histoire de la diffusion et de la lecture des ouvrages encyclopédiques du 18e siècle: quelques notes de bibliographie matérielle." Pp. 335–46 of *L'Encyclopedisme: actes du colloque de Caen, 12–16 janvier 1987*. Paris: Aux amateurs de livres, 1991.

Klancher, Jon P. *The Making of English Reading Audiences, 1790–1832*. Madison. WI: U. of Wisconsin Press, 1987. Pp. xi + 210; bibliography.

Rev. (favorably) by Paul Hamilton in *Notes and Queries*, 238 (1989), 403–04; by James Raven in *Review of English Studies*, 40 (1989), 125–26; in rev. article ("New Questions and New Approaches in the Study of the 'History of the Book'") by David A. Rawson in *ECLife*, 15 (1991), 103–12; (favorably) by John Stevenson in *English Historical Review*, 105 (1990), 496.

Klapp-Lehrmann, Astrid (comp. and ed.). *Bibliographie der Französischen Literaturwissenschaft*. Vol. 28: *1990*. Frankfurt am Main: V. Klostermann, 1991. Pp. 822; indices.

With period divisions for seventeenth- and eighteenth-century studies, and a general section with such headings as "Le livre et les bibliothèques"; reviews are offered for some works entered.

Kleinert, Annemarie. "L'histoire du *Journal de Berlin* (1740–1741), magazine politique et culturel." *Studies on Voltaire and the Eighteenth Century*, 284 (1991), 225–33.

Knopf, Sabine. "Der 'Verleger der Philanthropen.'" *Aus dem Antiquariat* (1991), A85–A87; illustrations.

Kókay, György. "A *Mindenes Gyüjtemy* Megjelenésének Körülményei és jellege." *Limes*, 2 (1990), 11–19.

Koppitz, Hans-Joachim: "Die Privilegierung von Klopstocks *Messias*–Ausgaben von 1780 (1781) durch Kaiser Joseph II. Für Werner Keller zum 60. Geburtstag am 16. Januar 1990." *Gutenberg-Jahrbuch*, 65 (1990), 205–12.

Korsten, F. J. M. "The Religious Controversy under James II: A Collection of Tracts and Pamphlets at Nijmegen University Library." *Lias*, 16 (1989), 61–79.

Besides surveying the controversy, Korsten describes the Nijmegen collection, listing its tracts and pamphlets.

Kosenina, Alexander. "Johann Jakob Engel (1741–1802): Bibliographie sèiner Werke und Briefe, zeitgenössischer Rezensionen und der Sekundärliteratur." *Das achtzehnte Jahrhundert*, 14 (1990), 79–121.

Kren, Claudia (comp.). *Alchemy in Europe: A Guide to Research*. (Garland Reference Library of the Humanities, 692.) London and New York: Garland Publishing, 1990. Pp. xiii + 130.

Rev. (favorably) by H. Lowood in *Choice*, 28 (1991), 1100; (favorably) by Marilyn Stark in *American Reference Books Annual*, 22 (1991), 706.
Entries 489–520 concern "Alchemy and Newton."

Kreutz, Jörg. "Aspekte des kurpfälzischen Verlags- und Pressewesens im 18. Jahrhundert: Eine Bilanz der Forschung." *Leipziger Jahrbuch zur Buchgeschichte*, 1 (1991), 229–40.

Krivatsy, Peter (comp.). *A Catalogue of Seventeenth-Century Printed Books in the National Library of Medicine*. Washington, D.C.: National Library of Medicine, 1989. Pp. xiv + 1315; bibliography.

Rev. (favorably) by Mordechai Feingold in *Isis*, 82 (1991), 180; by C. Webster in *Annals of Science*, 48 (1991), 193.

Kroeger, Karl (comp.). *Catalog of the Musical Works of William Billings*. (Music Reference Collection, 32.) Westport, CT: Greenwood Press, 1991. Pp. xx + 160; indices.

Kronick, David A. "Peer Review in 18th-Century Scientific Journals." *Journal of the American Medical Association*, 263 (March 9, 1990), 1321–22.

Kronick, David A. *Scientific and Technical Periodicals of the Seventeenth and Eighteenth Centuries: A Guide*. Metuchen, NJ: Scarecrow Press, 1991. Pp. xix + 332; bibliography; indices.

Kubów, Stefan. "Publications on the History of Books and Libraries in Poland, 1981–1988." *Libraries and Culture*, 25 (1990), 48–72.

Kuist, James M. "A Collaboration in Learning: *The Gentleman's Magazine* and Its Ingenious Contributors." *Studies in Bibliography*, 44 (1991), 302–17.

Kurscheidt, Georg, and Norbert Oellers. "Zum Verständnis poetischer Texte aus Varianten: Goethes und Schillers 'Tabulae votivae' und 'Xenien'." *Editio*, 4 (1990), 160–82; abstract in French.

Discusses the critical value of variant readings, too often overlooked, using examples from the two works of Schiller and Goethe.

Kwasitsu, Lishi. "Caribbean Publishing, 1711–1900: A Preliminary Subject Analysis." *Scholarly Publishing*, 22 (1991), 231–40.

Kwiatkowska, Magdalena. "Z dziejów biblioteki szkoly pijarskiej w Piotrkowie Trybunalskim, 1675-1833 (1864)." *Acta Universitatis Lodziensis: Folia Librorum*, 2 (1991), 75–96.

Labarre, Albert (comp.). *Répertoire bibliographique des livres imprimés en France au XVIIe siècle*. Vol. 15: *Artois, Flandre, Picardie: Abbeviulle, Aire-sur-la-Lys, Amiens, Arras, Beauvais, Bergues, Béthune, Bonnefontaine en l'hiérache, Boulogne-sur-Mer, Calais, Cambrai, Compiègne, Dunkerque, Laon, Maubeuge, Noyon, Saint-Quentin, Senlis, Soissons, Valenciennes; Douai (supplément)*. (Bibliotheca Bibliographica Aureliana, 111.) Baden-Baden and Bouxwiller: V. Koerner, 1987. Pp. 297; indices.

Laborde, Alice M. *La Bibliothèque du marquis de Sade au château de La Coste (en 1776)*. Geneva: Slatkine, 1991. Pp. 153; bibliography.

Labrosse, Claude. "Le Temps immédiat dans la presse parisienne de 1789." Pp. 109–20 in *L'Espace et le temps reconstruits: La Révolution française, une révolution des mentalités et des cultures?* Edited by Philippe Joutard. Aix-en-Provence: Université de Provence, 1990.

Labrosse, Claude, and Pierre Rétat. *Naissance du journal révolutionnaire, 1789*. (Librairie du bicentenaire de la Revolution Française.) Lyon: Presses U. de Lyon, 1989. Pp. 320; bibliography; illustrations.

Rev. in rev. article ("More Than Words: The Printing Press and the French Revolution") by Joan B. Landes in *Eighteenth-Century Studies*, 25 (1991), 85–98.

Laffitte, Marie-Pierre. "La Bibliothèque nationale et les 'conquêtes artistiques' de la Révolution et de l'Empire: les manuscrits d'Italie (1796–1815)." *Bulletin du bibliophile*, (1989), 273–323.

Lagrave, Jean-Paul de. "Fleury Mesplet: l'imprimeur des libertés." *Cap-Aux-Diamants*, 27 (1991), 30–33.

Laguna Platero, Antonio. "El Periodismo espagñol del siglo XVIII: Qué periodismo? El Caso del diario de Valencia." *Estudios de historia social*, 52–53 (1990), 283–94.

Lamonde, Yvan. *La Librairie et l'édition à Montréal, 1776–1920*. Montreal: Bibliothèque Nationale du Quebec, 1991. Pp. 198; bibliography; illustrations.

Landes, Joan B. "Review Essay: More than Words: The Printing Press and the French Revolution." *Eighteenth-Century Studies*, 25 (1991), 85–98.

Landwehr, John (comp.). *VOC [Verenigde Oostindische Compagnie] : A Bibliography of Publications Relating to the Dutch East India Company, 1602–1800*. Edited by Peter van der Kroght. Introduction by C. R. Boxer. Utrecht: HES Publishers, 1991. Pp. xlii + 840; illustrations; 16 plates (some colored).

Laserre, Paule. "Un Journal du 18e siècle: les Affiches de Lyon." *Rive gauche*, 119 (1991), 12–16.

Lause, Mark A. *Some Degree of Power: From Hired Hand to Union Craftsman in the Preindustrial American Printing Trade, 1778–1815*. Fayetteville, AR: U. of Arkansas Press, 1991. Pp. x + 261; appendices; bibliographic essay; illustrations; tables.

Lebédel, Claude. "Frédéric II de Prusse et les livres." *Bulletin du bibliophile*, (1989), 102–118.

Lee, Anthony W. "New Books and Articles on the Restoration and Eighteenth Century."
Johnsonian News Letter, 50–51 (1990/91), 45-59.

Items are arranged by subject; entries in the 1990/91 issue are undated and otherwise incomplete.

Lefanu, William. *Nehemiah Grew, M. D., F. R. S. A Study and Bibliography of his Writings*.
Winchester, Hampshire, U.K.: St. Paul's Bibliographies (distributed in North America
thorugh Detroit, MI: Omnigraphics), 1990. Pp. xviii + 182; bibliography; illustrations; plates.

Rev. (favorably) by Richard Burleigh in *The Book Collector*, 40 (1991), 124–26; by Michael Hunter in *TLS,* (Sep.
14, 1990), 984; (favorably) by Peter Murray Jones in the *British Journal for the History of Science*, 24 (1991), 255;
by C. Webster in *Annals of Science*, 48 (1991), 603–04.

Lehmstedt, Mark. "Die Geschichte einer Übersetzung. William Robertsons *Geschichte von
Amerika* (1777)." *Leipziger Jahrbuch zur Buchgeschichte*, 1 (1991), 265–97.

Leigh, Ralph A. *Unsolved Problems in the Bibliography of J.-J. Rousseau*. (1987 Sandars
Lectures in Bibliography at Cambridge.) Edited by J. T. A. Leigh. Cambridge and New
York: Cambridge U. Press, 1990. Pp. xi + 155. Cf. *ECCB*, n.s. 16, I:24.

Rev. (favorably) by Giles Barber in *Publishing History*, 30 (1991), 123–5; (with another book) by Jean-Daniel
Candaux in *TLS,* (Aug. 9, 1991), 28; by François Moureau in *Bulletin du bibliophile,* (1991), 464-65.

Lemaire, Claudine. "La Comtesse Anne-Philippine-Thérèse d'Yve, figure de proue de la
révolution brabançonne et grande bibliophile (1738–1814). *Archives et bibliothèques de
Belgique*, 61 (1990), 121–42.

Lemire, Maurice, with the assistance of Aurelien Boivin, et al (gen. ed.). *La vie littéraire au
Quebec*. Vol. 1: *1764–1805: La voix française des nouveaux sujets britanniques*. Sainte-
Foy: Les Presses de l'Université Laval, 1991. Pp. xix + 498; bibliography [403–73];
illustrations; indices [of persons, works, and periodicals]; portraits.

Lenman, Bruce P. "Some Recent Jacobite Studies" [review essay]. *Scottish Historical Review*,
70 (1991), 66–74.

Lescat, Philippe. *Méthodes et traités musicaux en France, 1660–1800. Réflexions sur l'écriture
de la pédagogie musicale en France, suivi de catalogues systématiques et chronologique, de
repères biographiques et bibliographiques*. Paris: Institut de Pédagogie Musicale et
Chorégraphique; La Villett, 1991. Pp. 239; bibliography; illustrations.

Le Tourneur, Pierre. *Preface du Shakespeare Traduit de l'anglais*. (Textes littéraires français.)
Edited by Jacques Gury. Geneva: Droz, 1990. Pp. 276.

Rev. (favorably) by Martine de Rougemont in *Dix-huitième siècle*, 23 (1991), 474–75.

Levine, Joseph M. *The Battle of the Books: History and Literature in the Augustan Age*. Ithaca,
NY: Cornell U. Press, 1991. Pp. xiv + 428; bibliography; illustrations; index.

Rev. by Karl Galinsky in *Libraries and Culture*, 28 (1993), 221–22; (favorably) by Lawrence Lipking in *New
Republic*, 205 (Sep. 30, 1991), 42–45.

Limbert, Claudia A. "The Poetry of Katherine Philips: Holographs, Manuscripts, and Early Printed Texts." *Philological Quarterly*, 70 (1991), 181–98.

Link, Viktor. "The First Operatic Versions of *Pamela.*" *Studies on Voltaire and the Eighteenth Century*, 267 (1989), 273–81.

Lisboa, Joao Luis. "Popular Knowledge in the 18th-Century Almanacs." *History of European Ideas*, 11 (1989), 509–13.

"The Literature of American Library History, 1987–1988" [review essay]. *Libraries and Culture*, 25 (1990), 543–74; bibliography

Lloyd, Andrew. "Early Atlases and Printed Books from the Manchester Geographical Society Collection: A Catalogue." *Bulletin of the John Rylands University Library of Manchester*, 73 (Summer 1991), 37–157.

Many eighteenth-century atlases and books are found in two separate chronological lists.

Lock, F. P. "Swift's Library: The Yale Copy of the Sale Catalogue Reconsidered." *The Book Collector*, 40 (1991), 31–50.

Rejects the view of Arthur Freeman that a handwritten list of 32 titles on a sale catalogue of Swift's library represents additional books owned by Swift, reiterating some points made by David Woolley in *Swift Studies* 1989; a rejoinder by Freeman follows, conceding some points (see above).

Lonçon, Pierre. *L'Édition rouergate aux XVIIe et XVIIIe siècle: répertoire bibliographique.* (Archives historiques du Rouergue, 22.) Rodez: Société des lettres, sciences et arts de l'Aveyron, 1991. Pp. 135; illustrations.

Lösel, Barbara, with assistance from Alfred G. Swierk. *Die Frau als Persönlichkeit im Buchwesen: Dargestellt am Beispiel der Göttinger Verlegerin Anna Vandenhoeck (1709–1787).* (Buchwissenschaftliche Beitrage aus dem Deutschen Bucharchiv München, 33.) Wiesbaden: Harrassowitz, 1991. Pp. viii + 229; bibliography (of Vandenhoeck imprints from 1750 to 1787 and of secondary sources); illustrations.

Lovett, Robert W., assisted by Charles C. Lovett. Robinson Crusoe: *A Bibliographical Checklist of English Language Editions (1719-1979).* (Bibliographies and Indexes in World Literature, 30.) Westport, CT: Greenwood, 1991. Pp. xxi + 305.

Annotated, with extensive introduction.

Luey, Beth, assisted by Kathleen Gorman. *Editing Documents and Texts: An Annotated Bibliography.* Compiled for the Association for Documentary Editing. Madison, WI: Madison House, 1990. Pp. xi + 291; frontispiece.

Rev. (favorably) by Henry Steffens in the *Journal of American History*, 77 (1991), 1475-76.

Lüsebrink, Hans-Jürgen, and Manfred Tietz (eds.). *Lectures de Raynal*: *L'*Histoire des deux Indes *en Europe et en Amérique au XVIIIe siècle. Actes du Colloque de Wolfenbüttel.* (Studies on Voltaire and the Eighteenth Century, 286.) Oxford: Voltaire Foundation at the Taylor Institution, 1991. Pp. viii + 399; index.

Contains the editors' introduction and 20 essays by diverse contributors, among which are several with bibliographical interest: Michèle Duchet's "L'*Histoire des deux Indes*: sources et structure d'un texte polyphonique" (9-16); Gianluigi Goggi's "Quelques remarques sur la collaboration de Diderot à la première édition de l'*Histoire des deux Indes*" (17-52); Michel Delon's "L'appel au lecteur dans l'*Histoire des deux Indes*" (53-66); Hervé Guénot's "La réception de l'*Histoire des deux Indes* dans la presse d'expression française (1772-1781)" (67-84); Manfred Tietz's "L'Espane et l'*Histoire des deux Indes* de l'abbé Raynal" (99-130); Jean Mondot's "La réception de Raynal en Allemagne: l'example de Wekhrlin" (189-204); Girolamo Imbruglia's "Les premières lectures italiennes de l'*Histoire philosophique et politique des deux Indes*: entre Raynal et Robertson" (235-51); Anthony Strugnell's "La réception de l'*Histoire des deux Indes* en Angleterre au dix-huitième siècle" (253-64); Olga Penke's "L'*Histoire des deux Indes* en Hongrie au siècle des Lumières" (265-86); Marian Skrzypek's "La réception de l'*Histoire des deux Indes* en Pologne et en Russie au dix-huitième siècle" (287-304); and Edoardo Tortarolo's "La réception de l'*Histoire des deux Indes* aux Etats-Unis" (305-328).

Macías Delgado, J. "La Biblioteca clandestina de un ilustrado en la oposición." *Hispania Sacra*, 87 (1990), 259–391.

Malaguzzi, Francesco. *Legatori e legature del Settecento in Piemonte.* (Biblioteca di "Studi piemontesi," 19.) Turin: Centro Studi Piemontesi, 1989. Pp. 183; illustrations; 46 photographic plates. Cf. *ECCB*, n.s. 16, I:25.

Rev. by François Moureau in *Dix-huitième siècle*, 23 (1991), 545.

Malo, Denis. "Diderot et la librairie: l'impensable propriété." *Recherches sur Diderot et sur l'Encyclopédie*, 10 (1990), 57–90.

Manevy, Alain. *Les Journalistes de la liberté et la naissance de l'opinion (1789–1793): Récit-essai sur les risques d'écrire.* Paris: B. Grasset, 1989. Pp. 255 + [v].

Mann, David D. "Checklist of Female Dramatists, 1660–1823." *Restoration and Eighteenth-Century Theatre Research*, 2nd ser., 5 (Summer 1990), 30–62.

Rev. (with additions and corrections) by Maureen E. Mulvihill in *The Scriblerian*, 24 (1991), 38.

Mannerheim, Ylva. "Charles de Geer: bokköpare i 1700-talets Sverige." *Biblioteksbladet* (1991), 76–78.

Manson, Michel. "Être enseignant en France de 1750 à 1800, J. C. Leroux et le *Journal d'éducation.*" *Revue d'histoire moderne et contemporaine*, 38 (1991), 462–72.

Mari, Michele. "Le tre *Iliadi* di Melchiorre Cesarotti." *Giornale storico della letteratura italiana*, 167 (1990), 321–95.

Rev. by Antonella Marini in *La Rassegna della letteratura italiana*, 95 (1991), 250–51.
On the extensive deletions, additions and revisions to the revised *La Morte di Ettore*, treating late eighteenth-century editions in detail.

Markworth, Tino. *Johann Gottfried Herder: A Bibliographical Survey, 1977–1987.* Hurth-Efferen: Gabel, 1990. Pp. 97.

Martens, Gunter. "Der wohlfeile Goethe: Überlegungen zur textphilologischen Grundlegung von Leseausgaben." Pp. 72–91 of *Edition als Wissenschaft: Festschrift für Hans Zeller.* Edited by Gunter Martens and Winfried Woesler. (Beihefte zu Editio, 2.) Tübingen: Niemeyer, 1991.

Martin, Angus. "Fiction and the Female Reading Public in Eighteenth-Century France: The *Journal des dames* (1759–1778)." *Eighteenth-Century Fiction*, 3 (1991), 241–58.

Martino, Alberto. *Die deutsche Leihbibliothek: Geschichte einer literarischen Institution (1756–1914).* (Beitrage zum Buch- und Bibliothekswesen, 298.) Index by Albert Martino with assistance of Georg Jager. Wiesbaden: Harrassowitz, 1990. Pp. xv + 1770; bibliography.

On commercial lending libraries run by booksellers.

Maslen, Keith. "Samuel Richardson's Books." *The Bibliographical Society of Australia and New Zealand Bulletin*, 12 (1988 [issued March 1990]), 85–89.

Maslen, Keith, and John Lancaster. *The Bowyer Ledgers: The Printing Accounts of William Bowyer Father and Son Reproduced on Microfiche with a Checklist of Bowyer Printing (1690–1777), a Commentary, Indexes, and Appendices.* London: The Bibliographical Society; New York: The Bibliographical Society of America, 1991. Pp. lxxv + 616; 70 microfiches.

Rev. by David McKitterick in *The Book Collector*, 40 (1991), 465–82; (favorably) by Calhoun Winton in *The Papers of the Bibliographical Society of America*, 85 (1991), 309–11.
An edition of four account ledgers, one at the Bodleian, and three at the Grolier Club in New York. The documents are reproduced in microfiche along with printed analytical indexes.

Mason, Laura. "Popular Songs and Political Singing in the French Revolution." *Princeton University Library Chronicle*, 51 (1991), 171–89.

Masseau, Didier. "L'Offensive des romanciers à la veille de la Révolution." Pp. 3–15 of *L'Écrivain devant la Révolution: 1780–1800, actes du colloque franco-italien de Grenoble.* Edited by Jean Sgard. Grenoble: U. Stendhal, 1990.

Massiet du Biest, Brigitte. "Les Bibliothèques des couvents d'hommes en 1790 dans le Morbihan: étude de quelques catalogues." Pp. 125–29 of *Charpiana: mélanges offerts par ses amis à Jacques Charpy.* Brest: Fédération des sociétés savantes de Bretagne, 1991.

Masson, Nicole. "La Bibliothèque d'un scélérat au XVIIIe siècle." *Bulletin du bibliophile,* (1989), 93–101.

Analysis of the library of a civil servant, circa 1770, for insights into contemporary tastes and private collections.

Mathes, W. Michael. "Mission Libraries of Baja California: 1773." *Dieciocho*, 13 (1990), 36–49.

On data from 1773 inventory of ten mission libraries, with tables on the most frequently listed writers.

Matteson, Robert S. "Archbishop William King and the Conception of his Library." *Library*, 13 (1991), 238–54.

Mauger, Michel. "Un Graveur breton de talent: Antoine François Ollivault (1731–1815)." Pp. 185–97 of *Charpiana: mélanges offerts par ses amis à Jacques Charpy*. Brest: Fédération des sociétés savantes de Bretagne, 1991.

May, James E., with the assistance of Nora J. Quinlan. *The Henry Pettit Edward Young Collection at the University of Colorado at Boulder Libraries: A Bibliography* [descriptive catalogue]. Boulder, CO: U. of Colorado Libraries, 1989. Pp. 86; frontispiece.

Rev. (favorably) by Stephen N. Brown in *Scriblerian*, 24 (1991), 86–87.

May, James E. "Scribleriana Transferred, 1988–1989." *The Scriblerian*, 24 (Autumn 1991), 91–101.

McDermott, Anne, and Marcus Walsh. "Editing Johnson's *Dictionary*: Some Editorial and Textual Considerations." Pp. 35–61 of *The Theory and Practice of Text-Editing: Essays in Honour of James T. Boulton*. Edited by Ian Small and Marcus Walsh. Cambridge and New York: Cambridge U. Press, 1991.

McEachern, Jo Anne E. (comp.). *Bibliography of the Writings of Jean Jacques Rousseau to 1800*. Vol. II: *Émile, ou de l'éducation*. Oxford: Voltaire Foundation at the Taylor Institution, 1989. Pp. ix + 473; bibliography; facsimiles; illustrations. Cf. *ECCB*, n.s. 15, I:7.

Rev. (favorably) by Jean H. Bloch in *Modern Language Review*, 86 (1991), 463–65; (with another work) by Jean-Daniel Candaux in *TLS*, (Aug. 9, 1991), 28; by P. Jimack in *French Studies*, 45 (1991), 81; (favorably) by Vivienne Mylne in *Notes and Queries*, 236 (1991), 118; by Charles Teisseyre in *Revue française d'histoire du livre*, 72–73 (1991), 314–15; by Raymond Trousson in *Dix-huitième siècle*, 23 (1991), 459.

McGann, Jerome J. *The Textual Condition*. Princeton, NJ: Princeton U. Press, 1991. Pp. xiv + 208.

While illustrating more general editorial principles, McGann provides an in-depth bibliographical and textual analysis of Blake's poetical publications.

McGuinness, Rosamond. "The *British Apollo* [1708–1711] as a Source of Musical Information." *British Journal for Eighteenth-Century Studies*, 14 (1991), 61–73.

McKitterick, David. "John Field in 1668: The Affairs of a University Printer." *Transactions of the Cambridge Bibliographical Society*, 9 (1990), 497–516.

McTeague, B. *Nature Illustrated: Flowers, Plants and Trees 1550–1900 from the Collections of the New York Public Library*. New York: Harry N. Abrams, 1989. Pp. 127; bibliography; illustrations (60 black and white; 46 color).

Rev. by E. C. Nelson in *Archives of Natural History*, 18 (1991), 411.

McVeagh, John. " 'Romantick' Ireland: Pococke's Tour of Cork and Kerry, 1758." *Erie/Ireland*, 25 (1990), 69–95.

Bishop Richard Pococke (1704–1765) published his tour of the Irish coast in 1752, but he did not publish travel manuscripts for tours in 1747 and 1758; a copy of the latter, now at the Bodleian, is here described in detail.

McWilliam, Neil, with Vera Schuster, Richard Wrigley, and Pascale Méker (eds.). *A Bibliography of Salon Criticism in Paris from the Ancien Régime to the Restoration, 1699–1827*. (Cambridge Studies in the History of Art.) Cambridge and New York: Cambridge U. Press, 1991. Pp. xx + 263; bibliography; indices.

Merian, Maria Sibylla [1647–1717]. *Das Insektenbuch. Metamorphosis insectorum Surinamensium. Nachdruck der Ausgabe Amsterdam 1707 nach dem Exemplar der Sächsischen Landesbibliothek Dresden*. With a note by Helmut Deckert. Frankfurt / Leipzig: Insel, 1991. Pp. 164.

Merland, Marie-Anne, with the assistance of Guy Parguez (comp.). *Répertoire bibliographique des livres imprimés en France au XVIIe siècle*. Vol. 16: *Lyon*. (Bibliotheca Bibliographica Aureliana, 117.) Baden-Baden: V. Koerner, 1989. Pp. 211; indices.

Rev. (with another volume in the series by Louis Desgraves) by Albert Labarre in *Bulletin du bibliophile*, (1989), 184–86.

Messenger, Ann. "Frances Sheridan and the Canon Then and Now." *Journal of Irish Literature*, 18 (1989), 55–58.

Meyer, Horst. "The Seventeenth-Century Book in German and England." *Publishing History*, 29 (1991), 81–83.

Summary of presentation to the Conference on the Renaissance Book in Britain (Warwick, 1990).

Meyer, V. "Catalogue de thèses illustrées in-folio soutenues aux XVIIe et XVIIIe siècles par des bordelais," *Revue française d'histoire du livre*, 21 (1991), 201–65; bibliography.

Meynell, Guy. "Books from Philip Miller's Library Later Owned by Sir Joseph Banks." *Archives of Natural History*, 18 (1991), 379–80.

Michaelson, Patricia Howell. "Women in the Reading Circle." *ECLife*, 13 (1989), 59–69.

Argues "that reading aloud was much more prevalent in the eighteenth century than we have believed, and second, that the reading of novels in the middle-class family circle was . . . patriarchal reading" (59–60).

Milhous, Judith, and Robert D. Hume. *A Register of English Theater Documents, 1660–1737*. 2 Vols. Vol. 1: *1660–1714*; Vol. 2: *1714–1739*. Carbondale, IL: Southern Illinois U. Press, 1991. Pp. xli + 521; [*3*] + 522–1079; appendices; calendar.

Rev. (favorably) by James K. Bracken in *Choice*, 29 (1991), 64.

Miguel Alonso, Aurora. "Del plan Pidal a la ley Moyano: Consolidacion de la Biblioteca de la Universidad Central." Pp. 681–701 of *Estudios históricos: Homenaje a los professores José Ma, Jover Zamora, y Vicente Palacio Atard*. Madrid: Universidad Complutense, 1990.

Monkman, Kenneth. "Books Sterne Owned?" *The Shandean*, 2 (1990), 215–25.

Moresi, Jean-Luc. "A propos d'une vente fameuse: La bibliothèque Emmery." *Cahiers Elie Fleur*, 3 (1991), 19–44.

Morgan, Paul. "Two Irish Bindings from the Workshop of A. B. King: English and Foreign Bindings 56." *The Book Collector*, 40 (1991), 407–11; 2 plates.

Morley, William F. E. *Queen Anne Pamphlets: An Annotated Bibliographical Catalogue of Pamphlet Publications . . . held in the Eighteenth-Century British Pamphlet Collection, Douglas Library, Queen's University: 1701–1714*. Kingston, Ontario: Douglas Library of Queen's U., 1987. Pp. xl + 264 + 10 leaves of plates; illustrations. Cf. *ECCB*, n.s. 14, I:6.

Rev. by Michael Treadwell in *The Scriblerian*, 24 (Autumn 1991), 90–91.

Moureau, François. *Le Roman vrai de l'Encyclopédie*. (Découvertes Gallimard Littérature.) Paris: Gallimard, 1990. Pp. 224.

Rev. by Robert Granderoute in *Dix-huitième siècle*, 23 (1991), 458.

Mozzarelli, Cesare, and Gianni Venturi (eds.). *L'Europa delle Corti alla fine dell'antico regime*. (Biblioteca de la cinquecento, 52.) Rome: Bulzoni, 1991. Pp. 575; illustrations; 42 plates.

Contains Francesca Fedi's "Leopoldo Cicognara e il problema del collezionismo" and Anna Giulia Cavagna's "Il libro del *Cortegiano* e le edizioni settecentesche."

Murray, Bill. "1789, The Press, The Revisionists and the Bourgeois Revolution." *The Australian Journal of French Studies*, 26 (1989), 260–71.

Myers, Robin. *The Stationers' Company Archive: An Account of the Records 1554–1984*. Winchester, Hampshire, U.K.: St. Paul's Bibliographies (distributed through Detroit, MI: Omnigraphics), 1990. Pp. xlvii + 376; appendices; indices; 8 plates; tables.

Rev. by Donald A. Barclay in *American Reference Books Annual*, 22 (1991), 266–67; (favorably) by William Baker in *Choice*, 28 (1991), 1296; (favorably) by C. Y. Ferdinand in *Publishing History*, 30 (1991), 127–29.

Neagles, James C. *The Library of Congress: A Guide to Genealogical and Historical Research*. Salt Lake City, UT: Ancestry, 1990. Pp. xii + 381; bibliography; illustrations. Cf. *ECCB*, n.s. 16, I:30.

Rev. (with reservations) by Donald E. Collins in *American Reference Books Annual*, 22 (1991), 166–67.

New, Melvyn. "A Manuscript of the Le Fever Episode in *Tristram Shandy*." *The Scriblerian*, 23 (1990/91), 165–74.

Newby, James Edward. *Black Authors: A Selected Annotated Bibliography*. (Garland Reference Library of the Humanities, 1260.) New York: Garland, 1990. Pp. xv + 720; bibliography.

Rev. (favorably) by G. T. Johnson in *Choice*, 28 (1991), 1620; (favorably) by Gail Leach in *Library Journal*, 116 (Feb. 1, 1991), 74.
Earliest references begin with 1773.

Nickell, Joe. *Pen, Ink, & Evidence: A Study of Writing and Writing Materials for the Penman, Collector, and Document Detective*. Forward by Charles Hamilton. Photographs from the Author's Collection by Robert H. van Outer. Lexington, KY: U. Press of Kentucky, 1990. Pp. ix + 229; bibliography; illustrations.

Rev. (favorably) in *Virginia Quarterly Review*, 67 (1991), 104.
A practical and well illustrated survey of writing instruments, ink, paper, penmanship, and diciphering and dating documents, with assistance from forensic analyst John F. Fischer.

Noçon, Peter. "Swift Translated: The Case of the Former GDR [German Democratic Republic]." *Swift Studies*, 6 (1991), 115–18.

Oellers, Norbert. "Die Heiterkeit der Kunst: Goethe variiert Schiller." Pp. 92–103 of *Edition als Wissenschaft: Festschrift für Hans Zeller*. Edited by Gunter Martens and Winfried Woesler. (Beihefte zu Editio, 2.) Tübingen: Niemeyer, 1991.

O'Keefe, Doris. "A Dublin Edition of the *Emblemata Horatiana*." *Long Room*, 36 (1991), 35–40; illustrations.

An April 1785 prospectus and early numbers of a translation by Elizabeth Grattan with engraved plates after Pierre Danet; with a subscribers list.

Olschki, Fiammetta (comp.). *Viaggi in Europa. Secoli XVI–XIX: Catalogo del fondo "Fiammetta Olschki."* (Gabinetto scientifico-letterario G. P. Vieusseux, 5.) Edited by Fiammetta Olschki; indexed by Simona Di Marco and Leo S. Olschki. Florence: Leo S. Olschki, 1990. Pp. x + 413; illustrations.

O'Malley, William T. (comp.). *Anglo-Irish Literature: A Bibliography of Dissertations, 1873–1989*. (Bibliographies and Indexes in World Literature, 26.) Westport, CT: Greenwood Press, 1990. Pp. xix + 299.

Rev. (favorably) by Robert Neville in *American Reference Books Annual*, 22 (1991), 497.

Ó Muirithe, Diarmaid. "'Tho' Not in Full Stile Compleat': Jacobite Songs from Gaelic Manuscript Sources." *Eighteenth-Century Ireland*, 6 (1991), 93–103.

Otto, Regine. "Zu aktuellen Problemen der Herder-Edition." *Editio*, 4 (1990), 148–59; abstract [in English].

On the three Herder "Studienausgaben" projects begun since 1984, each following different editorial principles, and how and why they need to cooperate.

Oury, G. M. "La vie intellectuelle dans la Congrégation de Saint-Maur: les bibliothèques au XVIIe siècles. Où entreposer les livres?" *Revue française d'histoire du livre*, 72–73 (1991), 163–200.

Ovenell, R. F. "Supplementary Notes on Ashmolean Catalogues." *The Bodleian Library Record*, 14 (1991), 97–98.

Overmier, Judith A. "Research Opportunities for Literary Scholarship in Medical History Collections." *Literary Research*, 14 (1989), 13–22; bibliography.

Pactor, Howard S. (comp.). *Colonial British Caribbean Newspapers: A Bibliography and Directory*. (Bibliographies and Indexes in World History, 19.) Westport, CT: Greenwood Press, 1990. Pp. xiii + 144.

Rev. (favorably) by Brian E. Coutts in *American Reference Books Annual*, 22 (1991), 385.

Paisey, David L. *Deutsche Buchdrucker, Buchhändler und Verleger (1701–1750)*. (Beiträge zum Buch- und Bibliothekswesen, 26.) Wiesbaden: Harrassowitz, 1988. Pp. xiv + 361. Cf. *ECCB*, n.s. 16, I:32.

Rev. (favorably) by John L. Flood in *The Book Collector*, 40 (1991), 110–13.
A alphabetical directory of printers, publishers, bookbinders, engravers, and others involved in the book trade, providing dates, places, and sometimes relationships for 3500 individuals.

Paisey, David. "Printed Books in English and Dutch in Early Printed Catalogues of German University Libraries." Pp. 127–48 of *Across the Narrow Seas: Studies in the History and Bibliography of Britain and the Low Countries: Presented to Ann E. C. Simoni*. Edited by Susan Roach. Forward by Mirjam M. Foot. Bibliography by Dennis E. Rhodes. London: British Library, 1991; checklist of 107 Dutch and 72 English books in eight university libraries.

Panetta, Marina. *Gli Arcani delle stelle. Astrologi e astrologia nella biblioteca casanatense*. (Mostre permanenti, 1.) Rome: Biblioteca Casanatense, 1991. Pp. 181; illustrations; 4 plates.

Panetta, Marina. *La "Libraria" di Mattia Casanate*. (Il Bibliotecario, n.s. 2.) Rome: Bulzoni, 1988. Pp. 248; bibliography.

Rev. by Giorgio Montecchi in *La Bibliofilia*, 92 (1990), 228–29.

Parks, Roger (ed.), with assistance of the Committee for a New England Bibliography. *New England: A Bibliography of Its History*. (Bibliographies of New England History, 7.) With historiographic essay by David D. Hall and Alan Taylor. Hanover, NH: U. Press of New England, 1989. Pp. lvi + 259.

Rev. (with Vol. 8: *New England: Additions to the Six State Bibliographies* [1989]) by Norman D. Stevens in *American Reference Books Annual*, 22 (1991), 193; (also with Vol. 8) by Sally Linden in *Library Journal*, 115 (August 15, 1990), 107–08.

With sources for the study of New England as a whole. Vols. 1–6 (already published by the Committee for a New England Bibliography) concern the six states in New England; Vol. 8 makes additions to those earlier volumes.

Parmentier, Jan. "Weyermans werk in de aanbieding bij de Brugse drukker Joseph de Busscher (1774-1777)." *Mededelingen van de Stichting Jacob Campo Weyerman*, 14 (1991), 41–46.

Partridge, Michael S. *The Duke of Wellington, 1769–1852: A Bibliography.* (Meckler's Bibliographies of British Statesmen, 10.) Westport, CT: Meckler, 1990. Pp. xii + 248; bibliography; 1 plate; portrait.

Rev. (favorably) by R. Nash in *Choice*, 28 (1991), 1104; (favorably) by Elizabeth Patterson in *American Reference Books Annual*, 22 (1991), 210–11.

Patterson, Diana. "Tristram's Marblings and Marblers." *The Shandean*, 3 (1991), 70–97.

Much general information on the process of marbling paper from the author of a dissertation on marbled paper.

Paultre, Roger. *Les images du livre. Emblêmes et devises.* Preface by Louis Marin. Paris: Hermann, 1991. Pp. xii + 206; 220 illustrations.

Pavercsik, Ilona. "Johann Gerhard Mauss és a pesti könyvkereskedelem színvonala a 18. század közepén, II." *Magyar Könyvszemle*, 106 (1990) 113–28.

Paz Rebollo, Maria Antonia. "Las fuentes informativas de la prensa española en la segunda mitad del siglo XVIII." *Estudios de historia social*, 52–53 (1990), 357–68.

Pearson, David. "Durham Cathedral Library, Cosin and Clarendon." *Durham University Journal*, 52 (1991), 91–92.

Pearson, David. "Elias Smith, Durham Cathedral Librarian (1633–1676)." *Library History*, 8 (1989), 65–73.

Pedley, Colin. "Blake's 'Tyger' and Contemporary Journalism." *British Journal for Eighteenth-Century Studies*, 14 (1991), 45–49.

Perlmann, Joel, and Dennis Shirley. "When Did New England Women Acquire Literacy?" *William and Mary Quarterly*, 48 (1991), 50–67.

Peters, Hubert J. M. (comp.). *The Crone Library: Books on The Art of Navigation Left by Dr. Ernst Crone to the Scheepvaart Museum in 1975 and Books on the Same Subject Acquired Previously. A Descriptive Special Catalogue with Annotations, Indexes, and an Introduction to the Catalogue.* (Bibliotheca Bibliographica Neerlandica, 26.) Amsterdam: De Graffe (for the Vereeniging Nederlandsch Historisch Scheepvaart Museum), 1989. Pp. lx + 805; bibliography; indices; maps; 54 plates.

Rev. (favorably) by Thomas R. Adams in *The Book Collector*, 40 (1991), 122–24.
Seven indices include authors, printers, places, variant place names, maps, artists, and shelf locations. There are 717 pre-1800 items.

Peters, Julie Stone. *Congreve, the Drama, and the Printed Word*. Stanford, CA: Stanford U. Press, 1990. Pp. xvi + 286; bibliography; illustrations.

Rev. by Paula Backscheider in *Studies in English Literature 1500–1900*, 31 (1991), 591, noting it is largely a study of print culture; (favorably) by E. D. Hill in *Choice*, 29 (1991), 100.

Petrucci Nardelli, Franca. *La Lettera e l'immagine: le iniziali "parlanti" nella tipografia italiana (secolo XVI–XVIII)*. (Biblioteca di bibliografia italiana, 125.) Florence: Olschki, 1991. Pp. 153; illustrations; 2 plates.

Petrucciani, Alberto. *Gli Incunaboli della Biblioteca Durazzo*. Genoa: Società Ligure di Storia Patria, 1988. Pp. 591; bibliography; illustrations; 24 plates (some color).

Rev. by M. Leembruggen in *Library*, 13 (1991), 281–84.

Petrucciani, Alberto. "Il libro a Genova nel Settecento. I. L'arte dei libri dai nuovi Capitoli (1685) alla caduta della Repùbblica aristocratica (1797)." *La Bibliofilía*, 92 (1990), 41–82.

Peyfuss, Max Demeter. *Die Druckerei von Moschopolis, 1731–1769: Buchdruck und Heiligenverehrung im Erzbistum Achrida*. (Wiener Archiv für Geschichte des Sklawentums und Osteuropas, 13.) Vienna and Koln: Böhlau, 1989. Pp. x + 256; illustrations; maps.

Rev. (with another book) in *Marginalien*, 124 (1991), 88.

Phillips, Michael. "Printing Blake's *Songs* 1789–94." *Library*, 13 (1991), 205–37; 8 color plates; 8 black/white plates.

Pia-Lachapelle, Léone. "L'évolution d'une bibliothèque publique fondée avant 1789, dans une petite ville de Bourgogne: Saulieu" [the books of Claude Sallier, 1737]. Pp. 39–44 in *Association bourguignonne des sociétés savantes, 58e congrès, Semur-en-Auxois, 15–17 mai 1987: Actes*. Dijon: A. B. S. S., 1990.

Pickering, Jennifer M. *Music in the British Isles 1700 to 1800: A Bibliography of Literature*. Edinburgh, Scotland: Burden and Cholij, 1990. Pp. xiv + 419.

Rev. (favorably) by Paula Backscheider in *Studies in English Literature 1500–1900*, 31 (1991), 579.

Pickering, O[liver]. S. "An Attribution of the Poem *The Town Life* (1686) to Charles Sackville, Earl of Dorset." *Notes and Queries*, 235 (1990), 296–97.

Attribution for this 1687 publication suggested by a manuscript note in Brotherton Library copy.

Pickering, O[liver]. S. "A New Database of Manuscript Verse: BCMSV." *The Seventeenth Century*, 6 (1991), 105–06.

An account of the database of manuscript verse at Leeds University Library, with a sample record, noting that the 35 manuscripts catalogued by January 1991 had produced 1400 records.

Pinault, Madeleine. "Sur les planches de l'*Encyclopédie* de d'Alembert et Diderot." Pp. 355–62 of *L'Encyclopédisme: actes du colloque de Caen, 12–16 janvier 1987.* Edited by Annie Becq. Paris: Aux amateurs de livres, 1991.

du Pineau, Gabriel-Joseph. *Dictionnaire angevin et français (1746–48) de Gabriel-Joseph Du Pineau: Édition critique d'après Paris, Bibl. nat., nouv. acq. fr. 22097.* Edited by Pierre Rézeau in collaboration with Jean-Paul Chauveau. (Matériaux pour l'étude des régionalismes du français, 4.) Paris: Centre Nationale de la Recherche Scientifique and Klincksieck, 1989. Pp. 469.

Rev. by Glynn Hesketh in *Modern Language Review*, 86 (1991), 1010.

Pittock, Murray. "New Jacobite Songs of the Forty-Five." *Studies on Voltaire and the Eighteenth Century*, 267 (1989), 1–75.

Rev. by Claire Lamont in *Scottish Literary Journal*, Supplement 37 (Winter 1992), 12–14.

Pollard, Mary Paul. *Dublin's Trade in Books 1550–1800: Lyell Lectures, 1986–87.* Oxford: Clarendon Press, 1990. Pp. xvi + 280; appendix [8 pp. from Daybooks for March-May 1685 of Samuel Helsham, Dublin bookseller]; graphs; illustrations; tables. Cf. *ECCB*, n.s. 16, I:33; 15, I:10–11.

Rev. (Favorably in an unsigned review presumably by editor Nicholas Barker) in *The Book Collector*, 40 (1991), 153–54; 157–58; 160–62; 165–66; and 168; by Lise Andries in *Dix-huitième siècle*, 23 (1991), 506–07; (favorably) by A. C. Elias, Jr., in *Eighteenth-Century Ireland*, 5 (1990), 198–200; by Keith Maslen in *Notes and Queries*, 236 (1991), 229–30; by Wesley McCann in *Linen Hall Review*, 8 (1991), 35.

Pollard, Mary Paul. *"Pity's Gift:* A Dublin Deception?" *Long Room*, 36 (1991), 13–16.

An apparent Dublin reprint, with false London imprint, of a 1798 collection for youth.

Popkin, Jeremy D. *News and Politics in the Age of Revolution: Jean Luzac's* Gazette de Leyde. Ithaca, NY, and London: Cornell U. Press, 1989. Pp. xiii + 292; bibliography; illustrations; tables. Cf. *ECCB*, n.s. 16, I:22.

Rev. by Nina Rattner Gelbart in *American Historical Review*, 96 (1991), 1206; (favorably) by Norman Hampson in *Journal of Modern History*, 63 (1991), 762–63; by Jeffrey A. Smith in *JQ: Journalism Quarterly*, 67 (1990), 608–09; by W. R. E. Velema in *Bijdragen en Mededelingen Betreffende de Geschiedenis der Nederlanden*, 106 (1991), 116–18.

Popkin, Jeremy D. *Revolutionary News: The Press in France, 1789–1799.* (Bicentennial Reflections on the French Revolution.) Durham, NC, and London: Duke U. Press, 1990. Pp. xx + 217; bibliography [187-209]; illustrations; index; tables. Cf. *ECCB*, n.s. 16, I:34.

Rev. by Lise Andries in *Dix-huitiéme siécle*, 23 (1991), 495; by Jeremy Black in *History: The Journal of the Historical Association*, 76 (1991), 511–12; (favorably) by Pascal Bourdon in *JQ: Journalism Quarterly*, 68 (1991), 860–61; by Ian Germani in *Canadian Journal of History*, 26 (1991), 111–12; by Lynn A. Hunt in *Journal of*

Interdisciplinary History, 21 (1991), 684–85; by Frank A. Kafker in *American Historical Review*, 96 (1991), 1205–06; in rev. article ("More than Words: The Printing Press and the French Revelution") by Joan B. Landes in *Eighteenth-Century Studies*, 25 (1991), 85–98.

Porter, A. N. (gen. ed.). *Atlas of British Overseas Expansion*. London: Routledge; New York: Simon and Schuster, 1991. Pp. x + 279; bibliography; explanatory texts by 15 contributors; maps.

Rev. (favorably) by Sandy Whiteley in *Booklist*, 88 (Nov. 15, 1991), 639.
Signed articles by many contributors. Separately issued in North American and Great Britain.

Provost, Foster. *Columbus: An Annotated Guide to the Scholarship on His Life and Writings, 1750–1988*. Detroit, MI: Omnigraphics, for the John Carter Brown Library, 1991. Pp. xxxii + 225; indices.

Rev. (favorably) by T. M. Izbicki in *Choice*, 28 (1991), 1764.

Quilici, Piccarda (ed.). *Carte decorate nella legatoria del '700 dalle raccolte della Biblioteca casanatense*. Rome: Istituto poligrafico e zecca dello Stato, 1989. Pp. 281; bibliography; colored illustrations; index.

Raabe, Mechthild (comp.). *Leser und Lektüre im 18. Jahrhundert: Die Ausleihbücher der Herzog August-Biliothek Wolfenbüttel (1714–1799)*. Vol. 1: Die Leser und ihre Lektüre; Vol. 2: Die sozialen Lesergruppen und ihre Lektüre; Vol. 3: Alphabetisches Verzeichnis der entliehenen Bücher; Vol. 4: Systematisches Verzeichnis der entliehenen Bücher. Forward by Paul Raabe. 4 vols. Munich and New York: K. G. Saur, 1989. Bibliography [Vol. 1, xcii-xciv]; illustrations.

Rev. (favorably) by Bärbel Raschke in *Leipziger Jahrbuch zur Buchgeschichte*, 1 (1991), 324–27; by Marianne Rumpf in *Zeitschrift für Bibliothekswesen und Bibliographie*, 38 (1991), 471–73.

Rancoeur, René (ed.). "Bibliographie de la littérature française (XVIe - XXe siècles): année 1989"; and "_____ année 1990." *Revue d'histoire littéraire de la France*, 90 (1990), 289–568 and 91 (1992), 289–568.

Eighteenth-century studies are covered in Vol. 90 (1990 but on 1989 imprints), 367–415; and Vol. 91 (1991 but on 1990 imprints), 367–410. To allow it to be issued separately from the volume, this issue (no. 3, May-June) is also separately paginated (280 pp.).

Real Academia de Ciencias Exactas, Físicas, y Naturales de Madrid, Biblioteca. *Catálogo de libros antiquos: siglos XV–XVIII: Real Academia de Ciencias Exactas, Fisicas y Naturales (Madrid)*. Madrid: La Academia, 1991. Pp. 443; bibliography; illustrations.

"Recent Books and Articles Received." *Swift Studies*, 4 (1989), 97–100; 5 (1990), 117–21; 6 (1991), 123–27.

Reddick, Allen. *The Making of Johnson's Dictionary (1746-1773)*. Cambridge and New York: Cambridge U. Press, 1990. Pp. xiii + 249; illustration. Cf. *ECCB*, n.s. 16, I:35.

Rev. (favorably) by W. B. Carnochan in *TLS,* (April 19, 1991), 9–10; by Christopher Hawtree in the *Times Educational Supplement,* (Feb. 22, 1991), 35; (favorably) by Elizabeth Hedrick in *Johnsonian News Letter*, 50, and 51, (1990/91), 5–6; (favorably) by Paul J. Korshin in *The Age of Johnson*, 4 (1991), 417–24.; and (favorably) by G. Scholtz in *Choice*, 28 (1991), 1488.

Rees, Eiluned. *Libri Walliae: A Catalogue of Welsh Books and Books Printed in Wales, 1546–1820.* 2 vols. Aberystwyth, Wales, U.K.: National Library of Wales, 1987. Pp. 923 + lxxxx; illustrations.

Rev. by G. Williams in *English Historical Review*, 106 (1991), 199–200.
Pp. i-lxxxx of Vol. 2 contain a 90-page essay, "The Welsh Book Trade Before 1820."

Rees, Eiluned. "The Merioneth Book-Trade, 1761–1820." *Journal of the Merionethshire Historical and Record Society*, 11 (1990), 49–58.

Rees, Eiluned. *The Welsh Book-Trade before 1820.* Aberystwyth, U.K.: National Library of Wales, 1988. Pp. cxx; illustrations; index.

Rees-Mogg, William. "Boswell and Adam Smith First Editions." *TLS,* (March 22, 1991), 25.

(Correspondence from Ian Ross in *TLS,* [May 10, 1991], 13).
"The collection history of Boswell and Adam Smith suggests 1900–19, low interest in books; 1920–29, bibliomania; 1930–59, depression in collecting; 1960–89, recovery, but to a level of activity well below the 1920s"

Reilly, Bernard. *American Political Prints, 1766–1876: A Catalog of the Collections in the Library of Congress.* Boston, MA: G. K. Hall, 1991. Pp. xxi + 638; bibliography; illustrations; indices.

Rev. (favorably) by J. D. Haskell, Jr., in *Choice* (1991), 578; by Stephen Rees in *Library Journal*, 116 (July 1991), 94; by James Rettig in *Wilson Library Bulletin*, 66 (1991), 118.

Répertoire d'imprimeurs-libraires, XVIe–XVIIIe siècles: état au 31 décembre 1990 (2000 notices). (Études, guides et inventaires, 9.) Edited by Madeleine Orieux and Jean-Dominique Mellot, under the direction of Odile Gantier. Paris: Bibliothèque nationale, 1991. Pp. viii + 306; bibliography; illustrations.

Rétat, Pierre. "Représentations du temps révolutionnaire d'après les journaux de 1789." Pp. 121–29 in *L'Espace et le temps reconstruits: La Révolution française, une révolution des mentalités et des cultures?* Edited by Philippe Joutard. Aix-en-Provence: U. de Provence, 1990.

Rétat, Pierre (ed.). *La Révolution du journal, 1788–1794.* Paris: Centre National de la Recherche Scientifique, 1989. Pp. 354; illustrations.

Rev. in rev. article ("More Than Words: The Printing Press and the French Revolution") by Joan B. Landes in *Eighteenth-Century Studies*, 25 (1991), 85–98.

Rhodes, D. E. (comp.). *Catalogue of Books Printed in Spain and of Spanish Books Printed Elsewhere in Europe before 1901 now in The British Library.* 2nd ed. London: British Library, 1989. Pp. viii + 294.

Rev. (favorably) by J. S. Cummins in *Modern Language Review*, 86 (1991), 761–62; (favorably) by Gustav Ungerer in *Huntington Library Quarterly*, 54 (1991), 275–79.

Rivet, Régis. "La bibliothèque interuniversitaire de médicine de Paris et son fonds ancien." *Mélanges de la bibliothèque de la Sorbonne*, 11 (1991), 121–29.

Rivington, Charles A. *"Tyrant": The Story of John Barber, 1675-1741: Jacobite Lord Mayor of London, and Printer and Friend to Dr. Swift.* York: William Sessions, 1989. Pp. viii + 311; illustrations; plates. Cf. *ECCB*, n.s. 16, I:36.

Rev. (favorably) by Joseph McMinn in *The Scriblerian*, 23 (1990/91), 278–79; by Murray G. H. Pittock in *British Journal for Eighteenth-Century Studies*, 14 (1991), 211.

Roach, Susan (ed.). *Across the Narrow Seas: Studies in the History and Bibliography of Britain and the Low Countries: Presented to Ann E. C. Simoni.* Forward by Mirjam M. Foot. Bibliography by Dennis E. Rhodes. London: British Library, 1991. Pp. xv + 223; bibliography; illustrations; maps; portraits.

Robinson, Gwen G. "The Punctuator's World: A Discursion, Part Five: Logic Takes Over, 1750–1800." *Courier*, 25 (1990), 85–125.

Continues a series of articles on the development of punctuation.

Roger, Philippe. "Repentirs de plume: l'échec du journalisme révolutionnaire selon Mercier et Louvet." *Revue d'histoire littéraire de la France*, 90 (1990), 589–98.

Roth-Wölfe, Lotte. "Der 'Musenhof' der Franziska von Hohenheim: Anmerkungen zur Person und Bibliothek der Herzogin von Württemberg." *Imprimatur*, 14 (1991), 177–89; illustrations.

Ruck, Peter (ed.). *Pergament: Geschichte, Struktur, Restaurierung, Herstellung.* (Historische Hilfswissenschaften, 2.) Sigmaringen, Germany: J. Thorbecke (distributed through Zaragoza: Avances de Pórtico Librerías), 1991. Pp. 480; bibliography; illustrations; plates.

Articles on parchment in English, French, and German, such as Michael Ryder's cited below.

Rudnicka, Jadwiga. "Biblioteka Stanislawa Augusta na Zamku Warszawskim: Dokumenty." *La Bibliothèque de Stanislas Auguste au château de Varsovie. Documents*. (Archiwum literackie, 26.) Wroclaw, Poland: Zaklad Narodowy im. Ossolinskich, 1988. Pp. 347; facsimiles.

Ruíz Martínez, Eduardo. *La Librería de Nariño y "Los Derechos del hombre."* Bogatá: Planeta, 1990. Pp. 503; bibliography.

Rupp, Paul Berthold. "Ein Emigrant und die Zensur: Anmerkungen zu der in Augsburg erschienenen französischsprachigen Zeitung *Bulletin politique d'Augsbourg.*" *Bibliotheksforum Bayern*, 19 (1991), 47–55; illustrations.

Ryder, Michael L. "The Biology and History of Parchment." Pp. 25–33 of *Pergament: Geschichte-Struktur-Restaurierung-Herstellung.* (Historische Hilfswissenschaften, 2.) Edited by Peter Rück. Sigmaringen, Germany: Thorbecke, 1991.

Sachse, Wieland. "Wirtschaftsliteratur und Kommunikation bis 1800: Beispiele und Tendenzen aus Mittelalter und Früher Neuzeit: Kaufmannsbücher, Enzyklopädien, Kameralistische Schriften und Statistiken." Pp. 199–215 of *Die Bedeutung der Kommunikation für Wirtschaft und Gesellschaft*. Edited by Hans Pohl. Stuttgart: Steiner, 1989. Pp. 485; illustrations.

Sadie, Julie Anne (comp.). *Companion to Baroque Music*. Forward by Christopher Hogwood. London: J. M. Dent, 1991; New York: Schirmer Books, 1991. Pp. xviii + 549; bibliography; illustrations; 10 maps; 23 musical examples; 16 plates.

Rev. (favorably) by Donald Burrows in *Early Music*, 19 (1991), 635–36; (favorably) by G. A. Marco in *Choice*, 30 (1992), 74.

Sahlin, Gunnar. "1700-talets lånebibliotek och den litterära publiken." Pp. 228–41 of *Bibliotek: Tradition och utveckling: Festskrift till Lars-Erik Sanner den 18 januari 1991*. Stockholm: Stockholms Universitetsbibliotek, 1991.

Santato, Guido. "Note sull' *Epistolario* alfieriano edito da Lanfranco Caretti." *Lettere italiane*, 42 (1990), 91–107.

Rev. by Paolo Marolda in *La Rassegna della letteratura italiana*, 95 (1991), 224; (with another book) by Antonella Marini in *La Rassegna della letteratura italiana*, 95 (1991), 251–52.

Sartori, Eva Martin, and Dorothy Winne Zimmerman (gen. eds.). *French Women Writers: A Bio-Bibliographical Sourcebook*. New York and Westport, CT: Greenwood Press, 1991. Pp. xxiii + 632; bibliographies; chronologies; indices [title and subject].

With signed biographical and critical sketches of authors ending with primary and secondary bibliographies. In Appendix 1, Julia Lauer-Chéenne provides "Situating Women Writers in French History: A Chronology"; Appendix 2 offers a list of authors by dates of birth.

Sauer, Helgard. "Gullivers Reisen: 1. Teil: Illustrationen von 1726–1843." *Illustration '63*, 28 (1991), 93–97.

Sauer, Helgard. "Illustrationen zu Swifts Roman 'Gullivers Reisen': ein Beitrag zur Entwicklungsgeschichte der Kinder- und Jugendbuchillustration seit dem 18. Jahrhundert." Diss. Dresden, 1990.

Saxe, Stephen O. "'Franklin' Common Press." *Printing History*, 12 (1990), 34–35; 1 illustration.

Saxe, Stephen O. "The Goodman Common Press: The Oldest American-Made Press [1787]" *Printing History*, 14 (1991), 28–29; 1 illustration.

Schille, Candy B. K. "Some Current Publications." *Restoration*, 15 (1991), 41–55.

Schlieder, Wolfgang. "Beiträge zur Geschichte der Papierherstellung in und um Leipzig." *Leipziger Jahrbuch zu Buchgeschichte*, 1 (1991), 53–116.

Schmelz, Reinhard. "Rokoko und Buchdruck in Leipzig." *Myosotis*, (1990), 15–26.

Schmilewski, Ulrich. *Verlegt bei [Johann Jacob] Korn in Breslau: Kleine Geschichte eines bedeutenden Verlages von 1732 bis heute.* Würzburg: Korn, 1991. Pp. 276.

Schoneveld, C. W. "The Eighteenth-Century Afterlife of John Locke's Writings in the Netherlands." *Documentatieblad Werkgroep achttiende eeuw*, 23 (1991), 3–22.

Schrader, Hans-Jürgen. *Literaturproduktion und Büchermarkt des radikalen Pietismus.* Göttingen: Vandenhoeck u Ruprecht, 1989. Pp. 635; bibliography.

Rev. (favorably) by Dominique Bourel in *Dix-huitième siècle*, 23 (1991), 516.

Schrijver, Emile G. L. "'Be-ôtiyyôt Amsterdam': Eighteenth-Century Hebrew Manuscript Production in Central Europe: The Case of Jacob ben Judah Leib Shamas." *Quaerendo*, 20 (1990), 24–62; illustrations; 8 plates.

Schweizer, K. W. "The Scottish London Papers at the Huntington Library: Material on the Rising of 1715." *Canadian Journal of History*, 26 (1991), 162–65.

Seary, Peter. *Lewis Theobald and the Editing of Shakespeare.* New York: Oxford U. Press; Oxford: Clarendon Press, 1990. Pp. xvi + 248. Cf. *ECCB*, n.s. 16, I:38.

Rev. (favorably) by Arthur Sherbo in *The Scriblerian*, 24 (1991), 80, who thinks this study the "last word, barring new documentary evidence," on Theobald's editing.

Selwyn, Pamela E. "Der Philosoph im Comptoir: Der Verlagsbuchhändler Friedrich Nicolai." *Börsenblatt für den deutschen Buchhandel*, 157 (1990), 48, Beih. Nr. 5, 37–42.

Rev. (with another book) in *Marginalien*, 124 (1991), 88.

Senser, Christine. *Die Bibliotheken der Schweiz.* (Elemente des Buch- und Bibliothekswesens, 13.) Wiesbaden: Reichert, 1991. Pp. 176.

A Sentimental Journey and the Index Librorum Prohibitorum." *The Shandean*, 3 (1991), 183–87; 4 illustrations.

Sessions, William K. *The First Printers in Waterford, Cork, and Kilkenny pre–1700.* York, UK: W. K. Sessions and Ebor Press, 1990. Pp. iv + 310; illustrations; indices; maps; portraits.

Rev. by Peter Isaac in the *Bulletin of the Printing History Society*, 31 (1991), 25.

Sgard, Jean (gen. ed.). *Dictionnaire des Journaux, 1600–1789.* 2 vols: Vol. I: *A-I.* Vol. II: *J-V.* (Dictionnaire de la presse, 1600–1789, 1–2.) Paris: Universitas; Oxford: The Voltaire Foundation at the Taylor Institution, 1991. Pp. xi + 1209; illustrations.

Shawcross, John T. "An Apparently Unrecorded Item in the Margaret I. King Library." *Kentucky Review*, 9 (Summer 1989), 97–98.

On an unrecorded edition of Rowe's *The Fair Penitent* found at the King Library of University of Kentucky.

Sherbo, Arthur. "John Nichol's Notes in the Scholarly Commentary of Others." *Studies in Bibliography*, 44 (1991), 318–22.

Sheridan, Geraldine. *Nicolas Lenglet Dufresnoy and the Literary Underworld of the* ancien régime. (*Studies on Voltaire and the Eighteenth Century*, 262.) Oxford: The Voltaire Foundation at the Taylor Institution, 1989. Pp. ix + 433; bibliography.

Rev. (favorably) by Sean O. Cathasaigh in *Modern Language Review*, 86 (1991), 1024–25; by J. Lough in *British Journal of Eighteenth-Century Studies*, 14 (1991), 106.

Sherry, T. F. "Early Irish Newspapers: Reporting Constitutional Conflict." *Notes and Queries*, 235 (1990), 299–301.

Coverage of the *Sherlock vs. Annesley* case before the Irish Lords in 1716 was too hot to cover until early 1719.

Shesgreen, Sean. *The Criers and Hawkers of London: Engravings and Drawings of Marcellus Laroon*. Stanford, CA: Stanford U. Press; Aldershot, Hampshire, U.K.: Scolar Press, 1990. Pp. xii + 252; bibliography; illustrations. Cf. *ECCB*, n.s. 16, I:39.

Rev. in *The Scriblerian*, 24 (1991), 84-85; (favorably) by Paula Backscheider in *Studies in English Literature (1500–1900)*, 31 (1991), 577–78; (favorably) by Alexander S. Gourlay in *Philological Quarterly*, 70 (1991), 397–99; (favorably) by Gary Harrison in *Huntington Library Quarterly*, 54 (1991), 79–84; (favorably) by David Mannings in *British Journal of Aesthetics*, 31 (1991), 380–81; by Ronald Paulson in *Eighteenth-Century Studies*, 24 (1990/91), 266–67; and (favorably) by David Wykes in *Notes and Queries*, 236 (1991), 387–88.

Shevelow, Kathryn. *Women and Print Culture: Construction of Femininity in the Early Periodical*. London and New York: Routledge, 1989. Pp. x + 235; bibliography; figures. Cf. *ECCB*, n.s. 16, I:39; 15, I:13.

Rev. (with other books) by Clare Brant in *Review of English Studies*, 42 (1991), 302–04.

Shirley, Betty Beinecke. *Read Me a Story–Show Me a Book: American Children's Literature 1690–1988 from the Collection of Betsy Beinecke Shirley. An Exhibition at the Beinecke Rare Book and Manuscript Library, Yale University*, October–December, 1991. Pp. 100; black-and-white and color plates.

The 21 sections have short essays of introduction to the illustrations of books; those relevant to eighteenth-century bibliography include chapters on ABC's and primers, fairy tales, poetry, colonial reading, chapbooks and etiquette books.

Shirley, Rodney W. *Printed Maps of the British Isles, 1650–1750*. Herfordshire, U.K.: Map Collection Publications; London: The British Library, 1987. Pp. 168; illustrations; maps. Cf. *ECCB*, n.s. 15, I:14–15.

Rev. (with another book) by Joan Winearls in *Papers of the Bibliographical Society of Canada*, 29 (1991), 81-84.

Shrader, Charles Reginald (ed.). *Reference Guide to United States Military History*. Vol. 1: *1607–1815*. New York and Oxford: Facts on File, 1991. Pp. x + 277; bibliography; illustrations; maps; ports.

Rev. by G. M. Getchell, Jr., in *Choice*, 29 (1991), 577–78; (favorably) by J. K. Sweeney in *Library Journal*, 116 (April 15, 1991), 86.

Simmons, Carl. "The Works (and Grace) of John Bunyan." *A Bookman's Weekly,* (14 January 1991), 97–101.

Simpson, Murray C.T. *A Catalogue of the Library of the Revd. James Nairn (1629–1678) bequeathed by him to Edinburgh University Library*. Edinburgh, Scotland: Edinburgh U. Library, 1990. Pp. 250.

Rev. by A. I. Dunlop in *University of Edinburgh Journal*, 35 (1991), 50; by J. Kidd in *Library Review*, 40 (1991), 57–58; and P. S. Morrish in *The Bibliotheck*, 15 (1990), 96–98.

Simpson, Murray C. T. "Some Aspects of Book Purchasing in Restoration Scotland: Two Letters from James Fall to the Earl of Tweeddale, May 1678." *Edinburgh Bibliographical Society Transactions*, 6 (1990), 2–9.

Sitter, John (ed.). *Eighteenth-Century British Poets: First Series*. (Dictionary of Literary Biography, 95.) Detroit: Gale, 1990. Pp. 436; illustrations.

Rev. (favorably) by Mark Y. Herring in *American Reference Books Annual*, 22 (1991), 493.

Smalley, Joseph. "The French Cataloguing Code of 1791: A Translation." *Library Quarterly*, 61 (1991), 1–14.

Smith, David. "The Popularity of Mme de Graffigny's *Lettres d'une Péruvienne*: The Bibliographical Evidence." *Eighteenth-Century Fiction*, 3 (1990), 1–20; bibliography ["Provisional Shortlist of Editions of Non-Dramatic Works by Mme de Graffigny"].

Smith, Margaret M. "Alexander Pope's Notes on William Wycherley." *Yale University Library Gazette*, 66 (1991), 26–32.

On notes now in the Osborn Collection at Yale University, transcribing some notes and comparing them to Joseph Spence's published adaptation of them.

Smith, Margaret M. *Index of English Literary Manuscripts*. Volume 3: *1700–1800*, Part 2: *John Gay-Ambrose Philips, with a First-Line Index to Parts 1 and 2*. London: Mansell Publishing (distributed through Rutherford, NJ: Publishers Distribution Center), 1989. Pp. xix + 375; 13 photographic facsimiles of autographs. Cf. *ECCB*, n.s. 15, I:14; 12, I:26–27.

Rev. (favorably) in *ANQ: American Notes and Queries*, 4 (1991), 218–29; (favorably) by J. D. Fleeman in *Notes and Queries*, 38 (1991), 390–92; by Ian Jack in *Review of English Studies*, 42 (1991), 429–30; by Philip R. Rider in *American Reference Books Annual*, 22 (1991), 479-80.

Somkúti, Gabriella. "Könyvgyüjö asszonyok a 18. Századi Magyarországon [Women Bookcollectors in Hungary in the eighteenth century]. *Könyvtáros*, 41 (1991), 290–96.

Sorgeloos, Claude. "L'analyse scientifique des imprimés anciens et l'histoire des idées: un cas de la fin du XVIIIe siècle: les *Mémoires historiques et politiques* de P. F. de Neny." *Archives et bibliothèques de Belgique*, 60 (1989), 9–34.

Sorgeloos, Claude. "La Bibliothèque des Etats de Hainaut." *Le Livre & l'estampe*, 37 (1991), 91–198.

Sorgeloos, Claude. "Le Livre dans les Pays-Bas autrichiens et à Liège: une esthétique rocaille." Pp. 139-150 (illustrations) of *Rocaille: Rococo*. (Études sur le XVIIIe siècle, 18.) Edited by Roland Mortier and Hervé Hasquin. Brussells: U. Libre de Bruxelles, Groupe d'études du XVIIIe siècle, 1991.

Soupel, Serge. "Lavieille, Hédouin, Leloir and the *Voyage Sentimental*." *The Shandean*, 2 (1990), 202–13; illustrations; 7 plates.

On three well illustrated nineteenth-century French translations of Sterne's *Sentimental Journey*, 1849, 1875, and 1884.

Speck, Bruce W. (comp.). *Editing: An Annotated Bibliography*. (Bibliographies and Indexes in Mass Media and Communication, 4.) Westport, CT: Greenwood, 1991. Pp. x + 295; indices.

Rev. (favorably) by S. Lehman in *Choice*, 29 (1991), 578.

Spector, Robert D. *Backgrounds to Restoration and Eighteenth-Century English Literature: An Annotated Bibliographical Guide to Modern Scholarship*. Westport, CT: Greenwood, 1989. Pp. xxiv + 553. Cf. *ECCB*, n.s. 16, I:41.

Rev. (Favorably and with another annotated bibliography) by Donald C. Mell in *The Scriblerian*, 23 (Spring 1991), 286–89.

Spector, Stephen (ed.). *Essays in Paper Analysis*. Washington, DC: Folger Shakespeare Library, 1987. Pp. 238; bibliography; illustrations. Cf. *ECCB*, n.s. 16, I: 41–42.

Rev. by Joyce M. Greening in *Analytical and Enumerative Bibliography*, 5 (1991), 89–92.

Spera, Lucinda. "Una Proposta editoriale d'oltralpe: La *Bibliothèque universelle des romans* e la sua traduzione italiana." *La Rassegna della letteratura italiana*, 95 (1991), 65–71.

Sporadora, David. "Bibliographical Essay." Pp. 425–53 of *The Idea of Progress in Eighteenth-Century Britain*. New Haven, CT, and London: Yale U. Press, 1990. Pp. xv + 464; illustrations.

Stanton, Judith Phillips. " 'This New-Found Path Attempting': Women Dramatists in England, 1660–1800." Pp. 325–54 of *Curtain Calls: British and American Women and the Theater, 1660–1820*. Edited by Mary Anne Schofield and Cecilia Macheski. Athens, OH: Ohio U. Press, 1991.

Rev. in *The Scriblerian*, 24 (Autumn 1991), 43.

Stedman, Preston. *The Symphony: A Research and Information Guide*. Vol. 1: *The Eighteenth Century*. (Music Research and Information Guides, 14.) New York: Garland, 1990. Pp. 343.

Rev. (unfavorably) by A. Peter Brown in *Music and Letters*, 72 (1991), 593–95; by C. A. Kolczynski in *Choice*, 28 (1991), 764.

Stenger, Gerhardt. "Deux manuscrits inconnus de Diderot: *Madame de la Carlière* et *Sur les Femmes*." *Dix-huitième siècle*, 23 (1991), 435–40.

Stern, Madeleine B. "Some French Revolutionary Imprints: Patterns from the Past." *Bulletin du bibliophile*, (1991), 164–72; 3 plates.

Stern, Martin, in collaboration with Beatrice Grob, Wolfram Groddeck, and Helmut Puff (eds.). *Textkonstitution bei mündlicher und bei schriftlicher Überlieferung: Basler Editoren-Kolloquium 19-22 März 1990, autor- und werkbezogene Referate*. Tübingen: Niemeyer, 1991. Pp. x + 225.

Among the relevant papers here are J. Golz's "Zur Textkonstitution von Schillers Gedichten" and W. Stark's "Überlegungen zum Nachschreibewesen im Lehrbetrieb des 18. Jahrhunderts (zu Kants Vorlesungen)."

Stewart, Philip. "On the 'Iconology' of Literary Illustration." Pp. 251–67 [7 of plates] in *Dilemmes du roman: Essays in Honor of Georges May*. (Stanford French and Italian Studies, 65.) Edited by Catherine LaFarge. Saratoga, CA: ANMA Libri, 1989.

Stitt, J. Michael, and Robert K. Dodge. *A Tale Type and Motif Index of Early U.S. Almanacs*. (Bibliographies and Indexes in American Literature, 14.) Westport, CT: Greenwood Press, 1991. Pp. xviii + 382; bibliography.

Provides a bibliography and content analyses of American almanacs 1777–1801.

Stoker, David. "The Early Booksellers and Printers of Kings Lynn." Pp. 76–105 of *Studies in the Provincial Book Trade of England, Scotland, and Wales before 1900: Papers Presented to the British Trade Index, Seventh Annual Seminar, Aberystwyth, 11–13 July 1989*. Edited by David A. Stoker. Aberystwyth, UK: Department of Information and Library Studies, University College of Wales, 1990.

Stoker, David. "Prosperity and Success in the Eighteenth-Century English Provincial Book Trade: The Firm of William Chase & Co." *Publishing History*, 30 (1991), 31–88.

Chase worked in Norwich from 1714 to 1741, after which his widow ran the business to 1750 and his son till 1781. Appendices contain book auction and catalogue sales information for 1721–1773; a bibliography of the press's printing and sales, 1710–1786; and Chase II's accounts to the Mayor's Court for paper stock, 1757–1759.

Storm van Leeuwen, Jan. "De Laatste Catalogus van de Stadhouderlijke Bibliotheek." *Documentatieblad Werkgroep achttiende eeuw*, 23 (1991), 83–102.

Streng, Jean C. "The Leiden Engraver Frans van Bleyswyck (1671–1746)." *Quaerendo*, 20 (1990), 111-36; illustrations; 5 plates.

Surrency, Erwin C. *A History of American Law Publishing*. Dobbs Ferry, NY: Oceana, 1990. Pp. 372; bibliography; index.

Rev. (favorably) by T. L. Bonn in *Choice*, 28 (1991), 1296–97.

Sutherland, Madeline. "Treinta y cuatro romances del siglo dieciocho en la Hemeroteca Municipal de Madrid." *Dieciocho*, 12 (1989), 20-33; bibliography.

Tagg, James. *Benjamin Franklin Bache and the Philadelphia* Aurora. Philadelphia, PA: U. of Pennsylvania Press, 1991. Pp. xiv + 431; bibliography.

Taillefer, Michel. "Le Journalisme de province pendant la Révolution française: l'exemple du midi toulousain." Pp. 65–90 of *Révolution et contre-révolution dans la France du Midi (1789–1799): travaux de recherche historique publies dans le cadre du Bicentenaire.* Edited by Jean Sentou. Toulouse: Presses Universitaires du Mirail, 1991.

Taylor, Thomas J. *Restoration Drama: An Annotated Bibliography.* (Magill Bibliographies.) Englewood Cliffs, NJ, and Pasadena, CA: Salem Press, 1989. Pp. vi + 156. Cf. *ECCB*, n.s. 16, I:43.

Rev. by Joseph Rosenheim in *Library Journal*, 115 (May 1, 1990), 84; (favorably) by James Edgar Stephenson in *American Reference Books Annual*, 22 (1991), 481.

Tebbel, John W., and Mary Ellen Zuckerman. *The Magazine in America, 1741–1990.* New York: Oxford U. Press, 1991. Pp. viii + 433; bibliography.

Rev. (favorably) by Mary Romano Marks in *Booklist*, 87 (June 15, 1991), 1946; (favorably) by Hiley Ward in *Editor and Publisher*, 124 (July 24, 1991), 22.

Thomas, David, and Arnold Hare (comps.). *Restoration and Georgian England (1600–1788).* Edited by David Thomas. Cambridge and New York: Cambridge U. Press, 1989. Pp. xxx + 460; bibliography; illustrations.

Rev. (with many reservations) by William J. Burling in *Scriblerian*, 24 (1991), 78–79; (favorably) by Brean S. Hammond in *British Journal of Eighteenth-Century Studies*, 14 (1991), 222.
Reproduces manuscript and printed sources for studying the theater.

Thomas, David H. "A Checklist of Major French Authors in Oxford Libraries: First Supplement." *Studies on Voltaire and the Eighteenth Century*, 260 (1989), 427–64.

Thomas, David H. "A Checklist of Major French Authors in Oxford Libraries: First Supplement." *Studies on Voltaire and the Eighteenth Century*, 266 (1989), 513–47.

Thomas, George-Michel. "Un bibliophile brestois au XVIIIe siècle: Joseph Tremblay." *Bulletin de la Société archéologique du Finistère*, 119 (1990), 225–31.

Thomas, Graham C. G. "George Whitefield and Friends: The Correspondence of Some Early Methodists." *National Library of Wales Journal*, 26 (1989–90), 251–280; 367–396 [to be continued].

This series of articles both indexes and reproduces 109 letters, 1737–39, by George Whitefield and his associations, found in a scribal manuscript volume at the National Library of Wales.

Thomson, Ann. "La Mettrie, lecteur et traducteur de Boerhaave." *Dix-huitième siècle*, 23 (1991), 23–29.

Tierney, James E. "A CD-ROM Subject Index to Pre-1800 British Periodicals." *The East-Central Intelligencer*, 5 (September, 1991), 8–13.

Contains a historical account of earlier efforts toward a subject index and offers a description and status-report for Tierney's own on-going project.

Todd, Christopher. *Political Bias, Censorship, and the Dissolution of the Official Press in Eighteenth-Century France*. (Studies in French Civilization, 8.) Lewiston, NY, and London: Edwin Mellen, 1991. Pp. ix + 431; bibliography; indices.

Todd, Janet (ed.). *British Women Writers: A Critical Reference Guide*. New York: Continuum, 1989. Pp. xx + 762.

Tortorelli, Gianfranco. *Studi di storia dell'editoria italiana*. Bologna: Patron editore, 1989. Pp. 177; biblography.

Tóth, Imre H. "Karcagújszállási-Carceus Mihály élete és Müvei." *Magyar Könyvszemle*, 107 (1991), 325–42.

Tóth, István György. "Nemesi könyvtárak Vas Megyében a 18. sz. második felében." *Történelmi szemle*, 32 (1990), 222–58.

Trattner, Jakobus. "Bücher aus dem Besitz Johann Michael Haydns in der Bibliothek von St. Peter." Pp. 187–93 of *Das Benedikterstift St. Peter zur Zeit Mozarts*. Salzburg: St. Peter, 1991.

Trenard, Louis (ed.). *Revue française d'histoire du livre: Les Bibliothèques au 18e siècle*. (Special issue of *RFHL*.) Bordeaux: Société des Bibliophiles de Guyenne, 1989. Pp. 387.

Rev. by Lise Andries in *Dix-huitième siècle*, 23 (1991), 451–52.

Trento, Angelo. "La Stampa periodica italiana in Brasile, 1765–1915)." *Il Veltro: Rivista della civiltà italiana*, 34 (1990), 301–15; with Italian, French, and English summaries.

Tucker, Louis Leonard. *Clio's Consort: Jeremy Belknap and the Founding of the Massachusetts Historical Society*. Boston, MA: Massachusetts Historical Society, 1989. Pp. xii + 149; bibliography; illustrations; 6 plates.

Rev. (favorably) by Frank C. Mevers in the *Journal of the Early Republic*, 10 (1990), 601–02.

Ulman, H. Lewis. "Discerning Readers: British Reviewers' Responses to Campbell's Rhetoric and Related Works." *Rhetorica*, 8 (1990), 65–90; abstract.

Unseld, Siegfried. *Goethe und seine Verleger*. Frankfurt am Main and Leipzig: Insel-Velag, 1991. Pp. 790; bibliography [1761–69]; illustrations (some colored); index.

Uphaus, Robert W. "Vicesimus Knox and the Canon of Eighteenth-Century Literature." *The Age of Johnson*, 4 (1991), 345–61.

Vakkari, Pertti. "Reading, Knowledge of Books, and Libraries as a Basis for the Conception of Scholarship in Eighteenth-Century Germany." *Libraries and Culture*, 26 (1991), 66–86.

Vandenhole, F. (comp.). *Inventaris van veilingcatalogi 1615–1914: met topografische, alfabetische en inhoudsindexen*. (Bijdragen tot de bibltheekwetenschap, 5.) 2 vols. Ghent: Rijksuniversiteit, Centrale Bibliotheek, 1987.

Rev. in *Quarendo*, 20 (1990), 74.
This list of art and book auction catalogues at the Ghent University Library provides date, place of auction, auctioneer, types of materials auctioned, length of catalogue, whether with or without prices and buyers, and shelfmark in the collection. Vol. 1 covers 1615–1897; Vol. 2: 1897–1914; the index is in Vol. 2.

Van der Haar, J. (comp.). *Schatkamer van de Gereformeerde theologie in Nederland (c. 1600– c. 1800): Bibliografisch onderzoek*. Veenendall, the Netherlands: G. Kool, 1987. Pp. 675; bibliography; indices.

Rev. (unsigned) in *Quaerendo*, 21 (1991), 78–79 [noting indices of publishers and locations for this survey of theological books at over 60 private collections].

Vander Meulen, David L. *Pope's Dunciad of 1728: A History and Facsimile*. Charlottesville, VA, and London: University Press of Virginia for the Bibliographical Society of the U. of Virginia and the New York Public Library, 1991. Pp. xviii + 174; facsimile illustrations.

Van der Woude, Corrie-Christine. "Veilingcatalogi als bron voor boekhistorisch onderzoek." *Documentatieblad Werkgroep achttiende eeuw*, 23 (1991), 47–57.

Van Dijk, Susan, and Dini Helmers. "Nederlandse Vrouwentijdschriften in de Achttiende Eeuw?" Pp. 71-88 of *Balans en Perspectief van de Nederlanse Cultuurgeschiedenis: De Productie, Distributie, en Consumptie van Cultuur*. Edited by J. J. Kloek and W. W. Mijnhardt. Amersterdam: Rodopi, 1991.

Van Galen, H. "De Recensent 1787–1793: Blauwe Beul van de Achttiende Eeuw." *Documentatieblad Werkgroep achttiende eeuw*, 23 (1991), 59–74.

Van Selm, Bert. "Dutch Book Trade Catalogues Printed before 1801 Now in the British Library." Pp. 54–66 of *Across the Narrow Seas: Studies in the History and Bibliography of Britain and the Low Countries: Presented to Ann E. C. Simoni*. Edited by Susan Roach. Forward by Mirjam M. Foot. Bibliography by Dennis E. Rhodes. London: British Library, 1991.

Varry, Dominique (gen. ed.). *Histoire des bibliothèques françaises*: Vol. 3: *Les Bibliothèques de la Révolution et du XIXᵉ siècle (1789–1914)*. Paris: Promodis, in conjuction with the Centre National des Lettres, 1991. Pp. xii + 671; bibliography; illustrations; indices [of names and places]; plates; register of illustrators.

Vercruysse, Jeroom. "The Publication of the *Oeuvres completes* [of Isabelle de Charrière]." *ECLife*, 13 (1989), 69–78.

Vincent, David. *Literacy and Popular Culture: England, 1750–1914*. Cambridge and New York: Cambridge U. Press, 1989. Pp. 372.

Rev. (favorably) by John Boli in *American Journal of Sociology*, 97 (1991), 569–71; (favorably) by Peter Gurney in *Sociological Review*, 39 (1991), 197–99; (mixed) by Richard A. Peterson in *International Journal of Comparative Sociology*, 32 (1991), 358–59; (favorably) in rev. article ("New Questions and New Approaches in the Study of the 'History of the Book'") by David A. Rawson in *ECLife*, 15 (1991), 103–12.

Von Arnim, Manfred. "Beiträge zur Einbandkunde I: "Ein Wappen-Einband Von (Jean?) Padeloup für Maria Leszczynska, ca. 1748." *Philobiblon*, 33 (1989), 39–40.

Wachs, Morris. "Voltaire's 'Regnante puero': The Date, the Title, and the French Original." *Studies on Voltaire and the Eighteenth Century*, 284 (1991), 107–13.

Wagner, Peter (ed.). *Erotica and the Enlightenment*. 1988. Reprinted, London: Paladin, 1990. Pp. xiv + 498; bibliography; illustrations; index. Reprinted in series Britannia Texts in English, 2. Frankfurt am Main and New York: Peter Lang, 1991. Pp. 366; bibliography; illustrations.

Rev. (mixed) by Pat Rogers in *Albion*, 23 (1991), 135–37.

Wagner, Peter. "Hogarth's Graphic Palimpsests: Intermedial Adaptation of Popular Literature." *Word and Image*, 7 (1991), 329–47; 32 illustrations.

Waldon, Freda Farrell. *Bibliography of Canadiana Published in Great Britain, 1519–1763 / Bibliographie des Ouvrages sur le Canada Publiés in Grande-Bretagne entre 1519 et 1763.* Revised and edited by William F. E. Morley. Ottawa: National Library of Canada; Toronto: ECW Press (distributed through North York, Ontario: U. of Toronto Press), 1990. Pp. lxv + 535; illustrations.

Rev. by W. J. Eccles in *The Papers of the Bibliographical Society of Canada*, 29 (1991), 54–57; by Virginia S. Fischer in *American Reference Books Annual*, 22 (1991), 517.

Walsh, Marcus. "Bentley Our Contemporary; or, Editors, Ancient and Modern." Pp. 157–85 of *The Theory and Practice of Text-Editing: Essays in Honour of James T. Boulton*. Edited by Ian Small and Marcus Walsh. Cambridge and New York: Cambridge U. Press, 1991.

Finds Richard Bentley's editorial principles comparable to those opposed by G. Thomas Tanselle et al. for neglecting the author's intentions.

Walther, Karl Klaus. *Britannischer Glückswechsel: deutschsprachige Flugschriften des 17 Jahrhunderts über England*. (Beitrage zum Buch- und Bibliothekswesen, 32.) Wiesbaden: Harrassowitz, 1991. Pp. vi + 246; facsimiles; illustrations; indices; 16 plates.

Walther, Karl Klaus. "Der Kupferstich als Medium–Literatur für Sammler um 1770." *Philobiblon*, 34 (1990), 309–20.

Waquet, Françoise. "Les savants face à leurs portraits, XVIIe-XVIIIe siècle." *Nouvelle de l'estampe*, 117 (1991), 22–28; illustrations.

Waquet, Françoise. "Protéger les livres, discipliner les lecteurs: Les *Avvertenze* de Gaetano Volpi (1756)." *Bulletin du bibliophile* (1991), 156–63.

Warner, Michael. *The Letters of the Republic: Publication and the Public Sphere in Eighteenth-Century America.* Cambridge, MA, and London: Harvard U. Press, 1990. Pp. xv + 205.

Rev. by C. E. Clark in the *William and Mary Quarterly*, 48 (1991), 311–13; by Hazel Dicken-Garcia in *Journal of the Early Republic*, 11 (1991), 103–04.

Waterston, Elizabeth, with Ian Easterbrook, Bernard Katz, and Kathleen Scott. *The Travellers–Canada to 1900: An Annotated Bibliography of Works Published in English from 1577.* Guelph, Ontario: U. of Guelph Press, 1989. Pp. viii + 321; illustrations.

Rev. by Barbara Belyea in *The Papers of the Bibliographical Society of Canada*, 29 (1991), 40-44; by Zbigniew Mieczkowski in *American Reference Books Annual*, 22 (1991), 186; (favorably except regarding illustrations) by William S. Peterson in *The Papers of the Bibliographical Society of America*, 85 (1991), 89; (favorably) by Donald H. Simpson in *The Book Collector*, 40 (1991), 269–71.

Wegehaupt, Heinz, with the editorial assistance of Ursula Henning (comp.). *Robinson und Struwwelpeter: Bücher für Kinder aus fünf Jahrhunderten: Katalog zur Ausstellung der Deutschen Staatsbibliothek Berlin.* Hildesheim: Olms, 1991. Pp. 176; illustrations.

Weissman, Stephen and Sarah Pogostin. *Henry Fielding, 1707–1754.* (Occasional List, No. 92.) New York: Ximenes Rare Books, 1991. Pp. 82 (approx.).

The detailed descriptions and estimations of scarcity in this sale catalogue of works by Fielding and his family members make it an indispensable tool.

Wiedemann, Konrad, with the assistance of Peter-Paul Schneider (comps.). *Die Bibliothek Friedrich Heinrich Jacobis: Ein Katalog.* (Friedrich Heinrich Jacobi, Dokumente zu Leben und Werk, 1–2.) Vols. 1–2. Stuttgart and Bad Canstatt: Frommann-Holzboog, 1989. Pp. xliv + 452; vi, 453–942.

Rev. of Vol. 1 by Rainer A. Bast and of Vol. 2 by Klaus Schreiber in *Zeitschrift für Bibliothekswesen und Bibliographie*, 38 (1991), 160–61 [Vol. 1] and 174–76 [Vol. 2].

Wilkie, Everett C., Jr. "The Authorship and Purpose of the *Histoire naturelle et morale des iles Antilles*, an Early Huguenot Emigration Guide." *Harvard Library Bulletin*, 2 (1991), 26–84.

Good survey of guidebooks to life in the colonies.

Wilkie, Richard W., and Jack Tager (eds.). *Historical Atlas of Massachusetts.* Amherst, MA: U. of Massachusetts Press, 1991. Pp. viii + 152; bibliography; illustrations; maps.

Rev. (favorably) by B. McCorkle in *Choice*, 29 (1991), 416; (favorably) by Charles Michaud in *Library Journal*, 116 (May 15, 1991), 77.

"Willam B. Todd: A Bibliography." Pp. 186–213 in *Essays in Honor of William B. Todd.* Compiled by Warner Barnes and Larry Carver. Austin, TX: Harry Ransom Humanities Research Center, 1991.

This festschrift for Professor Todd was also issued as nos. 3–4 of *The Library Chronicle of the U. of Texas*, 21 (1991).

Williams, Leigh, and Rosemarie Johnstone. "Updating Mary Wollstonecraft: A Bibliography of Criticism, 1976–1989." *The Bulletin of Bibliography*, 48 (1991), 103–07.

Willison, I. R. "Remarks on the History of the Book in Britain as a Field of Study within the Humanities, with a Synopsis and Select List of Current Literature." Pp. 94–145 in *Essays in Honor of William B. Todd*. Compiled by Warner Barnes and Larry Carver. Austin, TX: Harry Ransom Humanities Research Center, 1991. Pp. 215; illustrations.

This festschrift for Professor Todd was also issued as nos. 3–4 of *The Library Chronicle of the University of Texas*, 21 (1991).

Wilson, Jeffrey. "Bibliography Supplement, 1984–1989." *New Vico Studies*, 7 (1989), 162–91.

Wilson, Katharina M. (ed.). *An Encyclopedia of Continental Women Writers*. (Garland Reference Library of the Humanities, 698.) 2 vols. New York and London: Garland, 1991. Pp. xiii + 1389.

Winearls, Joan. *Mapping Upper Canada, 1780–1867: An Annotated Bibliography of Manuscript and Printed Maps*. Buffalo, NY, and Toronto, Ontario: U. of Toronto Press, 1991. Pp. xli + 986; bibliography; illustrations; indices.

Lists 10,000 maps, two-thirds of which are in manuscript.

Winship, Michael (ed.). *Bibliography of American Literature*. Vol. 8: *Charles Warren Stoddard to Susan Bogert Warner*. Compiled by Jacob Blanck. New Haven, CT: Yale U. Press, 1990. Pp. xxii + 519; illustrations.

Rev. (favorably) by Mary Jo Walker in *American Reference Books Annual*, 22 (1991), 460.
Only two of the 29 American authors covered in Vol. 8 wrote in the eighteenth-century: John Trumbull, 1750–1831 (345–57; 1 plate) and Royall Tyler, 1752–1826 (387–96; 1 plate).

Wittmann, Reinhard. *Geschichte des deutschen Buchhandels: Ein Überlick*. Munich: C. H. Beck, 1991. Pp. 438; illustrations.

Woesler, Winfried. "Edition und Kommentierung eines dienstlichen Briefes an Justus Möser." Pp. 62–71 of *Edition als Wissenschaft: Festschrift für Hans Zeller*. Edited by Gunter Martens and Winfried Woesler. (Beihefte zu Editio, 2.) Tübingen: Niemeyer, 1991.

Wolfe, Richard J. *Marbled Paper: Its History, Techniques, and Patterns: With Special Reference to the Relationship of Marbling to Bookbinding in Europe and the Western World*. Philadelphia, PA: U. of Pennsylvania Press, 1990. Pp. xvi + 245; 38 color plates; illustrations.

Reviewed by Geneviève Guilleminot-Chrétien in *Bulletin du bibliophile* (1991), 472–74; by S. F. Huttner in *Rare Books and Manuscripts Librarianship*, 5 (1990), 105–09; (favorably) by Bernard C. Middleton in *Library*, 13 (1991), 81–82; and Thomas D. Walker in *Library Quarterly*, 61 (1991), 117–18.

Woollam, Fiona. *Popular Literature in Eighteenth and Nineteenth Century Britain: A Listing and Guide to the Research Publications Edition* [at the British Library Vols. 2–3. Vol. 2: *The Sabine Bearing-Gould and Thomas Crampton Collections from the British Library*; Vol. 3: *The Barry Ono Collection* [of bloods and penny dreadfuls, at the British Library; reproduced on microfilm]. Woodbridge, CT, and Reading, U.K.: Research Publications, 1990, 1991.

Woods, C. J. "An Unnoticed Pamphlet by Charles O'Conor at Belanagare: *A Vindication of the Political Principles of Roman Catholics* (1761)." *Eighteenth-Century Ireland*, 6 (1991), 161.

Woudhuysen, R. R. "Dr. Johnson's Books." *TLS* (July 6, 1990), 728.

Zaslaw, Neal (ed.), with the assistance of William Cowdery. *The Complete Mozart: A Guide to the Musical Works of Wolfgang Amadeus Mozart.* New York: Norton, 1991. Pp. 351.

Rev. (favorably) by C. A. Kolczynski in *Choice*, 28 (1991), 1627; (favorably) by Timothy J. McGee in Library Journal, 116 (Jan. 1, 1991), 106 .

Zbikowska-Migón, Anna. *Historia Ksiazki w XVIII wieku: poczatki bibliologii.* Warsaw: Panstwowe Wydawnnictwo Naukowe, 1989. Pp. 399; bibliography.

Apparently reissued in 1990 by the same press in the series Ksiazku o ksiazce.

Zwigger, Steven N., and David Bywaters. "Politics and Translation: The English Tacitus of 1698." *Huntington Library Quarterly*, 52 (1989), 319–46.

Historical, Social,
and Economic Studies

Abercromby, James. *The Letter Book of James Abercromby, Colonial Agent: 1751–1773.* Edited by George Reese and John C. Van Horne. Richmond, VA: Virginia State Library and Archives, 1991. Pp. lvi + 471.

Adams, Geoffrey. *The Huguenots and French Opinion: The Enlightenment Debate on Toleration.* Waterloo, Ontario: The Canadian Corporation for Studies in Religion by Wilfrid Laurier U. Press, 1991. Pp. xiv + 336; bibliography; illustrations.

Over the course of the century between Louis XIV's revocation of the Edict of Nantes in 1685 and Louis XVI's decree of 1787 granting Protestants a measure of civil and religious liberty, the attitudes of French intellectuals toward the Huguenots underwent a profound transformation. Virtually universal support for the Revocation among Catholic thinkers in the late seventeenth century gave way to an increasing demand for greater religious toleration in general and for a restoration of basic civil rights to Protestants in particular. To illuminate this significant shift in elite opinion, Geoffrey Adams examines the writings of individual *philosophes* and explores the complex interplay of philosophical thought with ministerial politics. Its strength lies in its close, contextualized readings of individual texts by Enlightenment authors such as Montesquieu, Voltaire, Diderot, and Rousseau.

Adams explains Voltaire's evolution with particular skill. We meet him as the fiery young poet who, although he had little sympathy for the Huguenots' plight, fulminated against the Saint Bartholomew Day's Massacre in his 1723 epic *La Henriade*. With Adams' help, we watch Voltaire gradually develop into the pamphleteer-politician who, forty years later in the Calas Affair, crusaded ardently for Protestant equality before the law. Adams' analysis of Voltaire particularly brings to light a central paradox in the *philosophes'* views of French Protestantism. Many of them, including Voltaire and the Encyclopedists, sought for the Huguenots broader religious toleration and egalitarian civil treatment. Still, they remained critical of dogmatic theology and leery of the "superstitious" or intolerant qualities which Protestantism seemed to share with other forms of Christianity. The *philosophes*, deists for the most part, offered no ringing endorsement for Protestantism; indeed, the writings of Voltaire, Diderot, and other Encyclopedists sometimes satirized Calvinist theology or reiterated traditional criticisms of its subversive, anti-state qualities. Adams' carefully balanced exploration of these complexities in the *philosophes'* opinions offers both an account of the reception of their works by leading Calvinist thinkers and of that by conservative defenders of the Catholic monopoly.

The final section of the book traces the movement of the crusade from pamphleteering to pragmatic politics. By the 1770s, several of the king's ministers had assimilated the Enlightenment belief in the need for religious toleration; others recognized the problematic legal status of Protestant marriages. Adams concludes with a detailed analysis of the political circumstances, journalistic campaigning, and skillful maneuvering by Malesherbes, Breteuil, and Rulhiére in the mid-1780's, which ultimately convinced both the king and the Paris parlement to grant limited civil and religious rights to the Huguenots in 1787. If the strength of this book lies in its detailed treatment of evolving attitudes toward Protestantism, its weakness lies in Adams' reluctance to connect his specific analyses to broader questions. He might have clarified why this evolution came to pass or what it tells us more generally about the nature of the Enlightenment or the problematic character of attempts to reform the corporate structures of the late Old Regime. Likewise, comparisons to developing convictions regarding Judaism within France or religious toleration within the European community as a whole would have helped to place his analysis in a broader context. Adams has nonetheless crafted a useful and thorough study, which will be of interest to scholars of Protestantism, the Enlightenment, and French politics in the eighteenth century.—Suzanne Desan.

Åkerman, Susanna. *Queen Christina of Sweden and her Circle: The Transformation of a Seventeenth-Century Philosophical Libertine.* Leiden and New York: E. J. Brill, 1991. Pp. xv + 342; appendices; bibliography.

Susanna Åkerman's study of Queen Christina of Sweden reads in places like a postmodern tapestry of inter– and disconnected antiquarian tidbits and quotations, but it does contain nuggets of substance that reward the sufficiently patient reader. It is a shame, however, that the editors of the series—including Åkerman's doctoral adviser, Richard H. Popkin—did not intervene more forcefully to eliminate the numerous misspellings and other infelicities (beginning with "revelance" on p. xii and ending with "ar" for "år" on p. 331) that mar so many pages of this book.

Åkerman states late in her book that earlier treatments of Christina's life provide "an example of how a woman who acts in the political, theological, and juridical sphere came to be treated as an anomoly" (pp. 300–301). Early on in the book, she presents her own, radically new theories by taking issue with previous interpretations of Christina's abdication and conversion, arguing that her abdication must be seen as "[a] theologico-political act whereby [she] transmits her superior power to someone who . . . is better equipped to govern the military, whereas she as an unbound royalty can cause the formation of a new political constellation in Europe" and that her conversion was motivated by "[a] non-conformist deism combined with a Hermetic/neo-Platonic metaphysics as a basis for her self-image as an agent in European politics" (p. 6).

According to Åkerman, Christina's "search for a satisfactory religion, rooted in childhood doubts on the existence of hell, led her to the conclusion that religion is a political construction" (p. 291). She convincingly portrays the Swedish queen as a religious free-thinker (pp. 30–36) and discounts the influence on her thinking that has so frequently been attributed to René Descartes. Indeed, it turns out that the queen met Descartes only four or five times (p. 49), and Åkerman argues that he "did not have a deciding influence on Queen Christina's conversion, he had little to do with her skepticism, and his philosophy played no formative role in her decisions" (p. 44).

After dismissing religious motivations for the queen's abdication, Åkerman states that Christina "accepted genetical views that gave her comparable license to act as a divinely ordained monarch, even in absence of a throne" (p. 120) and believed that "Gothic genealogy had given her natural ties to the Spanish Habsburgs that she now could pursue for her own welfare and that of the rest of Europe" (p. 119). For these reasons she abdicated her throne and sought the recognition of Rome (through conversion to Catholicism) in order better to pursue "her enthusiastic involvement in political plans for a general peace between France and Spain" (p. 165). In Chapter 9, Åkerman links the timing of the queen's abdication to the eclipse of 1653, the comet of 1652, and the eclipse of 1654, all of which were much on the mind of European contemporaries and especially on the minds of the millenarians, who predicted that 1656 would witness "a sudden increase in catastrophes that would alter the entire political situation in Europe" (p. 163). Her presentation suggests that this context helps to explain both Christina's thinking and the way in which her abdication was viewed as being momentous by so many contemporaries.

Åkerman makes many interesting points and presents new data concerning both Christina's plans and how she was viewed in her own age, but her presentation is frequently circuitous and she never brings her arguments to satisfactory closure. This could have been a much better book had it been edited more expertly.—Michael Metcalf.

Alatri, Paolo. *L'Europa della successioni (1731–1748).* Palermo: Sellerio, 1989. Pp. 305.

Rev. (briefly) by Lelia Pessillo in *Studi francesi*, 34 (1991), 52–21.

Alexander, John K. *The Selling of the Constitutional Convention: A History of News Coverage*. Madison, WI: Madison House Publishers, 1990. Pp. x + 246. Cf. *ECCB*, n.s. 16, II: 50.

Rev. by P. J. Galie in *Choice*, 28 (1991), 1844.

Allen, Michael. *Western Rivermen, 1763–1861: Ohio and Mississippi Boatmen and the Myth of the Alligator Horse*. Baton Rouge, LA: Louisiana State U. Press, 1990. Pp. xiii + 261; illustrations; maps. Cf. *ECCB*, n.s. 16, II: 50.

Rev. by S. J. Bronner in *Choice*, 28 (1991), 1367.

Alotta, Robert I. *Another Part of the Field: Philadelphia's American Revolution, 1777–78*. Shippensburg, PA: White Mane Publishing Co., 1991. Pp. 133.

Altman, Ida, and James Horn (eds.). *'To Make America': European Emigration in the Early Modern Period*. Berkeley, CA, and Oxford: U. of California Press, 1991. Pp. vii + 251; maps; tables.

Anderson, Karen. *Chain Her by One Foot: The Subjugation of Women in Seventeenth-Century New France*. London and New York: Routledge, 1991. Pp. 247.

Arnold, Morris S. *Colonial Arkansas, 1686–1804: A Social and Cultural History*. Fayetteville, AR: U. of Arkansas Press, 1991. Pp. 232.

Arnebeck, Bob. *Through a Fiery Trial: Building Washington, 1790–1800*. Lanham, MD: Madison Books/National Book Network, 1991. Pp. 701.

Ashcraft, Richard (ed.). *John Locke: Critical Assessments, Vol. I*. (Critical Assessments of Leading Political Philosophers.) London: Routledge, 1991. Pp. ix + 341.

Ashcraft, Richard (ed.). *John Locke: Critical Assessments, Vol. II*. (Critical Assessments of Leading Political Philosophers.) London: Routledge, 1991. Pp. vi + 347.

Attwooll, Elspeth (ed.). *Shaping Revolution*. (Enlightenment, Rights, and Revolution Series.) Aberdeen, Scotland: Aberdeen U. Press, 1991. Pp. xviii + 214.

Ayling, Stanley. *Fox: The Life of Charles James Fox*. London: J. Murray, 1991. Pp. 271; illustrations; portraits.

Rev. by John Derry in *TLS*, (Oct. 25, 1991), 25.

Baecque, Antoine de. "L'Histoire de la Révolution française dans son moment herméneutique." *Dix-huitième siècle*, 21 (1991), 275–92.

Bailey, Thomas A., and David M. Kennedy (eds.). *The American Spirit: United States History as Seen by Contemporaries*. Vol. I. Lexington, MA, and Toronto: D. C. Heath, 1991. Pp. xv + 486 + xxii; illustrations; maps.

Bailyn, Bernard, and Philip D. Morgan (eds.). *Strangers within the Realm: Cultural Margins of the First British Empire*. Chapel Hill, NC, and London: U. of Chapel Hill Press for the

Institute of Early American History and Culture, Williamsburg, VA, 1991. Pp. 456; tables.

Rev. by J. A. Casada in *Choice*, 29 (1991), 336.

A collection of original essays concerning the interaction of "center" and "periphery" in the shaping of the British Empire. Starting with the incorporation of Scotland and Ireland on the "margins of Britain," the book proceeds to the "borderlands of the west," and an examination of the cultural transactions and political disputes involving British colonists, on the one hand, and Indians, Africans and African-Americans, West Indians, and Canadian French, Dutch and German-speaking populations, on the other. An additional dimension is provided by an essay on "the Scotch-Irish in British America," which points to the cultural heterogeneity of the colonists themselves. A final essay shifts the focus back to the "homeland," discussing the impact of the thirteen colonies on British society and politics.

Baker, Keith Michael. *Inventing the French Revolution: Essays on French Political Culture in the Eighteenth Century.* (Ideas in Context.) Cambridge and New York: Cambridge U. Press, 1990. Pp. x + 372; bibliography. Cf. *ECCB*, n.s. 16, II: 52.

Rev. (favorably) in rev. article ("An Enlightened Revolution?") by Robert Darnton in *New York Review of Books*, 38 (Oct. 24, 1991), 33–36; (with other works) by Colin Jones in *TLS,* (Mar. 29, 1991), 7–8.

Barny, Roger. *Le Comte d'Antraigues: Un Disciple aristocrate de J.-J. Rousseau. De la Fascination au reniement 1782–1797.* Oxford: The Voltaire Foundation at the Taylor Institution, 1991. Pp. vi + 261.

This case study of the comte d'Antraigues, a minor provincial aristocrat who, like many others of all social classes, fell for a while under the spell of Rousseau, is divided into two parts.

The first, dealing with d'Antraigues as a literary figure is, as one would expect from such an authoritative critic as Roger Barny, highly informative but unlikely to inspire one to delve into d'Antraigues's writings. This is not only because d'Antraigues followed Rousseau's ideas and themes, his mingling of fact and ficton, quite slavishly, but also because he was not a very good writer. Although Barny identifies areas in which d'Antraigues displayed a modicum of originality, for example, in his treatment of Nature, it seems to this reader that his departures from the tenets of his master constitute more a desperate and inauthentic attempt to carve out a niche for himself than the sincere expression of genuinely held differences.

By contrast, the second part of this monograph, the political evolution of d'Antraigues from radical to conservative, from disciple of Rousseau to follower of Burke, is fascinating on two levels. Through an examination of how this "seigneur" with egalitarian ideals started out as the most fervent proponent of the fundamental principles of the *Contrat social* and ended up by renouncing them, one can readily appreciate the extent to which so many of the "revolutionaries" became caught up, as they still are today, in the dilemmas involved in trying to reconcile Rousseauean theory and practice. The sovereignty of the people, the cornerstone of Jean-Jacques's system, turned out for d'Antraigues and for countless others to be hopelessly utopian, dangerous and consequently, undesirable.

Barny's most important observations in this second part have to do with the subtle ways in which Rousseau was used, as the Revolution progressed, not simply to justify one side against the other (the arguments about the democratic and totalitarian elements in his political philosophy still go on), but to characterize the disillusion felt by all sides as the difficulties in combining law and order with social justice, under any system, became increasingly apparent.

If the value of d'Antraigues's literary imitations of Rousseau may be questioned, no one can doubt the passion and sincerity displayed in his turning away from the political teachings of a master he had once so blindly worshipped. D'Antraigues story is, in some senses, the story of the Revolution itself, and Barny has told it well, here and, at much greater length, elsewhere.—Aubrey Rosenberg.

Bartlett, Beatrice S. *Monarchs and Ministers: The Grand Council in Mid-Ch'ing China, 1723–1820.* Berkeley, CA, and Oxford: U. of California Press, 1991. Pp. xxi + 417; appendices; bibliography; figures; frontispiece; map; tables.

Rev. (favorably) by H. T. Wong in *Choice*, 29 (1991), 943–44.
Parts 1–2 (i.e., the first half) concern the Eighteenth Century.

Bartoszewski, Wladyslaw, and Anthony Polonsky (eds.). *The Jews in Warsaw.* Oxford: Basil Blackwell in association with the Institute for Polish-Jewish Studies, 1991. Pp. xii + 392; maps; plates.

Bates, Samuel A. (ed.). *Records of the Town of Braintree, 1640–1793, Vol. 1–2.* (Heritage Classics.) Rupert, ID: Heritage Books, 1991. Pp. 939.

Baumgartner, Frederic J. *From Spear to Flintlock: A History of War in Europe and the Middle East to the French Revolution.* New York and Westport, CT: Praeger, 1991. Pp. xii + 355; illustrations; maps.

Baumier, Matthieu. "L'Organisation des hauts grades du Grand Orient de France. Le Grand chapitre général de France (décembre 1783–juillet 1787)." *LHS*, 21 (1991), 247–60.

Includes a list of chapters affiliated with the Grand Chapitre Général de France in 1787.

Bayard, Françoise, and Philippe Guignet. *L'Economie française XVIe, XVIIe et XVIIIe siècles.* (Synthèse et histoire.) Preface by Pierre Deyon. Gap, France: Ophrys, 1991. Pp. 264.

Bayle, Pierre. *Historical and Critical Dictionary: Selections.* Translated by Richard H. Popkin. Cambridge and Indianapolis, IN: Hackett Publishing Co., Inc., 1991. Pp. xl + 456; bibliography.

Beddard, Robert. *The Revolutions of 1688.* Oxford: Clarendon Press, 1991. Pp. 313.

Beier, A. L., David Cannadine, and James M. Rosenheim (eds.). *The First Modern Society. Essays in English History in Honour of Lawrence Stone.* Cambridge and New York: Cambridge U. Press, 1989. Pp. xxii + 654.

Rev. by Jeremy Black in *The Scriblerian*, 24 (1991), 89–90.

Bély, Lucien. *Les Relations internationales en Europe XVIIe et XVIIIe siècles.* (Thémis, Histoire.) Paris: Presses Universitaires de France, 1991. Pp. 768.

Bennett, Charles E., and Donald R. Lennon. *A Quest for Glory: Major General Robert Howe and the American Revolution.* Chapel Hill, NC: U. of North Carolina Press, 1991. Pp. xii + 205; bibliography; illustrations.

Berg, Maxine (ed.). *Markets and Manufacture in Early Industrial Europe.* London and New York: Routledge, 1990. Pp. xiv + 332; illustration; map. Cf. *ECCB*, n.s. 16, II: 54.

Rev. (with another work) by Peter Clark in *TLS*, (Oct. 11, 1991), 29.

Bergeron, David M. *Royal Family, Royal Lovers: King James of England and Scotland.* Columbia, MO, and London: U. of Missouri Press, 1991. Pp. x + 222; bibliography; illustrations.

Bergin, Joseph. *The Rise of Richelieu.* London and New Haven, CT: Yale U. Press, 1991. Pp. xiii + 282; bibliography; chronology; genealogies.

Bernard, Paul P. *From the Enlightenment to the Police State: The Public Life of Johann Anton Pergen.* Urbana, IL: U. of Illinois Press, 1991. Pp. xi + 252; bibliography.

Rev. (favorably) by P. Petschauer in *Choice*, 29 (1991), 646.

Johann Anton Pergen, Joseph II's minister of police, has a particularly nasty reputation: "a peculiarly bloody-minded policeman, unable to think in terms more complex than brutal repression when confronted with any sort of opposition to public authority," (p. x). Bernard, however, sees Pergen as "a man of considerable intelligence and sensitivity," who at least for part of his life embraced the reformist programs of the Enlightenment and who could even "defend positions diametrically opposed to those taken by the conservative opponents of Josephinian reform," (p. x). Certainly Bernard lightens the hitherto darkly brushed portrait of Pergen, although he ultimately cannot deny that under Joseph II and Francis II Pergen built and controlled a notorious system of *Kabinettsjustiz*, with closed, administrative proceedings, where charges of *Staatsverbrechen* prevailed. Nor can he conceal that Pergen's *Geheime Staatspolizei* remained far removed from the *Rechtsstaat* envisioned by legal reformers.

Bernard's careful discussion of Pergen's life, in particular his detailed analysis of the more infamous cases he was involved in, such as the Jacobin trials of the 1790s, does scrape a bit of the tarnish from Pergen's reputation, allowing a few glimmers of probity and compassion to shine through. But the true value of the book lies not it this partial rehabilitation of a rather dull imperial servant. More useful is Bernard's picture of Pergen as a type, as the quintessential careerist, a man of less than extraordinary abilities (except his truly great capacity for generating mountains of paper), who set out to make his way in the sprawling administrative world spawned by the many interests of the Habsburg. Pergen succeeded well enough in collecting positions and honors, but was perhaps unique in his ability to amass a huge salary and lucrative favors, ranging from pensions for himself to jewels for his wife, to godparents from the ruling family for his children. Fawning, wheedling, pleading, but also laboring hard to cultivate and please contacts and patrons (not the least important of whom was the all-powerful Kaunitz), Pergen mounted the ladder, rung by rung, occasionally sliding back, moving from post to post, waiting out displeasure in limbo, winning, losing, then winning once again in what must have been the common path trod by most eighteenth-century bureaucrats. Bernard reminds us that many qualities needed to make one's way were less than attractive, and that (as Hans Rosenberg observed years ago) the spoil system and meritocracy co-existed, and that merit without patronage went unnoticed and unrewarded.

Equally useful is Bernard's treatment of how Pergen's career intersected with several broad currents of eighteenth-century "reformism:" principally with educational reform and with the gradual separation of administration and justice. Particularly important in the realm of judicial reform was the slow movement toward a more modern concept of police in the last decades of the eighteenth century. Bernard traces out the gradual evolution of *Polizie* from an almost all-encompassing, expensive, and possibly utopian scheme for promoting the public good (as best articulated by academic representatives of the *Polizeiwissenschaften* such as Joseph von Sonnenfels and Johann Heinrich von Justi) to the more limited idea of police as an executory agency. Pergen and Joseph II, of course, constructed special variants of the latter: the political police and the secret police. And here, as well as in Bernard's treatment of Pergen's involvement in educational reform, I missed a discussion of these themes in a larger framework. What happened in Austria in education and in police reform was hardly unique and isolated, yet there is little explicit acknowledgement of the other work that has been done on both subjects. One misses, for example, any reference to James Van Horn Melton's *Absolutism and the Eighteenth-Century Origins of Compulsory Schooling in Prussia and Austria.* Of course, Bernard's subject is Pergen and not educational reform or police per se, but both sections would have benefitted from an inclusion of more of the recent historiography that had done so much to illuminate the politics and policies of late eighteenth-century German states.—Mary Lindemann.

Bernstein, Gail Lee (ed.). *Recreating Japanese Women, 1600–1945.* Berkeley and Los Angeles, CA: U. of California Press, 1991. Pp. xi + 340; figures; maps; tables.

This multidisciplinary collection of thirteen essays examines how Japanese women—usually stereotyped and consequently misinterpreted as an everlastingly submissive feminine ideal—were recreated, defined, and redefined over the last three hundred and forty-five years up till the end of the Second World War. The first part of the book focuses on the two-dimensional relationship between women and the family in the stem-family household *ie,* which is usually considered an embodiment of patriarchy, during the rigid federal Edo period governed by the Tokugawa *shogun* family (1600–1868). From a variety of perspectives, this book enables us to re-examine women in that era, whether known or unknown, as codes to comprehend different facets of women's lives in the Japanese history.

Questioning how a Japanese woman came to be defined as *ryosaikenbo* ("good wife, wise mother" 38), Kathleen S. Uno explores the reality that both productive and reproductive work by men, women, and children were well balanced and blended in the *ie* until the 1868 Meiji Restoration, when both industrialization and educational opportunities divided labor into two: public/productive work for men outside the home and domestic/reproductive work for women at home. Especialy farm women in the earlier era, according to Anne Walthall, had more flexible and varied roles than those in the Meije era. With demographic evidence, Laurel L. Cornall points out the paradox of elderly women's low mortality rate in their relationship with their daughters-in-law and grandchildren. Those three studies draw a picture of how, surprisingly, the *ie* was devoted to widening women's activities outside women's sphere in the preindustrial era, though it is difficult, as Walthall remarks, to draw a general conclusion because of socioeconomic and class differences.

Unlike unknown women, women publicly noted for their talents and achievements were small in number, yet could be found in the strictly male-dominated worlds of scholarship, art, and business. Jennifer Robertson's study of female disciples in *Shingaku* (Heart Learning), Patricia Fister's biographical research on a female poet–painter Ema Saiko, and Joyce Chapman Lebra's dicourse on a female sake brewer, Tatsu'uma Kiyo, present us another vision of women whose unconventional lives were ouside women's sphere within the *ie.* Their outstanding activities, however, were possible only with the financial support given by the *ie,* and more importantly with the other family members' understanding of and admiration for women's accomplishments. Whether they were praised or not, those remarkable women's inner conflicts, as Fister refers to Saiko's, must have been enormous enough to reexamine and reconsider.

The first part of this volume is so provocative that it naturally draws us into the second part which develops how Japanese women were therefore recreated in three eras, the Meiji, the Taisho, and the Showa, and the whole volume raises significant questions about the reality of contemporary Japanese women.—Masami Usui.

Bertrand, Michel. *Suffren: 1729–1788, de Saint-Tropez aux Indes.* Paris: Perrin, 1991. Pp. 334; illustrations.

Pierre-André de Suffren de Saint-Tropez has been the subject of more biographies than any other French sailor in history. At least a half dozen have appeared during the last score years alone. Yet, the florid, overweight, bad-tempered, courageous, patriotic, thoroughly professional bailli de Suffren never commanded more than fifteen ships of the line, won his fame and reputation in a secondary theatre of operations during three brief years, and exerted virtually no influence on his own sea service. In an age of idiosyncratic behaviour, however, Suffren was an original, which is part of the reason why his life continues to hold such fascination. But it is his success against perfidious Albion's navy during the great age of sail that chiefly attracts so many French naval historians.

Born into a family of lesser Provençal nobility, Suffren entered the navy at the age of fourteen. His early career, including time spent at Malta as a knight of the Order of St. John of Jerusalem, was unexceptional. He saw action during the mid-century wars, but only obtained his commission as *capitaine de vaisseau* in 1772. The interval of twenty-nine years since his entry into the navy was actually rather short; few officers rose so quickly in the service. Suffren subsequently served with distinction in American waters during 1778–79 and off the Atlantic approaches to the Mediterranean in 1780, but he was still a captain in March 1781, when he left Brest in command of five ships of the line on his voyage to glory. Three years later, Louis XVI would create a fourth office of Vice-Admiral of France for Suffren alone—it disappeared on his death—in recognition of his services in the Indian Ocean.

Michel Bertrand's biography is not based on any new evidence. Nor does it argue for any new interpretation of Suffren's life. Clearly intended for a popular audience, it is not a work of critical scholarship. The author relies on the work of earlier biographers but does not engage in source-criticism, and in view of the axes being ground by previous authors this is a serious weakness. Discussion of contested points is virtually non-existent and when it does occur, as in the case of Suffren's death, it only adds to previous calumny. This is unfortunate because the recent resurgence of interest in the great sailor's career has given rise to a better appreciation that is missing from this account.

It remains, nevertheless, an engaging read. The author, who is not an academic, served in the French navy and tells his tale well. He introduces the reader to some of the more controversial features of the story and to the complexity of Suffren's character. But while he displays a good feel for the sea, he is not so certain when he comes to the eighteenth century. Like Suffren, he is convinced of the primordial importance of naval battles. He does not question this and other common assumptions about military activity in international affairs. He focuses narrowly on events and passes up the opportunity to study the interplay of character and circumstances. Nor does he employ Suffren's career or personality as prisms by which to examine more critically either the service to which he devoted his life or the society that produced both. Readers will have to turn elsewhere for answers to such questions as whether the incompleteness of Suffren's campaign was chiefly due to the incompetence of his captains or to his own impetuosity and failure to explain his ideas clearly to them.—James Pritchard.

Bill, E. G. W. *Education at Christ Church Oxford 1660–1800*. Oxford: Clarendon Press, 1988. Pp. xii + 367.

Rev. by W. A. Speck in *The Scriblerian*, 23 (1991), 281–82.

Billings, Warren M. *Virginia's Viceroy: Their Majesties' Governor General: Francis Howard, Baron Howard of Effingham*. Lanham, MD: George Mason U. Press/U. Publishing Association, 1991. Pp. 152.

Black, Eileen (ed.). *Kings in Conflict: Ireland in the 1690s*. Belfast and Dufour, PA: Ulster Museum, 1990. Pp. xiv + 331.

Rev. (with another work) by Lionel K. J. Glassey in *The Scriblerian*, 24 (1991), 88–89.

Black, Jeremy. *A System of Ambition?: British Foreign Policy, 1660–1793*. (Studies in Modern History.) London and New York: Longman, 1991. Pp. xiv + 279; bibliography; maps.

Rev. (favorably) by P. K. Cline in *Choice*, 29 (1991), 50.

Black, Jeremy, and Jeremy Gregory (eds.). *Culture, Politics, and Society in Britain, 1660–1800*. Manchester, UK, and New York: Manchester U. Press, 1991. Pp. vii + 216.

These essays grew out of papers given at a colloquium held at Newcastle in September, 1989. It must have been an enjoyable occasion, for the general standard is high. If there is a common theme, it is perhaps that of a return to basics. Most of the English and Scots of the eighteenth century were Christians, most were members of the Church of England, and so on. We have perhaps been spending too much time and energy on minorities, and a return to the main stream may not be a bad idea.

But in another sense the authors are trying to get us to read things that, left to ourselves, we might skip. Paul Hammond wants us to read pamphlets and high literature. Jonathan Barry would like us to read provincial newspapers. Jeremy Gregory, concerned about the nature of Christianity in this period, wants us to "read" the churches themselves, for the slow creep of art works into Anglican buildings is taken as a sign that members of the

Establishment were less nervous about the dangers of popery than they had been before 1760. While that is true, the student of an earlier generation might have found the evidence in the history of Ireland, Nova Scotia, Gibraltar, or Minorca rather than in the slightly esoteric field of ecclesiastical decoration.

Colin Kidd reminds us that the Scots were Latinists. Or, at least, Scottish Episcopalians, early in the century. As time went on Latinity declined, even in Scotland. But we should be reading their Latin works if we want to have a true understanding of their world. Shearer West wants us to look at portraits, but with a discerning eye. The settings were contrived to make both the individual sitter and the aristocracy in general appear to be more secure and more serene than they really were. The famous painting of the children of George II playing musical instruments, with Kew as a backdrop, could not have been a happy occasion since the Prince of Wales and the Princess Royal did not speak to each other. Portraits of middle class sitters seem to be less traditional than those of portraits of the aristos. Roy Porter reminds us that the eighteenth century felt that civilization created sickness, at least for the fortunate. The rich could afford to overeat, to take drugs, and to go mad. When they had run to the end of their fortunes they could commit suicide, which was then called the "English sickness." This is another version of the myth of the noble savage. Noble savages tended in fact to die at nineteen, like people in the worst eighteenth century urban parishes, but the scholars of the time did not know that and hoped, as we all do, that the grass was greener on the other side. Jeremy Black points out that the men and women of the period read a great deal of history, including hack history, when they were not reading xenophobic and partisan novels about noble savages. The hack historians were moneymakers.

Each of the essays is entertaining, and the group encourages us to return to culture after two generations of overspecialization. But when and how is this to happen? Especially in this country, where students waste at least two years in high school and have to play catch-up. One wonders whether it is still possible to catch up. How to acquire taste, if the nearest serious museum is five hundred miles away? Or feel for the eighteenth century, among others, without a knowledge of the Bible? Or know the journals in a special field, as budgets are cut? Will these authors have no successors?—Stephan B. Baxter.

Black, Jeremy. *War for America: The Fight for Independence, 1775–1783.* New York: St. Martin's Press, 1991. Pp. x + 268; illustrations; maps.

Blackbourn, David, and Richard J. Evans. *The German Bourgeoisie: Essays on the Social History of the German Middle Class from the Late Eighteenth to the Early Twentieth Century.* London and New York: Routledge, 1991. Pp. xix + 348; tables.

Bliss, Robert M. *Revolution and Empire: English Politics and the American Colonies in the Seventeenth Century.* (Studies in Imperialism.) Manchester, UK, and New York: Manchester U. Press (distributed by St. Martin's Press: New York), 1990. Pp. xi + 300; bibliography. Cf. *ECCB*, n.s. 16, II: 56.

Rev. (favorably) by Mary K. Geiter in *TLS*, (Aug. 16, 1991), 9; by R. S. Schreiber in *Choice*, 28 (1991), 1198.

Bluche, François. *Louis XIV.* Translated and with a bibliography by Mark Greengrass of *Louis XIV* (Paris, 1986). New York: F. Watts; Oxford: Basil Blackwell, 1990. Pp. xvii +702; bibliography; illustrations, map. Cf. *ECCB*, n.s. 16, II: 56.

Rev. (severely and with another work) by Roger Mettam in *TLS*, (July 5, 1991), 23.

Blume, Helmut. *The German Coast During the Colonial Era, 1722–1803: The Evolution of a Distinct Cultural Landscape in the Lower Mississippi Delta during the Colonial Era, with Special Reference to the Development of Louisiana's German Coast.* Translated, edited and annotated by Ellen C. Merrill of *Die Entwicklung der Dulturlandschaft des Mississippideltal in kolonialer Zeit, unter besonderer Berücksichtigung der deutschen Siedlung* (Kiel, 1956).

Destrehan, LA: German-Acadian Coast, Historical and Genealogical Society, 1990. Pp. xiii + 165; bibliography; illustrations; maps. Cf. *ECCB*, n.s. 16, II: 56.

Rev. (favorably) by A. G. Tassin in *Choice*, 28 (1991), 1696.

Boesky, Amy. " 'Outlandish-Fruits': Commissioning Nature for the Museum of Man." *English Literary History*, 58 (1991), 305–30.

The diversity, breadth, and "classifications" of the early modern private collections like the *kunstkammer* are carried over into later, larger, national collections like the Ashmolean, the British Museum and the Vatican Collections.

Boia, Lucian (ed.), Keith Hitchins, Georg G. Iggers, and Ellen Nore (assoc. eds.). *Great Historians from Antiquity to 1800: An International Dictionary*. Sponsored by the Commission on the History of Historiography of the International Committee on the Historical Sciences. London and New York: Greenwood Press, 1989. Pp. xxiii + 417. Cf. *ECCB*, n.s. 15, II: 26.

Rev. (favorably) by Ronald H. Fritze in *American Reference Books Annual*, 22 (1991), 548.

Bonwick, Colin. *The American Revolution*. Basingstoke, UK: Macmillan; Charlottesville, VA: U. Press of Virginia, 1991. Pp. ix + 336; bibliography; maps.

Borsay, Peter. *The English Urban Renaissance. Culture and Society in the Provincial Town 1660–1770*. Oxford: Clarendon Press, 1989. Pp. xxii + 400. Cf. *ECCB*, n.s. 16, II: 57; 15, II: 26

Rev. by Brian Dietz in *The Scriblerian*, 23 (1991), 291–92.

Bossenga, Gail. *The Politics of Privilege: Old Regime and Revolution in Lille*. Cambridge and New York: Cambridge U. Press, 1991. Pp. xii + 263; bibliography; figure; tables.

Bourgin, Frank. *The Great Challenge: The Myth of Laissez-Faire in the Early Republic*. New York: George Braziller, 1989. Pp. xv + 223; bibliography. Cf. *ECCB*, n.s. 15, II: 27.

Bowen, H. V. *Revenue and Reform: The Indian Problem in British Politics, 1757–1773*. Cambridge and New York: Cambridge U. Press, 1991. Pp. xii + 204; bibliography, tables.

In 1767 the East India Company gained powers of revenue collection (called a *Diwani*) in the Indian region of Bengal. It thus assumed more of the functions of sovereignty in addition to those of trade. In 1773 the British Parliament passed a Regulating Act, which placed the Company under some measure of control by Westminster. H. V. Bowen's *Revenue and Reform: the Indian Problem in British Politics, 1757–1773*, argues a connection between those events and sets out to trace the linkage. An able monograph results, firmly based on Parliamentary and Company sources, which skillfully moves back and forth among Parliament, the cabinet of George III's ministers, the Company's General court, and its Board of Directors.

Although Bowen begins with scene-setting chapters on the period prior to 1767, the heart of his political narrative and analysis begins in 1767. The assumption of the *Diwani* by the Company set in train a series of problems. It held out the promise of a new and lavish revenue for *somebody*, hopes doomed to disappointment. It clouded the Company's relationship with the British government, for it prompted ministers and their parliamentary opponents to ask whether the Company received such revenue as a conqueror in its own right or as an agent of the British Crown. The *Diwani* soon coincided with a crisis in the Company's finances and because of the unclear jurisdictional position of the Company in Bengal (and because the Company had been given a monopolistic charter by the British domestic politics).

Bowen makes clear that the mingling of Company policy and domestic political rivalry affected imperial policy as well. The position of the company which ultimately led to the Boston Tea Party is clarified here. Bowen shows that the British government's concern with East India Company affairs remained chiefly financial (how to guarantee continuing revenue from the Company to the government), while "public opinion," convinced of East India Company corruption, made noise but had relatively little effect on the terms of the 1773 Regulating Act. On balance, he argues, the "Company's transition from trader to sovereign had been uncomfortable and, in many respects, unsuccessful" (p. 118), and so the 1773 Act would be only the first in a series of measures which transferred sovereignty from a shareholders' meeting to an imperial Parliament. He gives high marks to Lord North, both for able political maneuvering and for reasonable foresight into the longer-range issues that the Company's financial crisis raised.

The "Indian problem" in those years certainly did raise such issues, and Bowen explores some, hints at others, and leaves some implicit. How to secure the revenue surplus promised by the *Diwani*, and how to transfer it to Britain, were immediate questions in the late 1760s and early 1770s. But those questions implied a number of others, some of which cut to the core of all British imperial ventures. Could an "ideal form of imperial relationship: wealth without responsibility, and empire without expenditure" (p. 25)—be maintained? Could the Company or the Crown profit from imperial control, or would the related military expenses outrun the revenue received? Could an imperial position be consolidated which encouraged trade without further expansion of the frontiers and hence further costs? Would the "Anglicanization" of non-Europeans become an imperial responsibility? Could a Company (or a colony) be controlled from London, when it was six months away?

Bowen can only say that the years between 1767 and 1773 did not resolve such questions. His book therefore provides what are at most valuable pieces for some larger imperial puzzles. It ends with a measure which seems more a pause than a solution, and without the emergence of a coherent British policy toward its awkwardly-acquired Bengal territory.—Jo Hays.

Bowling, Kenneth R. *The Creation of Washington D. C.: The Idea and the Location of the American Capital*. Fairfax, VA: George Mason U. Press, 1991. Pp. xv +294; illustrations; maps.

Brading, D. A. *The First America: The Spanish Monarchy, Creole Patriots, and the Liberal State, 1492–1867*. Cambridge and New York: Cambridge U. Press, 1991. Pp. 761.

Brandon, William. *Quivira: Europeans in the Region of the Santa Fe Trail, 1540–1820*. Athens, OH: Ohio U. Press, 1990. Pp. xi + 33; bibliography; illustrations, maps. Cf. *ECCB*, n.s. 16, II: 59.

Rev. (with reservations) by M. L. Tate in *Choice*, 28 (1991), 840; 842.

Brown, Richard. *Society and Economy in Modern Britain, 1700–1850*. London and New York: Routledge, 1991. Pp. xvi + 473; figures.

Brunel, Françoise. "L'Acculturation d'un révolutionnaire: L'Exemple de Billaud-Varenne (1786–1791)." *Dix-huitième siècle*, 21 (1991), 261–74.

Bull, Kinloch. *The Oligarchs in Colonial and Revolutionary Charleston: Lieutenant Governor William Bull II and His Family*. Columbia, SC: U. of South Carolina Press, 1991. Pp. 415.

Burchell, R. A. (ed.). *The End of Anglo America: Historical Essays in the Study of Cultural Divergence*. Manchester, UK, and New York: Manchester U. Press, 1991. Pp. x + 214.

Burke, Edmund. *Writings and Speeches, Volume IX: I: The Revolutionary War, 1794–1797: II: Ireland*. Edited by R. B. McDowell. New York: Oxford U. Press; Oxford: Clarendon Press, 1991. Pp. xx + 724; appendices.

Burke, Thomas E., Jr. *Mohawk Frontier: The Dutch Community of Schenectady, New York, 1661–1710*. Ithaca, NY: Cornell U. Press, 1991. Pp. xvii + 252; bibliography; maps.

Burns, J. H., and Mark Goldie (eds.). *The Cambridge History of Political Thought, 1450–1700*. Cambridge and New York, NY: Cambridge U. Press, 1991. Pp. xii + 798; bibliography.

Burns, Michael. *Dreyfus: A Family Affair, 1789–1945*. New York: HarperCollins Publishers, 1991. Pp. xvi + 576; bibliography illustrations.

Cadle, Farris W. *Georgia Land Surveying History and Law*. Athens, GA: U. of Georgia Press, 1991. Pp. 688.

Calabria, Antonio. *The Cost of Empire: The Finances of the Kingdom of Naples in the Time of the Spanish Rule*. Cambridge and New York: Cambridge U. Press, 1991. Pp. xvii + 179; appendices; bibliography; figures; maps.

Callahan, North. *Thanks, Mr. President: The Trail-blazing Second Term of George Washington*. New York: Cornwall Books/Associated University Presses, 1991. Pp. 256.

Calloway, Colin G. (comp. and ed.). *Dawnland Encounters: Indians and Europeans in Northern New England*. Hanover, NH, and London: U. Press of New England, 1991. Pp. xiii + 296; bibliography; illustrations, maps (on lining papers), table.

Rev. by H. R. King in *Choice*, 28 (1991), 1836.

Colin Calloway's *Dawnland Encounters*, a compilation of documents pertaining to the encounter between Europeans and Native Americans in Northern New England during the colonial period, is divided into six chapters, each of which arranges in chronological order materials related to a specific theme. Beginning with "First Encounters," Calloway organizes the rest of his collection under the rubrics of religion, diplomacy, war, commerce, and captivity. In addition to his helpful introduction, Calloway intersperses the original materials with background commentary, most of which is very much to the point. And lest we forget the length and complexity of the history of Indian-European relations, the colonial segment of which this volume attempts to illuminate, Calloway includes a suggestive epilogue consisting of a very small selection of Henry David Thoreau's writings about his travels among Indians in Maine during the nineteenth century.

For the most part, Calloway does an admirable job of recovering the Indian voice that was routinely neglected in a previous mode of colonal historiography. The result is a much richer picture of the period that takes account of the linguistic, cultural, social, tribal, and national differences that both Indians and Europeans discovered and struggled with. In each section, Calloway attempts to place the materials in the context of the scholarship of the last dozen or so years, which has indeed transformed the way we examine our colonial past. In the chapter on captivity, for instance, Calloway includes writings from Europeans who willingly chose to remain with the Indians after they were given their freedom, and he also insists that we read these so-called captivity narratives in the context of Indians who were captured and brought to Europe against their will. My one criticism of the volume is that some selections are so short as to make me question the point of including them. Such a criticism is mitigated, however, by Calloway's own warning that "the volume is intended for general readers and as a starting point for student discussion rather than as a research work for scholars." And indeed, with its notes filled with basic bibliographic information, *Dawnland Encounters* would serve as an informative introduction for the general reader, or as an excellent text for a course in colonial American History or Literature.—Thomas Scanlan.

Calvert, Rosalie Stier. *Mistress of Riversdale: The Plantation Letters of Rosalie Stier Calvert, 1795–1821*. Edited by Margaret Law Callcott. Baltimore, MD: Johns Hopkins U. Press, 1991. Pp. 407.

Cannon, Garland. *The Life and Mind of Oriental Jones: Sir William Jones, the Father of Modern Linguistics*. Cambridge and New York: Cambridge U. Press, 1990. Pp. xix + 409; portrait. Cf. *ECCB*, n.s. 16, II: 61.

Rev. (favorably) by R. C. O'Hara in *Choice*, 29 (1991), 587.

Carroll, Patrick J. *Blacks in Colonial Veracruz: Race, Ethnicity, and Regional Development*. Austin, TX: U. of Texas Press, 1991. Pp. xv + 240; appendices; bibliography; figures; maps; tables.

Carr, Lois Green, Russell R. Menard, and Lorena S. Walsh. *Robert Cole's World: Agriculture and Society in Early Maryland*. Chapel Hill, NC: U. of North Carolina Press for the Instutute of Early American History and Culture, Williamsburg, Virginia, 1991. Pp. xxi + 362; appendices; bibliography; illustrations.

Carstens, Peter. *The Queen's People: A Study of Hegemony, Coercion, and Accommodation among the Okanagan of Canada*. Toronto, Ontario: U. of Toronto Press, 1991. Pp. xxvii + 333.

Celarie, Michel, and Christiane Constant-Le Stum. *Journal d'un bourgeois de Bégoux: Michel Célarie, 1771–1836*. (La France au fil des siècles.) Paris: Publisud, 1991.

Chandler, D. S. *Social Assistance and Bureaucratic Politics: The Montepíos of Colonial Mexico, 1767–1821*. Albuquerque, NM: U. of New Mexico, 1991. Pp. viii + 239; bibliography.

Chartier, Roger. *The Cultural Orgins of the French Revolution*. Translation by Lydia G. Cochrane of *Les Origines culturelles de la Révolution française* (Paris, 1991). (Bicentennial Reflections on the French Revolution.) Durham, NC, and London: Duke U. Press, 1991. Pp. xix + 239; bibliography. Cf. *ECCB*, n.s. 16, II: 63.

Rev. (favorably) in rev. article ("An Enlightened Revolution?") by Robert Darnton in *New York Review of Books*, 38 (Oct. 24, 1991), 33–36.
    Chartier does an impressive job of synthesizing post-revisionist scholarship on the origins of the French Revolution, but it suffers a little from an excessive reliance on Habermasian theory. Although he complements the recent syntheses by Doyle and Baker, his version of "political culture" pays too little attention to either Doyle's politics or Baker's intellectual culture to replace either one of them.—Dale K. Van Kley.

Chartier, Roger. *Les Origines culturelles de la Révolution française*. (L'univers historique Seuil.) Paris: Éditions du Seuil, 1991. Pp. 245.

Rev. (favorably and with other works) by Colin Jones in *TLS*, (Mar. 29, 1991), 7–8.

Chartier, Roger. *Le Origines culterelles de la Revolution française*. (L'univers historique Seuil.) Paris: Éditions du Seuil, 1990. Pp. 248.

Rev. (favorably) by Robert Forster *Eighteenth-Century Studies*, 25 (1991–92), 237–41.

Childs, John. *The Nine Years' War and the British Army, 1688–1697: The Operations in the Low Countries*. Manchester, UK: Manchester U. Press (distributed through New York: St. Martin's Press), 1991. Pp. vii + 372; maps.

Chisick, Harvey (ed.). *The Press in the French Revolution*. (Studies on Voltaire and the Eighteenth Century.) Oxford: The Voltaire Foundation at the Taylor Institution, 1991. Pp. viii + 423.

Christoph, P. R. (ed.). *Andros Papers: 1679–1680*. Vol. 3. (New York Historical Manuscripts Series, 28.) Translated from Dutch by C. T. Gehring. Syracuse, NY: Syracuse U. Press, 1991. Pp. xxix + 629.

Claghorn, Charles E. *Women Patriots of the American Revolution: A Biographical Dictionary*. Metuchen, NJ: Scarecrow Press, 1991. Pp. xviii + 499; illustrations.

Cohen, Robert. *Jews in Another Environment: Surinam in the Second Half of the Eighteenth Century*. (Brill's Series in Jewish Studies, 1.) Leiden and New York: E. J. Brill, 1991. Pp. xv + 350; bibliography.

Coldham, Peter Wilson. *Child Apprentices in America from Christ's Hospital, London 1617–1778*. Baltimore, MD: Genealogical Publishing, 1990. Pp. 163. Cf. *ECCB*, n.s. 16, II: 65.

Rev. by Donald E. Collins in *American Reference Books Annual*, 22 (1991), 415.

Coldham, Peter Wilson. *The Complete Book of Emigrants 1661–1699: A Comprehensive Listing Compiled from English Public of Those Who Took Ship to the Americas for Political, Religious and Economic Reasons; of Those Who Were Deported for Vagrancy, Roguery, or Non-conformity, and of Those Who Were Sold to Labour in the New Colonies*. Baltimore, MD: Genealogical Publishing, 1990. Pp. vii + 894. Cf. *ECCB*, n.s. 16, II: 65.

Rev. (favorably) by Carol Willsey Bell in *American Reference Books Annual*, 22 (1991), 416.

Connelly, Owen. *The French Revolution and the Napoleonic Era*. 2nd ed. Chicago, IL, and Fort Worth, TX: Holt, Rinehart and Winston, 1991. Pp. xiii + 400; bibliography; maps.

This is the second edition of a typical work of synthesis whose author has to be both a daredevil and a hard-working painstaker if he thinks he can escape the crossfire of punctilious critics. The writer claims that his final draft is based on the works of hundreds of scholars in the field whom he refers to only in the final bibliography, even though he gives them full credit in the quotations. "A magnificently complex overture to modern times" and "an epoch of incompatable drama" (p. 1): in the very first sentences of his book, Connelly has given us the gist of his argument. Even though the Revolution was "the Great Surprise" (p.ix), its roots in economic and social conditions and especially in the necessity of "a redefinition of the role of governments" (p. 2) are obvious and during its ten momentous years, "the issue of the balance between liberty and equality was basic to all the conflict" (p. 3) and perdured throughout the world during the next two centuries. A final victory for whom? For property holders, so thinks the author, as commercial and industrial capitalism was only in its infancy.

The ambiguity of the Napoleonic era is rightly emphasized by Connelly in that it established nationalism and nationalities as the principles of the subsequent redrawing of the European map. With Napoleon, the Revolution ceases being largely a French affair: "it blazed, it shocked, it was fixed for ever by trauma in the European mentality . . . Napoleon made the Revolution a crucial event in European and world history" (p. 351). The ultimate paradox of his reign lies in the fact that his work—both positive and negative—tolled the knell of European empires in the long run to replace them by the unsubmersible nations of today. The twelve chapters follow a strictly chronological order, even though French, European and world events are always judiciously covered and adequately linked to the main issue. Two turning points might have been emphasized more clearly: Varennes as the revelation of the duplicity of the king and of the new elites that called the flight an abduction and the *Cent Jours* that showed both a genuine fear of the return to the inequities of the Ancient Regime and a deep popular antipathy toward the restored monarchy. This volume must by warmly recommended for students as a starting point for budding scholars in the field.—Jean Rivière.

Cook, Alexandra Parma, and Noble David Cook. *Good Faith and Truthful Ignorance: A Case of Transatlantic Bigamy*. Durham, NC, and London: Duke U. Press, 1991. Pp. xvi + 206; bibliography; illustrations; maps.

Cranston, Maurice William. *The Noble Savage: Jean-Jacques Rousseau, 1754–1762*. Chicago, IL: U. of Chicago Press, 1991. Pp. xiv + 399.

Cronin, Thomas E. (ed.) *Inventing the American Presidency*. Lawrence, KS: U. Press of Kansas, 1989. Pp. xii + 404. Cf. *ECCB*, n.s. 15, II: 39.

Rev. by John Allphin Moore, Jr. in *Eighteenth-Century Studies*, 24 (1991), 369–71.

Crook, Malcolm. *Toulon in War and Revolution: From the* Ancien Regime *to the Restoration, 1750–1820*. (War, Armed Forces and Society.) Manchester, UK, and New York: Manchester U. Press, 1991. Pp. xii + 270; bibliography; maps; tables.

This is a valuable contribution to the growing literature on the provincial experience in revolutionary France. In a clear and concise fashion, Malcolm Crook brings us through the most important social and political trends shaping Toulon's history from the end of the Old Regime to the Restoration. While sensitive to the issue of class as an explanatory factor, Crook's work points up the importance of centralization and political rivalries for understanding the revolution. The site of an immense naval arsenal, Toulon revealed the impact of a militaristic state upon local society. The huge naval presence provided employment to one half of the city's adult male labor force, but also drove away other kinds of trade and manufacture. As a result, Toulon ended up as a virtual "company town" of the French navy. Before the Revolution, naval intendants gradually took over the city council's role in protecting and policing the town. The city became even more dependent on external grain supplies, and dock workers responded to the wage rhythms of war and peace. The most important political rivalries before 1789 were not between the aristocracy and bourgeoisie, but between naval and municipal elites.

Unsurprisingly, these tensions were played out repeatedly during the Revolution. The democritizing Revolution began as a two-pronged assault against the centralizing thrust of the naval administration and the oligarchic power of the municipality's local notables. The city's peculiar structure of taxation, which taxed foodstuffs heavily, and a new governmental policy of subcontracting on the dockyards exacerbated Toulon's economic crisis. After a brief experiment in 1789 with rule by a popularly constituted committee, a municipality was elected in 1790. Although less oligarchic than that of the old regime, it was recruited predominantly from the elite.

War, chronic grain shortages, unemployment in the dockyards, and intense political rivalries prevented stability from emerging. Toulon's Jacobins mobilized the sections, including many dock workers, to win power in the town council, but they set off a chain of difficult to control violence and retaliation. When inflation and food shortages continued, the lower classes grew restive, transferring their support to the old bourgeois notables and overthrowing the Jacobins. Although Toulon's "federalist" revolt had its roots in a local power struggle, it appeared treasonous to Parisian Montagnards. Toulon soon became a pawn of warring international enemies. Faced with a choice of surrendering to vindictive Montagnard armies or the British navy, it chose the British. When French armies reconquered the city, the Jacobins exacted savage revenge by executing approximately 1,000 townspeople.

But the city was too important to leave in ruins, and the central government immediately began rebuilding the arsenal. The legacy of the next period, from Thermidor to the Empire, was a victory for the navy. Poverty and sickness, as well as boom and bust cycles on the dockyards continued to inflict havoc on the local economy, but political stability gradually returned. Fiscal restraints public office to the well-off, but Napoleon was willing to work with both emigrés and Jacobins. The men of the Restoration were less ecumenical. After coming to power, they sacked many naval officers and replaced them with elderly aristocrats. The return to peace, furthermore, brought unemployment to the docks. This explains much of Toulon's support for Bonapartism. Coming to the end of his story, Crook finds Toulon more firmly integrated into the state than ever, more economically dependent upon the military, and politically apathetic.

Based on extensive archival research, this book will be helpful to those interested in naval history, urban and demographic history, the politics of the Midi, and the causes and consequences of the French Revolution.—Gail Bossenga.

Crouzet, François. *Britain Ascendant: Comparative Studies in Franco-British Economic History*. Translation by Martin Thom of *De la supériorité de l'Angleterre sur la France* (Paris, 1985). Cambridge and New York: Cambridge U. Press; Paris: Éditions de la Maison des sciences de l'homme, 1990. Pp. 514.

Rev. (favorably) by N. F. R. Crafts in *TLS*, (Apr. 12, 1991), 25.

Cummins, Light Townsend. *Spanish Observers and the American Revolution, 1775–1783*. Baton Rouge, LA: Louisiana State U. Press, 1991. Pp. xv + 229; bibliography.

Cunningham, Noble E. *Popular Images of the Presidency: From Washington to Lincoln*. Columbia, MO: U. of Missouri Press, 1991. Pp. 312.

Cutter, Donald C. *California in 1792: A Spanish Naval Visit*. (The American Exploration and Travel Series, 71.) London and Norman, OK: U. of Oklahoma Press, 1990. Pp. xv + 176; illustrations; maps; portraits. Cf. *ECCB*, n.s. 16, II: 86.

Rev. by G. J. Martin in *Choice*, 28 (1991), 1552.

Cutter, Donald C. *Malaspina and Galiano: Spanish Voyages to the Northwest Coast, 1791 and 1792*. Seattle, WA: Douglas and McIntyre, CN/U of Washington Press, 1991. Pp. 160.

Dandeker, Christopher. *Surveillance, Power and Modernity: Bureaucracy and Discipline from 1700 to the Present Day*. Cambridge: Polity; New York: St. Martin's Press, 1990. Pp. ix + 243. Cf. *ECCB*, n.s. 16, II: 67.

Rev. by J. Bearden in *Choice*, 28 (1991), 1193.

Daniel, Wallace L. *Gregorii Teplov: A Stateman at the Court of Catherine the Great*. (Russian Biography Series, 10.) Newtonville, MA: Oriental Research Partners, 1991. Pp. xiv + 194; bibliography; frontispiece.

Daniels, Roger. *Coming to America: A History of Immigration and Ethnicity in American Life*. New York: HarperCollins Publishers, 1990. Pp. xii + 450; bibliography; illustrations; maps; tables. Cf. *ECCB*, n.s. 16, II: 68.

Rev. (favorably) by E. Kohlman in *Choice*, 28 (1991), 1208.
   "Part I: Colonial America" (pp. 1–118) concerns the eighteenth-century.

Danieri, Cheryl L. *Credit Where Credit is Due: The* Mont-de-Piete *of Paris, 1777–1851*. (Modern European History: France.) London and New York: Garland Publishing, 1991. Pp. xii + 283; bibliography.

Dann, Uriel. *Hanover and Great Britain, 1740–1760: Diplomacy and Survival*. Leicester, UK, and London: Leicester U. Press, 1991. Pp. x + 174; bibliography.

Darnton, Robert. *Edition et Sédition. L'Univers de la littérature clandestine au XVIIIᵉ siècle*. Paris: Gallimard, 1991. Pp. 279.

Darnton, Robert. *The Kiss of Lamourette: Reflections in Cultural History*. London and New York: W. W. Norton, 1990. Pp. xxi + 393; bibliography; figures; illustrations. Cf. *ECCB*, n.s. 16, II: 68.

Darnton, Robert, and Daniel Roche (ed.). *Revolution in Print: The Press in France, 1775–1800*. Berkeley, CA: U. of California Press in collaboration with The New York Public Library, 1989. Pp. xv + 351; color plates; exhibition checklist; illustrations; tables. Cf. *ECCB*, n.s. 15, II: 39.

Rev. (favorably and with other works) by Colin Jones in *TLS*, (Mar. 29, 1991), 7-8; in rev. article ("More than Words: The Printing Press and the French Revolution") by Joan B. Landes in *Eighteenth-Century Studies*, 25 (1991), 85–98.

Davie, George. *The Scottish Enlightenment and Other Essays*. Edinburgh, Scotland: Polygon, 1991. Pp. 145.

Rev. (with another work) by Christopher Harvie in *TLS*, (Aug. 16, 1991), 20.
   Chapters 1–2, "The Scottish Enlightenment" (pp. 1–50) and "The Social Significance of the Scottish Philosophy of Common Sense" (pp. 51–85) concern the Eighteenth Century.

Davies, J. D. *Gentlemen and Tarpaulins: The Officers and Men of the Restoration Navy*. (Oxford Historical Monographs.) New York: Oxford U. Press; Oxford: Clarendon Press, 1991. Pp. xii + 270; appendices; bibliography.

Davis, David Brion. *Revolutions: Reflections on American Equality and Foreign Liberations*. (The William E. Massey Sr. Lectures in the History of American Civilization, 1989.) Cambridge, MA, and London: Harvard U. Press, 1990. Pp. vii + 130; notes. Cf. *ECCB*, n.s. 16, II: 68.

Rev. (with another work) by John Dunn in *TLS*, (May 31, 1991), 24.

Dicken-Garcia, Hazel. *To Western Woods: The Breckinridge Family Moves to Kentucky in 1793*. Rutherford, NJ: Fairleigh Dickinson U. Press (distributed through Cranbury, NJ, and London: Associated University Presses), 1991. Pp. 250; bibliography; illustrations; maps.

Dictionary of Canadian Biography, 1000–1900. 12 vols. Toronto, Ontario: U. of Toronto Press, 1991. Pp. 557.

Dickinson, William Calvin. *Sidney Godolphin, Lord Treasurer, 1702–1710.* Lewiston, NY: Edwin Mellen Press, 1990. Pp. 291. Cf. *ECCB*, n.s. 16, II: 70.

Dillon, Merton L. *Slavery Attacked: Southern Slaves and Their Allies, 1619–1865.* Baton Rouge, LA: Louisiana State U. Press, 1990. Pp. 300; bibliography. Cf. *ECCB*, n.s. 16, II: 70.

Rev. (with reservations) by J. Roper in *Choice*, 28 (1991), 1552–53.

Dodge, Meredith D., and Robert T. Kern (eds.). *Historical Dictionary of Modern Spain, 1700–1988.* London and New York: Greenwood Press, 1990. Pp. xxvi + 697; bibliography; chronology; maps. Cf. *ECCB*, n.s. 16, II: 71.

Rev. by Joyce Duncan Falk in *American Reference Books Annual*, 22 (1991), 116.

Doherty, J. E., and D. J. Hickey. *A Chronology of Irish History Since 1500.* Dublin: Gill and Macmillan, 1989; Savage, MD: Barnes and Noble Books, 1990. Pp. 395. Cf. *ECCB*, n.s. 16, II: 71.

Rev. (favorably) by K. L. Strohmeyer in *Choice*, 28 (1991), 753–754.

Donnachie, Ian, and George Hewitt. *A Companion to Scottish History: From the Reformation to the Present.* New York: Facts on File, 1989. Pp. 245; illustrations; maps; tables. Cf. *ECCB*, n.s. 16, II: 71; 15, II: 42.

Rev. by Christine E. King in *American Reference Books Annual*, 22 (1991), 533.

Drabkin, William. *Beethoven: Missa Solemnis.* Cambridge and New York: Cambridge U. Press, 1991. Pp. xiii + 118; bibliography; musical examples.

Drinker, Elizabeth Sandwith. *The Diary of Elizabeth Drinker.* 3 vols. Edited by Elaine Forman Crane, Sarah Blank Dine (assoc. ed.), Alison Duncan Hirsch, Arthur Scheerr (asst. eds.). and Anita J. Rapone (co-ed.,1982–86). Boston, MA: Northeastern U. Press, 1991. Pp. lxxv + 2398; bibliography.

Rev. (favorably) by T. D. Hamm in *Choice*, 29 (1991), 653–654.

Ducommun, Marie-Jeanne, and Dominique Quadroni. *Le Refuge Protestant dans le Pays de Vaud (fin XVIIᵉ—début XVIIIᵉ s): aspects d'une migration.* Geneva: Librairie Droz, 1991. Pp. 324; appendices; bibliography; illustrations; maps; tables.

Duden, Barbara. *The Woman Beneath the Skin: A Doctor's Patients in Eighteenth-Century Germany.* Translated by Thomas Dunlap. Cambridge, MA, and London: Harvard U. Press, 1991. Pp. x + 241.

The eighteenth century has emerged in recent historiography as a watershed for Western conceptions and perceptions of "the body." Barbara Duden makes an important contribution to our understanding of this paradigm shift. Duden's original German title begins with the words *Geschicte unter der Haut* ("history under the skin") and signals something the English title does not: her belief in the need to historicize "the body" in a way that includes the lived experience of its internal landscape lying "beneath the skin."

To give "the body" a history in this way challenges long-standing habits in which categories such as "nature," "the body," and "biology" remain fixed. What convinced Duden of the need to question "the self-evident manner in which we take the body for granted as an unchanging biological reality" (3) was her encounter with Johann Storch's eight volumes on "Women's Diseases," seven of which contain the diary-like case histories of women patients he compiled in the 1720s and 1730s. Duden leads one into the strange territory of corporeal complaint and treatment before the creation of the "disembodied" anatomical-physiological body "monopolized" by "scientific" medicine, forcing the rethinking of concepts like "health" and body perception. Her work has important implications for women's studies, making it difficult to view the relationship of women's bodies to reproduction as self-evident and unchanging.—Ruth Roach Pierson.

Earle, Peter. *The Making of the English Middle Class: Business, Society and Family Life in London, 1660–1730*. Berkeley and Los Angeles, CA: U. of California Press, 1989. Pp. xiv + 446. Cf. *ECCB*, n.s. 16, II: 73; 15, II: 43–44.

Rev. (with another work) by Daniel Statt in *Eighteenth-Century Studies*, 25 (1991–92), 264–71.

Eckelmeyer, Judith A. *The Cultural Context of Mozart's Flute: Social, Aesthetic, Philosophical.* Vol. I. (Studies in the History and Interpretation of Music, 34A.) Lewiston, NY: Edwin Mellen Press, 1991. Pp. viii + 329; bibliography; illustrations.

Eckert, Richard S. *"The Gentlemen of the Profession:" The Emergence of Lawyers in Mass., 1630–1810.* (Distinguished Studies in American Legal and Constitutional History, 5) [Rev. of thesis, U. of South Carolina, 1981], 1991. Pp. 556.

Edmonds, W. D. *Jacobinism and the Revolt of Lyon, 1789–1793.* New York: Oxford U. Press; Oxford: Clarendon Press, 1990. Pp. xi + 349; bibliography; maps. Cf. *ECCB*, n.s. 16, II: 73.

Rev. by D. C. Baxter in *Choice*, 28 (1991), 1200.

Edwardes, Michael. *The Nabobs at Home.* London: Constable, 1991. Pp. 192; illustrations; portraits.

Rev. (briefly) in *TLS*, (Oct. 11, 1991), 32.

Ehmer, Josef. *Heiratsverhalten, Socialstruktur, ökonomischer Wandel. England und Mitteleuropa in der Formationsperiode des Kapitalismus.* Göttingen: Vandenhoeck and Ruprecht, 1991. Pp. 320.

Ellis, Harold. *Boulainvilliers and the French Monarchy: Aristocratic Politics in Early Eighteenth-Century France.* Ithaca, NY: Cornell U. Press, 1988. Pp. 288. Cf. *ECCB*, n.s. 15, II: 44; 14, II: 33.

Rev. by Daniel Carroll Joynes in *Eightenth-Century Studies*, 24 (1991), 397–402.

English, Barbara. *The Great Landowners of East Yorkshire, 1530–1910.* London and New York: Harvester Wheatsheaf, 1990. Pp. x + 290; bibliography; illustrations; tables. Cf. *ECCB*, n.s. 16, II: 74.

Rev. (favorably) by Richard Ollard in *TLS*, (May 10, 1991), 6.

Erickson, Carolly. *To the Scaffold: The Life of Marie Antoinette.* New York: W. Morrow, 1991. Pp. 384; bibliography.

Rev. (favorably) by G. C. Bond in *Choice,* 29 (1991), 333; (briefly) by Margaret E. Guthrie in *New York Review of Books* (June 2, 1991), 20.

Estep, William R. *Revolution Within the Revolution: The First Amendment in Historical Context, 1612–1789.* Grand Rapids, MI: William B. Eerdmans Publishing Company, 1990. Pp. 212. Cf. *ECCB,* n.s. 16, II: 74.

Rev. by James E. Bradley in *The Journal of Church and State,* 33 (1991), 599–600.

Ewald, Janet J. *Soldiers, Traders, and Slaves: State Formation and Economic Transformation in the Greater Nine Valley, 1700–1885.* Madison, WI: U. of Wisconsin Press, 1990. Pp. xiii + 270; bibliography; maps. Cf. *ECCB,* n.s. 16, II: 75.

Rev. by R. T. Brown in *Choice,* 28 (1991), 1686.

Falvey, John, and William Brooks. *The Channel in the Eighteenth Century: Bridge, Barrier and Gateway: Transactions of the Anglo-French Colloquium held at the University of Southampton 20–23 September 1988.* (Studies on Voltaire and the Eighteenth Century, 292.) Oxford: The Voltaire Foundation at the Taylor Institution, 1991. Pp. vi + 422.

These excellent papers prove that the English Channel in the eighteenth century was a provocative and fruitful topic; peering across it to the Continent, the commentators have taken it literally, metaphorically, and imaginatively.

The Channel as physical reality unites four presentations. In "The Channel in the Clift family correspondence," Frances Austin explores how the waterway served as a means of alternative travel between Cornwall, Plymouth, and London for "humble country folk" (p. 105). Patricia Crimmin analyzes "The Channel's strategic significance: invasion threat, line of defence, prision wall, escape route," a blessing to the British barricaded behind it, a curse to French prisoners bent on getting out. William R. Jones details the trials and tribulations of venturing upon it in "The Channel and English writers: Johnson, Smollet, Fielding and Falconer." Georges Festa traces through travelers' accounts the ambivalent presence of Jersey and Guernsey in "Manche et permanence historique: les îles anglo-normandes dans la conscience des Lumières."

To bridge this physical separation was to cross to the other, the pleasure of contact varying according to the individual. Felix Paknadel analyzes a painting by a first-time traveler—arrested as a spy—in "Hogarth's *Gate of Calais*: myth and reality" and discovers more anti-French satire than accuracy. In "Channelling emotions: travel and literary creation in Smollett and Stearne," Frédéric Ogée finds that the irascible and isolated Smollett's *Travels* are, paradoxically, an incitement to stay home. Sterne, however, conceives a new kind of traveling in which exchange and non-verbal communication help overcome obstacles. K. E. Smith sees as foreign attractions escape from death and the admirable French talent for civilizing ordinary life in "Ordering things in France: the travels of Sterne, Tristram and Yorick."

But the Channel was also a metaphorical barrier which intellectuals did their best to surmount. Endi L. Stockwell shows in "The importance of the Channel in Prévost's life and work" that the abbé used his novels and his periodical *Le Pour et contre* to promote mutual understanding and thus "to *reduce* the distance between nations" (p. 44). In "Un exemple d'échanges france-anglais privilégiés: la correspondance entre Hans Sloane et l'abbé Bignon," Françoise Bléchet recounts the two distinguished academicians' trading of news of their respective scientific societies, as well as books and periodicals, between 1709 and 1741. More competitive in their eagerness to identify, describe, and name their discoveries were the scientists whom Georgia Beale follows in "Early French members of the Linnean Society of London, 1788–1802: initial encounters." Robert L. Dawson's "Books printed in France: the English connection" establishes French adoption of their rivals' typography and even language. William Hutchings suggests a modern approchement in "Boileau, Pope and the mock-heroic," liberating both poets from too-static neoclassical confines by insisting on their use of the dynamic, diverse, and simultaneous oxymoron.

The concluding article, "Montesquieu and the Dutch as a maritime nation," very fittingly takes the inquiry "out to sea": Sheila Mason closely examines the *Pensées*, the *Spicelège*, and the *Voyage en Hollande* to demonstrate "how central Montesquieu's study of Holland was to his formulation of the profile of the modern, commercial nation" (p. 183).—Josephine Grieder.

Faragher, John Mack (gen. ed.). *The Encyclopedia of Colonial and Revolutionary America*. New York and Oxford: Facts on File, 1991. Pp. viii + 484; illustrations; maps.

Rev. (favorably) by Ronald H. Fritze in *American Reference Books Annual*, 22 (1991), 504.

Farge, Arlette, and Jacques Revel. *The Vanishing Children of Paris: Rumor and Politics Before the French Revolution*. Translated by Claudia Miéville of *Logiques de la foule: l'affaire des enlèvements d'enfants Paris 1750* (Paris, 1988). Cambridge: Polity; Cambridge, MA: Harvard U. Press, 1991. Pp. 146; bibliography; map.

Farge and Revel provide us with a clear analysis of the impact of a rumor in mid-eighteenth century Paris and with the causes and consequences of such an event. A few children of the lower and middle classes were abducted from their parents on their way to school or when running errands. The public considered two interpretations of these abductions. The first was that the children were kidnapped in order to be sent to Louisiana, not so ludicrous an idea since voluntary emigrants were not rife. Second, they thought the kidnappings might provide necessary fresh blood for the king to bathe in and cure his leprosy. In the higher spheres, these abductions were considered as a way of controlling vagrants and decreasing juvenile delinquency. The *exempts* who were the representatives of the absolutist state were ready to deal with the problem of child vagrancy but met with the resistance of neighborhood *commissaires* who were reluctant to confront the mob.

In 1750, crowd control was still in its infancy and the uprisings resulted in the lynching of Constable Labbé. After an inquiry conducted by Councillor Severt from May 27 to July 28, 1750, four policemen were sentenced to a symbolic punishment—a reprimand and a small fine—and three rioters were sentenced to death and executed on August 3. Farge analyzes the whole episode as a turning point in the attitude of the people toward the king; the function was not challenged, but the person definitely was. The revolt was not a revolution, but a chasm seems to separate 1744, when people flocked to the churches to ask for the king's recovery, and the year 1750. Yet, the people already considered the monarch as too aloof and lacking dignity. Moreover, the struggle over Jansenism and its aftermath had given rise to the first movement of public opinion in French history. Such public opinion tended more and more to revile not so much the king as his entourage, courtiers, and mistresses. Quite rightly, the authors see in the episode told in the book an "anachronistic spasm of protest against the state's increasing grip on people's daily lives" (p. 131), especially against the government's attempts at controlling city mobs. The love of the French people for their king was no longer taken for granted. Farge's study stands as a concise masterpiece and cogent analysis of an apparently wayward movement telling us much of what people could already do and think and on what they could not yet achieve.—Jean Rivière.

Fauré, Christine. *Democracy Without Women: Feminism and the Rise of Liberal Individualism in France*. Translated by John Berks and Claudia Gorbman. Bloomington and Indianapolis, IN: Indiana U. Press, 1991. Pp. x + 198; bibliography.

Fauré's ambitious study of the link between liberalism and feminism (Introduction and six chapters) begins with Christine de Pizan in the fifteenth century and surveys the legal, political and social position of women in subsequent centuries.

François I, Marguerite d'Angoulême, John Calvin, Poullain de la Barre, Mademoiselle de Gournay and Montaigne, among others, contributed to the cause of "feminism." However, no substantial difference in women's subservient position occurred, even as *préciosité* valorized women and their *salons*. Attempting to strengthen a patriarchal monarchy, the state promoted religious institutions to educate women and secure their place within the private sphere. Proposals framed by Cartesian philosophy theoretically advocated sexual equality as a basis for legal, political and educational reform.

Chapter IV details the contributions of Montesquieu, Rousseau and Condorcet to liberal individualism, natural rights theories and the struggle for sexual equality. Montesquieu, a founder of modern liberal thought, conceptually bases liberty on law. In *The Spirit of the Laws*, his patriarchal analysis of the family valorizes marriage, fathers over mothers. Separating law from theology, influenced by John Locke, Montesquieu's views on women and the family were "retrograde" (79). While in the first half of the eighteenth century, "tyrannical monarchy was being challenged and religious plurality was being recognized," patriarchal authority went unchallenged, (80).

In Rousseau's *Discourse on Inequality*, gender based distinctions originate in the family. Favoring patriarchal power, Rousseau denies the mother equal authority over children. Underlying the concept of "modern natural right" is an "original principle of equality: with a different meaning for men and women. A woman's proper role as virtuous wife becomes her "inevitable fate" (89) and women's political existence is nullified.

While his position in the "Declaration of the Rights of Man" (1789) changes in the Constitutional Plan of 1793, Condorcet nevertheless advocated including women in public and political affairs. Though unfulfilled, Condorcet's "desire to emancipate women from the burden of their legal incapacities remained exemplary for the period" (99).

Chapter V, "Women and the French Revolution," documents Marie-Charlotte Pauline de Lézardière's political liberalism, Olympe de Gouges's fight for women's emancipation, Théroigne de Mérincourt's militaristic feminism and the conventional egalitarianism of Etta Palm d'Aelders. The male-dominated Revolution crushed "women's hopes" for equality and ultimately relegated them to the private sphere of home and family.

In her final chapter, Fauré emphasizes the Reformation's role in the articulation of sexual equality. While theories of "natural rights" aimed at restoring dignity to all human beings, they "failed to deal with women's condition, or to advance women's causes . . ." (134). Ramifications extending into the nineteenth and twentieth centuries are discussed.

Fauré's contextualization of her analysis within a philosophical amd historical framework at times detracts from the focus of her argument. This is a smooth translation of an informative, scholarly work of interest to specialists and laymen alike. An impressive, twenty-five page bibliography is included.—Felicia B. Sturzer.

Favre, Robert. "La Révolution: Mort et régénération ou la France 'Phénix'." *Dix-huitième siècle*, 21 (1991), 331–44.

Fissell, Mary E. *Patients, Power, and the Poor in Eighteenth Century Bristol*. (Cambridge History of Medicine.) Cambridge and New York: Cambridge U. Press, 1991. Pp. xii + 266; bibliography; figures; maps; tables.

Fleuriot, Jean Marie Jérome. *Voyage de Figaro en Espagne.* Presented and annotated by Robert Favre. Scoiété française d'Etude du XVIII siècle. Saint-Ètienne: Publications de l'Université de Saint-Ètienne, 1991. Pp. 105.

The title exploits the popularity of Beaumarchais's famous character from *Le Barbier de Séville*, who recently made his second appearance in *Le Mariage de Figaro*, just several months before the publishing of Fleuriot de Langle's book. Whether the author actually make the trip to Spain he describes has not been definitely settled; it is interesting to note, however, that a second volume which followed this one, *Tableau pittoresque de la Suisse . . .* (1790), seems to have taken some of the descriptions of cities from the first and substituted them with Swiss place names.

If there are some things he admires about Spain—the Spanish language, the beauty of some women, the countryside—there is much more criticism than praise of the country and its people offered by Fleuriot. The Spaniard is lazy and the siesta prove that Spaniards have always been among "les plus grands dormeurs du monde;"

the wine is poor: "il a un goût de souffre, de goudron, il est si noir, si épais, qu'il pourrait au besoin servir d'encre."
The government is bad, the ministers are terrible. As a good citizen of the Enlightenment, though, some of
Fleuriot's strongest attacks are made against the Church and the "fanatisme imbécile des Espagnols." Judgments
rendered by the Inquisition are unfair and arbitrary; often the person being burned has no idea what he has done but
the inquisitors have to answer to no one and, therefore, can kill without saying why. Although there is no
systematic philosophy being espoused, there is no doubt, at least where religion is concerned, what the author's
thinking is: "Cessons d'enfermer Dieu entre quatre murailles . . . démolissons nos églises; pénétrons tantôt,
arrêtons—nous au pied d'un rocher ou dans une plaine; et là, une fois par mois seulement, entonnons des hymnes,
disons notre chapelet, brûlons de l'encens et chantons les louanges de Dieu." The wealthy church and hypocritical
priests are not helping human brings to find their way to heaven; they are not necessary.

The random ideas sketched in the book are presented in just under ninety rubrics which make up the table of
contents. The author has a facility with words and has even created at least one neologism: *germicide*; two colors
introduced are *bleu mourant* and *prune Monsieur*. All is written "d'une sorte de verve cocasse . . . [p]arfois, à la
facilité d'un style fondé sur l'accujulation, l'énumération." In terms of critical apparatus, there is a preface, a
bibliography, critical comments dating from 1785 and 1786, a brief comparison of the opening pages of the 1784
edition with that of 1796 to show some odd juxtapositions, and some fifteen pages involving the controversy the
book caused with the ambassador of Spain and the banning of the book in France. There are no annotations by the
editor in the text and no index.—Donald C. Spinelli.

Flexner, James Thomas. *The Traitor and the Spy: Benedict Arnold and John André*. (New York
    Classics.) Syracuse, NY: Syracuse U. Press, 1991. Pp. xxiv + 453.

Includes new 3 p. foreword and new illustrations.

Floud, Roderick, Annabel Gregory, and Kenneth Wachter. *Height, Health, and History:
    Nutritional Status in the United Kingdom, 1750–1980*. (Cambridge Studies in Population,
    Economy, and Society in Past Time, 9.) Cambridge and New York: Cambridge U. Press,
    1990. Pp. xxi + 354; bibliography; figures; maps; tables. Cf. *ECCB*, n.s. 16, II: 76.

Rev. by John Burnett, *TLS* (Jan. 4, 1991), 4; by B. Osborne in *Choice*, 28 (1991), 1357–58.

Foner, Eric, and John A. Garraty (eds.). *The Reader's Companion to American History*. Boston,
    MA: Houghton Mifflin, Sponsored by the Society of American Historians, 1991. Pp. xxii +
    1226; maps; tables.

Fontana, Biancamaria. *Benjamin Constant and the Post-Revolutionary Mind*. London and New
    Haven, CT: Yale U. Press, 1991. Pp. xvii + 165.

De Fontenelle, Bernard le Bovier. *Oeuvres Complètes*. Tome II. Edited by Alain Niderst. Paris:
    Fayard. Corpues des oeuvres de philosophie en langue française, 1991. Pp. 437.

1686–1688, the years covered in the present volume make up a critical period in the life of young Fontenelle who
emerged from the provinces, conquered literary fame and was ready to become a member of the Académie française in
1691, of the Académie des sciences in 1679 (its perpetual secretary in 1699 for about forty years) and of the
Académie des inscriptions in 1701. Alain Niderst chose to publish the complete version of the *Entretiens sur la
pluralité des mondes*, as Fontenelle frequently revised and corrected the book in order to keep in touch with the latest
developments in astronomy. His *Histoire des oracles* was freely adapted from the Latin treatise by the Dutch writer
Anton Van Dale *De oraculis ethnicorum* (1683). In it, Fontenelle inaugurated a strategy which eighteenth century
philosophers were going to make popular: to use a criticism of ancient religions as a Trojan horse for a full attack
on Christianity. Even though it is one of the shortest texts in the volume, the *Digression sur les Anciens et les*

Modernes is the most revealing since Fontenelle's plea in favor of the Moderns was an attack against all systems that thought they could survive against the evidence of change. Even though he was a Cartesian, he admitted that two centuries from the time when he was writing, Descartes could be considered just as outmoded as Aristotle in 1686. His attack against Christianity is here indirect, but still potent: by supporting the Ancients, the Church defended permanence in the cultural field as it defended it in the realm of theology. If, on the other hand, Aristotle could be debunked, the challenge to religious dogma was not far behind. Apart from some monotonous eclogues, the three major texts in the book crown Fontenelle as the Modern *par excellence*. Alain Niderest's computer-aided make-up is perfect and based on the definitive 1757–1761 edition of Fontenelle's works.—Jean Rivière.

Forrest, Alan, and Peter Jones (eds.). *Reshaping France: Town, Country and Region during the French Revolution*. Manchester, UK, and New York: Manchester U. Press, 1991. Pp. viii + 258.

Alan Forrest and Peter Jones bring together many distinguished social historians of eighteenth-century France in this excellent collection of fifteen essays exploring the dynamic relations between the Revolution of 1789 and "town, country and region." Using a wide variety of approaches, the contributors examine social and professional groups (peasantry, urban laboring class, bourgeoisie, military), ideologies (agrarian radicalism, *sans-culotte* politics), formal and informal political practices (elections, municipal reforms, popular violence), and the transmission of political culture (language, the press) in the French Revolution.

Two articles give overviews of the Revolution's impact on the French economy. T. J. A. Le Goff and D. M. G. Sutherland, through a detailed analysis of the rural economy, show that the Revolution stymied growth in the countryside. Le Goff and Sutherland argue that "viewed from the perspective of probably most people who had to live through it, the Revolution was long and hard" (p. 76). In a parallel study of the urban economy, Paul Butel maintains that the Revolution, by bringing on war, foreign competition, and the Haitian slave revolt, wreaked havoc on cities and towns. Taken together, these essays present a negative picture of the Revolution. But a larger historical question remains: Why did so many rural and urban inhabitants support the Revolution when it caused them nothing but hardship?

Several historians use traditional social and political history to explore revolutionary *mentalités*. Colin Lucas, for example, discusses how revolutionaries differentiated between "bad" and "good" violence, indeed between riot and revolution, in their attempts to legitimize the founding moment of 1789. Peter Jones, in a case study of the Versaillais, examines how the issue of land distribution helped to politicize the peasantry. Isser Woloch, looking at the various attempts to reform local administration from 1789 to 1800, concludes that "administrative penetration of the countryside took a giant leap forward with the Revolution and then stalled" (p. 233).

The authors of the most original contributions in this collection use methods derived from cultural history, especially discourse analysis, to delve into the "psychology of Revolutionary politics" (p. 5). In a fascinating discussion of Marseille's bourgeoisie, William Scott argues that "even consideration of the 'economic' dimensions of the activities of the Revolutionary bourgeoisie must take into account questions of perception, *mentalité, moeurs*, of social and individual psychology" (p. 99). Deconstructing the cultural space between the real and the represented, Scott offers a sophisticated, socially-constructed portrayal of the relationship between the bourgeoisie and revolutionary politics, a relationship that escapes characterization in strict materialist terms. Michel Vovelle also examines the relationship between the bourgeoisie and the Revolution in a creative analysis of how the bourgeoisie represented peasants in popular iconography.

Focusing on key words, two historians provide rich studies of the revolutinary mind. Norman Hampson subtly examines how the concept of "nation" entered into the French consciousness, and led, somewhat paradoxically, to "both a fractured nation and a concept of national purpose" by the end of the Revolution (p. 24). Michael Sonenscher demonstrates "how artisans came to acquire the kind of political consciousness encapsulated by the term *sans-culotte*, so that, by 1792, the term had become one of the rhetorical resources of republican politics" (p. 111). Sonenscher's "social-constructionist" essay, in particular, is a model for social historians hoping to move beyond the moribund Marxist-revisionist debate.

The collection holds together very well, although it has two weaknesses. Ceri Crossley's article, a good discussion of the views of Bonald and Michelet on town and country, seems out of place in a book on the social history of the French Revolution. More problematic, especially given the near-comprehensiveness of topics and approaches covered in this collection, is the absence of a substantive discussion of gender in the Revolution, a topic that historians such as Darlene Levy, Olwen Hufton, and Suzanne Desan have brought to the center of current debates over the social history of the French Revolution. Nevertheless, this volume is a solid contribution to the study of the political culture of the French Revolution. Moreover, its essays will undoubtedly stimulate more work in the field, because, as Michael Sonenscher writes "much more remains to be discovered about the relationship between political vocabularies, political actors and political action before and during the French Revolution" (p. 118).—Bryant T. Ragan, Jr.

Fort, Bernadette (ed.). *Fictions of the French Revolution.* Evanston, IL: Northwestern U. Press, 1991. Pp. viii + 209.

The volume includes six essays presented at a Bicentennial Colloquium at Northwestern University in November, 1989. Bernadette Fort's introduction provides an elegant formulation and detailed synopsis of the main arguments of the contributors as well as an excellent analysis of how the authors engage techniques from psychoanalysis, narratology, feminist theory, semiotics and sociology to gain new insights into the ways in which the Revolutionaries exploited a variety of literary, religious, and mythological traditions to create the new political culture of the Revolution.

Despite differences in content, the first four essays interact with each other through their emphasis on the body as a privileged signifier in the Revolution's new culture. "In Refiguring the Body," Peter Brooks pursues connections between the new "aesthetics of embodiment, melodrama and revolutionary rhetoric" in Sylvain Maréchal's *Le jugement dernier des rois*, a political melodrama in which the morally unredeemable kings and queens of Europe, deposed on a desert island, tear each other to pieces until they are swallowed by flames from below. In "Revolutionary Activism and the Cult of Male," Thomas Crow deciphers two discourses in David's puzzling portrait *Bara*. David's attempt to figure a new image of outraged innocence and suffering and to link this image with Patriotism is also a reinterpretation of the *Endymion* of his deceased pupil Girodet.

Like Brooks, Jacques Revel and Patrice Higonnet rely on "second-rate literature" to formulate and validate their clams. Revel's excellent essay examined the role of pamphletary fiction in creation and staging the public hatred for Marie-Antoinette. Patrice Higonnet's less successful attempt to demonstrate connections and parallels between sentimental and political suicides in life and art before, during, and after the Revolution is perhaps due to the fact that is seems unnecessary to martial as much information, however interesting, as Higonnet does, to examine the reasons why joint suicides, so popular in sentimental, melodramatic fiction, did not become prevalent in the patriotic fiction produced in the totalitarian atmosphere of the Terror.

The fine essays of David Simpson, "The Revolution That Will Not Finish: Mythologies of Method in Britain," and François Furet, "The Tyranny of Revolutionary Memory," explore the Revolution's legacy. Simpson examines the endemic suspicion of systems and theories prevalent in contemporary English conservative political and critical prose in light of Burke's accounts of the Revolution in which he links radical Enlightenment philosophy to logic, theory and method. Simpson posits his work as a response to Furet's essay (itself a summary of the latter's monumental *La Révolution française: de Turgot à Jules Ferry (1770–1870)* in which Furet argues that the political diviseness caused by revolutionary models in the "language and consciousness informing French political life" has been overcome.

Despite this disagreement, all the contributors share a belief in the formative and directive power of language over history. Thus, the final essay by professor of theater Craig Kinzer on the staging of Stanislawa Pryzbyszewska's *The Danton Case* (1927) at the Colloquium provides a neat closure to the volume. The play, a criticism of the Communist appropriation of Jacobin rhetoric and ideals, attests to the ongoing myth-making power of the Revolution. Its presentation at the moment the Berlin Wall was coming down in the name of "democracy" must have appeared as a live enactment of many of the connections made in the preceding pages between history, rhetoric, art and the Revolution.—Carol Lazzaro-Weis.

Foster, Stephen. *The Long Argument: English Puritanism and the Shaping of New England Culture, 1570–1700*. Chapel Hill, NC: U. of North Carolina Press for the Institute of Early American History and Culture, Williamsburg, Virginia, 1991. Pp. x + 395; bibliography.

Rev. by B. R. Burg in *Choice*, 29 (1991), 186.

Frisch, Morton J. *Alexander Hamilton and the Political Order: An Interpretation of His Political Thought and Practice*. Lanham, MD: University Press of America, 1991. Pp. 118.

Fyfe, Christopher (ed.). *Our Children Free and Happy: Letters from Black Settlers in Africa in the 1790's*. Edinburgh, Scotland: Edinburgh U. Press (Distributed by New York: Columbia U. Press), 1991. Pp. x + 106; bibliography.

Gagliardi, John. *Germany Under the Old Regime, 1600–1790*. London and New York: Longman, 1991. Pp. ix + 453; bibliography; maps.

Garr, Daniel J. (ed.). *Hispanic Urban Planning in North America*. (Spanish Borderlands Series, 27). New York: Garland Publishing, 1991. Pp. xxiv + 471.

Garrison, J. Ritchie. *Landscape and Material Life in Franklin County, Massachusetts, 1770–1860*. Knoxville: TN: U. of Tennessee Press, in association with U. of Chicago Press, 1991. Pp. 314.

Gelbart, Nina Rattner. *Feminine and Opposition Journalism in Old Regime France: Le Journal des Dames*. Berkeley, CA: U. of California Press, 1987. Pp. xvii + 354; bibliography; illustrations. Cf. *ECCB*, n.s. 13, II: 63.

Rev. by Suellen Diaconoff in *Diderot Studies*, 24 (1991), 185–87.

Gelis, Jacques. *History of Childbirth: Fertility, Pregnancy and Birth in Early Modern Europe*. Translated by Rosemary Morris. Boston, MA: Northeastern U. Press, 1991. Pp. xvii + 326; bibliography; illustrations.

Gerbod, Paul. *Voyages au pays des mangeurs de grenouilles: La France vue par les voyageurs anglais du XVIIIᵉ siècle à nos jours*. Paris: Albin Michel, 1991. Pp. 417; illustrations.

Gianturco, Carolyn, and Eleanor McCrickard (eds.). *Alessandro Stradella 1639–1682): A Thematic Catalougue of his Compositions*. (Thematic Catalogue Series, 16.) Stuyvesant, NY: Pendragon Press, 1991. Pp. xxciii + 325; bibliography, illustrations.

Gilbert, Christopher. *English Vernacular Furniture, 1750–1900*. London and New Haven,CT: Yale U. Press for the Mellon Centre for Studies in British Art, 1991. Pp. viii + 294; appendices; bibliography; illustrations.

Gilmour, Ian. *Riot, Risings and Revolution: Governance and Violence in Eighteenth Century England*. London: Hutchinson, 1991. Pp. viii + 504; bibliography.

Giraud, Marcel. *A History of French Louisiana*. Vol. V: *The Company of the Indies, 1723–1731*. Translated by Brian Pearce. Baton Rouge, LA: Louisiana State U. Press, 1991. Pp. xiii + 517; maps.

Gragg, Larry. *A Quest for Security: The Life of Samuel Parris, 1653–1720*. (Contributions in American History, 142.) New York: Greenwood Press, 1990. Pp. xix + 214. Cf. *ECCB*, n.s. 16, II: 80.

Rev. by B. R. Burgg in *Choice*, 28 (1991), 1369.

Greaves, Richard L. *Enemies Under His Feet: Radicals and Nonformists in Britain, 1664–1677*. Stanford, CA: Stanford U. Press, 1990. Pp. xii + 324; bibliography. Cf. *ECCB*, n.s. 16, II: 80.

Rev. (with other works) by John Adamson in *TLS*, (June 7, 1991), 5–6; (favorably) by W. B. Robinson III in *Choice*, 28 (1991), 836.

Greene, Jack P., and J.R. Pole (eds.). *The Blackwell Encyclopedia of the American Revolution*. Cambridge, MA: Blackwell Reference, 1991. Pp. xvi + 845; bibliographies; illustrations; maps.

Not *one* bibliography but "about 180 bibliographical entries and a chronology of events."

Greene, Nathanael. *The Papers of General Nathanael Greene, Volume VI: 1 June 1780–25 December 1780*. Chapel Hill, NC, and London: The U. of North Carolina Press, 1991. Pp. xlviii + 693; appendices; chronology; frontispiece.

Green, Thurston. *The Language of the Constitution: A Sourcebook and Guide to the Ideas, Terms, and Vocabulary Used by the Framers of the United States Constitution*. Edited by Stuart B. Flexner. Westwood, CT: Greenwood Press/Greenwood Publishing Group Inc., 1991. Pp. xxviii + 1045.

Gregory, Desmond. *Minorca, the Illusory Prize: A History of the British Occupations of Minorca Between 1708 and 1802*. Rutherford, NJ: Fairleigh Dickinson U. Press; London and Toronto, Canada: Associated University Presses, 1990. Pp. 295; bibliography; illustrations; maps. Cf. *ECCB*, n.s. 16, II: 81.

Rev. by J. R. Breihan in *Choice*, 28 (1991), 1202.

Griffin, Patricia C. *Mullet on the Beach: The Minorcans of Florida, 1768–1788*. Gainesville, FL: U. North Florida Press in association with U. Presses of Florida and sponsored by the St. Augustine Historical Society, 1991. Pp. 219.

Grinde, Donald A., Jr., and Bruce E. Johansen. *Exemplar of Liberty: Native America and the Evolution of Democracy*. (Native American Politics Series, 3.) Los Angeles, CA: American Indian Studies Center, U. of California, Los Angeles, 1991. Pp. xxv + 320; bibliography; illustrations.

Gross, Hanns. *Rome in the Age of Enlightenment: The Post-Tridentine Syndrome and the Ancien Regime*. (Cambridge Studies in Early Modern History.) Cambridge and New York: Cambridge U. Press, 1990. Pp. x + 411; bibliography; illustrations; maps; tables. Cf. *ECCB*, n.s. 16, II: 81.

Rev. by K. F. Drew in *Choice*, 28 (1991), 1202

Guelzo, Allen C. *Edwards on the Will: A Century of American Theological Debate.* Middletown,
     CN: Wesleyan U. Press, 1989. Pp. xi + 349.

Rev. (with other works) by Darlene Harbour Unrue in *Religion & Literature*, 23 (1991), 87–90.

Gutiérrez, Ramón A. *When Jesus Came, the Corn Mothers Went Away: Marriage, Sexuality,
     and Power in New Mexico, 1500–1846.* Stanford, CA: Stanford U. Press, 1991. Pp. xxxi +
     414; bibliography; figures; map; tables.

Rev. (favorably) by M. L. Tate in *Choice*, 29 (1991), 186. "Part III: The Eighteenth Century" covers pages
141–336.
     This is an important book, not just for eighteenth-century studies in America, but for the entire range of
cultural, literary, historical and ethno-historical scholarship on Mexico and the U.S.. Guittérez, by taking seriously
the Pueblo peoples and cultures as well as the variety of Spanish peoples and cultures who contacted them in what
we now know as Mexico and the United States, has produced a stunning ethno-history of the first 350 years of
cultural contact that will reshape the standards for historical and possible even contemporary studies in this region.
     Guittérez focuses his study through a century-by-century study of the various cultures at the point of contact,
and how they affected each other—religiously, politically, culturally, economically—in the ensuing years. He
considers accommodations made by each culture to the other, and the defensive strategies the various groups used to
preserve their sense of identity. Using "marriage" as a key point for analysis, Guittérez is able to use marital
practices as a way of studying the key value patterns of the different groups, tracing how they formed alliances, who
they privileged and suppressed, gained and exchanged property and possessions, and how they formulated gender
relationships.
     Guittérez steers carefully away from evaluations; his work is impressively descriptive. Uninterested in proving
a particular culture "superior" to the other, either Spanish or Puebloan, makes this work impressively perceptive at
the "level of detail," and a much-needed balance for works that have tended to "take sides." For instance, Guittérez
argues that Puebloan philosophical emphasis on balance and harmony should not lead present-day scholars
uncritically to read these "as statements of fact." Rather, Guittérez cautions, we should understand that evocations of
balance and harmony were ritual counteractants to a human world threatened by social fragmentation.
     Reading cultural interaction metaphorically as a dialogue between equals—different groups but one neither better
not worse than others—enables Guittérez to closely examine not only the ways in which, say, Spanish Franciscan
practices assimilated aspects of Puebloan religious symbolism, but also how the cultures misunderstood each other
for the very fact that they read symbolism differently. Guittérez recounts, for example, how one day when a
Franciscan priest was exhorting the Puebloans to live monogamously, a woman who began preaching against it was
struck dead by a bolt of lightening. Although the priest was elatedly confident that the Pueblans would then see that
God had struck down the woman for her evil views, the Puebloans themselves understood something very different,
seeing the lightening not as a punitive, but as a germinative force. For them, the lightening bolt confirmed what
the woman had urged (73–74).
     The scope of his study allows Guittérez to trace the development of ideas about "race" in Spanish/Mexican
culture, which will be an important aspect for scholars trying to trace out theoretical and historical models for race as
a concept and a social apparatus. Guittérez argues that while most of the terminology and conceptual categories for
"race" were drawn by the Spaniards from the reconquest of the Moors, it was not until the mid 1700s that "race"
became a legally meaningful designation in New Mexico. His careful tracing out of links between notions of "race"
and honor ("claidad") inform each other during this period, in a way that differentiates Spanish American racism from
its Anglo-American version.
     In his Epilogue, Guittérez briefly discusses the entry of U.S. interests into New Mexico, drawing attention to
the similar cultural agendas and defensive strategies employed by the wave of Anglo-American settlers: "much as the
Spanish conquistadors and Franciscan friars had lambasted the idolatrous ways of their Indian subjects, so too the
nineteenth-century Protestant apostles of American democracy found in New Mexico a depraved people who
wallowed in promiscuity, whose devilish fandangos corrupted, and whose addiction to vice had created an indolent and

mongrel race." Believing, as had the Spaniards before them, that the people they encountered were ugly and lazy enabled the "white" settlers to ignore the claims of the indigenous peoples to both land and culture. Comparing the U.S. goddess Liberty in its symbolic function to the spanish Catholic Virgin Mary, Guittérez suggestively concludes his study be drawing attention to the feminized symbols that these two conquest cultures had wedded themselves to, and their implications for ongoing cultural conflicts and engagements in the U.S. southwest, today.—Dana D. Nelson.

Haber, Samuel. *The Quest for Authority and Honor in the American Professions, 1750–1900*. Chicago, IL, and London: The U. of Chicago Press, 1991. Pp. xiv + 478; illustrations.

Hackett, David G. *The Rude Hand of Innovation: Religion and Social Order in Albany, New York, 1652–1836*. New York and Oxford: Oxford U. Press, 1991. Pp. xv + 240; appendices; bibliography; maps; tables.

Haeger, John D. *John Jacob Astor: Business and Finance in the Early Republic*. (Great Lakes Books.) Detroit, MI: Wayne State U. Press, 1991. Pp. 365.

Hall, John Whitney (ed.), and James L. McClain (asst. ed.). *The Cambridge History of Japan*. Vol. 4: *Early Modern Japan*. Cambridge and New York: Cambridge U. Press, 1991. Pp. xxviii + 831; bibliography; figures; maps.

Hamilton-Phillips, Martha, and Robert P. Maccubbin. *The Age of William III and Mary II: Power, Politics and Patronage 1688–1702*. Williamsburg, VA: Grolier Club, Foger Shakespeare Library, and William and Mary, 1989. Pp. xxxii + 416. Cf. *ECCB*, n.s. 15, II: 72.

Rev. (with another work) by Lionel K. J. Glassey in *The Scriblerian*, 24 (1991), 88.

Hampson, Norman. *Saint-Just*. Cambridge, MA, and Oxford: Basil Blackwell, 1991. Pp. 245.

Rev. (favorably) by G. C. Bond in *Choice*, 28 (1991), 1829; (briefly) by Hilary Mantel in *TLS*, (Dec. 6, 1991), 12; (favorably) by Eugene Weber in *TLS*, (Feb. 15, 1991), 3–4.

Handrick, Wolfgang. *Die Pragmatische Armee 1741 bis 1743. Eine allierte Armee im Kalkül des Österreichischen Erfolgekrieges*. (Beiträge zur Militargeschichte, Band 30). Munich: Oldenbourg, 1991. Pp. xi + 350.

Hann, J. (ed. and trans.). *Missions to the Calusa*. (Ripley P. Bullen Series. Columbus Quincentenary Series.) Gainesville, FL: U. of Florida Press in association with Florida Museum of Natural History, U. Press of Florida and sponsored by the Florida Museum of Natural History, 1991. Pp. 460.

Series title changed from *Ripley P. Bullen Monographs in Anthropology & History*.

Harding, Richard. *Amphibious Warfare in the Eighteenth Century: The British Expedition to the West Indies, 1740–1742*. (Royal Historical Society Studies in History, 62.) Woodbridge, Suffolk, UK: Boydell Press, 1991. Pp. x + 248; bibliography; illustrations; maps.

Haring Fabend, Firth. *A Dutch Family in the Middle Colonies, 1660–1800*. New Brunswick, NJ: Rutgers U. Press, 1991. Pp. xviii + 326; bibliography; illustrations.

Rev. by G. W. Franz in *Choice*, 29 (1991), 508.

Harper, R. Eugene. *The Transformation of Western Pennsylvania, 1770–1800*. Pittsburgh, PA: U. of Pittsburgh Press, 1991. Pp. xx + 273; bibliography; illustrations; tables.

Harris, Frances. *A Passion for Government: The Life of Sarah, Duchess of Marlborough*. New York: Oxford U. Press; Oxford: Clarendon, 1991. Pp. viii + 421; bibliography; illustrations; portraits.

Countless biographical and historical works have recounted the lives of John and Sarah, Duke and Dutchess of Marlborough. Yet these works' individual and collective shortcomings are as great as they are numerous. In part this is due to the nature of the evidence. Ultimately they all rely largely on the great archive left by the ducal pair at Blenheim Palace. That archive, especially for the duke, consists largely of papers from his period of greatest glory, 1701–1711. Remarkably little survives from any other period. Moreover, the duke himself much of the more personal and intimate correspondence so that most of what remains is official and not revealing. The dutchess herself screened both her own and the duke's papers continually throughout much of her long life. The second factor that has compromised so much of what has been written about the two is that the papers were inaccessible to all but a chosen few until after World War II. To be sure the copious extracts made by Archdeacon Coxe were available in the British Library, but that was small consolation.

When the papers passed into public custody in 1973, British Library archivists sorted, organized, and published the papers with an admirably detailed index. One of those archivists has now utilized these resources and her own expertise to produce a long overdue and definitive account of the most colorful of all the Churchills, the first Dutchess of Marlborough. From the time her relationship with Queen Anne began to break down until her death nearly four decades later, the dutchess prepared apolgias, remonstrances, and justifications in bewildering and tedious prolixity. It is to Frances Harris' great credit that she has sorted, edited, dated, and organized these shards and that together with material in the archive as well as with other sources she has been able to weave a coherent, masterly narrative that does full justice to the indomitable, masterful, and indefatigable woman. May we hope that she will edit and publish the autobiographical accounts?

No previous work has interpreted so fully and revealingly Sarah's true role in the poltical controversies of Anne's reign. Harris accurately chronicles her limited and rapidly dwindling influence on the queen from the very outset of her reign. It was only through her husband and Godolphin that the dutchess was able to have some impact, and that was ultimately disastrous for the three of them and the Whig party she favored. Harris also delineates the use made of her by the Whigs to force their views on the ministry. In particular she explains the role of the dutchess' confidant, Arthur Maynwaring, and depicts him as a meddler and Whig agent whose advice was contrary to the best interests of herself and her family.

Yet Harris' most important accomplishment may be her account, the most detailed and most accurate yet published, of the dutchess' tempestuous and yet loving relationship with her husband, especially before and after Anne's reign, and her life after his death. Her role as the manager of the Marlborough fortune and the defender of its integrity, her combative and inevitably unhappy relationship with her children and their progeny, and the countless friendships she made and lost are laid out in graphic and fascinating detail. Harris has plumbed not only correspondence and contemporary gossip but bank accounts, property records, and court suits to create this superb biography. It is the most satisfying account of either the duke or dutchess yet to be written.—Henry L. Snyder.

Haslip, Joan. *Madame Du Barry: The Wages of Beauty*. London: Weidenfeld and Nicolson, 1991. Pp. viii + 213; illustrations.

Rev. (favorably) by Elizabeth Jennings in *TLS,* (Dec. 27, 1991), 20.

Hassen, Mohammed. *The Ormo of Ethiopia: A History, 1570–1860.* (African Studies Series, 66.) Cambridge and New York: Cambridge U. Press, 1990. Pp. xviii + 253; illustrations; maps. Cf. *ECCB*, n.s. 16, II: 83.

Rev. by E. E. Beauregard in *Choice*, 28 (1991), 831.

Haws, Robert J. (ed.). *The South's Role in the Creation of the Bill of Rights: Essays.* (Chancellor's Symposium Series, 1989.) Jackson, MS: U. Press of Mississippi, 1991. Pp. v + 186; bibliography.

Haycock, Lorna. *John Anstie of Devizes, 1743–1830: An Eighteenth-Century Wiltshire Clothier.* Phoenix Mill and Far Thrupp Stroud: Wiltshire Archaeological and Natural History Society in association with Alan Sutton, 1991. Pp. xii + 116; appendices; illustrations; select bibliography; tables.

Haythornthwaite, Philip J. *Invincible Generals: Gustavus Adolphus, Marlborough, Frederick the Great, George Washington, Wellington.* Bloomington and Indianapolis, IN: Indiana U. Press, 1991. Pp. 240; bibliography; illustrations.

Hayward, J. E. S. *After the French Revolution: Six Critics of Democracy and Nationalism.* (New York University Studies in French Culture and Civilization.) London: Harvester Wheatsheaf; Washington Square, NY: New York U. Press, 1991. Pp. xvi + 366; bibliography.

If Western scholarship since World War II has commonly posed the problem of why Germany failed to achieve a liberal democracy in the modern age, it has also questioned why modern France, home to the Declaration of the Rights of Man and Citizen, failed to sustain one. Plagued by periodic revolutionary upheavals, France changed political regimes nine times between 1789 and 1968. In *After the French Revolution*, Jack Hayward attempts to address this historical enigma by analyzing six nineteenth century "critics" of France's "founding myth of a liberal, democratic and national Revolution" (xii) ranging from the far right to the far left: the Catholic monarchist De Maistre, the counterrevolutionary utopian St. Simon, the liberal intellectuals Benjamin Constant and Tocqueville, the anarchist Proudhon, and the revolutionary insurrectionist Blanqui. Framing his work partly as a response to François Furet's most recent pronouncement that France's "République du centre" of the 1970s has finally brought the Revolution to a close, Hayward hopes to demonstrate the inherent precariousness of a model which sought to combine the rights of man with a unitary national democracy founded upon revolutionary innovation. Each of his designated critics, accordingly, manifests the frustrated political aspiration in modern France—be it through a return to royal absolutism, an advance toward a scientific or egalitarian utopia, or a pulralistic compromise—to terminate the Revolution.

For readers seeking reliable shorthand accounts of these six important post-revolutionary figures, Hayward offers solid if not ground-breaking summaries of their political thought and itineraries. The great virtue of this approach, moreover, is that while accepting the Anglo-American model of liberal democracy as a comparative norm, he nonetheless analyzes modern French political culture on its own terms. Accordingly, his interpretation of France's revolutionary tradition emphasizes the mercurial character of modern French politics—its idiosyncratic oscillation between centralized authoritarianism and revolutionary upheaval—without falling into the trap of assuming, as do many commentors on modern France, that whatever is not recognizably "liberal" in modern politics necessarily foreshadows totalitarianism. Hence while recognizing the intrinsically illiberal charcter of Rousseau's "general will," for example, or of Robespierre's "monolithic democracy," (30) he wisely absolves them both of responsibility for the horrors of twentieth-century politics.

In terms of its larger purpose, however, Hayward's work fails convincingly to illuminate the incapacity of modern France, at least until recently, to sustain a stable liberal–democratic policy. His introductory and concluding chapters, while commenting intelligently on the taming of the revolutionary myth, especially by De Gaulle and Mitterand, seem only tenuously connected to his six "representative intellectuals"—and indeed, he does not establish the "representative" status of the latter so much as assert it. As to which political traditions his chosen figures represent and how they relate to the volatility of the democratic-revolutionary model in modern France, Hayward offers only the barest of political family trees as the end of each chapter. His analysis, in short, leaves a gap between the realm of political ideas and practice, offering little explanation of how his designated critics and their supposed legacies mirrored and helped frame the dilemma of modern French politics. The problem would seem to stem from a contradiction between Hayward's ambitious—and laudable—desire to identify the broad political "myths" and intellectual traditions underlying France's post-revolutionary political culture, and his method, which is to construct individual intellectual biographies of his chosen figures and to trace the direct "influence" of each. His work might have been more convincing had it emphasized the myths and traditions themselves, and demonstrated how they have helped shape the political discourse of modern France.—Paul Cohen.

Hembry, Phyllis. *The English Spa 1500–1815. A Social History.* Cranbury, NJ: Fairleigh Dickinson, 1990. Pp. xiv +401. Cf. *ECCB*, n.s. 16, II: 84.

Rev. by Jeremy Black in *The Scriblerian*, 24 (1991), 82–83.

Henretta, James A. *The Origins of American Capitalism: Collected Essays.* Boston, MA, and Ithaca, NY: Northeastern U. Press in association with Cornell U. Press, 1991. Pp. xxxvii + 312.

Henricks, Thomas S. *Disputed Pleasures: Sport and Society in Preindustrial England.* (Contributions to the Study of World History, 28.) New York and Westport, CT: Greenwood Press, 1991. Pp. viii + 196; bibliography.

Hesse, Carla. *Publishing and Cultural Politics in Revolutionary Paris, 1789–1810.* Berkeley and Los Angeles, CA: U. of California Press, 1991. Pp. xvi + 296; appendices; illustrations; map; tables.

Based upon her Princeton dissertation, Carla Hesse's account of the vicissitudes of Paris publishing from the outbreak of the Revolution until the Napoleonic press law of 1810 is a dense and richly documented contribution to *l'histoire du livre* for a crucial yet curiously neglected period. Less interested in bibliographical matters or technological developments than she is in cultural transformations and legal issues, Hesse concurs with the views of Jürgen Habermas and Robert Darnton that "booty capitalist" booksellers initially diffused Enlightenment thought by challenging the corporate monopolies of the eighteenth-century French monarchy. As a consequence, liberal revolutionaries of 1789–90 opted for deregulation in seeking to complete the civic education of the French reading public. With the emergence of a free periodical press, journalism quickly flourished as the essential vehicle for this education. However, because Enlightenment culture had been primarily a bookish one, it was a major disappointment to the political elites of the early Revolution that, once they were no longer served by the old monarchy's inefficient system of privilege and exception, authors lost interest in educating the public. Moreover, by 1789 the liberated Paris book trade was virutally insolvent. Readers showed a preference for novels as opposed to *philosophie* and unprecendented numbers of publishers went bankrupt. Notions of what constituted literary property remained confused and the eighteenth-century epistemological conception of the author as a "privileged creature of the absolutist state" had not yet yielded place to one more appropriate for revolutionary times.

Just as it initiated a repressive policy toward rabble-rousing journalists, in 1793 the National Convention tried to revive the decadent book trade. Concerning authors, *conventionnels* issued a declaration of the rights of genius. As "civic heroes of public enlightenment," authors hereafter would be entitled to profit from their ideas during their lifetimes; at their deaths, however, their work became the property of the nation. Yet no precise definition immediately emerged of what ought to constitute the public domain. According to Hesse, only with Napoleon's regulation of 1810 did the contents of the domain achieve its modern "paratextual" identity. Hereafter, she believes, common texts would be subdivided into individualized *editions* based upon notes, format, paper, and prefaces. By monopolizing one or more of these editions and through rivalries over the establishment of a standard one, nineteenth-century publishers therefore re-emerged as the figures primarily responsible for preserving the nation's literary heritage.

Rich as Hesse's pioneering work is, certain of her assertions are both repetitive and open to challenge. More careful proofreading would have caught several embarrassing mistranscriptions. Her figures for the number of Paris book-guild masters for 1789 do not quite add up, and *capitation* tax assessments of of book guild members may be more indicative of their status than of their actual wealth. Hesse thoughtfully discusses the thorny issues of "text," "paratext," "edition," and "literary property," but she never quite resolves them. For example, she underestimates the influence of *permissions tacites* in the dethronement of an absolute conception of literary property and the subsequent evolution of a "limited" one defined by Condorcet and Sieyès. She is most convincing when she shows how revolutionary legislation did not necessarily confirm the author-enshrining priciples of Diderot (and Michel Foucault) but rather "combined an instrumentalist notion of the public good with a theory of authorship based upon natural rights" (122). Some final notes: Hesse's regulation/deregulation dates are slippery, and one can hardly call the National Convention's cultural policies until October 1794 *laissez-faire*. Furthermore, long before 1810 Old-Regime publishers fought over paratextual standards and living writers exploited them. Witness Rousseau's sale in 1761 of three separate "editions" of *La Nouvelle Héloise* and in paradoxical fashion, his attempt, just before his death, to posthumously control the texts of all his works by publicly disavowing every edition of his writings except the very first one.—Raymond Birn.

Hey, David. *The Fiery Blades of Hallamshire: Sheffield and its Neighbourhood, 1660–1740.* (Communities, Contexts, and Cultures: Leicester Studies in English Local History.) London and New York: Leicester U. Press, 1991. Pp. xx + 367; bibliography; figures; maps; tables.

This study of Sheffield cutlers is more than another English local history monograph. First, Hallamshire was neither parish nor county, but, arguably, a locally-sustained *pays*. If this region of ancient Northumbria retained a strong identity, it supports the community thesis expounded by the series editor, Charles Phythian-Adams. Second, Sheffield cutlery was famous in literature and marketplace. The history of this regional specialization provides a context for Adam Smith's discussion of the division of labor.

The first parts of the work—on geography, demography, and the cutlers' economy and social structure—are largely descriptive analyses of probate inventories and tax returns. Hallamshire was a region of mixed agriculture and small-scale industry. Joan Thirsk's or David Underdown's discussion of regional cultures would be relevant here, particularly given the pronounced Dissenter influence in this wood-pasture region. Sheffield cutlers largely regulated their own community, particularly after the last resident lord of the manor died in 1616. Though Geoffrey Chaucer mentions Sheffield "whittles," the industrial town had "much encreased" by the time of Daniel Defoe's *Tour* (p. 62). Local population rose in the early seventeenth century and rose rapidly in the early eighteenth. Apprenticeship registers show that few young men from outside Hallamshire sought fortunes making knives in Sheffield. Earlier marriages, rather than migration, account for the burgeoning population of this increasingly "smoky, industrial town" (p. 92). By the 1670s, Sheffield was uniquely specialized. Over half the men in the region registered their trade as a form of metalworking. Since in-migration was limited, Sheffield resembles a caste system of familial specialization more than a Smithian world of free individuals.

An intriquing chapter documents how the Sheffield cutlers combatted London dominance of the knife market (in part through false advertising). The metal trades became increasingly specialized—there were scissorsmiths, filesmiths, buttonmakers, razormakers, among others—in the same period that the cutlers pushed successfully for better navigation of the River Don, corroborating Smith's observation that market size determines specialization. By the eighteenth century, market needs in London, Virginia, Jamaica, and elsewhere determined the nailmakers' production calendar.

Like David Levine's and Keith Wrightson's *The Making of an Industrial Society: Whickam, 1560–1765* (1990), Hey documents a local "industrial revolution" that occurred over a long period. Unlike their study, he links

Sheffield's precocious industrialization to its Puritanism, reviving "[t]he Protestant work ethic" as an explanatory force (p. 286).

Hey's central thesis is that early modern Hallamshire was a distinct community, whose unitary social system was threatened neither by tensions between the governors and the governed nor by its widening links with the wider world. Such a consensual society is noteworthy given sweeping industrial and political changes looming in the nineteenth century. Hey's finding that Sheffield had little "serious crime" (p. 248) could be compared with Alan Macfarlane's similar but contested argument regarding late-seventeenth century Westmorland (*The Justice and the Mare's Ale*, 1981). Less convincing is Hey's argument that Sheffield was immune to the rage of party. The Dissenter-influenced cutlers were supposedly apolitical because they forsook their resident Whig squire to appeal to the country squire, Tory Sir John Reresby, when they needed clout during the Tory *revanche* of the 1680s, only to abandon Reresby at the Glorious Revolution. Such acumen enraged Reresby and, like a partisan dispute over the right to present a curate, suggests that Sheffield was closely tied to national politics. If the average Master Cutler was more *zoon politikon* than Hey would admit, he was also *homo economicu.* Despite the material success the cutlers experienced, there was no "urban renaissance" in dour, puritanical Sheffield (p. 280). The concluding chapters should be read by all students of early modern local history to ponder Hey's definition of community and his argument about how a culture is created and sustained.—Newton E. Key.

Hibbert, Christopher. *Redcoats and Rebels: The War for America, 1770–1781*. London: Grafton; New York: W. W. Norton, 1990. Pp. 375; bibliography; illustrations; maps. Cf. *ECCB*, n.s. 16, II: 85.

Rev. (with another work) by W. A. Speck in *TLS*, (May 31, 1991), 24.
American editions has subtitle: *The American Revolution Through British Eyes.*

Hickok, Eugene W., Jr. (ed.). *The Bill of Rights: Original Meaning and Current Understanding*. Charlottesville, VA: U. Press of Virginia, 1991. Pp. xii + 487; bibliography.

Rev. by L. Weinstein in *Choice*, 29 (1991), 668.

Hill, C. P. *Who's Who in Stuart Britain*. Revised and enlarged ed. (Who's Who in British History, 5.) Chicago, IL: St. James Press; London: Shepheard-Walwyn, 1988. Pp. xiv + 466; illustrations.

Rev. by S. A. Stussy in *Choice*, 28 (1991), 1616.

Hobsbawm, E. J. *Nations and Nationalism Since 1780: Progamme, Myth, Reality.* Cambridge and New York: Cambridge U. Press, 1991. Pp. viii + 191.

Holderness, B. A. (ed.). *Land, Labour, and Agriculture, 1700–1920: Essays for Gordon Mingary.* Rio Grande, OH: Hambledon Press, 1991. Pp. xxiv + 262.

Holsti, Kalevi J. *Peace and War: Armed Conflicts and International Order, 1648–1989.* (Cambridge Studies in International Relations, 14.) Cambridge and New York: Cambridge U. Press, 1991. Pp. xvii + 379; bibliography; figures; tables.

Holt, Mack P. (ed.). *Society and Institutions in Early Modern France.* Athens, GA: U. of Georgia Press, 1991. Pp. xxiii + 242.

Horle, Craig W. (ed.). *Records of the Courts of Sussex County, Delaware, 1677–1710, vol. I–II.* Philadelphia, PA: U. of Pennsylvania Press and sponsored by the Colonial Society of Pennsylvania and the Welcome Society of Pennsylvania, 1991. Pp. 1427.

Horle, Craig W., et. al. *Lawmaking & Legislators in Pennsylvania: A Biographical Dictionary, v. 1: 1682–1709.* Philadelphia, PA: U. of Pennsylvania Press, 1991. Pp. 880.

Hornstein, Sari R. *The Restoration Navy and English Foreign Trade, 1674–1688: A Study in the Peacetime Use of Sea Power.* (Studies in Naval History.) Berkeley, CA: Scholar Press; Brookfield, VT: Gower Publishing Co., 1991. Pp. 293.

Howard, Dick. *The Birth of American Political Thought, 1763–87.* Translation by David Ames Curtis of *La Naissance de la pensée politique américaine, 1763–1787* (Paris, 1987). Minneapolis, MN: U. of Minnesota Press, 1989; Basingstoke, UK: Macmillan, 1990. Pp. xxvi + 274; bibliography. Cf. *ECCB*, n.s. 16, II: 86.

Rev. by D. H. Rice in *Choice*, 28 (1991), 1565.

Howarth, Stephen. *To Shining Sea: A History of the United States Navy, 1776–1991.* London: Weidenfeld & Nicolson; New York: Random House, 1991. Pp. xv + 620; bibliography; illustrations; maps; portraits.

Rev. (favorably) by P. R. Schratz in *Choice*, 29 (1991), 353.

Hughes, Ann. *The Causes of the English Civil War.* (British History in Perspective.) New York: St. Martin's Press, 1991. Pp. vii + 211; bibliography.

Hughes, Lindsey. *Sophia, Regent of Russia, 1657–1704.* London and New Haven, CT: Yale U. Press, 1990. Pp. xvii + 345; bibliography; illustrations; portraits. Cf. *ECCB*, n.s. 16, II: 89.

Rev. (favorably) by J. T. Flynn in *Choice*, 28 (1991), 1546; (favorably) by Philip Longworth in *TLS*, (Mar. 22, 1991), 11.

Hunt, Lynn (ed.). *Eroticism and the Body Politic.* (Parallax: Revisions of Culture and Society.) Baltimore, MD, and London: Johns Hopkins U. Press, 1991. Pp. 242; illustrations.

The flyleaf of this collection of intriguing essays provides an accurate commentary upon the overall effect of the book: "Exploring the possibilities of a multidisciplinary approach, the volume shows that eroticism had an impact far beyond the usual confines of libertine or pornographic literature—and that politics included much more than voting, meeting, or demonstrating." Read in sequence and as a whole, the nine essays effectually interrogate the assumption that politics is an entity separate from the personal and the pornographic. Further, the essays problematize any implied distinction between the erotic and the pornographic. They show the multivalency of (particularly) the female body, which could, in editor Lynn Hunt's words, "stand for nurturance or corruption, for the power of desire or the need of domination, for the promise of a new order of the decay of an old one." To some extent such a demonstration of the multitude of meanings embodied by the female, such a blurring of expected categories, is possible precisely because of the country and era that the essays treat eighteenth- and nineteenth-century France. Yet these essays suggest, in compelling ways, that their methods might be extended to examinations of Western culture in other areas and other times.

Read in sequence, the essays seem somewhat disjointed in topic and method, some better and some worse. But generally the essays take an emancipating and insightful approach toward what has come to be called cultural studies.

The nine essays are grouped into three eras, so that three essays treat the eighteenth century, three treat Revolutionary France, and three treat the fin de siècle. Each group of three essays offers an essay by an art historian, one by a literary critic, and one by an historian. In three essays on eighteenth-century France, the problem of women in the public sphere is highlighted. Art historian Mary Sheriff's essay, "Fragonard's Erotic Mothers and the Politics of Reproduction," suggests the extent to which multiple "readings" of Fragonard, especially of his painting (usually called) *Visit to the Wet-Nurse*, emerge when considered against contemporary attitudes about wet-nursing. Anne Deneys discusses libertinism as a system of exchange defined in economic, ethical, and linguistic levels while examining Laclos in "The Political Economy of the Body in the *Liaisons dangereuses* of Choderlos de Laclos." Historian Sarah Maza treats the denigration effects of the 1785–86 Diamond Necklace Affair upon the representation of Marie Antoinette during the period before her execution.

The three essays that treat the eighteenth century are suggestive of the destabilized situation for women as the public arena shifted from the private dominance of women in public affairs (the women powerful in the court of Louis XV) to the public situation of the queen-as-outsider in French affairs. The gendered implications of the social tensions are clarified in the next set of essays that treat Revolutionary France. Vivian Cameron's essay, "Political Exposures: Sexuality and Caricature in the French Revolution," show the counter-revolutionary representation of the female body in the engraving, *Grande Débandement de l'armée anticonstitutionelle*. In Cameron's view, this engraving depiction of leading aristocratic women displaying their buttocks to the Austrian army shows the extent to which "the multiple discourses of eroticism, politics, rituals, Carnival, pornography, reproduction, [and] prostitution" are evidence of the shifting political base. Lynn Hunt's contribution, "The Many Bodies of Marie Antoinette: Political Pornography and the Problem of the Feminine in the French Revolution," picks up the same theme, pointing out that the multitude of representational meanings attributed to the body of Marie Antoinette effectually delimited women's public activity from the time of the Revolution onward. Hunt concludes that "The republican brothers who had overthrown the king and taken upon themselves his mantle did not want their sisters to follow their lead." Lucienne Frappier-Mazur's literary analysis, "The Social Body: Disorder and Ritual in Sade's *Story of Juliette*," confirms the situation, showing the extent to which Sade's work equated sexual power with social power and, because of the cultural association of the feminine with disgust, women became necessary victims.

The three essays on the late nineteenth century demonstrate a continued preoccupation by men to associate social tension with women's bodies, but they show as well how the terms of that preoccupation have shifted to prostitution and eroticism as examples of a complete commodification of human relation. In "The 'New Woman,' Feminism, and the Decorative Arts in Fin-de-Siècle France," Debora Silverman examines how the dual representations of women in the 1880s and 90s—the *femme féconde*, a maternal vision of interior femininity—coalesced in *La Parisienne*, the queen of the decorative arts that marked the entry to the Paris World Exhibition of 1900. In "Splitting Hairs: Female Fetishism and Postpartum Sentimentality in the Fin de Siècle," Emily Apter provides a feminist psychoanalytic reading of Maupassant's fictions, focussing on rituals of maternal bereavement and hypersensitivity. In the last essay of the collection, Anne M. Wagner, drawing upon commentaries of Rodin's work, discusses Rodin's reputation as a sexual "truth-teller," showing the representational situation in which the alternately shifting desires of both men and women are actualized.—Carla Mulford.

Huston, James A. *Logistics of Liberty: American Services of Supply in the Revolutionary War and After.* Newark, DE: U. of Delaware Press (distributed through Cranbury, NJ, and London: Associated University Presses), 1991. Pp. 373; bibliography; illustrations; maps.

Rev. (severely) by C. L. Egan in *Choice*, 29 (1991), 656.

Israel, Jonathan I. (ed.). *The Anglo-Dutch Moment: Essays on the Glorious Revolution and its World Impact.* Cambridge and New York: Cambridge U. Press, 1991. Pp. xvi + 502; frontispiece; maps; plates; tables.

The tercentenary of the Revolution of 1688 in Britain gave occasion for numerous scholarly gatherings, which in turn have resulted in such interpretive collections as *Liberty Secured?* (edited by J. R. Jones, Stanford: Stanford U.

Press, 1992), *By Force or By Default?* (edited by Eveline Cruickshanks, Edinburgh: John Donald Publishers, 1989), *The Revolution of 1688–1689* (edited by Lois G. Schwoerer, Cambridge: Cambridge U. Press, 1992), and *The Revolutions of 1688* (edited by Robert Beddard, Oxford: Clarendon Press, 1991). Among books of this sort, *The Anglo-Dutch Moment: Essays on the Glorious Revolution and Its World Impact*, which began life in tercentenary celebrations at the British Academy, has distinctive features.

Like some (but not all) of these recent volumes about the Revolution, this one insists on the British, and not only English, significance of the Revolution. Thus, after J. R. Jone's examination of James II's own highly innovative program and John Morrill's historiographical survey, which takes some revisionists to task for underestimating the impact of the Revolution, other essays explore the Revolution in Scotland, Ireland, and the American colonies. These essays—by the late Ian B. Cowan, D. W. Hayton, and Richard B. Johnson, respectively—all illustrate the paradoxical way in which a revolution, advertised as a defense of liberty, came in one way or another to increase the power of the state over society and the power of a central government over the peripheral territories it governed. Thus, while the Revolution may have shifted power from Crown to Parliament, it worked to solidify English dominance over its dependencies, near and far. As K. N. Chaudhuri and Jonathan Israel point out in another essay, the Revolution also helped to shift the balance of power among European competitors in Asia in favor of Britain.

However, as its title indicates, the book has a larger agenda, namely, insisting on the Dutch and, indeed, European dimension of the Revolution. It is indicative of the character of the volume that its guiding spirit is Jonathan I. Israel, a specialist in Dutch history, who edited and introduced the volume, contributed a key essay, and also co-authored three of the other fifteen essays in the volume. Israel is happy to endorse the current revisionist view that the British were at best ambivalent in the proceedings of 1688 since he sees the Dutch as the Revolution's efficient cause. Nor is he content to assign an important role to William of Orange alone. Backed by others in the volume, Israel insists that the Dutch state (that is, the States General and the States of Holland) in conjunction with William as Stadholder, requiring British aid for survival against the French, not only forwarded the revolution but assured its success through military intervention.

Various essays take up the international preconditions and consequences of the Dutch descent on Britain. The success of William of Orange's project depended on assembling a complicated alliance, which included the Elector of Brandenburg (treated by Wouter Troost) and the House of Savoy (treated by Robert Oresko). It involved careful military planning (discussed by Jonathan Israel and Geoffrey Parker) though as their contrast of William's invasion with the Spanish Armada of 1588 makes clear, luck was an important component. Luck is also and important theme in D. W. Jones's treatment of the economic circumstances that propelled the British military endeavors in the two decades after the Revolution: Jones argues that Britain was only able to pay for its wars because economic developments, both within Britain and elsewhere around the globe, were fortuitously, favorable. To the extent that this volume underscores the inadequacies of an Anglocentric version of the Revolution, its thrust is revisionist. But nothing in the volume detracts from the view propagated as long ago as 1688, that the Revolution was a turning point in the history of Britain.—Lawrence Klein.

Jackson, Guida M. *Women Who Ruled.* Santa Barbara, CA and Oxford: ABC–Clio, 1990. Pp. xii + 190; bibliography; illustrations. Cf. *ECCB*, n.s. 16, II: 88.

Rev. by D. Seaman in *Choice*, 28 (1991), 1290.
Includes twenty-two Eighteenth Century women from Anna (Russia) to Ulrica Eleanora (Sweden).

Jacob, Margaret C. *Living the Enlightenment: Freemasonry and Politics in Eighteenth-Century Europe.* New York and Oxford: Oxford U. Press, 1991. Pp. viii + 304; figures.

The last two decades have been an interesting time in Enlightenment scholarship. Historians have moved beyond interpretations of the movement as simply the work of a few great men, or as the intellectual reflection of a class struggle. Now the tendency is to see it as a great cultural upheaval in which thousands of men and women actively participated. In the process, many new veins of source material have been tapped, including the records of academies and the correspondence of publishing houses. Yet one of the most copious, and most international of these veins has remained relatively unexploited: the records of masonic lodges. While certain French historians have used them in order to plumb the origins of "revolutionary sociability," their relevance to the Enlightenment itself has received far less attention.

Now, Margaret C. Jacob has addressed this concern in a book that adds a great deal of color and texture to our picture of the European Enlightenment. Furthermore, she does it from an international perspective that is lamentably rare these days, displaying a mastery of several languages, historiographies, and sets of archives. Beginning in late seventeenth-century Britain, she shows how freemasonry evolved from its origins in artisan guilds and confraternities into societies of gentlemen imbued with the ideals of the parliamentary radicals of the 1640s. She then traces its diffusion on the continent during the eighteenth-century, concentrating on France and the Netherlands. Drawing, like so many recent Enlightenment scholars, on the work of Jürgen Habermas (although keeping feminist critiques in mind), she portrays masonic lodges as one of the most important sites in which a new "civic public sphere" evolved in the eighteenth century. From this sphere, absolute monarchies and their court societies were held up to standards of virtue developed in the private household. Criticizing Reinhart Kosselleck and François Furet, she argues that the lodges were neither hopelessly utopian, nor "machinelike" and dedicated to a search for ideological purity. If one takes masonic thought seriously, she insists, one discovers, underpinning a wide spectrum of opinions, a point of view that was resolutely radical in its secularism (sometimes eliding into materialism) and egalitarianism, but also generally pragmatic and "constitutionalist." In Jacob's view, masons treated their lodges as a sort of rational, democratic and egalitarian "counter-society" into which they could retreat, which they could contrast to the less perfect society outside, and from which they could launch broader projects of reform.

While impressive in its scope and generally convincing in its arguments, *Living the Enlightenment* has a few problems. On the editorial side, Jacob seems to have teetered between writing a general history of European freemasonry and a set of case studies, and the result is sometimes an organizational muddle. Also, too much of the fascinating source material is stuffed into footnotes. Conceptually, the book perhaps does not go far enough in acknowledging the tensions inherent in that elusive beast, the Enlightenment. This is a pity since, in Jacob's analysis, masonry seems to have straddled the fault lines between a Voltairean emphasis on conviviality and toleration of authoritarian regimes, and a Rousseauian obsession with moral purity and the need for universal social regeneration. One may also wonder about Jacob's protrayal of the lodges as "a shared and common experience that was civil and hence political" (p. 224). Surely the equation between the civil and the political was something that was being slowly *constructed* in the eighteenth century. Jacob seems to treat it as fully formed and self-evident to masons from the very start. Nonetheless, this book deserves a wide and appreciative audience.—David A. Bell.

Jenson, Joan M. *Promise to the Land: Essays on Rural Women.* Albuquerque, NM: U. of New Mexico Press, 1991. Pp. xii + 319; illustrations.

Job, Françoise. *Les Juifs de Nancy du XIIe au XXe siècle.* (Les Juifs de Lorraine.) Nancy: Presses Universitaires de Nancy, 1991. Pp. 172; illustrations.

Johnson, Nicola. *Eighteenth Century London.* London: HMSP Publications, 1991. Pp. 50; illustrations.

Johnson, Richard R. *John Nelson, Merchant Adventurer: A Life Between Empires.* New York and Oxford: Oxford U. Press, 1991. Pp. ix + 194; bibliography; illustrations; maps; portraits.

Rev. (favorably) by C. W. Wood, Jr., in *Choice,* 29 (1991), 341.

With this book Richard Johnson joins a small company of scholars of the early modern period who rightly insist upon writing the history of North America in its proper trans-Atlantic context. The subtitle *A Life Between Empires* not only signals Johnson's intent, but also captures his achievement.

Nelson himself (1654–1734) seems to have known just about everyone of consequence in the New England and New France of his day. Johnson notes that Nelson remained always a man of activity and business, was not given to reflection or musings, and left no detailed record of his thinking about the momentous changes he lived through. He began his life in a world Johnson limns succinctly, one in which European national identities and boundaries as yet counted for little in the North Atlantic. The belated consequences of the Thirty Years' War and the English Revolution and Restoration, however, changed all of that, for good. When Nelson arrived in North America in the late 1660s as a teenager, he quickly rose in the esteem of his uncle Sir Thomas Temple who made him deputy governor of Temple's proprietary colony in Acadia. The cession of Acadia to France ended this brief brush with political importance and Nelson resumed private life as a trader to Nevis, then by 1675 helped cement trade between Boston and French Acadia.

Significantly, Nelson secured social acceptance in Boston by joining the Ancient and Honorable Artillery Company, but never became a freeman and never voted, since he refused to relinquish his loyalty to the Church of England. Weathering the storms that destroyed the Stuarts' Dominion of New England, Nelson directed the siege of his old antagonist Edmund Andros who had in the 1670s pressed the issue of New York's eastern boundaries to the considerable discomfort of Nelson and other traders. Nelson's own vision for a revised Dominion, supported by other merchants, was firmly rejected by most New Englanders, and Nelson found himself pitted against the new governor Sir William Phips. Precisely because Nelson enjoyed significant personal connections with Acadia, he detested the manner in which the expedition against Port Royal in April 1690 ended with Phips breaking his pledge to the French that they could surrender honorably and then plundering Governor Meneval's personal belongings. By 1691, however, Nelson himself was captured by the understandably vindictive French, and spent the next seven years in captivity.

Had Nelson remained merely the prisoner of the French in Canada, his tale would still be interesting. Johnson recounts in detail, however, his aborted attempt to secure release, Phips's intentional neglect of his old enemy, and Nelson's eventual removal to close imprisonment in France as the planned invasion of New England and New York collapsed—because of Nelson, higher French authorities were sure. Released eventually because of the lobbying efforts of the merchant interest in New England, Nelson had first been acquainted with the Bastille, then confinement in England because of his unauthorized discussions with high French officials regarding the wisdom of colonial neutrality. Still convinced of the need for a viceroyalty of sorts to bind together the scattered and weak northern provinces, Nelson finally was able to rejoin his family in 1698.

Johnson fittingly closes his study by remarking that from this date until his death in 1734, Nelson retired into private life, his personal finances in ruin because of his long imprisonment. A distinct quality of *momento mori* surrounds Johnson's summing up of a life sacrificed in part for emerging empire. Dominated by personal relationships, not religious or political ideals, Nelson was both blessed and cursed with more vision of Britain's true interests in North America than most officials in Whitehall possessed before 1776. In short, a remarkable life; Johnson's interpretation, wittily, gracefully written, is highly recommended.—A. G. Roeber.

Jones, George Hilton. *Convergent Forces: Immediate Causes of the Revolution of 1688 in England.* Ames, IA: Iowa State U. Press, 1990. Pp. xvi + 218; bibliography. Cf. *ECCB*, n.s. 16, II: 89.

Rev. (severely) by C. Carlton in *Choice*, 29 (1991), 179.

Jonsson, Ulf, Christer Persson and Johan Söderberg. *A Stagnating Metropolis: The Economy and Demography of Stockholm, 1750–1850.* Cambridge and New York: Cambridge U. Press, 1991. Pp. xii + 234; bibliography; figures; tables.

Stockholm, as the majority of the 49 European towns outside Britain with a total population of at least 50,000 in 1750, or 70,000 in 1800, exhibited weak growth in the latter part of the eighteenth century. On the Continent, this was a period of inflation, rising agricultural prices, and a corresponding decline in real wages for urban dwellers. Stockholm declined industrially as well as commercially in a period of economic growth in the Swedish countryside and in smaller Swedish and Finnish towns, which expanded and enlarged their shares of domestic and foreign trade. This well-documented monograph is of particular interest to students of the comparartive demographic, social, and economic history of the European city between 1750 and 1800.—Ed Thaden.

Josselin, Ralph. *The Diary of Ralph Josselin, 1616–1683.* Edited by Alan Macfarlane. (Records of Social and Economic History: New Series III.) New York and Oxford: Oxford U. Press for The British Academy, 1991. Pp. xxiv + 727; appendices; illustrations.

Kaiser, David. *Politics and War: European Conflict from Philip II to Hitler.* Cambridge, MA: Harvard U. Press; London: Tauris, 1990. Pp. 435. Cf. *ECCB,* n.s. 16. II: 89.

Rev. by P. L. De Rosa in *Choice,* 28 (1991), 1363.
   Chapter 2: "The Age of Louis XIV" and Chapter 3: "The Revolutionary and Napoleonic Era" (pp. 139–270) concern the Eighteenth Century.

Kamen, Henry Arthur Francis. *Spain, 1469–1714: A Society of Conflict.* 2nd ed. New York: Longman, in association with Addison-Wesley Publishing Co., 1991. Pp. 307.

Kant, Immanuel. *Political Writings.* Edited by Hans Reiss. (Cambridge Texts in the History of Political Thought.) Cambridge and New York: Cambridge U. Press, 1991. Pp. xvi + bibliography.

Keay, John. *The Honorable Company: The History of the East India Company.* London: HarperCollins Publishers, 1991. Pp. xx + 475; bibliography; illustrations; maps.

Rev. by P. J. Marshall in *TLS,* (Oct. 11, 1991), 30.

Kempf, Thomas. *Aufklärung als Disziplinierung. Studien zum Diskurs des Wissens in Intelligenzblättern und gelehrten Beilagen der zweiten Hälfte des 18. Jahrhunderts.* (Cursus, Band 2.) Munich: Iudicium, 1991. Pp. 268.

Kershaw, Gordon E. *James Bowdoin II: Patriot and Man of the Enlightenment.* Lanham, MD: University Press of America, 1991. Pp. 327.

Kessell, J. L. (ed.). *Spanish Missions of New Mexico, 2: After 1680.* (Spanish Borderlands Sourcebooks, 18.) New York: Garland Publishers, 1991. Pp. xxii + 504.

Kirby, David. *Northern Europe in the Early Modern Period: The Baltic World, 1492–1772.* London and New York: Longman, 1990. Pp. xi + 443; bibliography; maps. Cf. *ECCB,* n.s. 16, II: 90.

Rev. by R. B. Barnes in *Choice,* 28 (1991), 1546.
   Part Three: "Sweden as a Great Power" and Part Four: "The Rise of Russia" (pp. 165–404) concern the Eighteenth Century.

Klein, Eric A. *Essays Commemorating the Bicentennial of the United States Constitution and the Bill of Rights: Looking Toward the Third Century.* Lanham, MD: University Press of America, 1991. Pp. 98.

Klepp, Susan E. (ed.). *"The Swift Progress of Population:" Documentary and Bibliographic Study of Philadelphia's Growth, 1642–1859.* (Memoirs of the American Philosophical Society, 187.) Philadelphia, PA: American Philosophical Society, 1991. Pp. 344.

Knight, Franklin W., and Peggy K. Liss (eds.). *Atlantic Port Cities: Economy, Culture, and Society in the Atlantic World, 1650–1850.* Knoxville, TN: The U. of Tennessee Press, 1991. Pp. xviii + 302; bibliography; illustrations.

Knupfer, Peter B. *The Union As It Is: Constitutional Unionism and Sectional Compromise, 1787–1861.* Chapel Hill, NC, and London: U. of North Carolina Press, 1991. Pp. xiv + 285; bibliography.

Koditschek, Theodore. *Class Formation and Urban-Industrial Society: Bradford, 1750–1850.* Cambridge and New York: Cambridge U. Press, 1990. Pp. xi + 611; illustrations. Cf. *ECCB*, n.s. 16, II: 91.

Rev. (favorably) by L. J. Satre in *Choice*, 28 (1991), 1690.

Kramnick, Isaac. *Republicanism and Burgeoise Radicalism: Political Ideology in Late Eighteenth-Century England and America.* Ithaca, NY, and London: Cornell U. Press, 1990. Pp. x + 304. Cf. *ECCB*, n.s. 16, II: 92–93.

Rev. by E. J. Eisenach in *Choice*, 28 (1991), 1382; (severely) by J. G. A. Pocock in *Eighteenth-Century Studies*, 25 (1991–92), 219–27.

Kuhn, Philip A. *Soulstealers: The Chinese Sorcery Scare of 1768.* Cambridge, MA, and London: Harvard U. Press, 1990. Pp. xiii + 299; bibliography; illustrations; maps. Cf. *ECCB*, n.s. 16, II: 93.

Rev. by E. H. Kaplan in *Choice*, 28 (1991), 1542.

Kusmer, Kenneth L. (ed.). *Black Communities and Urban Development in America, 1720–1990.* Vol. 1: *The Colonial and Early National Period.* New York: Garland Publishing, 1991. Pp. 308.

La Barre de Raillicourt, M. *Richelieu, le Maréchal libertin.* (Figures de proue.) Paris: Tallandier, 1991. Pp. 450.

Most of La Barre de Raillicourt's *Richilieu* is devoted to the Duke's love-life, and these amorous stories are quite boring. The readers have the impression that Richelieu went to bed with all the women of the eighteenth century. Perhaps, it would have been easier for the author to list only the women who had resisted. The explanation for his success is evident: Richelieu was a very handsome and rich aristocrat, with a pleasant personality and an extremely amorous temperament. In addition, he was always ready to start a new affair. It did not matter that he was a liar and a cheat, unable to fall deeply in love and even to keep a secret; the women were absolutely crazy about him: "Il se vante de ses conquêtes à qui veut l'entendre, il cite des noms, raconte ses aventures, ne respecte pas le bon ton et s'amuse de ses bonne fortunes" (p. 120).

    Richelieu was sent to the Bastille at the age of 15 because of his excessive gambling and womanizing. From then on, he craftily built his reputation by embellishing or even inventing some of his adventures. In an appendix, the author shows us how the Duke tried to hire several persons to write his autobiography to enhance and immortalize his reputation. Even if some of his stories were made up, it is true that women of all kinds adored him. Some died of love for him; others dueled because of him. Richelieu was 84 when he remarried for the third time with a woman nearly 50 years younger, spending the last eight years of his life surrounded by his wife's affection.

    The author points out that, although we remember Richelieu for his amorous adventures, this kind of reputation has hurt him during his life. While Louis XV was a close freind and enjoyed his company, the king never allowed him to realize his political ambition to rule France by naming him minister. It is possible that the Duke would have been a good politician: he demonstrated how clever and hard working he was during his ambassadorship in Vienna, and how tolerant he could be with the Protestants during his governorship in Guyenne. The reader has the feeling that, rather than half-wasting his life, under more favorable occurences, the Marshal of Richelieu could have accomplished as much as the Cardinal—his great-uncle.

This important work is very detailed and up to date on the people and events of the time. Most of the unpublished information on the Duke, his correspondence, and his diplomatic career, come directly from several archives. A large number of notes strengthen the carefully researched text, and some interesting appendices on Richelieu's wealth and on his biographies conclude it. While the notes and the bibliography are plentiful and highly instructive, many quotations with insufficient information of their origins are frustrating to the reader.—Philippe de Gain.

Labrosse, Claude, and Pierre Rętat. *Naissance du Journal Revolutionnaire, 1789*. Lyon: Presses Universitaires de Lyon, 1989. Cf. *ECCB*, n.s. 16, II: 94; 15, II: 66.

Rev. in rev. article ("More than Words: The Printing Press and the French Revolution") by Joan B. Landes in *Eighteenth-Century Studies*, 25 (1991), 85–98.

Lacey, Michael J. (ed.). *A Culture of Rights: The Bill of Rights in Philosophy, Politics, and Law: 1791 and 1991*. (Woodrow Wilson Center Series.) Cambridge and New York: Cambridge U. Press, 1991. Pp. 474.

Lachiver, Marcel. *Les années de misère. La famine au temps au Grand Roi 1680–1720*. Paris: Fayard, 1991. Pp. 573; bibliography; documents.

Since the publication of Pierre Goubert's *Louis XIV et vingt millions de Français* (Paris, 1966), historians of the seventy-two year long reign of the Sun King have had to take into account the vicissitudes of daily life among his subjects. Lachiver follows in this tradition with a double purpose: first, to show that the good old days were in most cases bad old days and that the reign witnessed the last episodes of widespread starvation in France. The author was lucky enough to have at his disposal the parish archives carefully kept by local priests since the 1667 Saint Germain-en Laye edict, the many diaries kept at the time by small landholders, *laboureurs*, and city dwellers and extensively published over the last century in local periodicals, the demographic studies of Alain Blum of the Institut national d'études démographiques on the evolution of the population during the reign of Louis XIV and the meteorological observations daily consigned at Saint-Maur by the botanist Louis Morin from 1676 to 1712.

With such primary sources completed by research in the Archives Nationales and the *Mémoires des Intendants*, Lachiver has achieved a study that will remain a landmark in historical demography. The narratives studied by the author are never taken at face value and he draws conclusions from them only if they are corroborated by other multiple sources. Starvation does not mean only the lack of food, but also the general debilitation of the body over years of undernourishment that favors the spread of epidemics. For instance, if actual starvation killed "only" half a million people in 1709, the 1719 epidemics can be considered long-term consequence of the 1709 famine over weakened bodies. War is considered as an aggravating factor, but cannot in itself account for the million and a half victims of the 1693–94 and the 1709 smaller hecatomb. The latter was due more to the high cost of grains than to actual shortage of them, a thing that was to be remembered for long in collective memory and explains the violent reactions of crowds during the *querre des farines* (1775). Moreover, public authorities had learnt the lessons from the 1693–94 disaster. A well-researched and legible book, Lachiver's *opus magnum* combines with the utmost felicity the findings of historians in the realm of medicine, agriculture and meteorology and the reflexions of a specialist of social history. His conclusion aptly compares the demographic ravages of the period with the fourteenth century bubonic plague epidemics, the difficult period from 1792 to 1815 and the World War I hecatomb.—Jean Rivière.

Lacorne, Denis. *L'invention de la république. Le modèle américain.* Paris: Hachette, 1991. Pp. 319; bibliography; chronology.

Starting with a study of the American Constitution as the quintessence of the political tenets of the Enlightenment, Denis Lacorne shows how the text was an exercise in practical republicanism that turned only by slow and incomplete stages into the emblem of an American democracy always in the making. The author considers that the very vagueness in which some of the real problems were referred to—for example calling the slaves "other persons" and not making any clear statement about the final power of the states and of the people—ensured its longevity. Had things been clearer, as in the 1861 Confederate Constitution, the document could not have been amended. Amendments and judicial review became therefore the breath of life which proved that the Holy Writ of American political life was not a dead scroll.

    Denis Lacorne does away with the myth of a new nation building its political practice on a tabula rasa. The 1787 compromise between the North and the South was based on the social and economic interests of both sections and on the paralyzing experience of the Articles of Confederation. The bloodiest war in American history took care of the legal problems of the "other persons," but another century was necessary for the Civil Rights Act (1964) and the Voting Rights Act (1965) to ban segregation everywhere in the United States and prevent the states from practically disenfranchising some of their citizens. With the *Roe v. Wade* decision of 1973, the "right to intimacy" was proclaimed by the U.S. Supreme Court in matters of abortion. In a system where the Supreme Court has got the final word over representative institutions, Lacorne thinks that the options must remain sufficiently open and that the intentions of the Founding Fathers were not once and for all consigned in a text enshrined in a sacred Ark. Had such a vision of American constitutionalism prevailed, Lincoln could not have emancipated the slaves by a proclamation, the Warren Court could not have overruled in 1954 the *Plessy v. Ferguson* 1896 decision and the Burger Court would have stopped short of any precise in its 1973 decision on abortion. The Constitution was adopted only 11 years after the Declaration of Independence. In the 1920s, Vernon Parrington already insisted on the value of both documents, as the spirit of the Declaration was often the engine behind the urge to amend the Constitution. Just as Bible exegetists had to cope with Darwinism or cling to the untenable positions of die-hard fundamentalists and lose everything, so flexible interpreters of the Constitution account for its longevity. Lacorne's book is a welcome scholarly contribution to a middle-of-the-road, yet tense and well-argumented interpretation of the American Constitution.—Jean Rivière.

Langford, Paul. *A Polite and Commercial People: England, 1727–1783, The New Oxford History of England.* New York: Oxford U. Press; Oxford: Clarendon, 1989. Pp. xx + 803. Cf. *ECCB*, n.s. 16, II: 94.

Rev. (with another work) by Daniel Statt in *Eighteenth-Century Studies*, 25 (1991–92), 264–71.

Langford, Paul. *Public Life and the Propertied Englishman, 1689–1798.* (The Ford Lectures, 1990.) New York: Oxford U. Press; Oxford: Clarendon, 1991. Pp. xiv + 608.

Rev. by John Cannon in *TLS,* (Oct. 11, 1991), 27.

    Paul Langford's aptly titled *Public Life and the Propertied Englishman, 1689–1798* explores the connection between the powers held and services performed by propertied people in eighteenth century England. Beginning with a sensitive and innovative account of "the propertied state of mind," Langford considers, in turn, the decline of both religious and party zeal by the middle decades of the century, the growth both of parliamentary and associational activity and importance, the growing centrality of real (as opposed to landed) property, the changing ways in which both rural and urban areas were ruled by local propertied men, and finally the beginnings of a transformation of the notion of nobility from being an attribute of inheritance to one of service. The scope and ambition of the work is commendable, the execution both bold and compelling. It is a book destined to be read, mined, attacked, and re-read many times.

    One of its most novel and most attractive qualities is its endeavour at combining the techniques and materials of social and political history. Because of its interest in governance, it combines a study of traditional political institutions, like Parliament, with less obvious, but perhaps even more important ones, like local boards of improvement and statutory associations of commissioners. The range of its scholarly sources is particularly impressive. For one thing, Langford's study is truly national, drawing from examples on materials found in widely dispersed record offices. In addition, he has read most of the memoirs, diaries, letter-books, novels and plays of the period. His filing system must be prodigious, for all this information is seamlessly and seemingly effortlessly brought to bear on the subject in question.

Secondly, Langford's is one of the few recent books that successfully attempts to connect the first thirty years of the eighteenth century with the last three decades. Although much still remains to be done, Langford's narrative provides the reader with some common threads to bridge the previously separate shores of eighteenth century scholarship.

In a book so successful, so comprehensive and so long, it seems a bit presumptuous to ask for yet more. However, I would have benefitted from two sorts of additional discussions; the first, on the nature of and effects of the press over the century, the second a recognition of propertied English*women*. Although Langford discusses several such women, a more explicit consideration of the ambiguities of gender and property would have been useful. If any source is slighted in this massive undertaking, it is the daily press, about which we still know lamentably little. And yet its role in the creation of a new public world, not only of discourse, but of action, must have been vital.

Public Life and the Propertied Englishman is a great, Christmas-pudding of a book, stuffed to bursting point with all sorts of plums. Though both nutritious and filling, it simultaneously piques the appetite for more, raising a host of new and important questions. It is a pioneer in what one hopes will become a new and invigorated historical area, the social history of political life.—Donna T. Andrews.

Larkin, John Francis (ed.). *The Trial of William Drennan: On a Trial for Sedition, in the Year 1794 and His Intended Defence.* Introduction by John Francis Larkin. Dublin: Irish Academic Press, 1991. Pp. 139.

Rev. (with another work) by Ian McBride in *TLS,* (June 21, 1991), 11.

Latham, Richard. *The Account Book of Richard Latham, 1724–1767.* Edited by Lorna Weatherill. (Records of Social and Economic History, 15.) New York and Oxford: Oxford U. Press for the British Academy, 1990. Pp. xxxix + 283; frontispiece. Cf. *ECCB,* n.s. 16, II: 94.

Rev. by A. W. Masters in *TLS,* (June 14, 1991), 32.

Law, Robin. *The Slave Coast of West Africa, 1550–1750: The Impact of the Atlantic Slave Trade on African Society.* (Oxford Studies in African Affairs.) New York: Oxford U. Press; Oxford: Clarendon Press, 1991. Pp. viii + 376; bibliography; illustrations; maps.

LeDonne, John P. *Absolutism and Ruling Class: The Formation of the Russian Political Order, 1700–1825.* New York and Oxford: Oxford U. Press, 1991. Pp. xviii + 376; bibliography.

This dense and fascinating book is rich in assertions about the emergence, nature, and fate of the Russian political and social system(s) in the eighteenth and earlier nineteenth centuries, with glances backward into the seventeenth (and even the sixteenth) centuries and forward into the twentieth. The author's overall purpose is to provide not only new or refreshed meaning for the concepts of ruling class, bureaucracy, absolutism, militarism, police, taxation, even justice and finance as they may apply to Russia in his period, to which end often familiar data are presented in original ways and models from the work of scholars in other fields—historians, sociologists, and others—are introduced. His ultimate purpose is to provide nothing less than a comprehensive *definition* of *the* modern Russian "political order" as it came into being in the reformative reigns of Peter the Great, Catherine the Great, and Alexander I. It was quite simply "a command structure governed by martial law" (p. 300); or again, more fully: "Russian society taken in its totality was thus a huge command structure in which social and family relationships were dominated by considerations of power . . . At all levels of such a society the tyranny of the superior was accepted because it justified the subordinate's tyranny over his own subordinates, leaving no room for the assertion of individual freedom, economic initiative, and social autonomy" (p. 17). In a typical aside (p. 312, n. 2) we are told that a certain C. Castoriadis, writing in the journal *Telos* in 1978–1979, "calls Russia a 'cynical society'." Some of the book's more stimulating if not outrageous assertions are thus aired, rather slyly. One misses however even a single quotation from that elegant, much-cited Russophobe of 1839, the Marquis de Custine.

John LeDonne's fellow Russian historians will often savor his polemics, his shrewd so to speak interlinear observations, his quite original suggestions, his withering wit. They will have to agree that he has illuminated much that was obscure in Russian governmental or administrative history and pointed to much that remains to be done in the field. They can only admire his comparative historical sallies and command of the relevant French and German literature, and be grateful for the wealth of historical detail and terminological clarification. Some of us, certainly, will admire the skill with which he has used legal and other official sources and applaud his unfashionable insistence on the importance of political history—even as we may resist carrying the point to his extremes (Russian history in effect as nothing but political history). Indeed few of LeDonne's colleagues, surely, will accept the implicit claim that in his often quite static, impersonal depiction of the multifarious operations and interruptions of noble "ruling class" and Imperial regime he has found the key to all of modern Russian history, or even that he has provided us with an entirely consistent or coherent argument to that effect. On the other hand, it should be emphasized that this is a solid, superbly interesting and useful work of history.—James Cracraft.

Legohérel, Henri. *L'économie des Temps modernes.* (Collection "Que Sais-Je?") Paris: PUF, 1991. Pp. 128; bibliography.

Largely devoted to the eighteenth century, Legohérel's epitome of a vast topic ranges from the great discoveries of the Renaissance to the Industrial Revolution. Whereas the sixteenth century asserted the predominance of commerce over industry and of Europe over the other continents, it also witnessed a profound disparity between the European powers sharpened by the growing nationalism of well-established states. The instability of the seventeenth century was due to the continental fight for predominance between France and the House of Austria with the United Provinces and England taking advantage of their useless feud. Europe then witnessed a definite slowing of capitalistic development with repeated financial and agricultural crises leading to demographic disasters. The eighteenth century was therefore the starting point of growth in the modern meaning of the word with England standing as an exemplar of successful development in spite of her limited economic and demographic resources. Legohérel insists on the financial, commercial and agricultural revolutions there, all of them harbingers of the extension of world trade and of British and European expansion world wide.

From 1750 onward, the stage was set for an Industrial Revolution combining division of labor and mass production, hence enormous productivity growth and a budding consumer society out of the reach, however, of the uprooted farmers and the exploited workers. The world-economy assumed a real existence by the end of the eighteenth century. Improvement of daily life and unequal social and national developments have ever since been part and parcel of the system. Legohérel's book sums up with clarity and a keen sense of contrasts the passage from a local subsistence economy to a core European system radiating all over the world. One unfortunate omission in the bibliography: Fernand Braudel's *Civilisation matérielle et capitalisme, XVe–XVIIIe siècle* (Paris, 1979).—Jean Rivière.

Leith, James A. *Space and Revolution. Projects for Monuments, Squares, and Public Buildings in France, 1789–1799.* Montreal and Kingston: McGill-Queen's U. Press, 1991. Pp. xvi + 363; appendices; bibliography; figures.

Revolutionary leaders used architecture and monuments in many different ways: first, they promoted the destruction of old monuments and symbols too closely linked with the old order, second, they encouraged the conversion of old monuments into new temples celebrating the virtues of the new regime, third, they erected new monuments to the glory of the Revolution, but the latter attempts were relatively small in number as the decade considered was too short a period and political vagaries too frequent. Even more important, though, was the positioning of the new buildings in the old urban planning which finally was hardly affected and the numerous projects that only materialized in the next century to provide the public with facilities such as parks, fountains, hospitals, libraries, theatres and museums, among others.

The main purpose of revolutionary leaders was "to eradicate the special status of the nobles and other legalized social distinctions" (p. 308) and in that connection James Leith challenges the revisionists' thesis according to which Ancien Régime nobles and upper bourgeois practically belonged to the same class. There was a definite egalitarian thrust into the plans of old or new architects and such thrust could not be achieved as long as the king remained in office and as long as the distinction between active and passive citizens persisted: the replacement of boxes by benches and seats in all theatres, the assembly halls and *temples décadaires* built in the shape of ampitheatres bear witness to that movement. This design reflected the idea of a loyal opposition. The first war memorial built in 1792 near the Ecole Militaire was a harbinger of the tens of thousands that were erected in the next two centuries. Dechristening and rechristening of streets and squares became less frequent over the next century and with the old regime, revolutionary, national and foreign names and symbols remaining in place and ceaselessly enriched over the years, Paris today stands as an epitome of French and world history and geography as no other city in the world. The author insists on the presence of hundreds of statues making up an "outdoor pantheon" (p. 312). Social purpose was the leitmotiv of revolutionary architects and James Leith makes us understand the nature of the new architecture and its political overtones in a book fraught with cogent and fresh analysis in addition to handsome and telling illustrations. Such an achievement will long stand as a classic in the field of revolutionary art.—Jean Rivière.

Lemire, Beverly. *Fashion's Favorite: The Cotton Trade and the Consumer in Britain, 1660–1800.* (Pasold Studies in Textile History, 9.) Oxford: Pasold Research Fund in association with Oxford U. Press, 1991. Pp. xi + 224; facsimiles; illustrations; map.

The study of mass consumption in early modern Britain has become a growth industry in recent years, with contributions from such historians as Joan Thirsk, Margaret Spufford, Lorna Weatherill and Carole Shammas. Beverly Lemire adds to this expanding volume a scrupulously researched and evocative study of the role popular interest in fashion came to play in the emergence of a mass market for cotton textiles, prior to the classic period of the Industrial Revolution, ca. 1780–1850.

Lemire places considerable emphasis on the fact that the growth of the home market prior to 1780 accompanied a democratization of fashion, stimulated by availability of a wide variety of cotton prints, and a growing homogeneity of demand along with a standardization of tastes nationally. She documents, using highly original archival material, the already well appreciated phenomena of the rise throughout the earlier part of the eighteenth century of a class of middlemen, (especially agents servicing Manchester firms); the proliferation of shops even in rural market towns; and the development by them of the use of standard prices. Her work thus confirms the observations of revisionist economic historians, who have stressed the continuities of economic growth in the industrial sector between the pre- and post-1780 periods, although in typically British empiricist style she makes scant reference to their work.

Lemire's study also possesses implications for assessing the quality of those changes in working class living standards occurring under industrialization, though she similarly declines to refer to the larger debate over the issue. Her view is nevertheless "optimistic," insofar as it draws upon the work of Peter Lindert and Jeffrey Williamson, if somewhat reflexively, while arguing that the spread of female and child labor produced the salutary effect of the increasing the disposable income of working class families. (Pessimists, in contrast, have concluded that this expansion of the labor force represented the spread of self-exploration among such families, which led in turn to their impoverishment).

The author is especially good at depicting the emergence of a domestic cotton manufacturing industry after 1721 and the innovative role played by the East India Company as midwife to its birth. The immense popularity of Indian cotton prints, imported by the East India Company, had eroded the traditional predominance of the woolen industry and led to calls from its representatives for protectionist legislation that, when finally enacted in 1721, appeared to return the economy to the status quo ante. But the absence of Indian competition after 1721 merely created opportunities for domestic entrepreneurs to fill the vacuum of consumer demand that the Indian trade had sharply whetted, while incidentally highlighting the foolhardiness of mercantilist restrictive practices. Thirsk and Spufford have shown that a ready-made trade in some clothing items had already existed by the beginning of the eighteenth century; Lemire demonstrates further that the East India Company stimulated its development on a massive scale, and by doing so signficantly promoted an already expanding trade in second-hand clothing. This second-hand trade, she demonstrates, had become much more widespread by the early 19th century than historians have hitherto appreciated. The expansion of a ready-made clothing trade had also given rise to the appearance of sweated labor on a sufficiently large scale as to establish continuity (once again) with the 19th century, a fact that might have led Lemire to qualify her earlier optimism regarding working class living standards under industrialization, though it does not.

Lemire is most original in her deployment of archival sources. Apart from her use of traditional materials, such as trade directories and newspaper accounts, she gleans from legal records (which document the kinds of goods stolen) examples of working class dress that are otherwise more difficult to obtain. She makes use of a small selection of surviving shopkeepers' records, which nevertheless give abundant detail on the types of goods purchased wholesale, as well as about the wide range of suppliers from diverse locales. Lemire exploits intensively the Sample Book of Barbara Johnson, which for over 60 years preserved illustrations of dress from a variety of printed media that had caught the collector's eye (not to mention examples of actual clothing fabric), in order to document how deep and widespread middle class concern for fashion had become, as well as how it had changed over time. Her use of telling quotations and examples provides much valuable texture, yet gives an excessively anecdotal and impressionistic quality to her presentation. Although her claims for the representativeness of her documents ring true, I found myself wishing for a statistical tabulation of their contents for the sake of better contextualization. This lament aside, Lemire has produced a valuable and very much welcomed study, which places the British "consumer revolution" as exemplified by its leading sector in a proper and timely long-term historical perspective.—Albion M. Urdank.

Lemay, Edna Hindie. *Dictionnaire des Constituants, 1789–1791.* Vol. I: *A-K.* Vol. II: *L-Y.* Paris: Universitas, 1991. Pp. lvii + 484; 437; bibliography.

Le Roy Ladurie, Emmanuel. *L'Ancien Régime, 1610–1770.* Vol. 3 of *Histoire de France Hachette.* Paris: Hachette, 1991. Pp. 456; illustrations.

Les Indes florissantes. Anthologie des voyageurs français (1750–1820). Préface by S. E. Idris Hassan Latif. Introduction, chronology, bibliography and glossary by Guy Deleury. (Bouquins.) Paris: Laffont, 1991.

Lesko, Kathleen M. *Black Georgetown Remembered: A History of its Black Community from the Founding of "The Town of George" in 1751 to the Present Day.* Washington, DC: Georgetown U. Press, 1991. Pp. 184.

Lever, Evelyne. *Marie-Antoinette.* Paris: Fayard, 1991. Pp. 236; bibliography.

Rev. by John Rogister in *TLS,* (Aug. 23, 1991), 6.

No Queen of France has been more written about than Marie-Antoinette and it was quite a feat for Evelyn Lever to try and find a new approach in the maze of conflicting interpretations. Marie-Antoinette emerged from them as a traitor or a victim: in no way, while reading the present book, do we feel that such was the dilemma the author had to solve. Each chapter is built around a particular part played by the queen: Austrian princess, dauphine, wife of an impotent king (in more than one sense of the word), willing or unwilling victim of intrigues, clumsy stateswomen, proud aristocrat and affectionate mother. The queen appears as fully faithful to her status insofar as she considers, just like the king, that her prerogatives are beyond question. A daughter of the Enlightenment—her brother Joseph II, the reformer emperor and elightened despot, had to repeal most of his reforms before his death in 1790—she conceived of the monarch as acting for the general welfare of his or her subjects and just like her husband she thought that only some power could be granted to the people and that none was theirs by right. Marie-Antionette was not mainly a character overwhelmed by events and intrigues beyond her power to alter or ward off. The stange love affairs she foolishly ran into, her dubious friendships and acquaintances, her lack of political flair and her compliance with the aims of her Austrian family which she never considered as being at odds with the interests of the French monarchy account for the hatred she inspired in the general public.

Had I to select one chapter in the book under review, I would choose the one dealing with Varennes, because the episode and its consequences are really *the* turning point in the history of the French Revoution. The king left Paris because he could not agree to sharing his power with the National Assembly and he wrote a manifesto clearly explaining his position which was read before the deputies who rallied, in spite of all proofs to the contrary, to the fiction of the abduction of the monarch. The feeling of respect toward the fleeing king cannot hide his subjects' determination to stop him and to obey the orders of the representatives of the National Assembly. The sight of the sovereign reentering Paris with his subjects keeping their hats on and his soldiers not standing to attention is a foreboding of the fall of the monarchy, whereas the returned king and queen immediately fall back into the routine of courtly etiquette as if nothing had happened. The narrative is always lively and fully informed. The bibliography of primary and secondary sources is well presented with a final section for the ten most authoritative biographies of the queen. Evelyne Lever's book is a valuable addition to her previously published biographies of Louis XVI (1985) and Louis XVIII (1988) by Librairie Arthème Fayard.—Jean Rivière.

Levine, David, and Keith Wrightson. *The Making of an Industrial Society: Whickham, 1560–1765.* New York: Oxford U. Press; Oxford: Clarendon Press, 1991. Pp. xviii + 456; bibliography; maps.

Rev. (with another work) by Peter Clark in *TLS,* (Oct. 11, 1991), 29.

Levine, Hillel. *Economic Origins of Antisemitism: Poland and Its Jews in the Early Middle Period.* London and New Haven: Yale U. Press, 1991. Pp. xiv + 271; bibliography; illustrations.

In attempting to answer the question of why the Polish and French revolutions differed "in their responses to the problem of the rights and status of Jews" (p. 232), Levine rumages through 2000 years of Polish history in search of the sources of a failure of modernization. At the same time, he seeks to establish how "Jewish activities in Poland from the sixteenth through the eighteenth centuries . . . saved a declining system and propped up a failing order" (p. 237). For Levine, the failure of modernization in Poland is the "matrix" of economic anti-semitism, which he sees as leading in the twentieth century to the erection of German death camps "on Polish soil" (p. 239).

Levine's account "is not free of the fashions of the marketplace of ideas and the spirit of the times" (p. xi). Thus along the way, he cites the works of Clifford Geertz, Fernand Braudel, Max Weber, Ferdinand Tönnies, and of course, Michel Foucault. Candidly admitting that "there is insufficient evidence to substantiate fully the argument" that he makes, Levine hopes that his "speculation will be useful as a guide for future research" (p. 80). For example, after detailing an incident of blood libel in the Ukranian town of Zhitomir in 1753, he treats us to several pages of speculation, which includes a reference to infanticide in England but no evidence of it in Poland. Yet, based on a study showing the Polish nobility kept an emotional distance from their children, Levine suggests "Polish child-care practices in this period may have found in the blood libel an actual and psychological resolution" (p. 185). Moreover, he finds that "the blood libel gave expression to associations between real and symbolic elements of everyday life as they were perceived by Polish Christians in their relation with Polish Jews" and proceeds to connect blood with money—both "media of circulation"—and grain produced by the serfs with alcohol made from grain and sold to the serfs by the Jews (p. 188).

Levine's argument ultimately hinges on his account of the place of Jews in the programs of Polish reformers at the end of the eighteenth century, programs that culminated in the Constitution of May 3, 1791, which according to Levine "legislatively defined [Jews] as nonpersons" (p. 238). Here, not for the first time, he does not speculate because of insufficient evidence to substantiate his argument but rather in spite of the evidence. Levine has not read widely in the Polish scholarship on the constitution that proliferated with the approach of its bicentennial. Although he notes that the Polish constitution resulted from a coup rather than a social revolution as in France, he draws no conclusions from this difference, such as the necessity of compromise on the part of the Polish advocates of reform. He points out the favorable international situation for Poland beginning in 1787 but seems unaware that this situation had radically changed for the worse even before the constitution passed.

Above all, Levine's narrow focus betrays him. Thus he concludes "Jews as indiviuals in Poland did not receive the rights guaranteed to other Poles" (p. 229). Yet neither the peasantry nor burghers outside of the royal towns had any specific rights guaranteed to them by the constitution. The constitution was a compromise reached by and for Polish nobles, one that reformers had to accept in view of the external threat to Poland, which resulted in the disappearance of the Polish state in 1795, a threat incomparable to anything faced by the French revolutionaries. What Levine says of the critics of Polish Jews can be said of his own study: "the difficulties in effecting changes in Poland in accordance with the Western pattern were largely ignored" (p. 236).

Although a footnote at the beginning of the chapter on the Polish reform movement speaks of the "paucity of internal sources on Jewish repsonses" (p. 191), Levine closes with the claim that the reforms "to many Jews appeared to be little more than wicked decrees" (p. 230). He therefore downplays Jewish support for the 1794 insurrection against intervention while commenting in a footnote that "Polish-Jewish historiography emphasizes, perhaps to an exaggerated degree, the enthusiasm of the Jewish masses for Kosciuszko and the insurrection" (p. 229). Indeed, in a study on the emancipation of the Jews of Poland, Arthur Eisenbach speaks of the heroic participation of the Jewish population in the defense of Warsaw in 1794. Published in Poland in 1988, Eisenbach's study may have appeared too late for Levine to consult it. But if he had, one senses that Levine would simply have cited it in a footnote and speculated further without letting it affect his argument.—John Kulczycki.

Levine, Joseph M. *The Battle of the Books: History and Literature in the Augustan Age.* Ithaca, NY, and London: Cornell U. Press, 1991. Pp. xiv + 428; illustrations; map.

Lewis, James A. *The Final Campaign of the American Revolution: Rise and Fall of the Spanish Bahamas.* Columbia, SC: U. of South Carolina Press, 1991. Pp. xi + 149; bibliography; illustrations; maps.

Rev. (favorably) by J. A. Gaglinao in *Choice*, 29 (1991), 183.

Lewis, Nelly Custis. *George Washington's Beautiful Nelly: The Letters of Eleanor Parke Custis Lewis to Elizabeth Bordley Gibson, 1794–1851.* (Women's Diaries & Letters of the Nineteenth-Century South.) Columbia, SC: U. of South Carolina Press, 1991. Pp. xxii + 287.

Liebermann, David. *The Province of Legislation Determined: Legal Theory in Eighteenth-Century Britain.* Cambridge and New York: Cambridge U. Press, 1989. Pp. xiii + 312.

Rev. (favorably) by Albert J. Schmidt in *Eighteenth Century Studies*, 24 (1991), 381–83.

Lindemann, Mary. *Patriots and Paupers: Hamburg, 1712–1830.* New York and Oxford: Oxford U. Press, 1990. Pp. vii + 339; bibliography; tables. Cf. *ECCB*, n.s. 16, II: 97–98.

Rev. by D. R. Skopp in *Choice*, 28 (1991), 1363.

Linebaugh, Peter. *The London Hanged: Crime and Civil Society in the Eighteenth Century.* Cambridge and New York: Cambridge U. Press; London: A. Lane/The Penguin Press, 1991. Pp. xxvii + 484; bibliography; illustrations; maps.

Rev. (severely) by John H. Langbein in *TLS,* (Oct. 11, 1991), 27.

Lines, Clifford. *Companion to the Industrial Revolution.* New York: Facts on File, 1990. Pp. x + 262; illustrations; maps. Cf. *ECCB,* n.s. 16, II: 98.

Rev. by Ronald H. Fritze in *American Reference Books Annual,* 22 (1991), 159; by E. Patterson in *Choice,* 28 (1991), 758; 760.

Livi-Bacci, Massimo. *Population and Nutrition: An Essay on European Demographic History.* Translated from Italian by Tania Croft-Murray. (Cambridge Studies in Population, Economy & Society in Past Time, 14.) Cambridge and New York: Cambridge U. Press, 1991. Pp. 149.

Longmate, Norman. *Island Fortress: The Defence of Great Britain, 1603–1945.* London: Hutcheson, 1991. Pp. xii + 580; bibliography; illustrations; maps.

Looney, J. J. *Princetonians: A Biographical Dictionary, 1791–1794.* Princeton, NJ: Princeton U. Press, 1991. Pp. 577.

Lucas, Colin (ed.). *Rewriting the French Revolution.* (The Andrew Browning Lectures, 1989.) New York: Oxford U. Press; Oxford: Clarendon Press, 1991. Pp. vii + 209.

Lucas, John. *England and Englishness.* Iowa City, IO: U. of Iowa Press, 1990. Pp. 227.

Rev. in *The Scriblerian,* 24 (1991), 82.

Lukowski, Jerzy. *Liberty's Folly: The Polish-Lithuanian Commonwealth in the Eighteenth Century, 1697–1795.* London and New York: Routledge, 1991. Pp. x + 316; bibliography; 8 illustrations; maps.

Rev. (favorably) by J. K. Hapak in *Choice,* 29 (1991), 179.

Lüsebrink, Hans-Jürgen, and Rolf Reichardt. *Die 'Bastille.' Zur Symbolgeschichte von Herrschaft und Freiheit.* Frankfurt: Fischer, 1990. Pp. 336.

Rev. by Jeremy D. Popkin in *Eighteenth-Century Studies,* 24 (1991), 506–08.

Luttrell, Barbara. *Mirabeau.* Carbondale, IL: Southern Illinois U. Press; London and New York: Wheatsheaf Harvester, 1990. Pp. ix + 307.

Rev. (favorably) by J. E. Brink in *Choice,* 29 (1991), 179–80; (briefly) by C. J. in *TLS,* (Aug. 2, 1991), 25.

MacArthur, E. Mairi. *Iona: The Living Memory of a Crofting Community, 1750–1914.* Edinburgh, Scotland: Edinburgh U. Press (distributed through New York: Columbia U. Press), 1990. Pp. vii + 260; appendices; bibliography; illustrations; maps. Cf. *ECCB,* n.s. 16, II: 100.

Rev. (favorably) by M. Cherno in *Choice*, 29 (1991), 334.

Madariaga, Isabel de. *Catherine the Great: A Short History*. London and New Haven, CT: Yale U. Press, 1990. Pp. viii + 240; bibliographical note; illustrations; map. Cf. *ECCB*, n.s. 16, II: 68.

Rev. (favorbly) by W. Bruce Lincoln in *TLS*, (Mar. 22, 1991), 11.
Isabel de Madariaga offers a much condensed and somewhat updated version of her magisterial Russia in the Age of Catherine the Great (Yale U. Press, 1981), one shorn of scholarly apparatus but concluding with a helpful bibliographical guide for students and non-specialists. As the previous was and remains the single best scholarly work on Catherine's reign, so the present book is and doubtless will long remain the best shorter introduction to the subject.—James Cracraft.

Magagna, Victor V. *Communities of Grain: Rural Rebellion in Comparative Perspective*. Ithaca, NY, and London: Cornell U. Press, 1991. Pp. xii + 279.

Maguire, W. A. (ed.). *Kings in Conflict: The Revolutionary War in Ireland and Its Aftermath, 1689–1750*. Belfast: Blackstaff, 1990. Pp. xiv + 203; facsimiles; illustrations (some colored); maps; portraits (some colored). Cf. *ECCB*, n.s. 16, II: 100.

Rev. (favorably) by H. T. Blethen in *Choice*, 28 (1991), 984.

Malone, Patrick M. *The Skulking Way of War: Technology and Tactics Among the New England Indians*. Lanham, MD: Madison Books/ National Book Network, 1991. Pp. 133.

Mancall, Peter C. *Valley of Opportunity: Economic Culture along the Upper Susquehanna, 1700–1800*. Ithaca, NY, and London: Cornell U. Press, 1991. Pp. xviii + 253; maps; tables.

Mangan, J. J. *The King's Favour: Three Eighteenth Century Monarchs and the Favourites Who Ruled Them*. New York: St. Martin's Press, 1991. Pp. xvi + 312; bibliography.

Mapp, Alf J. *Thomas Jefferson: Passionate Pilgrim: The Presidency, the Founding of the University, and the Private Battle*. Lanham, MD: Madison Books/National Book Network, 1991. Pp. 445.

Marlay, Ross, James S. Olson, William G. Ratliff, Joseph M. Rowe, Jr., and Robert Shadle (eds.). *Historical Dictionary of European Imperialism*. London and New York; Greenwood Press, 1991. Pp. xii + 782; appendices.

Marly, Diana de. *Dress in North America, the New World 1492–1800*. London and New York: Holmes & Meier, 1990. Pp. 221. Cf. *ECCB*, n.s. 16, II: 69.

Rev. by Michele Majer in *Eighteenth-Century Studies*, 25 (1991–92), 278–82.

Martres, Jean-Louis, Jean Béranger, Roland B. Simon, Jean-Louis Seurin, Christian Lerat, and James Ceaser (eds.). *Le discours sur les Révolutions*. 2 vols. Paris: Economica, 1991.

Each volume contains the essentials of papers presented on the bicentennial of the French Revolution. The volumes take two directions: first, there is a comparison between the American and the French Revolutions; second, the discourse on both revolutions and its consequences is related. The article by Merrill D. Peterson on Jefferson is particularly welcome because it shows how he influenced the drafting of the *Déclaration des droits de l'Homme* and derived lessons from the French experience that fed his quarrel with the Federalists. Toqueville rightly emphasized the long-term origins of the French Revolution in the centralization prevailing already under the absolute monarchy and of its American counterpart in the framing of ideas and mentalities linked to the Reformation and early Enlightenment (John Locke). Christian Lerat artfully shows how Franklin took advantage of the prevailing frankomania to promote American interests in the crucial years of the War of Independence. Other articles compare the religious experience of both revolutions showing how a rationalized form of religion was considered as going hand-in-hand with the revolutionary process and the separation between church and state in America, whereas in France the Catholic Church rejected the doctrine of human rights and openly condemned them in the nineteenth century. Paradoxically, the authority of the pope was reinforced and led to the proclamation of the dogma of papal infallibility in 1870.

The second volume starts with the possible influence of the American and French Revolutions and their ideals in other areas of the world, especially in Latin America and Africa and the comparison of both events is thrown in strong relief in such well-argumented articles as Dimitri-Georges Lavroff: *L'influence de la pensée américaine sur la Déclaration des Droits de l'Homme et du Citoyen de 1789*, Theodore Caplow's *Aspect militaire de deux révolutions*, and James Ceaser's *Les deux Révolutions*. Each article makes a distinct contribution to the main subject. One mission, however, the problem of slavery, might have provided us with facts and arguments for a comparative treatment of the problem in both countries. Of course, the problem was peripheral in France, but the discourse of French politicians could have been compared with that of their American counterparts. In fact, both the drafters of the American constitution and Bonaparte decided in favor of its preservation. But the problem goes further in American history as the indecision of the founding fathers and their successors finally led to the American Civil War which really was a second American Revolution. A comparison between a long American Revolution (1773–1877) and a long French Revolution (1789–1881) would be an appropriate subject for a new colloquium. But, within the traditional limits (1776–1787 and 1789–1799), both volumes make valuable, sound and most readable contributions to the subject at hand.—Jean Riviére.

McCusker, John J. *The Economy of British America, 1607–1789.* (Needs and Opportunities for Study Series.) Chapel Hill, NC: U. of North Carolina Press, sponsored by the Institute of Early American History and Culture, 1991. Pp. xxiv + 513; bibliography.

McEwan, Barbara. *Thomas Jefferson: Farmer.* Jefferson, NC: McFarland, 1991. Pp. xii + 219.

McKee, Christopher. *A Gentlemanly and Honorable Profession: The Creation of the U. S. Naval Officer Corps, 1794–1815.* Annapolis, MD: Naval Institute Press, 1991. Pp. xv + 600; bibliography; illustrations.

Rev. (favorably) by B. H. Groene in *Choice*, 29 (1991), 510.

McKnight, Stephen A. *The Modern Age and the Recovery of Ancient Wisdom: A Reconsideration of Historical Consciousness, 1450–1650.* Columbia, MO, and London: U. of Missouri Press, 1991. Pp. x + 162; bibliography; illustrations.

McLean, Marianne. *The People of Glengary: Highlanders in Transition, 1745–1820.* (McGill-Queen's Studies in Ethnic History, 9.) Montreal and Kingston: McGill-Queen's U. Press, 1991. Pp. xiii + 285; bibliography; illustrations; maps; tables.

The current preoccupation with ethnicity has greatly invigorated the field of immigration history. This study is one of the fruits of that development.

The book's focus is the interrelationship between western Inverness-shire and Glengarry County, Ontario, during the second half of the eighteenth century and the early decades of the nineteenth. The nexus that linked the two areas was established by successive waver of immigrants to Glengarry County between 1773 and 1820. The settlers who comprised those groups were impelled by the socio-economic innovations which transformed the Highlands after the suppression of the Jacobite rebellion in 1745, and rapidly integrated the Highlands into the capitalistic and commercial order that prevailed to the south. A new attitude was generated in the lairds by this integration. No longer regarding themselves as fiduciaries, administering their estates for the good of the clansmen, they now viewed land as a commodity from which they could enrich themselves by maximizing the potential profit. As a result, the clansmen developed a deep sense of disillusionment and betrayal; the bond between them and their chiefs was weakened. Moreover, they found it increasingly difficult to survive under the new economic conditions. Rising rents and agrarian changes, such as enclosure, crop rotation, and the substitution of sheep-raising for farming based on cattle, worsened their plight. So did evictions. All these changes combined with the pressure of population growth create will to emigrate. Those who left home sought to replicate the society and culture of the Highlands. They were eminently successful in achieving their objective.

The saga of this transplantation is deftly delineated by Marianne McLean. Beginning with a propaedeutic account of the socio-economic structure of the Highlands, she then presents as case histories the changes that structure underwent on two western Inverness-shire estates. Next she details the initial essay in colonization, 1773–1780. Then she considers the subsequent streams of emigration in 1785–1793, 1802–1803, and 1815. Finally, she examines in great detail the settlements established in Glengarry, Ontario, in 1784–1797 and 1797–1816.

McLean treats these matters with exemplary scholarship. Utilizing archival, published, and oral sources, she marshals the evidence with considerable skill. Thoroughly acquainted with the work of Bernard Bailyn, Eric Richards, and Malcom Gray, she duly considers their findings, accepting some of their interpretations, refuting others. Most notably, she effectively rebuts the widely entertained notion that the clearances did not induce emigration.

The competence of McLean's study makes it as useful as it it commendable. It will be of great value to students of the eighteenth century concerned with emigration, Scotland, or Canada.—J. Jean Hecht.

McLynn, Frank. *Crime and Punishment in Eighteenth-Century England.* London and New York: Routledge, 1989. Pp. xviii + 392. Cf. *ECCB*, n.s. 16, II: 104; 15, II: 77–78.

Rev. by Stuart Handley in *The Scriblerian*, 24 (1991), 83–84.

McMillen, Persis W. *Currents of Malice: Mary Towne Esty and Her Family in Salem Witchcraft.* Portsmouth, NH: P. E. Randall Publisher, 1990. Pp. xxiv + 603; illustrations; map. Cf. *ECCB*, n.s. 16, II: 105.

Rev. (severely) by E. W. Carp in *Choice*, 28 (1991), 1554–55.

Merlin, Hélène. "Figures du public au 18e siècle: Le Travail du passé." *Dix-huitième siècle*, 21 (1991), 345–56.

Meroney, Geraldine M. *Inseparable Loyalty: A Biography of William Bull.* Norcross, GA: Harrison Company, 1991. Pp. x + 232; illustrations; map; plates (endpaper fold-out).

Rev. by J. D. Born in *Choice*, 29 (1991), 657.

Merrick, Jeffrey W. *The Desacralization of the French Monarchy in the Eighteenth Century.* Baton Rouge, LA: Louisiana State U. Press, 1990. Pp. xiv + 196. Cf. *ECCB*, n.s. 16, II: 105.

Rev. (favorably) by James P. Gilroy in *The French Review*, 64 (1991), 1053–54.

Meyer, Jean. *Le Despotisme éclairé.* (Que Sais-Je?) Paris: Presses Universitaires de France, 1991. Pp. 128.

The phenomenon known as enlightened despotism concerned several categories of states: the large states of central and eastern Europe (Austria, Russia, Prussia), the smaller states of northern Europe (Denmark and Sweden), a host of small German states (Saxony, Bavaria, Hesse Kassel and Würtemberg) and southern states such as Spain, Portugal and Tuscany. Jean Meyer provides us with a useful synthesis, survey and appreciation of the subject. To him, the enlightenment in all these states was only an " 'auxiliary' means" (p. 55) for an end that was, especially in the case of the larger states, the preservation and reinforcement of the nation. Its two positive features were legal and religious reforms and all such states tried to promote a new legal order and religious tolerance or even with Joseph II a drastic curtailment of the power and influence of the Catholic Church. Enlightened despotism, however, had to rely on the power of the local landed gentry (junkers and boyard) and in many cases had to reinforce their power. In Russia, it even led to an extension and reinforcement of serfdom. It did not prevent an acute conflict between Prussia and Austria over Silesia that ended up only in 1866 with the final victory of Prussia at Sadowa and the realization by central European states of the growing influence of Russia. The enlightenment despots presided over the dismantlement of Poland.

In all countries, enlightened despotism meant a tacit compromise between the sovereign and traditional social forces in a period that witnessed the waning power of the baroque states of southern Germany, the decay of Italian city-states and the predominance of Russia and Prussia. Some sort of enlightened policy was, of course, conducted in each of these states, but it never succeeded in decreasing the causes of their fundamental rivalry. I would not go as far as Jean Mayer and say that the French Revolution stifled attempts at real reforms. In fact, in all cases, enlightened despotism was at most reformation from above and when these princes were confronted with real revolutions from the bottom in 1787 in the United Provinces and in 1790 in the Austrian Netherlands, in both cases these revolts were crushed by force, in the first case by Prussian and in the second by Austria. Jean Mayer presents us with a study that does not try to hide the fact enlightened despotism too often meant one ounce of enlightenment for one pound of despotism. One regrettable omission in the bibliography: the ground-breaking study of the late Robert Mandrou: *L'Europe absolutiste: raison et raison d'Etat* (Paris, 1977).—Jean Rivière.

Meyer, Jean. *La Noblesse française à l'époque moderne: 16e—18e siècles.* (Que sais-je?, 830.) Paris: Presses Universitaires de France, 1991. Pp. 128.

Meyer, Jean, André Corvisier, and Jean-Pierre Poussou. *La Révolution française.* 2 vols. Paris: PUF, collection Peuples et Civilisations, 1991. Pp. 1437; bibliography; chronology; indices.

A bicentennial trilogy of the French Revolution exists already with Michel Vovelle's *L'état de la France pendant la Révolution* (La Découverte, 1988), Albert Soboul's *Dictionnaire historique de la Révolution française* (PUF, 1989) and François Furet and Mona Ozouf's *Dictionnaire critique le la Révolution française* (Flammarion, 1989). The present volume will make a tetralogy. Jean Meyer, one of the best specialists of the European Enlightenment, André Corvisier, a scholar in military history, and Jean-Pierre Poussou, an economic historian united their talents to give us a new synthesis on the Revolution whose main originality lies in its putting in its due European and world perspective.

The closest attention is given everywhere to economic, social and demographic basic facts and details not only concerning France, but also every country in Europe and in the Americas. The relative "weight" of the protagonists whether in the French civil war or in the tug of war between France and Europe is critically assessed. The picture of pre-revolutionary and revolutionary Paris is a distinct masterpiece with apt comparisons with London. The religious question is rightly thrown into relief as the most distinct failure of the Constituante and of the following governments. The ravages of vandalism are balanced with the simultaneous creation of museums, a new concept in art appreciation. The two main social elements that took advantage of the Revolution are rightly described as the provincial petty bourgeoisie and the Parisian craftsment of the *faubourgs* both groups are considered as "les plus fragiles, intellectuellement et économiquement parlant" (p. 163) and are the harbingers of a France of local notables and small shopkeepers and aritsans. Due emphasis is given to the constant inferiority of the French navy and to the fact that the *levées en masse* could not dry up human resources in a nation where 42% of the population were under 20. In foreign policy, the French obsession with the House of Austria both under the *ancien régime* and during the Revolution hid the realities of the rise of Prussia and Russia. The greatest attention is given to intellectual sources and attitudes dutifully comparing them with the paltry political powers residing mainly in privileged and class-obsessed *parlements*. The authors number Louis XVI among the monarchs of the time that could not face such momentous upheavals: he was from the start, that is from the transformation of the Estates-General into an *assemblée constituante*, intent on stopping the overdue process of change.

Let us discuss the question of the *dérapage*. As the sovereign was the unwilling tool of the most momentous institutional changes that ever happened in France and was left enough clout—especially with his veto power—conflicts were bound to arise. Varennes in fact allowed the quesion of the control of the executive to move to the forefront. The authors emphasize the importance of the pornographic literature reviling the royal family and the nobles, but on the eye of Varennes, constitutional monarchy was the order of the day and republicanism a remote, impractical utopia better left to the Swiss cantons or the budding United States. The main consequences of Varennes were the split of the Jacobins between conservative Feuillants and legitimate Jacobins, the reviling of the king in caricature and the fact that the right clung adamantly to the fiction of the king's abduction even reinforcing his powers in the final draft of the constitution. The monarchy never recovered from Varennes, whereas "l'influence de la Révolution a été considérable à l'étranger. Elle fait parite du 'rayonnement' de la France, s'étant voulue modèle à jamais, fondatrice exemplaire des droits de l'homme et du citoyen" (p. 1195).

Yet, the authors draw a negative conclusion from the revolutionary turmoil. Such an assertion brings to mind two questions. First, all revolutionary decades are negative. Were the 1640s or 1650s in England positive? Was the Civil War (a "natural" sequel to the unresolved problems concerning the constitution of the United States) positive? did the Vendée, Lyon and Toulan, the most striking examples of mass revolutionary repression, suffer longer from their tragic fates than Ireland or the postbellum South? Second, if the ten-year balance sheet is altogether negative, can we say that things would have been better if the Revolution had not happened? The latter question is not answered in the book and the final references to Nazism, Stalinism and even the killing fields of Cambodia (why not add the genocide of American natives and the transatlantic slave trade?) are out of perspective: we all wish the French revolutionary decade could be deemed the most tragic event in history! In the index, we cannot find any reference to the Holy Alliance and only a passing one to the *Cent Jours* (p. 927), a reference to Lazre Carnot). True, both items are outside the revolutionary period, but the post-1815 Restoration is treated in six full pages, plus eight passing references. The final opinion on Napoleon is, in the contrary, terse and pungent: "un compomis mal taillé—et il ne pouvait en êntre autrement—entre ce que la France pouvait encore supporter de révolutionnaire et ce qu'elle pouvait encore supporter de régime royaliste" (p. 1147). No wonder Napolean's nephew was the first president of the Republic to be elected in 1848 in a contest where universal male suffrage had just been adopted. My critical remarks concern only some general perspectives I do not share with the authors, but their book is a magisterial addition to the collection *Peuples et Civilisations* and provides us with the most panoramic vista and the most accurate rendering of a cataclysmic and awe-inspiring decade.—Jean Rivière.

Miller, John Chester. *The Wolf by the Ears: Thomas Jefferson and Slavery*. Charlotesville, VA:
    U. Press of Virginia, 1991. Pp. 319.

Miller, Joshua I. *The Rise and Fall of Democracy in Early America, 1690–1789: The Legacy for
    Contemporary Politics*. University Park, PA: Pennsylvania State U. Press, 1991. Pp. 154.

Millican, Edward. *One United People: The Federalist Papers and the National Idea*. Lexington,
    KY: U. Press of Kentucky, 1990. Pp. x + 267; bibliography. Cf. *ECCB*, n.s. 16, II: 106.

Rev. by R. J. Vichot in *Choice*, 28 (1991), 856.

Mintz, Max M. *The Generals of Saratoga: John Burgoyne & Horatio Gates.* London and New Haven, CT: Yale U. Press, 1990. Pp. ix + 278; bibliography; illustrations; maps. Cf. *ECCB*, n.s. 16, II:106.

Rev. by C. R. Allen, Jr. in *Choice*, 28 (1991), 1212.

Mitchell, Robert D. (ed.). *Appalachian Frontiers: Settlement, Society, & Development in the Preindustrial Era.* Ithaca, NY, and Lexington, KY: U. Press of Kentucky in association with Cornell U. Press, 1991. Pp. 350.

Mitchison, Rosalind. *Coping with Destitution: Poverty and Relief in Western Europe.* (The 1989 Joanne Goodman Lectures.) Buffalo, NY, and Toronto: U. of Toronto Press, 1991. Pp. xvi + 94; bibliography.

Mollo, John. *Uniforms of the American Revolution in Color.* Illustrated by Malcolm McGregor. New York: Sterling Publishing, 1991. Pp. 228; colored illustrations.

Monkkonen, Eric H. (ed.). *The Colonies and Early Republic, v. 1–2.* 2 vols. (Crime and Justice in American History, 1.) Westport, CT: Meckler Books, 1991. Pp. 915.

Monod, Paul Kléber. *Jacobitism and the English People, 1688–1788.* Cambridge and New York: Cambridge U. Press, 1989. Pp. xvi + 408. Cf. *ECCB*, n.s. 16, II: 106; 15, II: 81.

Rev. by J. A. Downie in *Review of English Studies*, 42 (1991), 582–83; (with reservations) by David Hayton in *The Scriblerian*, 23 (1991), 279–81.

Mooers, Colin. *The Making of Bourgeois Europe: Absolutism, Revolution, and the Rise of Capitalism in England, France and Germany.* London and New York: Verso, 1991. Pp. vii + 208; bibliography.

With this brilliant book, both synthesis on existing scholarship and penetrating analysis, Colin Mooers has reinvigorated the "Great Debate" on the western transition from feudalism to capitalism. His work is, he tells us, a "theoretical clarification" of the issues of the Debate: dialogue with contemporary historians from Robert Brenner to Geoff Eley; critique of scholars from Maurice Dobb to Perry Anderson; challenge to (rejection of) revisionists from Alfred Cobban to François Furet. And it is, bluntly, a "rehabilitation" of Marx's linking of the origins and development of capitalism, and bourgeois revolutions in England and on the continent from the 17th to the 19th century.

In a wide-ranging first chapter Mooers establishes what Marx made so clear, what remains obscure to some, even Marxist historians: capitalism in England developing *within* the economic structures of feudal society, through the peasant petty commodity production on-going from the end of the 14th century. Peasant accumulation led to differentiation, to a rising "layer of richer peasants," the process accelerated by the inability of state and landowners to impose feudal restrictions, by the growing market for tenancies, by soaring prices for agricultural products and the general economic quickening through the 1500s. England by the 17th century presented Marx's "classic triadic pattern of capitalist farming:" great land-lords renting to capitalist farmers who hired as wage-laborers the by-now dispossesed small peasants. Out of this classic pattern of primitive accumulation came the coalition of social groups which overthrew the Stuart monarchy in the 1640s. And from the English Revolution emerged a "new type of state," which "allowed" the relatively "unfetted" capitalist production of the 18th and 19th centuries.

This "really revolutionary path"—Marx's phrase—can be traced only in England. Contradictory patterns, slow and uneven development on the continent, specifically in France and Germany, present the true test of Mooers' analyses. Could the French Revolution have been bourgeois, capitalist, when major social forces in the 1790s were explicitly anti-capitalist, when post-revolutionary settlements actually impeded capitalist transformation of the society? In the early modern formation of Prussian bureaucratic absolutism, in the ignominious liberal collapse in 1848, in bismarckian unification from on high—where in any part of this is a German bourgeois revolution?

Mooers' answers are conducted on a high level of the promised theoretical clarification, and grounded in authoritative control of French and German historical development. He insists (with Geoff Eley) on the distinction between class conscious revolutionary intent and the "deeper process on structural change." He concentrates (with Robert Brenner) on political power and the role of the state, whether absolutist or merely "parasitic," in capital formation. He stresses the impact and influence of the English world market, the internationalization of new forces and relations of production. But rather than a compressed review, his book demands attentive reading.—Margaret George.

Moorhead, Max L. *The Presidio: Bastion of the Spanish Borderlands.* London and Norman, OK: U. of Oklahoma Press, 1991. Pp. xvi + 288; bibliography; illustrations; maps.

Motley, Mark. *Becoming a French Aristocrat: The Education of the Court Nobility, 1580–1715.* Princeton, NJ: Princeton U. Press, 1990. Pp. x + 241; bibliography. Cf. *ECCB*, n.s. 16, II: 107.

Rev. by S. Fishman in *Choice*, 28 (1991), 1190; 1192.

Moziño, José Mariano. *Noticias de Nutka: An Account of Nootka Sound in 1792.* Edited and translated by Iris H. Wilson Engstrand. Seattle, WA: U. of Washington Press, 1991. Pp. liv + 142.

Munford, Clarence J. *Black Ordeal of Slavery & Slave Trading in the French West Indies, 1625–1715, v. 2: The Middle Passage and the Plantation Economy.* Lewiston, NY: Edwin Mellen Press, 1991. Pp. 362.

Munger, Donna Bingham. *Pennsylvania Land Records: A History and Guide for Research.* Wilmington, DE: Scholarly Resources in cooperation with the Pennsylvania Historical and Museum Commission, 1991. Pp. xxxiii + 240; maps.

Nader, Helen. *Liberty in Absolutist Spain: The Habsburg Sale of Towns, 1516–1700.* (The Johns Hopkins University Studies in Historical and Political Science, 108th series, 1.) Baltimore, MD: Johns Hopkins U. Press, 1990. Pp. xvi + 305; bibliography; illustrations; maps. Cf. *ECCB*, n.s. 16, II: 108.

Rev. (favorably) by R. L. Kagan in *Choice*, 28 (1991), 838.

Nagel, Paul C. *The Lees of Virginia: Seven Generations of an American Family.* New York and Oxford: Oxford U. Press, 1990. Pp. xiv + 332; illustrations; map. Cf. *ECCB*, n.s. 16, II: 109.

Rev. by J. Z. Rabun in *Choice*, 28 (1991), 844.

Nardinelli, Clark. *Child Labor and the Industrial Revolution.* Bloomington, IN: Indiana U. Press, 1990. Pp. x + 194; bibliography. Cf. *ECCB*, n.s. 16, II: 109.

Rev. by D. E. Moggridge in *Choice*, 28 (1991), 975–76.

Nash, Gary B., and Jean R. Soderlund. *Freedom by Degrees: Emancipation in Pennsylvania and Its Aftermath.* New York and Oxford: Oxford U. Press, 1991. Pp. xvi + 249; bibliography; illustrations; map.

Rev. (favorably) by R. Detweiler in *Choice*, 28 (1991), 1837–38.

Neal, Larry. *The Rise of Financial Capitalism: International Capital Markets in the Age of Reason.* (Studies in Monetary and Financial History.) Cambridge and New York: Cambridge U. Press, 1990. Pp. x + 278; bibliography; illustrations. Cf. *ECCB*, n.s. 16, II: 110.

Rev. (favorably) by Martin Ricketts in *TLS,* (Apr. 12, 1991), 25.

Nelson, Paul David. *William Tryon and the Course of Empire: A Life in British Imperial Service.* Chapel Hill, NC: U. of North Carolina Press, 1990. Pp. xiii + 250; bibliography; illustrations. Cf. *ECCB*, n.s. 16, II:110.

Rev. by J. L. McKelvey in *Choice*, 28 (1991), 1371.

New, Melvyn. " 'Scholia' to the Florida *Tristram Shandy* Annotations." *The Scriblerian*, 24 (1991), 105–06.

Newman, Peter R. *Companion to Irish History, 1603–1921: From the Submission of Tyrone to Partition.* New York and Oxford: Facts on File, 1991. Pp. xi + 244; maps.

Niderst, Alain. *Fontenelle.* Paris: Plon, 1991. Pp. 439; bibliography.

The centenarian of French literature (1657–1757), the forerunner of the Enlightenment—his longevity allowed him to see its full blossoming in the *Encyclopédie*—the nephew of Pierre and Thomas Corneille, the dabbler in minor genres never out of his depth either in the provincial libertine circles of Rouen or at court or in the successive salons he graced with his presence and wit from Ninon de Lenclos to Mme du Deffand, Fontenelle stands out as a unique figure. Alain Niderst, the renowned specialist of seventeenth century French literature, both a critic and editor of its best-known figures (Molière, Corneille, Racine) and its no less important libertines or pamphleteers (Saint-Evermond, Pierre Bayle) had written a most minute critical biography that every scholar of the period will have to consider. The author shows us both the complexity and uniqueness of Fontenelle's work. The kingdom of his Most Christian Majesty he describes was not the monolithic achievement of which Louvois in war and diplomacy and Bossuet in the religious field dreamt. In Rouen, before the fated abolition of the Edict of Nantes, there was still a fairly pluralistic society in which Protestants could belong to the highest circles before being forced into exile, martyrdom or abjuration. Niderst points out that the strength of anti-Calvinistic persecution diverted the attention of the powers that be from the apparently dutiful Catholics that were in fact libertines or unbelievers. He depicts Fontenelle's originality in three directions. First, Corneille's nephew with his *Entretiens sur la pluralité des mondes* (1686) sought to convince the general public of the superiority of Descartes, Galileo and Copernicus over Aristotle and Plato and appealed to the enlightened opinion of male and female aristocracy. He became the juggler of critical rationalism describing a universal system in which no fixed point of reference could be found and in which other inhabited worlds were likely to exist. Second, in his *La République des philosophes ou Histoire des Ajoiens* (Geneva, 1768), he built an ideal republic of materialists and atheists going well beyond the critical remarks of Fénelon's bestseller *Télémaque*. Third, in his *De l'origine des fables*, a treaty of social archeology to which Lévy-Bruhl and Lévi-Strauss paid tribute, he debunked the origins of all religions. The *roi Fontenelle* of the Regency, just as king Voltaire in the 1770s, was the witness of a long century in which he was born two years after the death of Gassende (1592–1655), the first deist libertine and in which he was able to encourage the talents of Helvétius

(1715–1771), the atheist. With the editorship of Fontenelle's *Oeuvres Complétes* (three volumes out of eight already published at Librairie Arthème Fayard's), Niderst is really *the* recognized Fontenelle scholar.—Jean Rivière.

Nokes, J. Richard. *Columbia's River: The Voyages of Robert Gray, 1787–1793.* Tacoma, WA: Washington State Historical Society/ Pacific Northwest Books, 1991. Pp. 352.

Noonkester, Myron C. "Gibbon in India." *Notes and Queries*, 236 (1991), 192.

William Carey, a Baptist missionary, disparaged his religious views in 1822.

O'Brien, Steven G. *American Political Leaders from Colonial Times to the Present.* Edited by Paula McGuire, James M. McPherson, and Gary Gerstle. Oxford and Santa Barbara, CA, 1991. Pp. xv + 473; illustrations.

O'Hagan, Timothy (ed.). *Revolution and Enlightenment in Europe.* (Enlightenment, Rights, and Revolution Series.) Aberdeen, Scotland: Aberdeen U. Press, 1991. Pp. xiv + 155.

Okie, Laird. *Augustan Historical Writing: Histories of England in the English Enlightenment.* Lanham, MD, and London: University Press of America, 1991. Pp. vii + 240; bibliography.

This informative and readable book charts the evolution of English historiography in the first half of the eighteenth century. Okie begins with a useful explanation of humanist historiography, which retained a belief in providential intervention well into the seventeenth century, and then moves on to explore the development of Enlightenment historiography with its distinctly modern style and secular emphasis. In discussing other attributes, such as the inclusion of economics and culture, as well as the ability to consider the progress of civilization as a whole, the author provides the backgroud for a close examination of several histories of England written during the Augustan period.

The book's greatest merit is the assessment of obscure historians many now cite but seldom read. The author convincingly demonstrates, contrary to many shibboleths on the subject, that credible English history in the eighteenth century did not begin with Hume as Hume himself wanted us to believe. In the first half of the century a host of historians prefigured Hume and occasionally surpassed him in their dedication to the sources.

Among others, Okie studies Clarendon and Burnet at the beginning of the century, and then the liberals John Oldmixon and Daniel Neal in addition to Thomas Salmon, who offered a Tory Rebuttal of the celebrated Whig of the 1730s, Rapin-Thoyras. While it is the case that Rapin's reputation as a Whig apologist originated with Hume's slanderous denunciation of Rapin as a party hack in the 1750s, it is also true that Rapin belived in the myth on an ancient constitution, which supposes that English Liberty developed steadily from medieval origins to the seventeenth century. The ancient constitution became the essence of the Whig view of English history, and Hume took great delight in denouncing Rapin for his support of this idea. In the decade before Hume, Thomas Carte, defender of the detested Jacobites, published a history that addressed only a limited audience; however, James Ralph and William Guthrie wrote histories that were well researched, well balanced and altogether secular. Their obscurity was in part the result of a tedious style.

Enter David Hume. His lucid, classical style and iconoclasm attracted readers all over Great Britain. With the publication of his history, the memory of his earlier defeats as a philosopher disappeared, and he occupied center stage as the great Enlightenment historian. Unfortunately the chapter on Hume is somewhat disappointing: clearly all roads have been leading to Hume, but the expected crescendo never appears. Rather than a thorough evaluation of Hume's contribution as an historian, which is significantly diminished by Okie's discovery that some of his predecessors were in some ways better historians, we see Hume's work as a general culmination of Enlightenment historiography: secular, skeptical and cultural. That Hume lifted passages wholesaled from men he denigrated as slavish monks lost in the sources is also in keeping with the typical profile of Enlightenment historians.

Okie's overall contribution to our understanding of those who preceded Hume is invaluable. The book serves the profession well by lending substance to vague and offhanded references concerning the works of important but lesser known historians of the Augustan period.—Victor G. Wexler.

Olson, Lester C. *Emblems of American Community in the Revolutionary Era: A Study in Rhetorical Iconology.* Washington, DC: Smithsonian Institution Press, 1991. Pp. xxi + 306; illustrations.

Onuf, Peter S. (ed.). *America and the World: Diplomacy, Politics, and War.* (New American Nation, 1775–1820, 9.) New York: Garland Publishers, 1991. Pp. 456.

Onuf, Peter S. (ed.). *American Culture, 1776–1815.* (New American Nation, 1775–1820, 12.) New York: Garland Publishers, 1991. Pp. 490.

Onuf, Peter S. (ed.). *American Society, 1776–1815.* (New American Nation, 1775–1820, 11.) New York: Garland Publishers, 1991. Pp. 531.

Onuf, Peter S. (ed.). *Congress and the Confederation.* (New American Nation, 1775–1820, 4.) New York: Garland Publishers, 1991. Pp. 444.

Onuf, Peter S. (ed.). *Establishing the New Regime: The Washington Administration.* (New American Nation, 1775–1820, 7.) New York: Garland Publishing, 1991. Pp. 458.

Onuf, Peter S. (ed.). *Federalists and Republicans.* (New American Nation, 1775–1810, 8.) New York: Garland Publishers, 1991. Pp. 383.

Onuf, Peter S. (ed.). *The Federal Constitution.* (New American Nation, 1775–1820, 5.) New York: Garland Publishers, 1991. Pp. 610.

Onuf, Peter S. (ed.). *Patriots, Redcoats, and Loyalists.* (New American Nation, 1775–1820, 2.) New York: Garland Publishers, 1991. Pp. 528.

Onuf, Peter S. (ed.). *Ratifying, Amending, and Interpreting the Constitution.* (New American Nation, 1775–1820, 6.) New York: Garland Publishers, 1991. Pp. 516.

Onuf, Peter S. (ed.). *The Revolution in the States.* (New American Nation, 1775–1820, 3.) New York: Garland Publishers, 1991. Pp. 527.

Onuf, Peter S. (ed.). *State and Local Politics in the New Nation.* (New American Nation, 1775–1820, 10.) New York: Garland Publishers, 1991. Pp. 580.

Oplinger, Jon. *The Politics of Demonology: The European Witchcraze and the Mass Production of Deviance.* Selinsgrove, PA: Susquehanna U. Press (distributed through Cranbury, NJ, and London: Associated University Presses), 1990. Pp. 311; bibliography. Cf. *ECCB*, n.s. 16, II: 111.

Rev. (with reservations) by D. M. Lowe in *Choice*, 28 (1991), 979–80.

Orosz, Joel J. *Curators and Culture: The Museum Movement in America, 1740–1870.* (History of American Science and Technology.) Tuscaloosa, AL: U. of Alabama Press, 1990. Pp. xii + 304; illustrations. Cf. *ECCB*, n.s. 16, II: 111.

Rev. by J. L. Cooper in *Choice*, 28 (1991), 1371.

Orth, John V. *Combination and Conspiracy: A Legal History of Trade Unionism, 1721–1906.* New York: Oxford U. Press; Oxford: Clarendon Press, 1991. Pp. xv + 207; appendices; bibliography.

Ousby, Ian. *The Englishman's England: Taste, Travel and the Rise of Tourism.* Cambridge and New York: Cambridge U. Press, 1990.

Rev. in *The Scriblerian*, 23 (1991), 284.

Owen, Robert. *A New View of Society and Other Writings.* London and New York: Penguin Books, 1991. Pp. xxxv + 385.

Pan, Lynn. *Sons of the Yellow Emperor: A History of the Chinese Diaspora.* Boston, MA, and London: Little/Brown, 1990. Pp. xvii + 408; 16 illustrations; maps. Cf. *ECCB*, n.s. 16, II: 112.

Rev. by H. T. Wong in *Choice*, 28 (1991), 1542.
The first two chapters (pp. 1–42) concern the eighteenth-century.

Pangle, Thomas L. *The Spirit of Modern Republicanism: The Moral Vision of the American Founders and the Philosophy of Locke.* Chicago, IL: U. of Chicago Press, 1988. Pp. x + 334. Cf. *ECCB*, n.s. 16, II: 112; 15, II: 88–89.

Rev. (with other works) by John Allphin Moore, Jr. in *Eighteenth-Century Studies*, 24 (1991), 363–69.

Pardailhé-Galabrun, Annik. *The Birth of Intimacy: Privacy and Domestic Life in Early Modern Paris.* Translation by Jocelyn Phelps of *La Naissance de l'intime: 3000 foyers parisiens XVIIe—XVIIIe siècles* (Paris, 1988). Oxford: Polity; Philadelphia, PA: U. of Pennsylvania Press, 1991. Pp. xiv + 241; 8 illustrations.

Parker, Stephen. *Informal Marriage, Cohabitation, and the Law, 1750–1989.* Basingstoke, UK: Macmillan, 1989; New York: St. Martin's Press, 1990. Pp. vii + 176. Cf. *ECCB*, n.s. 16, II: 113.

Rev. (Severely and with other works) by John Bossy in *TLS*, (Dec. 28, 1990–Jan. 3, 1991), 1393–94.

Percy, Carol. "Variation Between *-(E)TH* and *-(E)S* Spellings of the Third Person Singular Present Indicative: Captain James Cook's 'ENdeavor' Journal 1768–1771." *Neuphilologische Mitteillungen*, 92 (1991), 351–58.

Perrot, Philippe. *Le Corps féminin. Le Travail des apparences XVIIIe—XIXe siècles.* (Points. Histoire, 141.) Paris: Seuil, 1991. Pp. 288.

Pestana, Carla Gardina. *Quakers and Baptists in Colonial Massachusetts.* Cambridge and New York: Cambridge U. Press, 1991. Pp. 197.

Petit, Jacques-Guy, Nicole Castan, and Claude Faugeron. *Histoire des galères, bagnes et prisons: XIIIe—XXe siècles. Introduction à l'histoire pénale de la France.* Preface by Michelle Perrot. (Bibliothèque historique.) Toulouse: Privat, 1991. Pp. 368; illustrations.

Petterson, Merrill D., and Robert C. Vaughan (eds.) *The Virginia Statute for Religious Freedom: Its Evolution and Consequences in American History.* Cambridge and New York: Cambridge U. Press, 1988. Pp. xv + 373.

Rev. (with other works) by John Allphin Moore, Jr. in *Eighteenth-Century Studies*, 24 (1991), 363–69.

Philp, Mark (ed.). *The French Revolution and British Popular Politics.* Cambridge and New York: Cambridge U. Press, 1991. Pp. xii + 238.

Pittock, Joan H., and Andrew Wear (eds.). *Interpretation and Cultural History.* New York: St. Martin's Press, 1991. Pp. xvii + 296; 32 plates.

Pittock, Murray G. H. *The Invention of Scotland: The Stuart Myth and the Scottish Identity, 1638 to the Present.* London and New York: Routledge, 1991. Pp. ix + 198; bibliography.

Rev. by Bruce Lenman in *TLS*, (Jan. 31, 1991), 14.

Pollak, Martha D. *Turin, 1564–1680: Urban Design, Military Culture, and the Creation of the Absolutist Capital.* Chicago, IL, and London: The U. of Chicago Press, 1991. Pp. xxii + 391; illustrations.

Although the whole of the period covered in this book falls outside the chronological limits of eighteenth century studies, there are several aspects of it which are worth noting as relevant to urban and military studies of a later period. The central theme throughout the book is the relation of military culture and particularly military architecture to early modern city planning. Here the author has made a thorough search of sixteenth and seventeenth century planning proposals as well as a detailed study of the technical military treatises.

For those interested in early modern political culture, the sections on baroque festivals as expressions of representative sovereignty will be of interest. Finally, the concluding section describes minutely the final stages of construction which produced the finished city fortress that withstood the French siege of 1706. There is a formidable wealth of detail here, and architectual historians and urbanists will find it a rewarding study.—John P. Spielman.

Porter, Dorothy, and Roy Porter. *Patients and Doctoring in Eighteenth-Century England.* Stanford, CA: Stanford U. Press, 1989. Pp. 305.

Rev. by Antoinette Emch-Dériaz in *Eighteenth-Century Studies*, 25 (1991–92), 244–47.

Porter, Roy, and G.S. Rousseau (eds.). *Exoticism in the Enlightenment.* Manchester, UK: Manchester U. Press, 1990. Pp. 230.

Potash, P. Jeffrey. *Vermont's Burned-over District: Patterns of Community Development and Religious Activity, 1761–1850.* (Chicago Studies in the History of American Religion, 16.) Brooklyn, NY: Carlson Publishing, 1991. Pp. xiv + 277; bibliography.

Poyo, Gerald E., and Gilberto M. Hinojosa (eds.). *Tejano Origins in Eighteenth-Century San Antonio.* Illustrated by José Cisneros. Austin, TX: U. of Texas Press for the U. of Texas Institute of Texan Cultures at San Antonio, 1991. Pp. xxii + 198; bibliography; illustrations; maps.

Presser, Stephen B. *The Original Misunderstanding: The English, the Americans and the Dialectic of Federalist Jurisprudence.* Durham, NC: Carolina Academic Press, 1991. Pp. 272.

Proctor, Candice E. *Women, Equality and the French Revolution.* (Contributions in Women's Studies, 115.) New York: Greenwood Press, 1990. Pp. xiii + 210; bibliography. Cf. *ECCB*, n.s. 16, II: 117–18.

Rev. (with reservations) by J. E. Brink in *Choice*, 28 (1991), 1364.

Puglisi, Michael J. *Puritans Besieged: The Legacies of King Philip's War in the Massachusetts Bay Colony.* Lanham, MD: University Press of America, 1991. Pp. 244.

Quinn, Hartwell L. *Arthur Campbell: Pioneer and Patriot of the "Old Southwest."* Jefferson, NC: McFarland, 1990. Pp. viii + 199; illustrations. Cf. *ECCB*, n.s. 16, II: 119.

Rev. by C. R. Allen, Jr. in *Choice*, 28 (1991), 1372.

Ramsay, Clay. *The Ideology of the Great Fear: The Soissonnais in 1789.* (The Johns Hopkins University Studies in Historical and Political Science, 109th series, 2.) Baltimore, MD: Johns Hopkins U. Press, 1991. Pp. xxx + 311; bibliography; illustrations; maps.

Randall, Adrian. *Before the Luddites: Custom, Community and Machinery in the English Woollen Industry, 1776–1809.* Cambridge and New York: Cambridge U. Press, 1991. Pp. xvii + 318; bibliography; illustrations; maps.

Rev. (favorably) by G. F. Steckley in *Choice*, 29 (1991), 650.

Randall, Willard Sterne. *Benedict Arnold: Patriot and Traitor.* New York: W. Morrow, 1990. Pp. 667; bibliography; 24 illustrations. Cf. *ECCB*, n.s. 16, II: 120.

Rev. by E. W. Carp in *Choice*, 28 (1991), 844.

Reff, Daniel T. *Disease, Depopulation, and Culture Change in Northwestern New Spain, 1518–1764.* Salt Lake City, UT: U. of Utah Press, 1991. Pp. 330.

Reher, David Sven. *Town and Country in Pre-Industrial Spain: Cuenca, 1550–1870.* (Cambridge Studies in Population, Economy, and Society in Past Time, 12.) Cambridge and New York: Cambridge U. Press, 1990. Pp. xiv + 337; bibliography; illustrations. Cf. *ECCB*, n.s. 16, II: 120.

Rev. by R. L. Kagan in *Choice*, 28 (1991), 1212.

Reid, John Phillip. *The Concept of Liberty in the Age of the American Revolution.* Chicago, IL: U. of Chicago Press, 1988. Pp. viii + 224. Cf. *ECCB*, n.s. 14, II: 80.

Rev. (with other works) by John Allphin Moore, Jr. in *Eighteenth-Century Studies*, 24 (1991), 363–69.

Reid, John Phillip. *Constitutional History of the American Revolution: the Authority to Legislate.* Madison, WI: U. of Wisconsin Press, 1991. Pp. ix + 499. Cf. *ECCB*, n.s. 14, II: 80.

Reilly, Bernard. *American Political Prints, 1766–1876: A Catalog of the Collections in the Library of Congress.* Boston, MA: G. K. Hall, 1991. Pp. xxi + 638.

Rev. (favorably) by J. D. Haskell, Jr. in *Choice*, 29 (1991), 578.

Reinalter, Helmut (ed.). *Die Aufklärung in Österreich. Ignaz von Born und seine Zeit.* (Schriftenreihe der Internationalen Forschungsstelle "Demokratische Bewegungen in Mitteleuropa 1770–1850," Band 4.) Frankfurt am Main and New York: Peter Lang, 1991. Pp. 145.

Reinhardt, Steven G. *Justice in the Sarladais, 1770–1790.* Baton Rouge, LA, and London: Louisiana State U. Press, 1991. Pp. xxi + 301; bibliography.

Rétat, Pierre (ed.). *La Révolution du Journal, 1788–1794.* Paris: CNRS, 1989. Cf. *ECCB*, n.s. 15, II: 93.

Rev. in rev. article ("More than Words: The Printing Press and the French Revolution") by Joan B. Landes in *Eighteenth-Century Studies*, 25 (1991), 85–98.

Richards, Rhys. *Captain Simon Metcalfe: Pioneer Fur Trader in the Pacific Northwest, Hawaii and China, 1787–1794.* Edited by R. A. Pierce. (Alaska History, 37.) Fairbanks, AK: U. of Alaska Press; Kingston, Ontario: Limestone Press, 1991. Pp. 234.

Richarz, Monika (ed.). *Jewish Life in Germany: Memoirs from Three Centuries.* Translated by Sidney Rosenfeld and Stella P. Rosenfeld. Bloomington and Indianapolis, IN: Indiana U. Press, 1991. Pp. x + 484; glossary.

Richet, Denis. *De La Réforme à la Révolution: Naissance de la France moderne.* Preface by Pierre Goubert. Paris: Aubier, 1991. Pp. 584.

Rivington, Charles A. *"Tyrant" The Story of John Barber–Jacobite Lord Mayor of London, and Printer and Friend to Dr. Swift.* York, UK: William Sessions, Ltd., Ebor Press, 1990. Pp. viii + 311.

Rev. by Joseph McMinn in *The Scriblerian*, 23 (1991), 278–79.

Robbins, Christopher. *The Earl of Wharton and Whig Party Politics: 1679–1715.* (Studies in British History, 29.) Lewiston, NY, and Queenston, Ontario: Edward Mellen Press, 1991. Pp. x + 463; bibliography.

Roberts, Michael. "The Dubious Hand: The History of a Controversy." Pp. 144–203 of *From Oxenstierna to Charles XII: Four Studies*, by Michael Roberts. Cambridge and New York: Cambridge U. Press, 1991. Pp. 203.

Robinson, Enders A. *The Devil Discovered: Salem Witchcraft 1692*. New York: Hippocrene Books, 1991. Pp. xvii + 382; 16 illustrations.

Robinson, Richard (comp.). *United States Business History, 1602–1988: A Chronology*. London and New York: Greenwood Press, 1990. Pp. xii + 643. Cf. *ECCB*, n.s. 16, II: 123.

Rev. by Susan V. McKimm in *American Reference Books Annual*, 22 (1991), 130.

Roche, Daniel. *La Culture des Apparences: une histoire du vêtement, XVIIe–XVIIIe siècle*. Paris: Fayard, 1990. Pp. 549.

Rev. (favorably) by Orest Ranum in *Eighteenth-Century Studies*, 24 (1991), 524–31.

Rosner, Lisa. *Medical Education in the Age of Improvement: Edinburgh Students and Apprentices, 1760–1826*. Edinburgh, Scotland: Edinburgh U. Press/Columbia U. Press, 1991. Pp. 273.

Roudinesco, Elisabeth. *Théroigne de Méricourt: A Melancholic Woman during the French Revolution*. Translation by Martin Thom of *Théroigne de Méricourt: Une femme mélancolique sous la Révolution* (Paris, 1989). London and New York: Verso, 1991. Pp. x + 284; bibliography; 8 illustrations.

Rupolo, Wanda (ed.). *Voyage court, agréable et utile fait Mr. Eyrard*. Rome: Instituto Nationale di Archeologie e Storial dell'Arte, 1988. Pp. xx + 206.

Rev. by Jean-Paul de Nola in *Studi francesi*, 35 (1991), 152–53.
Edition of unpublished report of abbé François Eyrard (1741–1802) to the Bishop of Cahors, Mgr. Louis-Marie de Nicola on a trip to Italy in 1787.

Rutland, Robert Allen. *The Birth of the Bill of Rights, 1776–1791*. New ed. Boston, MA: Northeastern U. Press; Ithaca, NY: Cornell U. Press, 1991. Pp. 258.

Sa'adah, Anne. *The Shaping of Liberal Politics in Revolutionary France: A Comparative Perspective*. Oxford and Princeton, NJ: Princeton U. Press, 1990. Pp. xv + 248; bibliography. Cf. *ECCB*, n.s. 16, II: 126.

Rev. by C. A. Gliozzo in *Choice*, 28 (1991), 831.

Sabean, David W. *Property, Production, and Family in Neckarhausen, 1700–1870*. Cambridge and New York: Cambridge U. Press, 1991. Pp. xvi + 511; appendices; bibliography; tables.

Sacks, David Harris. *The Widening Gate: Bristol and the Atlantic Economy, 1450–1700*. (The New Historicism, 15.) Berkeley, CA, and Oxford: U. of California Press, 1991. Pp. xxvii + 464; bibliography; illustrations; tables.

Saul, Norman E. *Distant Friends: The United States and Russia, 1763–1867.* Lawrence, KS: U. Press of Kansas, 1991. Pp. xvi + 448; appendices; bibliography; illustrations; portraits.

Rev. (favorably) by G. E. Snow in *Choice*, 29 (1991), 505.
Chapters 1 "First Contacts for Distant Friends" and 2 "War and Peace" (ending with the War of 1812, pp. 1–91) concern the Eighteenth-Century.

Schaaf, Gregory. *Wampum Belts and Peace Trees: George Morgan, Native Americans, and Revolutionary Diplomacy.* Golden, CO: Fulcrum, 1990. Pp. xxiv + 278; bibliography; map; plate. Cf. *ECCB*, n.s. 16, II: 127.

Rev. by R. D. Edmunds in *Choice*, 28 (1991), 1556.

Schellinger, Paul E. (ed.). *St. James Guide to Biography.* Chicago, IL, and London: St. James Press, 1991. Pp. x + 870.

Schmalz, Peter S. *The Ojibwa of Southern Ontario.* Toronto, Canada: U. of Toronto Press, 1991. Pp. xv + 334; illustrations; map; portraits.

Rev. by D. Jacobson in *Choice*, 29 (1991), 190.

Schulze, Hagen. *The Course of German Nationalism from Frederick the Great to Bismarck, 1763–1867.* Translation by Sarah Hanbury-Tenison of *Der Weg zum Nationalstaat: deutsche Nationalbewegung vom 18. Jahrhundert bis zur Reichsgrundung* (Munich, 1985). Cambridge and New York: Cambridge U. Press, 1991. Pp. xiv + 174; bibliography; maps.

Rev. (favorably) by R. S. Levy in *Choice*, 29 (1991), 650–51.

Schweitzer, David. "The Destruction of Some Fox Papers." *Notes and Queries*, 236 (1991), 193.

By Rollo and Agatha Russell, perhaps with Sir G. O. Trevelyan's approval.

Schweizer, Karl. "Lord Bute and British Strategy in the Seven Years War: Further Evidence." *Notes and Queries*, 236 (1991), 189–91.

Scott, H. M. *British Foreign Policy in the Age of the American Revolution.* New York: Oxford U. Press; Oxford: Clarendon Press, 1990. Pp. xiii + 377; bibliography. Cf. *ECCB*, n.s. 16, II: 128–29.

Rev. (favorably) by J. Sainsbury in *Choice*, 28 (1991), 1831.

Setton, Kenneth M. *Venice, Austria, and the Turks in the Seventeenth Century.* (Memoirs Series, 192.) Philadelphia, PA: The American Philosophical Society, 1991. Pp. viii + 502.

While western Europeans wrangled over territorial and constitutional issues in the first half of the seventeenth century, the Venetian noble republic faced a renewed onslaught of Turkish power in the east. That tide rose with the conquest of Crete, then rushed on through Hungary to the gates of Vienna in 1683. The shift from the Mediterranean to the Danubian plains placed the Austrian Habsburgs on the front line against Islam.

Kenneth Setton's book, following upon his justly esteemed work on *The Papacy and the Levant*, tells in painstaking detail the story of these eastern conflicts and the convoluted diplomacy behind them. The main sources are manuscripts from the Venetian archives, and the story as Setton tells it reflects the view from the Adriatic. Some of these documents are quoted at length in the text, or given in full page footnotes in the original. The Austrian part of the Chronicle derives from published sources and secondary works.

This is "histoire événémentielle" in full spate, leaving no tale untold, no engagement unfought. What it does accomplish in a larger sense, however, is to put the eastern conflict between Venice and the Turks squarely in the context of the other great European conflicts at the end of the seventeenth century and the beginning of the eighteenth. The collaboration of Austria and Venice, with the urging and encouragement of the papacy, presented the Turks with two challenging fronts in the west: one in Hungary, the other in the lower Adriatic and the Morea. By 1718, when the treaty of Passarowitz confirmed Habsburg domination of the central Danube, the Venetian state had exhausted its resources trying to hold onto bases in the eastern Mediterranean. The Habsburgs won handsomely, the Venetians were left holding only a few bases guarding the entrance to the Adriatic. The commercial maritime empire of Venice shrank in wealth, while the city itself gradually settled into a magnificent tourist attraction sustained by small craft industry and nostalgia for a departed heroic age.—John P. Spielman.

Seaward, Paul. *The Restoration, 1660–1688.* (British History in Perspective.) New York: St. Martin's Press, 1991. Pp. vii + 173; bibliography.

Seward, Desmond. *Metternich: The First European.* New York: Viking Penguin Group, 1991. Pp. xviii + 300; bibliography.

Shaffer, Arthur H. *To Be an American: David Ramsay and the Making of the American Consciousness.* Columbia, SC: U. of South Carolina Press, 1991. Pp. x + 334; bibliography; illustrations.

Rev. by E. Cassara in *Choice,* 29 (1991), 190; 192.

Sheehan, James J. *German History, 1770–1866.* (The Oxford History of Modern Europe.) New York: Oxford U. Press; Oxford: Clarendon Press, 1989. Pp. xvii + 969; bibliography; maps; tables. Cf. *ECCB,* n.s. 16, II: 130.

Rev. (favorably) by R. S. Levy in *Choice,* 28 (1991), 987.
Parts I–II, "Eighteenth-Century Background" and "Germans and the French Revolution, 1789–1815," are found on pages 9–388.

Sheldon, Garrett Ward. *The Political Philosophy of Thomas Jefferson.* Baltimore, MD: Johns Hopkins U. Press, 1991. Pp. 174.

Sher, Richard B., and Jeffrey R. Smitten (eds.). *Scotland and America in the Age of the Enlightenment.* Princeton, NJ: Princeton U. Press, 1990. Pp. xii + 307; illustrations. Cf. *ECCB,* n.s. 16, II: 130.

Rev. by E. Cassara in *Choice,* 28 (1991), 1213.

Shoemaker, Robert B. *Prosecution and Punishment: Petty Crime and Law in London and Rural Middlesex, c. 1660–1725.* (Cambridge Studies in Early Modern British History.) Cambridge and New York: Cambridge U. Press, 1991. Pp. xviii + 352; appendices; bibliography; illustrations; tables.

Shrader, Charles Reginald (gen. ed.). *Reference Guide to United States Military History.* Vol. I: *1607–1815.* New York and Oxford: Facts on File, 1991. Pp. x + 276; illustrations; maps.

Rev. by G. M. Getchell, Jr. in *Choice*, 29 (1991), 577–78.

Silbey, Joel (ed.). *The Congress of the United States: Its Origins and Early Development.* (Congresses of the United States, 1789–1989, 1.) Brooklyn, NY: Carlson Publishing, 1991. Pp. 544.

Simard, Sylvain (ed.). *La Revolution au Canada Français.* Ottowa, Canada, and Paris: Les Presses de l'Université d'Ottowa, 1991. Pp. 442; illustrations.

Simmons, Marc. *Coronado's Land: Essays on Daily Life in Colonial New Mexico.* Albuquerque, NM: U. of New Mexico Press, 1991. Pp. 183.

Sismondi, J.-C.-L., Simonde de. *New Principles of Political Economy: of Wealth in Its Relation to Population.* Edited and translated from French by Richard Hyse. New Brunswick, NJ: Transaction Books, 1991. Pp. 658.

Smith, Alan K. *Creating a World Economy: Merchant Capital, Colonialism, and World Trade, 1400–1825.* Boulder, CO, and Oxford: Westview Press, 1991. Pp. viii + 318; bibliography.

Smith, Merrill D. *Breaking the Bonds: Marital Discord in Pennsylvania, 1730–1830.* (The American Social Experience Series, 21.) New York: New York U. Press, 1991. Pp. xv + 225; illustrations.

Smith, Murphy D. *"Realms of Gold": A Catalogue of Maps in the Library of the American Philosophical Society.* (Memoirs of the American Philosophical Society, 195.) Philadelphia, PA: American Philosophical Society, 1991. Pp. xxiii + 599; maps; 8 plates.

Solow, Barbara L. (ed.). *Slavery and the Rise of the Atlantic System.* Cambridge and New York: Cambridge U. Press; Cambridge, MA: W. E. B. DuBois Institute for Afro-American Research, Harvard U. Press, 1991. Pp. viii + 355; map.

Spadafora, David. *The Idea of Progress in Eighteenth-Century Britain.* New Haven, CT: Yale U. Press, 1990. Pp. xv + 464. Cf. *ECCB*, n.s. 16, II: 133.

Rev. (favorably) by Richard C. Wiles in *The Scriblerian*, 23 (1991), 274–75.

Spiel, Hilde. *Fanny von Arnstein: A Daughter of the Enlightenment, 1758–1818.* Translation by Christine Shuttleworth of *Fanny von Arnstein: oder, die Emanzipation; ein Frauenleben an der Zeitewende, 1758–1818* (Frankfurt am Main, 1962). Leamington Spa, UK: Berg, (distributed through New York: St. Martin's Press, 1991), 1990. Pp. x + 368.

Spiernburg, Pieter. *The Broken Spell: A Cultural and Anthropological History of Preindustrial Europe.* Translated by Herbert Rowen. New Brunswick, NJ: Rutgers U. Press, 1991. Pp. x + 313; bibliography; 4 illustrations.

Spiernburg, Pieter. *The Prison Experience: Disciplinary Institutions and their Inmates in Early Modern Europe.* London and New Brunswick, NJ: Rutgers U. Press, 1991. Pp. xii + 339; bibliography; figures; illustrations; tables.

Staves, Susan. *Married Women's Separate Property in England, 1660–1833.* Cambridge, MA: Harvard U. Press, 1990. Pp. ix + 290; bibliography. Cf. *ECCB*, n.s. 16, II: 134.

Rev. (with other works) by John Bossy in *TLS*, (Dec. 28, 1990–Jan. 3, 1991), 1393–94; by Lila V. Graves in *South Atlantic Review*, 56 (Sept. 1991), 108–110.

Steegmuller, Francis. *A Woman, A Man, and Two Kingdoms.* New York: Alfred Knopf, 1991.

Steele, Ian K. *Betrayals: Fort William Henry and the Massacre.* New York and Oxford: Oxford U. Press, 1990. Pp. viii + 250; bibliography; illustrations. Cf. *ECCB*, n.s. 16, II: 134.

Rev. (favorably) by R. D. Edmunds in *Choice*, 28 (1991), 993–94.

Stichweh, Rudolf. *Der frühmoderne Staat und die europäische Universität. Zur Interaktion von Politik und Erziehungssystem im Prozess ihrer Ausdifferenzierung (16.–18. Jahrhundert).* Frankfurt am Main: Suhrkamp, 1991. Pp. 427.

Stitt, J. Michael. *A Tale Type and Motif Index of Early U. S. Almanacs.* (Bibliographies & Indexes in American Literature, 14.) New York: Greenwood Press/Greenwood Publishing Group, Inc., 1991. Pp. 382.

Stokesbury, James L. *A Short History of the American Revolution.* New York: William Morrow & Co., 1991. Pp. 304.

Stone, Lawrence. *Road to Divorce: England 1530–1987.* New York: Oxford U. Press; Oxford: Clarendon Press, 1990. Pp. xxvii + 460; 32 illustrations. Cf. *ECCB*, n.s. 16, II: 134.

Rev. (with other works) by John Bossy in *TLS*, (Dec. 28, 1990–Jan. 3, 1991), 1393–94; by Keith Thomas in *New York Review of Books*, 38 (March 7, 1991), 30–33.

Subrahmanyam, Sanjay. *Improvising Empire: Portugese Trade and Settlement in the Bay of Bengal, 1500–1700.* New Delhi and Oxford: Oxford U. Press, 1990. Pp. xix + 269; maps. Cf. *ECCB*, n.s. 16, II: 134.

Rev. by N. R. Bennett in *Choice*, 29 (1991), 646.

Swanson, Carl E. *Predators and Prizes: American Privateering and Imperial Warfare, 1739–1748.* (Studies in Maritime History.) Columbia, SC: U. of South Carolina Press, 1991. Pp. xvii + 299; bibliography; illustrations; maps.

Rev. (favorably) by B. H. Gorene in *Choice*, 29 (1991), 192.

Sys, Jacques, (ed.). *Espace des Revolutions. Paris-Londres 1688–1848.* Lille: Université Charles-de-Gaulle, 1991. Pp. 157.

The space mentioned in the title of the book is not only geographical and political, but even more, dialectical and esthetic. I will concentrate on the problems of revolutions in England and France. The question is treated in two chapters on the Glorious Revolution—one on James II's personality as a monarch and as an individual, the second on 1688 as viewed by the French liberal Guizot—and in two chapters on de Bonald and Burke, the archetypes of counterrevolutionary thought in both countries. The study on James II is particularly illuminating and shows us that even though imbued with the ideal of absolute monarchy, Charles II's brother was the first sovereign to give English dissenters access to all the offices in the realm and the question asked is "Jacques II roi révoulutionnaire?." Guizot, Louis-Philippe's last prime minister, asks himself if France will find one day a process that could put an end for good and all to all revolutions, the same question being posed by Tocqueville. In French political liberal thought, 1688 stands as the archetypal revolutionary success, less emphasis being laid on the various stages that preceded it which were similar to the French Revolution (execution of a king, military dictatorship, bloody civil wars in Scotland and Ireland and so on).

De Bonald's *Théorie du pouvoir politique et religieux* (1796) is aptly considered as the first counterrevolutionary study and the article points out how the book views the turn of the century as a period in which "le temps est déboussolé, l'homme perdu, définitivement soumis à son seul juge, qui seul décidera du salut. La foi sauve, maintenant que l'histoire est perdue" (p. 85). A return to faith and order—and not the construction of a new system based on law and order—was the ulimate goal of de Bonald and Joseph de Maistre. In Burke's vision, the French Revolution stands as the dragon pursuing the women in labor in John's *Apocalypse*: "To us it is a Collosus which bestrides our channel. It has one foot on a foreign shore, the other upon the British soil" (*Works*, London, 1885, vol. V, p. 165) and all future sanitary cordon policies are legitimate. The present anthology is useful and well-researched but would need more of an initial presentation and final synthesis and more organic kinks between the different chapters.—Jean Rivière.

Szostak, Rick. *The Role of Transportation in the Industrial Revolution: A Comparison of England and France.* Montreal and Kingston: McGill-Queen's U. Press, 1991. Pp. 331; bibliography; figures; tables.

Historians have properly been wary of single causation, and Professor Szostak is no exception. Transportation serves as the ground-bass, the continuo, of this comparative discourse on the progress of aspects of eighteenth-century industrialization in France and England. With recurring insistence, Szostak gives the role of transportation its due, providing a structure for what becomes a richly detailed analysis that clarifies and revises much of what is known about eighteenth-century transportation in particular and the Industrial Revolution in general.

As is traditional, England and the iron and textile industries serve as the model for this study and receive the most detailed attention. What is less customary, and what gives special scope to the book, is the use of France and less well known industries, such as the metals trade, bleaching, and pottery, as control factors. This approach, together with the common reference point of transportation, provides a fresh look at the early process of industrialization. It also makes what the English achieved even more impressive than is generally accepted.

Szostak sees the Industrial Revolution as the result of four interrelated processes: increased regional specialization; the emergence of new industries; expanding production; and increased technological innovation. Eighteenth-century industrial development, whether in major enterprises such as textiles or in less well known ones such as nails or needles, was the product of these processes, each of which was affected by improvements in transportation. Szostak views transportation as instrumental in providing supplies necessary for growth and satisfying the demand necessary to sustain it. How important this is becomes clear in the comparison of English and French transportation facilities. Eighteenth-century improvements in England's transportation network—roads, canals, harbors—explain the rapid development of the four processes of industrialization there; the non-occurance of the same processes in France was the result of failure to improve French transportation significantly. Szostak's comparisons emphasize the theme of his book: though transportation improvements are not sufficient cause for industrial development, they are necessary for it.

Careful and judicious accumulation of detail sustains Szostak's thesis and provides a vivid account of the economic side of English and French societies in the eighteenth century. Szostak admits to being "decidedly in favor" of approaching economic history by looking at interesting historical questions and then choosing the most suitable tools for analyzing them (p. 233). He has command of the tools of analysis–for example, he begins with a consideration of recent literature on the Industrial Revolution and a discussion of Smithian and Schumpeterian theories of growth.

For Szostak, the Industrial Revolution is not a simple story to be explained by the steam engine or even railroads, but a matter of slow and not always recognized, interrelated efforts in many areas. Rather than being a cataclysmic process, industrial progress was an unfolding, often preceded and always expedited by improvements in transportation. The monuments to industrial growth, such as the steam engine, and industrial heroes, such as Watt or Boulton, are seen in a proper light, and the culmination of a long series of tinkerers and mechanics who provided the basics of technological change. Szostak sees the progress of development in the iron and textile industries as resting on improvemtns by unknown artisans. The Industrial Revolution, Szostak agress with Maxine Berg, "was an age of improvement" (p. 223).

Szostak believes that his analysis may be applied to other than the customary iron and textile industries. He himself applies it to pottery, in a sort of appendix to the present study, and expressed the hope other eighteenth-century industries will be investigated by others. Szostak has provided a fine example for them. In always touching base with transportation improvements, he has provided a coherent structure for his discussion, a structure greatly strengthened by the support he finds in eighteenth-century sources which comment on the necessity of transportation for economic growth. There is a sort of poignancy in the French sources, clearly aware of what was needed and of the success of the English example, clearly unable to do anything about the inadequacies of transportation in France. Such contemporary comments are powerful support for Szostak's thesis.

The book is carefully documented, with extensive explanatory endnotes. These have inherent interest but do not impede the argument or the narrative. What is undeniably a book with a thesis is really much more—a lively narrative which makes the reader reconsider an exciting century.—Charles A. Le Guin.

Tagg, James. *Benjamin Franklin Bache and the* Philadelphia Aurora. Philadelphia, PA: U. of Pennsylvania Press, 1991. Pp. xiv + 439.

Tatterfield, Nigel. *The Forgotten Trade: Comprising the Log of the "Daniel and Henry" of 1700 and Accounts of the Slave Trade from the Minor Ports of England, 1698–1725.* London: Jonathan Cape-Random Century Group, 1991. Pp. 416.

Thesing, William (ed.). *Executions and the British Experience from the Seventeenth to the Twentieth Century: A Collection of Essays.* Jefferson, NC: McFarland and Co., 1991. Pp. 192.

Rev. by Thomas Curley in *South Atlantic Review*, 56 (May 1991), 172–76.

Thomas, Clive S. *American Union in Federalist Political Thought.* (Political Theory & Political Philosophy.) [Rev. thesis, London School of Economics and Political Science, 1979.] New York: Garland Publishers, 1991. Pp. 288.

Thomas, Peter D. G. *Tea Party to Independence: The Third Phase of the American Revolution, 1773–1776.* New York: Oxford U. Press; Oxford: Clarendon Press, 1991. Pp. 357; bibliography.

Rev. (favorably) by Paul Langford in *TLS*, (Dec. 20, 1991), 12.
Concludes his trilogy on the British politics of the American Revolution. Cf. His *British Politics and the Stamp Act Crisis: The First Phase of the American Revolution, 1763–1767*, 1975. Cf. *ECCB*, n.s. 11: 97–98 and his *The Townshend Duties Crisis: The Second Phase of the American Revolution, 1767–1773*, 1987.

Thompson, E. P. *Customs in Common.* London: Merlin Press; New York: The New Press, 1991. Pp. xi + 547; 32 illustrations.

Thompson, F. M. L. (ed.). *The Cambridge Social History of Britain, 1750–1950.* Vol. I: *Regions and Communities.* Vol. II: *People and Their Environment.* Vol. III: *Social Agencies and Institutions.* Cambridge and New York: Cambridge U. Press, 1990. Pp. xv + 588; bibliography; tables; xv + 373; bibliography; xiii + 492; bibliography. Cf. *ECCB*, n.s. 16, II: 136.

Rev. (together with reservations) by F. Coetzee in *Choice*, 28 (1991), 982.

Tillson, Albert H., Jr. *Gentry and Common Folk: Political Culture on a Virginia Frontier, 1740–1789.* Lexington, KY: U. Press of Kentucky, 1991. Pp. 228; bibliography; illustrations.

Titus, James. *The Old Dominion at War: Society, Politics, and Warfare in Late Colonial Virginia.* (American Military History.) Columbia, SC: U. of South Carolina Press, 1990. Pp. xii + 213; bibliography. Cf. *ECCB*, n.s. 16, II: 136.

Rev. by H. M. Ward in *Choice*, 29 (1991), 343.

Todd, Christopher. *Political Bias, Censorship and the Dissolution of the "Official" Press in Eighteenth Century France.* (Studies in French Civilization, 8.) Lewiston, NY: Edwin Mellen Press, 1991. Pp. iv + 433.

Tracy, James E. (ed.). *The Rise of Merchant Empires: Long-Distance Trade in the Early Modern World, 1350–1750.* (Studies in Comparative Early Modern History.) Cambridge and New York: Cambridge U. Press, 1990. Pp. ix + 442; illustrations; maps. Cf. *ECCB*, n.s. 16, II: 136.

Rev. by R. O. Lindsay in *Choice*, 28 (1991), 838.

Troyansky, David G., Alfred Cismaru, and Norwood Andrews, Jr. (eds.). *The French Revolution in Culture and Society.* (Contributions to the Study of World History, 23.) New York: Greenwood Press, 1991. Pp. xvii + 221; bibliography.

The aim of the book is not so much to determine the part played by the French Revolution in changing or maintaining culture in its social context as to deal with the issue of the timing of change. Things changed, no doubt, but did they change before, during or after the revolutionary turmoil? As such, this volume is a broad-minded anthology of articles linking social and cultural history, combining old and new approaches, but always based on sound psychological and demographic studies and/or textual analysis and research in local halls of records. The work of dismantling ancien régime insititutions and mentalities is covered mainly in Part I, but Part II reminds us that the new democratic culture chose freely from the stock-in-trade of western culture and in Part III we see in many revolutionary cultural developments the harbinger of nineteenth century movements, mainly Romanticism. Part IV reveals not only the varieties of approaches taken by historians in order to understand eighteenth century France, especially in the study of crime, poverty and demography, but also puts in due relative perspective the novelty of the Revolution.

    Among the many symposia and colloquia devoted to the French Revolution around the bicentennial, the one held on the campus of Texas Tech University from 6 to 8 October 1988 was fully attuned to the new trend taken by Revolutionary history away from the cellar of historical determinism to the attic of mentalities and social behavior.

"This volume,"says Troynasky, "the product of individual specialists, is offered in the hope of seeing the Revolution whole" (p. xv). All articles make significant contributions to that purpose thanks to their impeccable scholarship and perfect sense of chronology. Being able to address such various topics as justice, contraception, the Revolutionary calendar or the influence of Figaro, among many others, and to sustain our interest throughout is in itself a welcome *tour de force*.—Jean Rivière.

Urlsperger, Samuel. *Detailed Reports on the Salzburger Emigrants who Settled in America, vol. 16, 1753–54.* Edited and translated from German by G. F. Jones. Athens, GA: U. of Georgia Press, 1991. Pp. 241.

Vann, Richard T., and David Eversley. *Friends in Life and Death: the British and Irish Quakers in the Demographic Transition.* (Cambridge Studies in Population, Economy and Society in Past Time, 16.) Cambridge and New York: Cambridge U. Press, 1991. Pp. xx + 283; figures; tables.

Van Ravenswaay, Charles. *Saint Louis: An Informal History of the City and Its People, 1764–1865.* Edited by Candace O'Connor. Champaign, IL: U. of Illinois Press; Missouri Historical Society, 1991. Pp. 568.

Veit, Helen E. (ed.). *Creating the Bill of Rights: The Documentary Record from the First Federal Congress.* Baltimore, MD: Johns Hopkins U. Press, 1991. Pp. xxiv + 323.

Venturi, Franco. *The End of the Old Regime in Europe, 1776–1789.* Vol. I: *The Great States of the West.* Vol. II: *Republican Patriotism and the Empires of the East.* Translation by R. Burr Litchfield of *Settecento riformatore.* Vol. IV: *La caduta dell'Antico Regime (1776–1789);* pt. 1: *I grandi stati dell'Occidente;* pt. 2: *Il patriottissmo repubblicano e gli imperi dell'Est* (Turin, 1984. Cf. *ECCB*, n.s. 11, II: 181.) Oxford and Princeton, NJ: Princeton U. Press, 1991. Pp. xiv + 455; 459–1044; 16 illustrations.

Rev. (favorably) by D. C. Baxter in *Choice*, 29 (1991), 182.

The Voyage of Sutil *and* Mexicana, *1792: The Last Spanish Exploration of the Northwest Coast of America.* Translated with an Introduction by John Kendrick of *Relación del viage hecho por las goletas* Sutil y Mexicana *en el año de 1792 para reconocer el Estrecho de Fuga.* (Northwest Historical Series, 16.) Spokane, WA: Arthur H. Clark Co., 1991. Pp. 260; illustrations; maps.

Ville, Simon P. *Transport and the Development of the European Economy, 1750–1918.* London: Macmillan; New York: St. Martin's Press, 1990. Pp. xiii + 252; bibliography; 12 illustrations. Cf. *ECCB*, n.s. 16, II: 138.

Rev. by B. Osborne in *Choice*, 28 (1991), 1548.

Vovelle, Michel. *Ideologies and Mentalities.* Translation by Eamon O'Flaherty of *Idéologies et mentalités* (Paris, 1982). Chicago, IL: U. of Chicago Press; Oxford: Polity Press, 1990. Pp. 263. Cf. *ECCB*, n.s. 16, II: 138.

Rev. (with reservations and with other works) by Colin Jones in *TLS*, (Mar. 29, 1991), 7–8.

Walthall, John A. (ed.). *French Colonial Archaeology: The Illinois Country and the Western Great Lakes*. Urbana, IL: U. of Illinois Press, 1991. Pp. 290; bibliography; illustrations; maps.

Ward, Harry M. *Colonial America, 1607–1763*. Englewood Cliffs, NJ: Prentice-Hall, 1991. Pp. xii + 436; bibliography; illustrations; maps.

Rev. by C. R. Allen, Jr. in *Choice*, 29 (1991), 343.

Washington, George. *Papers. Revolutionary War Series, 4: April–June 1776*. Edited by P.D. Chase. Charlottesville, VA: U. Press of Virginia, 1991. Pp. xxv + 589.

Wasmus, J. F. *An Eyewitness Account of the American Revolution and New England Life: The Journal of J. F. Wasmus, German Company Surgeon, 1776–1783*. Translated by Mary C. Lynne. (Contributions in Military Studies, 106.) New York: Greenwood Press, 1990. Pp. xxxiii + 311; illustrations. Cf. *ECCB*, n.s. 16, II: 139.

Rev. by J. C. Arndt in *Choice*, 28 (1991), 846.

Weddle, Robert S. *The French Thorn: Rival Explorers in the Spanish Sea, 1682–1762*. College Station, TX: Texas A&M U. Press, 1991. Pp. xi + 435; bibliography; illustrations; maps.

Weigley, Russell F. *The Age of Battles: The Quest for Decisive Warfare from Breitenfeld to Waterloo*. Bloomington, IN: Indiana U. Press, 1991. Pp. xviii + 579; maps.

Rev. (favorably) by P. L. de Rosa in *Choice*, 29 (1991), 507.

White, Richard. *The Middle Ground: Indians, Empires, and Republics in the Great Lakes Region, 1650–1815*. (Cambridge Studies in North American Indian History.) Cambridge and New York: Cambridge U. Press, 1991. Pp. xvi + 544; bibliography; illustrations; maps; tables.

White, Shane. *Somewhat More Independent: The End of Slavery in New York City, 1770–1810*. Athens, GA: U. of Georgia Press, 1991. Pp. xxix + 278; bibliography; maps.

Rev. (favorably) by K. Edgerton in *Choice*, 29 (1991), 192.

Whyte, Ian and Kathleen Whyte. *The Changing Scottish Landscape: 1500–1800*. London and New York: Routledge, 1991. Pp. 251; maps; plates.

Will, Pierre-Etienne. *Bureaucracy and Famine in Eighteenth-Century China*. Translation by Elborg Forster of *Bureaucratie et famine en Chine au 18e siècle* (Paris: 1980). Stanford, CA: Stanford U. Press, 1990. Pp. xiv + 364; bibliography; maps; tables. Cf. *ECCB*, n.s. 16, II: 140.

Rev. (favorably) by F. Ng in *Choice*, 28 (1991), 832.

Williams, Glyndwr, and Alan Frost (eds.). *"Terra Australis" to Australia*. Melbourne, Australia: Oxford U. Press in association with the Australian Academy of the Humanities, 1988. Pp. 242. Cf. *ECCB*, n.s. 16, II: 140.

Rev. by Michael Cartwright in *Eighteenth-Century Studies*, 24 (1991), 393–96.

Winearls, Joan. *Mapping Under Canada, 1780–1867: An Annotated Bibliography of Manuscript and Printed Maps.* Toronto, Canada: U. of Toronto Press, 1991. Pp. xli + 986.

Winius, George D., and Marcus P. M. Vink. *The Merchant-Warrior Pacified: The VOC (The Dutch East India Company) and its Changing Political Economy in India.* Delhi, Bombay and Calcutta: Oxford U. Press, 1991. Pp. 201; appendix; bibliography; illustrations.

Withey, Lynne. *Voyages of Discovery: Captain Cook and the Exploration of The Pacific.* Berkeley and Los Angeles, CA: U. of California Press, 1989. Pp. 512.

Rev. by Michael Cartwright in *Eighteenth-Century Studies*, 24 (1991), 390–93.

Withington, Ann Fairfax. *Toward a More Perfect Union: Virtue and the Formation of American Republics.* New York and Oxford: Oxford U. Press, 1991. Pp. xvi + 264; 18 illustrations; tables.

Woods, C. J. (ed.). *Journals and Memoirs of Thomas Russell, 1791–5.* Foreword by Marianne Elliott. Belfast: Irish Academic Press in association with the Linen Hall Library, 1991. Pp. 199.

Woodman, David C. *Unraveling the Franklin Disaster: Inuit Testimony.* (McGill-Queen's Series in Native & Northern Studies, 5.) Downsview, Ontario: McGill-Queen's U. Press/U. of Toronto Press, 1991. Pp. 390.

Woodward, R. L. *Princetonians: A Biographical Dictionary, 1784–1790.* Princeton, NJ: Princeton U. Press, 1991. Pp. lxiii + 577.

Main entry changed with 1784–1790 from author: Harrison, Richard A., to title.

Woolf, Stuart (ed.). *Domestic Strategies: Work and Family in France and Italy (1600–1800).* Cambridge and New York: Cambridge U. Press, 1991. Pp. viii + 207; bibliography; figures; tables.

Woolf, Stuart. *Napoleon's Integration of Europe.* London and New York: Routledge, 1991. Pp. ix + 319; appendix; bibliography; maps.

Stuart Woolf's *Napoleon's Integration of Europe* marks a major departure. It focuses less on military, high political or biographical history than comparable previous studies. Instead administrative structures and political culture are stressed, and more attention is given to annexed territories or satelites. It is based on secondary literature and thus the subject matter is often familiar, but the author's command of an enviable number of languages enables him to utilize sources not readily accesible to all scholars. Moreover Prof. Woolf's central theme of integration informs every passage.

The main lines of argument can be summarized as follows. The Enlightenment believed that universal principles of government could be applied to achieve progress. The Revolution descredited representative government, but faith in a uniform, rationalised model of administration based on statistical analyses remained, because this model was developed in France at the forefront of civilization. After military victories, application of the model became a means of attracting non-French elites to accept an Integrated Empire.

Working against integration were two main obstacles. Attempts to impose uniformity confronted the diversity of European traditions and practices; radical reform shocked sensibilities and threatened vested interests. Nevertheless it would appear that so long as it was stable, the Empire made steady progress against all resistance. More destructive were contradictions within Imperial policy as a whole. Napoleon's 'France first' priorities, especially in the Continental System, created economic dislocation and fostered incessant, burdensome warfare. Creation of a new nobility ruined one of the purported attributes of the model administration, balanced budgets, and undermined uniformity by creating intermediary bodies between the individual and the state.

Prof. Woolf has brought a very significant phenomenon to the forefront. It was not just French elites who saw the value of the new administrative model; the reforms of pre-1789 Enlightened despots, and contemporaneous reforms under Speranski and Czartoryske in Russia and Stein and Hardenberg in Prussia, all testify that this was a European-wide development. Although brief, the author's discussion of the relation of the Napoleonic model to subsequent nationalism, liberalism and integration is illuminating. In France, continued belief in the model was manifested in the efforts of Restoration prefects such as Malouet to maintain professionalism in the face of reactionary forces, and in the statistical reports of Villeneuve-Bargemont on the impact of industrialization at Lille.

In addition to the centrality of the new administrative model to state development, the very topic of integration makes this a work of broad interest. Passages on resistance and collaboration should sharpen our understanding of similarities and differences to the Nazi New Order. Historians of contemporary European integration will also find much to ponder, while Prof. Woolf's remarks concerning the extent of nationalism should prove an antidote to facile comparisons.

One can always quibble. The character of Napoleon permeates even in this non-biographical study, while the artisans remain rather faceless. There are numerous biographical sketches and quotations from statistical memoirs, but these are scattered in various parts of the book. A chapter on the chief proponents of integration might have been useful, especially had it explored to what extent such individuals were aware of the contradictions within general Imperial policy, and whether their belief in integration led them to criticize the destructive elements of incessant warfare and 'France first.' These comments are only suggestions for further consideration rather than criticisms. In short, this work is a major contribution to scholarship. It should stimulate new approaches to study of the Empire, while contributing to work in prior and subsequent periods.—R. S. Alexander.

Yarak, Larry W. *Asante and the Dutch, 1744–1873.* (Oxford Studies in African Affairs.) New York: Oxford U. Press; Oxford: Clarendon Press, 1990. Pp. xiv + 316; bibliography; illustrations; maps; tables. Cf. *ECCB*, n.s. 16, II: 141.

Rev. (favorably) by S. A. Harmon in *Choice*, 28 (1991), 1687.

Yiannias, John J. (ed.). *The Byzantine Tradition after the Fall of Constantinople.* Charlottesville, VA, and London: U. Press of Virginia, 1991. Pp. xiv + 354; figures.

Zagarri, Rosemarie (ed.). *David Humphrey's "Life of General Washington" with George Washington's "Remarks."* Athens, GA, and London: The U. of Georgia Press, 1991. Pp. lvii + 129; bibliography; illustrations.

Philosophy, Science, and Religion

Abelove, Henry. *The Evangelist of Desire: John Wesley and the Methodists*. Stranford, CA: Stanford U. Press, 1990. Pp. 136. Cf. *ECCB*, n.s. 16, III: 143.

Rev. by Richard E. Brantley in *Eighteenth-Century Studies*, 25 (1991) 250–54.

Adams, Geoffrey. *The Huguenots and French Opinion, 1685–1787: The Enlightenment Debate Over Toleration*. (Editions S.R, 1.) Waterloo: Wilfred Laurier U. for the Canadian Corporation for Studies in Religion, 1991. Pp. xiv + 335.

Åkerman, Susanna. *Queen Christina of Sweden and Her Circle: The Transformation of a Seventeenth-Century Philosophical Libertine*. Copenhagen and New York: E. J. Brill, 1991. Pp. xv + 339.

Albertini, Ippolito Francesco, and others. *Clinical Consultations and Letters by Ippolito Francesco Albertini, Francesco Torti, and Other Physicians*. University of Bologna MS 2089-1. Translated and annotated by Saul Jarcho. Boston: Francis A. Countway Library of Medicine, 1989. Pp. lxxxi + 356.

Rev. (favorably) by Richard F. Grady in *Bulletin of the New York Academy of Medicine*, 67 (1991), 399-401.

Alchon, Suzanne Austin. *Native Society and Disease in Colonial Ecuador*. (Cambridge Latin American Studies, 71.) Cambridge and New York: Cambridge U. Press, 1991. Pp. viii +151; bibliography; maps.

Appleby, John H. "Robert Dingley, F. R. S. (1710–1781), Merchant, Architect and Pioneering Philanthropist." *Notes and Records of the Royal Society of London*, 45 (1991), 139–154.

Ariew, Roger, and Peter Baker (eds.). *Revolution and Continuity: Essays in the History and Philosophy of Early Modern Science*. (Studies in Philosophy and the History of Philosophy, 24.) Washington, D.C: The Catholic U. of America Press, 1991. Pp. 222; bibliography.

Arkes, Hadley. *Beyond the Constitution*. Princeton, NJ: Princeton U. Press, 1990. Pp. 278. Cf. *ECCB*, n.s. 16, III: 144.

Rev. (favorably) by M. A. Foley in *Choice,* 28 (1991), 1566.

Arner, Robert D. *Dobson's Encyclopaedia: The Publisher, Text, and Publication of America's First Britannica, 1789–1803*. Philadelphia, PA: U. of Pennsylvania Press, 1991. Pp. 295.

Artigas-Menant, Geneviève. "La Vulgarisation Scientifique Dans *Le Nouveau Magasin Français* De Mme Leprince De Beaumont." *Revue d'histoire des sciences,* 44 (1991), 343–357.

Azouvi, François. "Magétisme animal. La Sensation infinie." *Dix-huitième siècle,* 21 (1991), 107–18.

Baily, Susan. *Saints, Goddesses and Kings: Muslims and Christians in South Indian Society, 1700–1900.* (Cambridge South Asian Studies, 43.) Cambridge and New York: Cambridge U. Press, 1989.

Rev. by André Padou in *Archives des sciences sociales des religions,* (1991), 216–17.

Barret-Kriegel, Blandine. *La Défaite de l'érudition.* Paris: Presses Universitaires de France, 1988.

Rev. by Emile Poulat in *Archives des sciences sociales des religions,* (1991), 222–23.

Barret-Kriegel, Blandine. *La République incertaine.* Paris: Presses Universitaires de France, 1988.

Rev. by Emile Poulat in *Archives des sciences sociales des religions,* (1991), 222–23.

Barret-Kriegel, Blandine. *Les Académies de l'histoire.* Paris: Presses Universitaires de France, 1988.

Rev. by Emile Poulat in *Archives des sciences sociales des religions,* (1991), 222–23.

Barret-Kriegel, Blandine. *Les Historiens de la monarchie.* Paris: Presses Universitaires de France, 1988.

Rev. by Emile Poulat in *Archives des sciences sociales des religions,* (1991), 222–23.

Barker, William S. "The Hemphill Case, Benjamin Franklin and Subscription to the Westminster Confession." *American Presbyterian,* 69 (1991), 243–56.

Barry, Jonathan, and Colin Jones (eds.). *Medicine and Charity Before the Welfare State.* (Studies in the Social History of Medicine.) London and New York: Routledge, 1991. Pp. x + 259; tables.

Baxter, Richard. *Calendar of the Correspondence of Richard Baxter.* Vol I: *1638–1660.* Vol. II: *1660–1696.* Edited by N. H. Keeble and Geoffrey F. Nuttall. Oxford: Clarendon Press, 1991. Pp. xl + 433.

Bechler, Zev. *Newton's Physics and the Conceptual Structure of the Scientific Revolution.* Boston, MA, and London: Kluwer Academic Publishers, 1991. Pp. xviii + 588; appendices; bibliography; figures.

Beddard, Robert (ed.). *The Revolutions of 1688.* (The Andrew Browning Lectures, 1988.) New York: Oxford U. Press; Oxford: Clarendon Press, 1991. Pp. 313.

Bell, James F. "The Late-Twentieth Century Resolution of a Mid-Nineteenth Century Dilemma Generated by the Eighteenth-Century Experiments on Ernst Chladni on the Dynamics of Rods." *Archive for History of the Exact Sciences*, 43 (1991), 273.

Benedict, Philip. *The Huguenot Population of France, 1600–1685: The Demographic Fate and Customs of a Religious Minority*. Philadelphia, PA: American Philosophical Society, 1991. Pp. ix + 164.

Benvenuto, Edoardo. *An Introduction to the History of Structural Mechanics, Pt.1: Statics and Resistance of Solids*. New York: Springer-Verlag, 1991. Pp. xxi + 306.

Benvenuto, Edoardo. *An Introduction to the History of Structural Mechanics, Pt. II: Vaulted Structures and Elastic Systems*. New York: Springer-Verlag, 1991. Pp. xxi + 245.

Set completed with this volume.

Berlin, Isaiah. *The Crooked Timber of Humanity: Chapters in the History of Ideas*. Edited by Henry Hardy. London: J. Murray, 1990; New York: A. A. Knopf, 1991. Pp. xii + 276.

Rev. by M. A Michael in *Choice*, 29 (1991), 295; (favorably) in article ("Paradise Lost") by Conor Cruise O'Brien in *New York Review of Books*, 38 (Apr. 25, 1991), 52; 54–60.

    Includes eight essays: "The Decline of Utopian Ideals in the West" (1978), "Giambattista Vico and Cultural European Thought" (1983), "Alleged Relativism in Eighteenth-Century European Thought" (1980), and "Joseph de Maistre and the Origins of Fascism" (published in *The New York Review of Books*, Sept. 27, Oct. 11, and Oct. 25, 1990).

Blamires, D. *Quakerism and its Manchester Connexions: An Exhibition Held in the John Rylands Library 6 February–23 May 1991*. 1991. Pp. 28.

Bloom, Allan (ed.), with the assistance of Steven J. Kautz. *Confronting the Constitution: The Challenge to Locke, Montesquieu, Jefferson, and the Federalists from Utilitarianism, Historicism, Marxism, Freudianism, Pragmatism, Existentialism. . . .* (AEI Studies, 496.) London and Washington, D.C.: American Enterprise Institute for Public Policy Research, 1990. Pp. xi + 552. Cf. *ECCB*, n.s. 16, III: 148.

Rev. (favorably) by R. J. Steamer in *Choice*, 28 (1991), 1223.

Bost, Hubert (ed.). *Genèse et enjeux de la laïcité*. Actes du Colloque de la Faculté de théologie protestante de Montpellier. Geneva: Labor et Fides, 1990.

Rev. by Hubert Bost in *Etudes thélogiques et religieuses*, 1 (1991), 158–59.

    Contains articles by Hubert Bost and Didier Poton on Elie Merlat and on Protestant loyalism to the monarchy at the time of the Edict of Nantes, by Jacques Proust on the Enlightenment philosophers views of the secularization of education, and by C. Langlois on the extent to which the French Revolution initiated a process of secularization.

Bostyn, Nicole, Michel Cloet, and Katrien de Vrees. *Repertorium van de dekenale visitatierverslagen betreffende de Mechelse kerkprovincie (1559–1801)*. Louvain: Centre Belge d'Histoire Rurale, 1989.

Rev. by Jan Art in *Archives des sciences sociales des religions*, (1991), 222–23.

Bowie, Andrew. *Aesthetics and Subjectivity: From Kant to Nietzsche.* Manchester, UK, and New York: Manchester U. Press (distributed in the U.S. and Canada through New York: St. Martin's Press), 1990. Pp. viii + 284. Cf. *ECCB*, n.s. 16, III: 148.

Rev. (favorably) by Nicholas Davey in *The British Journal of Aesthetics,* 31 (1991), 244–45; by N. Lukacher in *Choice,* 28 (1991), 946–47.

Bradley, James E. *Religion, Revolution, and English Radicalism: Nonconformity in Eighteenth-Century Politics and Society.* Cambridge and New York: Cambridge U. Press, 1990. Pp. xxi + 473; bibliography; figures; map; tables.

Rev. by John Adamson in *TLS,* (June 7, 1991), 5–6; (favorably) by P. K. Cline in *Choice,* 28 (1991), 1542.

Breen, Louise A. "Cotton Mather, the 'Angelical Ministry' and Innoculation." *Journal of the History of Medicine and Allied Sciences,* 46 (1991), 333–357.

Brégeon, Jean-Joël, and Reynald Sécher (eds.). *Gracchus Babeuf. La Guerre de la Vendée et le système de dépopulation.* Paris: Tallendier, 1987. Cf. *ECCB*, n.s. 16, III: 150.

Rev. by Emile Poulat in *Archives des sciences sociales des religions,* (1989), 325.

Bricker, Phillip and R. I. G. Hughes (eds.). *Philosophical Perspectives on Newtonian Science.* Cambridge, MA: MIT Press, 1990. Pp. vi + 248. Cf. *ECCB*, n.s. 16, III: 150.

Rev. by P. D. Skiff in *Choice,* 28 (1991), 954.

Brock, Peter. *The Quaker Peace Testimony, 1660 to 1914.* York, U. K: Sessions Book Trust (distributed through Syracuse, NY: Syracuse U. Press), 1990. Pp. viii + 387; bibliography; illustrations. Cf. *ECCB*, n.s. 16, III: 150.

Rev. by T. D. Hamm in *Choice,* 28 (1991), 1551.

Brooks, Randall C. "The Development of Micrometers in the Seventeenth, Eighteenth, and Nineteenth Centuries." *Journal for the History of Astronomy,* 22 (1991), 127–173.

Brown, Clifford. *Leibniz and Strawson: A New Essay in Descriptive Metaphysics. Introductions.* Munich: Philosophia Verlag; Vienna: Hamden, 1990.

A brilliant, methodical work dealing with a 1959 account of Leibniz by P. F. Strawson who demonstrated great vigor in confronting Leibniz with his great predecessors and with such modern philosophers as Bertrand Russell.

Brown, Richard. *Church and State in Modern Britain, 1700–1850.* London and New York: Routledge, 1990. Pp. xiii + 571; bibliography; illustrations. Cf. *ECCB*, n.s. 16, III: 150.

Rev. by J. R. Breihan in *Choice,* 29 (1991), 647.

Burns, J. H. with Mark Goldie. *The Cambridge History of Political Thought, 1450–1700.* Cambridge and New York: Cambridge U. Press, 1991. Pp. xii + 798; bibliography.

Rev. by Theodore K. Rabb in *TLS,* (Dec. 13, 1991), 26.

Burwick, Fredrick. *Illusion and the Drama: Critical Theory of the Enlightenment and Romantic Era*. College Station, PA: Pennsylvania State U. Press, 1991. Pp. 336.

Butler, Jon. *Awash in a Sea of Faith: Christianizing the American People*. Cambridge, MA: Harvard U. Press, 1990. Pp. 360.

Rev. by Patricia Bonomi in *The William and Mary Quarterly*, 48 (1991), 118–24; by Harvey Jackson in *Eighteenth-Century Studies*, 24 (1991), 386–90; by Richard W. Pointer in *The Catholic Historical Review*, 77 (1991), 331–32; by John E. Wilson in *Princeton Studies Bulletin*, 11 (1990), 189–91; by John F. Woolverton in *American Theological Journal*, 72 (1990), 473–76.

Campbell, Ted A. *The Religion of the Heart: A Study of European Religious Life in the Seventeenth and Eighteenth Centuries*. Columbia, SC: U. of South Carolina Press, 1991. Pp. xii + 218.

Rev. by Richard Muller in *Journal of Religion*, 73 (1991), 261–62.

Cantor, Geoffrey, and David C. Lindberg. *The Discourse of Light from the Middle Ages to the Enlightenment*. Los Angeles, CA: U. of California Press, 1985. Cf. *ECCB*, n.s. 11, III: 200.

Rev. by M. Elie in *Etudes philosophiques*, (1991), 123–28.
    Contains an article by G. Cantor that deals with Locke, William Law, and John Hutchinson (1674–1737).

Canup, John. *Tout of the Wilderness: The Emergence of an American Identity in Colonial New England*. Hanover, NH: Wesleyan U. Press, 1990. Pp. 303.

Rev. by Christopher Grasso in *Journal of Church and State*, 33 (1991), 617–18.

Capul, Maurice. *Infirmité et hérésie. Les enfants placés sous l'Ancien Régime*. Toulouse, France: Privat, 1990.

Rev. by Didier Poton in *Etudes théologiques et religieuses*, 1 (1991), 131–32.
    Part of the book deals with children abducted from their homes, in most cases, Protestants, to secure their religious "reeducation," a phenomenon that first manifested itself in 1615 but continued throughout the eighteenth century. A very interesting work which shows that the authorities perceived parish education to be a failure which had to be replaced by a more drastic system of substitution for family a total immersion in a school community.

Caruth, Cathy. *Empirical Truths and Critical Fictions: Locke, Wordsworth, Kant, Freud*. Baltimore, MD, and London: Johns Hopkins U. Press, 1991. Pp. viii +167.

Castellani, Carlo. "La Réception en Italie et en Europe du *Saggio di osservazioni microscopiche* de Spallanzani (1975)." *Dix-huitième siècle*, 23 (1991), 85–95.

Cavazza, Marta. *Settecento inquieto. Alle origini dell'istituto delle Scienze di Bologna*. Bologna, Italy: Il Mulino, 1990. Pp. 281.

Cazenobe, Colette. *Le Système du libertinage de Crébillon Laclos*. Oxford: The Voltaire Foundation at the Taylor Institution, 1991. Pp. viii + 161.

Chédozeau, Bernard. *La Bible et la liturgie en français.* Paris: Editions du Cerf, 1990.

The author traces the weakening of the Tridentine restrictions on reading the Bible in the vernacular to Benedict XIV's brief of 1757, and shows how the Port-Royal translation (1660–1720) opened the way to a wider knowledge of the Bible among the lay public.

Cheyne, George. *The English Malady, or A Treatise of Nervous Diseases of All Kinds (1733).* (Tavistock Classics in the History of Psychiatry.) Edited with an introduction by Roy Porter. London and New York: Routledge, 1991. Pp. li + xxxii + 370.

Rev. (favorably and with other works) by Richard Davenport-Hines in *TLS,* (Jan. 11, 1991), 20.

Chilcote, Paul Wesley. *John Wesley and the Women Preachers of Early Methodism.* Metuchen, NJ: Scarecrow Press, 1991. Pp. xii + 389.

Cholvy, Gérard. *La Religion en France de la fin du XVIIIᵉ siècle à nos jours.* Paris: Hachette, 1991.

Rev. by Emile Poulat in *Archives des sciences sociales des religions,* (1991), 243.
This is a synthesis of Cholvy's and Hilaire's *Histoire religieuse de la France contemporaine*, (3vols.), and includes an essay on the "Revolutionary shock."

Clemens, H. J. Th. *De Godsdienstigheid in de Nederlanden in de Spiegel van Katholische kerkboeken (1680–1840).* 2 vols. Tilbourg: Tilbourg U. Press, 1988. Cf. *ECCB*, n.s. 16, III: 153.

Rev. by Wilhem Frijhoff in *Archives des science sociales des religions,* (1989), 249–50.

Coggins, James. *John Smyth's Congregation. English Separatism, Menonite Influence and the Elect Nation.* Scottsdale, PA, and Waterloo: Herald Press, 1991.

Cohen, Claudine. "Benoît De Maillet et La Diffusion De L'Histoire Naturelle à L'Aube Des Lumières." *Revue d'histoire des sciences*, 44 (1991), 325–342.

Cohen, Robert. *Jews in Another Environment. Surinam in the Second Half of the Eighteenth Century.* Leiden: E.J. Brill, 1991.

Rev. by Régine Azria in *Archives des sciences sociales des religions*, (1991), 245–46.

Cook, Nobel David (ed.). "Secret Judgements of God": *Old World Disease in Colonial Spanish America: (Papers, 1988).* (Intl. Cong. of Americanists Selected Papers, 46, 1988. Civilization of the American Indian Series, 205.) Norman, OK: U. of Oklahoma Press, 1991. Pp. xxiii + 285.

Cook, Sir Alan. "Edmond Halley and Newton's *Principia.*" *Notes and Records of the Royal Society of London*, 45 (1991), 129–38.

Cooper, Carolyn C. "Making Inventions Patent." *Technology & Culture,* 32 (1991), 837–45.

Corrigan, John. "Catholick Congregational Clergy and Public Piety." *Church History*, 60 (1991), 210–22.

Corrigan, John. *The Prism of Piety: Catholic Congregational Clergy at the Beginning of the Enlightenment.* New York: Oxford U. Press, 1991. Pp. x + 197.

Cottret, Bernard. *Le Christ des Lumières. Jésus de Newton à Voltaire, 1660–1760. Jésus depuis Jésus.* Paris: Cerf, 1990.

Rev. by Hubert Bost in *Etudes théologiques et religieuses,* (1991), 134–35; by Emile Goichot in *Archives des sciences sociales des religions,* 74 (1991), 235.
  A study of the various images of Jesus in the writings of Newton, Locke, Toland, Woolston, Chubb, and Morgan in England, and of Meslier and Voltaire in France, with chapters on characterizations of Jesus and theology in the music of Bach, Handel, and in Wesleyan hymns.

Coward, David. *The Philosophy of Restif de la Bretonne.* Oxford: The Voltaire Foundation at the Taylor Institution, 1991. Pp. x + 878.

Crawford, Michael J. *Colonial New England's New Revival Tradition in Its British Context.* New York: Oxford U. Press, 1991. Pp. xi + 354.

Crawford, Michael J. "New England and the Scottish Religious Revivals of 1742." *American Presbyterian*, 69 (1991), 23–32.

Crawford, Michael J. *Seasons of Grace: Colonial New England's Revival Tradition in its British Context.* (Religion in America Series.) New York: Oxford U. Press, 1991. Pp. xi + 354; bibliography.

Rev. (favorably) by S.C. Pearson in *Choice*, 29 (1991), 1094; 1096.

Cristaudo, Wayne. *The Metaphysics of Science and Freedom: From Descartes to Kant to Hegel.* (Avebury Series in Philosophy.) Brookfield, VT: Avebury Publishing Group, an imprint of Ashgate Publishing Co., 1991. Pp. 187.

Cunningham, Andrew. "How the *Principia* Got its Name; or, Taking Natural Philosophy Seriously." *History of Science,* 29 (1991), 377–392.

Curry, Patrick. *Prophecy and Power: Astrology in Early Modern England.* Cambridge: Polity Press, 1989. Cf. *ECCB*, n.s. 15, III: 114.

Rev. by Jacques Maître in *Archives des sciences sociales des religions,* (1991), 248.

Dale, Andrew I. *A History of Inverse Probability from Thomas Bayes to Karl Pearson.* (Studies in the History of Mathematics and Physical Sciences, 16.) Berlin and New York: Springer-Verlag, 1991. Pp. xx + 495; bibliography; formulae.

Damerow, Peter, Gideon Freudenthal, Peter McLaughlin, and Jürgen Renn (eds.). *Exploring the Limits of Preclassical Mechanics: A Study of Conceptual Development in Early Modern Science: Free Fall and Compounded Motion in the Work of Descartes, Galileo, and Beeckman.* London and New York: Springer-Verlag, 1991. Pp. xii + 384; illustrations.

Daston, Lorriane. "Marvelous Facts and Miraculous Evidence in Early Modern Europe." *Critical Inquiry,* 18 (1991), 93–124.

Surveys various efforts to assess the doctrinary value, evidentiary force, and ultimate value of miracles as preternatural phenomena.

Davies, Catherine Glyn. *'Conscience' as Consciousness: The Idea of Self-Awareness in French Philosophical Writing from Descartes to Diderot.* Oxford: The Voltaire Foundation at the Taylor Institution, 1990. Pp. viii + 170. Cf. *ECCB*, n.s. 16, III: 155.

Rev. (favorably) by Phillip Robinson in *French Studies*, 45 (1991), 322–23.

Dawson, Virginia P. *Nature's Enigma: The Problem of the Polyp in the Letters of Bonnet, Trembley, and Réaumur.* Philadelphia, PA: American Philosophical Society, 1987. Pp. 266. Cf. *ECCB*, n.s. 14, III: 110; 13, III: 156–57.

Rev. (favorably) by Paul Ilie in *Eighteenth-Century Studies*, 24 (1991), 516–18.

Dear, Peter (ed.). *The Literary Structure of Scientific Argument: Historical Studies.* Philadelphia, PA: U. of Pennsylvania Press, 1991. Pp. vi + 211; figures; select bibliography.

Debus, Allen G. *The French Paracelsians: The Chemical Challenge to Medical and Scientific Tradition in Early Modern France.* Cambridge and New York: Cambridge U. Press, 1991. Pp. xvi + 247; bibliography; illustrations.

Dedieu, Jean-Pierre. *L'Administration de la foi. L'Inquisition de Tolède (XVIe–XVIIe siècles).* Madrid: Casa de Velásquez, 1989.

Rev. by Ricardo Sacz in *Archives des sciences sociales des religions,* (1991), 237–38.

Delon, Michel. *L'Idée d'énergie au tournant des lumières (1770–1829).* Paris: Presses Universitaires de France, 1988. Pp. 521. Cf. *ECCB*, n.s. 16, III: 156; 15, III: 115; 14, III: 111.

Rev. by Carmelina Imbroscio in *Studi Francesi*, 34 (1991), 478–79; by Pierre Malandain in *Revue des sciences humaines*, 222 (1991), 166–68.

Denig, Ludwig. *The Picture-Bible of Ludwig Denig: A Pennsylvania German Emblem Book.* Translated and edited by Don Yoder. 2 vols. New York: Hudson Hills Press in association with the Museum of American Folk Art and the Pennsylvania German Society (distributed through New York: Rizzoli International Publications), 1990. Pp. viii + 180; bibliography; [vol 2] unumbered text; 60 color plates; musical examples. Cf. *ECCB*, n.s. 16, III: 156.

Rev. by W. B. Miller in *Choice*, 28 (1991), 924.

Desan, Suzanne. *Reclaiming the Sacred: Lay Religion and Popular Politics in Revolutionary France.* (Wilder House Series in Politics, History & Culture.) Ithaca, NY, and London: Cornell U. Press, 1990. Pp. xv + 262. Cf. *ECCB*, n.s. 16, III: 156.

Deshen, Shlomo. *Les Gens du Mellah. La Vie juive au Maroc à l'époque précoloniale.* Paris: Albin Michel, 1991.

Rev. by Joëlle Allouche-Benayoun in *Archives des sciences sociales des religions*, (1991), 251.

Dinsmore, Charles E. (ed.). *A History of Regeneration Research: Milestones in the Evolution of a Science.* Cambridge and New York: Cambridge U. Press, 1991. Pp. x + 228; figures; illustrations; tables.

Ditchfield, G. M. "Priestly Riots in Historical Perspective." *Transactions of the Unitarian Historical Society*, 20 (1991), 3–16.

Dobbs, B. J. T. *The Janus Face of Genius: The Role of Alchemy in Newton's Thought.* Cambridge and New York: Cambridge U. Press, 1991. Pp. xii + 359; appendices; bibliography; illustrations.

Duchesneau, François. "La Physiologie mécaniste de Hoffman." *Dix-huitième siècle,* 23 (1991), 9–22.

Ducommun, Marie-Jeanne, and Dominique Quadroni. *Le Refuge Protestant dans le Pays de Vaud (fin XVIIe–début XVIIIe siècle): Aspects d'une migration.* (Publications pour l'Association suisse pour l'histoire de Refuge hugenot, 1.) Geneva: Droz, 1991. Pp. 324; appendices; bibliography; illustrations; maps; tables.

The first volume of the Swiss Association for the History of Huguenot Exile is a thoroughly researched and minutely detailed compendium of data drawn from the archives of fifteen Swiss communities in the canton of Vaud and the city Bern regarding their arrangements for the reception of French Protestants beginning with the 1680s, when Louis XIV's policies to impose Catholicism as the state religion of France became manifest; and 1704 when the refugees had either emigrated further or been naturalized. The volume, a synthesis of research on this period of Protestant emigration, offers precise documentation about the kind of planning local governments and institutions in Protestant Switzerland engaged in temporarily to sustain French and Piedmontese exiles on their way to more permanent homes in Germany, Holland, and England.

The twelve chapters, each written and documented by one of the two authors, each deals with a specific aspect of the refugee problem: the Protestant migration within Europe, their specific itinerary through Switzerland, timing (D. Quadroni); resettlement efforts (M.-J. Ducommun); organization of relief by towns, socio-economic profile of the refugees (D.Q.); relief funds, economic considerations, permanent settlement in Switzerland (M.-J. D.). The chapters are organized into four parts: 1. Overview of the Protestant exodus and arrival in Switzerland; 2. Aid to the refugees; 3. Economic policies of the Bern government; 4. Settlement and intergration of the French Huguenots in the canton of Vaud. Supported by a wealth of quantitative data in the form of tables and case histories, the principal observations document the swell of the refugee movement cresting in the summer of 1687, the straining of the resources of the well-organized Swiss charitable institutions; the resentment of local businesspeople, threatened by the competition of French Huguenot immigrants; the economic policy of the Bern government which tried to rejuvenate local industry by the influx of new skills, while encouraging the departure of those refugees who could not integrate into local economies; and the diverse socio-economic layers of the refugees and their unequal treatment by the Swiss governments and charitable institutions. The two researchers also discovered that during the Refuge, the Swiss authorities, as well as other host countries, notably the German states of Brandenburg and Wurtemburg, had to change their initial assumptions in the growing realization that most of the refugees were poor and became more so in exile. The unexpected resettlement expense caused England to withdraw its initial commitment to settle French Protestants in Ireland.

The book also shows how political changes and economic conditions during the French Protestant exodus affected their resettlement.

Although its aim is to document the plight of French Protestants, the book is valuable as a study of the institutions of Protestant Switzerland (Vaud) at the end of the 17th century.—Biruta Cap.

Duhem, Pierre Maurice Marie. *The Origins of Statics: The Sources of Physical Theory*. Translated by Grant F. Leneaux. (Boston Studies in the Philosophy of Science, 123.) Boston, MA, and Dordrecht, Netherlands: Kluwer Academic, 1991. Pp. 593.

Duranton, Henri. "La Diffusion d'Une Nouvelle Histoire: Les Avatars de Clio au XVIIIe Siècle." *Revue d'histoire des Sciences*, 44 (1991), 359–74.

Dutka, Jacques. "The Early History of the Factorial Function." *Archive for History of the Exact Sciences,* 43 (1991), 279.

Dworetz, Steven M. *The Unvarnished Doctrine: Locke, Liberalism, and the American Revolution*. Durham, NC, and London: Duke U. Press, 1990. Pp. x + 247; bibliography. Cf. *ECCB*, n.s. 16, III: 157.

Rev. (favorably) by P. Coby in *Choice*, 28 (1991), 1001.

Eddy, Richard. " 'Defended by an Adequate Power': Joshua Humphreys and the 74-Gun Ships of 1779." *The American Neptune,* 51 (1991), 173–94.

Eluerd, Roland. "Réaumur 'métallurgiste'." *Dix-huitième siècle*, 21 (1991), 293–306.

Ehrhardt, W. E. Schelling. *Leonbergensis und Maxilian II von Bayern Lehrstuden de Philosophie*. (Schellingiana, Bd. 2.) Stuttgart: Fromann-Hoolzboog, 1989.

English, John C. "John Wesley's Indebtedness to John Norris." *Church History*, 60 (1991), 55–69.

Erlichson, Herman. "Newton's First Inverse Solutions." *Centaurus*, 34 (1991), 345–65.

Euler, Leonhard. *Sol et Luna, 2*. Edited by C. Blanc. (Blanc's Leonhardi Euleri Opera Omnia. Series Secunda: Opera Mechanica et Astronomic, 24.) Boston, MA: Birkhauser, 1991. Pp. xxvii + 326; texts in Latin, German, English, and French.

Fabre, Gérard. "La Pests en l'absence de Dieu? Images votives et représentations du mal lors de la peste provençale de 1720." *Archives des science sociales des religions*, (1991), 141–58.

Contrary to the iconographic tradition of *ex-voto* images, those of the Marseilles-Provence plague of 1720–1722 do not show plague-striken cadavers and in fact tend to hide the existence of the plague ("evil") itself, as though its existence called into question the very existence of God, which was unthinkable. The author reviews the theses of Aries, Vovelle, and Dulumeau on the dynamics of "dechristianization" in France and their contribution to an explanation of the Marseilles reaction to the plague. The plague paved the way for a domination of Marseilles by two "charismatic" personalities, the Bishop Belsunce and the chevalier Roze who confronted the plague, risked death, led the resistance to it, and, along with other "charismatic" figures throughout Provence, in some fashion filled the void left in the public religious conscience by the retreat of God. The baroque code of piety proved itself insufficient to represent the plague because there had occurred an evolution of religious conscience.

Feingold, Mordechai (ed.). *Before Newton: The Life and Times of Isaac Barrow.* Cambridge and New York: Cambridge U. Press, 1990. Pp. xi + 380. Cf. *ECCB*, n.s. 16, III: 158.

Rev. by J.W. Dauben in *Choice*, 28 (1991), 800.

Ferreira, M. Jamie. *Skepticism and Reasonable Doubt: The British Naturalist Tradition in Wilkins, Hume, Reid, and Newman.* New York: Oxford U. Press; Oxford: Clarendon Press, 1986. Pp. xii + 255; bibliography. C.f. *ECCB*, n.s. 16, III: 159; 15, III: 116; 14, III: 113.

Rev. by John W. Yolton in *Studies in the Philosophy of the Scottish Enlightenment*, (1990), 303–06.

Field, Clive D. "Anti-Methodist Publications of the Eighteenth Century: A Revised Bibliography." *Bulletin of the John Rylands U. Library of Manchester*, 73 (1991), 159–280.

Fischer, Jabez Maud. *An American Quaker in the British Isles: The Travel Journals of Jabez Maud Fischer, 1775–1779.* Edited by Kenneth Morgan. (Records of Social and Economic History, British Academy: New Series, 16.) London: Oxford U. Press for the British Academy, 1991. Pp. xi + 300; facsimiles; illustrations; maps.

Fischer, Jean-Louis. "La Callipédie ou l'art d'avoir de beaux enfants." *Dix-huitième siècle,* 21 (1991), 141–58.

Fischer, Richard B. *Edward Jenner, 1749–1823.* London: A. Deutsch, 1991. Pp. 361; bibliography; frontispiece; 8 illustrations.

Rev. by Richard Davenport-Hines in *TLS,* (June 21, 1991), 5.

Fissell, Mary E. *Patients, Power, and the Poor in Eighteenth Century Bristol.* (Cambridge History of Medicine.) Cambridge and New York: Cambridge U. Press, 1991. Pp. xii + 266; bibliography; figures; maps; tables.

This work adds to the prevailing wisdom that an important change occurred in the medical profession and medical practice around the middle of the eighteenth century. Fissell's study focuses upon those changes as they unfolded at the Bristol Infirmary, and aims to place these within the appropriate social, economic, and historiographical contexts.

Fissell describes medical practice of the early eighteenth century as dominated by notions of sympathy and equilibrium, and by a concern with external symptoms; the effect of these beliefs was to empower patients to represent or even to treat their own diseases. She also provides an overview of the types of medical practitioners found in Bristol, and demonstrates the similarities of treatment regardless of the educational background or social status of the practitioner. The original role of Bristol Infirmary was to provide civic charity and poor relief. For this reason, a high number of those referred came from broken families, had out-of-wedlock pregnancies, or suffered from old age. Because medical treatment was so influenced by the charitable mission of the hospital, Fissell contends that the Bristol Infirmary must be placed in the context of changing attitudes towards poverty, charity, and changes in the view of the body itself. She uses the system of medical referral to demonstrate connections between these issues.

Changes within Bristol Infirmary occurred alongside broader transformations in medical practice over the eighteenth century. This change has been recently seen as one in which the patient became an object of study, subject to the authority of the medical practitioner. At Bristol, the surgeons played a crucial role in this shift. Their concern with external symptoms reduced patients to objects of anatomical study, and disregarded the patients' own accounts of their illness. The earlier notion of medicine as rooted in sympathy and equilibrium was relegated to popular, as distinct from elite, medicine.

This evolution occurred in Bristol not because of any one contest of medical views, or as a result of professional disputes. Instead, Fissell contends, a new role developed upon the surgeons as a direct result of a decline in the involvement of the Board of Governors in the management of the Infirmary. The surgeons thus appear as almost unconscious agents of fundamental change in medical practice, and the allocation of poor relief. Members of the Board of Governors became less involved, in part, because there were other venues for medical poor relief, and surgeons filled the void because of the decline in the practice of surgical apprenticeship, which created the concomitant need for hospital instruction.

This book adds to our understanding of early modern medical institutions, while corroborating the work of others, notably Roy Porter, on the changing nature of medicine over the eighteenth century. The author's discussion of early medicine, as opposed to later, elite medicine, is particularly persuasive. Some of the rich social and historiographical context for Bristol Infirmary is treated in a tantalizingly brief (and insubstantial) fashion, specifically the connections between Bristol Infirmary and the broader eighteenth-century context of medical practice, professionalization, and public charity. The author is much more successful in situating the Infirmary in the context of social and economic trends within Bristol itself.

One of Fissell's least persuasive assertions is that elite worries over the politically seditious character of Wesleyan Methodism were channeled into a crusade to suppress popular medicine. By the evidence she presents, concerted opposition to popular medicine arose prior to, and independantly of, concerns over religious dissent. Even in her account of the religious or "miraculous" aspects of reported cures, or the political aspects of practices such as the King's touch seem to be central, and any glancing blows at popular medicine peripheral. Another problem is that, for all of Fissell's insistence on the need to look at medicine from the patient's point of view, the voices of patients are rarely heard in this book. This of course is largely a problem of sources: the marginalization of patients' voices over the eighteenth century left its mark upon medical casebooks as well, as these were increasingly devoted to depicting the body and its symptoms, rather than individuals with particular stories.—Kathleen Wellman.

Fox, George. *George Fox Speaks for Himself.* Edited, selected, and introduced by Hugh McGregor Ross. York, UK: Sessions, 1991. Pp. 176.

Fraser, Craig G. "Mathematical Technique and Physical Conception in Euler's Investigation of the Elastica." *Centaurus,* 34 (1991), 211–41.

Fraunce, Abraham. *Symbolicae Philosophiae Liber Quartis et Ultimus.* New York: AMS Press, 1991. Pp. xxxi + 208; illustrations.

French, Roger (ed.). *British Medicine in an Age of Reform: [Papers, 1987].* (Wellcome Institute Series in the History of Medicine.) New York: Routledge, Chapman Hall, 1991. Pp. 260.

Fryer, Jonathan (ed.). *George Fox and the Children of Light.* London: K. Cathie, 1991. Pp. xxxii + 252.

Fuks-Mansfeld, R. G. *De Sefardin in Amsterdam tot 1795. Aspecten van een joodse minderheid in een Hollandse Stade.* Hilversum: Verloren, 1989. Cf. *ECCB,* n.s. 16, III: 159.

Rev. by Wilhelm Frijhoff in *Archives des sciences sociales des religions,* (1989), 262–63.

Furcha, E. J. *Truth and Tolerance. Papers from the 1989 International Symposium.* (ARC Supplement, 4.) Montreal: McGill-Queen's U. Press, 1990.

Rev. by Hubert Bost in *Etudes Thélogiques et religieuses,* (1991), 297.
Papers on Locke (J. Tully) and Bayle (B.M. Bracken).

Gardels, Nathan. "Two Concepts of Nationalism: An Interview with Isaiah Berlin." *New York Review of Books,* 38 (Nov. 21, 1991), 19–23.

Applies insights from Herder and Vico to the present " 'convulsive ingathering' of nations."

Gascoigne, John. *Cambridge in the Age of the Enlightenment: Science, Religion and Politics from the Restoration to the French Revolution.* Cambridge and New York: Cambridge U. Press, 1989. Pp. xi + 358. Cf. *ECCB*, n.s. 16, III: 160; 15, III: 116.

Rev. (favorably) by Lionel K. J. Glassey in *The Scriblerian,* 23 (1991), 282; (favorably) by Margaret C. Jacob in *Eighteenth-Century Studies,* 24 (1991), 375–78.

Gaulin, Michael. *Le Concept d'homme de lettres, en France, à l'époque de l'Encyclopédie.* (Harvard Dissertations in Romance Languages.) New York: Garland Publishing, 1991. Pp. vii + 198.

This handsome volume was originally a Harvard thesis, defended in 1973. Unfortunately, the text and bibliography have not been updated since then. Gaulin briefly mentions major contributions to the field which were not in print when the thesis was defended, but does not seem to have felt the need to revise his dissertation to include more recent studies in the field. Gaulin's primary objective is to examine a limited number of texts, including articles from *l'Encyclopédie*, which were published in the second half of the eighteenth century and which reflect widely held views of what a *homme de lettres* is or should be. In so doing, of course, he runs into a major problem of terminology: *gens de lettres, philosophe*, etc.

In the introduction, Gaulin sets out his reasons for choosing the texts which he then analyzes, one by one, in the following chapters. Chapter 1 is devoted to Duclos' *Considérations sur les moeurs de ce siècle* (1751), in which Duclos attempted to define the relationship between *the homme de lettres* and the *homme du monde*. In chapter 2, which analyses d'Alembert's *Essai sur les gens de lettres* (1753), Gaulin emphasizes d'Alembert's attempts to clarify the connection between the *philosophe* and the *homme de lettres*. Perhaps the most interesting chapter in the book is the third one, in which Gaulin discusses a number of relevant articles from the *Encyclopédie,* including d'Alembert's "Ecrivain" and Voltaire's "Gens de letteres." Gaulin's analysis of these articles and of their interrelationships allows him to piece together a fascinating picture of how the authors of the *Encyclopédie* saw the function of the writer in the middle of the eighteenth century. In addition, his discussion of Marmontel's article "Critique" (pp.100–101) provides useful insights into how the Encyclopédistes conceived the function of the literary critic.

The two remaining chapters deal with Grimm's *Correspondance littéraire* and two treatises by Malesherbes, *Mémoires sur la Librairie* (1759) and *Mémoire sur la liberté de la presse* (1788). Although Gaulin discusses the various elements of his corpus separately, he does make a number of very insightful comparisons between and among them, and manages to put together a coherent and in many ways highly successful synthesis of the many viewpoints he studies. This book is a useful contribution to the field, in that it brings together divergent opinions as to the role that an *homme de lettres* should play in society and thoroughly examines the common elements that exist among them. The delicate balance between textual analysis and social history which Gaulin strikes makes his monograph interesting from a methodological standpoint as well as with respect to the conclusions he reaches.—Richard G. Hodgson.

Gélis, Jacques. *History of Childbirth: Fertility, Pregnancy, and Birth in Early Modern Europe.* Translation by Rosemary Morris of *L'arbe et le fruit: la naissance dans l'Occident moderne XVIe–XIXe siècle* (Paris, 1984). Boston, MA: Northeastern U. Press; Cambridge: Polity Press with Oxford: Basil Blackwell, 1991. Pp. xvii + 326; bibliography; figures; 8 illustrations.

Gilain, Christian. "Sur l'Historie du Théorème Fondamental de l'Algèbre: Théorie des Équations et Calcul Intégral." *Archive for History of the Exact Sciences*, 42 (1991), 91–136.

Gilmour, Peter (ed.). *Philosophers of the Enlightenment*. Edinburgh, Scotland: Edinburgh U. Press, 1989. Pp. viii + 183. Cf. *ECCB*, n.s. 15, III: 117.

Goubert, Jean-Pierre. "Entre Ancien Régime et révolution. Les Chirurgiens vus par eux-mêmes (1790–1791)." *Dix-huitième siècle*, 21 (1991), 119–28.

Grell, Ole Peter, Jonathan I. Israel, and Nicholas Tyacke (eds.). *From Persectuion to Toleration: The Glorious Revolution and Religion in England*. New York: Oxford U. Press; Oxford: Clarendon Press, 1991. Pp. x + 443.

Gres-Gayer, Jacques M. *Théologie et pouvoir en Sorbonne. La Faculté de théologie de Paris et la bulle* Unigenitus *(1714–1721)*. (Mélanges de la Bibliotèque de la Sorbonne.) Paris: Klincksieck, 1991. Pp. 392.

Grmek, Mirko D. "La Réception du *De Sedibus* de Morgagni en France au 18e siècle." *Dix-huitième siècle*, 21 (1991), 59–73.

Groenendijk, L. F., and F. A. Van Lieburg. *Voor edeler staat geschapen. Levenen stervensbechrijvingen van gereformeerde kinderen en jengdigen uit 17e en 18e eeuw*. Leiden: J.J. Groen, 1991.

Rev. by Wilhem Frijhoff in *Archives des sciences sociales des religions*, (1991), 264.

Guicciardini, Niccolò. *The Development of Newtonian Calculus in Britain, 1700–1800*. Camdridge and New York: Cambridge U. Press, 1989. Pp. xii + 228; bibliography. Cf. *ECCB*, n.s. 16, III: 162; 15, III: 118.

Rev. (favorably) by J. McCleary in *Choice*, 28 (1991), 1174.

Guyon, Jeanne-Marie. *La Passion de croire*. Texts chosen and presented by Marie-Louise Gondal. Paris: Nouvelle Cité, 1990.

Rev. by Jacques Maître in *Archives des sicences sociales des religions*, 74 (1991), 252.
This is a fine collection of largely inaccessible texts of the seventeenth/eighteenth-century (1648–1717) mystic.

Haber, Samuel. *The Quest for Authority and Honor in the American Professions, 1750–1900*. Chicago, IL, and London: U. of Chicago Press, 1991. Pp. xiv + 478; bibliography; 4 illustrations.

Hall, Marie Boas. *Promoting Experimental Learning: Experiment and the Royal Society: 1660–1727*. Cambridge and New York: Cambridge U. Press, 1991. Pp. xiv + 207; bibliography.

Hall, Michael G. *The Last American Puritan: The Life of Increase Mather*. Middletown: Wesleyan U. Press, 1989. Pp. xv + 438.

Rev. (with other works) by Darlene Harbour Unrue in *Religion & Literature*, 23 (1991), 87–90.

Hamon, Léo (ed.). *Du Jansénisme à la laïcité. Le Jansénisme et les origines de la déchristianisation.* Paris: Editions de la Maison des Sciences de l'Homme, 1987. Cf. *ECCB*, n.s. 16, III: 163.

Rev. by Emile Poulat in *Archives des sciences sociales des religions*, (1989), 282.

Hamowy, Ronald. *The Scottish Enlightenment and the Theory of Spontaneous Order.* (The Journal of the History of Philosophy Monograph Series.) Carbondale, IL: Southern Illinois U. Press, 1987. Pp. xii + 65; bibliography. Cf. *ECCB*, n.s. 16, III: 163, 13, III: 166.

Hans-Heinz, Holz, Georges Labica, Domenico Losurdo, and Hans-Jörg Sandkuler (eds.). *Die französische Revolution: Philosophie und Wissenschaften.* Vols. I and II. (Annales der Internationalen Gesellschaft für dialektische Philosophie. Societas Hegeliana VI-VII.) Milan: Edizione Guerini e Associati, 1989 and 1990.

Harkányi, Katalin. *The Natural Sciences and American Scientists in the Revolutionary Era: A Bibliography.* (Bibliographies and Indexes in American History, 17.) New York: Greenwood Press, 1990. Pp. x + 510; appendices. Cf. *ECCB*, n.s. 16, III: 163.

Rev. (with reservations) by H. Lowood in *Choice*, 28 (1991), 1760.

Hart, James S. *Justice Upon Petition: The House of Lords and the Reformation of Justice, 1621–1675.* London and New York: HarperCollins Academic, 1991. Pp. 287; bibliography.

Heilbron, J. L. and W. F. Bynum. "Eighteen Ninety One and All That." *Nature*, 349 (1991), 9–12.

Heitsenrater, Richard P., and Albert C. Outler (eds.). *John Wesley's Sermons: An Anthology.* Nashville, TN: Abingdon, 1991. Pp. 231.

Helfand, William H. *The Picture of Health: Images of Medicine and Pharmacy From the William H. Helfand Collection.* (Philadelphia Museum of Art, Sept 21–Dec. 1, 1991.) Philadelphia, PA: Philadelphia Museum of Art; U. of Pennsylvania Press, 1991. Pp. 144.

Hembry, Phyllis. *The English Spa, 1560–1815: A Social History.* London: Athlone Press; Rutherford, NJ: Fairleigh Dickinson U. Press (distributed through Cranbury, NJ: Associated University Presses), 1990. Pp. xiv + 401; 16 illustrations; maps. Cf. *ECCB*, n.s. 16, III: 164.

Rev. (favorably) by G.M. Straka in *Choice*, 28 (1991), 1544.

Henderson, Adrienne Janice. *On the Distances Between Sun, Moon and Earth: According to Ptolemy, Copernicus, and Reinhold.* Leiden and New York: E. J. Brill, 1991. Pp. vii + 220; appendices; figures; tables.

Henkel, Willi (ed.). *Ecclesiæ memorial. Miscellanea in ornore del R. P. Josef Metzler, O. M. I., Prefetto dell' Archivo Segreto Vaticano.* Rome and Vienna: Herder, 1991.

This festschrift contains an inventory of papers of Clement XI concerning England, material on the nomination and suspension of D. M. Varlet as bishop of Babylon (1718–19), a paper on Jesuit missionaries in Malabar (1773–77), and another on missionaries along the Mississippi (1700).

Hilaire-Pérez, Liliane. "Invention and the State in 18th-Century France." *Technology & Culture,* 32 (1991), 911–31.

Hoffman, Paul. "L'Ame et les passions dans la philosophie médicale de Georg-Ernst Stahl." *Dix-huitième siècle,* 21 (1991) 31–43.

Hoinkes, Ulrich. *Philosophie und Grammatik in der französischen Aufklärung. Untersuchungen zur Geschichte der Sprachtheorie und französischen Grammatikographie im 18. Jahrhundert in Frankreich.* (Studium Sprachwissenschaft, 13.) Munster: Nodus Publikationen, 1991.

Holden, Christine. "Serving Tsar and King: George Tate, Admiral in the Russian Imperial Navy." *The American Neptune,* 51 (1991), 33–44.

Hölderlin, Friedrich. Bevestigter Gesang: *Die neu zu entdeckende hymnische Spädichtung bis 1806.* Edited by Dietrich Uffhausen. Stuttgart: J.B. Metzlerschem, 1989. Pp. xxxvi + 71.

Rev. (with reservations) by Emery E. George in *Journal of English and Germanic Philology,* 90 (1991), 605–10.

Hope, V. M. *Virtue by Consensus: The Moral Philosophy of Hutcheson, Hume, and Adam Smith.* Oxford: Clarendon Press, 1989. Pp. 166. Cf. *ECCB,* n.s. 15, III: 120.

Rev. by Paul Russell in *Ethics,* 101 (1991), 873–75.

Huet, Marie-Hélène. "Monstrous Imagination: Progeny as Art in French Classicism." *Critical Inquiry,* 17 (1991), 718–37.

Reconsiders the role of the mother's imagination in birth defects.

Hopkins, Fred W., and Donald G. Shomette. "The DeBraak Legacy: An Analysis of Eighteenth Century Rigging." *The American Neptune,* 51 (1991), 156–63.

Hutchinson, Keith. "Dormitive Virtues, Scholastic Qualities, and the New Philosophies." *History of Science,* 29 (1991), 245–78.

Hutchinson, Keith. "Idiosyncracy, Achromatic Lenses, and Early Romanticism." *Centaurus,* 34 (1991), 125–63.

Hutchison, Ross. *Locke in France.* Oxford: The Voltaire Foundation at the Taylor Institution, 1991. Pp. ix + 251.

Jacob, Margaret C. *Living the Enlightenment: Freemasonry and Politics in Eighteenth-Century Europe.* New York: Oxford U. Press, 1991. Pp. xiii + 304; bibliography; illustrations.

Jacobsen, Douglas G. *An Unprov'd Experiment: Religious Pluralism in Colonial New Jersey.* (Chicago Studies in the History of American Religion, 9.) Brooklyn, NY: Carlson Publishing, 1991. Pp. xx + 224; bibliography.

Jennings, Theodore W., Jr. *Good News for the Poor: John Wesley's Evangelical Economics.* Nashville, TN: Abingdon Press, 1990. Pp. 234.

Rev. by Henry H. Knight III in *Journal of Church and State*, 33 (1991), 312–13.

Jeremy, David J. (ed.). *International Technology Transfer: Europe, Japan, and the USA, 1700–1914.* Brookfield, VT: Gower, 1991. Pp. 253.

Johann Gottfried Herder: Language, Literature, & Enlightenment. Introduction by Wulf Koepe. (Studies in German Literature, Linguistics, and Culture, 52.) Columbia,SC: Camden House, 1990. Pp. 300.

Rev. by Helga Halbfass in *South Atlantic Review*, 56 (Nov. 1991), 112–115.

John Wesley's Sermons: An Introduction. Nashville, TN: Abingdon, 1991. Pp. 107.

Jolly, David C. *Maps in British Periodicals, Pt 2: Annuals, Scientific Periodicals & Miscellaneous Magazines, Mostly Before 1800.* Brookline, MA: David C. Jolly, 1991. Pp. 320.

Jolley, Nicholas. *The Light of the Soul: Theories of Ideas in Leibniz, Malebranche, and Descartes.* New York: Oxford U. Press; Oxford: Clarendon Press, 1990. Pp. x + 209. Cf. *ECCB*, n.s. 16, III: 168.

Rev. by C. J. Shields in *Choice*, 28 (1991), 793.

Kelly, John T. *Practical Astronomy During the Seventeenth Century: Almanac-Makers in America and England.* (Harvard Dissertations in the History of Science.) London and New York: Garland Publishing, 1991. Pp. vii + 319; appendices; bibliography; illustrations; tables.

Kervingant, Marie de la Trinité. *Des Moniales face á la Revolution française. Aux origines des Cisterciennes-Trappistines.* Paris: Beauchesne, 1989. Cf. *ECCB*, n.s. 16, III: 169.

Rev. by Jacques Olivier Boudon in *Archives des sciences sociales des religions*, (1991), 282.

King, Lester S. *Transformations in American Medicine: From Benjamin Rush to William Osler.* Baltimore, MD, and London: Johns Hopkins U. Press, 1991. Pp. 268.

Kloos, John. *"Feast of Reason/Flow of Soul*: Benjamin Rush's Public Piety." *American Presbyterian*, 69 (1991), 49–58.

Kottek, Samuel. "Texts and Documents 'Citizens! Do You Want Children's Doctors?' An Early Vindication of 'Paediatric' Specialists." *Medical History,* 35 (1991), 103–116.

Kulstad, Mark. *Leibniz on Appreciation, Consciousness and Reflection. Analytica.* Munich: Philosophia Verlag; Vienna: Hamden, 1991.

Lamb, Hubert, in collaboration with Knud Frydendahl. *Historic Storms of the North Sea, British Isles and Northwest Europe.* Cambridge and New York: Cambridge U. Press, 1991. Pp. xi + 204; bibliography; illustrations.

Lambert, Frank. "The Great Awakening as Artifact: George Whitefield and the Construction of Intercolonial Revival, 1739–1745." *Church History*, 60 (1991), 223–46.

Landers, John. "London's Mortality in the 'Long Eighteenth Century': A Family Reconstitution Study." *Medical History*, supplement 11 (1991), 1–128.

Landsman, Ned. "Evangelists and Their Hearers: Popular Interpretation of Revivalist Preaching in Eighteenth Century Scotland." *Journal of British Studies*, 282 (April 1989), 120–49.

Larson, Edward J. "Science in the American South Through the Eyes of Four Natural Historians, 1750–1850." *Annals of Science*, 48 (1991), 231–240.

Laurens, Henry et al. *Les Origines Intellectuelles De L'Expedition d'Egypte (1789–1801)*. Paris: Armand Colin, 1989. Cf. *ECCB*, n.s. 16, III: 170.

Rev. by Constant Hames in *Archives des sciences sociales des religions*, (1990), 285.

Lebrun, François (ed.). *La France religieuse. t. II: Du Christianisme flamboyant à l'aube des Lumiéres (XVIe-XVIIe siècles)*. Paris: Editions du Seuil, 1988. Cf. *ECCB*, n.s. 16, III: 171.

Rev. by Jean Séguy in *Archives des sciences sociales des religions*, (1989), 295.

Leibniz, Gottfried Wilhelm. *De l'horizon de la doctrine humaine- ʹαπο καταστσισ (La restitution universelle)*. Paris: Vrin, Collection de Textes Philosophiques, 1991.

Leibniz, Gottfried Wilhelm. *La monadologie*. Critical Edition by E. Boutroux. Preface by Jacques Rivelaygne. Paris: Le Livre de Poche, Collection Classiques de la Philosophie, 1990.

Levy, B. Barry. *Planets, Potions and Parchments: Scientific Hebraica from the Dead Sea Scrolls to the Eighteenth Century*. Buffalo, NY, and Montreal: McGill-Queens's U. Press for the Jewish Public Library, 1990. Pp. xii + 139; illustrations (some colored). Cf. *ECCB*, n.s. 16, III: 172.

Rev. by N. A. Greenburg in *Choice*, 28 (1991), 802; (favorably) by Barry Walfish in *SR*, 20 (1991). "Catalogue of an exhibition presented by the Jewish Public Library and held May-September, 1990 at the David M. Stewart Museum, Montréal."

Lovegrove, Deryck W. *Established Church Sectarian People: Itinerancy and the Transformation of English Dissent, 1780–1830*. Cambridge and New York: Cambridge U. Press, 1988. Pp. 254. Cf. *ECCB*, n.s. 16, III: 172.

Rev. by Jean Séguy in *Archives des sciences sociales des religions*, (1991), 270–71.

Lowood, Henry E. *Patriotism, Profit, and the Promotion of Science in the German Enlightenment: The Economic and Scientific Societies, 1760–1815*. London and New York: Garland Publishers, 1991. Pp. xvi + 445; bibliography; tables.

Lux, David S. *Patronage and Royal Science in Seventeenth-Century France: The Académie de Physique in Caen*. Ithaca, NY: Cornell U. Press, 1989. Pp. xiii + 199.

Rev. (with other works) by Jay Tribby in *Eighteenth-Century Studies*, 24 (1991) 519–24.

MacCannell, Juliet Flower. *The Regime of the Brother: After the Patriarchy*. London and New York: Routledge, 1991.

MacDonald, Michael, and Terence R. Murphy. *Sleepless Souls: Suicide in Early Modern England.* (Oxford Studies in Social History.) New York: Oxford U. Press; Oxford: Clarendon Press, 1990. Pp. xvi + 383; appendices; bibliography; figures; tables. Cf. *ECCB*, n.s. 16, III: 173.

Rev. (favorably) by John Bossy in *TLS*, (May 10, 1991), 5; (favorably) by G. M. Straka in *Choice*, 29 (1991), 180.

Maillard, Jean. *Louise du Néant ou Le Triomphe de la pauvreté de des humiliations (1732)*. Montbonnot St. Martin: Editions Jérôme Million, 1987. Cf. *ECCB*, n.s. 16, III: 173.

Rev. by Jacques Maître in *Archives des sciences sociales des religions*, (1990), 290.

Maïmon, Solomon. *Essai sur la philosophie transcendentale*. Presentation, translation, and notes by Jean-Baptiste Scherrer. Paris: Vrin, 1989.

Rev. by F. X. Chenet in *Etudes philosophiques*, (1991), 553–56.

Mandeville, Bernard. *La fable des abeilles*. 2nd part. Introduction by Paulette Carrive. Translated and with notes by Lucien Carrive. Paris: Vrin, 1991.

Marin, Louis. "The Figurability of the Visual: The Veronica or the Question of the Portrait at Port-Royal." *New Literary History*, 22 (1991), 281–96.

A translation by Marie Maclean of "Figurabilité du visuel: la Veronique ou la question du portriat à Port-Royal," *Nouvelle Revue de Psychanalyse*, 35 (1987).

Mason, H. T. (ed.). *Studies on Voltaire and the Eighteenth Century, 284*. Oxford: The Voltaire Foundation at the Taylor Institution, 1991. Pp. 397.

Mason, Stephen F. "Jean Hyacinthe De Magellan, F. R. S., and the Chemical Revolution of the Eighteenth Century." *Notes and Records of the Royal Society of London*, 45 (1991), 155–62.

Mayer, Jean. "Diderot Et Le Calcul Des Probabiliés Dans L'Encyclopédie." *Revue d'histoire des sciences*, 46 (1991), 158–77.

McBride, William M. " 'Normal' Medical Science and British Treatment of Scurvy, 1753–75." *Journal of the History of Medicine and Allied Sciences,* 46 (1991), 158–77.

McClelland, I. L. *Ideological Hesitancy in Spain 1700–1750*. (Publications of the Bulletin of Hispanic Studies: Textual Research and Criticism.) Liverpool, UK: Liverpool U. Press, 1991. Pp. viii + 152.

McConnell, Anita. "La Condamine's Scientific Journey Down the River Amazon, 1743–1744." *Annals of Science,* 48 (1991), 1–19.

McDermott, Gerald R. "Jonathan Edwards, the City on a Hill, and the Redeemer Nation: A Reappraisal." *American Presbyterian,* 69 (1991), 33–47.

McDowell, R. B. (ed.). *The Writings and Speeches of Edmund Burke.* Volume IX. I: *The Revolutionary War:* 1794–1797. II: *Ireland.* Oxford: Clarendon Press, 1991. Pp. xvii + 723.

McGuire, James R. "La Représentation du corps hermaphrodite dans les planches de *l'Encyclopédie.*" *Recherches sur Diderot et sur* l'Encyclopédie, 11 (1991), 109–29; illustrations.

Comments on a series of plates in Panckouke's 1776–1777 *Suite des planches.*

McKelvey, Susan Delano. *Botanical Exploration of the Trans-Mississippi West, 1790–1850.* (Northwest Reprints.) Portland, OR: Oregon State U. Press, 1991. Pp. 1200; maps.

McLoughlin, William G. *Soul Liberty: The Baptists' Struggle in New England, 1630–1833.* Hanover, NH: U. Press of New England for Brown U. Press, 1991. Pp. xiv + 336; bibliography.

Rev. by Kerry S. Walters in *Journal of the Early Republic,* 11 (1991), 546–48; by Tipson in *Choice,* 29 (1991), 611.

Meyer, Jean. *Le Despotisme eclaire* (Que sais-je?) Paris: Presses Universitaires de France, 1991. Pp. 128.

Generations of French students have relied upon the "Que sais-je?" collection in preparing for examinations in a wide diversity of fields. And francophone scholars have found many of the volumes equally useful; the best synthesize beautifully the most advanced research on the topic in question.

Jean Meyer is an eminent eighteenth-century specialist, and his study (Number 2586 in the series), ranks with or close to such volumes as Henri Michel's *Histoire de la Resistance* (number 429, 1950), and Georges LeFranc's *Le Front Populaire* (Number 1209, 1965). This is a lucid, elegantly written, judicious, and extremely informative work, with an introductory bibliography and a handy table listing the principal enlightened despots. Every page demonstrates vast knowledge and careful research.

The phenomenon of enlightened despotism is defined as precisely as is possible, since it often involved pragmatic responses on the part of rulers to unique historical situations. Meyer underscores its strong emphais on the notion of progress, and also the necessity inherent in enlightened despotism to be able to make rational predictions of an immediate future, based on precise estimates on one's own military and economic strength and that of one's enemy or enemies. Readers who share the common view that the modern bureaucratic phenomenon began with Baron Steins reforms in Prussia after 1806 will find convincing evidence that "le despotisme eclaire est le phenomene historique qui a generalise le fonctionnariat" (p.27).

Enlightened despotism is carefully located geographically in Central, Eastern, and Southern Europe. And Meyer situates it temporally as the dominant governmental system between approximately 1740 and 1789: "L'Europe du XVIIIe siecle est calla du despotism eclaire" (p.41).

The French revolution stopped it in its tracks, and what the Jacobins did not destroy, Napoleon eliminated.

Jean Meyer does not hide his preference for Maria-Theresa of Austria (rules 1740-1780), whom he views as the ideal-type enlightened despot. He argues forcefully that in the end Frederick the Great (ruled 1740-1786) perverted the essence of enlightened despotism, despite his fame, his military triumphs, his reputation as the quintessential

"Philosopher King," and his claim that he was only the "First Servant of the State."

There are a few printing errors, such as dating Frederick's first Silesian campaign as 1751, and the end of his reign as 1785. These will surely be corrected in future editions. Jean Meyer and the editiors at the Presses Universitaires de France would also be well advised to include maps outlining the boundaries of the enlightened despotisms, and how those boundaries shifted, especially as a result of the Silesian campaign of 1741. Meyer rightly views Frederick's undeniably daring gamble, taken so early in his reign, as key to the development of Prussia, Austria, and Russia as despotisms, if not always as enlightened as they advertised themselves to be.—David L. Schalk

Middleton, Arthur Pierce. "Prayer Book Revision Explained: Sermons on the Liturgy by Joseph Bend, Rector of St. Paul's, Baltimore 1791–1812." *Anglican and Episcopal History*, 60 (1991), 57–73.

Milanesi, Claudio. "La mort-instant et la mort-processus dans la médecine de la seconde motié du siècle." *Dix-huitième siècle*, 21 (1991), 171–90.

Miller Joshua. *The Rise and Fall of Democracy in Early America, 1630–1789*. University Park, PA: Pennsylvania State U. Press, 1991. Pp. xi + 154.

Rev. by R. Detweiler in *Choice*, 29 (1991), 510.

Modica, Massimo (ed.). *L'esetetica del* l'Encyclopédie. *Guida alla lettura*. (Universale idee.) Rome: Editori Riuniti, 1988. Pp. 240.

Rev. (briefly) by J. P. De Nola in *Studi francesi*, 34 (1991), 522–23.

Morris, G.C.R. "On the Identity of Jacques Du Moulin, F. R. S. 1667." *Notes and Records of the Royal Society of London*, 45 (1991), 1–10.

Mortureaux, Marie-Françoise. "De La Ressemblance Entre Les Mathématiques et 'L'Amore Dans Les Entretiens De Fontenelle'." *Revue d'histoire des sciences*, 44 (1991), 301–11.

Moses, Stéphan. *Spuren des Schrift. Von Goethe bis Celan*. Frankfurt am Main: Athenäum Verlag, 1987. Cf. *ECCB*, n.s. 16, III: 177.

Rev. by Dominique Bourel in *Recherches de sciences religieuses*, (1989), 457.

Moureau, François. "Condilllac et Mably: Dix lettres inédites ou retrouvées." *Dix-huitième siècle*, 21 (1991), 193–200.

Muchembled, Robert. *L'Invention de l'homme moderne. Sensibilités, mœurs de comportements collectifs sous l'Ancien Régime*. Paris: Fayard, 1988. Cf. *ECCB*, n.s. 16, III: 177.

Rev. by Emile Goichot in *Archives des sciences sociales des religions*, (1989), 309–10.

Muller, Philippe, and Daniel Schultess. *La Révolution française dans la pensée européene*. Neufchâtel and Lausanne: Presses Académiques and L'Age d'Homme, 1989.

Murphy, Lamar Riley. *Enter the Physician: The Transformation of Domestic Medicine, 1760–1860.* (History of American Science and Technology Series.) Tuscaloosa, AL: U. of Alabama Press, 1991. Pp. xxi + 312; bibliography; illustrations.

Néofontaine, Luc. *La franc-maçonnerie.* (Bref, 26.) Paris: Cerf; Fides, 1990.

Rev. by Jacques-Noël Pérès in *Etudes théologiques et religieuses,* (1991), 320.

Niderst, Alain. "Les *Lettres Anglaises* De Voltaire, Une Vulgarisation Méthodique et Imprudente." *Revue d'histoire des sciences,* 44 (1991), 313–323.

Northeast, Catherine M. *The Parisian Jesuits and the Enlightenment 1700–1762.* (Studies in Voltaire and the Eighteenth Century, 288.) Oxford: The Voltaire Foundation at the Taylor Institute, 1991. Pp. v + 261.

This volume provides a useful and sophisticated addition to our understanding of the relationship of religious thinking to the supposed irreligion of the Enlightenment. In the introductory chapter Catherine M. Northeast portrays an important aspect of the Jesuit presence in France prior to their expulsion in 1762, that is, as prolific men of letters. Centered in Collège Louis-le-Grand, in the hands of officially designated *scriptores* who devoted much of their energy to the official *Mémoires de Trévoux*, a cadre of Jesuit intellectuals participated actively in the intellectual life of France. Although the principal writers, such as Jean Hardouin and Isaac-Joseph Berruyer, are no longer familiar in most intellectual histories of the period, they were very much a part of the Parisian intellectual scene. They participated in the life of some of the salons, and their words and judgements reached a wide readership.

Moreover the author underscores the presence of certain elective affinities between the Jesuit approach to religious matters and that of the *philosophes*. The two parties shared deep antipathy to the Jansenist approach to religion and life, counted Pascal as a shared intellectual enemy, loved the theater, evinced an inclination to place an emphasis on human free will, and devoted significant attention to the possibility of a universal "natural" religion. Through the 1740s, therefore, Jesuit religious polemic tended to focus on the Jansenism of Pascal, the rationalism of Spinoza and Melbranche, and the skepticism of Pierre Bayle. Only in the 1750s did their attention turn primarily to contemporary *philosophes*.

In the meanwhile much energy was spent wrestling with the problems of their own positions: Just how universal was "natural religion" and what were the obligations of humans once they had access to Christian revelation? If religion and Christian revelation were not subject to rationalist proof, how reliable are the empirical proofs of miracles and prophecies (increasingly the principal intellectual battleground of an empiricist era)? If Biblical criticism in the manner of Richard Simon was useful in the battle againts Protestant Biblical literalism and the establishment of the authority of the Fathers and the Church, what were the limits of such criticism before it turned on the structure of belief itself?

The author thoroughly and sympathetically establishes the twists and turns, strengths and weaknesses, of these arguments. Although not always felicitous in organization, this volume marks a major step in re-establishing the importance of formal religious thought during the period of Enlightenment. As did R. R. Palmer's *Catholics and Unbelievers in Eighteenth-Century France* more than a half a century ago, it provides a significant corrective to the tendency to view the history of religion during the Enlightenment in the Voltairean mode, exclusively as a battle of reason against belief. One suspects such correctives will always be necessary.—Harry C. Payne.

Ojala, Jeanne A., and William T. Ojala. *Madame de Sévigné: A Seventeenth-Century Life.* (Berg Women's Series.) Providence, RI: Berg (distributed through New York: St. Martin's Press), 1990. Pp. 221. Cf. *ECCB,* n.s. 16, III:178.

Rev. (severely) by R. A. Picken in *Choice,* 28 (1991), 939.

Olson, Richard. *Science Deified & Science Defied: The Historical Significance of Science in Western Culture.* Vol. II: *From the Early Modrn Age through the Early Romantic Era, ca. 1640 to ca. 1820.* Berkeley, CA, and Oxford: U. of California Press, 1990. Pp. 445; bibliography; figures; illustrations; map; tables. Cf. *ECCB*, n.s. 16, III: 178.

Rev. by A. W. Masters in *TLS*, (July 26, 1991), 23; by J. L. McKnight in *Choice,* 29 (1991), 300.

Pantycelyn, William Williams. *Songs of Praises: English Hymns and Elegies of William Williams Pantycelyn.* Introduced by R. Brinley Jones. Felinfach: Llanerch, 1991. Pp. 124; illustrations.

Paulson, Ronald. *Breaking and Remaking: Aesthetic Practice in England 1700–1820.* New York: Rutgers U. Press, 1989. Pp. xiv + 363. Cf. *ECCB*, n.s. 16, III: 126.

Rev. (favorably) by Dabney Townsend in *The Journal of Aesthetic Art Criticism*, 49 (1991), 271–73.

Pellegrin, Nicole. "L'Uniforme de la santé. Les Médecins et la réforme du costume." *Dix-huitième siècle,* 21 (1991), 129–40.

Péronnet, Michel (ed.). *Protestanisme et Révolution. Actes du VIe colloque Jean Boisset.* Montpelier: Sauramp, 1990.

Rev. by Claude Lauriol in *Protestants on the Eve of Revolution;* by J. P. Donnadieu in the *Cahiers de doléances* of Lower Languedoc; by Daniel Ligou in *Montauban*; by B. Vogler in *The Attitudes of Alsacian Theologoans on the French Revolution.*

Pestana, Carla Gardina. *Quakers and Baptists in Colonial Massachusetts.* Cambridge and New York: Cambridge U. Press, 1991. Pp. xii + 197.

Peters, Henriette. *Mary Ward. Thre Personlichkeit und ihr Institut.* Innsbruck-Vienne: Tyrolia Verlag, 1991.

Pietro, Pericle di. "La Réception en Italie et en l'Europe du *Saggio di osservazioni microscopiche* de Spallanzani (1765)." *Dix-huitième siècle*, 21 (1991), 85–105.

Pointer, Richard W. "Recycling Early American Religion: Some Historiographical Problems and Perspectives." *Fid. et Hist*, 23 (1991), 31–42.

Pollock, John. *John Wesley.* London: Hodder and Stiughton, 1989. Pp. 256; 8 plates.

Porter, Roy. "Cleaning Up the Great Wen: Public Health in Eighteenth-Century London." *Medical History*, supplement 11, (1991), 61–75.

Porter, Roy (ed.). *The Medical History of Waters and Spas.* (*Medical History*, supplement 10.) London: Wellcome Institute for the History of Medicine, 1990. Pp. xii + 150; 12 illustrations; map; plans. Cf. *ECCB*, n.s. 16, III: 180.

Rev. (with other works) by Richard Davenport-Hines in *TLS*, (Jan. 11, 1991), 20.
    Six papers (pp. 23–101) concern the Eighteenth Century.

Poulouin, Claudine. "La Connaissance Du Passé Et La Vulgarisation Du Débat Sur Les Chronologies Dans *L'Encyclopédia.*" *Revue d'histoire des sciences*, 44 (1991), 392–411.

Pourciau, Bruce H. "On Newton's Proof That Inverse-Square Orbits Must be Conics." *Annals of Science*, 48 (1991), 159–172.

Powell, Thomas C. *Kant's Theory of Self-Consciousness*. Oxford: Clarendon Press, 1990. Pp. 268. Cf. *ECCB*, n.s. 16, III: 180.

Pratt, Herbert T. "Peter Crosthwaite: John Dalton's 'Friend and Colleague'." *Ambix*, 38 (1991), 11–28.

Priesner, Claus. *"Defensor Alchymiae* Zur Beweis- Und Rechtfertigungsstrstegie Bei Gabriel Clauder Und Friedrich Wilhelm Schröder." *Archives internationales d'histoire des sciences*, 41 (1991), 13–56.

Privateer, Paul Michael. *Romantic Voices: Identity and Ideology in British Poetry, 1789–1850*. Athens, GA: U. of Georgia Press, 1991. Pp. xvii + 257.

Pumfrey, Stephen. "Ideas Above His Station: A Social Study of Hooke's Curatorship of Experiments." *History of Science*, 29 (1991), 1–44.

Ranson, Patrick. *Richard Simon, ou du caractére illégitime de l'augustinianisme en théologie*. (La Lumiére du Thabor.) Lausanne and Paris: L'Age d'Homme, 1990.

Rev. by Emile Poulat in *Archives des sciences sociales des religions*, 74 (1991), 283–84.
　　Looking at the Bible critic Richard Simon from a Russian Orthodox point of view, the author seems to see him as a symbol of the reunion of Christians on the basis of pre-Augustinian Patristics.

Rappaport, Rhoda. "Fontenelle Interprets the Earth's History." *Revue d'histoire des sciences*, 44 (1991), 281–300.

Rappaport, Rhoda. "Italy and Europe: The Case of Antonio Vallisneri (1661–1730)." *History of Science,* 29 (1991), 73–98.

Rataboul, Louis J. *John Wesley, Un Anglican sans frontières 1703–1791*. Nancy: Presses Universitaires de Nancy, 1991. Pp. 239; bibliography.

The 88-year long life of John Wesley spans the whole eighteenth century and is by itself a refutation of the too common view of the Age of Swift and Voltaire as that of reason and sentiment. Rataboul's first important contemporary work in French on Wesley takes into account both the contents of Wesley's *Journal* edited by Nehemiah Curnock from 1909 to 1916 and of his *Diary* which unfortunately shows a gap of forty years between 1742 and 1781. Rataboul does not intend to supersede Luke Tyerman's *The Life and Times of the Rev. John Wesley* (London, 3 vols, 1870) and gratefully acknowledges his debt to it, but Tyerman's biography was more a hagiography than a scholarly rendering of Wesley's life. Too often considered as an unapproachable hero-saint or as a gullible quack, Wesley needs a biographer that "yields neither to summary defamation nor to complacent hagiography" (p. 17).
　　Just as all the other major figures of his age, Wesley was fond of experimental science, but his reactions often verged in quackery or pseudo-science. His forceful leadership cannot be denied but it often led to his breaking with his most faithful disciples (George Whitefield, the Countess of Huntingdon). His conservatism had a sobering

influence on social movements in the nineteenth century, but "primitive Methodists" (who seceded from the main branch in 1811) were very influential in the Chartist movement and in the development of trade unionism in Britain. His austere and rigid social and individual morality left a lasting imprint on the Victorian age. Though a non-conformist at heart, Wesley did not cut all formal ties with the Church of England and his only defiant action was to ordain ministers himself. Though it is absurd to claim with Curnock that Wesley saved Britain from popery at a time when Roman Catholics barely made up 1% of the total population, he and his disciples can be credited with two positive developments: they connected Britain with the powerful pietist movement that prevailed in Germany and Northern Europe helping keep religion alive in the Age of Reason and definitely linked English Protestantism to Arminianism which proclaimed that God had given every man and woman the possibility to choose freely between good and evil. William Booth, the founder of the Salvation Army (1878) and Lloyd George, the great liberal reformer, acknowledged their debt to him. The bicentennial of his death is aptly celebrated in Rataboul's tense, but clear, precise and objective study.—Jean Rivière

Reck, Andrew J. "Enlightenment in American Law. I, II, and III." *The Review of Metaphysics*, 44 (1991), 549–73; 44 (1991), 729–54; 45 (1991), 57–87.

In these three essays, Andrew Reck discusses the influences of the Enlightenment in Europe and America and the three major documents of the American legal system: the Declaration of Independence, the American Constitution, and the Bill of Rights. Professor Reck is not so naive as to think that such documents can be traced to a handful of influential philosophers. And a great many thinkers are discussed in his essays.

Nevertheless, in the first essay, Reck largely discusses Locke, Hutcheson, and Burlhmaqus, and their influence on the Declaration of Independence. In the second essay, the focus is on Locke and David Hume, and their influence on the Constitution. The third essay discusses the Bill of Rights, and traces much of its thought to two "dissenting" pastors, Richard Price and Joseph Priestly.

Reid, Thomas. *Practical Ethics*. Edited by Knud Haakonssen. Princeton, NJ: Princeton U. Press, 1990. Pp. 556. Cf. *ECCB*, n.s. 16, III: 181.

Rev. (briefly) by William L. Rowe in *Ethics*, 102 (1991), 187–88.

Reisse, Jacques, and Gisèle Van de Vyer (eds.). *Les Savants et la politique à la fin du XVIIIe siècle*. Vol. 7. Brussels: Éditions de l'université de Bruxelles, 1991. Pp. 95.

The slight collection of essays under review in this forum carries a title which does justice to each of the pieces inscribed therein. This collection forms part of the Etudes sur le XVIIIe siècle series brought out now for the better part of the past fifteen years or so by the Free University of Brussels. We have a very short introduction by our editors, six articles of varying lengths and complexities, and an "Annexe" of Condorcet's "Raisons qui m'ont empêché jusqu'ici de croire au magnétisme animal." The first piece, entitled "L'Heureux XVIIIe siècle," by Robert Devleeshouwer, is informal to the point of being chatty, and oddly enough does not mention at all the "pursuit of happiness" doctrine that was the eighteenth-century's most direct demonstration of the *topos*. The second, "Savants en politique, politique des savants" by Jean Dhombres, furnishes a fascinating inquiry into intellectual politics, which for this author culminates in the public manifestation into French culture of the metric system. Professor Dhombres delves smartly into why the Revolution's ideology led directly to the thwarting of the past's attempts to control time: not only did the calendar get disregarded but also did the sixty-minute hour and the twenty-four hour day fall victim to the Revolutionaries' zeal to overthrow that which was and to replace it with that which was to come. Here too, we come to grips with just why science flourished in the last decade of the eighteenth-century while literature and the arts languished upon heaps on mediocrity. "L'Enseignement des sciences," contributed by Bernard Maitte, deals specifically with how the scientific revolution radically altered what was taught in academies of all sizes, sending into dereliction Voltaire's quip upon leaving school: "Je savais du latin et des sottises," cited on page 45. We are provided a résumé of the founding of the Ecole Normale, the Ecole Polytechnique, the Ecoles Centrales all over France, Arts et Métiers, and all the rest– most of which can still today proudly lay claim to not a little scholarly prestige. The fourth article, this by Jean-Bernard Robert, provides a case study of one of the lesser-known luminaries of the day, Joseph Fourier, who is now recognized largely as the author of the 1822 *Théorie analytique de la chaleur*. The fifth, an excellent piece by Hervé Hasquin, sweeps over in a broad stroke "La Révolution et les sciences," which our author labels "the passion for the Universal." This particular essay is exemplary in the extensive scholarly apparatus which is affixed. Concluding the short collection is a two-page discursus entitled "Les Savants à l'école: le cas du Hainaut," by Claude Sorgeloos.

Anyone interested in the fascinating relationship between science, conceived in the broadest of terms, and the French Revolution would do well to consult this slight volume.—James F. Jones, Jr.

Religion, Révolution, Contre-Révolution dans le Midi, 1789–1799. Actes du Colloque international de Nîmes, Janvier 1989. Nîmes: Jacqueline Chamlon, 1990.

Rev. by Dider Poton in *Etudes théologiques et religieuses*, (1991), 135–37.
A remarkable colloquium about the variety of religious recations to the Revolution in a relatively poor and uneducated region of France.

Rey, Roselyne. "La Vulgarisation Médicale au XVIIIe Siècle: Le Cas des Dictionnaires Portatifs de Santé." *Revue d'histoire des sciences,* 44 (1991), 413–33.

Richey, Russell E. *Early American Methodism.* (Religion in America.) Bloomington, IN: Indiana U. Press, 1991. Pp. xix + 137; bibliography.

Ries, Julien. *Les études manichéennes. Des controverses de la Réforme aux découvertes du XXe siècle.* (Cerfaut-Lefort, 1.) Louvain-la-Neuve: Centre d'histoire des religions, 1988.

Rev. by Madeleine Scopello in *Etudes thélogiques et religieuses,* (1991), 449–50.
Part I treats views of Manicheanism from the middle of the thirteenth century to the end of the eighteenth.

Riley, Patrick. *Bossuet: Politics Drawn from the Very Words of Holy Scripture.* Cambridge and New York: Cambridge U. Press, 1991. Pp. 496.

Rivers, Isabel. *Reason, Grace, and Sentiment: A Study of the Language of Religion and Ethics in England, 1660–1780.* Vol I: *Whichcote to Wesley.* (Cambridge Studies in Eighteenth-Century English Literature and Thought, 8.) Cambridge and New York: Cambridge U. Press, 1991. Pp. xiii + 277; bibliography.

Rev. (severely) by Geoffrey Hill in *TLS,* (Dec. 27, 1991), 3–6.

Robinet, André. "La Conquête De La Chair De Mathématiques De Padoue Par Les Leibniziens." *Revue d'histoire des sciences,* 44 (1991), 201.

Rostow, W.W. *Theorists of Economic Growth from David Hume to the Present: With a Perspective on the Next Century.* New York: Oxford U. Press, 1990. Pp. xx + 712; bibliography; illustrations. Cf. *ECCB*, n.s. 16, III: 181.

Rev. by E. L. Whalen in *Choice,* 28 (1991), 826.

Roudinesco, Elisabeth. *Théroigne de Méricourt: Une femme mélancolique sous la Règvolution.* Paris: Seuil, 1989. Pp. 313; bibliography; illustrations.

Rev. (briefly) by Patricia Oppici in *Studi francesi*, 34 (1991) 531.

Rowe, William L. "Responsibility, Agent-Causation, and Freedom: An Eighteenth-Century View." *Ethics*, 101 (1991), 237–57.

In this paper, W. Rowe discusses the views of Thomas Reid on freedom and "agent-causation" to determine what sort of freedom is required for moral responsibility.

Rudko, Frances Howell. *John Marshall and International Law: Statesman and Chief Justice.* (Contributions in Political Science, 280.) New York: Greenwood Press, 1991. Pp. 145; bibliography.

Ruggles, Richard I. *A Country So Interesting: The Hudson's Bay Company and Two Centuries of Mapping, 1670–1870.* (Rupert's Land Record Society Series, 2.) Kingston, Ontario: McGill-Queen's U. Press, 1991. Pp. 300.

Ryan, W. F. "Scientific Instruments in Russia from the Middle Ages to Peter the Great." *Annals of Science*, 48 (1991), 367–84.

Sanger, Chesley W. " 'On Good Fishing Ground But Too Early for Whales I Think': The Impact of Greenland Right Whale Migration Patterns on Hunting Strategies in the Northern Whale Fishery, 1600–1900." *The American Neptune*, 51 (1991), 221–40.

Schaffer, Simon. "Self Evidence." *Critical Inquiry,* 18 (1991), 327–84.

The theatricality of natural philosophers, especially those working with electricity like Stephen Gray, Jean Antoine Nollet, and Mesmer, increased in importance as they took their evidence public.

Scheck, Florian. *Mechanics: From Newton's Laws to Deterministic Chaos.* Translation of *Mekanik: von den Newtonschen Gesetzen zum deterministischen Chaos* (Berlin, 1988). Berlin and New York: Springer-Verlag, 1990. Pp. xiv + 431; illustrations. Cf. *ECCB*, n.s 16, III: 183.

Rev. (with reservations) by C. A. Hewett in *Choice*, 28 (1991), 1688–70.

Schnädelbach, Herbert. *Vernunft und Geschichte. Vorträge und Abhandlungen.* (Surkamp Taschenbuch Wissenschaft , 683.) Frankfurt am Main: Suhrkamp, 1987.

Rev. by Michel Puech in *Etudes philosophiques,* (1991), 547–48.
    A collection of essays on reason and rationality in history, and the historicty of reason, questions connected with the philosophy of the Enlightenment.

Schneewind, J.B. "Natural Law Skepticism, and Methods of Ethics." *Journal of the History of Ideas,* 52 (1991), 289–308.

Most students are taught that in his theory of knowledge Kant tried to steer a middle course between rationalism and empiricism. In this paper Schneewind argues that Kant did much the same in ethics, steering between a sort of moral theory held by Joseph Butler on the one hand, and that of Francis Hutcheson and David Hume on the other.

Schwarzfuchs, Simon. *Du Juif à l'Israélite. Histoire d'une mutation (1770–1870)*. Paris: Fayard, 1989. Cf. *ECCB*, n.s. 15, III: 131.

Rev. by Martine Cohen in *Archive des sciences sociales des religions*, (1991), 296–97.

Scott, Geoffrey. *Gothic Rage Undone: English Monks in the Age of Enlightenment*. Stratton-on-the-Fosse, UK: Downside Abbey, 1991.

Segre, Michael. *In the Wake of Galileo*. New Brunswick, NJ: Rutgers U. Press, 1991. Pp. 192.

Seligman, Stanley A. "The Lesser Pestilence: Non-Epidemic Puerperal Fever." *Medical History,* 35 (1991), 89–102.

Sgard, Jean. *Dictionnaire des Jounaux: 1600–1789*. Vol I. & II. Oxford: The Voltaire Foundation at the Taylor Institution, 1991. Pp. xi + 1209; indices.

Shammas, Carole. *The Pre-Industrial Consumer in England and America*. New York: Oxford U. Press; Oxford: Clarendon Press, 1990. Pp. xi + 319; illustrations; map. Cf. *ECCB*, n.s. 16, III: 184.

Rev. by R. B. Lyman in *Choice*, 29 (1991), 505.

Shapin, Steven. " 'A Scholar and a Gentleman': The Problematic Identity of the Scientific Practitioner in Early Modern England." *History of Science*, 29 (1991), 270–327.

Sharman, Cecil W. *George Fox and the Quakers*. London: Quaker Home Service; Richmond, IN: Friends United Press, 1991. Pp. 255; illustrations; maps on lining pages.

Smith, A. Christopher. "William Ward, Radical Reform, and Missions in the 1790's." *American Baptist Quarterly*, 10 (1991), 218–44.

Snowiss, Sylvia. *Judicial Review and the Law of the Constitution*. London and New Haven, CT: Yale U. Press, 1990. Pp. ix + 228. Cf. *ECCB*, n.s. 16, III: 185.

Rev. by G. R. Urey in *Choice*, 28 (1991), 1567–58.

Spurr, John. *The Restoration Church of England, 1646–1689*. London and New Haven, CT: Yale U. Press, 1991. Pp. xvii + 445; bibliography.

Stafford, Barbara Maria. *Body Criticism: Imaging the Unseen in Enlightenment Art and Medicine*. Cambridge, MA, and London: Cambridge U. Press, 1991. Pp. xxiv + 588; bibliography; illustrations.

Stark, Suzanne J. "Sailors' Pets in the Royal Navy in the Age of Sail." *The American Neptune*, 51 (1991), 77–82.

Stewart, M. A. (ed.). *Studies in the Philosophy of the Scottish Enlightenment.* Vol. I. (Oxford Studies in the History of Philosophy,1.) New York: Oxford U. Press; Oxford: Clarendon Press, 1990. Pp. vii + 328. Cf. *ECCB*, n.s. 16, III: 186.

Rev. (briefly) by Sherry Kuhlman in *Ethics*, 102 (1991), 187.

Stroup, Alice. *A Company of Scientists: Botany, Patronage, and Community at the Seventeenth-Century Parisian Royal Academy of Sciences.* Berkeley, CA, and Oxford: U. of California Press, 1990. Pp. xv + 387.

Rev. (with another work) by Jay Tribby in *Eighteenth-Century Studies*, 24 (1991), 519–24.

Terisse, Michel. *Publication du dénombrement de l'abbé Expilly dans le dictionnaire des Gaules et de la France. Dénombrement de Provence.* Ais-en-Provence: Publications de l'Université de Provence, 1989. Pp. 199.

Rev. (briefly) by Carlo Cordié in *Studi francesci*, 35 (1991), 150.

Teysseire, Daniel. "Une Etape dans la constitution de la pédiatrie: L'*Encyclopédie méthodique*." *Dix-huitième siècle*, 21 (1991), 159–69.

The Restoration Church of England, 1646–1689. London and New Haven, CT: Yale U. Press, 1991. Pp. xvii + 445.

Thomson, Ann. "La Mettrie, lecteur et traducteur de Boerhaave." *Dix-huitième siècle*, 21 (1991), 23–29.

Tomaselli, Sylvana. "Reflections on the History of the Science of Woman." *History of Science*, 29 (1991), 185–205.

Trapnell, William H. *The Treatment of Christian Doctrine by Philosophers of the Natural Light from Descartes to Berkeley.* (Studies on Voltaire and the Eighteenth Century, 252.) Oxford: The Voltaire Foundation at the Taylor Institution, 1988. Pp. vi + 228; bibliography. Cf. *ECCB*, n.s. 15, III: 133; 14, III: 140.

Rev. by Paolo Alatri in *Studi francesi*, 33 (1989), 341; (favorably) by Sylviane Albertan-Coppola in *Revue d'histoire littéraire de la France*, 91 (1991), 96–97.

Tweddle, Ian. "John Machin and Robert Simson on Inverse-Tangent Series for [Pi]." *Archive for History of the Exact Sciences,* 42 (1991), 1–14.

Tweddle, Ian. "Some Results on Conic Sections in the Correspondence Between Colin McLaurin and Robert Simson." *Archive for History of the Exact Sciences*, 41 (1991), 285–309.

Un fonfateur dans la tourmente révolutionnaire. Pierre de Clorivière (1735–1820). Colloque du Centre Sèrves, 22–23 novembre 1985. (Christus, 131.) Paris: Hors série, 1986. Cf. *ECCB*, n.s. 16, III: 189.

Rev. by Danièle Hervien-Lèger in *Archives des sciences sociales des religions*, (1989), 267–68.

Unguru, Sabetai (ed.). *Physics, Cosmology, and Astronomy, 1300–1700: Tension and Accomodation.* (Boston Studies in the Philosophy of Science, 126.) Boston, MA, and Dordrecht: Kluwer Academic Publishers, 1991. Pp. viii + 321.

Valeri, Mark. "The Economic Thought of Jonathan Edwards." *Church History*, 60 (1991), 37–54.

Van Strien, C.D. "Recusant Houses in the Southern Netherlands As Seen by British Tourists, c. 1650–1720." *Religious History*, 20 (1991), 495–511.

Von Mücke, Dorothea E. *Virtue and the Veil of Illusion: Generic Innovation and the Pedagogical Project in Eighteenth-Century Literature.* Stanford, CA: Stanford U. Press, 1991. Pp. xiii + 331.

Vovelle, Michel. *The Revolution Against the Church: From Reason to the Supreme Being.* Translated by Alan José. Colombus, OH: Ohio State U. Press, 1991. Pp. viii + 214; appendices; bibliography; figures; tables. Cf. *ECCB*, n.s. 16, III: 186.

Wacjman, Claude (ed.). *Enfermer ou Guérir: Discours sur la folie à la fin du dix-huitième siècle.* (Société française d"etude du XVIIIᵉ siècle.) St. Etienne: Publications de l'Université de Saint-Étienne, 1991. Pp. 117; plates.

This volume is number five in the series "Lire le Dix-huitième siècle" published under the general editorship of Henri Duranton. Wacjman has supplied a useful introduction to both the general conditions concerning mental health during the period and a detailed presentation of the four texts he has chosen to present in extracted form, almost all of them completely unavailable in modern editions. First, Jean Colombier and François Doublet, *Instruction sur la manière de gouverner les insensés* (1785), which bases its prescriptions on the medieval theory of the four humors. Second, Guillaume Daignan, *Réflexions d'un citoyen* (ca. 1790–91) written for the Assemblée Nationale and advocating the integration of the medical and surgical communities, with hospitals serving as preventative centers as well as prisons. Third, Pierre-Jean-Georges Cabanis, *Quelques principes et quelques vues sur les secours publics* (1791–17993), written for the *Commission des Hôpitaux de Paris* and advocating isolation of the insane patients that had important architectural consequences. He also advised that the insanes should not be kept in chains. Finally, Philippe Pinel, *Traité médico-philosophique sur l'aliénation mentale ou la manie* (1800), the only one well known to modern researchers, that moves away from the theory of the four humors in favor of a new concept of the structure of the brain. Besides his legendary, and partly apocryphal, releasing of the insane from their chains at Bicêtre, Pinel insisted on a strictly controlled regimen of daily work and careful nutrition.

These four texts provide an excellent overview of the changes in attitude towards the insane in the last part of the eighteenth century and also provides a useful background to the innovative ideas of Pinel that are usually the only ones known to modern scholars.—Jean A. Perkins

Wake, William. *William Wake's Gallican Correspondence and Related Documents, 1716–1731.* Edited by Leonard Adams. (American U. Studies, Series VII: Theology and Religion.) 5 Vols. Frankfurt am Main and New York: Peter Lang, 1988–1991.

Rev. by Jacques M. Gres-Gayer in *The Catholic Historical Review*, 76 (1990), 864–65.

Waxman, Wayne. *Kant's Model of the Mind: A New Interpretation of Transcendental Idealism.* New York and Oxford: Oxford U. Press, 1991. Pp. 306.

Weinsheimer, Joel. *Philosophical Hermeneutics and Literary Theory*. London and New Haven, CT: Yale U. Press, 1991. Pp. xiii + 173.

Westerkamp, Marilyn J. *Triumph of the Laity: Scots-Irish Piety and the Great Awakening, 1625–1760*. New York: Oxford U. Press, 1988. Pp. 266. Cf. *ECCB*, n.s. 14, III: 141.

Rev. by James E. Bradley in *Eighteenth-Century Studies*, 24 (1991), 383–86.

Whiteside, D. T. "The Prehistory of the *Principia* from 1664–1686." *Notes and Records of the Royal Society of London,* 45 (1991), 11–61.

Wiltshire, John. *Samuel Johnson in the Medical World: The Doctor and the Patient*. Cambridge and New York: Cambridge U. Press, 1991. Pp. x + 293; bibliography; frontispiece.

Wykes, David L. "*The Spirit of Persecutors Exemplified*: The Priestly Riots and the Victims of the Church and King Mobs." *Transactions of the Unitarian Historical Society*, 20 (1991), 17–39.

Wyman, A. L. "Baron De Wenzel, Oculist to King George III: His Impact on British Ophthalmologists." *Medical History*, 35 (1991), 78–88.

Yardeni, Myraim. *Anti-Jewish Mentalities in Early-Modern Europe*. Lanham, MD, and London: University Presses of America, 1990.

Rev. by Régine Azria in *Archives des sciences sociales des religions*, 74 (1991), 307–08.
The author's theses leaves many questions unanswered.

Yeo, Richard. "Reading Encyclopedias: Science and the Organization of Knowledge in British Dictionaries of Arts and Sciences, 1730–1850." *Isis*, 82 (1991), 24–49.

The Fine Arts

Adas, Jane (ed.). *Corelli and His Contemporaries: Continuo Sonatas for Violin.* (Eighteenth-Century Continuo Sonata, 1.) New York: Garland Publishers, 1991. Pp. xx + 262.

Adas, Jane (ed.). *Early Eighteenth-Century French and German Masters: Continuo Sonatas for Violin.* (Eighteenth-Century Continuo Sonata, 3.) New York: Garland Publishers, 1991. Pp. xxii + 317.

Adas, Jane (ed.). *Early Eighteenth-Century Sonatas for Woodwinds: Continuo Sonatas for Woodwinds.* (Eighteenth-Century Continuo Sonata, 9.) New York: Garland Publishers, 1991. Pp. xxvi + 356.

Adas, Jane (ed.). *French and Italian Innovators: Continuo Sonatas for Violin.* (Eighteenth-Century Continuo Sonata, 4.) New York: Garland Publishers, 1991. Pp. xxi + 311.

Adas, Jane (ed.). *Late Eighteenth-Century Cello Sonatas: Continuo Sonatas for Cello.* (Eighteenth-Century Continuo Sonata, 8.) New York: Garland Publishers, 1991. Pp. xx + 311.

Adas, Jane (ed.). *Late Eighteenth-Century Masters: Continuo Sonatas for Violin.* (Eighteenth-Century Continuo Sonata, 6.) New York: Garland Publishers, 1991. Pp. xxii + 311

Adas, Jane (ed.). *Late Eighteenth-Century Sonatas for Woodwinds: Continuo Sonatas for Woodwinds.* (Eighteenth-Century Continuo Sonata, 10.) New York: Garland Publishers, 1991. Pp. xxiv + 331.

Adas, Jane (ed.). *Mid Eighteenth-Century Cello Sonatas: Continuo Sonatas for Cello.* (Eighteenth-Century Continuo Sonata, 7.) New York: Garland Publishers, 1991. Pp. 303.

Adas, Jane (ed.). *Mid Eighteenth-Century Masters: Continuo Sonatas for Violin.* (Eighteenth-Century Continuo Sonata, 5.) New York: Garland Publishers, 1991. Pp. xxii + 343.

Adas, Jane (ed.). *Veracini and His Contemporaries: Continuo Sonatas for Violin.* (Eighteenth-Century Continuo Sonata, 2.) New York: Garland Publishers, 1991. Pp. 273.

Agawu, V. Kofi. *Playing with Signs: A Semiotic Interpretation of Classic Music.* Princeton, NJ: Princeton U. Press, 1991. Pp. 154.

Albrecht, Theodore. "The Fortnight Fallacy: A Revised Chronology for Beethoven's *Christ on the Mount of Olives*, Op. 85, and Wielhorsky Sketchbook." *Journal of Musicological Research*, 11 (1991), 263–84; figures.

Anthony, James R. "Air and Aria Added to French Opera from the Death of Lully to 1720." *Revue de Musicologie*, 77 (1991), 201–19; musical examples; tables.

On the incorporation of Italian arias into French opera after the death of Lully. This paper identifies more than 30 such arias composed between 1691 and 1709, plus 17 composed and added to earlier operas after 1707.

Apel, Willi. *Italian Voice Music of the Seventeenth Century*. Edited by Thomas Binkley. (Music Scholarship and Performance.) Bloomington and Indianapolis, IN: Indiana U. Press, 1990. Pp. ix + 306. Cf. *ECCB*, n.s. 16, IV: 195.

Rev. by Matilde Catz in *Revue de Musicologie*, 77 (1991), 343–45; by M. Alexandra Eddy in *Notes*, 48 (1991), 516–18; by Eleanor Selfridge-Field in *Music and Letters*, 72 (1991), 583–86; by Richard Langham Smith in *Musical Times*, 132 (1991), 248–49.

Ashbee, Andrew (ed.). *Records of English Court Music*. Vol. V: *1625–1714*. Aldershot, UK, and Brookfield, VT: Scolar Press, 1991. Pp. xxi + 333.

Bach, Johann Sebastian. *Complete Organ Works in 10 Volumes*. Edited by Tamás Zászkliczky. Budapest: Editio Musica Budapest/Boosey and Hawkes, n.d.

Rev. by Stephen Daw in *Musical Times*, 132 (1991), 370.
Daw's review comments "This edition, for all its minor faults, is probably among the best we have."

Bach, Johann Sebastian. *Lutherische Messen: Missa in A-dur*, BWV 234. (Urtext der Neuen Bach-Ausgaba.) Kassel: Bärenreiter, 1987. Pp. 60; score.

Rev. by Jeanne Swack in *Notes*, 47 (1991), 946–48.

Bach, Johann Sebastian. *Mass, A major*, BWV 234; facsimile of the autographic [sic] score and continuo-part. Introduction by Oswald Bill and Klaus Häfner. Wiesbaden: Breitkopf & Härtel, 1985.

Rev. by Jeanne Swack in *Notes*, 47 (1991), 946–48.

Balthazar, Scott L. "Mayr, Rossini, and the Development of the Early *Concertato* Finale." *Journal of Musicological Research*, 116 (1991), 236–65; musical examples; tables.

Banks, C. A., and J. Rigbie Turner. *Mozart: Prodigy of Nature*. London: British Library; New York: Pierpont Morgan Library, 1991. Pp. 88; illustrations (some colored); map.

Rev. in rev. article ("A Conflict of Stories: The Irretrievable Likeness of the True Mozart") by Paul Griffiths in *TLS,* (Nov. 29, 1991), 3–6.

Barbieri, Patrizio. "Calegari, Vallotti, Ricati e le teorie armoniche di Rameau: priorità, concordanze, contrasti." *Rivista Italiana di Musicologia*, 27 (1991), 242–302; musical examples.

Barbieri, Patrizio. "Violin Intonation: A Historical Survey." *Early Music*, 19 (1991), 69–88; facsimiles; musical examples.

Patrizio Barbieri is a professor of electronics whose research specialty is the tuning of musical instruments. This study is both technical and practical.

Barcham, William L. *The Religious Paintings of Giambattista Tiepolo: Piety and Tradition in Eighteenth-Century Venice.* (The Clarendon Studies in the History of Art.) New York: Oxford U. Press; Oxford: Clarendon Press, 1989. Pp. xviii + 246; 18 illustrations (some colored). Cf. *ECCB*, n.s. 15, IV: 136.

Rev. (with reservations) by Nicolas Penny in *TLS,* (Mar. 1, 1991), 15; (favorably) by D. Pincus in *Choice*, 28 (1991), 922.

Barth, George. "Mozart Performance in the 19th century." *Early Music*, 19 (1991), 538–55; musical examples in facsimiles.

Barthélemy, Maurice. *Métamorphoses de l'opéra francais an siècle des Lumières.* Arles: Actes Sud, 1990. Pp. 143.

Rev. by Marie-Joseph Gaymard-Darde in *Research Chronicle of the Royal Musical Association*, 27 (1991–1992), 237–38; by Manuel Couvreur in *Revue Belge de Musicologie*, 45 (1991), 230–31.

Bashford, Christina. "Perrin and Cambert's 'Ariana, ou Le Mariage de Baccus' Re-Examined'." *Music and Letters*, 72 (1991), 1–16; figure; tables.

This work appeared in London in 1674.

Bates, Carol Henry. "The Early French Sonata for Solo Instruments. A Study in Diversity." *Research Chronicle of the Royal Musical Association*, 27 (1991–92), 71–98; table.

Bauman, Thomas. "Mozart's Belmonte." *Early Music*, 19 (1991), 556–63; musical examples; plates.

Bauman, Thomas. "Musicians in the Marketplace: The Venetian Guild of Instrumentalists in the Later 18th Century." *Early Music*, 19 (1991), 345–55; plates.

Bauman, Thomas. *W. A. Mozart: Die Entführung aus dem Serail.* Cambridge and New York: Cambridge U. Press, 1987. Pp. xiii + 141; musical examples. Cf. *ECCB*, n.s. 15, IV: 137; 14, IV: 148; 13, IV: 208.

Rev. by James P. Fairleigh in *Notes*, 47 (1991), 787–88; by Herbert Seifert in *Die Musikforschung*, 44 (1991), 378–79.

Bazzana, Kevin. "The Uses and Limits of Performance Practice in François Couperin's *Huitième Ordre*." *Musical Quarterly*, 75 (1991), 12–30; musical examples; tables.

Beauchamp, Pierre. *Le ballet des Fâcheux: Beauchamp's Music for Molière's Comedy.* Edited by George Houle. (Publications of the Early Music Institute.) Bloomington, IN: Indiana U. Press, 1991. Pp. 56; sheet music.

Beaussant, Phillippe. *Vous avez dit 'classique'? Sur la mise en scène de la tragédie.* Paris: Actes Sud, 1991. Pp. 146.

Rev. by Cécile Davy-Rigaux in *Research Chronicle of the Royal Musical Association*, 27 (1991–92), 238–39.

Beckwith, John (ed.). *Sing Out the Glad News: Hymn Tunes in Canada.* Toronto: Institute for Canadian Music, 1987. Pp. 166.

Rev. by Wallace McKenzie in *American Music*, 9 (1991), 104–06.
This book records the proceedings of a 1986 conference. Topics include hymn-singing of Canadian Indians, early 19th-century tunebooks, and fuging tunes.

Beethoven, Ludwig van. *The 32 Piano Sonatas in Reprints of the First and Early Editions, Principally from the Anthony van Hoboken Collection of the Austrian National Library.* Prefaces by Brian Jeffery. London: Tecla Editions, 1989. Pp. 700 in 5 volumes.

Rev. by William Drabkin in *Musical Times*, 132 (1991), 292–94.

Bellman, Jonathan. "Toward a Lexicon for the *Style hongrois*." *Journal of Musicology*, 9 (1991), 214–237; musical examples.

Includes some discussion of Haydn and Mozart works.

Benhamou, Reed. "Art et utilité. Les Ecoles de dessin de Grenoble et de Poitiers." *Dix-huitième siècle*, 21 (1991), 421–34.

Benton, Rita, and Jeanne Halley. *Pleyel as Music Publisher: A Documentary Sourcebook of Early Nineteenth-Century Music.* (Annotated Reference Tools in Music, 3.) Stuyvesant, NY: Pendragon Press, 1990. Pp. xxviii + 398.

Rev. by Hans Lenneberg in Journal of Musicological Research, 11 (1991), 143–44; by Richard Schaal in *Die Musikforschung*, 44 (1991), 380–81; by A. Devriès in *Revue de Musicologie*, 77 (1991), 129–31; by Corey Field in *Notes*, 47 (1991), 793–94.

Berke, Dietrich. "The *Neue Mozart-Ausgabe*." *Musical Times*, 132 (1991), 610.

Explains the beginning of this undertaking and the way it serves Mozart's music.

Bianchini, Gigliola, and Gianni Bosticco. *Liceo-Società Musicale 'Benedetto Marcello' 1877–1895: catalogo dei manoscritti (prima serie).* (" 'Historiae musicae cultores' biblioteca," xlvii.) Florence: Olschki, 1989. Pp. li + 335.

Rev. by Michael Talbot in *Music and Letters*, 72 (1991), 274–76.

Birtel, Wolfgang, and Christoph-Hellmut Mahling. *Aufklärungen. Studien zur deutsch-französischen Musikgeschichte im 18. Jahrhundert. Einflüsse und Wirkungen.* Vol. 2. (Annales Universitatis Saraviensis, 20.) Heidelberg: Carl Winter Universitätsverlag, 1986. Pp. 243; musical examples. Cf. *ECCB*, n.s. 12, IV: 223.

Rev. by Peter Rummenhöller in *Die Musikforschung*, 44 (1991), 288–90.

Birkmaier, Willi. "Das 'allererste' Mozartfest Wasserburg am Inn 8. August 1842." *Acta Mozartiana*, 38 (1991), 21–5.

Black, Leo. ". . . 'More than Authenticity'." *Musical Times*, 132 (1991), 64–65.

Compares interpretation of Mozart by Vienna Philharmonic and Claudio Abbado with more authentic performances.

Blezzard, Judith. *Borrowings in English Church Music 1550–1950*. London: Stainer and Bell, 1990. Pp. 224.

Rev. by Nigel Davison in *Music Review*, 52 (1991), 141–42; by Percy M. Young in *Music and Letters,* 72 (1991), 572–75.

Boecker, Max (ed.). *Mozart—Sein Leben und seine Zeit in Texten und Bildern*. Frankfurt am Main and Leipzig: Insel-Verlag, 1991.

Rev. by Gerhard Muller in *Beitrage zur Musikwissenschaft*, 33 (1991), 159–61.

Boismortier, Joseph Bodin de. *Cantatas by Joseph Bodin de Boismortier, 1689–1755: Cantates françoises à voix...*. Edited by David Tunley. (Eighteenth-Century French Cantata, 16.) New York: Garland Publishers, 1991. Pp. 166.

Bonds, Mark Evan. "Haydn, Laurence Sterne, and the Origins of Musical Irony." *Journal of the American Musicological Society*, 44 (1991), 57–91; bibliography; musical examples.

Just as Haydn's music often calls attention to its structural rhetoric by subverting formal conventions, Sterne's works often draw attention toward the act of reading. Such techniques had enjoyed a long tradition in literature, but represented a new aesthetic dimension in music.

Boomgaarden, Donald R., and Richard B. Nelson. "Johann Baptist Samber's (1654–1717) *Manuduction ad organum*: The First Modern Discussion of Fugue in German." *Journal of Musicological Research*, 11 (1991), 93–126.

Samber's treatise was published in Salzburg, 1704–1707.

Bowles, Edmund A. "The double, double, double beat of the thundering drum: The timpani in early music." *Early Music,* 19 (1991), 419–35; facsimiles; musical examples.

Branscombe, Peter. *W. A. Mozart: Die Zauberflöte*. (Cambridge Opera Handbooks.) Cambridge and New York: Cambridge U. Press, 1991. Pp. xv + 247; discography; illustrations; musical examples; select bibliography.

Rev. (favorably) in rev. article ("A Conflict of Stories: The Irretrievable Likeness of the True Mozart") by Paul Griffiths in *TLS,* (Nov. 29, 1991), 3–6.

Breitner, Karin (ed.). *Katalog der Sammlung Anthony van Hoboken in der Musiksammlung der österreichischen Nationalbibliothek*. Vol 7: *Joseph Haydn: Instrumentalmusik (Hob. II bis XI);* Vol. 8: *Joseph Haydn: Instrumentalmusik (Hob. XIV–XX/1)*. Herausgegeben unter der Leitung von Günter Brosche. Tutzing: Hans Schneider, 1989; 1990. Pp. xiii + 219; xiii + 180. Cf. *ECCB*, n.s. 16, IV: 200.

Rev. by Patricia Elliott in *Notes*, 47 (1991), 742–43.

Brito, Manuel Carlos de. *Opera in Portugal in the Eighteenth Century*. Cambridge and New York: Cambridge U. Press, 1989. Pp. xv + 254.

Rev. by Louise K. Stein in *Journal of the American Musicological Society*, 44 (1991), 322–43; by Robert Stevenson in *Notes*, 47 (1991), 740–42.

Britton, Allen Perdue, Irving Lowens, and completed by Richard Crawford. *American Sacred Music Imprints, 1698–1810: A Bibliography*. Worcester, MA: American Antiquarian Society (distributed through Charlottesville, VA: U. Press of Virginia), 1990. Pp. xvi + 798; appendices; bibliography; tables. Cf. *ECCB*, n.s. 16, IV: 201.

Rev. (favorably) by Dorothy E. Jones in *American Reference Books Annual*, 22 (1991), 1291; by Karl Kroeger in *Notes*, 48 (1991), 54–58.

Brown, Bruce Alan. *Gluck and the French Theatre in Vienna.* Oxford: Clarendon Press, 1991. Pp. xvii + 525; appendices; bibliography; musical examples; plates; tables.

Brown's work is a study of an eighteenth-century phenomenon, the French theater maintained by the Austrian Empress Maria Theresa between 1754 and 1764, to which Christoph Willibald Gluck made significant musical contributions. It is the most comprehensive work of its kind, consisting essentially of Brown's doctoral thesis submitted to the U. of California at Berkeley in 1986. The work is timely, for it is concerned with an area of musical research largely unexplored by scholars who write in English. That is one of the book's principal difficulties; only about 75 percent of the text is in English. Quotations from German or Italian sources are translated, with the original text given in footnotes. Quotes from French sources—and they inevitably comprise the essence of the discussion—are left in urtext, frequently leaving the reader the task of wading through and deciphering the cacography and macaronic mixtures that passed for French in Vienna during the era in question. Caveat lector!

The central thesis and eventual climax of the book involve the composition and first performances of Gluck's opus major, *Orfeo ed Euridice*, a collaboration with the poet Ranieri de' Clazabigi and a work which musical historians have conventionally termed a "reform opera"—athough what was reformed and how effectively have been bones of contention ever since. But that literary destination is not easily arrived at; as with many pilgrimages, the pilgrim arrives too exhausted from the journey to appreciate the moral—and merit—of his achievement.

After three chapters (107 pages—25 percent of the running text), the reader may wonder if this work bears a proper title; at that point the name of Gluck has been cited passim only five times. In chapter 4, entitled "Gluck and Concerts in the Burgtheater," the composer receives six additional transient mentions. Not till chapter 6 (p. 196), "Gluck and Opéra-Comique to 1760," does the protagonist appear on stage long enough for more than a momentary glimpse. Those facts illustrate the principal difficulty with this volume, viz., the author has covered his subject with so many minutiae that, from the density of the decorative foliage, the reader may have difficulty appreciating the nature of the forest, or even perceiving it.

The author's style is sometimes disturbing; for an historical account there is a good deal of supposition involved, e.g., "he was probably in Paris on and off . . . towards the end of the 1740s;" (p. 51); "it is quite possible that Count Durazzo subsidized the printing . . ." (p. 57). The pedantic vocabulary occasionally approaches burlesque, e.g., "Isabella of Parma successful parturition of a daughter" (p. 130). At times he leaves the reader adrift. How many readers will know what "the Parisian *Premier coup d'archet*" entails? Who will recognize in "gaming rooms for Pharaon" the card game known as faro in English-speaking lands?

On one occasion the author is tripped up by a type which—in a book dealing with the theater—can only be termed a Freudian slip, viz., "with the occupation of the Republic [of Genoa] by French troupes in 1746 (after Austrian forces had been expelled)" (p. 49). These are small slips, but there remains a genuine major oversight: Marian Hannah Winter's *The Pre-Romantic Ballet* is cited repeatedly but is not included in the bibliography. And, though not a major error, the author seems not to be aware that the terms "stage right" and "stage left" indicate directions from the perspective of the actor rather than the audience.

In the Nachwort to *Die Musik in Geschichte und Gegenwart*, general editor Friedrich Blume noted that one of his problems as editor was that "every author has the tendency to say everything possible about the subject on which he has worked, and as a rule that is more, often much more than an encyclopedia can use" (xiv; xxiii). While a specialized book such as this one might be with expected to be crammed to a greater density than a brief article with every pearl of wisdom that could possibly be useful, there comes a limit at which the mind repels further absorption. Following the words of Socrates to Meno, we must admit that men are wise by reason of what they know, yet it is obvious that knowledge—a head stuffed with facts, however numerous and relevant they may be—is not the same as wisdom. This volume may well prove to be a mine of information for those pursuing nuggets of information. For the searcher interested in tracing the phenomenon of the development of a Gallic style in a Teutonic court dominated by Italians and Italianate manners—or the philosophy which inspired or guided it—the mystery will remain as deep and arcane as ever.—Charles Michael Carroll.

Brown, Clive. "Historical Performance, metronome marks and tempo in Beethoven's symphonies." *Early Music*, 19 (1991), 247–58; musical example; tables.

Brown, Howard Mayer, and Stanley Sadie (eds.). *Performance Practice: Music after 1600.* (Norton/Grove Handbooks in Music.) New York: W. W. Norton & Co., 1990. Pp. 533.

Rev. by John Butt in *Historical Performance*, 4 (1991), 118–22; by George Houle in *Performance Practice Review*, 4 (1991), 71–75; by Albert R. Rice (seeking to enlarge upon or correct certain points with regard to woodwind and brass instruments) in *Performance Practice Review*, 4 (1991), 76–79.

Brown, Howard Mayer, and Stanley Sadie (eds.). *Performance Practice: Music before 1600.* (Norton/Grove Handbooks in Music.) New York: W. W. Norton & Co., 1990. Pp. 533.

Rev. by Timothy J. McGee in *Performance Practice Review*, 4 (1991), 64–70.

Brunel, Georges. *Tiepolo.* Paris: Fayard, 1991. Pp. 285; select bibliography.

Bryson, Scott S. *The Chastised Stage: Bourgeois Drama and the Exercise of Power.* (Stanford French & Italian Studies, 70.) Saratoga, CA: Anma Libri, 1991. Pp. vii + 125.

Buelow, George "Bach and the Concord-Discord Paradox." *Journal of Musicology*, 9 (1991), 343–57; musical examples.

Examines relationship between the solution of Bach's canon BWV 207, Vereinigte motto, *Concordia discors*, and the opening chorus of the secular cantata BWV 207, *Vereinigte Zweitract.* Concludes that intellectual fascination with "oxymoronic conundrum" is at the root of both works and suggests it also is of "decisive importance" in Bach's approach to the concerto genre.

Buelow, George (ed.). *Thorough-Bass Accompaniment according to Johann David Heinichen.* (Studies in Musicology, 84.) Ann Arbor, MI: UMI Research Press, 1986. Pp. xviii + 462. Cf. *ECCB*, n.s. 12, IV: 227.

Rev. by Philip Russom in *Performance Practice Review*, 4 (1991), 85–88.

Burney, Charles. *Memoirs of Dr. Charles Burney.* Edited from autograph fragments by Slava Klima, Garry Bowers, and Kerry S. Grant. Lincoln, NE: U. of Nebraska Press, 1988. Pp.

xxxiv + 233.

Rev. by Robert Ford in *Journal of Musicological Research*, 10 (1991), 285–87.

Burney, Charles. *The Letters of Dr. Charles Burney, Vol. 1.* Edited by Alvaro Ribeiro. New York and Oxford: Oxford U. Press, 1991. Pp. 500; illustrations.

Burnim, Kalman A., Philip H. Highfill, Jr., and Edward A. Langhans. *A Biographical Dictionary of Actors, Musicians, Dancers, Managers, and Other Stage Personnel in London, 1660–1800.* Vol. XIII: *Roach to H. Siddons.* Vol. XIV: *S. Siddons to Thynne.* Carbondale, IL: Southern Illinois U. Press, 1991. Pp. 416; illustrations.

Burrows, Donald. *Handel: Messiah.* (Cambridge Music Handbooks.) Cambridge and New York: Cambridge U. Press, 1991. Pp. x + 127; appendices; bibliography.

George Frideric Handel's *Messiah* is more than a musical masterpiece; it has attained, as Donald Burrows says "a 'classic' status among the artifacts of western culture" (p. vii). At Christmas season ensembles large and small, professional, amateur, and in between inundate us with the work—or more exactly with a rendering of Part One that always concludes with the "Halleluia Chorus" in spite of the fact that the chorus is supposed to end Part Two.

In the last thirty years, the so-called historical performance practices movement has tried to restore the work to a form that Mr. Handel would have recognized. We have come to realize, for example, that every time Handel revived *Messiah*, he altered it to accommodate changing casts of singers. Yet determining what was sung at any given occasion is often extremely difficult. Up to now, choir directors concerned about presenting the work in a more or less authentic form had to refer to Jens Peter Larsen's *Handel's Messiah: Origins, Composition, Sources* (1957) or Watkins Shaw's *A Textual and Historical Companion to Handel's Messiah* (1965). Both books, for all their merit, are daunting for any but the specialist and are now a bit dated.

Burrows' slim volume in the Cambridge Music Handbook series reflects the most recent research and provides sound guidance for those who would produce the work in one of its several authentic forms. At the same time, the music lover who would like to know more about Handel and *Messiah* will find a succinct history of English oratorio, a genre that Handel himself invented under circumstances and for reasons that remain unclear to this day, and a concise survey of the evolution of the genre to 1741 (Ch. 1). Burrows' Chapter 2 presents for the first time in English a clear and detailed chronology of the composition and the events leading up to the first performance of *Messiah* on 13 April, 1742. Though the Dublin performances of *Messiah* were hugely successful, the version performed seems to have been a compromise designed to accommodate the skills of the singers available in Dublin.

Chapters 3 and 4 describe Handel's first performances of the work in London (1743). At the beginning, *Messiah* gave rise to a public controversy because of scruples against presenting scripture in the mouths of professionals in the theatre. (As in the case of all of his English oratorios, Handel presented *Messiah* as an edifying theatrical entertainment). In addition and most surprising, the compiler of the libretto, Charles Jennens, was extremely disappointed with Handel's composition of "my Messiah." Burrows provides the texts of the public controversy and Jennens' private criticism and information about the contents of the various revivals in the composer's lifetime. Most welcome is the author's straightforward attempt to deal with the question "Handel's revisions: aesthetic choice or practical necessity?" and its consequences for "The early revisions" and "Handel's later revisions" (Pp. 40–44). Better still, Burrows recommends (a bit too diffidently for my taste) that one "avoid mixing 'early' and 'late' versions in modern performance" (p. 44), and suggests versions to adopt depending on the soloists available. Chapter 5 gives a summary history of the work in performance from Handel's death to the present day. It is here that the reader learns that only after 1770 does the chorus outnumber the orchestra; prior to that time, the reverse was true on almost all occasions. It is also from this date that amateurs participate in numbers in the chorus.

Chapters 6 and 7, "Design" and "Individual Movements" are excellent surveys of the textual basis of the work, analysis of the structure of the text, and Handel's setting of it. A final chapter discusses "Handel's Wordsetting" and its implications for performance. To get the full benefit of Burrows' insights in these chapters, the reader should either be quite familiar with *Messiah* or have a good full or vocal score at hand. The book does not include musical examples.

Appendices include a carefully edited text of the libretto of *Messiah* and a list and description of the three main manuscript sources for the work: Handel's autograph manuscript, the so-called conducting score, and the material prepared less than two years before Handel's death for the Foundling Hospital, to whom Handel willed the materials. In addition Burrows describes briefly the various other contemporary copies and printed libretti.—Howard Serwer.

Burrows, Donald, and Robert D. Hume. "George I, the Haymarket Opera Company and Handel's *Water Music*." *Early Music,* 19 (1991), 323–41.

Manuscripts in the archives of the Prince of Hanover supply interesting financial information and invite a reassessment of George I as opera patron.

Butler, Gregory. *Bach's Clavier-Übung III: The Making of a Print. With a Companion Study of the Canonic Variations on 'Von Himmel Hoch,' BWV 769.* (Sources of Music and their Inerpretation, Duke Studies in Music.) Durham, NC, and London: Duke U. Press, 1990. Pp. xiv + 140. Cf. *ECCB*, n.s. 16, IV: 201.

Rev. by John Butt in *Notes*, 48 (1991), 65–70; by Stephen Daw in *Musical Times*, 132 (1991), 196; by Richard Jones in *Music and Letters*, 72 (1991), 437–40.

Butt, John. *Bach Interpretation: Articulation Marks in Primary Sources of J. S. Bach.* (Cambridge Musical Texts and Monographs.) Cambridge and New York: Cambridge U. Press, 1990. Pp. xiii + 278; illustrations. Cf. *ECCB*, n.s. 16, IV: 201.

Rev. (favorably) by J. P. Ambrose in *Choice*, 28 (1991), 944; by Keith Elcombe in *Early Music*, 19 (1991), 285–87; by Peter Williams in *Music and Letters*, 72 (1991), 435–37.

Butt, John. *Bach: Mass in B Minor.* (Cambridge Music Handbooks.) Cambridge and New York: Cambridge U. Press, 1991. Pp. x + 116; bibliography; illustrations.

Butt, John. "Bach's Mass in B Minor: Considerations of Its Early Performance and Use." *Journal of Musicology*, 9 (1991), 109–23; musical examples.

Concludes that the function and early use of this *Mass* remain an enigma, with evidence that it was intended both as a legacy of musical achievement and for performance during Bach's lifetime.

Butt, John. "Improvised Vocal Ornamentation and German Compositional Theory–An Approach to 'Historical' Performance Practice." *Journal of the Royal Musical Association*, 116 (1991), 41–62; musical examples.

Campana, Alessandra. Mozart's Italian *buffo* singers." *Early Music*, 19 (1991), 580–83; plates.

Campbell, John. "The Unity of Time in *Athalie*." *Modern Language Review*, 86 (1991), 573–91.

Cannon-Brookes, Peter (ed.). *The Painted Word: British History Painting, 1750–1830.* Woodbridge, Suffolk: Boydell & Brewer, 1991. Pp. 139; bibliography; illustrations (some colored).

Cantagrel, Gilles, et al. *Guide de la musique d'orgue*. (Les Indispensibles de la Musique.) Paris: Fayard, 1991. Pp. 840; glossary.

Rev. by Marcelle Benoit in R*echerches sur la Musique française classique*, 27 (1991–92), 242–43.

Careri, Enrico. "The Correspondence between Burney and Twining about Corelli and Geminiani." *Music and Letters*, 72 (1991), 38–47; musical examples.

Carlier, Odile. "Testament et inventaire aprè dé cès de François Campion [c.1686–1748]." *Recherches sur la Musique française classique*, 27 (1991–1992), 203–18.

Carter, Stewart. "The String Tremolo in the 17th Century." *Early Music*, 19 (1991), 42–59; facsimiles; musical examples.

Carter, Tim. *W. A. Mozart:* Le nozzi di Figaro. (Cambridge Opera Handbooks.) Cambridge and New York: Cambridge U. Press, 1987. Pp. xii + 180; illustrations; musical examples. Cf. *ECCB*, n.s. 15, IV: 141; 14, IV: 152; 13, IV: 214.

Rev. by James P. Fairleigh in *Notes*, 47 (1991), 787–88.

Celletti, Rodolfo. *A History of Bel Canto*. Translated by Frederick Fuller. Oxford: Clarendon Press, 1991. Pp. 218; musical examples.

To undertake a discussion of *bel canto,* a notably vague term, is admirable in itself, and Celletti's concise study of this style of vocal composition provides a short, but thorough, history of early opera as well. Five chapters present the subject in an expanded chronological fashion. Chapter I, "The Cult of Bel Canto, Virtuosity, and Hedonism," introduces the philosophy of this style, while the following chapters focus on specific style periods, composers, and voice types.

Chapter II, "The Vocal Art of Baroque Opera," is an enlightening essay. Devoting special attention to Monteverdi, Celletti traces the evolution of vocal writing from its subservient role in early Florentine operas, to the more florid vocalism of early Roman operas, which became the standard for Italian opera until the later nineteenth century. Celletti analyzes the increasingly expressive, melismatic use of the voice, particularly in the roles of deities, royalty, and heroes. This florid style placed new demands on singers' technique and defined the public's tastes regarding voice types suitable for these characters.

Celletti begins his chronological investigation of *bel canto* with the operas of Monteverdi, Cavalli, Cesti, Legrenzi, Steffani, and Alessandro Scarlatti and concludes the chapter with the heart of the *bel canto* period, the operas of Handel. Celletti's enticing descriptions call the reader to search for recordings and live performances of these rarely-heard works. During this period characters were more profoundly drawn, elevating the importance of their arias and creating an explosion in vocalism. A fascinating and uncommon aspect to Celletti's treatment is his introduction to the singers for whom these arias were written. "Superstar" singers demanded music that heightened (or concealed) features of their instruments, and frequently popularized "their" compositional styles. For example, soprano Francesca Cuzzoni's gracefully ascending arcs in her upper range inspired Handel to compose exquisite arias for Cleopatra in *Giulio Cesare*.

Chapter III addresses "Particular Aspects of Baroque Opera." Celletti approaches "The Castrato and the Art of Singing in his Day" with an anatomical discussion and a description of the thrilling, if peculiar, traits of the voice. The author also compares music written for the castrato with music written for other voices in imitation of these unique singers. In "Tempest Arias" Celletti explains the function of these metaphorical arias in the development of vocal style. In comparing one's beating heart to the pounding of the ocean's waves, for example, the singer was given a greatly enhanced opportunity for dramatic singing. A brief discussion of "Buffo Roles" in early opera concludes this chapter.

In Chapter IV, "Rossini," Celletti leaps forward to the early nineteenth century, during which the term *bel canto* was coined. In the works of Rossini, Celletti marks the apex of the *bel canto* style. The reader is given an in-depth view of Rossini's philosophies of good singing, the state of singing in his day in Italy and elsewhere, and a rigorous analysis of his use of the voice in his operas. Celletti also offers an opinion which could explain Rossini's predilection for elevating the contralto voice (heretofore used for secondary roles) to a young, romantic, *buffo* lead in a virtuosic, *bel canto* style. Celletti poses the idea that in these voices Rossini was hearing the vocal possibilities of the castrati, whom he called ". . . the founders of the 'singing which is heard within the soul' . . . . The appalling decline of Italian *bel canto* began with their suppression."

The rise of the Italian operatic style of *verismo* brought about the death of *bel canto*, according to Celletti in "Death and Resurrection of Bel Canto." With the public's demand for realism, came an increasing impatience for the florid style of vocal writing. This chapter details the ideals of *bel canto* in contrast to those of *verismo*. Celletti places the burden and honor for the resurrection of *bel canto* on the head of one twentieth-century soprano, Maria Callas. In conclusion he describes the later twentieth-century resurgence of the operas of Rossini, Donizetti, Bellini and, to a lesser extent, the Baroque operas.

I highly recommend this book to all readers interested in the history of early opera, singing, and opera singers. The translation by Frederick Fuller is outstanding; the scholarly writing is presented in a fluid, conversational style that allows for enjoyable reading by musician and non-musician alike. Rodolfo Celletti's career as a writer and researcher on singing and singers is well represented by this work.—Judith Cline.

Chafe, Eric. *Tonal Allegory in the Vocal Music of J. S. Bach.* Berkeley, CA, and Oxford: U. of California Press, 1991. Pp. x + 449; bibliography; figures; musical examples.

Building on Gadamer's contemporary concept of philosophical hermeneutics and Kuhnau's Baroque approach, Eric Chafe seeks to develop the idea of a "heteronomous art" governed by theological concepts. Chafe's purpose is "to articulate Bach's particular version of the allegorical vision that was shared by all the arts of the age" (p. 8). He arrives at the idea of a "theological aesthetics—that is, an extensive analogical relationship between art and religion—as a fundamental aspect of the Lutheran Baroque tradition" (p. 9). Reminiscent of Suzanne Langer's sentiment of music as "the tonal analogue of the emotive life" (*Feeling and Form*, 1953, p. 27), Chafe portrays Bach's music as the tonal analogue of Lutheran theology.

Chafe's discussions provide extremely valuable and original insights. He explores the developing eighteenth-century concept of the circle of keys in order to show how the tonal plans of various works (ascent, descent, descent/ascent, ascent/descent) reflect their theological character. In contrast to Friedrich Smend, Chafe argues for a different musico-theological character in the *St. John* and *St. Matthew Passions* (p. 139). He traces clearly the developmental differences both theologically and musically during the composition of these two works (*St. Matthew Passion* in terms of Lutheran Orthodoxy and *St. John Passion* in terms of biblical emphasis). Chafe skillfully navigates heretofore uncharted theological, musicological, and theoretical channels in Bach studies.

Chafe implies that Bach's Lutheran Baroque musical culture followed the medieval hermeneutical approach of differentiating various levels of meaning: 1) the literal-historical; 2) the allegorico-theological; 3) the tropological; and 4) eschatological (pp. 33–34). [Chafe passes over the fact that Luther himself repudiated this medieval approach: "I consider the ascription of several senses to Scripture to be not merely dangerous and useless for teaching but even to cancel the authority of Scripture whose meaning ought to be always one and the same." (*Werke*, Weimar Ausgabe [1883—], Vol. 40, p. 567).] Building on the numerological work of Smend, Chafe then applies these various levels of meaning, especially the allegorico-theological, to music.

In several instances, Chafe's conclusions appear as the worst case of eisegesis (reading in one's own ideas). For example, he avers that the "Ach" of the Bach goblet "expresses the theology of the cross, Luther's basic definition of the theology of faith, of the necessary tribulation endured in the present life through faith in Christ and hope for the future life of fulfillment" (p. 34). Again he *interprets* the "allegorical character" of the F minor sinfonia: "Interpretation of the number twenty-one would emphasize it as a multiple of seven and three, cosmic and Trinitarian numbers that confirm the eternal, while fourteen is the multiple of seven and two, representing a mixture of the universal and the human, imperfect . . . " (pp. 43–44).

Selective treatment of Bach's music also introduces bias into his conclusions. Chafe deals primarily with works that he feels "feature a clearly patterned and purposive overall arrangement of keys in conjunction with detailed planning at other levels" (p. 125). Although he deals extensively with the *St. Matthew* and *St. John Passions*, he includes less than half of the cantatas, treats briefly a number of other choral and instrumental works, and devotes less than four pages to the *Mass in B Minor*. At times he is forced to do some clever explaining in the works that he does address: "And Bach—deliberately, I am sure—reverses the relative allegorical meanings of the sharps and flats from the recitative (sharp direction, positive; flat, negative) . . ." (p. 217).

A concise and clear introduction to Chafe's thought is provided in his 1981 article, "Key Structure and Tonal Allegory in the Passions of J. S. Bach: An Introduction" (*Current Musicology*, Vol. 31, pp. 39–54). John Butt notes that Chafe's publications "have enjoyed a high profile in Bach scholarship during the last decade," particularly in "American musicological circles," although they have not been as well received in Germany (*Music and Letters*, May, 1993, Vol. 74/2, pp. 289–90).

At the very least, Chafe's work shows that there is a strong correlation between the theology of the words and the expressiveness of the music in much of the texted music of J. S. Bach. The music does articulate and amplify the theological content and emphasis of the words. Although it does not supply the linchpin for its allegorical thesis, Chafe's book is the best (and most extensive) treatment in English in recent years of the relationship between Bach's theology and his music. It should be read and discussed.—Allen P. Schantz.

Charlton, David. *Grétry and the Growth of Opéra Comique*. Cambridge and New York: Cambridge U. Press, 1986. Pp. xii + 371. Cf. *ECCB*, n.s. 13, IV: 214; 12, IV: 230.

Rev. by Charles Dill in *Notes*, 48 (1991), 82–84.

Clark, J. Bunker. *The Dawning of American Keyboard Music*. (Contributions to the Study of Music and Dance, 12.) New York: Greenwood Press, 1988. Pp. xxii + 411.

Rev. by John H. Baron in *Notes*, 47 (1991), 743–47.

Clark, Stephen L. (ed.). *C. P. E. Bach Studies*. Oxford: Clarendon Press, 1988. Pp. xv + 346. Cf. *ECCB*, n.s. 15, IV: 142; 14, IV: 153.

Rev. by Leta Miller in *Notes*, 47 (1991), 743–47.

Classical Music and Its Origins. Consultant Editors: Denis Arnold, Roger Blanchard, and H. C. Robbins Landon. New York and Oxford: Oxford U. Press, 1989. Pp. 320.

Rev. by George R. Hill in *Notes*, 48 (1991), 84–85.

Clement, Albert. " 'Alsdann ich gantz freudig sterbe . . .'. Zu J. S. Bach's Deutung des 24/16 Taktes." *Musik und Kirche*, 61 (1991), 303–11; musical examples.

Colley, Linda. *Crown Pictorial: Art and the British Monarchy*. London and New Haven, CT: Yale Center for British Art, 1991. Pp. iii + 45; illustrations.

Conti, Giovanni (ed.). *Celebrando J. S. Bach: Atti delle celebrazioni in onore di J. S. Bach nel 300 anniversario della nascta (Como 20.12.1985–19.1.1986)*. Commune di Como: Centro Studi e Ricerche Musicale, 1989. Pp. 73.

Rev. by Malcolm Boyd in *Music and Letters*, 72 (1991), 441–42.

Cooke, Nym. "William Billings [1746–1800] in the District of Maine, 1780." *American Music*, 9 (1991), 243–59; figure; musical example.

Cooper, Barry. *Beethoven and the Creative Process*. New York: Oxford U. Press; Oxford: Clarendon Press, 1990. Pp. x + 325; facsimiles; musical examples; tables. Cf. *ECCB*, n.s. 16, IV: 204.

Rev. by Tallis Barker in *Music Review*, 52 (1991), 308–12; by William Drabkin in *Musical Times*, 132 (1991), 294–95; by Nicholas Marston in *Music and Letters*, 72 (1991), 601–05.

Cooper, Barry (ed.). *The Beethoven Compendium: A Guide to Beethoven's Life and Music*. London and New York: Thames & Hudson, 1991. Pp. 351; bibliography; genealogical tables; 16 illustrations; musical examples; portraits.

Rev. by C. Isaac in *Choice*, 28 (1991), 1318; by Douglas Johnson in *TLS*, (May 3, 1991), 16.

The Beethoven Compendium is a comprehensive collection of well-edited essays by Barry Cooper (general editor), Anne-Louise Coldicott, Nicholas Marston, and William Drabkin. Cooper states that their aim "is to provide a compendium of information on every significant aspect of Beethoven and his music," a goal which is achieved with some notable exceptions. Cooper asserts that "the emphasis has been on presenting hard, factual data in concise form, rather than lengthy and eloquent commentary . . ." (p. 9). With this in mind, it is somewhat disturbing to see the reference in the opening "Calendar of Beethoven's Life, . . ." that in 1770 ca. March "Beethoven's life begins." Is this a subtle insertion of pro-life propaganda? At best, it is out of place in a scholarly text, and certainly should not be included in a calendar of events. Selected essays also are marred by an over-abundance of subjective commentary.

The book is divided into thirteen sections. The first three are quick reference guides, including the above-mentioned "Calendar," "Beethoven's Family Tree," and "Who's Who of Beethoven's Contemporaries" (Cooper). The next section, "Historical Background," includes essays on politics (Coldicott), intellectual currents and patronage, and the artist in society (Marston), and a very useful, detailed guide to the currency units in use and their respective values throughout much of Beethoven's lifetime (Cooper). Additional writings which illuminate Beethoven's musical milieu are included in "Musical Background." "Evolution of the Classical Style, 1750–1800" (Coldicott), is less than comprehensive and occasionally lapses into subjective commentary akin to linear notes for a CD. The essays on the influence of Beethoven's style (Cooper), Beethoven's musical environment (Coldicott), and music copying and publishing (Cooper) are clearly written, and the discussion of Beethoven's patrons and commissions is informative and greatly enhanced by pertinent biographical data found in the earlier "Who's Who."

Beethoven's personality and life are illuminated by two sections: "Beethoven as an Individual" and "Beethoven's Beliefs and Opinions." In the former, Coldicott makes several well-documented contributions on Beethoven's appearance, character, personal relationships, and an especially interesting essay on his often inaccurate perception of his financial affairs. Also included are essays on Beethoven's residences and travel, his daily routine, composing habits, contemporaneous views of Beethoven as a pianist, conductor, and teacher, and his illnesses, deafness, and death. This part features 21 plates of authentic portraits including oil paintings, pencil drawings, engravings, and the Beethoven memorial statue in Bonn. "Beethoven's Opinions and Outlook," by Barry Cooper, focuses on Beethoven's attitudes on religion, politics, literature, and philosophical ideas, as well as his documented opinions of himself and other composers.

Sources for Beethoven's life and works—letters, conversation books, sketches, etc.—are skillfully discussed by Marston in "Biographical and Musical Source Material." Also included are several thorough essays by Cooper. The essays on the diaries and other documents include useful information about the 1827 auction catalogue of Beethoven's musical effects, contracts, documents relating to Beethoven's litigation over the guardianship of his nephew, Karl, newspaper announcements, and a reprint of the entire "Heiligenstadt Testament." Further essays on the autograph scores, the corrected copies and copyists, first editions, and manuscript paper and handwriting include a brief outline of the outstanding work of Douglas Johnson, Alan Tyson, and Robert Winter on the Beethoven sketchbooks. "A Conspectus of Beethoven's Music" by Drabkin includes concise, easily readable information on the stylistic periods, traditional elements of Beethoven's style, harmony and tonality, counterpoint, orchestration, and musical form.

The superlative section on the music itself is prefaced by a numerical list of works. This is followed by individual entries for each work arranged by genre, listing title, instrumentation, details of original publication, dedications or commissions if applicable, and critical notes. Each genre is preceded by an introductory overview of Beethoven's contributions to the genre with additional information on instruments and performance practice where appropriate.

The volume concludes with a short section on "Performance Practice in Beethoven's Day," followed by several essays on contemporaneous and posthumous assessments of Beethoven's life and music, performance styles since Beethoven's time, and Beethoven's place in music history. The final section includes a "selected" bibliography, information on Beethoven biographers, editions, analytical studies, biographies, catalogues, and indexes.

While *The Beethoven Compendium* is not entirely successful in its attempt to cover the entire range of Beethoven's life and music, it is certainly a worthwhile addition to the libraries of Beethoven scholars and enthusiasts alike.—Theresa Bogard.

Coover, James. *Music at Auction: Puttick and Simpson (of London), 1794–1971.* (Detroit Studies in Music Bibliography, 60.) Warren, MI: Harmonie Park Press, 1988. Pp. xxiii + 528; facsimiles; plates; tables. Cf. *ECCB*, n.s. 16, IV: 205.

Rev. by Michael C. Finkelman in *Journal of the American Musical Instrument Society*, 17 (1991), 137–40.

Cormack, Malcolm. *The Paintings of Thomas Gainsborough.* Cambridge and New York: Cambridge U. Press, 1991. Pp. xvi + 182; colored illustrations.

Courbois, Philippe. *Cantatas by Philippe Courbois, 1705–1730: Cantates françoises à I. et II. voix.* Edited by David Tunley. (Eighteenth-Century French Cantata, 14.) New York: Garland Publishers, 1991. Pp. 280.

Couvreur, Manuel. "La Collaboration de Quinault et Lully avant la *Psyché* de 1671." *Recherches sur la Musique française classique*, 27 (1991–92), 9–34.

Cowart, Georgia (ed.). *French Musical Thought, 1600–1800.* (Studies in Music, 105.) Ann Arbor, MI: UMI Press, 1989. Pp. vi + 258. Cf. *ECCB*, n.s. 15, IV: 144.

Rev. by James R. Anthony in *Journal of Musicological Research*, 10 (1991), 306–10.

Cresti, Renzo. *Aldo Clementi. Studio monografico e intervista.* (Musicalia, 2.) Milan: Suvini Zerboni. 1990.

Cusic, Don. *The Sound of Light: A History of Gospel Music.* Bowling Green, OH: Bowling Green State U. Popular Press, 1990. Pp. iv + 267; bibliography. Cf. *ECCB*, n.s. 16, IV: 206.

Rev. by W. K. Kearns in *Choice*, 28 (1991), 1319.

Dahlhaus, Carl. *Klassische und Romantische Musikästhetik.* Laaber: Laaber-Verlag, 1988. Pp. 512; illustrations.

Rev. by Robert P. Morgan in *Journal of Musicological Research*, 11 (1991), 127–31.

Dahlhaus, Carl. *Ludwig van Beethoven und seine Zeit*. (Gro e Komponmisten und ihre Zeit.) Laaber: Laaber-Verlag, 1987. Pp. 320; musical examples. Cf. *ECCB*, n.s. 13, IV: 218.

Rev. by Glenn Stanley in *International Review of the Aesthetics and Sociology of Music*, 22 (1991), 203–16.

Dahlhaus, Carl. *Ludwig van Beethoven: Approaches to His Music*. Translation by Mary Whittall of *Ludwig van Beethoven und seine Zeit* (Laaber, 1987). New York: Oxford U. Press; Oxford: Clarendon Press, 1991. Pp. xxviii + 254; 16 illustrations.

Damschroder, David, and David Russell Williams. *Music Theory from Zarlino to Schenker: A Bibliography and Guide*. (Harmonologia Series, 4.) Stuyvesant, NY: Pendragon Press, 1990. Pp. xlii + 522. Cf. *ECCB*, n.s. 16, IV: 206.

Rev. by Burdette L. Green in *Fontis Artis Musicae*, 38 (1991), 340–41.

Davies, Peter J. "Mozart's Death: A Rebuttal of Karhausen. Further Evidence for Schönlein-Henoch Syndrome." *Journal of the Royal Society of Medicine*, 84 (1991), 737–40.

Davies, Peter J. *Mozart in Person: His Character and Health*. Westport, CT: Greenwood Press, 1989. Pp. xxviii + 272. Cf. *ECCB*, n.s. 16, IV: 206; 15, IV: 145.

Rev. by John A. Rice in *Notes*, 47 (1991), 1128–30; by P. Grahame Woolf in *Musical Times*, 132 (1991), 196–97.

Dean, William. *Essays on Opera*. New York: Oxford U. Press; Oxford: Clarendon Press, 1990. Pp. x + 323; 12 illustrations; musical examples; tables. Cf. *ECCB*, n.s. 16, IV: 206.

Rev. by John Rosselli in *TLS*, (Mar. 1, 1991), 16.

Dean, Winton. "A New Source for Handel's 'Amadigi'." *Music and Letters*, 72 (1991), 27–37; musical examples.

Dell'Antonio, Andrew. "Classic and Romantic Instrumental Music and Narrative." *Current Musicology*, 48 (1991), 42–50.

Dell'Era, Tommaso. *e Mozart*. Brindisi: Schene, 1991.

De Marly, Diana. *Dress in North America*. Vol. I: *The New World, 1492–1800*. London and New York: Holmes & Meier, 1990. Pp. xiii + 221; appendices; bibliography; illustrations (some colored).

Rev. (favorably) by M. F. Morris in *Choice*, 29 (1991), 186.
    Includes the following: "La Novelle France," pp. 61–84; "The English Colonies, 1689–1774," pp. 85–130; and "The United States and Canada, 1775–1800," pp. 131–72.

Demoris, René. *Chardin, la chair et l'objet*. Paris: Adam Viro, 1991.

De Place, Adaïde. *La Vie musicale en France au temps de la Révolution*. Paris: Fayard, 1989.

Rev. by Patrick Taïeb in *Research Chronicle of the Royal Musical Association*, 27 (1991–92), 243–45.

De Ruiter, Jacob. *Der Charakterbegriff in der Musik: Studien zur deutschen Ästhetik der Instrumentalmusic 1740–1850.* (Beihefte zum *Archiv für Musikwissenschaft*, xxix.) Stuttgart: Steiner, 1989. Pp. 314. Cf. *ECCB*, n.s. 15, IV: 146.

Rev. by Bernard Harrison in *Music and Letters*, 72 (1991), 287–90.

Dibelius, Ulrich. *Mozart-Aspekte.* Expanded edition. (Deutscher Taschenbuch-Verlag.) Munich: GmbH and Co. KG, 1991.

Rev. by Friedrich Dieckmann in *Beiträge zur Musikwissenschaft*, 33 (1991), 151–53.

Dieckmann, Friedrich. *Die Geschichte Don Giovannis. Werdegang eines erotischen Anarchisten.* Frankfurt am Main and Leipzig: Insel-Verlag, 1991.

Rev. by Gerd Rienäcker in *Beiträge zur Musikwissenschaft*, 33 (1991), 57–59.

Dox. "Samuel Felsted of Jamaica." *American Music Research Center Journal*, 1 (1991), 37–46; musical examples; plates.

Felsted composed *Jonah*, "America's first oratorio." Written in Jamaica and published in London in 1775, it was revived on the east and west coasts in 1980. The AMRC at the University of Colorado at Boulder will sponsor the publication of the performing edition.

Drabkin, Willam. *Beethoven: "Missa Solemnis."* (Cambridge Music Handbooks.) Cambridge and New York: Cambridge U. Press, 1991. Pp. xiii + 118; musical examples.

Duron, Jean. "Marc-Antoine Charpentier: *Mors Saülis et Jonathae–David et Jonathas*, de l'histoire sacrée à l'opéra biblique." *Revue de Musicologie*, 77 (1991), 221–68; musical examples.

Highlights the process whereby Charpentier composed both an oratorio (an Italian genre) and a tragedy set to music (a French genre) on the same subject only a few years apart.

Dürr, Alfred. *Bachs Werk vom Einfall bis zur Drucklegung.* (Jahrausgabe 1988 der Internationalen Bach-Gesellschaft Schaffhausen.) Wiesbaden: Breitkopf & Härtel, 1989. Pp. 43.

Rev. by John Butt in *Notes*, 48 (1991), 65–70.

Eckelmeyer, Judith A. *The Cultural Context of Mozart's Magic Flute: Social, Aesthetic, Philosophical.* Vol. I & II. (Studies in the History & Interpretation of Music, 34A & 34B.) Lewiston, NY: The Edwin Mellen Press, 1991. Pp. viii + 329; bibliography; illustrations; viii + 475.

This book is the result of long-standing, wide-ranging research on Mozart's penultimate opera. The first volume presents the author's arguments and findings, while the second comprises three Appendices—a facsimile and translation of the original libretto (Ignaz Alberti, 1791) alongside an English translation of the words Mozart actually set; a reprint and translation of letters exchanged between the Emperor Joseph II and Baron Gottfried van Swieten, and a facsimile and translation of Ignaz von Born's 1784 "Über die Mysterien der Ägyptier" from the first issue of the *Journal für Freymaurer (Journal for Freemasons)*. This last has long been recognized as a source for some of the details of the ritual of Sarastro's brotherhood in the *Magic Flute*, but it has not been easily available in

English. For this contribution we should be grateful.

Eckelmeyer is primarily interested in putatively direct influences on the libretto and the cultural and political meanings or effects of the work. Her chief argument involves the use of Rosicrucian elements in addition to the long-acknowledged Masonic, Egyptian, and fairy-tale influences; she claims the opera is shot through with elements traceable to this philosophical system, ranging from a millenarian sensibility and the endorsement of "experiential wisdom" to references to alchemy and metallurgy, and identification of the first scene's monster as a serpent. She argues that several members of Mozart's extended social circle had some contact with Rosicrucian-influenced aspects of Freemasonry, with mineralogical or metallurgical pursuits, and/or with the radical politics of the Illuminati.

On the basis of the breadth and arcane allusions in the opera, and as a result of information she has uncovered about the members of Mozart's circle, Eckelmeyer suggests that the libretto was composed essentially by a committee whose agenda was primarily social and political rather than artistic. Her discoveries about members of Mozart's circle are not, on the whole, problematic, and substantiate some of the more general information in, for example, Peter Branscombe's handbook on the opera (Cambridge University Press, 1991), and Volkmar Braunbehrens' *Mozart in Vienna*. However, her assertions about direct influence on the opera present difficulties, even though she presents her work quite frankly as speculation.

Gottfried van Swieten's putatively central role in the creation of the work is a case in point. His connection to the Bach chorale tune for the two armed men seems unproblematic, though unprovable. However, Eckelmeyer also claims that he was crucial in influencing the arcane references and general value system of the opera; although he was the only person in Mozart's circle with sufficiently wide interests and talents to affect the opera substantively, this claim is riddled with difficulties. Eckelmeyer establishes that during van Swieten's tenure as Prefect of the Court Library, the collection included books on Rosicrucianism, that van Swieten was likely to have known about them, but also that he did not endorse those texts of a "superstitious" nature. One is led to ask whether, if he explicitly distanced himself from arcane religious practices, it is likely that he would have pressed Mozart to embody them in his opera. However, Eckelmeyer says that he may not have considered alchemy "superstitious," and thus might have helped Mozart with the relevant allusions. This claim, made solely on the basis that he did not remove alchemical texts from the Imperial collection, is flimsy at best. Finally, she argues that van Swieten's librettistic contribution to Haydn's *Creation* is evidence of earlier involvement with *Magic Flute*. This argument is based on the comparable utopian vision of the two works, on van Swieten's librettistic competence, (which may indicate previous experience), and on his praise for Mozart's treatment of the German translation of Handel's *Messiah* (further evidence for van Swieten's interest in texts with utopian or millenarian endings). To argue that *Creation* bears some relation to *Magic Flute* seems fair enough, as several commentators have noted, but to stretch a feeling that both works belong to the same cultural climate into an argument that they share a librettist seems, at the very least, unhelpful.

I have borne in on this example not merely to dispute the point about van Swieten, which, after all, remains speculative, but to demonstrate Eckelmeyer's characteristic mode of argumentation. As in the argument just described, she typically maintains conclusions or assumptions that contradict evidence that she herself has produced.

Some difficulties of the book might have been ameliorated with careful editing—misspellings like "portentious" (Preface) should simply have been caught by a careful editor. But the attempt to settle the meaning of a complex work of art through methods Eckelmeyer herself describes as akin to criminal investigation may be doomed from the outset, since the clues offered by art can legitimately point in many directions. Eckelmeyer's attempt both to acknowledge the many layers of *The Magic Flute* and to solve a single puzzle about authorship and influence raises some interesting philosophical and political questions about Central Europe in the late eighteenth century, but it does not provide much new insight into Mozart's and Schikaneder's opera.—Mary Hunter

Edge, Dexter. "Mozart's Fee for *Così fan tutte*." *Journal of the Royal Musical Association*, 116 (1991), 211–35; figures; tables.

Edmonds, Mary Jaene. *Samplers & Samplemakers: An American Schoolgirl Art, 1700–1850*. Los Angeles, CA: Los Angeles County Museum of Art; New York: Rizzoli, 1991. Pp. 168; illustrations (some colored).

Edwards, George. "The Nonsense of an Ending: Closure in Haydn's String Quartets." *Musical Quarterly*, 75 (1991), 227–54; musical examples.

Egerton, Judy. *Wright of Derby*. London: Tate Gallery; New York: The Metropolitan Museum of Art, 1990. Pp. 291; illustrations (some colored). Cf. *ECCB*, n.s. 16, IV: 208.

Rev. (favorably) by J. Riely in *Choice*, 29 (1991), 269.

Eggebrecht, Hans Heinrich. "Thomaskantor Bach." *Musik und Kirche*, 61 (1991), 63–72; photographs of organs.

An Eighteenth Century Musical Chronicle: Events 1750–1799. Compiled by Charles J. Hall. (Music Reference Collection, 25.) New York: Greenwood Press, 1990. Pp. ix + 177.

Rev. by George R. Hill in *Notes*, 48 (1991), 84–85.

Eisen, Cliff. *New Mozart Documents: A Supplement to O. E. Deutsch's Documentary Biography*. London: Macmillan; Stanford, CA: Stanford U. Press, 1991. Pp. xvii + 192; bibliography; 8 illustrations; musical examples.

Rev. (with reservations) in rev. article ("A Conflict of Stories: The Irretrievable Likeness of the True Mozart") by Paul Griffiths in *TLS,* (Nov. 29, 1991), 3–6.

In the preface to this volume, Cliff Eisen points out that " 'documentary' biography was for all intents and purposes [Otto Erich] Deutsch's invention." Deutsch's *Mozart: die Dokumente seines Lebens*, published in 1961, drew together in chronological order all known documents about Mozart's life and music. Included as "documents" were references found in newspaper reviews and advertisements, concert programs and announcements, theater contracts and registers, title pages of Mozart's published works, and selected correspondence. Published by the Internationale Stiftung Mozarteum, Salzburg, in conjunction with the *Neue Mozart-Ausgabe*, the biography appeared in an English translation in 1965, published by Stanford University Press.

Eisen's supplement, issued by the same publisher in 1991, the Mozart bicentenary, contains 241 new documents. The majority of the documents came to light in late eighteenth-century journals such as Carl Friedrich Cramer's *Magazin der Musik* and the *Allgemeine musikalische Zeitung*. Others appeared in the memoirs of Charles Burney and in the correspondence of members of the British nobility, or were uncovered in civil and ecclesiastical archives. Documents in a foreign language are translated into English, and a complete list of the sources consulted, both manuscript and printed, is listed at the end of the volume. Included as an appendix is a translation of the 17 Addenda and Corrigenda to Deutsch's biography that were published in 1978 by Joseph Heinz Eibl.

Like Deutsch, Eisen lists the documents in chronological order, but in a slightly different format. In place of a brief annotation for each document, Eisen includes 1) a source citation, 2) a commentary on the historical importance of each document, and 3) a listing of the available secondary literature. His detailed and informative commentary is particularly helpful in dispelling many of the myths about Mozart that arose during his tours of Europe as a child prodigy, when he was an object of unprecedented interest, and then again after his early death at the age of 35. Unlike Deutsch, Eisen separates the documents into two categories "to reflect the ways in which Mozart documents have been used: as direct evidence for Mozart's life and works, or as the basis for 'reception' studies organized on national, regional, or local lines" (p. xiii). The reception documents he lists by place of origin: German-speaking Europe, French (Paris), and British (London). Dividing the documents in this way, while it may achieve Eisen's purpose, often proves disadvantageous to the reader. For it is only when the reception entries are placed alongside those from the inner circle that a complete picture of a particular event or musical work begins to emerge.

Although the new documents do not dramatically alter our view of the composer or his music, they contribute to Mozart's biography in various ways. Many of the documents offer evidence about when and where specific works were performed. In some cases, the evidence comes in the form of a concert program, and, in other cases, a newspaper notice. An example of the latter is a report of a performance of Mozart's *Die Entführung* in Vienna in 1784; previously, the last documented performance dated from 1782. Several documents answer questions about the authenticity of a work. An entry in a catalogue in Sigmaringen, Germany, for example, allows Eisen to identify the Symphony in D major, K.Anhh.219, a work of questionable attribution, as a piece composed by Wolfgang's father Leopold. Other documents shed light on the dissemination of Mozart's works. As Eisen points out, compiling a documentary biography is an ongoing process, and it is to be hoped that Eisen himself eventually will undertake not only an additional supplement, but also a complete revision of Deutsch's biography. Meanwhile, the present supplement will enrich our understanding of a composer who is one of the pivotal figures of the late eighteenth century, as well as serve as a valuable resource for eighteenth-century studies.—Don O. Franklin.

Eisen, Cliff. "The Old and New Mozart Editions." *Early Music*, 19 (1991), 513–32; facsimiles; musical examples.

Everett, Paul. *The Manchester Concerto Partbooks*. 2 vols. New York: Garland Publishers, 1989.

Rev. by Barry Cooper in *Early Music*, 19 (1991), 643–45.

Fabris, Dinko. "Fourth Biennial Conference on Baroque Music. Egham, Surrey, England, 19–22 July, 1990." *Journal of Musicology*, 9 (1991), 269–273.

Fein, Fiona Morgan, and Neal Zaslaw (eds.). *The Mozart Repertory: A Guide for Musicians, Programmers and Researchers*. Ithaca, NY, and London: Cornell U. Press, 1991. Pp. xvii + 157.

Feist, Romain. "Èléments maçonniques dans la musique religieuse de Franz-Xaver Richter." *Revue de Musicologie*, 77 (1991), 108–16; musical examples.

Fitch, Donald. *Blake Set to Music: A Bibliography of Musical Settings of the Poems and Prose of William Blake*. (University of California Publications in Catalogs and Bibliographies, 5.) Berkeley and Los Angeles, CA: U. of California Press, 1990. Pp. xxix + 281.

Rev. by Brian N. S. Gooch in *Notes*, 48 (1991), 107–08.

Fleischhauer, Günter. "Hamburg, 18. Bis 21, Oktober 1990: 1. Internationales Telemann-Symposium Hamburg." *Die Musikforschung*, 44 (1991), 363–64.

Flothuis, Marius. "The Neue Mozart-Ausgabe: A Retrospect." *Early Music*, 19 (1991), 533–37; facsimiles; musical examples.

Ford, Boris (ed.). *The Cambridge Guide to the Arts in Britain*. Vol. V: *The Augustan Age*. Cambridge and New York: Cambridge U. Press, 1991. Pp. x + 374; bibliography; illustrations.

Rev. (briefly and with reservations) by SW in *TLS*, (Nov. 8, 1991), 32.

Ford, Charles. *Così? Sexual Politics in Mozart's Operas*. Manchester, UK, and New York: Manchester U. Press (distributed through New York: St. Martin's Press), 1991. Pp. 262; bibliographic references.

The erotically charged, quasi pornographic cover illustration for Charles Ford's study, subtitled "Sexual Politics in Mozart's Operas" suggests that the pages within will be as tantalizing as its cover: a graphic rendering of an eighteenth-century couple portrayed at the moment of sexual bliss. Yet throughout Ford's exploration of how Mozart created musical spheres of male and female desire runs a rather too conceptual approach to sexuality. In Ford's own words, his "discourse of the erotic allows not space for inter-personal transcendence—and that of love allows no space for the excitements of the flesh" (p. 8).

Indeed, there are precious few examples of the latter, despite the fact that in their rebellion against Christian notions about chastity, many Enlightenment figures celebrated an anticipated 'joy of sex' in the liberated world to come. Ford does touch briefly on this sexual optimism in his discussion of Enlightenment sexuality, citing a profound belief and trust in the passions by figures such as Diderot, Hume, and Rousseau, their rejection of the doctrine of original sin and the pall of guilt it cast on sexuality. Moving on to the rampant libertinage of the period, however, Ford shifts to the ideas of Sade, who, together with Laclos' arch-libertine, Valmont, articulate the Enlightenment's darker sexual beliefs. Throughout, it is Sade and Laclos to whom Ford returns to underscore the essential sexual dichotomy: the subject/object, the will-to-power of men, i.e: Sade, ". . . every man wants to be a tyrant when he fornicates" (p. 29), and the general passivity of women, i.e: Countess Almaviva in Mozart's *Figaro*, Dorabella in *Così*.

For Ford, sonata form gave composers a musical tool with which to delineate that dichotomy through ". . . the equation of dominant modulation with reason, assertion, and striving, and, on the other hand, subdominant modulation with feeling and yielding . . . " (p. 52). Mozart, too, tends to characterize masculinity in his operas with a driving, more aggressive rhythmic and modulatory instability, i.e: "contextually aberrant, dotted rhythm" for Giovanni's "proud acceptance of the stone man's invitation" (p. 120), or Ferrando's "exuberant broken arpeggiations of the dominant area in the context of a broad . . . middleground ascent" in *Così* as a "powerful celebration of the strong, active desires of Enlightened masculinity" (p. 131). On the other hand, "Mozart's feminine music, with its fluid a-periodicity and decorative prolongation of single pitches and arpeggios, reflects . . . [a] lack of persona—the music of the dangerously inward and amorphous realms of Enlightenment feelings—the music of femininity" (pp. 139–40).

When Fiordiligi, in *Così*, returns to the tonic, but in the "wrong register," after a rather interesting development section (p. 161), Ford sees this as a failure to find her "authentic 'natural' feminine voice range, rather as if she were imitating that moral freedom, which is really the sole prerogative of Enlightenment masculinity," an idea repeated over and over again (p. 161). Ford's principle exception to this rule of male dominance and moral assertiveness is Susanna in *Figaro*, for her music "which he fits the analysis." For readers who are not musicologists, the book is virtually inaccessible. At the same time, Ford's analysis of Enlightenment attitudes toward sexuality misses the very real complexity of the debate, while relying far too heavily on Sade and Laclos as sexual spokesmen for the age. One almost feels that the very male and female stereotypes which many Enlightenment figures (especially Diderot) challenged so vigorously prevail here throughout.

Most of all, Ford fails to convey Mozart's exquisite reverence for the sensual, his rendering of the great and timeless mystery of human love and sexuality in his operas. For years writers and critics have understood this without being able to tell us why. For all his complex analyses, neither has Ford. Perhaps one might paraphrase his quotation from W. Mann that Giovanni's sexually ambivalent Anna "deserves to be pleasantly raped" (p. 185). Ford should, perhaps, be "pleasantly edited" so that this most interesting topic would become more accessible to his readers.—D. Tishkoff.

Fort, Bernadette (ed.). *Fictions of the French Revolution.* Evanston, IL: Northwestern U. Press, 1991. Pp. vii + 209.

Foster, Donald H. *Jean-Phillipe Rameau: A Guide to Research.* (Garland Composer Research Manuals, 10.) London and New York: Garland Publishers, 1989. Pp. xiii + 292. Cf. *ECCB*, n.s. 15, IV: 148.

Rev. by Bruce Gustafson in *Notes*, 47 (1991), 739–40; by Graham Sadler in *Music and Letters*, 72 (1991), 103–05.

François-Sappey, Brigitte. *Alexandre P. F. Boëly (1785–1858). Ses ancêtres. Sa vie. Son oeuvre Son temps.* Paris: Aux Amateurs des Livres, 1989. Pp. 627. Cf. *ECCB*, n.s. 15, IV: 148.

Rev. by Norbert Dufourcq in *Recherches sur la Musique francaise classique*, 27 (1991–92), 245–46; by Cl. Knepper in *Revue de Musicologie*, 77 (1991), 133–361.

François-Sappey, Brigitte. "Le Personnel de la Musique royale. De l'avènement de Louis XVI à la chute de la Monarchie (1774–1792)." *Recherches sur la Musique française classique*, 27 (1991–92), 185–99.

Franklin, Don O. "The Carnegie Manuscript and J. S. Bach." *Bach*, 22 (1991), 5–15; facsimile; figure; musical examples.

Freeman, Robert N. *The Practice of Music at Melk Abbey.* (Österreichische Akademie der Wissenschaftenm Philosophisch-Historische Klasse, Sitzungs-Berichte, 548. Veröffentlichungen der Kommission für Musikforschung, 23.) Vienna: Verlag der Östereichischen Akademie der Wissenschaften, 1989. Pp. 523. Cf. *ECCB*, n.s. 15, IV: 148.

Rev. by Merritt C. Nequette in *Notes*, 47 (1991), 802–03.

Froberger, Johann Jacob. *Diverse . . . Partite, 2 parts (Mainz, Bourgeat, 1693, 1696); 10 Suittes de Clavessin (Amsterdam, Mortier, n.d.).* Facsimile edition with introduction by Robert Hill. (17th Century Keyboard Music, 4.) London and New York: Garland Publishers, 1988. Pp. xiv + 39 fols. + 25 fols. + 38 pp.

Frohlich, Martha. *Beethoven's 'Appasionata' Sonata.* (Studies in Musical Genesis and Structure.) New York: Oxford U. Press; Oxford: Clarendon Press, 1991. Pp. viii + 204; bibliography; musical examples.

Fruehwald, Scott. *Authenticity Problems in Joseph Haydn's Early Instrumental Works: A Stylistic Investigation.* (Monographs in Musicology, 8.) Stuyvesant, NY: Pendragon Press, 1988. Pp. viii + 275. Cf. *ECCB*, n.s. 16, IV: 209; 15, IV: 150; 14, IV: 161–62.

Funtenberger, Verena. "Zwangsneurotiker oder Juxfigur." *Acta Mozartiana*, 38 (1991), 52–7.

Gambassi, Osvaldo. *Il Concerto Palatino della Signoria di Bologna: cinque secoli di vita musicali a corte (1250–1797).* Florence: Leo S. Olschki Editore, 1989. Pp. viii + 734. Cf. *ECCB*, n.s. 15, IV: 150.

Rev. by Keith Polk in *Journal of the American Musicological Society*, 44 (1991), 328–32.

Garden, Greer. "*Les Amours de Vénus* (1712) et le *Second Livre de cantates* (1714) de Campra." *Revue de Musicologie*, 77 (1991), 96–107; musical example.

Garrett, Elisabeth Donaghy. *At Home: The American Family, 1750–1870.* New York: H. N. Abrams, 1990. Pp. 304; illustrations (some colored). Cf. *ECCB*, n.s. 16, IV: 209.

Rev. by S. J. Diomici in *Choice*, 28 (1991), 842–43, by Linda Pollock in *TLS*, (Mar. 22, 1991), 21.

Garrison, J. Ritchie. *Landscape and Material Life in Franklin County, Massachusetts, 1770–1860.* Knoxville, TN: U. of Tennessee Press, 1991. Pp. xix + 314; bibliography; illustrations; maps.

Gärtner, Heinz. *Constanze Mozart: After the Requiem.* Translated by Reinhard G. Pauly. Portland, OR: Amadeus Press, 1991. Pp. 238; bibliography; illustrations.

After the death of Wolfgang Amadeus Mozart in December 1791, the composer's young widow, Constanze (1762–1842), searched for another composer to complete the unfinished *Requiem* for delivery to Count Franz Walsegg, who had commissioned it in memory of his wife. The *Requiem* was completed by Franz Xaver Süssmayer and passed off as entirely Mozart's work. Although the work should have been the patron's exclusive property, Constanze was able to profit further by supplying copies of the score for other performances and even for publication. She was the source of much of the confusion that arose about the work's commission and completion.

For Heinz Gärtner, the *Requiem* story that unfolds in this book is almost exclusively the story of Constanze and her remarkable transformation from the spoiled "little wife" into a capable businesswoman, shrewd and daring in her manipulations of the Mozart legacy. Gärtner's original title is descriptive: *Mozarts Requiem und die Geschäfte* ["business affairs"] *der Constanze Mozart* [Munich, 1986]. Reinhard Pauly has softened the title in translation, as he questions the traditional German view of Constanze. "In her defense," he writes in his preface, "it should be noted that . . . she was left with two small children to raise"—Karl, aged seven, and Franz Xaver Wolfgang, five months old. With no means of support, "she took charge of her destiny with remarkable strength of character" (p. 10). Given the rapid rise in popularity of Mozart's music, her desire to derive some tangible benefit from this is understandable, Pauly believes.

The book covers the period from 1791 through the deaths of Constanze in 1842 and the younger son Wolfgang in 1844, ending with the death of Karl in 1858; each of these deaths was commemorated by a performance of the *Requiem.* In thirteen chapters, Gärtner describes and analyzes what Constanze and others did, or might have done—with the *Requiem* and with other manuscripts and sketches as well. He considers reported events, facts, rumors, and personal motives in the light of documentary evidence and almost 200 years of interpretative scholarship. A final chronological listing of events provides a highly useful summary of what has been narrated in detail.

Gärtner finds precedents for Constanze's shrewdness in the circumstances of the marriage; he mentions the persistent rumors that she, her mother, and her guardian had schemed to entrap into marriage the unsuspecting and love-smitten Mozart. Under Constanze's influence, the composer became increasingly distant from his father Leopold, who had opposed the marriage, and even from his elder sister Maria Anna ("Nannerl"), later Reichsfreyin (baroness) von Berchtold zu Sonnenburg. Constanze, Gärtner observes, gave no evidence of profound understanding of her husband's works; she was not enough of a musician to have been an inspiration, a kind of Muse. At her husband's death, she did not accompany the hearse to the cemetery, visit the grave even belatedly, or mark it, if only with a simple cross. Widowed at age 29, and with limited perspective, Constanze viewed the music as basically of material value to be dealt with according to the laws of supply and demand. She also may have wished to make up for hardships she had suffered during her marriage.

She gave unreliable, even false, information to her husband's friend Professor Franz Niemtschek of Prague, who wrote the first extensive Mozart biography. She had other "puppets" in her show, moving them as she pleased—the musician Abbé Maximilian Stadler among them. In the publisher Gottfried Christoph Härtel, she met her match, Gärtner asserts. She also had dealings with the Offenbach publisher Johann André, Härtel's rival. In 1825, Gottfried Weber, jurist, serious musical amateur, and author of books on music, questioned the authenticity of the *Requiem* and called for an exhaustive comparison of information and sources. Constanze's second husband, Georg Nikolaus Nissen, collected massive amounts of new materials for a Mozart biography. Published by Constanze in 1828, after his death, its 500 pages came to be called, condescendingly, a "monumental pile of raw material" (p. 177).

Gärtner provides extensive illustrations, including protraits of principal figures, facsimiles of manuscripts and drawings, photos, and paintings of important locations and scenes. Extensive notes cite original source materials, including correspondence, diaries, and journals of the day, many of which are published here in English for the first time.—Deborah Hayes.

Giacobello, Sebastiano. *Una stagione operistica (1793–94) al Teatro Santa Cecilia di Palermo ricostruita attraverso documenti inediti d'archivo.* Palermo: Flaccovio, 1990.

Gianturco, Carolyn, and Eleanor McCrickard (eds.). *Alessandro Stradella, 1639–1682: A Thematic Catalogue of His Compositions.* (Thematic Catalogues Series, 16.) Stuyvesant, New York: Pendragon Press, 1991. Pp. xxviii + 325; bibliography; indices; plate.

In this carefully documented catalogue, Stradella scholars Carolyn Gianturco and Eleanor McCrickard organize the musical incipits for all of Alessandro Stradella's compositions that can be identified at the present time. Stradella was active in Rome and Genoa, and briefly also in Venice and Turin. A minor aristocrat, he enjoyed the support and patronage of the leading Maecenas of the period. Stradella's operas, oratorios, cantatas, and instrumental works were well received and continued to be performed for several years after his death—an unusual practice for that time. Stradella, evidently, was held in high esteem by his contemporaries and today is considered one of the most significant composers of his era. Nevertheless, Stradella's repute, and his enduring appeal to historians and musicians alike, has been due far less to the merits of his music than to the salacious scandals produced by his frequent amorous intrigues and the mysterious circumstances of his murder. (The instant popularity of Friederich von Flotow's opera *Alessandro Stradella*, 1844, therefore is not surprising.)

In this work Gianturco and McCrickard are concerned only with Stradella the musician, and have researched their subject extensively. Their meticulous scholarship is evident in their detailed indexes, concordances, and cross references, in their comprehensive annotations, and in their painstaking efforts to rectify the errors and misattributions of earlier Stradella thematic catalogues. Musical incipits are provided for each work, with scoring and/or instrumentation, and lists of all sources. Where relevant, alternate titles, publications, concordances, literary sources, and performance details are indicated also.

The heart of any thematic catalogue, of course, is in the disposition and treatment of the musical incipits and, unfortunately, it is precisely this aspect of Gianturco's and McCrickard's catalogue that is most problematic. Stradella's music is clearly tonal and is organized metrically with measures and bar lines. Nevertheless the (prevailing) tonality of each work is not identified by keys (or modes), nor are measure totals (indicative of the relative length of the composition, movements, acts, etc.) provided for any of the works. Since the editors did examine each composition in manuscript or facsimile, the omission of key designations and measure counts is especially puzzling.

The incipits themselves seem to have been severely restricted in length and scope, possibly to reduce the length of the catalogue. Instrumental works are identified with musical incipits, in score, for each movement. Incipits for the vocal works, however (cantatas, operas, oratorios, etc.), are limited to the opening measures of the introductory Sinfonia (if any) and to the opening bars of the first texted music, regardless of dramatic function; i.e., if the first texted music is recitative, a musical incipit for the aria or ensemble that follows in *not* provided. Subsequent "closed form" in the vocal works (e.g., arias, duets, trios, etc.) are cited only with text incipits and a description of the scoring, rather than with musical incipits. The incipits themselves have been arranged elegantly on the page, but they are inconsistent in length and musically annoying, as the quotations usually break off just *before* a logical pause or cadence—even when the musical context indicates this is only a note or two away. To be wished for also, in this catalogue, is that the editors had identified the vocal parts not only by generic designations ("S[oprano]," "A[lto]," etc.), but also by the respective ranges (e.g., d'-g"). (See, for example, Gene E. Vollen, *The French Cantata: A Survey and Thematic Catalog.* Ann Arbor, MI: UMI Research Press, 1982.)

Gianturco's and McCrickard's diligence and thoroughness in preparing this catalogue is evident throughout, and particularly so in the comprehensive data they have provided for almost every work cited. In future editions of this catalogue, however, the editors are strongly urged to complement their many annotations, performance details, and intermittent text synopses (all listed under "Remarks") with brief summaries of *each* text, and with more *musical* information for each work. Inconsistencies notwithstanding—and some of these may have resulted simply from inadequate proof-reading—Gianturco and McCrickard have compiled an exemplary and much needed catalogue of Stradella's music, a catalogue that will be invaluable to anyone working in this field.—Gloria Eive.

Gidwitz, Patricia Lewy. " 'Ich bin die erste Sängerin': vocal profiles of two Mozart sopranos." *Early Music*, 19 (1991), 556–79; musical examples; plates.

Gilbert, Christopher. *English Vernacular Furniture, 1750–1900.* (Studies in British Art.) London and New Haven, CT: Yale U. Press for the Paul Mellon Centre for Studies in British Art, 1991. Pp. viii + 294; bibliography; illustrations (some colored).

Rev. (favorably) by J. Risley in *Choice*, 29 (1991), 429.

Girardi, Michele, and Franco Rossi. *Il Teatro La Fenice: Cronologia degli spettacoli 1792–1936.* Venice: Albrizzi, 1989. Pp. xxxi + 493.

Rev. by Julian Budden in *Music and Letters*, 72 (1991), 448–50.

Girouard, Mark. *The English Town: A History of Urban Life.* London and New Haven, CT: Yale U. Press, 1990. Pp. 330; illustrations (some colored). Cf. *ECCB*, n.s. 16, IV: 210.

Rev. by J. R. Breihan in *Choice*, 28 (1991), 983.

Glanville, Philippa, and Jennifer Faulds Goldsborough. *Women Silversmiths, 1685–1845: Works from the Collection of The National Museum of Women in the Arts.* New York: Thames & Hudson; Washington, DC: The National Museum of Women in the Arts, 1990. Pp. 176; illustrations (some colored). Cf. *ECCB*, n.s. 16, IV: 210.

Rev. (favorably) by G. A. Anderson in *Choice*, 28 (1991), 767; 770.

Goertzen, Chris. "Compromises in Orchestration in Mozart's *Coronation* Concerto." *Musical Quarterly*, 75 (1991), 148–73; musical examples.

Goldgar, Bertrand A. "Why Was *Eurydice* Hissed.?" *Notes and Queries*, 236 (1991), 186–88.

Because of a joke about the Gin Act.

Grave, Floyd K., and Margaret G. Grave. *Franz Joseph Haydn: A Guide to Research.* (Garland Composer Resource Manuals, 31.) New York: Garland Publishers, 1990. Pp. xi + 451; appendices.

Rev. by Peter Brown in *Music and Letters*, 72 (1991), 595–97; by Denis McCaldin in *Musical Times*, 132 (1991), 349–50; by Robert Skinner in *American Reference Books Annual*, 22 (1991), 1272; by R. L. Wick in *Choice*, 28 (1991), 789.

Gries, Christian. "(. . .)Es zeigen die Pfoten, es zeigen die Säulen . . ." *Acta Mozartiana*, 38 (1991), 25–34; plates.

Grimm, Hartmut. "Berlin auf dem Wege zu Mozart und Haydn." *Beiträge zur Musikwissenschaft*, 33 (1991), 126–34.

Groce, Nancy. *Musical Instrument Makers of New York: A Directory of Eighteenth- and Nineteenth-Century Urban Craftsmen.* (Annotated Reference Tools in Music, 4.) Stuyvesant, NY: Pendragon Press, 1991. Pp. xxi + 200.

Gruber, Gernot. *Mozart and Posterity.* Translation by R. S. Furness of *Mozart und die Nachwelt* (Salzburg, 1985). London: Quartet, 1991. Pp. ix + 277; illustrations.

Rev. in rev. article ("A Conflict of Stories: The Irretrievable Likeness of the True Mozart") by Paul Griffiths in *TLS,* (Nov. 29, 1991), 3–6.

Guitton, Isabelle. "Un Avatar de l'oratorio en France à la veille de la Révolution. L'Hiérodrame." *Dix-huitième siècle*, 21 (1991), 407–19.

Gustafson, Bruce, and David Fuller. *A Catalogue of French Harpsichord Music 1699–1780.* Oxford: Clarendon Press, 1990. Cf. *ECCB*, n.s. 16, IV: 211.

Rev. by John Kitchen in *Journal of the Royal Musical Association*, 116 (1991), 312; by Howard Scott in *Musical Times*, 132 (1991), 395.

Haberkamp, Gertraut. *Die Erstdrucke der Werke von Wolfgang Amadeus Mozart.* (Musikbibliographische Arbeiten, 10/I–II.) 2 vols. Tutzing: Hans Schneider, 1986. Pp. 495; 388. Cf. *ECCB*, n.s. 13, IV: 227; 12, IV: 244.

Rev. by Jean Gribensik in *Revue de Musicologie*, 77 (1991), 349–51.

Hall, Charles J. (comp.). *An Eighteenth-Century Musical Chronicle: Events 1750–1799.* (Music Reference Collection, 25.) London and New York: Greenwood Press, 1990. Pp. ix + 177. Cf. *ECCB*, n.s. 16, IV: 212.

Rev. (favorably) by Allie Wise Goudy in *American Reference Books Annual*, 22 (1991), 1258.

Harnoncourt, Nikolaus. *Baroque Music Today: Music as Speech, Ways to a New Understanding of Music*. Translated by Mary O'Neill. Portland, OR: Amadeus Press, 1988. Pp. 205. Cf. *ECCB*, n.s. 15, IV: 152; 14, IV: 163.

Rev. by Pamela L. Poulin in *Notes*, 47 (1991), 1120.

Harris, Eileen, assisted by Nicholas Savage. *British Architectural Books and Writers, 1556–1785.* Cambridge and New York: Cambridge U. Press, 1990. Pp. 571.

Rev. (favorably) by William Park in *The Scriblerian*, 24 (1991), 86.

Harris, Ellen T. (ed.). *The Librettos of Handel's Operas*. 13 vols. New York: Garland Publishers, 1989. Cf. *ECCB*, n.s. 15, IV: 152.

Rev. by Mary Ann Parker in *Notes*, 47 (1991), 1120–22.

Hasquin, Hervé, and Roland Mortier (eds.). *Études sur le XVIIIe siècle: Rocaille. Rococo.* Vol. XVIII. Brussels: Éditions de l'Université de Bruxelles, 1991. Pp. 173; plates.

Hastings, Baird. *Wolfgang Amadeus Mozart: A Guide to Research*. (Garland Composer Resource Manuals, 16; Garland Reference Library of the Humanities, 910.) New York: Garland Publishers, 1989. Pp. xxx + 411. Cf. *ECCB*, n.s. 16, IV: 212; 15, IV: 153.

Rev. by John Rice in *Notes*, 47 (1991), 1128–30.

Hatten, Robert. "On Narrativity in Music: Expressive Genres and Levels of Discourse in Beethoven." *Indiana Theory Review*, 12 (1991), 75–98; figures; musical examples.

Haydn Symphonies 1761–63, Reihe 1, Band 3, full score. Edited by Jorgen Braun and Sonja Gerlach. Munich: Henle, n.d.

Rev. by Denis McCaldin in *Musical Times*, 132 (1991), 448.
This is the latest volume in the authoritative Joseph Haydn *Werke* project.

Haynes, Bruce. "Beyond Temperament: Non-keyboard Intonation in the 17th and 18th Centuries." *Early Music*, 19 (1991), 357–81; facsimiles.

Heartz, Daniel. *Mozart's Operas*. Edited and with contributing essays by Thomas Bauman. Berkeley, CA, and Oxford: U. of California Press, 1990. Pp. xvi + 363; bibliography; illustrations; musical examples; portraits. Cf. *ECCB*, n.s. 16, IV: 212.

Rev. (with reservations) in rev. article ("Radical, Conventional Mozart") by Charles Rosen in *New York Review of Books*, 38 (Dec. 19, 1991), 51–54; 56–59; in rev. article ("A Conflict of Stories: The Irretrievable Likeness of the True Mozart") by Paul Griffiths in *TLS*, (Nov. 29, 1991), 3–6; by K. Pendle in *Choice*, 28 (1991), 1496; by Mary Hunter in *Notes*, 48 (1991), 486–88); by Alec Hyatt King in *Musical Times*, 132 (1991), 568; by Paul Robinson in *Historical Performance*, 4 (1991), 58–60.

Heartz, Daniel. "Susanna's hat." *Early Music*, 19 (1991), 585–89.

Heintze, James R. *American Music before 1865 in Print and on Records: A Biblio-Discography*. Rev. ed. (I.S.A.M. Monographs, 30.) Brooklyn, NY: Institute for Studies in American Music, Conservatory of Music, Brooklyn College of the City U. of New York, 1990. Pp. xiii + 248. Cf. *ECCB*, n.s. 16, IV: 212.

Rev. by L. Smith in *Choice*, 28 (1991), 1290.

Heller, George N., and Jere T. Humphreys. "Music Teacher Education in America (1752–1840): A Look at One of Its Sources." *College Music Symposium*, 31 (1991), 49–58.

Heller, Karl. *Vivaldi. Cronologia della vita e dell'opera*. (Studi di musica veneta. Quaderni vivaldiani, 6.) Florence: Olschki, 1991.

Helm, E. Eugene. *Thematic Catalogue of the Works of Carl Philipp Emanuel Bach*. London and New Haven, CT: Yale U. Press, 1989. Pp. xxvii + 271. Cf. *ECCB*, n.s. 15, IV: 153.

Rev. by Gregory S. Johnston in *Music Review*, 52 (1991), 79–80; by Horst Leuchtmann in *Fontis Artis Musicae*, 38 (1991), 78–79; by Leta Miller in *Notes*, 47 (1991), 743–47.

Heyer, John Hajdu (ed.). *Jean-Baptiste Lully and the Music of the French Baroque. Essays in Honor of James R. Anthony.* Cambridge and New York: Cambridge U. Press, 1989. Pp. xiv + 328. Cf. *ECCB*, n.s. 16, IV: 213.

Rev. by Robert Ford in *Notes,* 47 (1991), 737–39.

Hill, Robert (ed.). *Keyboard Music from the Andreas Bach Book and the Möller Manuscript.* (Harvard Publications in Music, 16.) Littleton, MA: Harvard U. Dept Music/Harvard U. Press, 1991. Pp. xlvii + 210.

Hitchcock, H. Wiley. *Marc-Antoine Charpentier.* (Oxford Studies of Composers, 23.) New York and Oxford: Oxford U. Press, 1990. Pp. xi + 123; musical examples. Cf. *ECCB*, n.s. 16, IV: 213.

Rev. by James R. Anthony in *Notes*, 48 (1991), 480–82; by Richard Langham Smith in *Musical Times*, 132 (1991), 711; by R. Wood in *Choice*, 28 (1991), 944.

Hochstein, Wolfgang, Reinhard Wiesend, and Renate Wutta (eds.). ('Schriftenreihe der Hasse-Gesellschaften in Hamburg-Bergedorf und München'.) Stuttgart: Carus, 1990. Pp. 48. Cf. *ECCB*, n.s. 16, IV: 213.

Rev. by Raymond Monelle in *Music and Letters*, 72 (1991), 276–77.

Hodges, Sheila. "Venanzio Rauzzini [1746–1810]: The First Master for Teaching in the Universe." *Music Review*, 52 (1991), 12–30; facsimiles; musical example.

Hofmann, Klaus. "Zur Tonartenordnung der Mohannes-Passion von Johann Sebastian Bach." *Music und Kirche*, 61 (1991), 78–86.

Holmes, Mary Tavener. *Nicholas Lancret, 1690–1743.* Edited by Joseph Focarino. New York: H. N. Abrams in collaboration with the Frick Collection, 1991. Pp. 167; illustrations (some colored).

Honolka, Kurt. *Papageno: Emanuel Schikaneder, Man of the Theater in Mozart's Time.* Translated by Jane Mary Wilde. Edited by Reinhard G. Pauly. Portland, OR: Amadeus Press, 1990. Pp. 236. Cf. *ECCB*, n.s. 16, IV: 214–15.

Rev. by Donald Henderson in *Music and Letters*, 72 (1991), 599–601.

Horn, Wolfgang. *Die Dresdner Hofkirchenmusik 1720–1745: Studien zu ihren Voraussetzungen und ihrem Repertoire.* Kassel: Bärenreiter; Stuttgart: Carus-Verlag, 1987. Pp. 232. Cf. *ECCB*, n.s. 15, IV: 154; 13, IV :232.

Rev. by Brian W. Pritchard in *Notes*, 48 (1991), 79–81.

Hume, Robert D., and Judith Milhous (comps. and eds.). *A Register of English Theatrical Documents, 1660–1737.* Vol. 1: *1660–1714.* Vol. 2: *1714–1737.* Carbondale, IL, and London: Southern Illinois U. Press, 1991. Pp. xxxiv + 521; 522–1079.

Rev. (favorably) by J. K. Bracken in *Choice*, 29 (1991), 64.

Hunt, John Dixon, and Peter Wilis (eds.). *The Genius of the Place: The English Landscape Garden, 1620–1820*. 3rd ed. Cambridge, MA, and London: MIT Press, 1988. Pp. xx + 391; bibliography; illustrations. Cf. *ECCB*, n.s. 14, IV: 165.

Rev. by Douglas Chambers in *The Scriblerian*, 23 (1991), 284–86.

Hunt, John N. "The Blanchets, Parisian Musical Instrument Makers of the 17th and 18th Centuries: A Biographical Sketch." *Recherches sur la Musique française classique*, 27 (1991–92), 113–29; family tree.

Hunter, David. "The Publishing of Opera and Song Books in England, 1703–1726." *Notes,* 47 (1991), 647–85; tables.

Huygens, Christiaan. Le Cycle Harmonique *(Rotterdam 1691) and* Novus Cyclus Harmonicus *(Leiden 1724), with Dutch and English Translations*. Edited by Rudolf Rasch. (Tuning and Temperament Library, 6.) Utrecht: The Diapason Press, 1986. Pp. 183. Cf. *ECCB*, n.s. 12, IV: 251.

Rev. by Douglas Leedy in *Notes*, 47 (1991), 1103–06.

Jackson, Roland. *Performance Practice, Medieval to Contemporary: A Bibliographic Guide*. (Music Research and Information Guides, 9; Garland Reference Library of the Humanities, 790.) London and New York: Garland Publishers, 1988. Pp. xxix + 518. Cf. *ECCB*, n.s. 15, IV: 155; 14, IV: 166.

Rev. by Cynthia J. Cyrus in *Fontis Artis Musicae*, 38 (1991), 147–48; by Pamela L. Poulin in *Notes*, 47 (1991), 1174.

Jackson Stops, Gervase (comp.). *An English Arcadia, 1600–1990: Designs for Gardens and Garden Buildings in the Care of the National Trust*. Washington, DC: American Institute of Architects Press in association with the British National Trust, 1991. Pp. 160; illustrations (some colored).

Jacobs, Helmut C. "Jean Nicolas Bouilly (1763–1842) und die Genese des Leonorenstoffes. 'Léonore ou L'amour conjugal' als 'Fait historique' der Revolutionszeit." *Archiv für Musikwissenschaft,* 48 (1991), 199–216.

Jaffe, Irma B. (ed.). *The Italian Presence in American Art, 1760–1860*. New York: Fordham U. Press; Rome: Istituto della Enciclopedia italiana, 1989. Pp. xvii + 250; 36 color illustrations, 160 black & white. Cf. *ECCB*, n.s. 16, IV: 216; 15, IV: 155.

Rev. by Damie Stillman in *Eighteenth-Century Studies*, 25 (1991–92), 247–50.

Jander, O. "La profetica conversazione al termine della scena presso il ruscello." *Rivista Italiana di Musicologia*, 27 (1991), 303–46; musical examples.

On Beethoven's "Pastoral" Symphony.

Jenne, Natalie, and Meredith Little. *Dance and the Music of J.S. Bach*. Bloomington and Indianapolis, IN: Indiana U. Press, 1991. Pp. x + 352; appendices; bibliography; musical examples.

Dance has been a major influence on musical style in virtually all cultures, across all time periods. One of our more stylized dance types, French noble dance, was codified through notation first published in 1700. Disseminated internationally and studied by anyone of culture from the 1650s on, this style not only formed the roots of classical ballet, but also generated the Baroque instrumental suite. Little and Jenne have addressed the need for more study of the influence of French dance on Bach's music, especially for the performer rendering Bach's music the way it would have been performed in the 18th century. Following the work of their Stanford mentor, Putnam Aldrich, the authors address structure and style in this music, focussing on rhythmic and metric aspects of composition.

The authors' combined experiences qualify them to tackle this multidisciplinary subject. Little's 1967 dissertation was a pioneer study of Lully's dance music and Jenne teaches harpsichord and Baroque performance practice. Their coverage is comprehensive, encompassing all of Bach's 195 movements titled as dances plus 103 untitled movements. The titled dances also are discussed in the analysis chapters. In Part I, a 30-page summary of dance practice in France and Germany within broader cultural contexts, one notes the singular, Parisian focus of French dance, in contrast to the many German courts where French dance was à la mode. Part I also defines terminology and methodology for discussing Bach's dance music. The book's greatest contribution to the subject is in the 175 pages of Part II, where this methodology is applied to each French dance type in Bach's music, one dance per chapter: bourrée, gavotte, minuet, etc. These discussions are richly illustrated with original choreographies, views of dancers, quotations from contemporaneous theorists, and musical examples by Bach and others.

Modern criticism clearly requires more explicit terminology for French Baroque music and dance. This work is a step in that direction, but not the final solution. The authors' goal has been a "new set of analytic tools" (p. ix) to discuss dance music with more precision. But has their critical vocabulary really succeeded? The book is intended primarily for practitioners (with harpsichordists probably benefiting most), but will dancers be interested in the detailed analyses of musical metrical structure, which often diverges from the dance structure? The authors do urge readers "not to intellectualize rhythm" too much (p. x), but is much feeling communicated through these written analyses alone, which obviously speak so illuminatingly to the authors? This topic could be enhanced by an accompanying audio or video tape of performances to help the reader feel the insight which the analyses reveal.

While the authors analyze each dance type systematically, their historical methods are not as critical, or perhaps it is just the language used. Phrases such as "Bach *would have* encountered French . . . music" (p. 3) leaves one questioning whether this is a historical fact. Also, the origins of terminology could be clarified further. For example, are the terms "beat," "pulse," and "tap" historically based? Finally, while theorists of the past assigned gender to musical cadences (the feminine was always the weak cadence), these terms do not need to reappear in our more objective vocabulary of the 1990s.

The format of the volume could also be clearer. Both "Figures" and "Examples" can contain scores and both are indispensable for understanding the detailed analyses discussed in the text. This makes it difficult to know where to turn in search of illustrations. Also the oblong format of Appendix A makes it awkward to refer to while reading. Footnote and bibliography format is also confusing. Although the bibliography includes many Germanic sources on French dance often left out of studies of French dance, it might be more useful if divided between historical and modern sources.

What conclusions will the reader draw? Who will the book enlighten—harpsichordist, dancer, scholar of Baroque music, general reader? My experience suggests that performing musicians first want to know how to do specific Baroque dance steps and at what tempo. As this book illustrates, there is no simple nor singular answer to those questions, but that conclusion could have been stated much more clearly by the authors. However, the overall goal of addressing an important part of Bach's repertoire is as noble as the dance style it explains. The volume is important, but also must be used carefully.—Barbara Coeyman.

John, David G. *The German Nachspiel in the Eighteenth Century*. Buffalo, NY, and Toronto: U. of Toronto Press, 1991. Pp. xii + 411; bibliography.

John Nash: A Complete Catalogue. Photographs and Text by Michael Mansbridge. Introduction by John Summerson. New York: Rizzoli, 1991. Pp. 336; illustrations (some colored); plans; portraits.

Rev. (briefly) in rev. article ("Architecture") by Martin Filler in *New York Times Book Review,* 96 (Dec. 1, 1991), 12.
    British edition, *John Nash: An Illustrated Catalogue of Works*, was published at Oxford by Phaidon Press in 1991.

Johnston, Gregory S. "Rhetorical Personification of the Dead in 17th-Century German Funeral Music." *Journal of Musicology*, 9 (1991), 186–213; figures.

Examines Heinrich Schültz's *Musikalische Exequien* (1636) and three works by Michael Wiedemann (1693) to demonstrate the shared rhetorical aims of music and oratory in the Mutheran funeral ceremony."

Johnstone, H. Diack, and Roger Fiske (eds.). *Music in Britain. The Eighteenth Century.* (The Blackwell History of Music in Britain, 4.) Cambridge, MA, and Oxford: Blackwell Reference, 1990. Pp. xvii + 534; bibliography; musical examples. Cf. *ECCB*, n.s. 16, IV: 216.

Rev. by W. Metcalfe in *Choice*, 29 (1991), 114.

Joly, Jacques. *Dagli Elisi all'Inferno: il melodramma tra Italia e Francia dal 1730 al 1850.* (Discanto/Contrappunti, xxvii.) Florence: La Nuova Italia, 1990. Pp. 295.

Rev. by John Rosselli in *Music and Letters*, 72 (1991), 589–90.

Jones, Peter (ed.). *Philosophy and Science in the Scottish Enlightenment.* Edinburgh, Scotland: John Donald Publishers, 1988. Pp. vii + 230.

Rev. by Malcolm Jack in *Eighteenth-Century Studies*, 24 (1991), 371–73.

Jones, Richard. "Further Observations on the Development of *The Well-Tempered Clavier II*." *Musical Times*, 132 (1991), 607–09

A sequel to Jones' article listed below.

Jones, Richard. "Stages in the Development of Bach's *The Well-Tempered Clavier II*." *Musical Time*s, 132 (1991), 441–46; musical examples.

Scholarly discussion of the preparation of Jones new edition which will be published by the Associated Board of the Royal Schools of Music.

Jorgensen, Owen. *Tuning: Containing the Perfection of Eighteenth-Century Temperament, the Lost Art of Nineteenth-Century Temperament, and the Science of Equal Temperament, Complete with Instructions . . . .* Ann Arbor, MI: Michigan State U. Press, 1991. Pp. xxiii + 798.

Kagen, Susan. *Archduke Rudolph: Beethoven's Patron, Pupil, and Friend.* Stuyvesant, NY: Pendragon Press, 1988. Pp. xxiv + 353. Cf. *ECCB*, n.s. 16, IV: 217; 14, IV: 167.

Rev. by Mary Sue Morrow in *Journal of Musicological Research*, 11 (1991), 134–39.

Karhausen, L. R. "Contra Davies: Mozart's Terminal Illness." *Journal of the Royal Society of Medicine*, 84 (1991), 734–36.

Keller, Hermann. *Thoroughbass Method: With Excerpts from the Theoretical Works of Praetorius, Niedt, Telemann, Mattheson, Heinichen, J. S. And C. P. E. Bach [and others] and Numerous Examples from the Literature of the Seventeenth and Eighteenth Centuries.* Translated and edited by Carl Parrish. New York: Columbia U. Press, 1990. Pp. 97. Cf. *ECCB*, n.s. 16, IV: 218.

Kenyon, Nicholas (ed.). *Authenticity and Early Music. A Symposium.* New York and Oxford: Oxford U. Press, 1988. Pp. xv + 219. Cf. *ECCB*, n.s. 16, IV: 218; 15, IV: 156; 14, IV:167.

Rev. by Dieter Gutknecht in *Die Musikforschung*, 44 (1991), 284; by David Schulenberg in *Current Musicology*, 48 (1991), 78–87.

Keyes, George S. *Mirror of Empire: Dutch Marine Art of the Seventeenth Century.* Cambridge and New York: Cambridge U. Press; Minneapolis, MN: Minneapolis Institute of Arts, 1990. Pp. xiv + 444; illustrations (some colored). Cf. *ECCB*, n.s. 16, IV: 218.

Rev. (favorably) by A. Golahny in Choice, 28 (1991), 925; (favorably) by Margarita Russell in *TLS,* (Sept. 20, 1991), 20.
    "Published in connection with the exhibition held at the Minneapolis Institute of Arts, Sept. 23–Dec. 31, 1990; The Toledo Museum of Art, Jan. 27–Apr. 21, 1991 [and] the Los Angeles County Museum of Art, May 23–Aug. 11, 1991."

Kimball, G. Cook. "The second Theme in Sonata Form as Insertion." *Music Review*, 52 (1991), 279–93; figures; musical examples.

Refers to Riepel and Marx.

Kimbell, David. *Italian Opera*. (National Traditions of Opera.) Cambridge and New York: Cambridge U. Press, 1991. Pp. xvii + 684; bibliography; illustrations; map; musical examples.

Rev. (severely and with another work) by Roger Park in *TLS,* (Dec. 13, 1991), 18.
    "Part III: Opera seria" (pp. 179–279) and "Part IV: The Tradition of Comedy" (pp. 280–387) concern the Eighteenth Century.

Kinderman, William (ed.). *Beethoven's Compositional Process*. (North American Beethoven Studies, 1.) Lincoln, NE, and London: U. of Nebraska Press in association with the American Beethoven Society and the Ira F. Brilliant Center for Beethoven Studies, San Jose State U., 1991. Pp. xii + 195; musical examples.

King, Richard G. "Handel's Travels in the Netherlands in 1750." *Music and Letters*, 72 (1991), 372–86; plates.

Examines documents that raise "new questions about his connections in Holland, in particular, with his former pupil, Princess Anne."

Kintzler, Catherine. *Poétique de l'opéra français de Corneille è Rousseau. collection 'Voies de l'histoire.* (Culture et société.) Editions Minerve, 1991. Pp. 583.

Rev. by Françoise Escal in *International Review of the Aesthetics and Sociology of Music*, 22 (1991), 109–11.

Klakowich, Robert. "Scocca pur: Genesis of an English Ground." *Journal of the Royal Musical Association*, 116 (1991), 63–77; facsimiles; musical examples; tables.

This ground was published in Henry Playford's *The Second Part of Musick's Hand-maid* (1689).

Klefisch, Walter. "Mozart und der 'Zeitgeist'." *Acta Mozartiana*, 38 (1991), 6–7.

Knepler, Georg. "Mozart als Herausforderung." *Beiträge zur Musikwissenschaft,* 33 (1991), 111–25; muscial examples.

Knepler, Georg. *Wolfgang Amadé Mozart. Annäherungen.* Berlin: Henschel, 1991.

Rev. by Friedrich Dieckmann in *Beiträge zur Musikwissenschaft*, 33 (1991), 151–53.

Knights, Francis. "Some Observations on the Clavichord in France." *Galpin Society Journal*, 44 (1991), 71–76; tables.

Konrad, Ulrich. "Bemerkungen zu Problemen der Edition von Mozart-Skizzen." *Die Musikforschung*, 44 (1991), 331–55.

Koogje, Anneke J. "Anne Longeau, première chanteuse du Théâtre française de la Haye (1788–1793)." *Recherches sur la Musique française classique*, 27 (1991–92), 163–84; appendices.

Kordes, Gesa. "Self-Parody and the 'Hunting Cantata,' BWV 208–An Aspect of Bach's Compositional Process." *Bach*, 22 (1991), 35–57; muscial examples; tables.

Kornhauser, Elizabeth Mankin, with Richard L. Bushman, Stephen H. Kornhauser, and Aileen Ribeiro. *Ralph Earl: The Face of the Young Republic.* Hartford, CT: Wadsworth Atheneum; New Haven, CT: Yale U. Press, 1991. Pp. xiii + 258; bibliography; illustrations (some colored).

Kremer, Joachim. "Schulische Musikunterricht zwischen 1766 und 1825." *International Review of the Aesthetics and Sociology of Music*, 22 (1991), 29–46.

Kroeger, Karl. "Johann Sebastian Bach in Nineteenth-Century America." *Bach*, 22 (1991), 33–42.

Kroeger, Karl (comp.). *Catalog of the Musical Works of William Billings.* (Music Reference Collection, 32.) New York: Greenwood Press, 1991. Pp. xx + 160.

Kropfinger, Klaus. *Wagner and Beethoven: Richard Wagner's Reception of Beethoven.* Revised translation by Peter Palmer of *Wagner und Beethoven* (Regensburg, 1974). Cambridge and New York: Cambridge U. Press, 1991. Pp. xi + 288; bibliography; musical examples.

Krummacher, Friedrich. "Bach als Zeitgenosse. Zum historischen und aktuellen Verständis von Bachs Music." *Archuv für Musikwissenschaft*, 48 (1991), 64–83.

Krummacher, Friedrich. "Bachs frühe Kantaten im Kontext der Tradition." *Die Musikforschung*, 44 (1991), 9–32; musical examples.

Lacour, Pierre. *Notes et souvenirs d'un artiste octogénaire, 1778–1798*. Edited by Philippe Le Leyzour and Dominique Cante. Bordeaux: Musée des Beaux-Arts de Bordeaux et William Blake and Co., 1989. Pp. 151.

Rev. by Carlo Cordié in *Studi francesi*, 35 (1991), 147.

Ladewig, James. "Bach and the *Prima prattica*: The influence of Frescobaldi on a Fugue from the *Well-Tempered Clavier*." *Journal of Musicology*, 9 (1991), 358–75; musical examples.

Bach's assimilation of *prima prattica*, particularly ricercar style, is demonstrated by comparing Frescobaldi's *Ricercar primo* (1615) with Bach's Fugue in C# Minor (*WTC!*). Just as Frescobaldi's *oeuvre* balances *prima prattica* and *seconda prattica* styles, so the vital use of this older style by Bach and his German forbears is seen as a counterbalancing and unifying factor throughout the Baroque.

Lafler, Joanne. *The Celebrated Mrs. Oldfield: The Life and Art of an Augustan Actress*. Carbondale, IL: Southern Illinois U. Press, 1989. Pp. xii + 243. Cf. *ECCB*, n.s. 16, IV: 219; 15, IV: 156.

Rev. (with another work) by Nancy Cotton in *The Scriblerian*, 23 (1991), 264–65.

Landon, H. C. Robbins. *1791 Mozarts letztes Jahr*. Munich: Deutsche Taschenbuch-Verlag, 1991.

Landon, H. C. Robbins. *Mozart and Vienna*. London: Thames and Hudson; New York: Schirmer Books and Maxwell Macmillan International, 1991. Pp. 208; illustrations; portraits; select bibliography.

Rev. (severely) by C. Isaac in *Choice*, 29 (1991), 604; by Lindsay Kemp in *Musical Times*, 132 (1991), 569.
    Even at first glance, H. C. Robbins Landon's *Mozart and Vienna* promises to be another in his series of excellent Mozart studies, works valued by music scholars and appreciators alike. To a late-eighteenth-century music historian, Landon's rich chronicle of Mozart's four sojourns to Vienna (1762, 1767–1768, 1773 and 1781–1791; chapters 1, 2, 3, and 6), which are based on contemporaneous letters, diaries, newspapers, and biographies, provides an illuminating context for Mozart's relationship with various Habsburgs in Vienna and Milan. Notable are Landon's myriad of peripheral references in chapter 2 (1767–8), in which an opera scholar may well hang on every word, in view of the storehouse of information. Landon's assortment of sources are eminently helpful with regard to opera, court celebrations, impresarios, singers, and composers, and underscore those political and financial exigencies that dictated Mozart's limited participation in the Viennese repertory. Landon's overview of the *Sturm und Drang* movement (chapter 4) is valuable for its succinctly-drawn explanation of the movement's origins and eventual infusion into musical style, an easy task for the author of the monumental Haydn chronicles.
    As Landon states in chapter 5 ("Mozart and Vienna in the 1780s"), a reconstruction of Viennese life during Mozart's final decade in Vienna "is not as difficult a task as it might at first appear," with the wealth of contemporaneous paintings, engravings, and source materials evidenced in Landon's diverse selection of thirty two illustrations and instructive captions. Scholars, both cultural historians and musicologists, and those simply

interested in Mozart and Vienna will benefit from Landon's attractive volume and clear prose.

While Landon's contextual overview of musico-political Vienna—into which Mozart attempted to assimilate—is valuable for its concise gathering of Mozart's Viennese journeys, it may well be that the main attraction is Landon's abridged, English translation of Johann Pezzl's *Skizze von Wien* ("Sketches of Vienna," chapter 5). Originally published in six installments between 1786 and 1790, Landon's 138-page transcription of Pezzl's history of Viennese cultural life, institutions, and contemporaneous events provides an invaluable cultural context. As Landon explains, bracketed information—explanatory interpolations, commentary, supplemental information, and corrections—is offered as an aid to the reader. This information includes, for example, Landon's revision of Pezzl's figures for circulating newspapers during this period (p. 156), as well as summaries of omitted or abridged portions of the complete text, available in the 1923 reissue of Pezzl's original version edited by Gustav Gugitz and Anton Schlosser.

Pezzl, a former Mason, was a supporter of many of Joseph II's reforms, which accounts for his sometimes lengthy and biased discussions (monasteries, toleration edicts, Enlightenment theories, penal code reforms, consumption of goods, etc.). The broad appeal of Pezzl's sketches lies in its contextual overview for the music historian and quick reference for the cultural historian (population data, ethnic and religious representations, consumption of goods, income, etc.). Pezzl's observations on fashion, politics, the Viennese social strata, leisure, prostitution, criminal laws, holidays, worship, police, burials, and animal baiting represent only a sampling of his commentary.

Pezzl's limited discussion of Italian and German opera and the National Theater accurately reflects the limited public who could afford to attend the opera. Pezzl's list of the five most popular operas in Vienna in 1787 does not exactly accord with Viennese opera historian Otto Michtner's statistical index, but instead isolates those "pieces which have received the most general applause," which corroborates recent scholars' research. (Curiously, one reviewer complained that Pezzl had not singled out Mozart's operas, but why should he, for Pezzl's list confirms the domination of Italian composers who overshadowed Mozart.) Significantly, Pezzl's comment that the National Theater served as "a school for manners" is borne out in his detailed analysis of Viennese class structure from Emperor to chamber maids, which is reflected in both the social and operatic hierarchy. (Pezzl's description of the exacting differences between chamber and ladies' maids underscores the distinction between Mozart's Susanna [*Le nozze di Figaro*] and Despina [*Così fan tutte*].) The Viennese disdain for Parisian taste and culture runs through much of Pezzl's commentary, ranging from subtle understatement to outright ridicule. Landon's chronological approach is made all the more effective by Pezzl's sketches, which set up Landon's final and most profound chapter ("Mozart's stay in Vienna, 1781–1791, and its ramifications"), in which he posits why Mozart remained in Vienna despite the rapidly-shifting political and artistic reforms under Leopold II. The single liability to Landon's stunning work may be its title, which does not disclose its wealth of source materials.—Kay Lipton

Landon, H. C. Robbins. *Mozart and the Masons: New Light in the Lodge "Crowned Hope."* Paper back edition, with a new Preface and minor corrections. London: Thames and Hudson, 1991. Pp. 72.

Rev. by I. Grattan-Guinness in *Music Review*, 52 (1991), 306.

Landon, H. C. Robbins (ed.). *The Mozart Compendium: A Guide to Mozart's Life and Music.* London: Thames and Hudson; New York: Schirmer Books, 1990. Pp. 452; illustrations.

Rev. (briefly and favorably) by Peggy Constantine in *New York Times Book Review*, (Mar. 10, 1991), 16; (favorably) by C. A. Kolczynski in *Choice*, 21 (1991), 1619–20; by Linda L. Tyler in *Music and Letters*, 72 (1991), 447–48.

LaRue, Jan. *A Catalogue of 18th-Century Symphonies, Vol. 1: Thematic Identifies.* Bloomington, IN: Indiana U. Press, 1988. Pp. xvi + 352. Cf. *ECCB*, n.s. 16, IV: 220; 14, IV:169.

Rev. by Sterling Murray in *Notes*, 47 (1991), 1122–24.

Leaver, Robin A. "New Light on the Pre-History of the Bach Choir of Bethlehem." *Bach*, 22 (1991), 24–34.

Ledbetter, David (ed.). *Continuo Playing According to Handel: His Figured Bass Exercises.* (Early Music Series, xii.) New York and Oxford; Oxford U. Press, 1990. Pp. [vi] + 106. Cf. *ECCB*, n.s. 16, IV: 220.

Rev. by Peter Williams in *Music and Letters*, 72 (1991), 586–87.

Le Huray, Peter. *Authenticity in Performance: Eighteenth-Century Case Studies.* Cambridge and New York: Cambridge U. Press, 1990. Pp. xvii + 202. Cf. *ECCB*, n.s. 16, IV: 220.

Rev. by George Houle in *Performance Practice Review*, 4 (1991), 208–10.

Le Maître, Edmond. "Les soucres des Plaisirs de l'Isle enchantée." *Revue de Musicologie*, 77 (1991), 187–200; appendices; bibliography.

Entertainment arranged by Louis XIV for the queen in 1664. This is seen as the greatest event in the musical history of Versailles, as Lully, Molière, amd Benserade joined efforts to present several days of festivities. The author has brought together and described all available documents.

Lenoir, Yves (ed.). *Documents Grétry dans les collections de la Bibliothèque Royale Albert Ier.* Brussels: Bibliothèque Royale Albert Ier, 1989. Pp. 183. Cf. *ECCB*, n.s. 16, IV: 221.

Rev. by Charles Dill in *Notes*, 48 (1991), 82–84.

Leppert, Richard. *Music and Image: Domesticity, Ideology, and Sociocultural Formation in Eighteenth Century England.* Cambridge and New York: Cambridge U. Press, 1988. Pp. xvi + 248. Cf. *ECCB*, n.s. 16, IV: 221; 15, IV: 158; 14, IV: 169.

Rev. briefly by Maureen Egan in the *Journal of Aesthetics and Art Criticism*, 49 (1991), 104; (favorably) by Claudia L. Johnson in *The Scriblerian*, 23 (1991), 268–69.

Le Rougetel, Hazel. *The Chelsea Gardener: Philip Miller, 1691–1770.* London: Natural History Museum Publications; Portland, OR: Sagapress in association with Timber Press, 1990. Pp. 212; colored plates. Cf. *ECCB*, n.s. 16, IV: 221.

Rev. by D. H. Pfister in *Choice*, 28 (1991), 1158.

Lester, Joel. *Between Modes and Keys: German Theory, 1592–1802.* (Harmonologia Series, 3.) Stuyvesant, NY: Pendragon Press, 1989. Pp. xxv + 240. Cf. *ECCB*, n.s. 15, IV: 158.

Rev. by Douglas Leedy in *Notes*, 47 (1991), 1103–06; by Benito V. Riviera in *Journal of Music Theory*, 35 (1991), 267–82; musical examples.

Levey, Michael. *The Later Italian Pictures in the Collection of Her Majesty the Queen.* 2nd ed. Cambridge and New York: Cambridge U. Press, 1991. Pp. lxx + 396; bibliography; catalogue; plates.

Levin, Robert D. *Who Wrote the Mozart Four-Wind Concertante?* Stuyvesant, NY: Pendragon Press, 1988. Pp. xviii + 472. Cf. *ECCB*, n.s. 14, IV: 171.

Rev. by Richard Maunder in *Journal of the Royal Musical Association*, 116 (1991), 136–39.

Lindgren, Lowell. "Musicians and Librettists in the Correspondence of Gio. Giacomo Zamboni [c.1724] (Oxford, Bodleian Library, MSS Rawlinson Letters 116–138)." *Research Chronicle of the Royal Musical Association*, 24 (1991), 1–186.

Linfield, Eva. "Formal and Tonal Organization of a 17th-Century Ritornello/Ripieni Structure." *Journal of Musicology*, 9 (1991), 145–164; figures; musical examples.

Concentrates on Schültz's "Sämann" from *Symphoniae Sacrae III* (1650), but suggests links between this work and the eighteenth-century concerto.

Litten, Julian. *The English Way of Death: The Common Funeral Since 1450.* London: R. Hale, 1991. Pp. xvii + 254; appendices; illustrations (some colored).

Rev. (with another work) by Liam Hudson in *TLS*, (June 21, 1991), 28.

Llewellyn, Nigel. *The Art of Death: Visual Culture in the English Death Ritual, c. 1500–c.1800.* London: Reaktion Books in association with the Victoria and Albert Museum, 1991. Pp. 160; bibliography; illustrations (some colored); portraits.

Rev. (with another work) by Liam Hudson in *TLS*, (June 21, 1991), 28.

Lockwood, Lewis. "Performance and 'authenticity'." *Early Music*, 19 (1991), 501–06; facsimiles.

London, Justin. "Metric Ambiguity (?) in Bach's Branderburg Concerto No. 3." *In Theory Only*, 11 (1991), 21–53; musical examples.

Lough, John. "Lemonnier's Painting, 'Une Soirée chez Madame Geoffrin en 1755'." *French Studies*, 45 (1991), 266–78; illustration.

Shows that the famous painting is but a valueless fabrication.

Low, Donald A. *The Scots Musical Museum, 1787–1803.* Vols. 1–2. Portland, OR: Amadeus Press and Timber Press, 1991. Pp. 800.

Lühning, Helga, and Sieghard Brandenburg. *Beethoven: Zwischen Revolution und Restauration.* Bonn: Beethoven-Haus, 1989. Pp. 308. Cf. *ECCB*, n.s. 16, IV: 222.

Rev. by Theodore Albrecht in *Notes*, 47 (1991), 1130–31.

Luppi, Andrea. *Lo specchio dell'armonia universale: Estetica e musica in Leibniz.* (Collana di filosofia, xxxvii.) Milan: Franco Angeli, 1989. Pp. 198.

Rev. by Bojan Bujic in *Music and Letters*, 72 (1991), 431–32.

Luppi, Andrea, and Maurizio Padoan. *Statuti della musica: Studi sull'estetica musicale tra Sei e Ottocento.* (Contributi musicologici del Centro Ricerche dell'A. M. I. S.–Como, vi.) Como:

Antiquea Musicae Italicae Studiosi, 1989. Pp. 175.

Rev. by Bojan Bujic in *Music and Letters*, 72 (1991), 431–32.

MacDonogh, Giles. *Brillat-Savarin: The Judge and His Stomach.* London: J. Murray, 1991. Pp. viii + 248.

Macheski, Cecilia, and Mary Anne Schofield. *Curtain Calls: American and British Women in the Theatre, 1670–1820.* Athens, OH: Ohio U. Press, 1991. Pp. 375; illustrations.

Macmillan, Duncan. *Scottish Art, 1460–1990.* Edinburgh, Scotland: Mainstream Publishing, 1990. Pp. 432; bibliography; illustrations (some colored). Cf. *ECCB*, n.s. 16, IV: 222.

Rev. (with another work) by Duncan Thomson in *TLS,* (Apr. 5, 1991), 23.
    Chapters 4–8 (pp. 73–164) concern the Eighteenth Century.

Mahaut, Antoine. *A New Method for Learning to Play the Transverse Flute.* Translated and Edited by Eileen Hadidian. (Publications of the Early Music Institute.) Bloomington, IN: Indiana U. Press, 1989. Pp. xii + 73. Cf. *ECCB*, n.s. 15, IV: 160.

Rev. by Edgar H. Hunt in *Galpin Society Journal,* 44 (1991), 180–81; by David Lasoki in *Notes,* 47 (1991), 1150–53.

Maier, Hans. "Mozart in seinen Briefen." *Acta Mozartiana,* 38 (1991), 71–9.

Majers, J. F. B. C. *Josepf Friedrich Bernard Caspar Majers Neueröffneter Theoretisch- und Praktischer Music-Saal (Nuremberg, 1741).* Facsimile edn., introduced by Eitelfriedrich Thom. (Kultur- und Forschungsstätte Michaelstein.) Blankenburg/Michaelstein, n.d. Pp. [xii] + 117 + [ii].

Rev. by Pamela L. Poulin in *Music and Letter*s, 72 (1991), 587–89.

Malloch, William. "Bach and the French Ouverture." *Musical Quarterly,* 75 (1991), 174–97.

Mangsen, Sandra. "*Ad libitum* Procedures in Instrumental Duos and Trios." *Early Music,* 19 (1991), 28–40.

Covers the period 1600 through 1675.

Marchal, Roger. *Madame de Lambert et son milieu.* Oxford: The Voltaire Foundation at the Taylor Institution, 1991. Pp. xvii + 798.

Marshall, Robert L. "Bach and Mozart: Styles of Musical Genius." *Bach,* 22 (1991), 16–32; musical examples.

Marston, Nicholas. "Approaching the Sketches for Beethoven's 'Hammerklavier' Sonata." *Journal of the American Musicological Society,* 44 (1991), 404–50.

Places loose leaves in a tentative order and identifies desk sketches, thus laying foundations for future study.

Martin, Peter. *The Pleasure Gardens of Virginia from Jamestown to Jefferson.* Oxford and Princeton, NJ: Princeton U. Press, 1991. Pp. xiv + 240; bibliography; illustrations; maps.

Marty, Jean-Pierre. *The Tempo Indications of Mozart.* London and New Haven, CT: Yale U. Press, 1988. Pp. xvi + 279. Cf. *ECCB*, n.s. 15, IV: 160; 14, IV: 173.

Rev. by Thomas Bauman in *Performance Practice Review*, 4 (1991), 96–100.

Massip, Catherine. "Airs Français et italiens dans l'édition français, 1643–1710." *Revue de Musicologie*, 77 (1991), 179–85.

Assesses the degree of Italian influence on French vocal music in the late 17th and early 18th centuries. French airs in the Italian style are seen as forerunners of the first cantatas published in France.

Mather, Betty Bang, with Dean M. Karns. *Dance Rhythms of the French Baroque: A Handbook for Performance.* (Music: Scholarship and Performance.) Bloomington, IN: Indiana U. Press, 1987. Pp. xiv + 334. Cf. *ECCB*, n.s. 14, IV: 173; 13, IV: 239.

Rev. by Shirley Wynne in *Notes*, 47 (1991), 789–90.

Maunder, Richard. "J. C. Bach and the Early Piano in London." *Journal of the Royal Musical Association*, 116 (1991), 210–10; muscial examples.

McCormick, Thomas J. *Charles-Louis Clérisseau and the Genesis of Neoclassicism.* Cambridge, MA: MIT Press; New York: Architectural History Foundation, 1990. Pp. xiv + 284; appendices; illustrations. Cf. *ECCB*, n.s. 16, IV: 223.

Rev. (favorably) by R. W. Liscombe in *Choice*, 28 (1991), 1773.

Meier, Adolf. *Thematisches Werkverzeichnis der Kompositionen von Johannes Sperger (1750–1812).* (Dokumentationen: Reprints, xxi.) Kultur- und Forschungsstätte Michaelstein: Institut für Auffürungspraxis, Michaelstein/Blankenburg, 1990. Pp. 90.

Rev. by Mary Térey-Smith in *Music and Letters*, 72 (1991), 592.

Mercier-Ythier, Claude. *Les Clavecins.* Preface by Jane Favier. Paric: Éditions Vecteurs, 1990. Pp. 263; illustrations.

Rev. by Marcelle Benoit in *Recherches sur la Musique française classique*, 27 (1991–92), 240–41.

Miggiani, Maria Giovanna. *Il Fondo Giustiniani del Conservatorio 'Benedetto Marcello': catalogo dei manoscritti e della stampe.* (" 'Historae musicae sultores' biblioteca," li.) Florence: Olschki, 1990. Pp. lvi + 613.

Rev. by Michael Talbot in *Music and Letters*, 72 (1991), 274–76.

Miller, Lillian B., and David C. Ward (eds.). *New Perspectives on Charles Willson Peale: A 250th Anniversary Celebration.* Pittsburgh, PA: U. of Pittsburgh Press for the Smithsonian Institution, 1991. Pp. xviii + 317; 89 illustrations.

Rev. (favorably) by R. L. McGrath in *Choice*, 29 (1991), 1773.

Milliot, Slyvette. "Du nouveau sur Jean Rousseau, maître de musique et de viole (1644–1699)." *Recherches sur la Musique française classique*, 27 (1991–92), 35–42.

Milner, Anthony. "British Music–A Misunderstood Tradition." *Musical Times*, 132 (1991), 496–97.

Continuation of Milner's reappraisal of British achievements. This article covers "from Purcell to the end of the 19th century."

Morana, Frank. "The Lost Dedication Copy of *Partita 1*: Bach as Poet?" *Bach*, 22 (1991), 12–23; musical examples; plates.

Morris, David. *Thomas Hearne and His Landscape*. London: Reaktion Books, 1989. Pp. vii + 152; illustrations (some colored). Cf. *ECCB*, n.s. 16, IV: 225; 15, IV: 163.

Rev. (favorably) by J. Riely in *Choice*, 28 (1991), 926.

Morrow, Mary Sue. *Concert Life in Haydn's Vienna: Aspects of a Developing Musical and Social Institution*. (Sociology of Music, 7.) Stuyvesant, NY: Pendragon Press, 1989. Pp. xxii + 552. Cf. *ECCB*, n.s. 16, IV: 225; 15, IV: 163.

Rev. by Thomas Leibnitz in *Fontis Artis Musicae*, 38 (1991), 82; by W. Dean Sutcliffe in *Musical Times*, 132 (1991), 135–36; by Murl Sickbert in *Notes*, 47 (1991), 1124–26.

Mortier, Roland, and Hervé Hasquin (eds.). *Fêtes et musiques révolutionaires: Grétry et Gossec*. (Études sur le XVIII siècle, xvii.) Brussels: Éditions de l'Université de Bruxelles, 1990. Pp. 215. Cf. *ECCB*, n.s. 16, IV: 225.

Rev. by David Charlton in *Music and Letters*, 72 (1991), 290–92; by Marie-Joseph Gaymard-Darde in *Revue de Musicologie*, 77 (1991), 351–53; by Charles Dill in *Notes*, 48 (1991), 82–84.

Mosser, Monique, and Georges Teyssot (eds.). *The Architecture of Western Gardens: A Design History from the Renaissance to the Present Day*. Translation by Anthony Bland, Wendy Dallas, Barbara Mellor, Paul Vincent, and Sebastian Wormell of *L'architettura dei Giardini d'Occidente* (Milan, 1990). Cambridge, MA: MIT Press; London: Thames & Hudson, 1991. Pp. 543; illustrations (some colored); plans.

Rev. by J. Mordaunt Crook in *TLS*, (July 5, 1991), 14.
Includes "Part Three: Picturesque, Arcadian and Sublime: The Age of Enlightenment," pp. 203–350.

Mozart-Jahrbuch. Vols. 1–2. (Internationale Stiftung Mozarteum Salzburg.) Kassel: Bärenreiter Verlag, 1991. Pp. 1 + 558; 559 + 1113.

This journal celebrates the Mozart bicentennial with articles too numerous to list individually. Articles in German, French, or English.

Mozart, Wolfgang Amadeus. *Mozart Speaks: Views on Music, Musicians and the World Drawn from the Letters of Wolfgang Amadeus Mozart and Other Early Accounts*. Selected and with commentary by Robert L. Marshall. New York: Schirmer Books; Don Mills, Ontario, Canada: Collier Macmillan Canada, 1991. Pp. xxxi + 446; illustrations.

Rev. (favorably) in rev. article ("Radical, Conventional Mozart") by Charles Rosen in *New York Review of Books*, 38 (Dec. 19, 1991), 51–54, 56–59.

Mozart, Wolfgang Amadeus. *Mozart's Thematic Catalogue: A Facsimile, British Library, Stefan Zweig MS 63*. Translation of *Verzeichnüss aller meiner Werke*. Introduction and transcription by Albi Rosenthal and Alan Tyson. Ithaca, NY: Cornell U. Press; London: British Library, 1990. Pp. 57 + 43; bibliography; colored frontispiece; illustrations; musical examples. Cf. *ECCB*, n.s. 16, IV: 226.

Rev. (with exhibitions and memorabilia) by Robert Craft in *New York Review of Books*, 38 (Aug. 15, 1991), 57–58; (favorably) in rev. article ("A Conflict of Stories: The Irretrievable Likeness of the True Mozart") by Paul Griffiths in *TLS,* (Nov. 29, 1991), 3–6.

Mozart, Wolfgang Amadeus. *The Mozart Violin Concerti: A Facsimile Edition of the Autographs*. Edited by Gabriel Banat. New York: Raven Press, 1986. Cf. *ECCB*, n.s. 15, IV: 163; 12, IV: 267.

Contains K.207, 211, 216, 218, 219, 261, and 261a.

Mozart's Thematic Catalogue (British Library, Stefan Zweig MS63): A Facsimile. Introduction and transcription by Albi Rosenthal and Alan Tyson. London: British Library, 1990. Pp. viii + 59 + ff.45. Cf. *ECCB*, n.s. 16, IV: 226.

Rev. by Alec Hyatt King in *Music and Letters*, 72 (1991), 597–99; by John A. Rice in *Notes*, 48 (1991), 484–86.

Muller, Julia. *Words and Music in Henry Purcell's First Semi-Opera, 'Dioclesian': An Approach to Early Music through Early Theatre*. (Studies in the History and Interpretation of Music, xxviii.) Lewiston, NY: Edwin Mellen Press, 1990. Pp. 507. Cf. *ECCB*, n.s. 16, IV: 226.

Rev. by Andrew Pinnock in *Music and Letters*, 72 (1991),432–35.

Muraro, Maria Tereas, and David Bryant (eds.). *I vicini di Mozart*. 2 vols. Florence: Olschki, 1989. Pp. ix + 707.

Rev. by Mary Hunter in *Music and Letters*, 72 (1991), 283–86.

Myers, Mary L. *French Architectural and Ornament Drawings of the Eighteenth Century*. New York: Metropolitan Museum of Art (distributed through New York: H. N. Abrams), 1991. Pp. xxx + 224; illustrations (some colored).

Nagel, Ivan. *Autonomy and Mercy: Reflections on Mozart's Operas*. Translated by Marion Faber and Ivan Nagel of *Autonomie und Gnade* (Munich, 1985). Cambridge, MA, and London: Harvard U. Press, 1991. Pp. 151.

Rev. (favorably) in rev. article ("A Conflict of Stories: The Irretrievable Likeness of the True Mozart") by Paul Griffiths in *TLS,* (Nov. 29, 1991), 3–6; (favorably) in rev. article ("Radical, Conventional Mozart") by Charles Rosen in *New York Review of Books,* 38 (Dec. 19, 1991), 51–54; 56–59.
    This compact, critical reflection on the politics of and around Mozart's operas is divided into three discursive sections: "Mercy and Autonomy," "Pamina's Three Deaths; or the Happy Ending," and "Son and Father: On Kleist's Last Play." These are interrupted by two "readings"; brief thoughts and aperçus that form a wayward counterpoint to the discursive sections with subjects as diverse as "singing for mercy" and "time and space." Although not a scholarly book, it is clearly informed by a wide-ranging and intimate knowledge of the German literary and philosophical tradition. Nagel treats a bewildering array of topics in quick succession, from the formation and meaning of the operatic canon to the disposition of voice-types in opera seria; from the relation of law (*Recht*) to revenge (*Rache*) to the nature and meaning of Mozart's codas. A review cannot do justice to its dense but

quixotic tapestry of ideas; nevertheless, Nagel's general approach can usefully be considered.

Nagel is at his best when he addresses the political content and implication of Mozart's operas; his assumption that these works take on issues of power and justice is a happy corrective to the notion of Mozart as the quintessentially apolitical composer. He starts by showing the inevitable connection of mercy with power and traces its occurrence through the operas. The moment that animates this discussion is the point in *La clemenza di Tito*, when the Emperor pardons Sesto, who has plotted to kill him. Nagel points out the depoliticization of the notion of mercy in this moment, relating it to the waning power of sovereigns and the decline in opera seria—a decline exaggerated here as elsewhere. Autonomy, as the opposite to mercy, is figured as self-realization; Pamina's assertion (*Magic Flute*) that she will tell the truth to Sarastro is the moment that seems to have stimulated Nagel's interest. This discussion is far less successful than the discussion of mercy, partly because Nagel conveniently ignores the fact that, shortly after thrilling to the idea of The Truth, Pamina pleads to Sarastro that her participation in the plot against him was compelled, and partly because Nagel's other principal example of autonomy is the pair of lovers in *Die Entführung aus dem Serail*, whose successful union is as much the result of lucky circumstance as of self-determination. Indeed, convenient omissions are rather too common throughout the book.

One of the main virtues of Nagel's arguments is that they suggest new and fruitful points of contact between operas. Thus, as far as mercy is concerned, of *Figaro* (in which the originally middle-class Countess pardons her aristocratic husband) can be seen as an inversion of *La clemenza di Tito* (in which the magnanimous emperor pardons Sesto for plotting against him. The comparison I found most provocative was the relation of Pamina as she leads Tamino through the final trials of his initiation into the brotherhood to Beethoven's eponymous Fidelio (Leonora) as she saves her husband Florestan. The general relation between *Fidelio* and *The Magic Flute* has long been recognized, but Nagel sees an almost subversive feminist message in these operas (and in Goethe's *Iphigenia*), in which the true representative of autonomy is not the brave hero, but rather "the weakest of creatures," whose dramatic actions and vocal presence represent a new sort of subjectivity.

This is thought on a grand scale—stimulating but also infuriating. Many of Nagel's points are innocent of particular examples, which makes them all but meaningless unless one has been thinking along the same lines. In addition there is a stunning disregard for any but the most lofty intellectual context. If the subject is rescue operas, for example, as when Pamina and Leonora are compared, then surely the French tradition, and now-forgotten operas like Paer's *Camilla*, should be invoked to avoid the impression that only the canonized masters (Goethe, Mozart, Beethoven) could suggest the subjective implications of the move from monarchism to something more like democracy. It may be that the canonical works embody this move more fully and resonantly than the now-forgotten pieces, but it misrepresents even their greatness to write as if they relate only to each other, and not to the circumstances in which they were written. In short, there is much in this book to admire, but at least as much to beware of.—Mary Hunter.

Nagel, Ivan. *Autonomie und Gnade. Über Mozarts Opern.* Munich: Deutschen Taschenbuch-Verlag, Bärenreiter-Verlag, 1991.

Rev. by Gerd Pienäcker in *Beiträge zur Musikwissenschaft*, 33 (1991), 155–57.

Nettheim, Nigel. "How the Young Schubert Borrowed from Beethoven." *Musical Times*, 132 (1991), 330–31; musical examples.

Explores relationship between Beethoven's Op. 13, Movt. I., and Schubert's *Fantasie* (D.48) and others.

Neumann, Frederick. "How fast should Classical minuets be played?" *Historical Performance*, 4 (1991), 3–13; musical examples.

Neumann, Frederick. *New Essays on Performance Practice.* Ann Arbor, MI: UMI, 1989. Pp. x + 257. Cf. *ECCB*, n.s. 15, IV: 164.

Rev. by Erich Schwandt in *Performance Practice Review*, 4 (1991), 85–95; by Thomas Binkley in *Notes*, 48 (1991), 482–84.

Neumann, Frederick. "The Vibrato Controversy." *Performance Practice Review*, 4 (1991), 14–27.

Argues in favor of vibrato. Quotes primary sources and discusses other interpretations of the passages quoted.

Newman, William S. *Beethoven on Beethoven: Playing his Piano Music his Way.* New York: W. W. Norton, 1988. Pp. 336. Cf. *ECCB*, n.s. 14, IV: 176.

Rev. by Barry Cooper in *Performance Practice Review*, 4 (1991), 106–08.

North, Roger. *Roger North's* The Musicall Grammarian, *1728.* Edited with Introductions and Notes by Mary Chan and Jamie C. Kassler. (Cambridge Studies in Music.) Cambridge and New York: Cambridge U. Press, 1990. Pp. xvii + 305; bibliography; illustrations; musical examples. Cf. *ECCB*, n.s. 16, IV: 226.

Rev. by Curtis Price in *TLS,* (May 10, 1991), 15; Correspondence from Mary Chan and Jamie C. Kassler in *TLS,* (June 14, 1991), 17.

Noske, Frits. *Music Bridging Divided Religions. The Motet in the Seventeenth-Century Dutch Republic.* (Paperbacks on Musicology, 10.) 2 vols. Wilhelmshaven: Florian Noetzel Verlag, 1989. Pp. 548.

Rev. by Rudolf A. Rasch in *Tijdschrift van de Vereniging voor Nederlandse Muziekgeschiedenis*, 41 (1991), 135–40.

O'Grady, Deidre. *The Last Troubadours: Poetic Drama in Italian Opera 1597–1887.* London: Routledge, 1991. Pp. xiii + 236.

Rev. by John Rosselli in *Music and Letters*, 72 (1991), 589–90.

Orel, Alfred. "Mozart in der Kunstanschauung Franz Grillparzers." *Actas Mozartiana,* 38 (1991), 1–6.

O'Shea, John. *Was Mozart Poisoned? Medical Investigations into the Lives of the Great Composers.* New York: St. Martin's Press, 1991. Pp. xiii + 247; appendices; illustrations; tables.

Rev. (briefly) by Harold C. Schonberg in *New York Times Book Review,* (June 2, 1991), 20.

Osthof, Wolfgang, and Reinhard Wiesend (eds.). *Bach und die italienische Musik/Bach e la musica italiana.* (Quaderni, xxxvi.) Venice: Centro Tedesco di Studi Veneziani, 1987. Pp. 220. Cf. *ECCB*, n.s. 13, IV: 243.

Rev. by Malcolm Boyd in *Music and Letters*, 72 (1991), 441–42.

Owen, Sue. " 'Partial Tyrants' and 'Freeborn People' in *Lucius Junius Brutus.*" *Studies in English Literature 1500–1900*, 31 (1991), 463–82.

The theme, plot, character of Brutus, and handling of the crowd and the Royalist mark the play as decidedly radical.

Page, Janet, and Dexter Edge. "A Newly Uncovered Autograph Sketch for Mozart's 'Al Desio di chi t'Adora', K.577." *Musical Times*, 132 (1991), 601–06; facsimile; transcription.

Palisca, Claude V. *Baroque Music.* (Prentice-Hall History of Music Series.) Englwood Cliffs, NJ: Prentice-Hall, 1991. Pp. 356.

Paquette, Daniel (ed.). *Aspect de la musique baroque et classique à Lyon et en France. (Lyon et la musique du XVI au XX siècle.)* Lyon: Presses universitaires de Lyon, Éditions à Coeur Joie, 1989. Pp. 255.

Rev. by Nathalie Berton in *Revue de Musicologie*, 77 (1991), 345–48.

Pascal, Jean-Noël. *La fable au Siècle des Lumières: 1715–1815: Anthologies des successeurs de la Fontaine, de La Motte à Juffret.* (Société française d'Etude du XVIIIᵉ siècle.) Saint-Étienne: Publications de l'Université de Saint-Étienne, 1991. Pp. 142.

Pascual, Beryl Kenyon de. "Two Features of Early Spanish Keyboard Instruments." *Galpin Society Journal*, 44 (1991), 94–102; figures; plates.

Pendle, Karin (ed.). *Women & Music: A History.* Bloomington, IN: Indiana U. Press, 1991. Pp. x + 358; bibliography; illustrations; musical examples.

"Performance Practice Bibliography (1990)." *Performance Practice Review*, 4 (1991), 227–66.

Includes author, subject, and theorist indices. Early eighteenth century, 242–47; late eighteenth century, 248–251.

Pergolesi, Giovanni Battista. *Livietta e Tracollo (la contadina astuta): intermezzi.* Edited by G. Lazarevich. Translated from Italian by C. C. Russell. (His Complete Works, 6.) New York: Pendragon Press, 1991. Pp. xxix + 91.

Pérouse de montclos, Jean-Marie. *Versailles.* Translated from French by John Goodman. Photography by Robert Polidori. New York: Abbeville, 1991. Pp. 424; colored illustrations.

Rev. (briefly and favorably) in rev. article ("Architecture") by Martin Filler in *New York Times Book Review*, 96 (Dec. 1, 1991), 12.

Peterman, Lewis E., Jr. "Michel Blavet's Breathing Marks: A Rare Source for Musical Phrasing in Eighteenth-Century France." *Performance Practice Review*, 4 (1991), 186–98; musical examples.

Blavet (1700–1768), a composer and virtuoso flautist, was particularly interested in clarifying musical phrasing. Peterman has analyzed over 1,000 notated breathing marks in 99 compositions and sorted them into 15 different contexts, such as dance patterns and hemiolia rhythms.

Picker, Martin. *Henricus Isaac: A Guide to Research.* (Garland Composer Resource Manuals, 35. Garland Reference Library of the Humanities, 897.) New York: Garland Publishing, 1991. Pp. 308.

Pickering, Jennifer M. "Printing, Publishing and the Migration of Sources: The Case of Carl Stamitz." *Fontis Artis Musicae,* 38 (1991), 130–38; table.

In this case migration was the result of multiple publication by different publishers. Plates enables reprints. Within a year of publication in London, works were known in Paris, Amsterdam, and Berlin. Shows the importance of development of printing techniques in migration of new music.

Picton, Howard J. *The Life and Works of Joseph Anton Steffan (1726–1797): With Special Reference to his Keyboard Concertos.* (Outstanding Dissertations in Music from British Universities.) 2 vols. New York: Garland Publishers, 1989. Pp. xvi + 613. Cf. *ECCB*, n.s. 15, IV: 166.

Rev. by Brian W. Pritchard in *Notes*, 48 (1991), 81–2.

Pirrotta, N. *Don Giovanni in musica. Dall' "Empio punito" a Mozart.* Venice: Marsilio, 1991.

Rev. by E. Rosand in *Revista Italiana di Musicologia*, 27 (1991), 387–94.

Plank, S. E. "Monmouth in Italy: L'Ambitione Debellata." *Musical Times*, 132 (1991), 280–84; musical examples.

Vitali's oratorio considered sgainst political background of Monmouth's Rebellion (1685).

Platoff, John. "Tonal Organization in 'Buffo' Finales and the Act II Finale of 'Le nozze di Figaro'." *Music and Letters*, 72 (1991), 387–403; musical examples; tables.

Proceeds from the premise "that the structure of the drama provides a more accurate guide to undersatnding tonal structure in an operatic finale than do the abstract formal schemes of instrumental music."

Pollack, Howard. "Seventh Symposium on Literature and the Arts." *Current Musicology*, 48 (1991) 51–55.

Pollack, Howard. "Some Thought on 'Clavier' in Haydn's Solo *Claviersonaten*." *Journal of Musicology*, 9 (1991), 74–91.

Addresses questions of when Haydn began to write for fortepiano and what instrument(s) he had in mind prior to that time. Line of argument favors clavichord.

Pollens, Stewart. "Three Keyboard Instruments Signed by Cristofori's Assistant, Giovanni Ferrini." *Galpin Society Journal*, 44 (1991), 77–93; plates; tables.

Porter, Andrew. "*Messiah*: Two New Perspectives." *Historical Performance,* 4 (1991), 95–100; facsimile.

Porter, David H. "The Structure of Beethoven's Diabelli Variations, op. 120–Again." *Music Review*, 52 (1991), 294–98.

Porter, Susan L. *With an Air Debonair: Musical Theatre in America, 1785–1815.* Washington, DC: Smithsonian Institution Press, 1991. Pp. xiv + 631; bibliography; illustrations.

A welcome adjunct to the current upswing in American musical research is the reappearance of many forgotten native styles in today's repertoires. At any meeting of the Sonneck Society, the national organization devoted to American music, performances of these recaptured art forms abound, ranging from traditional Native American dances to nineteenth-century parlor music for voice and guitar. Past editor of *The Sonneck Society Bulletin*, Susan L. Porter, has illuminated another potential venue of historical performance in her book, *With An Air Debonair: Musical Theatre in America, 1785–1815.*

Departing from the broader historical gamuts of her predecessors Oscar G. Sonneck and Julien Mates, Porter spotlights a thirty-year period in the history of the American musical theatre. Her concentrated historical account is then embellished with elaborate performance details, gleaned in part from over seventy eighteenth- and nineteenth-century periodicals and newspapers that appear in her bibliography. Her address of Musical Theatre is admirably balanced between the two artistic components implied by the genre, but the essential function of music in all theatrical entertainments of the time is clearly maintained.

Following a historical overview that begins in the early eighteenth century, the subsequent chapters cover genres and styles, the relationship of the parts to the whole, theatres, "ttrimming" such as stage machinery, actors and acting traditions, singers and songs, and the orchestra. Along the way, the reader becomes acquainted with many of the colorful personalities that peopled the stages of the era. Musical areas such as ornamentation and instrumentation receive particular attention. Theatre historians will find interest in lighting, costuming, and acting traditions' "Problems of Pronunciation" (pp. 278ff.) will delight etymologists and sociologists alike.

One of Porter's stated aims was "to make all the information available in a . . . readable format" (p. xi), a goal adeptly realized. The essentially practical writing exudes good humor and genuine fondness for the theatre and the time period. Occasional lapses into the colorful jargon of the age (e.g., "hapless heroines held in harems," p. 35), only draw the reader further into the era when florid elocution was preferable to rhetorical restraint. Vivid anecdotes cause the nostalgic lover of history to yearn for the days when a "raging" sea, fashioned of flat, parallel rows of painted waves (p. 129) would evoke a heartfelt warning from a zealous sea captain in the audience.

Appendix A, "A Preliminary Checklist of Musical Entertainments Performed in the United States, 1785–1815," is arranged alphabetically by title and comprises nearly eighty; each entry then lists composers, librettists, genres, and premieres. Specific genre distinctions such as operatic farce or melodramatic romance are especially helpful, as they clarify the contemporaneous practice of applying the term "opera" to "anything that had music as its focus" (p. 23). Notwithstanding the author's acknowledged gaps, contradictions, and inconsistencies (p. 425), the catalog is a valuable contribution to musical and theatrical literature. The second appendix, "Musical Theatre Performances in Five American Cities, 1801–1815," covers activity in Baltimore, Boston, Charleston, New York, and Philadelphia.

Porter's final chapter, "The Modern Performance" addresses the musician's instinctual desire to witness these art forms in production. The call to revive them is a natural and welcome consequene to such a wealth of historical detail; however, the author relates the demands of modern repertory performance in unvarnished form. For musicians, the preparation of idiomatic orchestral parts from the most common published format, a piano reduction, will present a substantial challenge. Actors face a somewhat different dilemma in rendering authentic performances. Regarding the area of "attitude," Porter states, "What may seem to us today to be parody or exaggeration was actually total sincerity" (p. 421). A respect for the historical tradition therefore demands that modern actors override the temptation to lampoon the picturesque speech and demeanor of circa-1800 characters.

One criticism of Porter's expert achievement is that her table of recommended works is merely a list of the eleven pieces most frequently performed between 1785 and 1815 (p. 413). In preparing a monography such as this, the author must certainly have identified a few works that held the greatest promise for revival. With her unique perspective in the field, Porter's musical judgement would have provided a valuable tool in the selection of candidates for re-enactment.

Perhaps the egalitarian spirit of American musical research, one that reminds the scholar that all artifacts of our culture instruct us about ourselves, prevented Susan L. Porter from voicing her own preferences. That spirit is equally present in her excellent admonition: "One sure way to guarantee the failure of a modern performance is to treat the work as something esoteric, of great historical value but understandable only by scholars and the cultural elite" (p. 419). The reader is therefore challenged, not only to explore these forms of musical theatre, but to make them accessible as well.—Kay Norton.

Pommier, Édouard. *L'Art de la liberté: doctrines et débats de la Révolution française.* (Bibliothèque des histoires.) Paris: Gallimard, 1991. Pp. 504; bibliography; plates.

Poulin, Pamela. "Niedt's *Musicalische Handleitung,* Part I and Bach's 'Vorschriften und Grundsätze'." *Music Review,* 52 (1991), 171–89; musical examples.

Niedt's work is especially important because of his direct connection with J. S. Bach.

Powell, John S. "La *Sérénade* pour *Le Sicilien* de M.-A. Charpentier et le crépuscule de la comédie-ballet." *Revue de Musicologie,* 77 (1991), 88–96; muscial examples.

Ratner, Leonard G. "Topical Content in Mozart's Keyboard Sonatas." *Early Music*, 19 (1991), 615–19; musical examples.

Rehm, Wolfgang. "Ideal and Reality: Aspeckt of the *Neue Mozart Ausgabe*." *Notes*, 48 (1991), 11–19.
Rehm, Wolfgang. " 'Neue Mozart-Ausgabe'." *Acta Mozartiana*, 38 (1991), 45–9.

Thoughts at the conclusion of their edition of the works.

Rice, John A. *W. A. Mozart*, La Clemenza di Tito. (Cambridge Opera Handbooks.) Cambridge and New York: Cambridge U. Press, 1991. Pp. xii + 181; bibliography; discography; illustrations.

Rev. in rev. article ("A Conflict of Stories: The Irretrievable Likeness of the True Mozart") by Paul Griffiths in *TLS*, (Nov. 29, 1991), 3–6.

Rice, Paul F. *The Performing Arts at Fountainebleau from Louis XIV to Louis XVI*. (Studies in Music, 102.) Ann Arbor, MI: UMI Research Press, 1989. Pp. xiii + 299. Cf. *ECCB*, n.s. 15, IV: 168.

Rev. by Lois Rosow in *Notes*, 47 (1991), 1119–20.

Richards, Jeffrey H. *Theater Enough: American Culture and the Metaphor of the World Stage, 1607–1789*. Durham, NC, and London: Duke U. Press, 1991. Pp. 335.

"My point," Jeffrey H. Richards states near the end of this provocative study of the figure of theater in early America, is "that the peculiar circumstances of American settlement produced a culture that was at once poor in playhouses but rich in figural stages" (294). Indeed, the landscape of colonial America from Virginia to Massachusetts was so "poor in playhouses" that no contemporary scholars have thought fit to cast more than passing glances at its theater or theatrical language. The genius of Richards' study is that, by pursuing the cultural meaning of stage metaphors in the discourse of colonial Americans rather than a history of stage productions or dramatic texts, he opens a new window upon the American colonial condition. *Theater Enough* locates the origins and development of an idea of American exceptionalism in the figurative use of theater by colonial America's foremost writers, including John Smith, Cotton Mather, John Adams, and Mercy Otis Warren. At a time when the academy seems most interested in resurrecting non-traditional voices, Richards turns to traditionally important writers but finds in them a discourse, indeed a world, that we have lost.

The first quarter of *Theater Enough* contains a historical overview of the various formulations of theater metaphors, from Plato's tragicomic conception of life to the English Puritans' demonization of theater and the theatrical life, with a variety of interesting and, occasionally, unpredictable stops along the way. This is an unusual beginning for a book concerned with American literature; Richards wants to resist any notion that the American discourse he is investigating in the other three-quarters of his book springs fully formed from Puritanism or from the landscape or from the expanding frontier, either in the seventeenth century or beyond. Stage metaphors are part of the baggage brought to America by both the Puritans in New England and the cavaliers in Virginia. Though not entirely successful in this opening gambit–for most of what is said merely recapitulates the work of other scholars on the history of theater and theatrical language–Richards is correct to resist a narrow, naive, isolationist version of American exceptionalism. His notion of how American discourse comes to differ from Britain's is grounded in a close analysis of the way in which the two diverge in the seventeenth and eighteenth centuries: "despite the intellectual and cultural dependence of the colonies on Britain," he summarizes, "the conceptions of figural theater differ significantly between the two societies–and those differences ultimately reflect the political and ideological rifts that lead to revolution" (179). Having established the traditional Western uses of stage metaphors in the first quarter of his book, Richards then moves on in several chapters to analyze John Smith's various narratives, the court transcripts of Anne Hutchinson's trial, and Cotton Mather's sermons and histories, finding in each of these bodies of texts an innovative cultural use of stage metaphor. Richards shows quite clearly how and why colonial writers brought theatrical tropes with them, and he shows that the process of modifying those tropes for new cultural circumstances began immediately upon debarking.

Methodologically, Richards uses the insights in their respective fields of Kenneth Burke, Kai Erikson, Victor Turner, and Clifford Geertz. Throughout the study, he emphasizes the cultural use of the metaphor of theater, its usefulness within specific, colonial cultures as a way of organizing and ordering experience: "the language of theater and tragedy provides for Americans in times of crisis an instrument by which disorder can be ordered, the purity of mission enhanced, individuals praised or condemned, and the workings of Providence made manifest before a spectating world" (144). So, for example, Cotton Mather in *Magnalia Christi Americana* (1702) can, through the metaphors of theater, exalt the American colonial enterprise within the British empire; so, for example, the founding fathers and mothers can in the late eighteenth century "reconstitute reality" (218) in the crisis leading up to the American Revolution.

The entire second half of Richards' study focuses on the American Revolution. Richards is at his best here, perhaps because the era is so much richer in stage metaphors, perhaps because having slowed down the pace of his investigation he finally has the leisure to explore these stage metaphors in more complex and subtle ways. What Richards shows us is remarkable in its explanatory power: "no theater smaller or less dynamic than the streets, battlefields, and political halls of America can impel or compel the people to action" in the 1770s (258). In the rhetoric of our founding fathers and mothers, Richards locates a "cause" for the American Revolution that parallels and complements recent arguments for the cultural power of both republicanism and Lockean individualism in British North America in the late eighteenth century. Richards' colonist write to cope with reality, and in the process–a process he traces in the second half of *Theater Enough*–they create a new reality, one worth dying for. Appropriately, *Theater Enough* ends in 1789, at a point when the "theater of Providence was no longer theater enough" (296) in America, and when the rise of individualism, romanticism, and representative democracy were on the verge of initiating an order of things different from the one imagined and experienced by the Revolutionary generation.

The problems in *Theater Enough* are few. As I suggested above, the early chapters of the study are synthetic and derivative; I found myself hurrying through them to get to the chapters dealing with colonial culture. I also found gaps in Richards' historical survey of colonial America: though he is quite perceptive in his analyses of the works of John Smith, John Winthrop, Cotton Mather, and the entire Revolutionary generation, Richards says relatively little about the mid-seventeenth century and the first two-thirds of the eighteenth. How theatrical tropes are used in the years between Cotton Mather's *Magnalia Christi Americana* and Mercy Otis Warren's closet dramas of the 1770s is not entirely clear. But these are quibbles, really: in its range, its clear and jargon-free prose, its discovery of these lost metaphors of colonial discourse, its relentless pursuit of the various meanings of stage metaphors of colonial discourse, *Theater Enough* is an excellent critical study. It will take place alongside several other recent, important studies–Michael Warner's *The Letters of the Republic* (1990), David Shield's *Oracles of Empire* (1990), William Dowling's *Poetry and Ideology in Revolutionary Connecticut* (1990), and Jay Fliegelman's *Declaring Independence* (1993)–that grapple with the many meanings of the Enlightenment in colonial America and attempt to represent those meanings to a twentieth-century audience.—Stephen Carl Arch.

Richards, Kenneth, and Laura Richards. *The Commedia dell'Arte: A Documentary History*. Cambridge, MA, and Oxford: Basil Blackwell for the Shakespeare Head Press, 1990. Pp. xxi + 346; bibliography; illustrations. Cf. *ECCB*, n.s. 16, IV: 229.

Rev. (with reservations and with another work) by Peter Holland in *TLS*, (Apr. 12, 1991), 15.

Rienäcker, Gerd. "Einleitung in die Ouvertüre der 'Zauberflöte." *Beiträge zur Musikwissenschaft*, 33 (1991), 97–110.

Rifkin, Joshua. "More (and Less) on Bach's Orchestra." *Performance Practice Review*, 4 (1991), 5–13.

A reply to Hans-Joachim Schulze's "Johann Sebastian Bach's Orchestra: Some Unanswered Questions" in *Early Music*, 17 (1989), 3–15, which argued for "a certain opulence of sound."

Ringer, Alexander (ed.). *The Early Romantic Era: Between Revolutions: 1789 and 1848*. (Music and Society.) Englewood Cliffs, NJ: Prentice Hall, 1991. Pp. x + 325; chronology; illustrations.

Music and Society, an eight-volume set under the general editorial direction of Stanley Sadie, is the latest in a long tradition of studies that attempt to encompass the full spectrum of Western music. This set aims particularly at cross-cultural associations, at showing "in what context, and as a result of what forces—social, cultural, intellectual"—musical works or types of music came into being. In the Preface, Sadie emphasizes that point:

> The intention is to view musical history not as a series of developments in some hermetic world of its own but rather as a series of responses to social, economic and political circumstances and to religious and intellectual stimuli. We want to explain not simply *what* happened, but *why* it happened, and why it happened when and where it did (p. x).

The reader will proceed in the individual volumes with the clear expectation of cultural history—of a guide to the complex interrelations of music and those forces from which it cannot be separated.

The title of the volume under review leads one to assume that romanticism will be a factor, as will revolutions, since these provide the temporal boundaries; if size of print is to be taken as an indicator, the discussion of romanticism will predominate. After an introductory chapter by Ringer, the book proceeds geographically through the major musical centers of Europe, including Paris, Vienna, Berlin, Dresden, Leipzig, Italy, London and Moscow, and then on to the new world, first to the United States, and finally Latin America. Each chapter is richly illustrated with paintings, drawings and documents in facsimile pertaining to the discussion at hand.

Those searching for cultural history will be disappointed, since it ends with Ringer's survey in the first chapter. Beyond that one finds little other than description of musical activities, fascinating and informative to be sure, but hardly the wealth of cross-cultural interrelationships promised by Sadie in the Preface. In the chapter following the introductory survey, labeled "Paris: Centre of Intellectual Ferment," one searches in vain amid the descriptions of musical life for a single intellectual idea. Authors of the subsequent chapter drop the pretense, sparing us the expectation of such matters, as their titles are more reflective of their archival approaches.

While the title of the book uses the word "romantic" in bold type, one is again struck by the virtual absence of discussion of romanticism after the first chapter. A treatment of romanticism in music would have had to be predicated on a consideration of literature, but literary matters are scrupulously avoided. Here the geographical organization of the volume worked to its disadvantage; we are told, for example, that Vienna was a non-literary city, which is true, but that should not prevent a discussion of Schubert and romanticism. The author's interest in poets from another locale, Protestant northern Germany, did not, it appears, fit with the format of the book. Borrowed terms of periodization such as "baroque" or "classical" tend to miscarry when applied to music, but "romantic" could actually be useful. Its application here since avoided in discussion, was either a dogged adherence to textbook terminology, or an attempt at egalitarianism—to render the classification "romantic" as inept as the other terms of periodization.

In a book associated with a television series from the mid 1980s entitled *Man and Music*, one should presumably not be surprised that women (even notable women such as Clara Wieck or Fanny Mendelssohn) have no place, either in their relationship to the solo keyboard repertory, or to the romantic literature that gave birth to art song. One is also puzzled why a volume defining itself by social revolutions should focus almost exclusively on the musical activities of the wealthy classes, ignoring the enormous range of music making including folk song and popular music in Europe. At the end of the Preface Sadie notes that

> musical histories have never enjoyed the appeal to a broad, intelligent general readership in the way that histories of art, architecture or literature have done: these books represent an attempt to reach such a readership and explain music in terms that may quicken their interest (p. x). While this volume contains much interesting information about the musical life of various cities, the readership searching for music within cultural history will not find fulfillment here.—David P. Schroeder.

Robinson, Michael F. *Giovanni Paisiello, a Thematic Cataloque of his Works, vol. 1: Dramatic Works*. (Thematic Catalogues Series, 15.) Stuyvesant, NY: Pendragon Press, 1991. Pp. xxv + 591.

Robinson, Sidney K. *Inquiry into the Picturesque*. Chicago, IL, and London: U. of Chicago Press, 1991. Pp. xiv + 180; bibliography.

Rosand, Ellen. *Opera in Seventeenth-Century Venice: The Creation of a Genre*. Berkeley, CA: U. of California Press, 1991. Pp. xxii + 684; bibliography; illustrations.

Rev. (favorably) by R. Miller in *Choice*, 29 (1991), 605.

Rosenblum, Sandra P. *Performance Practices in Classic Piano Music*. (Music Scholarship and Performance.) Bloomington, IN: Indiana U. Press, 1988. Pp. xxviii + 516. Cf. *ECCB*, n.s. 16, IV: 230, 15, IV: 170; 14, IV: 179.

Rev. by Kenneth Drake in *Notes*, 48 (1991), 518–21.

Roucher, Eugenia. "À propos de Jean Brunet [1688–1747], huissier ordinaire des ballets du roi." *Recherches sur la Musique française classique*, 27 (1991–92), 201–02.

Saccamano, Neil. "The Sublime Force of Words in Addison's 'Pleasures'." *English Literary History*, 58 (1991), 83–106.

Considers the dynamics between the rhetorical and natural established connections with melancholy.

Sachs, Barbara. "Scarlatti's *tremulo*." *Early Music*, 19 (1991), musical examples.

Sadie, Julie Anne (comp. and ed.). *Companion to Baroque Music*. London: J. M. Dent, 1990; New York: Schirmer Books, 1991. Pp. xviii + 549; bibliography; illustrations; maps; musical examples.

Rev. by Donald Burrows in *Early Music*, 19 (1991), 635–36.

Saint Lambert, Monsieur de. *A New Treatise on Accompaniment, with the Harpsichord, the Organ, and with Other Instruments*. Edited and Translated by John S. Powell. Bloomington. IN: Indiana U. Press, 1991. Pp. vxii + 155; musical examples.

Salomon, Joseph-François. *Medeé et Jason: Tragédie en musique*. Edited by Leslie Ellen Brown. (French Opera in the 17th & 18th centuries, 28.) Stuyvesant, NY: Pendragon Press, 1991. Pp. xlvii + 286.

Saumarez Smith, Charles. *The Building of Castle Howard*. Chicago, IL: U. of Chicago Press; London: Farber, 1990. Pp. xviii + 221; illustrations; plans; portraits. Cf. *ECCB*, n.s. 16, IV: 231.

Rev. by D. J. R. Bruckner in *New York Times Book Review*, 96 (Jan. 6, 1991), 19.

Schachter, Carl. "20th-century Analysis and Mozart Performance." *Early Music*, 19 (1991), 620–26; musical examples.

Scheurer, Timothy E. *Born in the U.S.A.: The Myth of America in Popular Music from Colonial Times to the Present*. (Studies in Popular Culture.) Jackson, MS. U. Press of Mississippi, 1991. Pp. xi + 280; bibliography; discography.

Rev. by R. D. Cohen in *Choice*, 29 (1991), 605.

Schmitz, Hans-Peter. *Quantz heute: Der "Versuch einer Answeisung, die Flöte traversiere zu spielen" als Lehrbuch für unser Musizieren.* Kassel: Bärenreiter, 1987. Pp. 83. Cf. *ECCB*, n.s. 13, IV :251.

Rev. by David Lasoki in *Notes*, 47 (1991), 1150–53.

Schroeder, David P. *Haydn and the Enlightenment: The Late Symphonies and Their Audience.* New York: Oxford U. Press; Oxford: Clarendon Press, 1990. Pp. x + 219; bibliography; music. Cf. *ECCB*, n.s. 16, IV: 232.

Rev. (severely) by C. Isaac in *Choice*, 28 (1991), 1650; by Jean Jeltsch in *Revue de Musicologie*, 77 (1991), 348–49; by David Wyn Jones in *Music and Letters*, 72 (1991), 440–41.

Schulze, Hans Joachim, and Christoph Wolff. *Bach-Compendium. Analytisch-bibliographisches Repertorium der Werke Johann Sebastian Bachs.* Vol. 1, Parts 2, 3 and 4: *Vokalwerke II.* Leipzig: Edition Peters, 1987, 1988, 1989. Pp. 421–820; 821–1144; 1145–1724; musical examples. Cf. *ECCB*, n.s. 15, IV: 171; 14, IV: 181.

Rev. by Frank Mund in *Beiträge zur Musikwissenschaft*, 33 (1991), 79–81.

Schumann, Joachim. "Anton Peter Graf Przichovsky von Przichovitz, Fürstenbischol von Prag." *Acta Mozartiana*, 38 (1991), 7–13; plate.

Scott, Virginia. *The Commedia dell'Arte in Paris, 1644–1697.* Charlottesville, VA: U. Press of Virginia, 1990. Pp. xii + 459; bibliography; illustrations. Cf. *ECCB*, n.s. 16, IV: 232.

Rev. (favorably and with another work) by Peter Holland in *TLS*, (Apr. 12, 1991), 15.

Selfridge-Field, Eleanor. "Instrumentation and Genre in Italian Music, 1600–1670." *Early Music*, 19 (1991), 61–67; facsimiles; table.

Selfridge-Field, Eleanor. *The Music of Benedetto and Alessandro Marcello: A Thematic Catalogue with Commentary on the Composers, Repertory, and Sources.* New York: Oxford U. Press; Oxford: Clarendon Press, 1990. Pp. 517. Cf. *ECCB*, n.s. 16, IV: 233.

Rev. by Graham Dixon in *Early Music*, 19 (1991), 283–85.

Shawe-Taylor, Desmond. *The Georgians: Eighteenth-Century Portraiture and Society.* London: Barrie & Jenkins, 1990. Pp. 239; illustrations (some colored). Cf. *ECCB*, n.s. 16, IV: 233.

Rev. (with another work and with reservations) by Shearer West in *TLS*, (Jan. 18, 1991), 16.

Sheriff, Mary D. *Fragonard: Art and Eroticism.* Chicago, IL: U. of Chicago Press, 1990. Pp. 253; illustrations. Cf. *ECCB*, n.s. 16, IV: 233.

Rev. (favorably) by Bernadette Fort in *Eighteenth-Century Studies*, 24 (1991), 408–13.

Shesgreen, Sean (ed.). *The Criers and Hawkers of London: Engravings and Drawings by Marcellus Laroon.* Brookfield, VT: Scolar Press, 1990. Pp. xii + 252. Cf. *ECCB*, n.s. 16, IV: 233.

Rev. in *The Scriblerian*, 24 (1991), 84; by David Wykes in *Notes and Queries*, 236 (1991), 387–88.

Shive, Clyde S., Jr. "*National Martial Music and Songs*, A Musical First." *American Music*, 9 (1991), 92–101; facsimiles.

This collection comprises six poems, two marches, and three songs. It is the first extant publication in the Unites States to include a set of instrumental parts, and the first compilation of music of a national character to be printed in America (1809).

Siegele, Ulrich. " 'I had to be Industrious . . .' Thoughts about the Relationship between Bach's Social and Musical Character." Translated by Gerhard Herz. *Bach*, 22 (1991), 5–12.

Siegele, Ulrich. " 'Ich habe fleißig sein müssen . . .'. Zur Vermittlung von Bachs sozialem und musikalischem Charakter." *Musik und Kirche*, 61 (1991), 73–78.

Signorile, Marc. "Les Maîtres de chapelle du chapitre cathédral de Saint-Trophime d'Arles aux XVI et XVIII siècles." *Recherches sur la Musique française classique*, 27 (1991–92), 43–70; appendices; plates.

Smeed, J. W. *Don Juan: Variations on a Theme*. London and New York: Routledge, 1990. Pp. xi + 190. Cf. *ECCB*, n.s. 16, IV: 234.

Rev. by Julien Rushton in *Music and Letters*, 72 (1991), 286–87.

Smith, Dawn L., and Anita K. Stoll (eds.). *The Perception of Women in Spanish Theater of the Golden Age*. Cranbury, NJ: Bucknell U. Press; London and Toronto: Associated University Presses, 1991. Pp. 276; plate.

Smithers, Don L. *The Music and History of the Baroque Trumpet before 1721*. Revised second edition. Carbondale, IL: Southern Illinois U. Press, 1988. Pp. 352. Cf. *ECCB*, n.s. 14, IV: 182.

Rev. by M. T. Wright and Andrew Pinnock in *Galpin Society Journal*, 44 (1991), 188–91.

Sohm, Philip L. *Pittoresco: Marco Boschini, His Critics, and Their Critiques of Painterly Brushwork in Seventeenth- and Eighteenth-Century Italy*. (Cambridge Studies in the History of Art.) Cambridge and New York: Cambridge U. Press, 1991. Pp. xvi + 276; bibliography; illustrations (some colored).

Solomon, Maynard. *Beethoven Essays*. Cambridge and New York: Harvard U. Press, 1988. Pp. xi + 375. Cf. *ECCB*, n.s. 14, IV: 182.

Rev. by Tallis Barker in *Music Review*, 52 (1991), 306–08.

Somfai, László. "Mozart's first thoughts: The Two Versions of the Sonata in D Major, K284." *Early Music*, 19 (1991), 601–13; facsimile; musical examples; plate.

Spitzer, John. "The Birth of the Orchestra in Rome–An Iconographic Study." *Early Music*, 19 (1991), 2–27; illustrations.

Staffieri, Gloria. "L'Athalie di Racine e l'orotorio romano alla fine del XVII secolo." *Revue de Musicologie*, 77 (1991), 291–310; tables.

Investigates the position of oratorio within the pattern of French influence in late 17th-century Italian musical theatre. Analysis of three Roman oratorios derived from Racine's "Athalie" (1691) leads to the conclusion that Roman oratorio is probably the first genre in Italian musical theatre upon which reform efforts were attempted.

Stafford, Barbara Maria. *Body Criticism: Imaging the Unseen in Enlightenment Art and Medicine*. Cambridge, MA: MIT Press, 1991. Pp. xxi + 587; bibliography; illustrations.

Stafford, William. *The Mozart Myths: A Critical Reassessment*. Stanford, CA: Stanford U. Press, 1991. Pp. viii + 285; illustrations.

Rev. in rev. article ("A Conflict of Stories: The Irretrievable Likeness of the True Mozart") by Paul Griffiths in *TLS,* (Nov. 29, 1991), 3–6.
    British edition has the title, *Mozart's Death: A Corrective Survey of the Legends* (London: Macmillan Academic and Professional, 1991).

Stauffer, George B. (ed.). *The Forkel-Hoffmeister and Kühnel Correspondence: A Document of the Early 19th-Century Bach Revival*. New York: C. F. Peters, 1990.

Stedman, Preston. *The Symphony: A Research and Information Guide*. Vol. 1: *The Eighteenth Century*. (Music Research and Information Guides, xiv.) London and New York: Garland Publishers, 1990. Pp. xviii + 343. Cf. *ECCB*, n.s. 16, IV: 235.

Rev. by Peter Brown in *Music and Letters*, 72 (1991), 593–95.

Steiger, Renate. "SVAVISSIMA [sic] MUSICA CHRISTO. Zur Symbolik der Stimmlagen bei J. S. Bach." *Musik und Kirche*, 61 (1991), 318–24; facsimile; photo of organ.

Steptoe, Andrew. *The Mozart-Da Ponte Operas: The Cultural and Musical Background to "Le Nozze di Figaro," "Don Giovanni," and "Così fan tutti."* Oxford: Clarendon Press, 1988. Pp. 273. Cf. *ECCB*, n.s. 15, IV: 174; 14, IV: 183.

Rev. by James P. Fairleigh in *Notes*, 47 (1991), 1126–28.

Stinson, Russell. *The Bach Manuscripts of Johann Peter Kellner and his Circle: A Case Study in Reception History*. (Sources of Music and Thier Intrepretation/ Duke Studies in Music.) Durham, NC, and London: Duke U. Press, 1990. Pp. xvi + 184. Cf. *ECCB*, n.s. 16, IV: 235.

Rev. by John Butt in *Notes*, 48 (1991), 65–70; by Stephen Daw in *Musical Times*, 132 (1991), 196; by Richard Jones in *Music and Letters*, 72 (1991), 440–41.

Talbot, Michael. *Tomaso Albinoni: The Venetian Composer and His World*. New York: Oxford U. Press; Oxford: Clarendon Press, 1990. Pp. vi + 308; appendices; illustrations; musical examples. Cf. *ECCB*, n.s. 16, IV: 235.

Rev. by A. S. Coussot in *Revue de Musicologie*, 77 (1991), 129–31; by R. Freedman in *Choice*, 28 (1991), 1321.

Talbot, Michael. *Vivaldi. Fonti e letteratura critica*. Traduzione di Luca Zoppelli. (Studi di musica veneta. Quaderni vivaldiana, 5.) Florence: Olschki, 1991.

Tarasti, Eero. "Beethoven's *Waldstein* and the Generative Course." *Indiana Theory Review*, 12 (1991), 99–140; figures; musical examples.

Tatlow, Ruth. *Bach and the Riddle of the Number Alphabet.* Cambridge and New York: Cambridge U. Press, 1991. Pp. xiii + 186; bibliography; illustrations.

Rev. by Malcolm Boyd in *TLS,* (July 19, 1991), 16.

Tatlow, Ruth. *Bach and the Riddle of the Number Alphabet.* (Symbolism in Music.) Cambridge and New York: Cambridge U. Press, 1991. Pp. xiii + 186; appendices; bibliography; illustrations; musical examples.

Rev. by J. P. Ambrose in *Choice,* 29 (1991), 460.

Temperley, Nicholas. "Haydn's tempos in *The Creation.*" *Early Music,* 19 (1991), 235–45; tables.

Temperley, Nicholas. *Haydn: The Creation.* (Cambridge Music Handbooks.) Cambridge and New York: Cambridge U. Press, 1991. Pp. vii + 135; appendices; bibliography.

Temperley, Nicholas (ed.). *The London Pianoforte School 1766–1860: Clementi, Dussek, Cogan, Cramer, Field, Pinto, Sterndale, Bennett, and Other Masters of the Pianoforte.* 20 vols. New York: Garland, 1984–87. Cf. *ECCB,* n.s. 13, IV: 258.

Rev. by R. Larry Todd in *Journal of the American Musicological Society,* 44 (1991). 128–136.

Teplow, Deborah A. *Performance Practice and Technique in Marin Marais' 'Pièces de viole'.* (Studies in Musicology, 93.) Ann Arbor, MI: UMI Research Press, 1986. Pp. xii + 156. Cf. *ECCB,* n.s. 12, IV: 289.

Rev. by Frank Traficante in *Performance Practice Review,* 4 (1991), 80–84.

Thayer, Alexander Wheelock. *Salieri, Rival of Mozart.* Edited by Theodore Albrecht. Kansas City, MO: The Philharmonia of Greater Kansas City, 1989. Pp. xx + 186. Cf. *ECCB,* n.s. 16, IV: 236; 15, IV: 175.

Rev. by Donald Gill in *Performance Practice Review,* 4 (1991), 202–07.

Todd, R. Larry, and Peter Williams (eds.). *Perspectives on Mozart Performance.* (Cambridge Studies in Performance Practice, 1.) Cambridge and New York: Cambridge U. Press, 1991. Pp. xiv + 246; musical examples.

Rev. (with reservations) in rev. article ("A Conflict of Stories: The Irretrievable Likeness of the True Mozart") by Paul Griffiths in *TLS,* (Nov. 29, 1991), 3–6.

This book represents a major contribution to the field of Mozartean performance studies, with articles representing all major foci of the performance practices discipline. Studies of improvisation, cadenzes, instrumental technique, and treatises represent familiar areas of inquiry. The articles by the two editors, however, suggest a broader definition of the field. R. Larry Todd's examination of the ways in which Mendelssohn's familiarity with Mozart's music affected both his own compositions and his performance of Mozart in a fortunate blend of performance practices and reception history. Peter Williams' examination of how a particular musical formula, the chromatic fourth, was used by Mozart, and how it might have been heard and understood, illuminates a part of the musical language that already had a long history. In using it, Mozart was situating himself within an established tradition.

The essays by Katalin Kosmolós and Jaap Schröder are of particular value. Komolós' study of Mozart's extempore pianism gleans constructive and formal principles from his surviving preludes, fantasias and variation sets; her discussion of such Mozartean approaches as melodic ornamentation in the Adagio style (39–40), and his 'brilliant' style (40–41) will be valued by students of improvisation. Schröder begins by identifying those aspects of string writing that were characteristic of Mozart's era (clarity and brightness, intensity without tension, slower bow speed, tempi closer to the human pulse, and so on), and then points out the ways in which modern string technique and performance style work to obscure them. As with the Komolós essay, Schröder's clear discussion of principles serves to illuminate key aspects of a historical performance aesthetic to merit close study by all with an interest in performance, "historical" and "modern" alike.

Traditional performance studies are represented by two founders of the field, Paul Badura-Skoda and Frederick Neumann. Neumann, an indefatigable polemicist, takes as his starting-point an article by Will Crutchfield discussing the prosodic appoggiatura, an ornament traditionally added to certain types of vocal lines, notably those that end with a feminine cadence and a descending leap of a third. Neumann and Crutchfield both agree that such a thing existed, but the (heated) disagreement concerns frequency and appropriate circumstances. Paul Badura-Skoda's essay on Mozart's trills is more problematic, beginning with his premise: he posits a close musical relationship between Mozart and Clementi, citing "their common Italianate musical culture" (an oversimplification) and proceeds to draw conclusions about Mozart's trills from Clementi's piano treatise (1801), which had been published a decade after Mozart's death, and was probably intended primarily for students and amateurs. In the course of the ensuing case-by-case series of instructions, Badura-Skoda quotes Hummel's piano treatise (1828) to illustrate Mozartean practice and asserts, "this rule is also valid for Beethoven and Brahms" (p. 18) with no further explanation.

Cadenzas are addressed by Eduard Melkus and Christoph Wolff. Melkus concerns himself with cadenzas for the violin concerti, summarizing principles set down by Badura-Skoda and his wife Eva (*Interpreting Mozart at the Keyboard*, London, 1961), examining representative didactic cadenzas from the classic era, and finally addressing the needs of the violin as opposed to the piano. Wolff's essay outlines the stylistic changes evident in surviving cadenzas Mozart wrote for his piano concerti, identifying the progression from the freer, largely unmetered, improvised Salzburg type to the later, more worked-out sort favored by Viennese audiences. This insight is highly valuable, but a major problem arises when Wolff, discussing Mozart's later cadenzas for his early *Concerto in D major*, K. 175, states that "consequently, we do not possess any original cadenzas for this concerto in its original Salzburg version; they should be recreated in the proper *non mesuré* manner" (p. 238). The unanswered question: how important should stylistically appropriate cadenzas be for us in Mozart concerti, since Wolff himself demonstrated that they clearly were not of great importance *for Mozart himself*? This issue is central to the way we view later cadenzas by such figures as Beethoven, Brahms, Busoni, and Glenn Gould; Wolff's innocuous "should be" hides a crucial issue.

Space constraints unfortunately prohibit a treatment of Jean-Pierre Marty's discussion of Mozart's tempo indications from an interpretive perspective and Robin Stowell's historical overview of Leopold Mozart's violin treatise and its revisions by later editors, though both certainly merit close reading. This is an attractive book (though marred by a handful of unfortunate editorial errors), clear and well laid-out, and will be of great value not only to performers of Mozart's music, but also to those with an interest in performance practices and eighteenth-century musical culture in general.—Jonathan Bellman.

Tomlinson, Janis A. *Francisco Goya: The Tapestry Cartoons and Early Career at the Court of Madrid.* Cambridge and New York: Cambridge U. Press, 1989. Pp. xiii + 273; 152 figures. Cf. *ECCB*, n.s. 16, IV: 236.

Rev. by Ann Glenn Crowe in *Eighteenth-Century Studies*, 25 (1991–92), 274–78.

Tromlitz, Johann George. *The Virtuoso Flute Player.* Edited and translated by Ardel Powell. (Cambridge Musical Texts and Monographs.) Cambridge and New York: Cambridge U. Press, 1991. Pp. xxviii + 338; bibliography.

Ardel Powell's translation of Johann George Tromlitz's *Detailed and Thorough Tutor for Playing the Flute* (*Ausführlicher und gründlicher Unterricht die Flöte zu spielen*) presents an accessible view of musical performance in 1791. It is valuable to modern flutists, one-keyed flute specialists, and scholars and performers of late eighteenth-century music. Further, Tromlitz's strong opinions on a variety of musically related topics permit us to share in the life of one of Germany's most prominent flutists, teachers, and instrument designers.

Tromlitz's treatise appeared thirty-nine years after Quantz's famous *Essay of a Method for Playing the Transverse Flute* (1752) and Tromlitz assumes his readers' familiarity with the earlier work. Yet Tromlitz frequently differs from and fervently disagrees with Quantz, suggesting that his treatise reflects an age in which the galant was no longer considered a new style. Important, too, is the fact that twenty-five years have passed since Edward R. Reilly's translation of Quantz's *Essay*, regarded as the "classic" of baroque music instruction. Powell frequently refers to Reilly's Quantz, citing specific instances where a given subject is treated in the earlier work and implying that the modern reader will keep a copy of the *Versuch* at hand. Powell therefore abdicates the role of interpreter, deferring to Reilly's interpretative notes and introduction. Because Powell's commentary is so limited and incomplete, there is some implication that this version of Tromlitz's treatise does not stand entirely on its own.

The *Unterricht* is an extremely full work, by both eighteenth-century and modern standards. Following a Foreword in which Tromlitz justifies the need for a treatise subsequent to Quantz's, and an Introduction on attitudes towards teaching, learning, and virtuosity, fifteen chapters unfold. The traverso player will find Chapter 3, on fingering, extremely detailed; it contains numerous valuable possibilities for superior intonation, an issue which Tromlitz contends has not been dealt with satisfactorily, even by Quantz. Chapter 8, on articulation, is especially revealing to performers on the one-keyed flute, since Tromlitz specifies tonguing syllables in relation to a whole piece, unlike Quantz, who applied the patterns to the bar only. Here Tromlitz sets down thirteen "rules for playing," each quite complicated and carefully illustrated with valuable examples. Also rich in detail and examples are chapter 10, on essential ornaments, and chapter 12, on fermatas and cadenzas, which serve as excellent sources for stylistically accurate performance. Chapter 14, on discretionary ornaments, can be appreciated by all modern performers who have struggled to learn the art of embellishing a melody. These musical examples prove to be worth the cost of the entire volume; Tromlitz presents a melody, first embellishes it with essential ornaments and a few discretionary ones, next outlines the main notes of the melody with appropriate harmonies in both figures and chords, and finally illustrates some variations on the melody in three different versions of discretionary ornamentation. Working through this exercise is a rewarding enterprise; we are given a full, fifty-one measure *adagio* movement, including an *ad libitum* fermata. Tromlitz's solutions are vibrant, intricate, and ornate. In chapter 15 Tromlitz summarizes and reinforces his attitudes regarding the roles of pupil and master. It is obvious that Tromlitz has attempted to provide the "complete" tutor, from fundamentals to the diverse possibilities for varying an adagio in the Italianate fashion.

Powell's translation is in a comfortable, informal, and tightly-paced style; it is quite readable and very clear, and in this regard is somewhat more successful than Reilly's work with the Quantz's treatise. His annotations are almost entirely limited to clarifying the original German. Eileen Hadidian's well-documented introduction is a highlight of the edition; she presents biographical information, draws important comparisons with the Quantz *Versuch*, addresses the issue of flute construction, and evaluates the treatise as a source for late eighteenth-century performance style.

My major criticism is that the title, *The Virtuoso Flute-Player,* is never satisfactorily explained. Powell's introduction notes that Tromlitz addresses the work to the aspiring virtuoso, and in the dedication there is a reference to the formation of the virtuoso through proper guidance of the student. Yet the thread of Tromlitz's comments throughout does not consistently address the virtuoso, especially in the eighteenth-century sense of the term; if anything, his remarks are somewhat derogatory towards "so-called virtuosos." Thus the original title seems to have been altered for superficial reasons.—Leslie Ellen Brown.

Tyler, James, and Paul Sparks. *The Early Mandolin: The Mondolino and the Neapolitan Mandoline.* (Early Music Series, 9.) New York and Oxford: Oxford U. Press, 1989. Pp. x + 186. Cf. *ECCB*, n.s. 15, IV: 175.

Rev. by Donald Gill in *Performance Practice Review*, 4 (1991), 202–07.

Tyler, Linda L. " 'Zaide' in the Development of Mozart's Operatic Language." *Music and Letters*, 72 (1991), 214–35; musical examples; table.

Composed in 1779 and 1780, just before *Idomeneo*, this unfinished work proved a testing ground for many experiments that were to find a place in Mozart's operatic style.

Tyson, Alan. *Mozart: Studies of the Autograph Scores*. Cambridge, MA: Harvard U. Press, 1987. Pp. 381. Cf. *ECCB*, n.s. 15, IV: 175; 14, IV: 187; 13, IV: 258–59.

Rev. by Peter Cahn in *Die Musikforschung*, 44 (1991), 377–78.

Valenti, Fernando. *A Performer's Guide to the Keyboard Partitas of J. S. Bach*. London and New Haven, CT: Yale U. Press, 1989. Pp. 136. Cf. *ECCB*, n.s. 16, IV: 238; 15, IV: 175.

Rev. by Howard Schott in *Musical Times*, Vol. 132 (1991), 82.

Valentin, Erich. " 'Neben-Jubilare' 1991." *Acta Mozartiana*, 38 (1991), 49–51.

Valentin, Erich. " 'Meister aller Meister'." *Acta Mozartiana*, 38 (1991), 69–71.

Van Acht, Robert, Vincent Van den Ende, and Hans Schimmel. *Dutch Recorders of the 18th Century [in the Collection of The Hague Gemeente Museaum]*. Celle: Moeck Verlag, 1991.

Rev. by Jeremy Montagu in *Early Music*, 19 (1991), 636–41.

Van Reigen, Paul Willem. *Vergleichende Studien zur Klaviervariationstechnik von Mozart und seinen Zeitgenossen*. Buren: Frits Knuf, 1988. Pp. 261.

Rev. by Katherine Douglas in *Musical Times*, 132 (1991), 346–48.

Vaughan, William. *L'art du XIXe siècle, 1780–1850*. Paris: Citadelle, 1989.

Rev. by Laurent Gambarotto in *Etudes thélogiques et religieuses*, (1991), 137–138.
Deals with the passage from the rigorous neoclassicism of the Enlightenment to the romanticism of the nineteenth century.

Vendrix, Phillipe. "Pierre-Jean Burdette, archéologue de la musique grecque [during the 17th and 18th centuries]." *Recherches sur la Musique française classique*, 27 (1991–92), 99–111; musical examples.

Vernooij, A. *Het rooms-katholieke devotielied in Nederland vanaf 1800*. Utrecht: Nederlands Institut voor Kerkmusiek, 1990. Pp. 170.

Rev. by Jan Valkestijn in *Tijdschrift van de Vereniging voor Nederlandse Muziekgeschiedenis*, 41 (1991), 71–73.

Viano, Richard J. "By invitation only. Private Concerts in France during the second half of the Eighteenth Century." *Recherches sur la Musique française classique*, 27 (1991–92), 131–62.

Vidler, Anthony. *Claude-Nicolas Ledoux: Architecture and Social Reform at the End of the Ancien Régime*. Cambridge, MA, and London: MIT Press, 1990. Pp. xiv + 446; bibliography; illustrations; plans. Cf. *ECCB*, n.s. 16, IV: 239.

Rev. (with reservations) by Margaret and Patrice Higonnet in *TLS*, (Feb. 22, 1991), 14–15.

Vlaadingerbroek, Kees. "Faustina Bordoni Applauds Jan Alensoon [1683–1769]: A Dutch Music-Lover in Italy and France in 1723–4." *Music and Letters*, 72 (1991), 536–51.

Based on his diary of almost 500 pages. Includes observations on church, chamber, and theatre music.

Wacjman, Claude (ed.). *Enfermer ou Guérir: Discourse sur la folie à la fin du Dix-huitième siècle.* Société française d'Etude du XVIIIᵉ siècle. Saint-Étienne, France: Publications de l'Université de Saint-Étienne, 1991. Pp. 117.

Waddy, Patricia. *Seventeenth-Century Roman Palaces: Use and the Art of the Plan.* Cambridge, MA: MIT Press; New York: Architectural History Foundation, 1990. Pp. xiii + 456; illustrations. Cf. *ECCB*, n.s. 16, IV: 239.

Rev. by J. I. Miller in *Choice*, 28 (1991), 1477.

Walter, Meinard. "Gotteserfahrung in der Musik?–J. S. Bachs musikalische Sparche des Glaubens." *Musik und Kirche*, 61 (1991), 312–18.

Wang, Fang-yü, and Richard M. Barnhart. *Master of the Lotus Garden: The Life and Art of Bada Shanren (1626–1705).* Edited by Judith G. Smith. [Exhibition] 22 August–28 October, The Asian Art Museum of San Francisco; 25 January–24 March 1991, Yale U. Art Gallery. New Haven, CT: Yale U. Art Gallery/Yale U. Press, 1990. Pp. 299; appendices; illustrations (some colored). Cf. *ECCB*, n.s. 16, IV: 240.

Rev. (favorably) by J. O. Caswell in *Choice*, 28 (1991), 1299.

Webster, James. Analysis and the Performer: Introduction." *Early Music*, 19 (1991), 590–91; plate.

Webster, James. *Haydn's "Farewell" Symphony and the Idea of Classical Style.* (Cambridge Studies in Music Theory and Analysis.) Cambridge and New York: Cambridge U. Press, 1991. Pp. xix + 402; bibliography; frontispiece; musical examples.

Wendorf, Richard. *The Elements of Life: Biography and Portrait-Painting in Stuart and Georgian England.* New York: Oxford U. Press; Oxford: Clarendon Press, 1990. Pp. xxi + 308; illustrations (some colored). Cf. *ECCB*, n.s. 16, IV: 240.

Rev. by Mordechai Feingold in *Choice*, 28 (1991), 839–40; (with another work) by Shearer West in *TLS*, (Jan. 18, 1991), 16.

Werner, Klaus G. " '. . . Das größte in der Art, was ich gamacht habe.' Gedanken zu den Kopfsätzen der Orchestersinfonien von C. P. E. Bach." *Archiv für Musikwissenschaft*, 48 (1991), 64–83.

West, Shearer. *The Image of the Actor: Verbal and Visual Representation in the Age of Garrick and Kemble.* New York: St. Martin's Press, 1991. Pp. xii + 191; bibliography; illustrations.

Rev. by J. W. Lafler in *Choice*, 29 (1991), 295.

Wheelock, Gretchen A. "Engaging Strategies in Haydn's Opus 33 String Quartets." *Eighteenth-Century Studies*, 25 (1991), 1–30; musical examples.

Draws the audience into the "conversation" among the players.

Whitmore, Philip. *Unpremeditated Art: the Cadenza in the Classical Keyboard Concerto.* Oxford: Clarendon Press, 1991. Pp. xx + 227; bibliography; figure; illustrations; tables.

At the beginning of his study of the cadenza in the classical keyboartd concerto, Philip Whitmore quotes the definition of a cadenza from Johann Joachim Quantz in *Nersuch einer Anweisung die Flöte zu spielen* (1752): "that extempore embellishment created, according to the fancy and pleasure of the performer, by a concertante part at the close of a piece on the penultimate note of the bass, that is, the fifty of the key of the piece." From this starting point, Whitmore traces, in Part I of his study, the evolution of the cadenza in the classical keyboard concerto from a brief single-line melodic ornament to a longer idiomatic passage, often designed to display the skill of the soloist. Such ad libitum cadenzas were not always specifically related to the compositions into which they were inserted, but sometimes did develop and comment on one or more themes of the parent composition. By the early nineteenth century, composers seldom allowed a cadenza "according to the fancy and pleasure of the performer." In their piano concertos, they either included an obligatory cadenza or provided no place for a cadenza. Typically, virtuosic display was emphasized in all the solo passages, and thus a brilliant ad libitum cadenza, an attractive characteristec of the late eighteenth-century concerto, became unnecessary.

In Part II of the monograph, cadenzas in the keyboard concertos of the principal composers of the Classical Era are examined in detail. Since cadenzas ostensibly were improvised, and thus unique to a single performance, Whitmore's task is not simple. He makes use of three types of evidence: the relatively infrequent comments and recommendations in instructional treatises; contemporary scores and performance materials that indicate where a cadenza should be inserted, how it is introduced, and how the soloist signals its conclusion to the accompanying ensemble; and extant cadenzas written out by important compser-performers of the period. By far the most informative sources are these written cadenzas. They are surprisingly abundant and reveal quite clearly what composers and audiences expected.

A large number of cadenzas, many by unnamed composers, were published for the use of students and amateurs. More important are the numerous surviving manuscript cadenzas by C. P. E. Bach, Haydn (?), Mozart, Beethoven, Hummel, and other celebrated musicians of the time. Some of these cadenzas are known to have had a pedagogical purpose. Others are thought to be transcripts of cadenzas improvised in specific performances, and some may have been written in advance and presented to audiences as if invented on the spot. Among Mozart's written-out cadenzas are several for concertos that he reserved for his own use. The cadenzas he himself played were perhaps not always wholly "unpremeditated."

Beethoven's piano concertos present a useful bench mark in the history of the cadenza in the keyboard concerto. About three years after the completion of his *Piano Concerto No. 4*, Beethoven wrote cadenzas for the first movements of each of his first four concertos (three for *Concerto No. 4*). He also wrote two cadenzas for the last movement of *Concerto No. 4*, and cadenzas for the piano version of his *Violin Concerto* and for the Mozart *Piano Concerto in D minor*, K. 466. At about the same time, he wrote his *Piano Concerto No. 5*, the "Emperor" Concerto. In the score of this, his last concerto, Beethoven included an obligatory cadenza that performers can neither omit nor replace. Like Beethoven, virtually all later composers allow no inserted cadenzas in their concertos. Whitmore's discussion of Beethoven's treatment of the cadenza and the factors related to his rejection of the ad libitum cadenza is one of the most interesting portions of his book.

Whitmore does not attempt to instruct performers as to the type of cadenza appropriate in present-day performances of classical concertos, though he does suggest that the cadenzas written for the Mozart concertos by composers such as Hummel, Moscheles, and Reinecke might now be considered "stylistically incongruous." He neither recommends improvised cadenzas over pre-composed insertions designed to sound extemporaneous, nor defines the boundaries of a soloist's obligation to reflect in the cadenza the style of the concerto itself. Nonetheless, his documentation of the variety of cadenza practices in the last half of the eighteenth century and his conveniently organized lists of the written cadenzas by C. P. E. Bach, Mozart, and Beethoven, can help performers to be effective colloaboators with the classical composers whose concertos they choose to play, but also can help other readers to be discerning listeners.—Herbert Livingston.

Williams, Simon. *Shakespeare on the German Stage.* Vol. I: *1586–1914.* Cambridge and New York: Cambridge U. Press, 1990. Pp. xiii + 245; bibliography; illustrations. Cf. *ECCB*, n.s. 16, IV: 240.

Rev. by J. E. Gates in *Choice*, 28 (1991), 791.
    Chapters 1–5 (pp. 1–107) concern Shakespeare in eighteenth-century Germany.

Wind, Barry. *Genre in the Age of the Baroque: A Resource Guide.* (Garland Reference Library of the Humanities, 1382.) New York: Garland Publishers, 1991. Pp. xxvi + 178.

Winter, Robert S. "Of Realizations, Completions, Restorations and Reconstructions: From Bach's *The Art of Fugue* to Beethoven's Tenth Symphony." *Journal of the Royal Musical Association*, 116 (1991), 96–126; appendix with musical examples; table.

Wolf, Eugene K. "On the History and Historiography of Eighteenth-Century Music: Reflections on Dahlhaus's *Die Musik des 18.Jahrhunderts.*" *Journal of Musicological Research*, 10 (1991), 239–255.

Described as a review article.

Wolf, Eugene K., and Edward H. Roesner. *Studies in Musical Sources and Style: Essays in Honor of Jan LeRue.* Madison, WI: A-R Press, 1990. Pp. xii + 555

Wolff, Christoph. *Bach: Essays on His Life and Music.* Cambridge, MA, and London: Harvard U. Press, 1991. Pp. xiv + 461; bibliography; figures; indices; map; musical examples; tables.

Rev. by J. P. Ambrose in *Choice*, 29 (1991), 294.
      In the century following Spitta's monograph on the life of J. S. Bach, the source repertory of the Leipzig Archive has nearly doubled. Subsequent investigations by Schweitzer (1905), Terry (1928), Steglich (1935), Geiringer (1966), and Boyd (1983), while incorporating this new information, are nevertheless built upon Spitta's sometimes flawed assumptions.
      Christoph Wolff's *Bach* represents a long-overdue critical re-evaluation by one of the world's preeminent Bach connoisseurs—the scholar who recently restored to the repertory such lost works as the fourteen canons on the "Goldberg" ground and the thirty-three pre-Weimar preludes. Here Wolff collects twenty-five years of essays, half of them in English for the first time. Wolff's essays read as well as his insights; conclusions (and speculations) are cogent, sometimes brilliant, but always eloquent.
      In "Outlines of a Musical Portrait" Wolff sketches a man supremely driven, organized, equipped, and disciplined. Bach orchestrated his career, Wolff contends, with the same finesse as a concerto. Contrary to the popular portrait of a provincial cantor, swallowed by the routine of his own musical orbit, Wolff's Bach absorbs the nationalistic, stylistic, historical, and theoretical idioms of greater Europe. Wolff focuses our attention anew upon Palestrina (*stile antico*), Reinken (North German school), and Vivaldi (concerted style), whose influences surely have been underestimated.
      In "New Sources: Broadened Perspectives," Wolff weaves into the picture a tapestry of recently discovered manuscripts, significant both as restored repertory, and for our understanding of previously-known works. Yale University's Lowell Mason manuscript 4708, for example, not only provides an important repository of works—thirty-three chorale preludes dating perhaps as far back as Ohrdruf—but also permits Wolff to discern the influence of distant relation Johann Michael Bach upon the nascent compositional efforts of Sebastian.
      The recently discovered *Handexemplar* of the *Goldberg Variations* Wolff calls "the most important Bach source that has come to light in a generation" (p. 163). He proposes that they substantiate Bach's preoccupation with monothematicism during his last decade, an interest in modern trends which coincides with a seemingly paradoxical study of *stile antico*.
      Wolff discloses a Mass by Dresden composer von Wilderer that Bach may have parodied in the first *Kyrie* of his *B minor Mass*. He also reveals that the aggrandized version of *Ein feste Burg* is historically improper to this cantata; it was not authorized by Johann Sebastian's eldest son, Wilhelm Friedemann, although Friedemann did add trumpets and timpani in two movements adapted to a different text.
      In "Old Sources Revisited: Novel Aspects," Wolff disabuses the reader of more traditional Bachiana by demonstrating that the chorale, *Wenn wir in Höchsten Nöthen sein*, was not a deathbed utterance, but was added to the *Art of Fugue* to compensate for editorial haste (or inability to decipher the conclusion of the preceding *Fuga a 3 Soggetti*). Wolff also contends that the latter composition was not terminated following the BACH exposition in

the exigency of imminent demise, since Bach had been revising the fugues of his "last" *tour de force* for nearly a decade.

"Concepts, Style and Chronology" probes the formal dimensions of Bach's late works.   In these thought-provoking discussions, Wolff concludes that the cyclic dispositions of these works "emanate apparently from the thought that the microcosmic order must be mirrored in a macrocosmic order in rational correspondence" (p. 358).

In "Early Reception and Artistic Legacy," Wolff revisits Bach's contemporaries in their comments upon composition, criticism, analysis, and aesthetics. Because Bach declined to describe himself or his work in prosaic terms, these reflections provide illuminating insights into the mind of this great composer.

Wolff's thematic format allows him a depth of exposition more substantive than that of his chronologically-minded counterparts. Yet, the strength of his format is also its weakness, for in his frames and proofs, Wolff inevitably admits several redundancies: the Scheibe-Birnbaum controversy is mentioned at least four times, while the problem of order in the *Art of Fugue* receives scrutiny twice. Readers with these interests might have been assisted by a synthesis of ideas that are scattered hither and yon.

It is perhaps a measure of the significance of Wolff's tract that he is able to speculate, while simultaneously chipping away the accretions of myth surrounding the monolith, without dimming Bach's hallowed reputation among musicians. To the contrary, the reader of these essays will—inasmuch as Wolff attempts to carve an image breathing neither flattery nor flatulence—still see the halo, somewhat unctuous, but undimmed.—Timothy A. Smith.

Wollenberg, Susan. "Schumann's Piano Quinitet in E flat: The Bach Legacy." *Music Review*, 52 (1991), 299–305; figures; musical examples.

Yearbook of Interdisciplinary Studies in the Fine Arts. Edited by William E. Grimm, and Michael B. Harper. Pittsburgh, PA: Mellen Press, Vol. 1 (1989).

Rev. by Jonathan Sturm in *Indian Theory Review*, 12 (1991), 206–11.

Zahn, Robert V. "Autographe Johann Sebastian Bach im Besitz von C. F. G. Schwenke (1767–1822)." *Musik und Kirche*, 61 (1991), 332–38.

Zaslaw, Neal. *Mozart's Symphonies: Context, Performance Practice, Reception.* Oxford: Clarendon Press, 1989. Pp. 617. Cf. *ECCB*, n.s. 16, IV: 241; 15, IV: 179.

Rev. by Peter Brown in *Music and Letters*, 72 (1991), 277–83; by Malcolm S. Cole in *Performance Practice Review*, 4 (1991), 211–17; and by Gretchen Wheelock in *Historical Performance*, 4 (1991), 55–57.

Zaslaw, Neal. "Vibrato in Eighteenth-Century Orchestras." *Performance Practice Review*, 4 (1991), 28–33.

Argues against vibrato except as an ornament. Quotes and interprets primary sources. Cites Greta Moens-Haenen's *Das Vibrato in der Musik der Baorck: ein Handbuch zur Aufführungspraxis für Vokalisten und Instrumentalisten.* Graz: Akademische Druck- und Verlagsanstatt, 1988.

Zaslaw, Neal (ed.). *The Classical Era: From the 1740s to the End of the 18th Century.* (Man and Music.) Basingstoke, UK: Macmillan, 1989 [1990]. Pp. x + 416. Cf. *ECCB*, n.s. 16, IV: 241; 15, IV: 170.

Rev. by Julian Rushton in *Music and Letters*, 72 (1991), 443–45.

Zaslaw, Neal (ed.) with William Cowdery. *The Complete Mozart: A Guide to the Musical Works of Wolfgang Amadeus Mozart.* New York: Mozart Bicentennial at Lincoln Center/W.W. Norton, 1990. Pp. xv + 351; illustrations. Cf. *ECCB*, n.s. 16, IV: 241.

Rev. (favorably) by C. A. Kolczynski in *Choice*, 28 (1991), 1627; by Malcolm Miller in *Musical Times*, 132 (1991), 568–69; by John A. Rice in *Notes*, 48 (1991), 484–86.

Zaslaw, Neal, and Fiona Morgan Fein (eds.). *The Mozart Repertory: A Guide for Musicians, Programmers and Researchers.* Ithaca, NY: Cornell U. Press, 1991. Pp. xvii + 157.

Rev. by Malcolm Miller in *Musical Times*, 132 (1991), 568–69.

Zeigler, Frank. *Wolfgang Amadeus Mozart: Autographenverzeichnis.* (Deutsche Staatsbibliothek. Handschrifteninvertare, 12.) Berlin: Deutsche Staatsbibliothek, 1990. Pp. xii + 62.

Rev. by John A. Rice in *Notes*, 48 (1991), 484–86.

Zelenka-Dokumentation: Quellen und Materialen. Compiled by Wolfgang Horn and Thomas Kohlhase in association with Ortrun Landmann and Wolfgang Reich. 2 vols. · Wiesbaden: Breitkopf und Härtel, 1989. Pp. 368.

Rev. by Brian W. Pritchard in *Notes*, 48 (1991), 79–81.

Zelenka, Jan Dismas. *Missa ultimarum secunda: Missa Dei Filii*, ZWV 20: *Litanaiae Lauretanae "Consolatrix afflictorum,"* ZWV 151. Edited by Paul Horn and Thomas Kohlhase. (Das Erbe deutscher Music, Bd. 100; Abteilung Motette und Messe, Bd. 13.) Wiesbaden: Breitkopf & Härtel, 1989. Pp. 197; critical commentary; facsimiles; score.

Rev. by John Eric Floreen in *Notes*, 47 (1991), 944–46.

Zelenka, Jan Dismas. *Missa Omnium Sanctorum.* Edited by Wolfgang Horn; *Litaniae Lauretanae Salus infirmorum.* Edited by Thomas Kohlhase. (Das Erbe deutscher Musik. Bd. 101; Abteilung Motette und Messe, Bd. 14.) Wiesbaden: Breitkopf & Härtel, 1989. Pp. 274; critical commentary; facsimiles; score.

Rev. by John Eric Floreen in *Notes*, 47 (1991), 944–46.

Zimmerman, Franklin B. *Henry Purcell: A Guide to Research.* New York: Garland, 1988. Pp. vi + 333. Cf. *ECCB*, n.s. 16, IV: 241; 15, IV: 180.

Rev. by Irena Cholij in *Musical Times*, 132 (1991), 138; by Robert Ford in *Journal of Musicological Research*, 10 (1991), 283–5.

Literary Studies

Abbot, Scott H. *Fiction of Freemasonry: Freemasonry and the German Novel.* Detroit, MI: Wayne State U. Press, 1991. Pp. 240.

Abraham, Lindy. *Marvell and Alchemy.* Aldershot, UK: Scolar Press, 1990. Pp. xi + 634.

Rev. (with reservations) by Elizabeth Mackenzie in *Notes and Queries,* 236 (1991), 386–87.

Ahrens, Rüdiger. "The Political Pamphlet: 1660–1714. Pre-and post-revolutionary Aspects." *Anglia,* 109 (1991), 21–43.

Airakisinen, Timo. *Of Glamour, Sex, and De Sade.* Wakefield, NH: Longwood Academic, 1991. Pp. 220.

Alkon, Paul K. *Origins of Futuristic Fiction.* Athens, GA: Georgia U. Press, 1987. Pp. xii + 341; illustrations. Cf. *ECCB,* n.s. 16, V:244; 15, V:182; 14, V:192; 13, V: 263.

Rev. by Jacques Prévot in *Revue d'histoire littéraire de la France,* 91 (1991), 108–09.

Andresen, Julie Tetel. *Linguistics in America, 1769–1924: A Critical History.* (Routledge History of Linguistic Thought Series.) London and New York: Routledge, 1990. Pp. vi + 308.

Rev. by W. D. Miller in *Choice,* 28 (1991), 1302.
    Chapter One is titled "In the Beginning (1769–1815): The Political Conception of Language" (pp. 22–67).

Andries, Lise. *La Bibliothéque bleue au dix-huitiéme siécle: une tradition editoriale.* Oxford: The Voltaire Foundation at the Taylor Institution, 1989. Pp. vii + 211.

Rev. (with reservations) by Peter France in *French Studies,* 45 (1991), 324–25; (with reservations) by Marie-Dominique Leclerc in *Revue d'histoire littéraire de la France,* 91 (1991), 977–79; by Renée Waldinger in *The French Review,* 65 (1991), 123–24.

Anselment, Raymond A. *Loyalist Resolve: Patient Fortitude in the English Civil War.* Cranbury, NJ: Associated U. Presses; Newark, DE: U. Of Delaware Press, 1988. Pp. 233.

Rev. (with reservations) by Ann Baynes Coiro in *Journal of English and Germanic Philology,* 90 (1991), 561–63.

Apostolidès, Jean-Marie. "Le paradoxe de l' *Encyclopédie.*" *Stanford French Review,* 14 (1990), 47–64.

Auroux, Sylvain, Dominique Bourel, and Charles Porset (eds.). *L'Encyclopédie, Diderot L'esthétique. Mélanges en Hommage à Jacques Chouillet (1915–1990)*.   Paris: Presses Universitaires de France, 1991. Pp. 334.

The editors of this testimonial volume honoring a leading Diderot scholar have assembled an impressive array of twenty-seven articles effectively reflecting his three main areas of interest. The volume, which opens with a photograph of his honor, also comprises an affectionate tribute in the modest form of an "Avant-propos" by the editors, a fascinating and moving "Entretien avec Jacques Chouillet," held two months before his death, which highlights the life and career of a French "universitaire" who was also intimately involved in the political turmoils, battles, and wars of our century, a bibliography of his publications by Anne-Marie Chouillet, his wife and able collaborator, a list of subscribers, and even a helpful index.

As is appropriate, Diderot occupies center stage in the articles. Within the limitations of this review, individual contributions can only be briefly commented upon. In the section titled "Diderot, La Philosophie, L'Esthétique," which has the largest number of contributions, Lucette Pérol delves into the Encyclopedist's political thought, Roland Mortier evokes the image of Diderot through Grétry's memoirs, Larry Bongie ponders the relationship between Diderot and Condillac, Anthony Strugnell reexamines Diderot's part in anglomania in eighteenth-century France, and Gianluigi Goggi focuses on Diderot and Russia through the testimony of a contemporary travel journal held by Georges-Louis Schmid, a Swiss man of letters. Michel Baridon brings fresh insights on the scientific imagination in the *Rêve de d'Alembert*, Simon Davues reflects on the theme of law and justice in Diderot's works of fiction, Pierre Rétat analyzes Diderot's self-representation in his letters to Sophie Volland, Lynn Salkin Sbiroli recalls the importance of image and metaphor in Diderot's scientific writings, Philip Stewart emphasizes the close relationship between Diderot's theory and practice in the theater and painting through his obsessive interest in the unseen observer, Marian Hobson deals with Diderot's generally overlooked interest in architecture, Béatrice Didier reminds us that Diderot, the atheist and materialist, nevertheless had a strong appreciation for religious painting, and Marc Buffat elaborates on Jacques Chouillet's ideas concerning Diderot's dramatic poetics. Georges May brings together the unexpected pair of Horace, the Latin poet and artist, and Orou, the main protagonist of *Supplément au Voyage de Bougainville*, Jean Sgard delves on what he calls "la beauté convulsive" of *La Religieuse*, while Jean Deprun cites four little-known but revealing testimonies by Catholics whose credibility in such matters is unimpeachable in order to demonstrate that Diderot's novel was by no means unfairly slanted against monastic life. The last contribution to this section, titled "Vandoliana," is by François Moureau, and it inventories a Vandeul library preserved in one of the residences owned by the family until the beginning of this century. Thanks to its present-day owners, the author of this article was able to spend two days sorting through the remaining volumes.

In the section titled "L'Encyclopédie, Les Lumières, L'Esthétique," there are two articles specifically devoted to science. Jean Ehrard shows how the initial centrality of the unitary concept of the tree of knowledge evolved toward the notion of a "labyrinthe inextricable" that only future generations would be able to untangle, and Haydn Mason assesses Voltaire's strategy in his article "Inoculation" and the role it played in the eventual victory of the pro-inoculists.

In view of Jacques Chouillet's own interests, it is hardly surprising that five contributions deal with the *Encyclopédie* and aesthetics. Anne Becq reminds us that one cannot find an overriding theory of aesthetics in the *Encyclopédie* and that an entry specifically devoted to this topic only appeared in the 1776 *Supplément*, which she analyzes in the context of Baumgarten's *Aesthetica* and Sulzer's *Allgemeine Theorie der schönen Künste*. Paul Sardin deals with the brief and heretofore overlooked article "Laideur," which he insightfully contrasts with the famous article "Beau"; Catherine Kintzler compares Rousseau's articles "Cadence" in the *Encyclopédie* and in his own *Dictionnaire de musique*; Madeleine Pinault shows how frequently such authors or articles on the visual arts as Watelet, Jaucourt, and Paul Landois, cited the great French seventeeth-century artists, notably Poussin, Le Sueur, Jouvenet, and especially Le Brun; and Aurélio deals with the idea of dramatic and novelistic dialogue in the articles on poetics contributed by Marmontel, which he would eventually gather together in his *Eléments de littérature*. Three other articles in this section respectively deal with good taste and pedagogy, by Robert Granderoute, with cladestine literature and the diffusion of anti-religious ideas in the first half of the eighteenth century, by Ann

Thomson, and with a by now forgotten academic "discours" by Jean-Henri Lambert, "Des Secours mutuels que peuvent se prêter les sciences solides et les belles-lettres," by Martin Fontius.

This substantial *festschrift* will be of interest to the historian of ideas, the literary critic, the *dix-huitiémiste*, and the aesthetician, and is indeed a fitting tribute to the outstanding *Diderotiste* and French intellectual it honors.—Gita May.

Baader, Renate (ed.). *Das Frauenbild im Literarishen Frankreich vom Mittelalter bis zur Gegenwart.* (Wege der Forschung, 611.) Darmstadt: Wissenschaftliche Buchgesellschaft, 1988. Pp. vi + 386. Cf. *ECCB*, n.s. 14, V:192.

Rev. by D. Williams in *French Studies*, 45 (1991), 110–11.

Baasner, Frank. *Der Begriff "sensibilité" im 18. Jahrhundert. Aufsteig und Niedergang eines Ideals.* (Studia Romanica, 69.) Heidelberg: Carl Winter, 1988. Pp. 425.

Rev. by Paul H. Meyer in *Recherches sur Diderot et sur l'Encyclopédie*, 11 (1991), 158–61.

Backscheider, Paula R. "Recent Studies in Restoration and Eighteenth Century." *Studies in English Literature: 1500–1900*, 31 (1991), 569–614.

Backscheider, Paula, (ed.). *Restoration and Eighteenth-Century Dramatists; First Series.* (Dictionary of Literary Biography, 80.) Detroit, MI: Gale Research Press, 1989. Pp. xi + 397. Cf. *ECCB*, n.s. 16, V:247; 15, V:183.

Rev. by Richard H. Dammers in *The Scriblerian*, 23 (1991), 261–63; by Jean Hamard in *Études anglaises*, 44 (1991), 343.

Backscheider, Paula, (ed.). *Restoration and Eighteenth-Century Dramatists: Second Series.* (Dictionary of Literary Biography, 84.) Detroit, MI: Gale Research Press, 1989. Pp. xix + 456.

Rev. by Linda M. Hill in *South Atlantic Review*, 56 (1991), 113–14.

Bacon, Jon Lance. "Wives, Widows, and Writings in Restoration Comedy." *Studies in English Literature: 1500–1900*, 31 (1991), 427–44.

Frequent comparisons of women to texts reflect the anxieties of males and the legal status of wives and widows.

Baehr, Stephen Lessing. *The Paradise Myth in Eighteenth-Century Russian Literature: Utopian Patterns in Early Secular Russian Literature and Culture.* Stanford, CA: Stanford U. Press, 1991. Pp. xiv + 308; appendices; figures; selected bibliography.

The Paradise Myth in Eighteenth-Century Russian Literature is rich with literary and historical facts derived from diverse sources which reflect the spirit of old and new times, moods of various writers, and the clashing opinions of critics. Dr. Baehr discusses Russian secular literature of the century that witnessed the last years of the reign of Peter the Great, weathered the "Time of Toubles" (when one tsar or tsarina was succeeded by another), and came to an end during the rule of Catherine the Great. The majority of the analysis refers to the Russian literature under Catherine II (1762 1796). The author advocates "the integration of Russian and Western ideals of paradise in many diverse areas of the eighteenth century" (13) and maintains that the panegyric and utopian kinds of literature (along with traditional satire) were widespread in the secular society of eighteenth-century Russia.

The "secular" literature, as it appears in the monograph, accounts only for the works written by the authors close to or influenced by the imperial court. In these discussed works the praise of the "enlightened rule" of Catherine the Great was sometimes balanced by moderate critique of the tsarina: advise and warnings filtered into propagandistic utopia (120). The author justly compares a panegyric poet of the period with the "court jester" (160), for the satire is to be understood in the context of praise. However, another kind of secular literature with utopian patterns extant in the eighteenth century has no imprint on this monograph. That literature (oral and written) was created in the spheres removed from the court's influence and was connected with the rebellion of 1773–1775. After much wandering and suffering, E. Pugachev, the legendary leader of the rebellion and the subject of tales and songs (some of which represent him as tsar Peter III) comes back to Russia in order to regain his "lawful" throne and restore Russia to its perfect paradisiacal state. Though this rebellious literature was officially prohibited during the reign of Catherine II, it was so popular that even in the mid nineteenth century it was still part of the oral tradition. Thus, the same utopian patterns that contributed to the praise of Catherine II presented a dangerous foil for her in the mythical image of the "good" but uncrowned "tsar." Lack of discussion of the secular literature outside the ruling spheres deprives the monograph of analyzing how the paradisal myth in eighteenth-century Russia was not only propagandistic, but also rebellious.

Another problematic aspect is that while in chapter 5 Baehr emphasizes the Masonic ideas for the nobility in 18th-century Russia, he fails to articulate major contrasts and similarities with other current ideologies and beliefs presented earlier in the book. For example, Baehr states that the four works by M. M. Kheraskov, *The Golden Wand* (1782), *Vladimir Reborn* (1785), *Cadmus and Harmonia* (1789), and *Polydorus: The Son of Cadmus and Harmonia* (1794), "reflect the general beliefs dominating much Masonic literature: that paradise is within the self; that only the virtuous person can achieve it; and that this achievement requires significant self-knowledge, self-improvement, and self-sacrifice" (100). The general Masonic beliefs enumerated here are characteristic not only of Masonic literature. For every branch of religion it would be untenable to say that Paradise is just physical, that it welcomes unrepentent sinful souls, and that it can be achieved without sacrifice and self-improvement. In other words, to make the proof of Masonic influence upon the literature in question conclusive, it is desireable to demonstrate clearly how the features in discussion are not Byzantine, Orthodox, or Muscovite, and how and why they are exclusively Masonic.

At the same time, specialists in Russian studies will find here a wonderful source of diverse facts about paradise patterns, and a bibliography that extends from the eighteenth century well into the twentieth. Up to this point, the paradise motives per se have been little discussed in Soviet criticism and in Russian studies abroad. This monograph breaks ground for further research and will be of great interest to those who want to deepen their knowledge of religious motives and utopia in Russian literature. Baehr's work will add to the dialogue in mixed American-Russian arenas where it has the potential to suddenly spotlight otherwise evasive issues of socio-historical character.—Elena Khalturina.

Barber, Giles, and C. P. Courtney (eds.). *Enlightenment Essays in Memory of Robert Shackleton.* Oxford: The Voltaire Foundation at the Taylor Institution, 1988. Pp. xxix + 335. Cf. *ECCB*, n.s. 16, V:248; 14, V: 193.

Rev. (with another work) by Sheila Mason in *Modern Language Review*, 86 (1991), 209–10.

Barny, Roger. *Études Textuelles 1*. (Centre de Recherches Jacques-Petit, 56.) Paris: Annales Littéraires de l'Université de Besançon 454 (distributed through Paris: Les Belles Lettres), 1991. Pp. 212.

What ties this short collection of eight essays together is a common focus on some major writings of the brightest of the eighteenth century's "lumières." One essay is devoted to a reading of Candide's encounter with the Bulgars, one to the opening of Montesquieu's *L'esprit des lois*, another to the lake scene in Rousseau's *La Nouvelle Héloïse*, still another to a passage from the beginning of *Les Confessions,* and finally, three essays to Diderot's *Le Neveu de Rameau*. A reading of La Fontaine's "Le Gland et la Citrouilee" is the odd essay out.

The essay's origin as lecture notes is obvious. The presentation of arguments is at times schematic with details or points to be developed elliptically referred to in parenthetical notes. A disclaimer at the beginning of the volume explains that these essays are the result of a prolonged pedagogical experience: preparation for the C.A.P.E.S, Agrégation etc. In part they are geared to a non-specialist readership. Barny makes observations at times that would be self-evident to an eighteenth-century scholar, but are not necessarily so to a student. He notes, for example, that the novel was a sort of non-genre that was considered both vulgar and morally suspect. Yet despite their pedagogical thrust, the essays are rewarding for the seasoned "dix-huitièmiste." Barny's interpretations are richly informed and often ingenious.

As the title of the collection suggests, the essays take the form of that quintessentially French academic exercise—the "explication de texte." At the hands of a master this exercise is both learned and thoroughly up-to-date. A common technique prevails throughout: Barny pulls on one detail or thematic strand until the whole text unravels. His reading of Rousseau's *Confessions*, for example, focuses on the remark: "Je sentis avant de penser." Thus a seemingly offhand remark reveals, on close inspection, the relationship between two distinct projects: the autobiographical and the philosophical. Rousseau's privileging of sensory experience allies him to sensualist philosophical currents yet also leads him to conceive of consciousness of the self in utterly unique terms. In *Les Confessions*, as in the work as a whole, personal mythography is interwoven with theoretical preoccupations.

Several of the essays in this collection are complementary. Rousseau's presentation of himself in *Les Confessions* contrasts nicely, for example, with a caricature of him in (*Le Neveu de Rameau*). The portrait, which Barny analyzes in the course of a discussion on genius, is only partially unflattering for, as Diderot himself sees it, both the Nephew and Jean-Jacques serve as an ironic conscience to the bad faith of the Enlightenment. These essays demonstrate that a good explication can open up not just a particular passage, but an entire *oeuvre*. They also show the vigorous workings of the dialectic of the Enlightenment.—Nanette LeCoat.

Bate, Jonathan. *Shakespearean Constitutions: Politics, Theatre, Criticism 1730–1830.* Oxford: Clarendon Press, 1989. Pp. xiii + 234. Cf. *ECCB*, n.s. 15, V:184–85.

Rev. by R. S. White in *Notes and Queries*, 236 (1991), 111–12.

Baym, Nina. "Between Enlightenment and Victorian: Toward a Narrative of American Women Writers Writing History." *Critical Inquiry*, 18 (1991), 22–41.

American women writers born before 1790 were "enabled by an Enlightenment republicanism whose tenets guaranteed women intellectual parity with men and offered them the chance to serve their nation if they developed their minds."

Beasley, Faith E. *Revising Memory: Women's Fiction and Memoirs in Seventeenth-Century France.* London and New Brunswick, NJ: Rutgers U. Press, 1990. Pp. xi + 288; bibliography. Cf. *ECCB*, n.s. 16, V: 249.

Rev. (favorably) by R. A. Picken in *Choice*, 29 (1991), 451.
"Analyz[es the] texts of the Duchesse de Montpensier, Madame de Lafayette, and Madame de Villedieu to offer 'an alternative narrative of the past, a particular history designed to undermine the patriarchal, official history advanced by the Sun King, Louis XIV'."

Becq, Annie (ed.). *L'Encyclopédisme.* Actes du Colloque de Caen (12–16 January 1987). Paris: Aux Amatuers de livres, (distributed through Paris: Klincksieck), 1991. Pp. 592.

The publication of the *Nouvelle Encyclopédie Diderot* was the pretext for an important colloquium organized by Professor Annie Becq of the University of Caen in January, 1987. The acts have now been collected in a handsome volume published in 1991. The purpose of the colloquium was to study past versions of encyclopedism as well as its future.

Creating an encyclopedia involves first the process of gathering together past and present knowledge, followed by an analysis and a reflection of the various components of knowledge. Lastly encyclopedists view as their mission the spreading of knowledge, both for their contemporaries and for future generations.

Professor Becq and the colloquium participants present a wide array of reflections on the origins of the concept of the encyclopedia, its significance, and its methodological execution. This ambitious undertaking examines various facets of encyclopedism; in particular, it sheds light on its relationship with theology, philosophy, religion, and political power.

Although Chinese scholars were pioneers, their encyclopedias were ignored by the occident until the arrival of Jesuits. In the western world, Isidore de Seville produced vast compilations in the seventh century followed in the tenth century by Arabic scholars. Averroes (twelfth century) followed suit in the medical field. Medieval encyclopedism is the topic of an outstanding article by the greatly missed Michel de Boüard. As for the Renaissance, it lacked an innovative spirit, and the concept of an "arbor scientarum" was to prevail only with Bacon and Leibniz. The eighteenth century is viewed as "the" century of encyclopedias: Chambers in England, Diderot and d'Alembert in France and Zedler and his huge work in Germany. In the nineteenth century, encyclopedias multiply.

As is the case with every colloquium, the one held in Caen did not claim to be exhaustive, and the critical approaches and the methodologies of the participants varied greatly. Therefore, rather than presenting a systematic reflection of the art of creating an encyclopedia, this volume offers a wide choice of articles on numerous aspects of the problem. This multiplicity of approaches makes for an outstanding collection indeed. Worthy of a special mention are the articles by Franz Kafker: "La Place de l'Encyclopédie dans l'histoire des encyclopédies," Charles Porset: "L'Encyclopédie et la question de l'ordre: réflexions sur la lexicalisation des connaissances au XVIIIe siecle," Dominique Lecourt: "De l'Encyclopédie des 'Lumieries' à la Nouvelle Encyclopédie Diderot," and Madeleine Pinault: "Sur les plances de l'Encyclopédie."

Beisel, Inge. *Asthetischer Anspruch und Narrative Praxis. Sur Koautorschaft des Lesers in Französischen Romanen des 18 Jahrhunderts.* (Erlanger Romanistische Dokumente und Arbeiten.) Tübingen: Stauffernburg Verlag, 1991. Pp. 254.

Rev. by Paul H. Meyer in *Recherces sur Diderot et sur l'Encyclopédie*, 13 (1992), 161–63.

Bell, Ian A. *Literature and Crime in Augustan England.* London and New York: Routledge, 1991. Pp. viii + 250; bibliography; 12 illustrations.

Rev. by P. D. McGlynn in *Choice*, 29 (1991), 276.

As every eighteenth-century initiate knows, crime was as pervasive in the novels, plays, and even poems of the age of Anne and Walpole as it was on the streets of London. Until recent times, an empirical and perhaps simplistic model of historical research presented this literature as "a kind of window on the past, offering reliable access to lost worlds" (p. 21). This book repudiates such unproblematical access. Working within the new historicist emphases as understood by Gramsci, Foucault, and Raymond Williams, Ian Bell has produced a refreshing study on the intersection of sociology and aesthetics.

While stressing the role of ideology and politics in the literature, Bell has not fallen into the trap of so many new historicists of disregarding the unique function of literature of this period (as well as every other), which is both to disseminate and resist ideology. In the context of crime, Bell argues that "literature explored the mismatching of law and morality, isolating and exploiting paradoxes and ironies which the univocal body of statute sought to ignore or suppress" (p. 27). He thus repudiates the claims of neo-Marxists that high culture, especially canonical works, is a conservative force within the contending ideologies of a society.

Bell's goal, to celebrate literature's unique ability to reveal the fissures and skirmishes within culture, is mostly realized in a series of close inspections of canonical pieces by Hogarth, Defoe, Gay, Swift, Pope, Lillo, and Fielding, as well as lesser-known material by Blackstone, Dunton, and anonymous Grub Street hacks. Bell, though, refuses to be pigeonholed among the humanists or post-modernists. On the one hand, he asserts that "literary treatments of crime are clearly not motivated exclusively by literary or formal considerations . . . but by more stealthy deep seated social needs and imperatives" (p. 61). On the other hand, "it would be wrong, of course, to deny that forms of writing and genres establish their own momentum" (p. 61). While sounding occasionally like an epigone of Foucault with the fashionable jargon of "discourse," "class interests," and the like, Bell affirms the power of genius by such adjectives as "creative" (applied to the Swift poem) or "tantalisingly brilliant" (applied to Gay's *Beggar's Opera*, of which he can scarcely disguise his relish).

In the period's ambivalences about causes and cures for crime, Bell shows how artists as diverse as Johnson and Hogarth create a dialectic or double perspective on crime. In "London" Johnson offers a paradox: "London is at once the center of the most developed modern civilization, and the baffling apogee of proliferating crime and corruption" (p. 48). In *Industry and Idleness*, Hogarth, while seeming to endorse severe punishment for crime, creates a skeptical, comic treatment of morality, thus complicating a simple message. The homiletic emerges in irony, and different meanings "contend for authority."

In the last chapter, with the curious title, "Fielding and the Discipline of Fiction," probably his most persuasive, Bell demonstrates how Fielding could be a conservative (Bell often calls him "reactionary") demanding severe punishment and less compassion, and yet at the same time, in his novels, could finely dissect the ideology of the ruling classes, with their obsession for property (think of Squire Western) and desire to hang malefactors. This is the "Discipline" of the title: "Fielding replaces [in *Joseph Andrews*] the transparently fallible legal structure described within the tale with the superior discipline of comic fiction, where the magisterial author may overcome the obduracy of the world, and dispense justice, exercise restraint, or allocate and administer punishment and reward, as he thinks fit" (p. 209). This amounts to a truism really, but Bell never alludes to the obvious formal requirements of fiction of the eighteenth century (codified by Thomas Rymer), that the author end his story with poetic justice. So formalism, specifically repudiated by Bell as not being a motivating factor for the author, plays after all a crucial role when the critic is confronted with a real textual crux.

This is not the only ideological fissure of interest to Bell; throughout the book, he is concerned with the "blatant savagery of the Augustan penal code" (p. 188). He argues à la Nietzsche that there is no objective data about crime. The fear of it, exaggerated by those ideologically motivated and in positions of power, is the real problem, and that fear pushes the propertied to manipulating and augmenting the penal code so as to make it harsher and more violent. Unfortunately, Bell, sharing a failing common to some new historicists, makes no comparisons with other European societies or with England of the past, but rather with an idealized vision of the modern welfare state. Had he compared the rule of law in Great Britain, even in its rudimentary, eighteenth-century condition, with the Inquisition in Southern Europe, French tyranny, and the chaos of Eastern Europe, he might have mitigated his attack on the complacent celebrators of English law like Blackstone. For another example, in his chapter focusing on women, Bell makes no mention of the elimination of witch burning in this period. His treatment of "the double standard" rehearses a feminist litany of suffering and oppression, again without looking at historical context, but only at recently established radical feminist values; "The apparent case for the tenderness and vulnerability of women was a way of legitimizing their disenfranchisement, and providing them a very limited repertoire of acceptable behavior" (p. 98). But when had they ever possessed the franchise? And what was their status in comparison to previous eras? Clearly ideology is a knife that cuts two ways.

Though Bell's approach to the intertwining of sociology and literature is vulnerable, it is often insightful and occasionally brilliant, for instance, in the sections on Pope's and Swift's punitive satire, in which the rhetoric and imagery often reflect the penal code or expose its gaps.—Arthur J. Weitzman.

Bell, Maureen, George Parfitt, and Simon Shepherd. *A Biographical Dictionary of English Women Writers, 1580–1720*. Boston, MA: G.K. Hall; London: Harvester Wheatsheaf, 1990. Pp. xxvi + 298. Cf. *ECCB*, n.s. 16, V:250.

Rev. by N. Knipe in *Choice*, 28 (1991), 749; by Lynn F. Williams in *American Reference Books Annual*, 22 (1991), 1183.

Bem, Jeanne. *Le Texte traversé: Corneille, Prévost, Marivaux, Musset, Dumas, Nerval, Baudelaire, Hugo, Flaubert, Verlaine, Laforgue, Proust, Giraudoux, Aragon, Giono.* (Travaux et recherches des universités rhénanes, 6.) Paris: Champion, 1991. Pp. 211.

Bendjebbar, André. "Le Théâtre angevin pendant la Révolution (1789–1799)." *Revue d'histoire du théâtre,* 43 (1991), 136–46.

Studies all aspects of theater in the provincial town of Angers during the French Revolution.

Bernstein, Stephen. "Form and Ideology in the Gothic Novel." *Essays in Literature,* 18 (1991), 151–65.

From 1764 to 1820, the genre was cohesive, with a courtship narrative and a family secret, both of which respond to the insights of Foucault.

Bevis, Richard W. *English Drama: Restoration and Eighteenth Century, 1660–1789.* London and New York: Longman, 1988. Pp. xiii + 341. Cf. *ECCB,* n.s. 15, V:186; 14, V: 196.

Rev. by Laura Morrow in *The Scriblerian,* 23 (1991), 263–64.

Bhalla, Alok. *The Cartographers of Hell: Essays on the Gothic Novel and the Social History of England.* New Delhi: Sterling Publishers (distributed through New York: Apt Books), 1991. Pp. x + 182.

This book is one of a growing number of studies linking the gothic novel to social and political realities of an age of unease, revolution, and repression. Alok Bhalla's central argument sees the gothic as "an attempt to expose the underside of eighteenth and nineteenth-century cultural and social order—the illogical, the brutal, the coercive, and predatory aspects of a society" (p. 14). He offers three points of focus for his exposé: pastoralism, structure, and gothic settings.

The dark side of the pastoral landscape is the subject of the second chapter, which centers upon Mary Shelley's *Frankenstein* and James Hogg's tales of the Scottish peasantry. More generally, Bhalla encourages us to see the demonic pastoral in the background of a range of works that offer glimpses of rural lives governed by misery and exploitation. His third chapter links the fragmented narratives of the gothic novel with the culture's loss of moral and spiritual direction. It offers a searching critique of a variety of critical approaches that catalogue gothic novels—by theatrical properties, by signs, by structural models—but ignore the historical moment that generated the phenomenon. An examination of Hogg's *Justified Sinner* and Maturin's *Melmoth* connects disjointed narrative structures to communities of duress and dispossession at specific moments in time. The fourth chapter weighs nostalgia against skepticism in its account of ruins and cathedrals in the gothic novel. The ideal of the sacred community collapses into loss of faith as hallowed spaces become venues of corruption and religions become infatuated with political and social power. The result is the coercion, superstition, and bigotry so apparent in the pages of Radcliffe, Lewis, and Maturin.

Bhalla's study affirms repeatedly that gothic novels are historically specific: they are not escapist fantasies but imaginative projections of late eighteenth and early nineteenth-century political realities of division and tyranny. His study is mainly literary and could be supplemented by studies of the repressive nature of the three decades of gothicism and Romanticism when agrarian and commercial gentries prolonged their power and profit with the help of arrests and arraignments, trials and transportations, sponsored by government and abetted by an aggressive and political church.

Bhalla's work is marred by three tendencies: it claims too much for its theories, ascribes too much influence to a notion it calls Augustan, and confuses rationalism with ideological conservatism. Of course the reader longs for more historical evidence to substantiate some claims. But, to adapt its own metaphor, the book is an outline sketch rather than a survey map. It is richly suggestive of directions for further research. One can forgive much in a work that assails the formalist endeavor to abstract the gothic novel from its moment of generation, that makes credible links between the gothic novel and the Romantic poem, that offers endnotes full of the fascinating and the bizarre, that features prose free from jargon and self-protective obscurities, prose that even rises to luminousness. If only the gothic novel could continue to be discussed at this level.—Kenneth W. Graham.

Biard, Michel. "La Scène angevine dans la carrière théâtrale de Jean-Marie Collot d'Herbois, (1774–1776)." *Revue d'Histoire du théâtre*, 43 (1991), 119–27.

Contrary to what is usually believed, Collot d'Herbois was very successful in Angers, both as an actor and an author.

Biletzki, Anat. "Richard Johnson: A Case History of Eighteenth-Century Pragmatics." *Historiographica Linguistica*, 18 (1991), 281–99.

Johnson was the only grammarian of the time who "comes close to an explicit rendering of moods akin to speech acts and based on language use."

Bilton, Peter, George Bisztray, Barbara Day, Bogdan Mischiu, Laurence Senelick, and Karyna Wierzbicka-Michalska (eds.). *National Theatre in Northern and Eastern Europe, 1746–1900.* (Theatre in Europe: A Documentary History.) Cambridge and New York: Cambridge U. Press, 1991. Pp. xxx + 480; bibliography; illustrations.

The second volume of the series "Theatre in Europe" certainly fills a gap: it documents the coming into existence of a number of national theatres both in Northern and in Eastern Europe from the mid-eighteenth to the late nineteenth century. Among the wide variety of documents assembled in this book are royal edicts, censors' reports, pieces of contemporary theatre criticism, actors' personal letters and letters to public institutions, instructions for applicants to drama schools, architects' plans, financial reports and many others. The expert choice of documents comprises "canonized" texts and pictures as well as source material which is known less and, in part, not easy to come by. All documents are given in remarkably careful and readable translations into English.

The main chapters of this "documentary history," which is meant to be "representative" much rather than "comprehensive" (p. xxvi), are devoted to Denmark, Sweden, Norway, Poland, the Czech land, i.e. Bohemia and Moravia, Hungary, Rumania and Russia. Some of the smaller cultures of Northern and Eastern Europe, Latvia, Lithuania, Estonia and others, are also taken into consideration within the highly instructive "General introduction" (pp. 6-13). Each of the main chapters again consists of a short introduction providing political and social background, information about the more "advanced" theatre cultures (France, Italy, England, Austria, and Germany) which serve as models etc. The documents and other source materials are arranged according to systemic aspects such as "legislation and administration," "the audience" and "censorship." Many of the source texts are given together with short explanations and bibliographical notes.

The last sections of the book contain bibliographical material for each of the theatre cultures represented in this publication. They also contain an index combining names and subject matter. The choice of titles assembled in the bibliographies clearly shows the expertship of the team responsible for this book.

It seems to be inevitable that this genre of "documentary history," here and there, contains specific remarks which are not fully comprehensible to non-experts, or which seem to be fully in line with information given in other parts of the book. For example: The authors justly emphasize that, as a rule, the emergence of national theatres coincides with a growth of influence of middle-class society. In the "General Introduction" the situation in Poland is described in the following way: "In the absence of an influential middle-class, which all but disappeared during the interminable warefare of the seventeenth century, a national theatre was likely to emerge" (p. 8). Obviously, this "influential middle class" was still lacking in Poland, when Boguskawski (1757–1820) gained fame as the "Father of the Polish theatre." In this instance it might have been helpful to explain that new strata from within Polish nobility, i.e. members of the low *szlachta*, who were discovering the theatre as a place for entertainment and communication. To give another example: Readers not acquainted with the history of Czech theatre during the period of "National Revival" may be somewhat at a loss when they read a sentence like this: "let us not complain that these pieces are too long with regard to the limited time allocated to our Czech plays" (p. 249). Here, it might have been helpful to explain the so-called "two-hours'-rule" according to which performances in Czech, no matter whether they were based on translations or on original Czech plays, had to be limited to two hours play time. Of course, such additional information is to be found in the bibliographies.

To sum up, this unique "documentary history" will be of great help to anybody dealing with Comparative Theatre Studies in Europe. The book ought to have a wide distribution.—Brigitte Schultze.

Bishop, Lloyd. *Romantic Irony in French Literature from Diderot to Beckett*. Nashville, TN: Vanderbilt U. Press, 1989. Pp. xi + 238.

Blain, Virginia, Patricia Clements, and Isobel Grundy (eds.). *The Feminist Companion to Literature in English: Women Writers from the Middle Ages to the Present*. London: Batsford; New Haven, CT: Yale U. Press, 1990. Pp. xvi + 1231; illustrations. Cf. *ECCB*, n.s. 16, V: 252.

Rev. (with reservations) by Helen McNeil in *TLS*, (Jan. 18, 1991), 8; by N. Knipe in *Choice*, 28 (1991), 912; correspondence from Editors Blain, Clements, and Grundy in *TLS*, (Mar. 1, 1991), 13; reply from Helen McNeil in *TLS*, (March 8, 1991), 13; correspondence from Janet Todd, *TLS*, (March 15, 1991), 13.

Bléchet, Françoise. *Les ventes publiques de livres en France, 1630–1750: Répertoire des catalogues conservés à la Bibliothèque Nationale*. Oxford: The Voltaire Foundation at the Taylor Institution, 1991. Pp. 256; bibliography; illustrations; indices.

The scholarly value of book auction catalogues as sources of information not readily obtainable elsewhere has long been recognized, especially by those who work with manuscripts of the Medieval period. Yet their potential remains largely unrealized due to a lack of biographical control, minimal forms of indexing, and a general failure of academic institutions to realize their importance and systematically collect them. Thus any work which provides an *entrée* to an important collection is especially welcome, and the Voltaire Foundation is to be congratulated for publishing Mme Bléchet's annotated list of French book auction catalogues from 1630 to 1750 held by the Bibliothèque Nationale. It contains an extensive interpretive introduction, a chronological catalogue, a list of manuscript and printed sources, and several useful indices.

The earliest European book auction (at least the earliest for which a catalogue survives) was held in Leiden in 1599. The practice spread quickly throughout Europe although the first surviving English catalogue is 1676. The earliest in this catalogue is 1630 and describes in only twelve pages the manuscripts and books of Jacobus Goilus, a Professor of Oriental languages and Mathematics at the University of Leiden. The sale, however, was held in Paris and the descriptions of each item must have been very brief indeed. One of the difficulties of using early catalogues is attempting to identify exactly a book or manuscript from a tantalizing, but inadequate description.

A primary use of book auction catalogues is, of course, the tracing of provenance and the identification of particular books in particular collections. Under 1673 in this catalogue is a description of the sale of the library of Gui Patin, Dean of the Faculty of Medicine at Paris and the life-long friend of Gabriel Naudé, librarian to Cardinal Mazarin and author of the first treatise of modern academic librarianship, the *Advis pur dresser une bibliotheque* of 1627. Patin published little but wrote a great many letters and was closely acquainted with most of the great figures of his time. In 1701, thirty years after his death and almost fifty after the death of Naudé, was published *Nandaena at Patiniana*, a series of anecdotes from the conversations of the two friends. Patin's sale catalogue is a primary source for any biographical or critical study of him.

Recently attempts have been initiated by various organizations to locate, bring under bibliographical control and provide partial indexing for collections of book auction and antiquarian bookseller's catalogues, using machine-readable cataloguing techniques. Models have been provided by the Getty Museum's Scipio project for catalogues of art and by the Philadelphia Area Consortium of special Collections Libraries project, which applies similar techniques to book catalogues. Francoise Bléchet's work will assuredly be used eventually for a similar project. In the meantime, it is very useful to have it available in a handsome hard-copy volume.—Richard Landon.

Boccage, Anne-Marie du. *La Colombiade, ou la foi portée au Nouveau Monde, 1756*. Paris: Coté-femmes, 1991. Pp. 240; bibliography.

Nowadays, when both Columbus and feminism vie for scrutiny, the reprinting of *La Colombiade*, first published in 1756, is well-timed, since this is by a woman and presents an attitude of mind which still challenges consideration.

Anne-Marie du Boccage, a name now almost unknown, was a prominent social and intellectual leader in Paris, from 1733 to the end of her long life. Her charm and erudition led the best thinkers of her time to help form her celebrated salon and to become lasting friends of its extraordinarily gifted hostess. Voltaire, with whom she corresponded and visited, despite their divergent outlooks, heralded her poetry, calling its author "*la Sapho de Normandie*" and "*la gloire de son sexe et de la France*." At 39, Anne-Marie made public her view of feminism in a five-act tragedy, *Les Amazones*, published, performed, and translated into Italian, in 1749, its immediate success winning for its playwright the nick-name "l'Amazone." Anne-Marie's budding fame as writer sprang into full bloom with her *Colombiade*, 1765, which was received enthusiastically in France and successively translated into Portuguese, German, and Italian.

While this ten-canto epic embodies several features typical of the genre, they do not constitute the poem's gist. A wealth of novel facts is so independently mingled with conventional epic functions, as to make the poet's modern mind seem unconsciously in revolt against her old-fashioned poetic vehicle. Hence the poem's subtitle is misleading, the propagation of religion being almost absent, whereas endless homage is paid to the beauty and intelligent simplicity of innocent savages before being perverted by corrupt Christians. Every feature of the eighteenth century dream of America as paradise regained (never mind a few demons) is conveyed, with hope yet fear, hope for a New World of virtuous peace, yet fear lest that world should eventually duplicate the monstrosities of the Old. Anne-Marie's Columbus sets out to improve the New World, not as a missionary, but as a man of science, capable of introducing a host of techniques where none existed. Although tempted, misled, and finally combated by Vascona, a powerful Amazon, he persists in his errand of guiding humanity forward. Two ambiguities are thus clarified: "*foi*" in the subtitle is really faith in material progress and the heroism of "*Colombiade*" stands for the possible but not inevitable triumph of that faith.

Readers who find epic poetry chore or bore will be suprised and delighted by the eminent readability of *La Colombiade's* alexandrines, cleverly informative, elegantly descriptive, often unsentimentally moving.

The diabolical side of the Columbus story, scarcely touched on by the author, is effectively accounted for in a vivid foreward by Milagros Palma, while the editor, Catherine Jardin, contributes an enlightening preface on Anne-Marie and her poem, as well as lucid notes to the *Colombiade's* lavish but sometimes elliptically expressed data.

Useful biographical and bibliographical lists enhance this scholarly edition.—Robert Finch.

Boerner, Peter, and Sidney Johnson (eds.). *Faust Through Four Centuries: Retrospect and Analysis; Vierhundert Jahre Faust: Rückblick und Analyse*. Tübingen: Max Niemeyer, 1989. Pp. xiii + 272.

Rev. by Stuart Atkins in *Journal of English and Germanic Philology*, 90 (1991), 291–93.

Boiscareis, Mercedes, and Alicia Yllere. *Narrativa francesa en el siglio XVIII*. Madrid: Edit, 1988. Pp. 448.

Rev. by Josette Chéry-Sobolewski in *Revue d'histoire littéraire de la France*, 91 (1991), 103–04.

Bold, Alan. *Scotland: A Literary Guide*. London: Routledge, 1989. Pp. ix + 327.

Rev. by Christine E. King in *American Reference Books Annual*, 22 (1991), 474.

Bombelles, Marc de. *Journal de Voyage en Grande Bretagne et en Irlande 1784*. Transcription, Introduction, and Annotation by Jacques Gury. (Studies on Voltaire and the Eighteenth Century, 269.) Oxford: The Voltaire Foundation at the Taylor Institution, 1989. Pp. x + 370; bibliography; maps. Cf. *ECCB*, n.s. 15, V:188.

Rev. by Paolo Alatri in *Studi francesi*, 35 (1991) 153.

Bonnerot, Olivier H. *La Perse dans la littérature et la pensée français au XVIIIe siècle: De l'image au mythe*. Paris: Librarie Honoré Champion, 1988. Pp. 379; illustrations. Cf. *ECCB*, n.s. 16, V:254; 15, V:188; 14, V:200.

Rev. by Luca Pietromarchi in *Studi francesi*, 34 (1991), 521–22.

Bonnet, Jean-Claude (ed.). *La Carmagnole des muses: l'homme de lettres et l'artiste dans la Révolution*. (Librairie du Bicentenaire de la Révolution Française.) Paris: Colin, 1988. Pp. 425.

Rev. by Malcolm Cook in *Modern Language Review*, 86 (1991), 730.

Boursier, Nicole, and David Trott (eds.). *The Age of the Theatre in France; L'Age du Théâtre en France*. Alberta and Edmonton, Canada: Academic Printing & Publishing, 1988. Pp. 374; charts; illustrations. Cf. *ECCB*, n.s. 14, V: 256.

Rev. (favorably) by Donald C. Spinelli in *The French Review*, 64 (1991), 1037–38.

Bouysse, Alain. "Les Habits de Persée 1770." *Revue d'historie du théâtre*, 43 (1991), 231–41; illustrations.

Thanks to archival material, it is possible to study the costumes used in the performance of Lully's *Persée* at the wedding of the future Louis XVI.

Bowden, Betsy. *Eighteenth-Century Modernizations from the Canterbury Tales*. Rochester, NY: Boydell & Brewer; Woodridge, UK: D.S. Brewer, 1991. Pp. xx + 263; bibliography.

Betsy Bowden's *Eighteenth-Century Modernizations from the Canterbury Tales* is a welcome addition to the recently discovered field of post-Chaucerian Chaucer studies. Coming hard on the heels of Piero Boitani's *The European Tragedy of Troilus* (1989) and Barry Windeatt's *Chaucer Tradition* (1990), *Eighteenth-Century Modernizations* supplements these informative and analytical essays by providing scholars who are interested in actually working in the field with an addition of forty-five eighteenth-century texts that "have not seen print for two centuries, thus excluding those by Pope and Dryden" (p. x). These forty-five tales are, with the exception of those by Thomas Betterton (a probable psuedonym for Pope), either anonymous or the work of minor authors such as William Lipscomb and George Ogle. The collection includes modernizations of most of the *Canterbury Tales* (only the *Knight's, Wife's, Pardoner's*, and *Parson's Tales* are missing), but the eighteenth-century modernizers seem to have favored the fabliaux: the *Miller's, Reeve's*, and *Shipman's Tales* check in with four translations each. Bowden accompanies her texts with biographical sketches, minimal footnotes and printing histories, as well as a theoretical and practical introduction, and an extensive bibliography.

Bowden's anthology is invaluable in that it makes these texts easily available for further study. However, I would advise approaching her theoretical introduction cautiously. She limits her definition of reception aesthetics and reader-response criticism to the search for "Zeitgeist," thereby sidestepping the modern critical theories altogether, and in the process, missing an opportunity of using them in ways that could be especially valuable to this anthology, to illuminate how individual "retellings" function in their political and cultural contexts. Furthermore, her claim that twentieth-century Chaucer scholars have not examined their own "prejudices and pre-conceptions" (p. xi) or observed "the extent to which the late-twentieth century academic context controls interpretation" (p. xii) fails to take into account much of the recent work done on medievalism and Chaucer studies in the academy, most notable that of Carolyn Dinshaw, Elaine Tuttle Hansen, and Lee Paterson.

One final note of caution. Bowden's bibliography manifests a tendency that seems to be common in eighteenth-century Chaucer studies: medieval scholars cite their fellow medievalists, eighteenth-century scholars and other eighteenth centuryists. Thus Bowden, a medievalist, misses several important works on Chaucer in the eighteenth century. Even though she cites some earlier works on Dryden and Pope, notably absent are Earl Miner's, Judith Sloman's, and Cedric Reverand's books on Dryden, each of which deals extensively with his modernizations of Chaucer. This oversight implies that there is little or no dialogue between two groups of critics working on the same body of texts. Perhaps Bowden's edition, published in a series of *Chaucer Studies* and reviewed here, will help to initiate this dialogue.—Susan Aronstein.

Bradby, David (ed.). *Landmarks of French Classical Drama: Corneille: The Cid; Racine: Phaedra; Moliere: Tartuffe; Marivaux: The Lottery of Love; Beaumarchais: The Marriage of Figaro.* London: Methuen Drama, 1991. Pp. xxxi + 393.

Braudy, Leo *Native Informant: Essays on Film, Fiction, and Popular Culture.* New York and Oxford: Oxford U. Press, 1991. Pp. x + 304; 14 illustrations.

Leo Braudy takes a risk in presenting a collection of essays and book reviews, all published between 1968 and 1989, characterizing his venture as an "effort to stand between the scholarly and the amateur" (p. 10), and congratulating himself for his perspicacity in writing on popular culture when it lacked academic validation. The epigraph to Raymond Williams notwithstanding, Braudy seems unaware of cultural studies or its repute within academia. Despite his contention that his essays "are held together by some constant themes," the real justification for presenting this collection is, as he admits, "the fact that [he] wrote them all" (p. 8). In my view, the risk he takes (and loses), then, is not his decision to write about the "border" (p. 9) areas of culture from a personal vantage, but rather that I discover no development in Braudy's thought precisely during the era of such remarkable achievements in cultural analysis. His interest in "suppressed autobiography" and "the nature of character and identity" itself barely suppresses his apparent obsession with his own autobiography; this may account for his presentation of essentialist and universalist notions of subjectivity and culture as though they had not formed the center of a critical storm for these past two decades. By the time I reach his proposition that "Defoe . . . seems to define personal identity simultaneously as a structuring and merchandising of the private self" (pp. 121–11), we heartily wish this author of *The Frenzy of Renown: Fame and Its History* had himself provided more reticence and less merchandising.

Several essays are devoted to eighteenth-century subjects that, despite Braudy's claims to the contrary, demonstrate his adherence to a traditional canon and traditional values. Three—on Gibbon, the sentimental novel, and Johnson's *Preface*—lack substance; of the others, two discourse at some length on the unexceptionable thesis that the eighteenth-century novel embodies in its characterizations a repsonse to "the newly perceived problems of self-definition" (p. 153). "Penetration and Impenetrability in *Clarissa*" (1974) collects some philosophical texts from Hobbes, Locke, and Hume to support its claim that "*Clarissa* explores and helps define the cultural moment when the self-willed isolation of the individual that insures a security against the world becomes first an opposition between self and society and finally a mutually exclusive definition of the images of male and female" (p. 158). And the essay entitled "Daniel Defoe and the Anxieties of Autobiography" (1973) argues that Defoe's "first-person novels change the basic nature of autobiography . . . through their compelling delineation of the mystery at the heart of human personality" (p. 124). Oddly, only the earliest of these essays on eighteenth-century literature, "*Fanny Hill* and Materialism" (1970), offers any continuing interest, insofar as its discussion of Cleland's use of La Mettrie's *L'Homme machine* seems to provide an example of proto-new historicism.—Molly Anne Rothenberg.

Breuer, Horst. *Historische Literaturpsychologie: Von Shakespeare bis Beckett.* Tübingen: Francke, 1989. Pp. 227.

Rev. by Kurt Tetzeli von Rosador in *Modern Language Review,* 86 (1991), 1004–06.

Brönnimann-Egger, Werner. *The Friendly Reader: Modes of Cooperation between Eighteenth-Century English Poets and Their Audience.* Tübingen: Stauffenburg, 1991. Pp. 120.

Brophy, Elizabeth Bergen. *Women's Lives and the Eighteenth-Century English Novel.* Tampa, FL: U. of South Florida Press (distributed through Gainesville, FL: U. Presses of Florida), 1991. Pp. ix + 291; bibliography; illustrations.

Rev. by R. G. Brown in *Choice,* 29 (1991), 438; by Patricia Meyer Spacks in *Christianity and Literature,* 41 (1991), 85–6.

Not the eighteenth-century English novel as a whole but a particular kind of English novel and novelist, and a particular reading of the genre, are the focus here. Samuel Richardson, Henry Fielding, Charlotte Lennox, Sarah Scott, Clara Reeve, and Frances Burney are the novelists. The writers and their works are arrayed against a large body of primary sources, most often consisting of excerpts from letters, diaries, and journals, in a process intended to demonstrate the extent to which these novelists succeeded at portraying "life in its true state"—or, as Elizabeth Bergen Brophy reminds us, what Samuel Johnson said the English novel was doing.

Brophy's project is undeniably ambitious: she intends both to assess how accurately a representative group of novels might have portrayed what she defines as the "a*verage* eighteenth-century woman" (p. 2), and to determine to what extent—and in what way—the "responsible realism" (p. 2) of the post-Richardsonian novel might have exerted influence over female readers. Brophy argues that determining these relationships between the novel and social life has both an intrinsic value and the potential to help explain the role of realism in the emerging genre. Judging a novel's relative realism and moral intent also provides criteria for judging the work, Brophy contends, "criteria that the age itself continually posited" (p. 233).

A clear *telos* surfaces in Brophy's methodology, in her approach to what she concedes in an understatement is a "rather literal realism" (p. 234) and in her decided assumptions about, for example, the novel's potential efficacy: "Fiction reflects the values of its time, to be sure, but just as importantly, it creates them" (p. 234). Within this tightly ordered context, Brophy's organization is straightforward and well-delineated, and her prose highly readable. Indeed, the book is at times *too* readable; it segues so effortlessly from primary materials to the novels that the distinction between texts is deliberately and almost seamlessly concealed, a process that raises methodological questions of its own. Meanwhile, the bulk of manuscript material is augmented by such printed sources as conduct manuals and other published non-fiction, and while Brophy considers only novels from 1740–1799, the non-fiction spans a considerably wider period. These juxtapositions cause occasional confusion, since the date of primary materials is neither always immediately evident nor immediately relevant to the novels—as, for example, the interjection of Mary Astell's *A Serious Proposal to the Ladies* (1694) into a discussion of later eighteenth-century fiction. Brophy approched what must have been considerable taxonomic and logistical difficulties with a topical organization that divides both kinds of texts into chapters on daughters, courtship, wives, and spinsters and widows. This schema also seems too convenient, and may have invited some of the indiscriminateness with which fiction and non-fiction merge.

The reader who does not share Brophy's methodological or theoretical assumptions can find that her manuscript excerpts, which are consistently interesting, nevertheless imply a wholly different social commentary than the one Brophy endorses. Moreover, discovering that novels resembled real life sometimes seem to consist of a series of tautological and self-evident insights; Richardson, Lennox, and Reeve all showed unhappy marriages, Brophy writes, while the "journals of Sarah Cowper are evidence that such marriages indeed existed in reality" (p. 197). Elsewhere, we find from the letters of one Charles Pratt that some men *did* prefer sensible women and discover that the dialogue of fictional protagonists sometimes sounds like the letters real women wrote.

Considering Brophy's two previous works on Richardson, her preference in *Women's Lives* for that writer and for *Clarissa,* which she terms "the century's most powerful feminist text" (p. 238), may be understandable. It is unfortunate, however, that not only Fielding but the five women novelists Brophy considers thus emerge as less efficacious voices for women—and this aside from their call for a "radical reassessment" (p. 267) of women's position. Readers looking for a reading that is radical, or for that matter for a reassessment, will not find it here, despite the good primary sources.—Christine Blouch.

Brouard, Arends Isabelle. *Vies et images maternelles dans la littérature française du dix-huitième siècle.* Oxford: The Voltaire Foundation at the Taylor Institution, 1991. Pp. ix + 465.

Brown, Leslie Ellen, and John Yolton (eds.). *Studies in Eighteenth-Century Culture, 17.* East Lansing, MI: Colleagues Press, 1987. Pp. xii + 371.

Rev. by Paul-Gabriel Boucé in *Modern Language Review,* 86 (1991), 392–93.

Brown, Leslie Ellen, and John Yolton (eds.). *Studies in Eighteenth-Century Culture, 18.* East Lansing, MI: Colleagues Press, 1988. Pp. xii + 516.

Rev. by J. A. Downie in *Review of English Studies,* 42 (1991), 442–43.

Brown, Marshall. *Preromanticism.* Stanford, CA: Stanford U. Press, 1991. Pp. xiv + 500; bibliography.

Marshall Brown's splendid book differs from virtually all other treatments of his subject in its insistence not on the continuites between the Romantics and their predecessors but rather on the discontinuities. Brown eschews the familiar practice of enumerating the ways in which the literary lights of the second half of the eighteenth century prefigured, and gradually melded with, the dramatic burst of creative, intellectual, political, social, spiritual, and philosophical energy customarily designated as Romanticism. Instead, he examines the ways in which these figures were specifically "*not yet* Romantic" (p. 2). Dismissing immediately a number of venerable myths about what is meant by "pre-Romanticism," Brown forthrightly confronts the curious, inescapable, but too often unremarked, phenomenon of the odd silences—about themselves and their writings—that characterize the most prominent literary figures of the later eighteenth century.

   Brown argues that most of the major literary figures subsumed under the term "Pre-romantics" (his survey begins with Gray's "Eton College Ode" and ends with a long chapter on Wordsworth) betray both overtly and implicitly in their writings considerable and increasing dissatisfaction with the available means of, and vehicles for, expression. This dissatisfaction produced in the latter half of the century increasing numbers of shorter and less immediately prestigious literary events (i.e. "masterpieces") than did the eras that preceded and followed. Moreover, major writers chose for the most part (even Dr. Johnson is only a partial exception) not to write about literature and language, leaving the task to frequently unimaginative academics (like Hurd) and rhetoricians (like Blair). "Masterpieces" like Gray's "Elegy" are infrequent and, typically, comparatively brief (*Tristram Shandy* seems an exception, but Brown argues that in its own way the ultimate brilliance of this piecemeal production becomes fully apparent only in the final several pages). The bursting of the great literary dam at the century's end produced an astonishing profusion of masterworks from giants like Kant and Wordsworth, a phenomenon that reflects the emerging era's discovery of new ways to write, new ways to express both self and feeling and, in the process, a new sort of compact between writer and reader. This new, more personal, intimate discourse becomes the hallmark of Romanticism, a freeing of tongue and pen that liberates the individual writer from the conviction among the pre-Romantics that increasing diversity—of subject, of genre, of style—taken together with a need for literature to address ideas and ethics in some coherence of expression and, by a sort of de facto logic, paralyzed the writer when it came to "great" tasks. In grappling with this paralysis the pre-Romantics did not in fact "pave the way" for Romanticism, as the venerable myth would still have it; but they did generate an array of physical, textual artifacts that enable us more clearly to recognize what separated them from their successors, and why.

Brown acknowledges critical debts to Derrida, Foucault, and Serres, as well as to various formalist and structuralist critics, but notes as well the less immediately fashionable influences of late nineteenth-century scholars like Burkhardt, Taine, and Wölfflin, each of whose influence is visible in the broadly interdisciplinary methodology that underlies the book. Indeed, the cosmopolitan, cross-disciplinary nature of the discussion elevates the book beyond the "mere" set of separate close readings (of Gray, Cowper, Goldsmith especially, Sheridan, Sterne, Wordsworth, and others) for which Brown self-effacingly prepares the reader. The readings are subtle and penetrating, and the book itself perhaps the most coherent and compelling analysis of the multiplicity of pressures—literary and extra-literary—that came to bear on the writer in the latter part of the eighteenth century. Moreover, the nature of the cultural fabric that is so carefully examined in this long and learned book (the bibliography covers twenty-seven pages) comes, by the end, to reveal why the startling eloquence of self-expression of a Kant or a Wordsworth necessarily marked the irreversible crossing of a literary and cultural divide. Finally, the author wears his erudition lightly; the book is written elegantly and with a delightful absence of the clouds of jargon that have obscured the critical light of far too many contemporary literary studies.—Stephen C. Behrendt.

Brown, Robert H. *Nature's Hidden Terror: Violent Nature Imagery in Eighteenth-Century Germany.* (Studies in German Literature, Linguistics, and Culture, 69.) Columbia, SC: Camden House, 1991. Pp. 148; bibliography.

The ancient Chinese philosophers and poets of the T'ang Dynasty often commented on how the business of man finds reflection in the "business" of nature. Nearly a millenium later on another continent, during the European Enlightenment, the reflective relationship between nature and human society perplexed and stimulated yet another group of brilliant thinkers and writers. Fortunately, Robert H. Brown's concise monograph, *Nature's Hidden Terror: Violent Nature Imagery in Eighteenth-Century Germany*, does a good job of sorting out and clarifying some of the often complex interactions between man and nature as they are represented in German philosophy and literature of the *Aufklärung*.

The short first chapter, "Nature Imagery and Social Change," introduces us to the difficulties inherent in the Enlightenment view of nature: namely, much early eighteenth-century scientific discovery optimistically proclaimed the ability of man to dispel all of nature's mysteries; yet natural catastrophes and disasters occasionally dampened such an enthusiastic spirit, producing tension between man's desires and his limitations. At the same time, in a seemingly unrelated sphere, sweeping upheavals in the social structures presaged great social change; the steady deterioration of the old aristocracy and the rise to power of the "new bourgeoisie" upset the old order, producing the birthpangs of a new social system. Brown skillfully avoids positing a cause and effect relationship between natural catastrophe and social change, but he creatively contends that three of the era's most prominent authors–Gerstenberg, Goethe, and Schiller—used violent upheaval in nature as a means to express the pressures and tensions of *social* upheaval as they impacted the individual.

Before launching into literary analysis, Brown offers in his second chapter, a fascinating explanation for why such (metaphoric) usage of nature became possible at this time. He begins by tracing the evolution of eighteenth-century thought on nature in the most prominent philosophers of the period (Pope, Voltaire, Rousseau, Kant), and he views reactions to the Lisbon earthquake of 1755 as emblematic of a profound shift in the philosophic attitude towards nature. Commenting on Pope's *Essay on Man* (1736), Brown argues that the *early* Enlightenment view was very optimistic, holding to the belief that "Whatever is, is right" (Pope, line 294); natural wonders, though occasionally inexplicable and sometimes seemingly disastrous, occur for profoundly logical or rational reasons, even if such reasons are not readily available to human cognition. But such an optimistic belief couldn't last for long, and philosophical cynics such as Voltaire questioned Pope's belief; even less flamboyantly skeptical critics, such as Herder, began to wonder about the nature of a "divine Providence" or "reasonable Nature," especially in the wake of the Lisbon disaster. Eventually, with Kant's critiques and Rousseau's writings, the optimistic view of nature as essentially benevolent gave way to an emphasis on human perception; "The new discourse on nature . . . articulated knowledge of the physical world in terms of human faculties of perceiving, feeling, and organizing reality" (Brown, 54); the inability to create or locate solid explanations for the sometimes terrifying mysteries of nature turned into a meta-critical exploration of how we empirically perceive the physical world we try to explain.

It is this emphasis on perception, (Brown calls this the "triumph of empiricism" [132]), which freed "[m]an [to become] the primary measure of reality" and is in opposition to his "age-old reliance on revealed truth" (132). Such a shift allowed late eighteenth-century authors to concentrate on individual experience and to view nature and the physical world as filtered through such experience; as Brown states, "[N]ature could be used to explore personality, individuality, and subjectivity[,] . . . a way of articulating the concrete experiences and aspirations of isolated individuals on the fringes of traditional corporative society: the new bourgeoisie" (54–55).

For instance, in a chapter on Goethe's *Die Leiden des jungen Werthers* (1774), Brown argues that severe social changes affecting the individual find reflection in how the individual characters perceive and depict their natural surroundings; he summarizes thusly in the concluding chapter:

The hopelessness of this situaion is signified by the transformation in the novel of the idyllic into violent nature imagery. Citing Alexander Pope and Klopstock respectively, Werther and Lotte envision a timeless corporative harmony in idyllic nature at the falling brook and after the storm. This vision is undermined by Werther's own discourse of individual identity on the fringes of corporative society, which transforms nature from a scene of eternal life into an eternally consuming monster. The mergence of demonic nature signals the displacement of harmonious corporative hierarchies by a violent struggle among isolated individuals and competing interests in a new and frightening social order (135).

With additional chapters on Gerstenberg's *Ugolino* (1767) and Schiller's *Die Räuber* (first staged in 1782), Brown ultimately argues that "[t]he seamy underside of modern capitalist society—its uncertainly, alienation, and brutal marketplace logic—emerges in late eighteenth-century writings in the fearful form of wild or violent nature imagery, . . . display[ing] a hidden fear of corresponding processes of modern change and a secret yearning for the security of lost corporative ties" (136).

Overall, the individual chapters of literary analysis are well done in that they offer an intelligent explanation of the complex relationship between social change and the artistic figuring of nature. Likewise, the historical survey in chapter two of the evolution in Enlightenment philosophical thought vis-á-vis nature is an excellent and much-needed overview. It is the connection Brown makes between eighteenth-century empiricism and the use of nature in literature which some readers may find theoretically shaky; the relationship betwen a philosophical interest in subjectivity and the use of nature to express the concerns of the subjective individual is not entirely worked out. But Brown's text draws together many aspects of the eighteenth century—novels, social change, drama, and philosophy—that deserve closer comparative attention; Brown's success is that he brings these diverse areas of study together in an intelligent, readable manner.—Jonathan Alexander.

Bryson, Scott S. *Chastised Stage: Bourgeois Drama and the Exercise of Power*. (Stanford French & Italian Studies, 70.) Saratoga, CA: Anma Libri, 1991. Pp. vii + 125.

Scott Bryson begins his study of the dramatic theories of Diderot, Mercier, Beaumarchais, and Restif de la Bretonne by offering a provocative set of parallels and encounters between their theatrical innovations and the penal reforms proposed by Beccaria and others. In the reformers' view, violent executions drew public attention, but remained extraordinary, repellent events that could not properly touch their spectators and thereby deter them from other crimes; the well-governed prisoner for life, however, would invite identification and an internalized sense of the law. Similarly, theoreticians of the bourgeois stage aimed at assuring a profound identification of spectator and spectacle that would lead to the reshaping of the audience within the plays' moral universe. In both cases a new mode of representation, judicial or theatrical, produces a more disciplined, self-regulating subject.

Bryson approaches his subject with a reading of the play which served as a manifesto for the *drame bourgeois*, Diderot's *Fils naturel*, as well as passages in his *Salons* that reinforce the authority of the spectacle on the spectator. Two further chapters draw on a number of theorists and on the writings of theater architect Claude-Nicholas Ledoux, to look at various elements of the new dramaturgy: the use of tableau, characterization by "condition," the importance of the audience's affective participation, the transparency of the plot. Bryson's analysis is strongest in his treatment of Mercier's *Du théâtre* and Restif's *Le Mimographe* and *Le Pornographe*, in which the coercive potential within the reformist imaginary is disturbingly evident. The conclusion discusses the persistence into the Revolution of the issues raised by theatrical and judicial reform.

The main theoretical model for Bryson's study is Foucault's *Discipline and Punish*; like Foucault, Bryson offers a powerful demystifying critique of the means by which the subtle ramifications of social control institute themselves in the most ostensibly progressive discourse. On the other hand, the disadvantages of such an approach are apparent as well: by so thoroughly aligning himself with the dark, "disciplinary" model, Bryson often tends to read all forms of identification and persuasion as coercion, and fails to appreciate the potential for mobility and resistance to authority that is implicit in many of the texts of his study, notably Diderot's. The reading of *Le Fils naturel*, for instance, conflates the father's rigid, absolute notion of truth, with the son's more mutable, contingent, and relational understanding that will form the basis of his dramatic poetics. Bryson also tends to read his theoreticians as extensions of one another, underscoring a point in Diderot by referring to Mercier, and thereby obscuring the significant differences among their programs.

Even with these reservations, however, I find much to admire in this study: the strength and clarity of the writing, the attention to detail in the analyses, and the importance of its overall project in our ongoing rereading of the Enlightenment. Unmasking their ruses of power is nevertheless only one side of that rereading, for otherwise we miss the paradoxes and complexities both of the historical period and its philosophical legacy.—Julie C. Hayes.

Burnim, Kalman A., Philip H. Highfill Jr., and Edward A. Langhans. *A Biographical Dictionary of Actors, Actresses, Musicians, Dancers, Managers, and Other Stage Personnel in London, 1660–1800*. Vol. XIII: *Roach to H. Siddons*. Vol. XIV: *S. Siddons to Thynne*. Carbondale, Il, and Edwardsville: Southern Illinois U. Press, 1991. Pp. 396; frontispiece; illustrations: 438; frontispiece; illustrations.

With these latest volumes of the *Biographical Dictionary*, begun in 1973, the compilers have not only pushed this massive project closer to completion, but they also have continued the same high standards users have come to expect. The principal figures in Volume XIII, *Roach to H. Siddons*, are the Sheridans, who take up more than fifty pages. The father of the theatrical family is Thomas (twenty-one pages), his son Richard Brinsley (twenty pages), and his daughter-in-law Elizabeth Linley (ten+ pages). His wife Frances (1724–1766), a dramatist in her own right, is given some attention (XIII:353–54) under Thomas's entry.

The volume begins, however, with one of Reynold's portraits of Mary "Perdita" Robinson (1758–1800). The seventeen-page entry about her tells the story of a talented actress, singer, and playwright who, after a liaison with the Prince of Wales, managed to survive the remainder of her life, plagued by poverty and ill health. Users of the *Biographical Dictionary* will find the same format as in previous volumes: entries begin with a biography, which includes comments by contemporaries; this is followed by an evaluation of the individual's contribution to the stage; the final part of the entry is a list of known portraits (for example, there are more than eighty of Mary Robinson).

Important but lesser known figures illustrate the range in this volume, which included the singer Anastasia Robinson (c. 1692–1755, four pages), the scene designer Michael Angelo Rooker (1746?–1801, five pages), and actress, novelist, playwright, editor, and educator Susanna Rowson (c. 1762–1824, three+ pages). Here also are dancer and choreographer Marie Salle (1707–1756, four pages), impresario Johann Peter Salomon (1745–1815, three+ pages), and sceneographer Giovanni Servandoni (1695–1766, four pages). The volume concludes with Henry Siddons (1774–1815, six pages) and his wife Harriet Siddons (1783–1844, four+ pages).

Volume XIV, *S. Siddons to Thynne*, begins with Gainsborough's well-known portrait of Sarah Siddons, followed by a sixty-six page entry tracing the rise of her career from being a strolling player on the provincial boards to becoming reigning actress of the London theater. The iconography runs to 387 items. The remainder of the volume includes the poet Christopher Smart (1722–1771, six+ pages), as an actor, manager, and playwright; the essayist and sometime playwright Sir Richard Steele (1672–1729, eleven pages), as a theater manager; as well as actor and manager William Smith (1730–1819, fourteen pages), singer and actress Ann Selina Storace (1765–1819, ten pages), and scene painter James Thornhill (1675–1734, seven pages).

One strength of the continuing publication of the *Biographical Dictionary* is that the authors have made corrections to their previous volumes: for example, "We erroneously stated in our notice of William Brereton that she [Sarah Siddons] acted Jane Shore for him on 19 August 1784" (XIV:14). She was, they later discovered, indisposed. Oversights in the *London Stage* have been amended, and new information that has come to light has been added. Useful cross-references, such as that on XIV:15, remind us to see a previously reproduced picture—in this case Sarah Siddons and John Philip Kemble playing *Macbeth* on VIII: 364. On XIV:186, there is a reference to a reproduction on IX:33 of William Smith playing Charles Surface.

There are a few typographical errors. For instance, on XIV:23, the beginning of paragraph five should read "1798–99" instead of "1788–99." Sarah Siddon's second child Sarah Martha (called Sally) was born in 1775, not 1755 (XIV:33). Her third child, Maria, was born in 1779, not 1799 (XIV:33). The errors are few and, more important, these volumes contain a wondrous amount of detail, from where actors lived in different parts of their careers to the amount of money they made in their benefit nights. I look forward with relish to the remaining volumes in the series and to its completion. The compilers of this most useful compendium—Highfill, Burnim, and Langhans—have again provided us with a wealth of theatrical information. Theirs is a Herculean job, which scholars and theatrical historians will find useful for many years to come.—David D. Mann.

Burwick, Frederick. *Illusion and the Drama: Critical Theory of the Enlightenment and Romantic Era*. College Station, PA: Pennsylvania State U. Press, 1991. Pp. 336.

Traces the debate over illusion from Johnson to Coleridge.

Cafarelli, Annette Wheeler. *Prose in the Age of Poets: Romanticism and Biographical Narrative from Johnson to DeQuincey*. Philadelphia, PA: U. of Pennsylvania Press, 1990. Pp. vii + 301. Cf. *ECCB*, n.s. 16, V:256–57.

Rev. by Mark Parker in *South Atlantic Review*, 56 (May 1991), 140–42; by Donald Sultana in *Notes and Queries*, 236 (1991), 394–95.

Canfield, J. Douglas. *Word as Bond in English Literature from the Middle Ages to the Restoration*. Philadelphia, PA: U. of Pennsylvania Press, 1989. Pp. xviii + 338. Cf. *ECCB*, n.s. 15, V:191–92.

Rev. by Derek Hughes in *The Scriblerian*, 23 (1991), 275–76; by John P. Zomchick in *Eighteenth-Century Studies*, 25 (1991–92), 241–44.

Canning, George, and John Hookman Frere. *Poetry of the Anti-Jacobin (1799)*. Introduction by Jonathan Wordsworth. (Revolution and Romanticism, 1789–1834.) New York and Oxford: Woodstock Books, 1991. Pp. xii + 240 (in mixed paginations).

Facsimile reprint of the satirical poems originally appearing in *The Anti-Jacobin; Or, Weekly Examine*r, spoofing the desire for undefinable latitude and extravagence" and the "aspiration after shapeless somethings" that were to characterize Romantic poetry (and aiming specifically at Schiller, Goethe, Coleridge, Godwin, and Erasmus Darwin). Includes *The Rovers* (probably by Frere), featuring such memorable verse as: "Whene'er with haggard eyes I view / This dungeon that I'm rotting in, / I think of those companions true / Who studied with me at the U / -niversity of Gottingen / -nivesity of Gottingen."

Caraher, Brian G. *Wordsworth's Slumber and the Problematics of Reading*. University Park, PA: Pennsylvania State U. Press, 1991. Pp. viii + 280.

Carlson, Susan. *Women and Comedy: Rewriting the British Theatrical Tradition*. Ann Arbor, MI: U. of Michigan Press, 1991. Pp. xii + 388; bibliography.

Susan Carlson's *Women and Comedy: Rewriting the British Theatrical Tradition* reads like a cautionary tale to those who have embraced, perhaps too enthusiastically, the idea that comedy has provided a privileged site of empowerment for women. Positioning her argument firmly within the emerging body of critical work on the relationship between gender and genre, and also within the current debate on how to discriminate between the revolutionary and the reactionary, or between texts that liberate the female subject and those that contain the female subject, Carlson sets out to demonstrate that "for several hundred years, comedy's welcoming of women has been comprised by the genre's structural checks against women's power" (p. 3). Indeed, Carlson goes so far as to argue not only that female characters in comedy have been compromised by its generic structure, but that the "genre does more to reduce than to enlarge female power" (p. 15). Finally, she argues that "both the critics who applaud comedy's women and those who look past them rarely, if ever, have studied the connections between the women and the assumptions by which critics define comedy" (p. 15). It is perhaps in this area and in her correction of this deficiency that Carlson makes her greatest contribution to the field of drama studies.

The text is divided into two parts; the first, entitled "Women *in* Comedy," is the most relevant for students of the Restoration and the eighteenth century. In this section Carlson examines the status of female characters in comedy through readings of what she considers representative works. Claiming in Chapter 1 that "women in comedy . . . are constrained primarily by comedy's inversion and ending" (p. 23), Carlson applies this thesis to Shakespeare's *As You Like It* (Chapter 2), Congreve's *The Way of the World* (Chapter 3), as well as to Shaw's *The Philanderer* (Chapter 4), and Ayckbourn's *Women in Mind* (Chapter 5). In Part Two, entitled "Women *Writing* Comedy," Carlson turns to an emerging counter-tradition, a feminist transformation comedy that has its fruition in twentieth-century drama but that really begins with Aphra Behn. Discussing Behn's *The Lucky Chance*, Carlson stresses the significance to women's concerns of "her loose conception of plot; . . . her less-than-resolved ending; her direct and substantive treatment of women's sexuality as it is tied to women's sense of self; and her recognition of the power women may gain from one another" (p. 152).

In Part One, then, Carlson's main argument is that comic inversions of gender roles serve only to reify the male-female division and that the returns to order of comic endings, especially insofar as they are traditionally articulated through the institution of marriage, have greater import and impact than the temporary representations of what Natalie Davis has termed "women on top." While this argument supplies a necessary and timely corrective to critical readings that celebrate the transformations without regard to the final, repressive moments of closure, Carlson, like many recent critics, seems to move too far in the opposite direction, too readily dismissing the disruptive ironies and conflicts that often inform those closing moments. While Carlson is clearly aware of the recent feminist work, which argues that inversions of the male-female roles necessarily involve some modification of binary gender systems, she does not fully engage with it or with the questions it raises for her own argument.

Nevertheless, for students of Restoration drama Carlson's strong reading of Congreve's *The Way of the World*, in which she argues that the valorization of Millamant in critical literature as a powerful woman outweighs her actual presence in the play, is certainly worth heeding as an important warning against a too enthusiastic and narrow search for heroic female figures in literary history. Moreover, while Carlson's greatest strength lies in her knowledge of contemporary women's theatre, readers in earlier periods can enjoy the benefits of a carefully organized study as well as an outstanding bibliography to find the portions of the text most relevant to their own work. Finally, by selecting the structures of comedy as the focal point of her study, Carlson does much to raise our awareness of, and to shed light on, the kinds of conventional codes that constrain women and which, far too often, have been rendered either invisible or merely benign in other studies of the genre.—Lisa A. Freeman.

Carretta, Vincent. *George III and the Satirists from Hogarth to Byron*. Athens, GA: U. of Georgia Press, 1990. Pp. xviii + 389. Cf. *ECCB*, n.s. 16, V:258–59.

Rev. (with another work) by Herbert M. Atherton in *The Scriblerian*, 23 (1991), 269–71.

Castle, Terry. "Contagious Folly: An Adventure and Its Skeptics." *Critical Inquiry*, 17 (1991), 741–72.

Recounts and examines the encounter at Versailles of Charlotte Anne Moberly and Eleanor Jourdain with personages and events from August 10, 1792.

Cazenobe, Colette. *Le Système du libertinage de Crébillon à Laclos.* (Studies on Voltaire and the Eighteenth Century, 282.) Oxford: The Voltaire Foundation at the Taylor Institution, 1991. Pp. 444.

There can be no question that this volume will become an indispensable resource for the flourishing field of studies on libertinism. Cazenobe's is a painstaking (at times exhausting) meditation on libertinism as a project to denigrate and diminish the idea of love, thus to exalt freedom from fleshly constraints, a strategy viewed as a human dilemma, at times liberating, at others productive of pain and confusion. The smallest nuances of the politics of sexuality in selected novels by Crébillon, Richardson and Laclos are seized upon and scrutinized by this study.

Characterizing Crébillon's as a "libertinage d'esprit," Cazenobe roots his hero's will to sexual power in his terror of love as a dance of nature, leading both sexes, like amoebae, into blind combinations and recombinations. The most ingenious section of the Crébillon analysis concentrates in his libertine's relationship to government, which resembles intriguingly his methods with women. In *Ah, quel conte!*, the minister reflects that one must always address men as if one believed in virtue, while acting as if one did not. For the profoundly cynical Crébillon, culture's complexity, jerry-built over a barbarous human nature, ceaselessly, therefore comically, murders possibility.

Cazenobe hampers her treatment of Richardson's *Clarissa Harlowe* by tying it to a discussion of its first translations into French, by Prévost and by Tourneur. Her own perceptions never predicated on the English original nor much informed by the voluminous critical corpus in English on Richardson's *oeuvre*, remain telling. Building on insights gleaned from Crébillon, Cazenobe finds *Clarissa*'s insistent cleavage between body and soul an enrichment of the probelmatics of libertinism. The early translations washed away *Clarissa*'s "grandeur luciférienne" and its sustained mood of profanation of the sacred.

Cazenobe's treatment of the *Liaisons dangereuses* argues ably its view of the novel as one of rationalized libertinism. She reads Valmont as the work's master plotter, not as Merteuil's victim. To the question of whether or not Valmont loves, Cazenobe responds that he does, yet in Racinian fashion, hates, too; whereas Merteuil remains incapable of love. *Les Liaisons* demonstrates the vilifying effects of passion, even as it illustrates how indissociable the techniques of love are from its mystique. Ratiocination, in the novel, obscures the total unreason of its game, which replaces God with man. Eschewing answers to questions she herself raises—why libertinism at that particular moment? What, if anything, linked the novelistic libertine ethos with the times? —Cazenobe defends her exclusion of Sade from her study.

Her libertines, she claims, still need social order, religion, and law, so as to flout and scorn their power. Arguably, Sade remains, with his insistent blasphemies, within this continuum. Perhaps it is rather the contrast in tone that distinguishes Sade from them most decisively: an aura of melancholy ultimately emerges from the works of Cazenobe's three authors, a sign of their failed quest to escape from slavery to the flesh. Sade, precisely, claims to have won that battle. All the same, for both Sade and the others, Cazenobe's pertinent formula works: "Le libertinagem c'est la manière la plus moderne de faire le brave contre Dieu." Visibly, she has carried off a major attempt to cast more light from literature than is usual upon our vexing sexual conundrums.—Madelyn Gutwirth.

Chamoiseau, Patrick, and Raphaël Confiant. *Lettres créoles: Tracées antillaises et continentales de la littérature: Haiti, Guadeloupe, Martinique, Guyane, (1635–1975)*. Paris: Hatier, 1991. Pp. 225; illustrations, plates.

Chapin, Chester. "The Poems of Abel Evans 1679–1737." *Notes and Queries*, 236 (1991), 178–81.

Christie, John, and Sally Shuttleworth (eds.). *Nature Transfigured: Science and Literature, 1700–1900*. Manchester UK, and New York: Manchester U. Press, 1989. Pp. vi + 226.

Rev. by T. R. Wright in *Review of English Studies*, 42 (1991), 446-47.

Clark, Lorraine. *Blake, Kierkegaard, and the Spectre of Dialectic*. Cambridge and New York: Cambridge U. Press, 1991. Pp. xii + 238; bibliography.

Lorraine Clark proposes that Blake and Kierkegaard rejected both their earlier reconciliatory dialectics (epitomized in Hegel's "both/and" model), substituting a dramatically exclusive "either/or" model. For Blake—and this book is principally about Blake rather than Kierkegaard—this meant abandoning earlier attempts to construct a mythology that held the contraries in a sustained dialectical tension that preserved both, a system that, Clark says, "abstracted from and hence destroyed his ideal of life" (p. 7). No longer would Blake attempt to confine Orc and Urizen, Prolific and Devourer, Desire and Reason, to an ongoing *pas de deux*. Rather, Clark argues, Blake shifted his model radically, introducing in the form of the Spectre the concept of the Negation, the formal, concretized embodiment of Error that must be *rejected*, not accomodated or redeemed. In short, Blake would adopt a more decisively fundamentalist position, arguing (and citing Jesus Christ as one prototype) that the just individual must separate the sheep from the goats, Truth from Error, and embrace the former and repudiate entirely the latter. In this formulation, the Contraries become not merely polar opposites to be reconciled, but rather components of two alternative perspectives on the external and internal, the eternal and the physical, universe. One is the "true" perspective. The other, the erroneous, Blake now embodies in the Spectre that encompasses simultaneously both the despairing, reductionist threat and the potentially liberating invitation.

For Blake, according to Clark, the crucial moment in the shift from the earlier epistemology to the more complex and more comprehensive later one came with Blake's three-year stay at Felpham with his erstwhile patron William Hayley. This ambivalent relationship prefigured the ambiguity of Los's relationship with his spectre. Initially grateful for Hayley's well-intentioned efforts on his behalf, Blake came to see in their relationship a mortal threat to his own original vision. Recasting Hayley's pattern of conformity and convention as an irreconcilable Negation, Blake evolved from this impasse his notion of the Spectre. Like Blake, Los rages against his Spectre at times and at other times pities him. In either case, in the later works Los seems unable to perform his visionary task without the Spectre, who becomes "somehow his indispensible tool for recreating the lost eternity" (p. 54). For all his fulmination against Hayley—and Clark curiously fails to discuss this directly—Blake owed much of the psychological conviction embodied in his later mythological system to his tortured relationship with Hayley. The crisis of consciousness and aesthetics precipitated by the struggles at Felpham in fact "made" the mature Blake by forcing him to recast his mythological system in a way that rejected the initial "both/and" conciliatory approach to dialectic in favor of the apocalyptic "either/or" whose culmination is visible in the culmination of *Jerusalem*.

The key to Blake's new system, Clark proposes, is a "new dialectic of perspective" (p. 82) in which all Contraries—and all phenomena of physical and imaginative or visionary life—are understood to possess both true forms and false forms. The false forms are those arising from excesses both of reason and of passion (as opposed to the earlier formulation in which, as in *The Marriage of Heaven and Hell*, Reason is entirely pernicious and Desire entirely healthy), and these must be distinguished from their true forms. This means rearranging the old dialectical opposition of reason and passion into a new opposition between truth and error. The struggle is not now between "two contraries within a single systematic dialectic (two parts within a larger whole) but between two entire dialectics (or two wholes)" (p. 82). This new dialectic Clark describes as more "a dialectic of *exclusive perspectives* than of *inclusive contraries*" (p. 82). The ensuing discussion of *Milton* and *Jerusalem* puts this important distinction to good use in a new reading of the Spectre's function in Blake's later works. Whether it is ultimately necessary to devote so much space in this study to Kierkegaard in order to justify the ways of Blake to readers remains unclear, but the new insight on Blake's philosophical and psychological system generated by Clark's consideration of the analogy proposed between Kierkegaard and Blake is well worth having in any case.—Stephen C. Behrendt.

Cole, Lucinda. "(Anti)Feminist Sympathies: The Politics of Relationship in Smith, Wollstonecraft, and More." *English Literary History*, 58 (1991), 107–40.

The male-based discourse of sympathy enables these writers to constitute community and structure feeling to their own advantage.

Collé, Charles. *La Veuve*. Montpellier: Editions Espace 34, 1991. Pp. 80.

Conacher, D. J., Barbara Kerslake, Pia Kleber, C. J. McDonough, Damiano Pietropaolo, and Michael Sidnell (eds.). *Sources of Dramatic Theory*. Vol. I: *Plato to Congreve*. Cambridge and New York: Cambridge U. Press, 1991. Pp. x + 317; bibliography.

A selection of excerpts from major theoretical writings, thoughtfully annotated, "intended for the use of students of drama and theatre," but for the most part restricted to students of specifically designed courses in drama, such as the graduate seminar at the University of Toronto where this volume apparently originated. The limitation of this work lies not only in the inevitable distortions caused by excision, but also in the extremely restricted size of the excerpts—two and a half pages of Rymer's *Short Views*, about a third of Dryden's *Essay of Dramatick Poesie*, two pages from Saint-Evremond's "On Ancient and Modern Tragedy"—scarcely enough to give a representative idea of the author's positions and ultimately insufficient to the needs of advanced students and scholars alike.

Conger, Syndy McMillen (ed.). *Sensibility in Transformation: Creative Resistance to Sentiment from the Augustans to the Romantics*. Rutherford, NJ: Fairleigh Dickinson, 1990. Pp. 235; bibliography; frontispiece; illustrations. Cf. *ECCB*, n.s. 16, V: 259–60.

Rev. by Alistair M. Duckworth in *The Scriblerian*, 23 (1991), 244–47.

Cope, Kevin L. *Criteria of Certainty: Truth and Judgement in the English Enlightenment*. Lexington, KY: The U. Press of Kentucky, 1990. Pp. viii + 224; bibliography. Cf. *ECCB*, n.s. 16, V:261.

Rev.(favorably) by James L. Thorson in *Rocky Mountain Review of Language and Literature*, 45 (1991), 254–55; by J. Wilkinson in *Choice*, 28 (1991), 1482.

Coughlin, Edward V. *Nicasio Alvarez de Cienfuegos*. Boston, MA: Twayne Publishers, 1988. Pp. 129.

Rev. by Monroe Z. Hafter in *Eighteenth-Century Studies*, 24 (1991), 396–97.

Couturier, Maurice. *Textual Communication: A Print-Based Theory of the Novel*. London and New York: Routledge, 1991. Pp. xii + 251; bibliography.

In assessing the importance of printing and the materiality of the text in the history of the novel, critics as diverse as Marshall McLuhan and Walter Ong have emphasized the crucial role of technology in the emergence of the new literary form. The aim of Maurice Couturier's new study is to develop their arguments, and to "analyse the structures of the industry which manufactures and marketed the novels in order to show how the novelist, through his narrative strategies, managed to solve the communication problems he had to face" (p. ix). In his remarkably confident book, which ranges from the earliest days of printing through to the post-modernist avant-garde, Couturier is unabashed by the many challenges he faces, identifying his highly idiosyncratic cocktail of materialist history, reader-oriented study, and narratology as "textual communication" criticism. He is eager to establish an innovative approach, and there are skirmishes aplenty amid the argument, with Genette, with Lacan, with the "pragmaticians" Grice, Austin, Strawson, and Searle, and with Palo Alto psychologists, before the main sweep of the author's own position takes over.

Couturier's first chapter, on the history of printing before the eighteenth century, is readable and fair, but adds little of significance to the standard account in Lucien Febvre and Henry-Jean Martin's *L'Apparition de livre* (1958). Later, with equal care, Couturier borrows from such excellent sources as Elizabeth L. Eisenstein's *The Printing Press as an Agent of Change* (1979) and John Lough's *Writer and Public in France from the Middle Ages to the*

Present Day (1978), and for all its protestations of novelty, his narrative treads familiar ground. When he comes to what he calls "the bookhood of the novel" (p. 52), however, the argument becomes more original, even if that originality is bought at the expense of conventional scholarly caution. Drawing on Murray Cohen's *Sensible Words: Linguistic Practice in England 1640–1785* (1977), Couturier looks at the representation of punctuation and typography in a number of novels, discusses the title page and prefaces, and offers an extended account of *Tristram Shandy* as a complex exercise in the problematics of communication. There are clear expositions in this section of the book, but it is disappointing to see the reader and the writer continually cited as "he," "him," "his," and other gender-specific terms.

Couturier then goes on to give a higly schematic account of the "many births of the novel" before moving on to twentieth-century concerns. It is with these post-modernist extravaganzas that his heart really lies, and his book will be of more interest to later specialists than to scholars of the eighteenth century. His historical account of eighteenth-century fiction is at its best when it reprises its named sources, and weaker when less firmly supported, making it useful primarily for non-specialists. When dealing with the development of the early novel, it does not stand up well against the more subtle and intricate accounts offered recently by Lennard J. Davis, Michael McKeon, and especially J. Paul Hunter. So although it does not please me to be so unwelcoming to a book of undeniable vigor, intelligence, and boldness, I cannot find much here to recommend itself to scholars.—Ian A. Bell.

Cowan, Bainard, and Joseph G. Kronick (eds.). *Theorizing American Literature: Hegel, the Sign, and History.* Baton Rouge, LA, and London: Louisiana State U. Press, 1991. Pp. ix + 294.

Cox, Jeffrey N. "Ideology and Genre in the British Anti-revolutionary Drama of the 1790s." *English Literary History*, 58 (1991), 579–610.

These neglected texts are important to "the ideological struggles of the day" and to literary history.

Craft, Catherine A. "Reworking Male Models: Aphra Behn's *Fair Vow-Breaker*, Eliza Haywood's *Fantomina*, and Charlotte Lennox's *Female Quixote*." *Modern Language Review*, 86 (1991), 821–38.

These "subversive female stories and tales picture heroines who are in control, both of themselves and of the men around them"; "they topple the male stereotypes of women."

Craig, George, and Margaret McGowan (eds.). *Moy qui me voy: The Writer and the Self from Montaigne to Leiris.* Oxford: Clarendon Press, 1989. Pp. xi + 228.

Rev. by Edward Hughes in *Modern Language Review*, 86 (1991), 664–66.

Crossan, Greg. "John Clare's Last Letter." *Notes and Queries*, 236 (1991), 319.

Cummings, Katherine. *Telling Tales: The Hysteric's Seduction in Fiction and Theory.* Stanford, CA: Stanford U. Press, 1991. Pp. xiv + 298.

Rev. (with another work) by Patricia Meyer Spacks in *Modern Language Quarterly*, 52 (1991), 217–21.

Telling Tales deals with narratives of seduction in tales told by three psychoanalytic theorists—Freud, Lacan, and Derrida—and in three novels: *Clarissa*, *Bleak House*, and *Tender is the Night*. There are two chapters on *Clarissa*, to which this review is confined: one in an "Interlude: 'Between the Acts,' " and one on "Clarissa's 'Life with Father.'" The "Interlude" chapter differs from the remainder of the work in being avowedly fictional. It presents Clarissa in the company of the homicidal Papin family—Christine, Lea, and their mother Aimee—as well as Lovelace in the company of Lacan. The importance of the Papins, two of them murderers and all three clearly deranged, lies less in their resemblance to Clarissa than in that their case, like hers, has "engaged expert male attention" (p. 69), the hermeneutic ministrations of Lacan, here compared to those of Lovelace and Belford in *Clarissa*. Imitating the early Derrida, particularly the Derrida of *Glas*, in its abundance of wordplay and neologisms, and announcing its topics through such alliterative subheadings as "The Perverse 'Pere' " and "Paranoid Poetics," the "Interlude" resembles William Warner's *Reading 'Clarissa'* (1979) in playing fast and loose with Richardson's text. Cummings acknowledges an indebtedness to Warner; both believe that *Clarissa* is "partially about a hermeneutic struggle," and both oppose Terry Castle's view of Clarissa as a "hermeneutic casualty," although, Cummings contends, Warner's response originates "in an identification with Lovelace, mine in a kinship with Clarissa" (pp. 88; 95).

If all of *Telling Tales* were written in the mode of this "Interlude," it would, I believe, be a better book. Unconfined by historical constraints, Cummings could exercise her imagination as she pleased, and readers could enjoy the tales she tells. Regrettably, however, the chapter on *Clarissa* makes claims that can be tested, and many of these claims are demonstrably false. Cummings declares, for example, that Richardson's "late additions and emendations" to *Clarissa* (presumably those of the second and third editions) "attempt to impose a single reading—the villain—upon Lovelace and its opposite upon Clarissa—the saint" (p. 93). This old chestnut of Richardson criticism is belied by the evidence of the text; the hundreds of pages of revisions in *Clarissa* are too diverse and complex to impose any single reading on anything. Cummings also writes of Lovelace's "desire to sire his 'twin,'" sharing "Clarissa with his son, as her son" (p. 119); the scene in question, however, depicts Clarissa nursing twin sons sired by Lovelace, with no suggestion that either one is twin to his father. Another odd claim by Cummings is that the name of the brothel-keeper, Sinclair, is a homophone: "when voiced by an English speaker, it functions rather adroitly to cast Clarissa in(to) the French figure of 'St. Claire' " (p. 123). Rather, the name St. Claire would be voiced as Sinclair; there is a homophone, but not the one Cummings envisages.

In a brief epilogue, Cummings writes of "relating," "staging," and "configuring" the story of her book, concluding that "in more than one sense, my narrative has therefore been perverse" (p. 280). *Telling Tales*, however, is not perverse enough. Rewriting *Clarissa* is a time-honored pursuit, first practiced by one of Richardson's correspondents, Lady Echlin, whose genteel alternative ending avoided Clarissa's rape. It is when it ceases to rewrite and attempts instead to interpret *Clarissa* that the inadequacies of *Telling Tales* become apparent.—Peter Sabor

Dabydeen, David. *Hogarth, Walpole and Commercial Britain*. London: Hansib, 1987. Pp. 167.

Rev. (with another work) by Herbert M. Atherton in *The Scriblerian*, 23 (1991), 269–71.

Dahl, Erhard. "Der Wertkomplex 'Arbeit' in den englischen Kinderbuchausgaben des *Robinson Crusoe* zwischen 1719 und 1860." Pp. 30–39 of *Vom Wert der Arbeit: Zur literarischen Konstitution des Wertkomplexes "Arbeit" in der deutschen Literatur (1770–1930)*. Edited by Harro Segeberg. Tübingen: Niemeyer, 1991. Pp. xi + 423; illustrations.

Damrosch, Leopold. *Fictions of Reality in the Age of Hume and Johnson*. Madison, WI: U. of Wisconsin Press, 1989. Pp. x + 262. Cf *ECCB*, n.s. 15, V: 196.

Rev. by Eric Rothstein in *Modern Philology*, 89 (1990–91), 280–83.

Darnton, Robert. *Edition et sédition: L'Univers de la littérature clandestine au XVIIIe siècle*. (Essais.) Paris: Gallimard, 1991. Pp. 278.

Edition et sédition is the first book written directly in French by Robert Darnton even though all his best works were translated into French. The pun in the original French title has got its exact equivalent in English, but Cranton insists on the fact that *Edition et sédition* must not be understood as "Edition *ergo* Sédition" (p. 6). The author traced the diffusion of clandestine literature in eighteenth-century France through the files of the Société typographique de Neuchâtel (STN), a Swiss Protestant publishing firm: thousands of letters were scrutinized by

Darnton both in the Bibliotèque publique et universitaire de Neuchâtel and in the Archives nationales in Paris. Through them, we are able to reconstruct the whole strategy of the publishing firm (with anti-Catholic overtones), its commercial networks, and its marketing devices.

Darnton is not content with scrutinizing the strategy of one firm. He shows us in the most vivid details the way in which smugglers, hawkers and even the most honorable publishers and booksellers took part in the trade and how the best-known authors (Voltaire, Rousseau, Diderot, etc.) saw part of their work circulating in clandestine editions. Most of the clandestine books and libels dealt with anti-religious, erotic, political and utopian themes. Barnton makes a close analysis of three books: *Thérèse philosophe* (attributed to Jean-Baptiste de Boyer, marquis d'Argens) is a *roman galant* showing us that sexual pleasure is a natural thing ordained by God for our own happiness, but which must be governed by reason, "un lélange de spinozisme vulgaire et d'épicurisme mondain dirigé surtout contre l'Eglise catholique" (p. 187). *L'An 2440* by Louis-Sébastien Mercier, also famous as the author of the *Tableau de Paris* introduces us to a new world in which political satire and mawkish scenes lead to a society ruled by reason and sentiment. It reminds us of Edward Bellamy's *Looking Backward* (1888), an American bestseller. *Les Anecdotes sur Mme la comtesse Du Barry* by Matthieu-François Pidansat de Mairobert is a compilation of gossip and anecdotes gleaned from various sources, purporting to show that France is run by the king's mistresses.

The final outcome of a clandestine literature made necessary by censorship is that all the slanders it contains remain unchallenged. They are therefore believed by people who think that, if a book cannot be openly published, it is because it tells an embarrassing truth. Together with Roger Chartier's *Les origines culturelles de la Révolution française* (already reviewed in *ECCB*), such a rich and fascinating book throws new light on the relation between reading and political conscience, but Darnton is aware of the chasm between "une opinion publiquement partagée et l'engagement collectif dans l'action" (p. 214).—Jean Rivière.

Davies, Catherine G. *Conscience as Consciousness: The Idea of Self-Awareness in French Philosophical Writing from Descartes to Diderot.* (Studies on Voltaire and the Eighteenth Century, 272.) Oxford: The Voltaire Foundation at the Taylor Institution, 1990. Pp. 170.

Rev. by Didier Gil in *Recherches sur Diderot et sur l'Encycolpédie*, 10 (1991), 163–64; by Norbert Sclippa in *Eighteenth-Century Studies*, 24 (1991), 551–52.

Davis, Gwenn, and Beverly A. Joyce (comps.). *Poetry by Women to 1900: A Bibliography of American and British Writers.* Buffalo NY, and Toronto: U. of Toronto Press, 1991. Pp. xxiv + 340; bibliography.

Davis, Nina Cox. *Autobiography as Burla in the* Guzmán de Alfarche. Lewisburg: Bucknell U. Press; London and Toronto: Associated University Presses, 1991. Pp. 153; bibliography.

Dédéyan, Charles. *Télémaque ou la Liberté de l'Esprit.* Paris: Librairie Nizet, 1991. Pp. 344; appendices; bibliography.

DeGategno, Paul J. *James Macpherson.* Boston: G. K. Hall, 1989. Pp. 224.

Rev. by David H. Radcliffe in *South Atlantic Review*, 56 (Nov. 1991), 105–08.

de Grazia, Margreta. *Shakespeare Verbatim: The Reproduction of Authenticity and the 1790 Apparatus.* New York: Oxford U. Press; Oxford: Clarendon Press, 1991. Pp. 270; bibliography; 8 illustrations.

DeJean, Joan. *Tender Geographies: Women and the Origins of the Novel in France.* (Gender and Culture). New York: Columbia U. Press, 1991. Pp. xii + 297; bibliography; illustrations.

Delany, Mary. *Letters from Georgian Ireland: The Correspondence of Mary Delany, 1731–68.* Edited by Angélique Day. Foreword by Sybil Connolly. Belfast, Ireland: Friar's Bush Press, 1991. Pp. viii + 303; bibliography; chronology; 16 color plates; 66 illustrations.

Mary Delany (1700–1788) was born in Wiltshire, the eldest daughter of Colonel Bernard Granville, brother of George, Lord Lansdowne, a friend of Pope and Swift. Important in Tory government circles in the early eighteenth century, the Granvilles lost favor with the accession of the Whigs in 1714; and Mary, her parents, her two brothers, and her younger sister retired to a quiet country life in Buckland in Gloucestershire. As a young girl, Mary was taken into the household of her paternal aunt in London and acquired there her education and the social graces such an education provided.

When Mary was seventeen, her paternal uncle persuaded her to marry Alexander Pendarves, a political associate of his and a man many years her senior. Though the marriage was uncongenial, Mary faithfully performed her wifely duties. Perhaps fortunately for her happiness, Pendarves died in 1724, leaving her, however, with so little income that she had to rejoin her uncle's family at Longleat in Wiltshire. Although she was under some family pressure to remarry, she resisted, and to recover from a disappointment in love at this time, she paid a visit lasting over a year to the Dublin home of an intimate friend, Anne Donnellan. There she met Patrick Delany (1686–1768), a graduate of Trinity College, a clergyman of the Church of Ireland, and then Chancellor of St. Patrick's, Dublin. Delany was married. When Mary was in Dublin in 1731–32, she met him frequently in her close circle of friends, and her letters of those years indicate a growing interest in him. After Mary returned to London, she kept her correspondence with her Irish friends, and when Delany's wife died in 1741, he wrote Mary asking her to marry him. Although her family disapproved, Mary accepted him, and they were married in 1743, he being fifty-nine, she being forty-four. Through family influence, she managed to secure the Deanery of Down for him, and they left for Ireland in 1744. From then until her husband's death in 1768, her life was spent chiefly in Ireland. After Delany's death, she returned to England, living first in a house in St. James's Place, and from 1785 on, in a "grace and favor" house in Windsor, granted to her along with a pension from George III and Queen Charlotte. At the time of her death, Edmund Burke wrote of her: "She was not only the woman of fashion at the present age, but she was the highest bred woman in the world, and the woman of fashion of all ages."

This collection of Mary Delany's letters records her impressions of people, places, social events, and Dublin society, including her years in northern Ireland as wife of the Dean of Down. She was devoted to her husband, her "dear D. D.," to her family, to her wide circle of friends (including not only Swift, but Hannah More and Frances Burney), and to her house and garden. In addition to the interest of Mary's lively letters, and the insight they throw on the Ireland of her day, this book also includes many color plates and black-and-white drawings of hers and of her flower colleagues, which induced Sybil Connelly, one of Ireland's foremost fashion designers of today, to stage a major exhibition of Mary's collages in the United States. These flower portraits, executed in cut paper, and begun in her old age, are now in the British Museum Prints and Drawings Collection. When next you visit Britain, take a look at them. One color illustration of a wild rose, *rosa canina*, drawn by Mary on June 25, 1777, is a little beauty.—Edna L. Steeves.

Delon, Michel. *L'Idée d'énergie au tournant des lumières (1770–1829).* Paris: Presses Universitaires de France, 1988. Pp. 521.

Rev. by Carmelina Imbroscio in *Studi francesi*, 34 (1991), 478–79; by Hans-Jürgen Lüsebrink in *Lendemains*, 16 (1991), 158–59.

Denham, Robert D. (ed.). *Visionary Poetics: Essays on Northrop Frye's Criticism.* New York: Peter Lang, 1991. Pp. ix + 161.

Denham, Robert D. (ed.). *The World in a Grain of Sand: Twenty-Two Interviews with Northrup Frye.* New York: Peter Lang, 1990. Pp. 300.

Didier, Béatrice. *Écrire la Révolution, 1789–1799.* (Écriture.) Paris: Presses Universitaires de France, 1989. Pp. 318. Cf. *ECCB*, n.s. 15, V:200.

Rev. by Malcolm Cook in *Modern Language Review*, 86 (1991), 730–31.

Didier, Béatrice, and Jacques Neefs (eds.). *La Fin de l'ancien régime: Sade, Rétif, Beaumarchais, Laclos. Manuscrits de la Révolution I.* Saint-Denis: Presses Universitaires de Vincennes, 1991. Pp. 203.

The subjects, though not altogether evident from the title page, are manuscripts-sources, repertoires, and uses. "Du vrai travail," in Didier's words. The papers emanate from a colloquium, one of an ongoing series, sponsored by the *centre d'étude des manuscrits* of Université de Paris VIII. Except for inherent common problems in dealing with manuscripts, which thus are more or less the main focus in such a collection, the authors discussed are connected only by chronological proximity.

Some of the papers detail references that no one who is not immersed in the same precise material would read straight through. But from such technical considerations we branch out, especially in the case of Sade, to how and where the manuscripts were collected and, questions of the importance of particular texts (above all correspondences) and aspects of their genesis. Particularly interesting from the point of view of the history of texts are the complementary contributions of the editor who was prosecuted for publishing Sade's complete works and the one who introduced them to Pléiade. The former, Jean-Jacques Pauvert, describes the complex history, which he calls a "combat de deux siècles," leading from highly limited availability to the eventual procurement of Sade's texts for the general public. The latter, Michel Delon, emphasizes editorial problems: punctuation, italics, variants and so forth.

Almost all of what remains is devoted to Restif and Beaumarchais. Although a number of Restif manuscripts are extant, none of them relates to the texts that are most read. Beaumarchais' have principally to do with his political and commercial activities. These varied papers furnish us with a mise au point of the status of these collections as well as those of Laclos.—Philip Stewart.

Donato, Clorinda, and Kathleen Hardesty Doig. "Notices sur les auteurs des quarante-huit volumes de 'Discours' de l'*Encyclopédie* d'Yverdon." *Recherches sur Diderot et sur l'*Encyclopédie, 11 (1991), 133–41.

Dopheide, Theodor. *'Satyr the true medicine': die Komödien Thomas Shadwells.* Frankfurt am Main and New York: Peter Lang, 1991. Pp. 275.

Dotoli, Giovanni. *Letteratura per il popolo in Francia (1600–1750): proposte di lettura della "Bibliotèque bleue."* (Biblioteca della ricerca. Mentalità e scrittura, 4.) Fasano, Italy: Schena, 1991. Pp. 405; bibliography; 96 illustrations.

Rev. in rev. article ("Women in Retreat") by Benedetta Craveri in *New York Review of Books*, 38 (Dec. 19, 1991), 67–71.

Until recently the history of literature has, like art history, been built on what may be called the master-piece aesthetic combined, since the Enlightenment, with a theory of progress. This meant essentially a history of taste, or taste of the élite and, believing the criticism by women, a male-dominated view of literary and art history. Considerations and studies in the history of the book, of readership as against authorship, of distribution and the history of the press, have altered this long traditional history of high art and culture. But these recent modifications are as nothing compared with the suggestions implied by Dotoli's excellent study of the *Bibliothèque bleue*.

This bibliothèque bleue is a rather vast collection of what in English are referred to as chap books: cheaply printed, on cheap paper, with rough illustrations when such there are, and covered in blue wrappers and mostly printed in Troyes, though there were other provincial presses which brought some of these books out. They were mostly distributed by itinerant booksellers or *colporteurs*. It was a literature written for and read by and heard by the people, including those who could not read but could listen in the evening by the fire, or in some inn or even in catechism. Indeed, as Dotoli points out and stresses, this was a species of oral tradition written down to be heard, written in a style for the ear rather than the eye, a literature for a public rather than silent and individual reading. The books which made up this vast collection can be found from the XVIth into the early XIXth century. New ones were being written into the early eighteenth century. They were forbidden under the Second Empire but continued to be read in the country. I recall my grandmother still read *le Messager boiteux* which was published in Basel. The collections reflected all the preoccupations of life against women, medicinal herb books to novels of chivalry to social satire and histories, grammmars, etc.

As Dotoli continually stresses, the importance of these books lies in their capacity to allow one to penetrate the mentality of the people, not the elites, not court and town, but the poor in the country, the artisans in towns, even small country nobility, small merchants, the semi-educated. What it shows is a persistence of a medieval and baroque mentality even while the world stage seems dominated by so called Classicism and Enlightenment. This was the voice of Sancho Panza, that of the experience of a hard life against the illusions and art of polite society. Dotoli says suggestively that it was to the French people what the commedia dell'arts was to the Italians. It implies that our traditional literary history illuminates but a small space of what could be a far more varied type of history of the human imagination and mentality. Certainly this is not the "best that has been thought and written," though Dotoli says there are masterpieces in this bibliothèque bleue, but it is a precious source for those who would know the obverse of polite letters, of the Grand Siècle, of the Enlightenment.

Dotoli has founded his research not only on the texts of the Bibliothèque bleue, many well illustrated here, but has also used the latest research in this growing field of investigation. The result is not only an excellent study but a first rate and very useful bibliography.—R. G. S.

Dowling, William C. *The Epistolary Moment: The Poetics of the Eighteenth-Century Verse Epistle.* Princeton, NJ: Princeton U. Press, 1991. Pp. 220; bibliography.

William C. Dowling's excellent book provides an account of eighteenth-century English poetry based on the theoretical implications of the Augustan verse epistle, the "dominant poetic mode of its age" (p. 9). Building on the work of Raymond Williams and Isaac Kramnick, as well as J. G. A. Pocock and selected formalist critics, Dowling contends that "Pope and Swift and Gay demand to be seen in this [Marxist] light because they were carrying out a proto-Marxist critique of early capitalism" (p. 15). Given this thesis, it is surprising to see no mention whatsoever of Laura Brown's *Alexander Pope* (1985), a book that presented Pope as sympathetic, if not complicit, with the commodity culture of nascent capitalism. Indeed, Dowling's point is so diametrically opposed to Brown's thesis that his argument may be seen as an all but explicit attempt to rescue Pope (and his friends) from her charges.

For Dowling the story of eighteenth-century poetry is the story of the verse epistle as the poetic attempt to escape Lockean solipsism, Walpolean corruption, and the credit economy by creating a moral community that the implied reader is invited to share with the poet and the explicit addressee of the epistle. The usual strategy of the verse epistle is to declare "its autonomy from the corrupt world" in order to offer to its audience "a moral choice between that world and its own ideal commonwealth" (p. 61). The Augustan audience constituted by this choice thus emerges in Dowling's argument as a sort of shadow government. Within this shadowy ideal commonwealth, "civic virtue" is transposed "from the sphere of action to that of discourse" (p. 64), the aristocracy is expected "to serve its country through personal example" (p. 66), and "qualities that we now tend to consider 'merely' aesthetic or stylistic were inseparable from morality" (p. 72). "The mob in Augustan writing," as Dowling puts it, "is a moral rather than a social category, and one becomes a member not by thinking wrongly but by refusing to think. . . . Augustan audience is thus always imagined as a reader or readers who are drawn out of the vulgar and into the patrician world" (pp. 80–81). The role of satire in this project is to unmask "the deceptions of the new society" so that "delusion will ultimately evaporate and the commonwealth emerge into visibility" (p. 83).

However, this whole project ultimatelty undermines itself, according to Dowling, because "having founded its discourse on the presumed moral authority of aristocratic speech, and having created an interior landscape in which the country house and the *otium* scene operate as objectifications of aristocratic values," Augustan poetry "summons an audience now endowed with aristocratic sensibility out of the timeless world of a universal human community and into a poetic world that, for all its own ideality, is governed by an uncompromising system of social and class distinctions" (p. 96). This paradox brings about the collapse of the Augustan epistolary project and results in a return to and embracing of solipsism, under the banner of Shaftesburian moral connoisseurship and Addisonian politeness. Dowling concludes his discussion by questioning the notion of "pre-Romanticism," positing an internalization of the *otium* landscape, the scene of contemplation and retirement from a corrupt world, rather than an internalization of quest romance (as Harold Bloom has called it). The madness of Chatterton marks not the beginning of Romanticism (and thus is not "pre-Romantic") but the failure and end of the Augustan confrontation with solipsism.

For a book that devotes considerable attention to classical verse and to poems like Denham's *Cooper's Hill*, there is at least one important omission. Dowling suggests several times that the issues under consideration are literary extensions of the English Civil War, yet he nonetheless fails to mention at all Milton's great Latin epistolary elegiacs, *Ad Patrem* and *Ad Carolum Diodatum, Ruri Commorantem*, nor any of Milton's epistolary sonnets. Milton's epistle to Diodati would be particularly useful here, concerned as Milton is with Diodati's reception in the country (the scene of *otium* retirement), and the sort of life appropriate for different poetic aspirations.

Despite its omissions, Dowling's book provides insightful analysis of major poems as well of poems less often discussed, all within the context of English social and economic change in the eighteenth century. Moreover, its implications should prove useful in establishing lines of continuity between, for example, Pope's epistles and the Romantic conversation poems.—R. Paul Yoder.

Dowling, William C. *Poetry and Ideology in Revolutionary Connecticut*. Athens, GA: U. of Georgia Press, 1990. Pp. xix + 167; bibliography. Cf. *ECCB*, n.s. 16, V:266.

Rev. by D. D. Knight in *Choice*, 28 (1991), 1636.

Draper, James P., and James E. Person, Jr. (eds.). *Literature Criticism from 1400 to 1800: Excerpts from Criticism from the Works of Fifteenth-, Sixteenth-, Seventeenth-, and Eighteenth-Century Novelists, Poets, Playwrights, Philosophers, and Other Creative Writers, from the First Published Critical Appraisals to Current Evaluations*. Volume 15. Detroit, MI, and London: Gale Research, 1991. Pp. xiii + 570; illustrations.

Drury, John (ed.). *Critics of the Bible, 1724–1873*. Cambridge and New York: Cambridge U. Press, 1989. Pp. ix + 204. Cf. *ECCB*, n.s. 16, V: 267; 15, V:200–01.

Rev. by Virginia Ramey Mollenkott in *Christianity and Literature*, 41 (1991), 76–78.

Dugaw, Dianne. *Warrior Women and Popular Balladry 1650–1850*. (Cambridge Studies in Eighteenth-Century English Literature and Thought, 4.) Cambridge and New York: Cambridge U. Press, 1989. Pp. 233. Cf. *ECCB*, n.s. 15, V:201.

Rev. (favorably) by Kathy Howlett in *The Scriblerian*, 23 (1991), 282–84; (with another work) by Anne Williams in *Eighteenth-Century Studies*, 24 (1991), 402–08.

Duggan, Margaret M. *English Literature and Backgrounds 1660–1700: A Selective Critical Guide*. (Garland Reference Library of the Humanities, 711.) 2 vols. London and New York: Garland, 1990. Pp. xxv + 1160; indices. Cf. *ECCB*, n.s. 16, V:267.

Rev. by Robert D. Spector in *The Scriblerian*, 24 (1991), 87–88.

Duval, Gilles. *Littérature de colportage et imaginaire collectif en Angleterre à l'époque des Dicey: 1720–v. 1800.* Bordeaux: Presses Universitaires de Bordeaux, 1991. Pp. 745.

Edmiston, William F. *Hindsight and Insight: Focalization in Four Eighteenth-Century French Novels.* University Park, PA: Pennsylvania State Press, 1991. Pp. xii + 208.

William Edmiston's study of focalization in the memoir-novel is a masterfully executed *mise au point* of the question of viewpoint in first-person narratives in the French eighteenth century. Lucidly interweaving narratological theory, literary criticism, and personal analyses of narrative practice, he demonstrates convincingly, contrary to traditional critical opinion, that there are just as many focal options and strategies available to the first-person narrator as to the third-person narrator. Edmiston bases his study on a combination of prominent narratological positions, including, principally, Genette's defintion and tripartite concept of focalization, Chon's distinction between "external" (narrator's viewpoint) and "internal" (character's viewpoint) focalization, and Vitoux's notion of delegated focalization.

   Hindsight and Insight includes in-depth studies of focalization in four well-known novels: *Les Egarements du coeur et de l'esprit*, *Le Paysan parvenu*, *Manon Lescaut*, and *La Religieuse*. In each of the four chapters, Edmiston demonstrates first how the narrator establishes a point of view, then discusses the focal choices of the narrator, and, finally, analyses how the narrator delegates focalization to the experiencing self and to others. The study as a whole tends to emphasize, on the one hand, "focal variation between the narrating self and the experiencing self" (15) in each of the works, especially a marked tendency toward "constant" narration, that is, interal focalization which intentionally blends, indeed confuses, the viewpoints of narrator and character. Each novel offers, however, a separate "case-study" in focalization. Crébillon's novel exhibits, for instance, a greater degree of "dissonant" narration than the others, the narrator maintaining an ironic distance from himself as hero through the use of nonfocalization (omniscient psychological insights). In *Le Paysan parvenu*, the focalization of the narrator and hero are frequently coalesced, and Marivaux's use of verb tenses produces a curious temporal ambiguity which tends to draw both the narrator and reader into the diegetic world of the characters. Des Grieux is the most manipulative narrator, delegating focalization to create flattering perspectives on the hero, but, as Edmiston demonstrates, he is not "unreliable," from a purely narratological standpoint. Suzanne, on the other hand, the narrator of *La Religieuse*, is shown to be fundamentally unreliable due to her refusal to admit knowledge that she necessarily possessed retrospectively. This "denial of cognitive privilege" (103) by the narrator is considered by Edmiston to be an intentional narrative technique, "perhaps the boldest and most innovative of many techniques used by Diderot to achieve consonant self-narration, to effect a convincing integration of the narrating self and the experiencing self, and to efface the boundary between story and discourse" (131).

   As in the case of Suzanne's several denials of retrospective knowledge, considered by many to be technical errors on the part of Diderot, Edmiston argues that the obvious infractions of convention in first-person narrative,. such as flashes of inexplicable omniscience, should not be viewed as technical weaknesses at all. These infractions should be seen, in fact, as "creative innovations, striving to overcome the bondage of convention and to attain a narrational freedom not shared by the autobiographer—or at least by the historian" (145). Whether or not the reader accepts this viewpoint, Edmiston's study, which includes an appendix on the evolution of theories of focalization, ending with an interesting revision of Genette's typology of focalization as applied to first-person narration, is an illuminating contribution to the existing body of narratological theory and practice.—Alan J. Singerman.

Ellis, Frank H. *Sentimental Comedy: Theory and Practice.* (Cambridge Studies in Eighteenth-Century English Literature and Thought, 10.) Cambridge and New York: Cambridge U. Press, 1991. Pp. xviii + 228; 7 illustrations.

Among the most obvious virtues of this new monograph by Frank Ellis is its clarity of design and purpose. The introductory chapter on "Theory" poses and answers three questions: "What is sentimental?", "What is comedy?", and

"What is sentimental comedy?" The following eight chapters, entitled collectively "Practice," analyze eight plays dating from 1696 to 1793 that are "most frequently called sentimental" (p. xiii). After a brief concluding chapter, complete texts of two of these plays, William Whitehead's *The School for Lovers* (1762) and Elizabeth Inchbald's *Every One Has His Fault* (1793), are appended.

The middle chapters, discussing particular plays and playwrights, are strong, the pithy accounts of biography and stage history particularly well-informed. Ellis introduces Cibber's *The Careless Husband* (1704), for example, by traversing the alcoholic origin of Cibber's association with Henry Brett, the complex marital history of Brett's wife (Cibber's model for Lady Easy), the influence of the Duke of Argyll on Cibber's dialogue, and the personal and professional circumstances of Anne Oldfield, Cibber's leading lady (pp. 34–35). In addition to providing detailed and fascinating information, these chapters offer clear and comprehensive analyses. Ellis elucidates, for example, the systematic parallels and contrasts in Cumberland's *The West Indian* (1771). His readings can also be richly suggestive, as in his account of Moore's *The Foundling* (1748), where, he observes, the action is "interior," of the mind (p. 60).

Unfortunately, the introductory chapter places the author's unarguable knowledge and insight in a theoretical context that is assumed and asserted rather than systematically reasoned. For instance, Ellis glosses over the epistemological complexities of sentimentality, moving in a single paragraph from describing it in terms of "pity for all humanity," to Christian charity, to "almost . . . a physical attribute," to "universal benevolence," to Hutcheson's "*disinterested ultimate Desire* of the Happiness of others" (pp. 5–6). In addition, the general discussion of comedy, drawn chiefly from Northrop Frye, is extraneous to Ellis's analysis of sentimental comedy, which consists primarily of an inductively derived list of "subjects treated sentimentally" in the eighteenth century: women, parents, children, "the lower orders: servants, peasants, foreigners, the poor," money, the emotions, and so on (pp. 10–11). By defining the "sentimental attitude" toward each of these subjects in isolation, Ellis precludes discussion of many of the most compelling issues raised by sentimental literature, among them, the intricate interdependence of sentimentality, theology, and ethics. Similarly, Ellis's pronouncements that women and the "lower orders" are "upgraded" ignore such issues as the troubling prominence of female suffering in sentimental texts and the class bias of the apparently egalitarian rhetoric of sentiment (pp. 10–14).

Ironically, Ellis is more condescending toward sentimental drama than those scholars who question its humanitarian motives and effects. He begins the book with a psychological study that approaches sentimentality as an illness; he frequently and uncritically borrows the mocking language of Goldsmith (p. 10 and *passim*); and he repeatedly characterizes sentimental attitudes as "nonsense" (p. 7 and *passim*). It is hardly surprising that he concludes only "lesser figures" like Steele and Cumberland present sentimental attitudes without satirizing them (p. 119). Like Bernbaum and Sherbo before him, Ellis assumes a distinction between historical importance and "social utility," on the one hand, and aesthetic value and extra-literary truth on the other, which keeps him from recognizing the full and complex significance of sentimental drama (p. 123).

Strangely, the author's refusal to take his subject seriously also helps redeem this idiosyncratic study, for the tone is refreshingly breezy. Self-importance gives way to verve and humor as Ellis deadpans, "The truth can be concealed no longer. Sir Richard Steele was also a reformer . . . " (p. 48). Readers' disappointment in his predictably modest conclusions will be mitigated by his droll presentation: "Sentimental comedy exists. This will be particularly good news for . . . graduate students writing dissertations on sentimental comedy" (p. 117). More important than Ellis's humor, however, is the fact that eight of ten chapters are devoted to informed discussions of individual plays. Thus, however one might regret its theoretical deficiencies, *Sentimental Comedy* remains valuable as an entertaining and learned account of the eighteenth-century drama, dramatists, and theater history Ellis knows so well.—Peggy Thompson.

Engell, James. *Forming the Critical Mind: Dryden to Coleridge*. Cambridge, MA, and London: Harvard U. Press, 1989. Pp. xii + 322. Cf. *ECCB*, n.s. 16, V:268; 15, V:202–03.

Rev. (with another work) by Allan Ingram in *Modern Language Review*, 86 (1991), 404–06; by Ira Konigsberg in *Journal of English and Germanic Philology*, 90 (1991), 439–42.

Erlebach, P. "Das dichterische Selbstverständnis von John Keats und der Bezug zur poetologischen und zur geistesgeschichtlichen Entwicklung des 18. und 19. Jahrhunderts." *Mitteilungen des Verbandes deutscher Anglisten*, 2:2 (1991), 23–35.

Everett, Barbara. *Poets in Their Time: Essays on English Poetry from Donne to Larkin.* Oxford: Clarendon Press, 1991. Pp. viii + 264.

Barbara Everett's book contains three articles of interest to *ECCB* readers. In "The Shooting of the Bears: Poetry and Politics in Andrew Marvell," she presents a remarkable evaluation of Marvell's "Horatian Ode upon Cromwell's Return from Ireland," explaining that it was conceived as a private poem, and though political, it is not as public as Marvell's other occasional verse. She discusses Marvell's metrical effects and contends his "best poems lie within a territory that charts out the transition from one field to the other" (p. 60).

Another fine essay by Everett, "Rochester: The Sense of Nothing," shows Rochester's ability to transcend the social fashion. She relates how Rochester's transmutation of the Hobbesian idea of time in his verse transcends social form, and she further demonstrates how the smoothness of Rochester's poems is interspersed with flaws or "disjunctions of language" like "minute cracks that beautify crackleware ceramics." Thus Rochester creates the elegance of a "social surface" and "shatters" it with an obscenity, thereby creating two opposed poles." Everett's brilliant essay shows how obscenity in Rochester, far from making him a pornographic poet, represents a transcendence: "for in obscenity, . . . the extreme of verbal and emotional nothingness is reached" (p. 104).

Finally, there is "Tibbles: A New Life of Pope" in which Everett argues for the facts of history in biography rather than the biographer's own "sympathetic romanticism." Although, she tells us, Maynard Mack's recent definitive biography on Pope is an artwork in itself as well as "a thoroughly readable and enjoyable book," there remains "room to voice a few regrets." In revealing Mack's inclination to romanticize, Everett refers to his oversight of historical facts surrounding two reproduced portraits, custard pie, and the name "Tibbald." She further argues that "slips" and uses of "incompatible" references to other writers do not help the reader to see Pope's life better. This essay is very informative, especially as it bears on the ongoing debate over whether biographers are correct to allow their personal criticism to enter the factual history surrounding a life.—Ron May.

Farrell, Michèle Longino. *Performing Motherhood: The Sévigné Correspondence.* Hanover, NH, and London: U. Press of New England, 1991. Pp. viii + 302; bibliography.

Feingold, Richard. *Moralized Song: The Character of Augustan Lyricism.* New Brunswick, NJ: Rutgers U. Press, 1989. Pp. viii + 223; appendices. Cf. *ECCB*, n.s. 15, V:204–05.

Rev. (severely) by P. E. Hewison in *Notes and Queries*, 236 (1991), 233–34; by Douglas Lane Patey in *English Language Notes*, 29 (1991), 85–88.

Fietz, Lothar. "Zur Genese des englischen Melodramas aus der Tradition der bürgerlichen Tragödie und des Rührstücks: Lillo, Schröder, Kotzebue, Sheridan, Thompson, Jerrold." *Deutsche Vierteljahrsschrift für Literaturwissenschaft und Geistesgeschichte*, 65:1 (1991), 99–116.

Fissell, Mary E. *Patients, Power, and the Poor in Eighteenth-Century Bristol.* (Cambridge History of Medicine.) Cambridge and New York: Cambridge U. Press, 1991. Pp. xii + 266; bibliography; figures; maps; tables.

This work adds to the prevailing wisdom that an important change occurred in the medical profession and medical practice around the middle of the eighteenth century. Fissell's study focuses upon those changes as they unfolded at the Bristol Infirmary and aims to place these within the appropriate social, economic, and historiographical contexts.

Fissell describes medical practice of the early eighteenth century as still dominated by notions of sympathy and equilibrium, and by a concern with external symptoms; the effect of these beliefs was to empower patients to represent or even to treat their own diseases. She also provides an overview of the types of medical practitioners found in Bristol, and demonstrates the similarities of treatment regardless of the educational background or social status of the practitioner. The original role of Bristol Infirmary was to provide civic charity and poor relief. For this reason, a high number of those referred came from broken families, had out-of-wedlock pregnancies, or suffered from old age. Because medical treatment was so influenced by the charitable mission of the hospital, Fissell contends that the Bristol Infirmary must be placed in the context of changing attitudes toward poverty, charity, and changes in the view of the body itself. She uses the system of medical referral to demonstrate connections between these issues.

Changes within Bristol Infirmary occurred alongside broader transformations in medical practice over the eighteenth century. This change has been recently seen as one in which the patient became an object of study, subject to the authority of the medical professional, and in which authority was transferred from the patient to the medical practitioner. At Bristol, the surgeons played a crucial role in this shift. Their concern with external symptoms reduced patients to objects of anatomical study, and disregarded the patients' own accounts of their illness. The earlier notion of medicine as rooted in sympathy and equilibrium was relegated to popular, as distinct from elite, medicine.

This evolution occurred in Bristol not because of an open contest of medical views, or as the result of professional disputes. Instead, Fissell contends, a new role devolved upon the surgeons as a direct result of a decline in the involvement of the Board of Governors in the management of the Infirmary. The surgeons thus appear as almost unconscious agents of fundamental change in medical practice, and the allocation of poor relief. Members of the Board of Governors became less involved, in part, because there were other venues for medical poor relief, and surgeons filled the void because of the decline in the practice of surgical apprenticeship, which created the concomitant need for hospital instruction.

This book adds to our understanding of early modern medical institutions, while corroborating the work of others, notably Roy Porter, on the changing nature of medicine during the eighteenth century. The author's discussion of early medicine, as opposed to later, elite medicine, is particularly persuasive. Some of the rich social and historiographical context for the Bristol Infirmary is treated in a tantalizingly brief (and insubstantial) fashion, specifically the connections between Bristol Infirmary and the broader eighteenth-century context of medical practice, professionalization, and public charity. The author is much more successful in situating the Infirmary in the context of social and economic trends within Bristol itself.

One of Fissell's least persuasive assertions is that elite worries over the politically seditious character of Wesleyan Methodism were channeled into a crusade to suppress popular medicine. By the evidence she presents, concerted opposition to popular medicine arose prior to, and independently of, concerns over religious dissent. Even in her account the religious or "miraculous" aspects of reported cures, or the political aspects of practices such as the King's touch, seem to be central, and any glancing blows at popular medicine peripheral. Another problem is that, for all of Fissell's insistence on the need to look at medicine from the patient's point of view, the voices of patients are rarely heard in this book. This of course is largely a problem of sources: the marginalization of patients' voices over the eighteenth century left its mark upon medical casebooks as well, as these were increasingly devoted to depicting the body and its symptoms, rather than individuals with particular stories.—Kathleen Wellman.

Flynn, Carol Houlihan. *The Body in Swift and Defoe*. (Cambridge Studies in Eighteenth-Century English Literature and Thought, 5.) Cambridge and New York: Cambridge U. Press, 1990. Pp. viii + 231. Cf. *ECCB*, n.s. 16, V:270–71.

Rev. by Kirk Combe in *Notes and Queries*, 236 (1991), 544–45; by Everett Zimmerman in *The Scriblerian*, 24 (1991), 51–52.

Folkenflik, Robert. "The Heirs of Ian Watt." *Eighteenth-Century Studies*, 25 (1991–92), 203–17.

Considers works by Armstrong, Davis, Bender, Castle, and McKeon.

Formigari, Lia. *L'esperienza e il segno: la filosofia del linguaggio tra Illuminismo e Restaurazione*. Rome: Editori Riuniti, 1990. Pp. 280.

Rev. by Lori D. Repetti in *Eighteenth-Century Studies*, 24 (1991), 504–06.

Fort, Bernadette (ed.). *Fictions of the French Revolution*. Evanston, IL: Northwestern U. Press, 1991. Pp. viii + 209.

Given its title, it is not inappropriate that this volume should be reviewed by a literature professor and not a historian. The notion that fiction has formed our understanding of the French Revolution is central to all the essays in the book. While this may not please all historians, it does stimulate the student of literature who already suspects how close literature and history really are.

In her introductory essay, Bernadette Fort makes a succinct argument for history as fiction. She explains this revisionist perspective in part by noting that the historian marshalling documents and interpreting them resembles the novelist shaping events or imagining settings and dialogues. Not only is history writing (and thus an experience mediated through discourse and not the events themselves), but the French Revolution is itself more and more a written event. It was (re)told and (mis)interpreted by its participants, not to mention the legions of historians who followed them, as they argued over the meaning of the events they were enacting. The Revolution is both word and deed, events and the retelling of events, and thus easily subject to fictionalization.

Fort is not advocating, of course, any simplistic view that we do not know *what* has happened in the past. Rather we do not know—or more accurately, our knowledge changes from generation to generation—how to account for what has happened. So we fictionalize in order to best explain the events we choose to study.

Rather than touch on each of these seven essays lightly, I would prefer to concentrate on three that illustrate in practice what Fort has described in the abstract. Peter Brook argues that oratory and theater were hyperbolic genres that exclude compromise and deal only with sharp extremes. He then reads this melodramatic rhetoric onto historical bodies. Crimes were seen in terms of bodies that had to be punished. Marie Antionette and Mme Roland were accused of bodily, i.e. sexual, crimes. The beheading of Louis and the desecration of the royal tombs at Saint-Denis were culminating examples of that rhetoric of violence since the bodies punished were royal and the most sacred in France.

Bodies appear in two other essays, one on painting, the other on the public image and vilification of the queen. For Thomas Crow, David's *The Death of Bara* can best be understood as a fiction. David was commissioned by the Convention to commemorate the thirteen-year-old Bara killed in the Vendée. Embellished with republican details, his story became a myth David wanted to capture in paint. Crow demonstrates how David's disturbingly erotic figure borrowed the pictorial syntax of two of his students, Drouais and Girodet, and capitalized on another well-known narrative about French republican virtue beseiged in the French art academy in Rome. For the Revolution this androgynous nude was understood as suffering, patriotic virtue. As these fictional supports were forgotten, however, *Bara* became a puzzle, no longer a public statement about the Revolution but a private work centered on a sexually ambiguous body. Jacques Revel deals with the scurrilous pamphlets that attacked Marie-Antoinette in the mid-70s and 80s. This supposedly marginal literature reveals deep social anxieties. The threat posed by women invading the body politic (the queen's meddling in her husband's politics) was compounded by fears about the loss of sexual differences (lesbianism). Revel shows how preposterous exaggerations needed only the slightest hint of plausibility, often furnished by the libels' own intertextuality, to be believed. This fictional corpus, comprised of stories repeating the same sexual accusations, literally created a paper queen that replaced the real one in the mind of the people.

The term "fiction" can then be accurately applied to the historical objects these essays study. But it can also refer to the essays themselves, for they too are "fictional" in the partial readings they propose. More than she might have wished, Fort proves that history is a fiction of several times and places, first when it happened and then when it was written down. And fiction is best judged not by its truth value but by the force of its argument and the willingness of its reader to suspend disbelief.—Peter V. Conroy, Jr.

Foster, Gretchen M. *Pope Versus Dryden: A Controversy in Letters to* The Gentleman's Magazine *(1789–91)*. (English Literary Studies, 41.) Victoria, B.C.: U. of Victoria Press, 1989. Pp. 156. Cf. *ECCB*, n.s. 15, VI:382–83.

Rev. by James A. Winn in *The Scriblerian*, 23 (1991), 258–59; (with reservations) by David Womersley in *Notes and Queries*, 236, (1991), 235–36.

Fournier, Nathalie. *L'Aparte dans la théâtre français du 17e siècle au 20e siècle*. (Bibliothèque de l'information grammaticals, 21.) Louvain: Peeters, 1991. Pp. 380.

Fowler, Alastair (ed.). *The New Oxford Book of Seventeenth-Century Verse*. New York and Oxford: Oxford U. Press, 1991. Pp. xlv + 831.

Rev. (severely, with another work) by Donald Davie in *TLS*, (Dec. 27, 1991), 6–7.

Fox, Christopher. *Locke and the Scriblerians: Identity and Consciousness in Early Eighteenth-Century Britain*. Berkeley, CA: U. of California Press, 1989. Pp. x + 174.

Rev. by Kevin Cope in *South Atlantic Review*, 56 (May 1991), 137–140; by Carolyn Williams in *Modern Language Review*, 86 (1991), 669–70.

Fox, Christopher (ed.). *Teaching Eighteenth-Century Poetry*. New York: AMS Press, 1990. Pp. 445. Cf. *ECCB*, n.s. 16, V:271–72.

Rev. (favorably) by Robert D. Lund in *The Scriblerian*, 24 (1991), 71–73; (briefly) by Alfred Lutz in *English Language Notes*, 28 (1991), 81–82; by Peter Sabor in *Eighteenth-Century Studies*, 25 (1991–92), 271–74.

Fox, Dian. *Refiguring the Hero: From Peasant to Noble in Lope de Vega and Calderón*. (Penn State Studies in Romance Literatures.) University Park, PA: Pennsylvania State U. Press, 1991. Pp. xiii + 242; bibliography.

Franklin, Colin. *Shakespeare Domesticated: The Eighteenth-Century Editions*. Aldershot, UK: Scolar Press, 1991. Pp. xiv + 246; 24 illustrations; 16 plates.

Colin Franklin is an antiquarian bookseller who collects editions of Shakespeare's works. Here he presents a rather offhand commentary on the eighteenth-century editions and on certain of that century's commentators on Shakespeare, focusing on the production and contents of the editions, and on the issues as quarrels that divided their editors and critics. The result is often fascinating and sometimes insightful; but, given its subject, the book is curiously ambivalent about scholarship and editing, perhaps reflecting Franklin's own bookseller's bias (the Tonsons, for example, are termed "martyrs to editors").

Franklin first surveys the editions from Rowe to the "third variorum" of 1821, giving some editions only a paragraph of comment, none more than two or three pages. A longer chapter, "The Editors and their Prefaces," by and large goes over ground already covered, more thoroughly, by Sherbo in *The Birth of Shakespeare Studies* (1986) and by others. Three subsequent chapters deal with "Styles in Editing" (an uncritical but entertaining account of the editors as editors), "The Growth of Apparatus" (a helpful discussion of the appearance, over time, of indices, glossaries, and the like), and "Illustrations" (perhaps the most original and substantial section). The final chapter, "The Fable and the Moral," is in part an attempt to argue that "Shakespeare's treatment of his plots ('fables') and the presence or absence of moral purpose" (p. 225) were the chief preoccupations of eighteenth-century Shakespeare critics, a thesis that Franklin's own considerably disorganized evidence does not appear to support.

One of the underlying problems with this book is the absence of a central thesis. A further difficulty comes from Franklin's haphazard approach, as revealed in this telling description of his preparations for writing the book: "it was not difficult to assemble the collection [of edition] I was seeking; thus it has been possible to enjoy an 18th-century experience of reading and writing at home. My chief sources are those editions, a few 18th-century critics, and the 17 volumes of Nichols' *Literary Anecdotes* and *Literary History*" (p. 6). Nor is it clear who Franklin intends his audience to be: this is neither a scholarly work nor an introduction to the subject. Its organization is casual and repetitious, the documentation uneven, the index porous, the spelling inconsistent ("Nichol Smith" and "Nicol Smith" by turns). Franklin admits that he made no attempt to be inclusive—either of editions or of critics—but the absence of any reference to (for example) Dennis, Hurd, Sewell, Whalley, or Young gives me pause.

All of which is sad to report because the topic is an important one and Franklin clearly has much to say about it. But his enthusiasm for Shakespeare and old books does not compensate for such shortcomings. Go then to Franklin in a holiday spirit, for entertainment rather than edification.—Leslie F. Chard.

Fullard, Joyce (ed.). *British Women Poets 1660–1800: An Anthology*. Troy, NY: Whitson, 1990. Pp. ix + 608. Cf. *ECCB*, n.s. 16, V:272–73.

Rev. by Daniel Albright in *The Scriblerian*, 24 (1991), 45–47.

Gamez, Anne, and Merry-Hugues Duracher. "L'Art dramatique et la mort de Beaurepaire à Verdun (1792–1873)." *Revue d'histoire du théâtre*, 43 (1991), 147–61.

Interesting article which analyses six different plays (Oct. 14, 1792; Nov. 23, 1792; Feb. 3, 1793; June 14, 1793; March 1806 and Nov. 23, 1872) on the suicide at Verdun of the commander of the town, Nicolas Beaurepaire (1740–1792) on Sept. 2, 1792.

Glen, Duncan. *The Poetry of the Scots: An Introduction and Bibliographical Guide to Poetry in Gaelic, Scots, Latin, and English*. Edinburgh, Scotland: Edinburgh U. Press, 1991. Pp. xxxi + 149; indices.

'A chield's amang you, taking notes': so might Burns, on behalf of Scots poets using their several poetic languages, salute this enterprise. Glen's book offers useful starting information about Scottish history, language use, criticism and theory, also printed sources, and thereafter sections devoted to poets grouped chronologically, with an additional section on ballads. Within each section there are bibliographical entries for individual poets, with comments on collections and editions that the author believes have contributed to a "literary tradition of Scottish poetry." Glen recognizes that it is difficult to define such a thing, but he seems to mean a tradition formed by poets working in the Scottish lowlands dialect (Lallans), which was a court language until 1603 when James VI went south to rule England as well as Scotland. Afterwards, Lallans had to compete with the powerful influence of southern standard English. Part of the story, of course, deals with the efforts of Allan Ramsay, Robert Fergusson, and Robert Burns to revive Lallans as a poetic language in the eighteenth century and expand its resources to accomodate the intellectual and consumer revolutions of their day. Glen provides some guidance about this, but his book needs to be supplemented with recent work on the Scottish Enlightenment and the crisis occasioned for poets wishing to respond to the ideals of that movement. Scholars should turn to the annual newsletters of the Eighteenth-Century Scottish Studies Society—*Eighteenth-Century Scotland* (Dept. of Humanities, New Jersey, Institute of Technology, Newark, NJ 07102, 1987)—for information about current debates over the creation and criticism of literature in Enlightened Scotland. An additional source of information not mentioned by Glen is the quarterly review periodical, *Books in Scotland* (The Ramsey Head Press, 15 Gloucester Place, Edinburgh EH3 6EE, Scotland).

Glen's stance to his subject matter is that of a follower of "Hugh MacDiarmid" (alias C. M. Grieve, 1892–1978), whose modernist poetry from the 1920s on recreated Lallans to cope with themes of impressive intellectual range. This orientation gives a forceful air of polemic to the criticism, but it results in neglect of important poetry: that of the eighteenth-century Anglo-Scots, so to speak, e.g., James Thomson, Robert Blair, and James Beattie, on whom we need a careful study. Though there are good entries on poets in Scotland writing in

Latin and Gaelic—the renaissance in the second tongue in the eighteenth century, in particular, gets its due (pp. 69–75)—no helpful information is provided about the "Ossian" publications of James Macpherson, which are important artistic creations and had an immense impact on Europe: see *Ossian Revisited*, edited by Howard Gaskill (1991). Further, the nationalistic argument of Glen's book needs to be revised and supplemented in the light of Robert Crawford's *Devolving English Literature* (1992), a bracing treatment of the invention of "English literature" in eighteenth-century Scotland, with an excellent account of what this did to the writing of poetry and criticism in that country.—Ian S. Ross.

Goldsmith, Elizabeth C. (ed.). *Writing in the Female Voice: Essays on Epistolary Literature.* Boston, MA: Northeastern U. Press, 1989. Pp. xiii + 296. Cf. *ECCB*, n.s. 15, V:209.

Rev. (favorably) by Mary Trouille in *Eighteenth-Century Studies*, 25 (1991), 106–10.

Goodden, Angelica. *The Complete Lover: Eros, Nature, and Artifice in the Eighteenth-Century French Novel.* Oxford: Clarendon Press, 1989. Pp. vi + 329; bibliography. Cf. *ECCB*, n.s. 16, V:275; 15, V:210–11.

Rev. (briefly) by Pierluigi Ligas in *Studi francesi*, 34 (1991), 521.

Goodman, Dena. "The Hume-Rousseau Affair: From Private *Querelle* to Public *Procés*." *Eighteenth-Century Studies*, 25 (1991–92), 171–201.

Traces "the process by which a private matter became a public affair, readers became writers, and the reading public played its role as the tribunal of public opinion."

Grafton, Anthony. *Defenders of the Text: The Tradition of Scholarship in the Age of Science, 1450–1800.* Cambridge, MA: Harvard U. Press, 1991. Pp. 330; bibliography.

Rev. (favorably) by C. W. Clark in *Choice*, 29 (1991), 334; (favorably) by Oswan Murray in *TLS*, (Aug. 16, 1991), 5.

Graham, Elspeth, Hilary Hinds, Elaine Hobby, and Helen Wilcox (eds.). *Her Own Life: Autobiographical Writings by Seventeenth-Century Englishwomen.* London and New York: Routledge, 1989. Pp. 250; bibliography. Cf. *ECCB*, n.s. 16, V:276; 15, V:211.

Rev. by Shannon Murray in *English Language Notes*, 29 (1991), 97–98.

Graham, Kenneth W. (ed.). *Gothic Fictions: Prohibition/Transgression.* New York: AMS Press, 1989. Pp. xviii + 292; plates. Cf. *ECCB*, n.s. 15, V:211.

Rev. (with another work) by David Richter in *Modern Language Review*, 86 (1991), 174–77.

Green, Katherine Sobba. *The Courtship Novel, 1740–1820: A Feminized Genre.* Lexington, KY: U. Press of Kentucky, 1991. Pp. vii + 184; frontispiece.

Rev. (with reservations) by D. Landry in *Choice*, 29 (1991), 94.

Greer, Margaret Rich. *The Play of Power: Mythological Court Dramas of Calderón de la Barca.* Princeton, NJ: Princeton U. Press, 1991. Pp. xii + 256; bibliography; illustrations; plates (one colored).

Guibert, Noëlle, and Jacqueline Razgonnikoff. *Le Journal de la Comédie Française 1789–1799. La Comédie Française aux trois couleurs*. Paris: Sides Emprientes, 1989. Pp. 336; 160 illustrations.

Rev. (favorably) by Rose Marie Moudouès in *Revue d'histoire de théâtre*, 43 (1991), 378.

Guilhamet, Leon. *Satire and the Transformation of Genre*. Philadelphia, PA: U. of Pennsylvania Press, 1989. Pp. xii + 200. Cf. *ECCB*, n.s. 16, V:278; 15, V:213; 14, V:217; 13, V:307.

Rev. by Edward A. Bloom in *Eighteenth-Century Studies*, 24 (1991), 512–16.

Haggerty, George E. *Gothic Fiction/Gothic Form*. London and University Park, PA: Pennsylvania State U. Press, 1989. Pp. xii + 194. Cf. *ECCB*, n.s. 16, V:278; 15, V:213–14.

Rev. (with another work) by David Richter in *Modern Language Review*, 86 (1991), 174–77.

Hagstrum, Jean H. *Eros and Vision: The Restoration to Romanticism*. Evanston, IL: Northwestern U. Press, 1989. Pp. xx + 290; 26 illustrations. Cf. *ECCB*, n.s. 16, V:278; 15, V:214–15.

Rev. by G. S. Rousseau in *The Scriblerian*, 23 (1991), 231–33; (with another work) by Fiona J. Stafford in *Review of English Studies*, 42 (1991), 266–69.

Hall, Dennis R. "A Sign of the Human Condition: George Campbell on Grammatical Purity." *English Language Notes*, 28 (1991), 16–22.

For Campbell grammar is an emblem of purity and a mark of humanity.

Hamilton, Alexander. *The History of the Ancient and Honorable Tuesday Club*. Edited by Robert Micklus. 3 vols. Chapel Hill, NC, and London: U. of North Carolina Press for the Institute of Early American History and Culture, Williamsburg, VA, 1990. Pp. cv + 444; illustrations; musical examples: ix + 423: viii + 421; appendices; illustrations; musical examples.

Rev. (with reservations) by A. W. Masters in *TLS*, (April 21, 1991), 28.

Handler, Richard, and Daniel Segal. *Jane Austen and the Fiction of Culture: An Essay on the Narration of Social Realities*. (The Anthropology of Form and Meaning.) Tucson, AZ: U. of Arizona Press, 1990. Pp. x + 175.

Rev. by T. Loe in *Choice*, 28 (1991), 1130.

Hardin, James (ed.). *Reflection and Action: Essays on the Bildungsroman*. Columbia, SC: U. of South Carolina Press, 1991. Pp. xxvii + 504; bibliography.

Hardin, James, and Christopher E. Schweitzer (eds.). *German Writers in the Age of Goethe, 1789–1832*. (Dictionary of Literary Biography, 90.) Detriot, MI, and London: Gale Research, 1989. Pp. xi + 435; illustrations. Cf. *ECCB*, n.s. 15, V:215.

Rev. by Valerie R. Hotchkiss in *American Reference Books Annual*, 22 (1991), 1235.

Hardin, James, and Christopher E. Schweitzer (eds.). *German Writers from the Enlightenment to Strum und Drang, 1720–1764.* (Dictionary of Literary Biography, 97.) Detriot, MI, and London: Gale Research, 1990. Pp. x + 399; illustrations.

Rev. (favorably) by J. H. Spohrer in *Choice*, 28 (1991), 913.

Hare, A., and D. Thomas (eds.). *Restoration and Georgian England, 1660-1788.* (Theatre in Europe: A Documentary History.) Cambridge and New York: Cambridge U. Press, 1989. Pp. xxx + 460.

Rev. by William J. Burling in the *Scriblerian*, 24 (1991), 78–79; by David Roberts in *Notes and Queries*, 236 (1991), 110–11.

Hayes, Julie Candler. *Identity and Ideology: Diderot, Sade and the Serious Genre.* West Lafayette, IN: Purdue U. Press, 1991. Pp. xiv + 186.

With this work, Hayes seeks to correct longstanding critical neglect of the serious genre, reframing traditional definitions of the form frequently known as the *drame bourgeois* and proposing a new understanding of its significance in terms of its "fusion of social reality and contemporary philosophy in a particular concept of the self." Her study offers a working theory of the *drame* and an examination of two important writers within the context of that theory, along with a substantial bibliography, an appendix of plot summaries, and an index.

Hayes establishes her theoretical bases in her first chapter, "Of Sensibility and Sociability," beginning with the influence of empiricism, sensationalism, and sensibility on the notion of self presented in the *drame*. Drawing on the work of social historians, her investigation of genre reveals, not a portrayal of the individual autonomy habitually associated with the rise of the bourgeoisie, but a definition of identity in terms of the individual's place in the social network. Politically, this relational identity is seen to represent the importation not the domestic setting of the marketplace structure of exchange and interdependency characteristic of the bourgeois public sphere; aesthetically, a spatialization of identity is motivated by the search for a new approach to dramatic characterization on the part of post-Molière playwrights, exemplified by La Chaussée and Graffigny.

Devoting her second chapter to Diderot, Hayes examines his innovative characterization by *condition* and his substitution of the *tableau* for the *coup de théâtre* as manifestations of a theater based on absorption of the individual into the familial and social structure. Here, consideration of the importance of *rapports* in his other works, as well as discussion of the probelmatical nature both of the authority of the fathers in his plays and of his own "paternal" authority as writer and theoretician, support Hayes's contention that his dramatic works are to be seen "not as an aberration among the author's total output, but . . . as partaking of the same structures and concerns that characterize the 'mainstream' works."

In chapter four, Hayes likewise argues for the close links between Sade's theater and his other writings. In Sade's *drames*, as in Diderot's, family relationships are central, but Sade blurs rather than clarifies those relationships, undermining any harmonious social integration by allowing structures of incest and parricide to dominate. Characterized by obsessive observation yet perversion of the genre's conventions, Sade's is "the move that brings the system down."

Chapter three, positioned between the discussion of literary paternity and patricide, explores the ideology of "The Equivocal Genre," whose attempt to replace the old regime of comedy and tragedy was emblematic of its potential for subversion of the social order. Hayes proceeds here by analyzing, not the plays themselves, but contemporary critical reaction to them. While these are revealing, this approach sheds only indirect light on the works of the genre's other practitioners, which must also be examined to verify her theory. Still, Hayes's book not only contributes to Diderot and Sade scholarship, but demonstrates that further study of the serious genre is warranted and that such study can refine our understanding of the French Enlightenment.—Bonnie Robb.

Herman, Jan. *Le Mensonge romanesque: Paramètres pour l'étude du roman épistolaire en France*. (Faux-Titre, 40.) Amsterdam: Rodopi; Leuven, Belgium: Leuven U. Press, 1989. Pp. 245. Cf. *ECCB*, n.s. 16, V:281; 15, V:216.

Rev. by Regina Bochenek-Franczakowa in *Studi francesi*, 34 (1991), 522; by Ronald C. Rosbottom in *Modern Language Review*, 86 (1991), 718–19.

Herr, Mireille. *Les Tragédies bibliques au XVIIIᵉ Siécle*. Paris and Geneva: Champion-Slatkine, 1988. Pp. 268; appendices; bibliography; indices. Cf. *ECCB*, n.s. 15, V:216; 14, III:117.

Rev. (with reservations) by Guillaume Robichez in *Revue d'histoire littéraire de la France*, 91 (1991), 252.

Hill, Geoffrey. *The Enemy's Country: Words, Contexture and Other Circumstances of Language*. (Clark Lectures, 1986.) New York: Oxford U. Press; Oxford: Clarendon Press; Stanford, CA: Stanford U. Press, 1991. Pp. xiv + 153.

Rev. (with another work) by Donald Davie in *TLS*, (Dec. 27, 1991), 6–7.

Hinnant, Charles H. "Song and Speech in Anne Finch's *To the Nightingale*." *Studies in English Literature, 1500–1900*, 31 (1991), 499–513.

The speaker's inability to achieve "spontaneity" revises the "triumphalist assumptions" of earlier poets but does not anticipate Romantic transformation. The poem transcends generic limitations of gender.

Hohendahl, Peter Uwe. *A History of German Literary Criticism, 1730–1980*. (Modern German Culture and Literature.) Lincoln, NE and London: U. of Nebraska Press, 1988. Pp. viii + 479. Cf. *ECCB*, n.s. 16, V:282.

Rev. (favorably) by Steve Giles in *Modern Language Review*, 86 (1991), 801–03.

Howells, Robin. "Structure and Meaning in the *Incipit* of Marivaux's Comedies." *Modern Language Review*, 86 (1991), 839–51.

The first two scenes in each of the 35 extant comedies prepare for the play that followed it: "The Duo; Distinction and Commonality; Project or Test; Disguise or Trick; Metadiscourse."

Howland, John W. *The Letter Form and the French Enlightenment: The Epistolary Paradox*. (American University Studies, Series II: Romance Languages and Literature, 126.) Frankfurt am Main and New York: Peter Lang, 1991. Pp. vi + 192; bibliography.

Interest in writing and reading letters developed in France in the eighteenth century. Private correspondences began to be published and fictitious ones soon followed. By the time of the Revolution, "almost any kind of prose composition can be found in epistolary form." While much has been written on the literary uses of the letters, it has mostly been limited to the study of its novelistic applications. By studying all letters, the author hopes to contribute to a better understanding of "the forces at work in the intellectual culture" of the French Enlightenment and "achieve a more comprehensive view of how the letter functions as a prose form."

After a brief history of the letter (from Cicero on) he deals with the striking popularity of the letter form in eighteenth-century France, and why it should be so specific to the period. The Enlightenment, although fascinated by the individual is especially intrigued by what the individual has in common with his peers. And there is no better way for the individual to share his thoughts and feelings, express the uniqueness of his character, and at the same time emphasize the link between him and other men, than through a letter, as it invited a response and suggests exchange.

He distinguishes three dominant, and not exclusive, categories of missives. The "letter from abroad" reflects the new mobility of the French, their curiosity for exploring foreign lands, and their willingness to share their observations with those left behind. The contemporary reader is asked to adopt a new perspective in relation to the conventions with which he is familiar, an undertaking very destabilizing to established authority. The "philosophical letter" is a report on its author's search for the causes of something he has observed, the expression of his desire to be useful. But the most widespread use of the epistolary form, the most typical of the period, is in the novel. Although fiction is almost never called *roman*, it flourished as never before, with its new ambition to express an individual's vision of reality, to show his most confidential and intimate behavior, his most secret motivations, his most subtle emotions. The personal letter seems the perfect tool for such an endeavor, and many of the period's most popular fictions are *romans par lettres*.

At the same time, "paradox and contradiction are the hallmarks of the use of the form in eighteenth-century France." Letter writers can manipulate their readers and mold public opinion. It soon became obvious that most of the letters from abroad were not composed by travelers, that philosophical ones were sometimes "just as dogmatically authoritarian as the self-proclaimed truths they criticize," and that letters in the novel, far from being accurate insight into the soul, could disguise their sender's ulterior motives. These paradoxes happen also to be those of the Enlightenment whose utopian dreams could not be fulfilled by reality.

On the whole, John W. Howland is successful in carrying out his stated objectives, and *dix-huitièmistes* should find in his book an instructive read.—Claude Roquin.

Hühn, Peter. "Outwitting Self-Consciousness: Self-Reference and Paradox in Three Romantic Poems." *English Studies: A Journal of English Language and Literature* (Lisse, Netherlands), 72 (1991), 230–45.

Hunt, Lynn (ed.). *Eroticism and the Body Politic*. (Parallax: Re-visions of Culture and Society.) Baltimore, MD, and London: Johns Hopkins U. Press, 1991. Pp. 242; illustrations.

Hunter, J. Paul. *Before Novels: The Cultural Contexts of Eighteenth-Century English Fiction*. New York: W. W. Norton, 1990. Pp. xxiv + 421; bibliography. Cf. *ECCB*, n.s. 16, V:282–83.

Rev. (favorably) by P. D. McGlynn in *Choice*, 28 (1991), 1485; (with reservations) by Maximillian E. Novak in *TLS*, (Jan. 25, 1991), 8; (with another work) by Alexander Pettit in *Modern Language Quarterly*, 52 (1991), 210–15; by Philip Stevick in *The Scriblerian*, 24 (1991), 52–54.

Ingram, Allan. *The Madhouse of Language: Writing and Reading Madness in the Eighteenth Century*. London and New York: Routledge, 1991. Pp. vi + 206; bibliography.

This pleasant, well-written monograph deals chiefly with language—the language of psychiatrists, the language of nonprofessional writers about madness, and most importantly, the language of mad people themselves. Embroidering this central theme is a history of what passed for psychiatry in the eighteenth century. Allan Ingram has read widely and well. He gently takes the reader through the observations of Willis and Sydenham at the time of the Restoration into the explosion of literature about madness (chiefly melancholia) after 1700, citing Sir Richard Blackmore, Nicholas Robinson, George Cheyne, et al., even taking the reader down to 1792 when John Birch applied electric shock therapy to the heads of his patients.

Ingram is on target in the controversy between William Battie who was the first physician at St. Luke's Hospital for Lunaticks and whose principles of treatment were in direct opposition to those of the Monro family who manages Bethlehem Hosptial. Battie's *Treatise on Madness* (1758) is the key text for mid eighteenth-century psychiatry, a major step in the humane treatment of the confined. Ingram's exposition is sensitive to the nuances and ramifications of the controversy. Yet Battie provides no case histories, nor does he deal directly with the language used by his patients.

Ingram is most effective when he deals with the literature produced by patients suffering from mental disorders. He quotes Thomas Gray's letter to Richard West in which Gray proposes the term "leucocholy" to describe his own situation, and he presents briefly such familiar "mad poets" as Collins, Cowper, Smart, and James Carkesse, and even William Blake. His comment on Blake merits citation: "Blake's work represents madness canonised: alternative arrangements that are no longer regarded as alternative." It is a fitting epitaph on the frustrations and oppression experienced by the mad in the course of endlessly renewed engagements with conventional perceptions of insanity and conventional forms of the English language.

But Ingram's range is not encyclopedic. He fails to mention Anne Finch, Countess of Winchilsea, whose poem *The Spleen. A Pindaric Poem* (published anonymously in 1701, then under the author's name in 1709) contains not only a fine description of her symptoms but also the important couplet:

The Cause indeed is a defect in Sense;
But still the Spleen's alleged, and still the dull pretense.

Nor does he mention William Stukeley's Gulstonian lecture of 1722 *Of the Spleen, &c.* The only allusion to Samuel Johnson gives his *Dictionary* definition of "rave" and a passing allusion to his astronomer in *Rasselas*. Yet Johnson's own melancholia and his response to it in his writings are a mine of information about the use of language in relation to madness. Ingram does cite Boswell's episodic melancholia as revealed in his letters to his friend William Temple, but he does not explore several relevant essays in Boswell's column written under the pseudonym The Hypochondriack that appeared in *The London Magazine* from 1777 to 1783. Inclusion of these, especially Johnson and Boswell, would have enriched the book.— William B. Ober, M.D.

Jack, Malcolm. *Corruption & Progress: The Eighteenth-Century Debate.* New York: AMS Press, 1989. Pp. xii + 240.

Rev. (with another work) by M. M. Goldsmith in *The Scriblerian*, 23 (1991), 251–54.

Janowitz, Anne. *England's Ruins: Poetic Purpose and the National Landscape.* Cambridge, MA, and Oxford: Basil Blackwell, 1990. Pp. viii + 211. Cf. *ECCB*, n.s. 16, V:283–84.

Rev. (with reservations) by Philippa Tristram in *Notes and Queries*, 236 (1991), 269–70.

Jensen, Joan M. *Promise to the Land: Essays on Rural Women.* Albuquerque, NM: U. of New Mexico Press, 1991. Pp. xii + 319; illustrations.

With this collection, historian Joan M. Jensen delivers on her promise to show that "the lives of rural women were [and are] central to the development of American history" (xi). Jensen interweaves "staunchly academic" historical essays (xi) with family histories and biographical and autobiographical accounts to describe the experiences of ethnically diverse rural women from various regions of the United States. Jensen's discerning use of interdisciplinary methodologies uncovers the histories of women, from the seventeenth through the late twentieth century, largely ommitted from traditional historical records. While roughly half of the essays are available in other publications, the seventeen essays in this volume, taken together, present an original and eloquent argument for the diversity, the texture and the breadth of rural women's history. In her introduction, Jensen notes the desire of "women, on and off the farm" to discover "a usable past" (26). *Promise to the Land* provides a past that is eminently usable not only for the "broad public," for other rural historians and for rural development policymakers (the three audiences for whom, according to Jensen, rural historians write), but also, in more and less direct ways, for scholars of eighteenth-century American history and culture.

Describing her experience in communal farming in the early 1970s as the inciting incident for her research on farm women, and opening with an historical overview of the periods, issues, institutions, practices and women's lives which constitute the study, Jensen then divides her book into five parts: I) Autobiography and Biography; II)

Oral History, Iconography and Material Culture; III) Rural Development; IV) Rural Social Welfare; and V) Rural History. As these section titles suggest, the brilliance of Jensen's work lies in her skill in discovering various points of entry into histories made "invisible" (170) by a dearth of direct documentation and, then, in building from what begins as an extremely specific set of questions and conditions to be a complex account of broad social, political and economic patterns of change. This insistence upon the relationship between local specificity and larger historical processes operates within and among the essays in this volume. The art of plastering the fire-place building practiced by twentieth-century Hispanic women in New Mexico provides an opening, for instance, for Jensen's investigation of seventeenth-century Pueblo women's use of traditional building skills to construct churches at the behest of Spanish friars. Her essay "reimage[s] the lives of Pueblo women during the first century of Spanish contact . . . allow[ing] a sharper picture of these women as social agents to emerge" (72) within the context of the "*reconquista* tradition" of Christianizing, Hispanicizing and resettling indigenous peoples to make them more "like European workers" (118).

In her introduction, beginning with the eighteenth century, Jensen delineates the historical evolution of differences in property rights and access to power and familial wealth among rural women, as determined by geographical location, class position, ethnicity and economic or marital status. Native American women and women living under the rule of French and Spanish law in the western regions, she points out, had significantly more control of the land than did eastern women, until Anglo-American common law came to dominate the western states. In this essay, Jensen also explores the changing conditions created by the institutions which determined the forms of eighteenth-century women's labor: marriage, slavery, indenture, and tenancy. Thus, while the majority of Jensen's essays focus primarily on the nineteenth and twentieth centuries, her approach is, from the outset, to trace the conditions within which women lived and worked over time in order to document and evaluate the shifting forces that have given shape to rural women's collective history.

Part II of the book provides the author's most detailed accounts of eighteenth-century rural women (for a more in-depth study of eighteenth-century rural women see Jensen's *Loosening the Bonds: Mid-Atlantic Farm Women, 1750–1850*. New Haven, CT: Yale U. Press, 1986). Exploring the ramifications of Euro-American colonization, Jensen begins by documenting the control of land and agriculture possessed by Seneca women prior to and during the eighteenth century in New York. She reveals the Quakers, along with other missionaries, to have aided the U.S. government's imperialist project, by "retraining" Seneca men and women according to the Euro-American gender division of labor. These missionaries, male and female, were instrumental in dismantling the matrilineal mode of agricultural production at the center of Seneca economy and culture; yet, citing records of Seneca women's active political role as tribal representatives well into the nineteenth century, Jensen makes clear these women's determination to defend their traditional relation to the land and to tribal governance. The volume and variety of work, responsibilities and skills of enslaved African American women, are detailed in a chapter recounting the life's work of Rachel Burke in nineteenth-century Maryland. Along with a brief, but informative, discussion of enslaved black workers in the eighteenth century, Jensen's description of enslaved black women's lives and labor in the early nineteenth century serves as an important model and a point of comparison for future investigations of eighteenth-century African American women's history. Jensen's ground-breaking essays, "Butter Making and Economic Development on Mid-Atlantic America, 1750–1850" and "Cloth, Butter, and Boarders: Women's Household Production for the Market" show that the study of "specific agricultural tasks performed by women" yield sources for documenting women's work, and, also provide proof of the crucial role played by rural women in the transition from a subsistence economy to a market economy between 1750 and 1850 (170).

Having established the range, significance and wealth of materials available for the study of rural women's history, Jensen closes her collection by suggesting an exciting (and somewhat overwhelming) array of questions posed by recent scholarship that remain to be answered—including numerous avenues of research open to eighteenth-century scholars. Arming us with questions to answer and historical and scholarly sources to consult, Jensen sends us off to continue the work for which she has so expansively prepared the way.—Kristie Hamilton.

John, David G. *The German "Nachspiel" in the Eighteenth Century*. Buffalo, NY, and Toronto: U. of Toronto Press, 1991. Pp. xii + 412; appendices; bibliography.

Conventional scholarship that delineates the evolution of eighteenth-century German dramatic presentation usually promotes the following considerations: transitions in performance ". . . from itinerant groups to permanent theatres; from extemporized performance to controlled acting; from improvised scenario to text-based drama; [and] from unrestricted expression to censorship and control" (290). David G. John supports these general features with his comprehensive analysis into the art of *Nachspiel* (literally "afterpiece," a shorter show following a longer performance). Recognizing that the *Nachspiel* largely remains a neglected theatrical expression in scholarship, similar to an absence of studies into the "satyr plays" of the Ancient Greek stage, John nevertheless contends that the establishment and growth of the *Nachspiel* illustrate well the overall nature of German drama during the eighteenth century.

In presenting the grand scope of *Nachspiel* expression, John provides a useful annotated bibliography of theatrical activity in selective cities (Berlin, Frankfurt am Main, Gotha, Hamburg, Munich, Vienna, and Weiman); actors and managers (Caroline Johann Friedrich Schönemann, and Konrad Ernst Ackermann); and recognizable performance traditions (Italian *commedia dell'arte* and German stock characters) that contribute to the *Nachspiel* stage. John supplements his historiography by including three previously unpublished *Nachspiel* (*Der falsche Verdacht, Das lustige Elendt*, and *Die Bauern*).

After developing historical and textual features, John's study turns largely positivistic, as he categorizes 114 *Nachspiel* into six recognizable groups: *Nachspiel* based on French or foreign models; *Nachspiel* in 2–3 acts; *Nachspiel* connected to a previous work; *Nachspiel* with song, music, and dance; *Nachspiel* with traditional comic elements; and *Nachspiel* with serious thematics or social criticism. John adopts this approach to reach a practical definition of the *Nachspiel* during the eighteenth century. He argues that *Nachspiels* before 1770 generally feature one central comic figure, improvisation beyond the text, connections to a previous work, and entertainment over serious presentation. After 1770, the genre no longer emphasizes one central comic character, although extemporized comedy remains, no longer depends upon a previous work, and no longer excludes serious themes. John marks the year 1770 as the period when *Nachspiel* become more literary than during previous decades and when standing theatres surpass in importance the stages of traveling troupe performance.

The changing venues carry a challenge to the traditional expression of *Nachspiel* by redirecting the extemporization into more standard acting techniques. Managers and directors replace fragment scenarios with fixed texts to create greater harmony in acting. Unified acting techniques become a point of emphasis for both "elitist" practitioners and court officials: rules allow authority figures to exercise control over performers. In addition to the contributions of Johann Gottsched, Gotthold Lessing, and Konrad Ekhof, John explores the impact of Goethe on acting. As the first real director, *Regisseur*, of the German stage, Goethe codifies many theatre practices with the hand of an autocratic dictator who commands complete responsibility for the final stage work (233). Extemporization did continue; however, the *Nachspiel* at the end of the eighteenth century begins to emphasize standard acting techniques.

Nachspiel in the late-eighteenth century exhibit the Enlightened *Zeitgeist*, or tenets of the intellectual "spirit of the times," as the genre becomes principally a vehicle for social commentary, criticism, and education (235) over its traditional use as an instrument for entertainment. After this transition, government censorship presses *Nachspiel* into reform. John presents an engaging example of the piece *Die Martinsgänse*, with censor and director deletions and additions. This example immediately leads one to recognize that an author's intent often succumbs to the regulations of local government. John's analysis reminds readers that published texts reveal only part of the dramatic experience from past centuries. Readers must discern between the author's original message and authority's mandidated reforms.

This book's value is clearly its status as perhaps the only study to offer a comprehensive analysis of the *Nachspiel* as independent genre. Beyond this consideration, John's work additionally assumes multiple functions: theatre history, source of primary texts, textual analysis, social and culture history, and genre theory. The appendices also provide a valuable collection of 136 *Nachspiel* titles, with document information and plot summaries, and a general historiography of performance activities. A significant result of John's choice of adopting various strategies and approaches is an informative, engaging, and lucid presentation of many aspects of the eighteenth-century *Nachspiel*. John's analysis does not redirect the traditional presentation of eighteenth-century theatre; his study does reintroduce the expression of *Nachspiel* as a popular and pervasive albeit overlooked art form of the German stage.—Gregory J. Dykhouse.

Jones, Vivien (ed.). *Women in the Eighteenth Century: Constructions of Femininity*. (World and Word Series.) London and New York: Routledge, 1990. Pp. xii + 258. Cf. *ECCB*, n.s. 16, V:284–85.

Rev. (favorably) by Kathy Howlett in *The Scriblerian*, 24 (1991), 73–74; by April London in *Review of English Studies*, 42 (1991), 611–12.

Kafker, Frank A., with Serena L. Kafker. *The Encyclopedists as Individuals: A Biographical Dictionary of the Authors of the* Encyclopédie. (Studies on Voltaire and the Eighteenth Century, 257.) Oxford: The Voltiare Foundation at the Taylor Institution, 1988. Pp. xxx + 430. Cf. *ECCB*, n.s. 16, V:285; 14, V:221–22.

Rev. by Peter Jimack in *Modern Language Review*, 86 (1991), 458–59; (favorably) by John Pappas in *Revue d'histoire littéraire de la France*, 91 (1991), 100–01; (briefly) by Paolo Alatri in *Studi francesi*, 34 (1990), 142.

Kahn, Madeleine. *Narrative Transvestism: Rhetoric and Gender in the Eighteenth-Century Novel*. Ithaca, NY, and London: Cornell U. Press, 1991. Pp. 172; bibliography.

In her book, Madeleine Kahn develops her theory of "narrative transvestism," defined as a "process whereby a male author gains access to a culturally defined female voice and sensibility but runs no risk of being trapped in the devalued female realm. Through narrative transvestism the male author plays out, in the metaphorical body of the text, the ambiguous possibilities of identity and gender" (p. 6). Kahn contends that these "ambiguous possibilities" are central concerns of the novel, for she reads the novel not only as an expression of its author's identity, but also as a narrative about the creation of that identity. Early eighteenth-century England, she argues, saw the destabilization of "an entire binary epistemological structure" (male/female, author/reader, reality/fiction); amidst the period's yearning for a return to the balance and stability of binarism, "the novel emerged as a form designed for the exploration of the undefined realm between the poles" (p. 159). Narrative transvestism does for the male author what cross-dressing does for the transvestite: it reasserts his masculinity. By transgressing the binary oppositions of gender, male authors create "a coherent narrative self" (p. 151).

  The bulk of Kahn's book presents, as illustrations of her theory, close readings of two novels, Defoe's *Roxana* and Richardson's *Clarissa*. Interpreting *Roxana* as the "authorial story of creation" (p. 102), Kahn examines how Defoe exploits the female voice in order to create his own masculine, textual authority. Roxana's attempts to become a "Man-Woman" mirror Defoe's own narrative transvestism; the close relationship between identity and narrative can be seen in the threat posed by Roxana's daughter, Susan. Susan's insistence on defining Roxana within the clearly feminine role of "mother" puts a stop to Roxana's narrative. In reading *Clarissa*, Kahn discusses the assortment of authors, readers, impersonators, and editors—both within the novel and outside it—involved in Richardson's masculine appropriation of the female voice. For Clarissa, as for Roxana, being female means being silent, being a mere body (or body of text) subject to masculine intervention and interpretation. Kahn's concluding chapter briefly discusses why Cleland's *Fanny Hill* ought to be excluded from the category of transvestite narrative.

  Kahn's method is theoretically diverse; as her authorities, she cites Freud, Havelock Ellis, Bakhtin, Foucault, Thomas Laquer, Ian Watt, Michael McKeon, Christopher Hill, Lawrence Stone, and Stephen Greenblatt, to name a few. Her own close readings, however, hail unmistakingly from the school of reader-response; so, for example, we are told: "because Defoe isn't an obviously ironic metanarrative presence, we lose track of him. We see only the narrator creating—more of less convincingly—the tale, not the author creating both narrator and tale"

(p. 62). In a similar universalist vein, Kahn regularly indulges in pronouncements about the nature of literary endeavor that are at best problematic, e.g. "one becomes an author, and in particular an author of fiction, because one can imaginatively create through language a more passionate, more expressive, more vivid and more enduring self than by any other means" (p. 57). Equally bothersome, her argumentation is not always convincing. The importance of binary oppositions to her model occasionally causes her to invent them where they cannot be found (e.g., her discussion of foolish marriages and old maids, p.81), and her readings are sometimes forced. For example, because Clarissa describes being deprived of pen and ink as an "act of violence," Kahn puzzlingly concludes, "Clarissa rightly sees this as a violation of her body" (p. 139). Still, taken overall, Kahn's work furthers a valuable discussion about the role played by gender in narrative authority and literary history.—Wendy Motooka.

Kamuf, Peggy. *Signature Pieces: On the Institution of Authorship*. Ithaca, NY, and London: Cornell U. Press, 1988. Pp. 237.

Rev. by James F. Jones, Jr. in *Eighteenth-Century Studies*, 24 (1991), 373–75.

Kay, Carol. *Political Construction: Defoe, Richardson, & Sterne in Relation to Hobbes, Hume & Burke*. Ithaca, NY, and London: Cornell U. Press, 1988. Pp. xiv + 286. Cf. *ECCB*, n.s. 16, V:285; 15, V:221; 14, V:222–23.

Rev. by John Mullan in *Journal of English and Germanic Philology*, 90 (1991), 427–30; (with another work) by John Richetti in *Modern Language Review*, 86 (1991), 396–98.

King, John N. with assistance from Robin Smith. "Recent Studies in Protestant Poetics." *English Literary Renaissance*, 21 (1991), 283–307.

Kittel, Harald. "Revolutionäre Formen perspektivischen Erzählens in einem quasi-autobiographischen Ich-Roman: William Godwin's *Caleb Williams*." Pp. 34–53 of *Frühe Formen mehrperspektivischen Erzählens von der Edda bis Flaubert*. Edited by Armin Paul Frank, and Ulrich Mölk. Berlin: E. Schmidt, 1991. Pp. ix + 166.

Klein, J. "Mathematics of Desire: On the Meaning of Darker Movements in English Eighteenth-Century Literature and the Fine Arts." Pp. 210–293 of *Erotica and the Enlightenment*. Edited by P. Wagner. Frankfurt am Main and New York: Peter Lang, 1991. Pp. 368; illustrations.

Kohl, S. "Kulturtypologie und englischer Barock: Zur Rechtfertigung eines Epochenbegriffs." Pp. 981–94 of *Europäische Barock-Rezeption. Wolfenbütteler Arbeiten zur Barockforschung 20, Teil 2*. Edited by K. Garber. Wiesbaden: Harrassowitz, 1991. Pp. xiv + 1365; illustrations.

Korshin, Paul J. (ed.). *The Age of Johnson: A Scholarly Annual*. Vol. IV. New York: AMS Press, 1991. Pp. xv + 493.

Kowaleski-Wallace, Elizabeth. *Their Fathers' Daughters: Hannah More, Maria Edgeworth, and Patriarchal Complicity*. New York and Oxford: Oxford U. Press, 1991. Pp. xi + 235; bibliography.

See *Edgeworth* in sec. 6 for review.

Kroll, Richard W. F. *The Material Word: Literate Culture in the Restoration and Early Eighteenth Century*. Baltimore, MD, and London: Johns Hopkins U. Press, 1991. Pp. xxii + 420.

Rev. (favorably) by Alfred Lutz in *English Language Notes*, 29 (1991), 88–90.

Scholars of epistemology and language in the England of the seventeenth and eighteenth centuries have been (mis)led, especially by the pioneering work of R. F. Jones, to believe that an earlier, essentially superstitious methodology yielded to one based on a *plain style* that aimed at an immediacy between scientific observer and the observed. Richard Kroll sets out to revise that interpretation by demonstrating that contemporary philosophers of language, epistemology, politics, and "science" in its broadest sense made no such claim, but instead treated knowledge as something mediated through conventional signs, negotiated, provisional. Kroll insists on the preciseness of the term *neoclassical*, for he sees as the methodological paradigm during this period a revised and revitalized neo-Epicureanism, formulated especially by Gassendi (in opposition to the rationalism of Descartes), absorbed by English thinkers in exile in Paris during the Interregnum, and developed by their successors both in and out of the Royal Society. To me the most exciting aspect of his thesis is Kroll's argument concerning the political consequences of this neoclassical methodology: contrary to received opinion, politics do not determine method nor vice versa; thinkers of different political persuasions often adopt this essentially skeptical, hypothetical method which is employed to discredit extremists both on the far right (Catholics, monarchists) and on the far left (Dissenters, Levellers).

At the same time, Kroll really *does* acknowledge specific political connections: the discursive method he described mystifies its deployment as the hegemonic discourse of an apparent centrist position; rationalism and earlier scholasticism are discredited as supporting the absolutism of tyranny or the anarchy of radicalism. Nicely dissecting Dryden's "Epistle to Dr. Charleton," Kroll admits that "the rhetoric of moderation is a form of mystification, because to exclude Aristotle is to make an exception fatal to the claims of moderation, and Dryden becomes as much of a tyrant as is 'Aristotle,' a wielder of centralized power. . . . Dryden's poem asserts its own cultural superiority to other texts embodying different epistemological and social motives, and that it seeks to silence" (p. 36).

Ironically, the same thing can be said of Kroll's own reading of "Absalom and Achitophel" (Chapter 9). In a book arguing with obvious sympathy for a contingent methodology, one that yields not absolute truth but arguments of probability, Kroll begins this reading with the exclusionary and therefore academically if not culturally superior stance that "few of Dryden's modern critics have grasped *the* significance of *Absalom and Achitophel*'s ending" (p. 306, emphasis mine). Interestingly, Kroll omits reference to interpretations of the poem's ending as rhetorical (especially Dustin Griffin's well-known piece and Michael Conlon's 1989 follow-up to the earlier piece cited by Kroll) and to readings exploring the poem's ambiguity (especially those by Ruth Salvaggio, Michael McKeon, and me). These silences imply a superiority in an only apparently contested arena. Some possible contenders were not invited.

Kroll's stance in this last chapter underscores another problem with the book. Its own method seeks its legitimation not from other literary scholars—indeed, a good deal of the history of neoclassical criticism, from the influence of the French doctrine of rules to Pope's great synthesis in "An Essay on Criticism," is omitted from his otherwise provocative reading of that history in Chapter 8—but from historians of science, epistemology, political theory, and language. Thus Kroll attempts to ground his study in endless footnotes, which often interrupt sentences and which carry on a sub-textual argument with those scholars. The material of this *Material Word* is abstruse enough, without the annoyance of constant interruption, often for what proves to be digressive.

My criticisms notwithstanding, Kroll's book is an excellent example of the new history of ideas which has been transformed by cultural studies. Kroll cites such influential thinkers as Foucault, Kuhn, Derrida, and Geertz. Volosinov, Bakhtin, Raymond Williams, and the American new historicists also appear to have been silently influential. Kroll has ably and amply demonstrated that the neoclassical skeptical method is related to our modern conception of the social construction of language and meaning.—J. Douglas Canfield.

Landry, Donna. *The Muses of Resistance: Laboring-Class Women's Poetry in Britain, 1739–1796*. Cambridge and New York: Cambridge U. Press, 1990. Pp. ix + 325; bibliography; illustrations.

Rev. by Chris Baldick in *TLS*, (Feb. 22, 1991), 8; (with reservations) by K. P. Mulcahy in *Choice*, 28 (1991), 1486.

Langbauer, Laurie. *Women and Romance: The Consolations of Gender in the English Novel*. (Reading Women's Writing.) Ithaca, NY, and London: Cornell U. Press, 1990. Pp. xii + 271; bibliography. Cf. *ECCB*, n.s. 16, V:289.

Rev. (with reservations) by S. A. Parker in *Choice*, 28 (1991), 1639–40.

Larson, Catherine. *Language and the Comedia: Theory and Practice*. Lewisburg: Bucknell U. Press; London and Toronto: Associated U. Presses, 1991. Pp. 181; bibliography.

L'Art du théâtre. Mélanges en hommage à Robert Garapon. Paris: Presses Universitaires de France, 1991. Pp. 448.

Includes the following articles on the eighteenth century: Guichemerre, Roger, "*La Princesse de Carizme* de Lesage: L'Adaption d'un conte persan au théâtre de la foire"; Coirault, Yves, "L'Affaire Quesnel à la manière de Racine (1720): " 'Ah' Que vois-je, Seigneur . . . ?"; Menant, Sylvain, "Le Comique dans ou *La Méchant* de Gresset"; Mortier, Roland, "Marivaux a ou 'la petite merveille.' Notes sur une satire littéraire."

Leacock, John. *The First Book of the American Chronicles of the Times, 1774–1775*. Edited by Carla Mulford. Newark, DE: U. of Delaware Press, 1987. Pp. 130. Cf. *ECCB*, n.s. 13, V:320.

Rev. (with another work) by Christopher Looby in *Modern Philology*, 88 (1990–91), 446–48.

Leerssen, Joseph Theodoor. *Mere Irish & Fíor-Ghael: Studies in the Idea of Irish Nationality, Its Development and Literary Expression Prior to the Nineteenth Century*. Amsterdam and Philadelphia, PA: John Benjamins, 1986. Pp. xvii + 535.

Rev. (favorably) in *The Scriblerian*, 24 (1991), 81–82.

Lepape, Pierre. *Diderot*. (Grandes Biographies Flammarion.) Paris: Flammarion, 1991. Pp. 448; plates.

This biography by the book critic of the Parisian *Le Monde* is strikingly different from André Billy's *Vie de Diderot* (1932; rev. ed. 1943) aimed at the same kind of reading public. Billy's Diderot is a cheerful raconteur, the toast of Parisian *salons*, kind to the point of naiveté. Lepape's revisionist portrayal, written in *fin de siècle*, introspective Paris, is not one of a happy *philosophe*. His Diderot is haunted by the specters of the Bastille and the dungeon of Vincennes, a fear that Lepape emphasizes by devoting his entire first chapter to Diderot's early imprisonment in Vincennes. Lepape also hastens to warn his readers that the generous *philosophe* is capable of playing dirty tricks on his friends (15). His apparent joviality conceals persistent doubts about his professed image as a profound thinker (157), and the famous crisis of 1758-59, with the desertion of his main collaborators on the *Encyclopédie*, reinforces this lack of self-esteem. Lepape's Diderot remains deeply torn between two worlds, the provincial Langres of his roots and his childhood, and Parisian *salon* society which never completely embraced him (143-44).

But Lepape can also show great sympathy for his subject. Diderot repeatedly comes out on top in comparisons with Voltaire and Rousseau: he is rated as sincerely eager to enlighten the masses, while Voltaire limits enlightenment to the upper classes for fear of social explosion, and Rousseau is far more interested in delving into his inner self than improving society (202). Lepape stresses that the recent celebration of the bicentennial of the French Revolution focussed rather unfairly on Voltaire's and Rousseau's utopias, ignoring Diderot's more complex but more realistic message (197-98).

Lepape's story of Diderot's twenty years of epic struggles to bring the *Encyclopédie* to fruition compels his reader's admiration. Out of nineteen chapters, ten are devoted wholly or in large part to the *Encyclopédie*, resulting, however, in scant attention given to Diderot's other work. Lepape's major emphasis also causes him to skip rather hastily over Diderot's early years in Paris, without mentioning, for instance, his three years of study at the University of Paris, an important element in the *philosophe*'s intellectual development.

The volume is marred by several unfortunate misspellings of proper names: Mme de Puisieux is repeatedly spelled as Puiseux, Bordeu as Brodeu, Mme Madin of *La Religieuse* as Nadin, and the physiocrat Quesnay becomes Quesnel. The month of Diderot's arrest is given as January instead of July, and the critical apparatus has been poorly handled.

While Arthur Wilson's impressive *Diderot* (1972) remains the most reliable reference source for serious research, Lepape's volume provides a useful and often entertaining introduction to the *philosophe*, from a contemporary French viewpoint.—Huguette Cohen.

Lessenich, Rolf P. *Aspects of English Preromanticism.* Köln: Böhlau, 1989. Pp. xii + 490.

Rev. (Severely and with another work) by Fiona J. Stafford in *Review of English Studies*, 42 (1991), 266–69.

Le Tourneur, Pierre. *Préface de Shakespeare, traduit de l'anglois.* Edited by Jacques Gury. (Textes littéraires francais, 379.) Geneva: Droz, 1990. Pp. 276; illustrations. Cf. *ECCB*, n.s. 16, V:291.

Rev. by J. Lough in *French Studies*, 45 (1991), 466–67.

Levi, Peter. *The Art of Poetry.* London and New Haven, CT: Yale U. Press, 1991. Pp. 336.

Levine, Joseph M. *The Battle of the Books: History and Literature in the Augustan Age.* Ithaca, NY, and London: Cornell U. Press, 1991. Pp. xv + 429; frontispiece; illustrations.

The outline of the story told in this book will be familiar to many readers, from their having read Swift's *Battle of the Books* with the usual notes about the participants and the issues. But there is considerably more to know about the debate between the ancients and the moderns around the turn of the eighteenth century, in which Swift's role becomes relatively small. Levine tells the story in detail, with a steady eye on what the participants understood—or did not understand—the "battle" to be about.

Levine discusses the debate in two parts, the debate over "Literature" and the debate over "History." There is some overlapping, as one might expect in a discussion of writers who didn't differentiate between these disciplines as we do, but at issue in both sections are competing sets of attitudes toward the materials one inherits from the past.

With respect to the literary texts, Levine describes how Willliam Temple came to write his "Essay upon Ancient and Modern Learning," publications that constituted the first skirmish. Temple and Wotton's assumptions about literature, like the titles of their essays, were more alike than different, but they disagreed over the quality of literary production that might be expected from their contemporaries. Temple, the "ancient," regarded literature to be imitative and doubted that his contemporaries could equal, let alone surpass their predecessors; Wotton, the "modern," optimistic that literature is cumulative, thought that he could see further than his ancestors by standing on their shoulders. The parties to the debate became aligned as wits and pedants, each group with its own culture, distinguished especially by whether they saw the values in Homer's epics to be timeless or contingent.

The complexities and paradoxes of the debate are revealed in the discussions of Alexander Pope and Richard Bentley, each of whom is the focus of two chapters. Levine frequently offers insightful guesses about Pope's frame of mind as the poet goes about translating Homer without much knowledge of Greek, or lifts a comment from Madame Dacier, or is forced to recognize that recovering certain aspects of Homer requires more than poetic intuition. Bentley is shown to have limitations, too, but Levine sees him less as the pedant of Pope's later *Dunciad* than as the admirable "Newton of classical philosophy" (p. 64). Later in life, however, when Bentley hurriedly applies his methods to a "modern" poem, Milton's *Paradise Lost*, Bentley does seem to be making a fool of himself. Where readers will be startled—as Pope would be—is at the end of the chapter on "Bentley's Milton," where Levine speculates that Bentley may have meant his comments on Milton ironically, that "we should perhaps be laughing with him!" It is difficult to accept but interesting to imagine that the arrogant Bentley was trying to provoke his enemies to use his own philosophical methods to find fault with his readings of Milton, in order to win from the ancients a "grudging admission that modern historical scholarship, however lowly and pedantic, was after all indispensable to the reading of a historical text" (pp. 262–63).

The second part of Levine's book, on history, begins with a chapter called "History and Theory." This is not a cerebral discussion of the instability of a text or the fiction-like qualities of historical narrative, but of the theory as it was understood around 1700. Levine tells the story of the writing of the first "modern" English histories, with considerable attention to John Horsley's *Britannia Romana* in 1731, as awareness was growing that the same complex issues were at stake with English texts as with Greek ones. Indeed, Levine concludes, before either side won the "battle of the books," the arguments were transformed so that the old quarrel disappeared.

The existence of this book is testimony that victory went to the moderns, for Levine's work exemplifies extensive, thoughtful and scrupulously documented use of source materials in the best philological tradition. Specialists will already know some of what they are being told about "the Augustan Age," but ideas about literature in this period—and the history of its history—have never been in sharper focus.—James R. Aubrey.

Lim, C. S. "A Postdating for OED from William Dodd's Beauties of Shakespeare (1752)." *Notes and Queries*, 239 (1991), 188–89.

Logé, Tanguy. "Baroque et classicisme: Le XVIIIe siècle face au Père Le Moyne." *Studi francesi*, 35 (1991), 25–34.

Explains why the epic of Father Pierre Le Moyne (1602–1671) entitled *Saint-Louis, ou la sainte couronne reconquise* (1653, new edition 1658 in the complete works 1671) was so popular in France in the eighteenth century.

Logé, Tanguy. "Le Théâtre comique sous le Consulat et l'Empire: Pour ou contr le rire." *Revue d'histoire du théâtre*, 43 (1991), 312–30.

Detailed study of plays once very popular but now almost forgotten which concluded: "Ainsi entrevoit-on, à la fin de l'Empire, des horizons nouveaux."

Londré, Felicia Hardison. *The History of World Theater*. Vol. II: *From the English Restoration to the Present*. New York: Continuum, 1991. Pp. xii + 644; bibliography; frontispiece; illustrations.

Felicia Londré states her aims clearly and usually achieves them. She says in her "Preface" that she is interested in "interconnecting elements," in theater's relationship to "politics, religion, economics, science, and sociocultural norms," in "audience demographics, the theatre's system of patronage or management, the physical facility, the intellectual context articulated by critics and theorists, and so on" (p. viii). She does well at placing seventeenth-and eighteenth-century theatrical activity (some 200 pages) in its historical context, though only specialized works dealing with particular times and places can do that thoroughly enough to make us feel we were there.

Writing a good history of the theater is almost impossible. If the result is readable, it is often criticized for not being sufficiently scholarly. If it is scholarly, it may be useful but unreadable. Londré was saddled with yet another problem: writing a work to complement Margot Berthold's *Weltgeschichte des Theaters* (1968, translated in

1972), the first 477 pages of which have just been reprinted as the companion volume to Londré's work. So Londré had to include the English court theater of Indigo Jones, the Restoration, and new coverage of the eighteenth century and later, but not the seventeenth-century continental theater. The result is an odd compilation which cannot stand alone, that may rule out its use in theater history courses, the justification for most such publications. There is a large market for texts: at least ten came out during the 1980s.

There are several kinds of theater histories: comprehensive, fact-laden works such as Oscar Brockett's—now in its sixth edition, the standard for advanced theater history courses, and a very useful reference work; or surveys like Phyllis Hartnoll's (not her *Oxford Companion* but the inexpensive *Theatre, A Concise History*)—uncluttered with factual details, illustrated in black-and-white and color, and aimed at the layman or survey courses in the arts; or such handsome coffee table volumes as that by Robin May—non-scholarly, and not designed for academic use, illustrated with historical pictures and colorful photographs of current productions. Londré's work is an account of the first kind, but has some characteristics of the other two.

Londré's book is smoothly written in those parts where it goes into some depth, but it bogs down, as so many histories do, when it dutifully provides shopping lists of names, dates, and places of secondary importance. It has an extensive bibliography, but many primary source quotations in the text are not documented. It is well illustrated, but many pictures are small, and, as in most scholarly histories, there is no color. Londré seems most comfortable dealing with material that is alive and well–with play texts and theaters still standing–and less confortable with performers of the past. Her volume sometimes is best as a history of dramatic literature; quotations of plays are rare, but Londré is good at recounting plots, just as she is good at summarizing periods. She gives good coverage to women in the theater (Mlle Guimard and her private theater, ignored in most histories, is a fine example), but Asian coverage is restricted to contemporary theater, since, again, Berthold has already covered the ground.

There are some mixed-bag paragraphs (see pp. 58, 73, and 180 for examples). And occasionally Londré errs: she gets a Dryden title wrong on page 25 but right on page 31, calls the Earl of Dorset Brockhurst instead of Buckhurst on page 26, has Mrs. Siddons on page 94 making a debut in 1755 with Garrick, and claims first mention on page 127 of Czech and Polish theaters that were illustrated in Baur-Heinhold's *Barock Theatre* in 1966.—Edward A. Langhans.

Lowe, Lisa. *Critical Terrains: French and British Orientalisms*. Ithaca, NY, and London, : Cornell U. Press, 1991. Pp. xii + 216; bibliography.

Lucas, John. *England and Englishness: Ideas of Nationhood in English Poetry 1688–1900*. Iowa City, IO: U. of Iowa Press, 1990. Pp. 227; bibliography. Cf. *ECCB*, n.s.16, V:293–94.

Nikolaus Pevsner's *The Englishness of English Art*, though not a conceptual model for Lucas's study of the poetry of Pope, Goldsmith, Blake, Wordsworth, Shelley, Clare, and Tennyson (and others in fewer pages), comes to mind as a parallel volume: both books attempt to define that which is distinctive about a national medium, and both read as a set of lectures. Lucas's facade, however, seems not so deeply secured by scholarly foundations, though it is perhaps even more neatly polished. In fact, Lucas's style is unpretentious, unacademic, and sprightly. The prose is oral prose, and the chapter endings have the touch of *Masterpiece Theatre:* e.g., chapter one on Pope ends, "But other, contemporary, poets refuse to identitfy with his pessimism. For them self-interest is in the national interest. This points us to the next chapter" (tune in next week); or, taking leave of the "Contesting Voices" of Duck, Thomson, Gray, Collins, Macpherson, and Burns, chapter two Cookes up another Sunday night sign off: "But one poet had a much sharper sense than his contemporaries of what was at issue. He is the subject of the next chapter." There's something refreshing about this chumminess, but it's too tidy. Tidiness, in fact, is the book's weak point: that same weakness is a virtue, however, if, as one might surmise, these chapters are really lectures. Hurrah, in that case, for the continuation of the tradition manifested at its best in Harold C. Goodard's *The Meaning of Shakespeare* (1951)—wise words distilled from decades of lecturing.

Pevsner's book was written from years of archival county research, and Goddard's, from more than three decades lecturing at Swarthmore–whereas Lucas's attempt to identitfy the "Ideas of Nationhood in English Poetry" springs full-blown from merely *brief* and *facile* encounters with only two (albeit fine) modern statements about nationalism–Anthony Giddens's *The Nation State and Violence* (1985) and Ernest Gellner's *Nations and Nationalism* (1983)–and then proceeds, to cite but one example of its tidy method, to discuss Augustinism in English poetry without benefit of either Weinbrot's *Augustus Caesar in 'Augustan' England* (1978) or Erskine Hill's *The Augustan Idea in English Literature* (1983). Ideas about republicanism and civic virtue are applied to Shadwell and Dryden without our being given any sense that, e.g., Pocock ever wrote a word that might have helped us to a deeper understanding of the relation of those ideas to those authors. The scholarly literature on ideas of liberty, or on the Horatian verse epistle, is similarly hammocked, left swinging unread in the breeze. An endnote claims that the history of the illustrated editions of *Paradise Lost,* "still awaits its historian," a breezy, perhaps dismissive, comment that wafts rights over recent work of several scholars; and the main text, which instructs us that Thomas Gray and William Collins "have not been properly appreciated," whistles *Dixie* as it passes by recent criticism. The frequency of such authoritative pronouncements unmitigated by authoritative documentation unauthorizes the author. Why do learned scholars write learned books and articles if not even other scholars, and lecturers, read them, or, if they do, come to inter their good before they are dead?

The tidy-flaw manifests itself in other ways. For example, inasmuch as an endnote identitfies the ideological bases of Walter Bagehot's and Santayana's attacks on Browning, we expect Lucas to identify the ideological bases of the poets he discusses; but his broad brush strokes do not build up much detail. Other criticism has found a way to combine broad strokes with fine detail, so it can be done: Margaret Doody's *The Daring Muse* (1985) does so on virtually every page, as does Marshall Brown's *Preromanticism* (1991), the endnotes to which are an analytical guide through a bibliographical maze on each subject he has touched on.

To examine some exemplary passages: 1., on what Lucas rightly sees as the accomodation of "civilising values of friendship" (p.3) in Pope's poetry, read David Morris's uncited *Alexander Pope: The Genius of Sense* (1984) for a superior account; 2., page 49 gives a questionable impression of the relation between Smart and Gray, ignoring that Gray wrote to Smart (though the letters do not survive), early on thought Smart outrageous and not in full control; 3., because Lucas neither argues the case nor perceives a need to enter into an ongoing critical debate, those who are more skeptical will not be convinced by Lucas's assertions that Gray's "Elegy" is an "'innocent' reading of the actual labour and social relations of the vale" (p.45).

Even though Lucas does not sustain a complex argument, his hunches are often enlightening, and his style, engaging, neither of which can be said for many who have chosen to write more scholarly–but less wise–books. As a lecturer, Lucas must be a significant teacher; however, as an author, he may miss his audience, for colleagues–though enjoying the read–may find it quicksilverish.—Robert Maccubbin.

Mackie, Erin. "Desperate Measures: The Narratives of the Life of Mrs. Charlotte Clarke." *English Literary History*, 58 (1991), 841–65.

Reads the fiction with the autobiography and against the constraints of recent feminist criticism.

Maguire, Nancy Klein. "Regicide and Reparation: The Autobiographical Drama of Roger Boyle, Earl of Orrery." *English Literary Renaissance*, 21 (1991), 257–82.

Five self-indicating plays about the regicide combine history, biography, therapy, and exorcism.

Maillard, Jacques. "Le Théâtre à Angers au XVIIIe siècle." *Revue d'histoire du théâtre*, 43 (1991), 107–118.

Based on archival material; interesting addition to what we already know on theater in the provinces in eighteenth-century France.

Malarte, Claire-Lise. *Perrault a travers la critique depuis 1960: bibliographie annotée*. (Biblio 17, 47.) Paris and Seattle, WA: Papers on French Seventeenth-Century Literature, 1989. Pp. xv + 80.

Rev. by Robin Howells in *Modern Language Review*, 86 (1991), 455–56.

Mann, Maria A. *La Mère dans la littérature française 1678–1831*. (American University Studies, Series 2. Romance Languages and Literature, 92.) Frankfurt am Main and New York: Peter Lang, 1989. Pp. 289; bibliography. Cf. *ECCB*, n.s. 15, V: 228.

Rev. (severely) by Peter Jimack in *French Studies*, 45 (1991), 81–82.

Mant, Richard. *The Simpliciad (1808)*. Introduction by Jonathan Wordsworth. (Revolution and Romanticism, 1789–1834.) New York and Oxford: Woodstock Books, 1991. Pp. xi + 51, in mixed paginations.

A facsimile reprint of Mant's satirical attack on Wordsworth, Southey, and Coleridge, following hard upon Jeffrey's review of *Thalaba* in 1802 and occasioned by Wordsworth's *Poems in Two Volumes* of 1806. Though it neither rises nor sinks to the level of *The Dunciad*, *The Simpliciad* nevertheless reminds us that to proponents of the old decorum, the Romantic revolution could look comical. Lacking the force of his idols, Dryden and Pope, Mant still scores a few points, especially when demonstrating that a love for the simple and commonplace can to some appear simple and commonplace.

Maravall, José Antonio. *Utopia and Counterutopia in the "Quixote."* Translated by Robert W. Felkel. Detriot, MI: Wayne State U. Press, 1991. Pp. 255; bibliography.

Marazzini, Claudio. *Storia e coscienza della lingua in Italia dall'Umanesimo al Romanticismo*. Turin, Italy: Risenberg & Sellier, 1989. Pp. 267.

Rev. (Favorably) by Michael T. Ward in *Historiographia Linguistica*, 18 (1991), 384–87.

Marshall, James. *The Surprising Effects of Sympathy: Marivaux, Diderot, Rousseau, and Mary Shelley*. Chicago, IL: U. of Chicago Press, 1988. Pp. 286. Cf. *ECCB*, n.s. 16, V:297; 15, V:229.

Rev. by Robert Morrissey in *Modern Philology*, 88 (1990–91), 320–24.

Martz, Louis L. *From Renaissance to Baroque: Essays on Literature and Art*. Columbia, MO, and London: U. of Missouri Press, 1991. Pp. xiii + 277; bibliography; frontispiece (colored); 39 illustrations.

Mason, H. T. (ed.). *Transactions of the Seventh International Congress on the Enlightenment*. (Studies on Voltaire and the Eighteenth Century, 263–65). Oxford: The Voltaire Foundation at the Taylor Institution, 1989. Pp. 1796.

Rev. by D. Williams in *Modern Language Review*, 86 (1991), 965–66.

Mauser, Wolfram. "Poesie der Erscheinung: Zur Rhetorik des 'glückseligen Körpers' in der Aufklärungsliteratur: Ein Versuch." Pp. 73–84 of *The Enlightenment and its Legacy: Studies in German Literature in Honor of Helga Slessarev*. Edited by Sara Friedrichsmeyer, and B. Becker-Cantarino. Bonn: Bouvier Verlag, 1991. Pp. 227; bibliography; illustrations.

Mazauric, Claude. "Sur le *Dictionnaire critique de la Révolution française* [1988] de F[rançois]. Furet et M[ona]. Ozouf." *Stanford French Review*, 14 (1990), 85–103.

McGlathery, James M. *Fairy Tale Romance: The Grimms, Basile, and Perault.* Champaign, IL: U. of Illinois Press, 1991. Pp. 240.

McGowan, Ian (ed.). *St. Martin's Anthologies of English Literature.* Vol. III: *The Restoration and Eighteenth Century (1660–1798).* New York: St. Martin's Press, 1991. Pp. 612.

McIntosh, Carey. *Common and Courtly Language: The Stylistics of Social Class in Eighteenth-Century British Literature.* Philadelphia, PA: U. of Pennsylvania Press, 1986. Pp. viii + 168. Cf. *ECCB*, n.s. 14, V:229; 13, V:328; 12, V:352–53.

Rev. by B. D. H. Miller in *Review of English Studies*, 42 (1991), 239–40.

McKenzie, Alan T. *Certain, Lively Episodes: The Articulation of Passion in Eighteenth-Century Prose.* Athens, GA: U. of Georgia Press, 1990. Pp. 265. Cf. *ECCB*, n.s. 16, V:299–300.

Rev. (favorably) by James G. Juroe in *Christianity and Literature*, 41 (1991), 83–85; by Ann Van Sant in *The Scriblerian*, 23 (1991), 267–68.

McNeil, David. *The Grotesque Depiction of War and the Military in Eighteenth-Century English Fiction.* London and Toronto: Associated University Press; Newark, DE: U. of Delaware Press, 1990. Pp. 229.

Rev. by Melvyn New in *The Scriblerian*, 24 (1991), 62–64.

Messenger, Ann (ed.). *Gender at Work: Four Women Writers of the Eighteenth Century.* Detroit, MI: Wayne State U. Press, 1990. Pp. 164. Cf. *ECCB*, n.s. 16, V:302–03.

Rev. (severely) by B. Kowaleski-Wallace in *Choice*, 28 (1991), 1779.

Milhous, Judith, and Robert D. Hume (eds.). *A Register of English Theatrical Documents 1660–1737.* Carbondale, IL: Southern Illinois U. Press, 1991. Pp. xiii + 521; appendices.

The work of Hume and Milhous on Restoration and early eighteenth-century theatrical history and practice requires no introduction to readers of the *ECCB*. Working together and at times apart, they have in such works as *Vice Chamberlain Coke's Theatrical Papers, 1706–1715*, and Milhous's *Thomas Betterton and the Management of Lincoln's Inn Fields, 1695–1708*, begun to lay down an accurate foundation for the study of the drama of that period. This intention is aligned with Hume's critical writings, (including *The Development of English Drama in the Late Seventeenth Century*), which typically attempt to correct what Hume perceives as critical misconceptions about the drama, from 1660, to, roughly, the time of Fielding.

Their present work is "a first attempt at a chronological list of all documents related to the management and regulation of the theater in England from the reopening of the playhouse in 1660 to the passage of the Licensing Act in 1737." They term their work "a descriptive checklist," and they proceed season by season, printing titles and descriptions of significant documents pertaining to the theatrical situation. Their purpose is to provide a tool, a kind of handbook, designed to "lead scholars to documents that may be of use to them," and to "facilitate the identification and publication of new theatrical documents" (p. ix). The authors work from standard sources such as *The London Stage*, Leslie Hotson's *The Commonwealth and Restoration Court Stage, 1660–1702*, and other important works, plus their own searches of the Public Record Office. They have no illusions that their present work offers a complete account, but maintain, rightly, that it provides the working scholar with a valuable tool for research in theatrical history.

Hume and Milhous present chronologically all known documents concerning the management and government regulation of theater in England, primarily London, between 1660 and 1737, both printed material and manuscripts. Each item is dated, its source and location noted, and a brief description of its content recorded. For example, on 9 July, 1660 a crucial document is cited: "Order for a grant to Killigrew to erect a company." The source is the State Papers in the Public Record Office and the gist of the document is quoted: Killigrew is given permission "to erect one Company of players which shall be our owne Company." The authors comment on the document more generally: "The basic terms of the proposed grant are spelled out: Killigrew may select performers; build a theater; set prices; eject mutinous persons," and they note that Killigrew's will be one of two companies, the other being that of Davenant. They cite a modern reprint of the document; the excerpt they print is found in Hotson.

Many of the documents are crucial to an understanding of the development of the theater of the time: "Submission of the actors to Herbert's authority" (the actors agree to pay Sir Henry Herbert, the Master of the Revels, for licensing new plays); "Order against Disturbing the Cockpitt by soldiers"; "King's comedians sworn." Some are trivial, but amusing and interesting: "Warrant for fencing at the Red Bull"; "Hall theater fitted for rope dancing." Indeed, there is a good deal of fun and local color obtainable *passim*. For example, for the season of 1660–61, among a list of miscellaneous theatrical expenses incurred by the Revel's Office, we find 1s 6d for "a Chamberpott for the Players." We may feel that we are getting to the heart of things. There are endless applications and orders for "Six Scones for the Passages that are dark," "New matting ye degrees in one of ye boxes at ye Cockpit," "Setting up one partition for Mr. Johnson at ye Cockpit . . . with a doore in it. "There are lists of players, contractual agreements, lawsuits, sales of shares in the companies, warrants for this and that ("Warrant to arrest unlicensed drummers, trumpeters, and fife players"), repairs to walls, and "Two curtains made and seats covered in the Cockpit." The documents lead us to a sense of the daily working life of the theaters, with the sounds of hammers and unliscensed fifes as well as the rhetorical bombast from the stage itself. Easy to use and agreeable to skim, this work will take its place aside the volumes of *The London Stage* as a basic tool for theatrical studies.—Anthony Kaufman.

Miller, Jane. *Seductions in Reading and Culture*. Cambridge, MA, and London: Harvard U. Press, 1991. Pp. 194.

Rev. (with another work) by Patricia Meyer Spacks in *Modern Language Quarterly*, 52 (1991), 217–21.

Minerva, Nadia. *Il Diavolo. eclissi e metamorfosi nel Secolo dei Lumi. da Asmodeo a Belzebù.* (Biblioteca di Lettere e Arti. Sezione: Letteratura Straniera. Il portico, 91.) Ravenna: Longo Editore, 1990. Pp. 219. Cf. *ECCB*, n.s. 16, V:203–04.

This stimulating study is neither a straight history of the Devil during the Enlightenment nor a study of its various demonologies but an original combination of the two. Focussing on France, with some attention to Italy, Minerva shows how the Devil, broadly speaking, lost ground, became increasingly spiritualized, and turned into a literary character between Louis XIV's Edict of 1682, defining witchcraft as the exploitation of credulity, and the appearance in 1772 of Jacques Cazotte's ambiguous *Diable Amoureux*. She displays a keen sense of the cultural, institutional and theological resonances of debate and scholarship on the Devil of the past three centuries such as J. B. Russell, H. A. Kelly, Alfonso di Nola and especially Max Milner, who introduces the volume. Her deft reading of medical and theological treatises on demons demonstrates their interdependence. She elucidates the moderate scepticism of Christian thinkers like Malebranche and Muratori who blamed intense belief in Satan on ignorant clergy and laity who forgot biblical assurances that his kingdom has been destroyed and he himself been bound in the abyss until the end of time. Her work on Italian figures such as Girolamo Tantarotti (1751) follows in the tradition of Franco Venturi's *Settecento Riformatore*. The heart of her book is a wonderfully sympathetic reading of the *Traité sur les apparitions des esprits et sur les revenants de Hongrie, de Moravie etc.* (1751) by the Benedictine scholar Augustin Calmet responding to Voltaire's criticism of an earlier work. She adds considerable nuance and depth to Voltaire's portrait of Calmet as one whose erudition overshadowed his critical sense, and finds the two often in agreement. She views the period as unified field rather than the clash of two armies. In Calmet's wake Nicholas Lenglet-Dufresnoy published two multi-volume treatises (1751-52) positing, in effect, two devils: the picturesque character in fables and a less fearsome "real" devil. Minerva argues that his lucid, still relevant pathology of the diabolic imagination constitutes an epistemological rupture splitting the history of the Devil into two parts. In the following decades the initially Voltairean Cazotte mediated to subsequent generations a tantalizingly ambiguous "Devil in love." Cazotte is a sort of prophet who replaced the colorful medieval devil with an austere, troubled sense of collective and individual guilt. A brilliant last chapter on the Jacobin Devil surveys the "mythology" of the French Revolution as seen by protagonists and later historians. Minerva shows how satanic myth permeated stories of the Revolution and how both sides employed satanic symbolism. She raises and partially answers a large question: why after the eclipse and metamorphoses of the Devil should all sides eagerly seize on such metaphors? Her last sentence remarks that the diabolical metaphor "tells the truth" for so many. That metaphor, one imagines, also tells the truth for her, but rather differently than it did for, say, De Maistre. A book from her on Devil in the Revolution would, one also imagines, be even more enlightening than this splendid study.—John Ahern.

Modica, Massimo (ed.). *L'Estetica dell'Encyclopedie. Guida alla lettura.* (Universale idee.) Rome: Editori Riuniti, 1988. Pp. 240. Cf. *ECCB*, n.s. 14, V:232.

Rev. by J. P. de Nola in *Studi francesi*, 34 (1991), 522–23.

Mohr, Hans-Ulrich. "Rollen, Normen, Werte, Welt—und Gesellschaftsmodelle in Literatur und Rechtswesen (mit Beispielen zum englischen Schauerroman)." Pp. 205–27 of *Erzählte Kriminalität: Zur Typologie und Funktion von narrativen Darstellungen in Strafrechtspflege, Publizistik und Literatur zwischen 1770 und 1920.* Edited by Jörg Schönert et al. Tübingen: Niemeyer, 1991. Pp. xi + 682.

Moore, Leslie E. *Beautiful Sublime: The Making of Paradise Lost, 1701–1734.* Stanford, CA: Stanford U. Press, 1990. Pp. xii + 235. Cf. *ECCB*, n.s. 16, V:304–05.

Rev. by Francis C. Blessington in *The Scriblerian*, 23 (1991), 289–90; by Anne K. Krook in *Eighteenth-Century Studies*, 24 (1991), 549–51.

Moriarty, Michael. *Taste and Ideology in Seventeenth-Century France.* Cambridge and NY: Cambridge U. Press, 1988. Pp. x + 232.

Rev. by Lionel Gossman in *Modern Language Review*, 86 (1991), 205–08.

Mortier, Roland. *Le cour et la raison: recueil d'études sur le dix-huitième siècle.* Bruxelles: Editions de l'université de Bruxelles; Oxford: Voltaire Foundation; Paris: Universitas, 1990. Pp. x + 540; illustrations. Cf. *ECCB*, n.s. 16, V:305–06.

Rev. (favorably) by Jean Sgard in *Recherches sur Diderot et sur l'Encyclopedie*, 11 (1991), 166–68.

Mullan, John. *Sentiment and Sociability: The Language of Feeling in the Eighteenth Century.* Oxford: Clarendon Press, 1988. Pp. 272. Cf. *ECCB*, n.s. 15, V:236; 14, V:234–35.

Rev. (favorably) by Melvyn New in *The Scriblerian*, 23 (1991), 247–50.

Munsters, Wil. *La Poétique du pittoresque en France, de 1770-1830.* Geneva: Droz, 1991. Pp. 219; plates.

The complex history of *pittoresque* as a word, style, and poetics is ably presented in Wil Munsters' perceptive study. Well before the exemplary picturesque of Victor Hugo's *Les Orientales* and prior to the pre-romantic prose of Rousseau, Bernardin de Saint-Pierre and Chateaubriand, the picturesque was already an important element of eighteenth-century descriptive poetry.

Focusing upon the period from 1700 when the word *picturesque* first appeared in the context of painting as a lexical borrowing from Italian (*pittoresca*: relative to a painter, to painting), Munsters documents in his first chapter the semantic evolution of the word which itself becomes an index of eighteenth-century sociocultural and aesthetic tastes. Initially a technical term in the jargon of painting, *pittoresque* escaped its narrow categorization and acquired secondary meanings and aesthetic value through metonymy, referring to the subjects of painting and to the particular form of beauty represented, which reflected the new artistic sensibility of the eighteenth century and its taste for the unusual, piquant detail. Spurred by the proliferation in France of the *jardin a l'anglaise* with its varied and irregular landscape in the second half of the century and fostered by aesthetic treatises linking painting to poetry by Abbe Du Bos (1719) and Ch. Batteux (1746), the picturesque emerged from its restricted use in the context of art to become a visual reality and a literary theme.

Already associated with a new genre of travel narrative ("le voyage pittoresque"), the picturesque received its most complete literary expression in the descriptive poems of Saint-Lambert (*Les Saisons* 1769), Roucher (*Les Mois* 1779) and Delille (*Les Jardins* 1782), which celebrate the varied, unexpected delights of picturesque gardens. However, as Munsters points out in his analysis of these texts, there is a paradox between the poets' desire to paint *un pictura poesis* and their practice of observing *le bon usage* of classical poetry. Constrained by the artificial purification of literary vocabulary, stock epithets and conventional metaphor, their verse is marked by an ambivalence deriving from their effort to reconcile a new aesthetic privileging the particular with the classical doctrine of *le beau ideal*. Only Delille succeeded in painting for the ear if not the eye through imitative harmony and, together with his disciple Roucher, he extended the lexicon of poetry to include the literal, lowly and technical word to describe concrete reality. Although Delille was the scapegoat of the Romantics, he preceded them in the renewal of poetic language and the rediscovery of nature.

If "descriptive" and "picturesque" were equivalent terms at this point in time, both challenged classical notions of beauty in their concerns with irregularity and capricious detail. Munsters traces their semantic evolution from a relation of synonymy to antonymy when descriptive poetry fell out of favor at the end of the eighteenth century to the benefit of *pittoresque*. Because of its positive associations with art and a concrete, plastic reality, *pittoresque* gained the ascendancy and denoted not just a style but a genre.

The overwhelming success of the poetics of the picturesque in early Romanticism and its sustained influence well into the nineteenth century have tended to obscure the origins of the theory in the preceding century. Wil Munsters' study has effectively located the *pittoresque* within the aesthetic doctrines and poetic practices of the eighteenth century.—Maxine G. Cutler.

Myers, Sylvia Harcstark. *The Bluestocking Circle: Women, Friendship, and the Life of the Mind in Eighteenth-Century England.* Oxford: Clarendon Press, 1990. Pp. xvii + 342; bibliography; illustrations. Cf. *ECCB*, n.s. 16, V:306–07.

Rev. by A. E. Jones, Jr., in *Choice*, 28 (1991), 1488; by Christine Salmon in *Notes and Queries*, 236 (1991), 547–48.

Nardo, Anna K. *The Ludic Self in Seventeenth-Century English Literature*. Albany, NY: State U. of New York Press, 1991. Pp. x + 263; bibliography.

Contains a chapter on Marvell's lyric poetry, seen as expressions of a self striving to escape childhood narcissism and apparently never quite making it. Along with the selves that don't manage to emerge, and selves that are fed as well as devoured by external forces they both seek and avoid, Nardo examines play as a strategy whereby the author distances himself from the experience he describes while simultaneously participating in it. Nardo's psychoanalytic approach tends to describe what is already well known rather than make new insights available. That Marvell often avoids clean resolutions, that he is given to paradox, contradiction, evasiveness, and irony (not as different from play as Nardo would like to think), is unlikely to surprise scholars of Marvell.

Nokes, David. *Raillery and Rage: A Study of Eighteenth Century Satire*. Brighton, UK: Harvester Press, 1987. Pp. xii + 211. Cf. *ECCB*, n.s. 13, V:336–37.

Rev. by Raman Selden in *Modern Language Review*, 86 (1991), 393–95.

Nokes, David, and Janet Barron. *An Annotated Critical Bibliography of Augustan Poetry*. New York: St. Martin's, 1989. Pp. xl + 158.

Rev. (with another work) by Donald C. Mell in *The Scriblerian*, 23 (1991), 286–89.

Nordloh, David J. (ed.). *American Literary Scholarship: An Annual, 1989*. Durham, NC, and London: Duke U. Press, 1991. Pp. xix + 504; indices.

Nussbaum, Felicity. *The Autobiographical Subject: Gender and Ideology in Eighteenth-Century England*. Baltimore, MD, and London: Johns Hopkins U. Press, 1989. Pp. 288. Cf. *ECCB*, n.s. 16, V:308; 15, V:237.

Rev. by B. Kowaleski-Wallace in *Eighteenth-Century Studies*, 24 (1991), 534–37; by Jeffery A. Portnoy in *The Scriblerian*, 23 (1991), 276–78; (severely) by David Womersley in *Essays in Criticism*, 41 (1991), 339–46.

Nutall, A. D. *The Stoic in Love: Selected Essays on Literature and Ideas*. London, and New York: Harvester Wheatsheaf, 1989. Pp. xii + 209.

Rev. (favorably) by Robert Craver in *Notes and Queries*, 236 (1991), 238–39.

Oppici, Patricia. *L' Idea di "bienfaisance" nel settecento francese: o il laccio di Aglaia*. Preface by Corrado Rosso (storia e critica della idee, 14.) Pisa: Goliardica, 1989. Pp. 328. Cf. *ECCB*, n.s. 15, V:239.

Rev. (briefly) by Carlo Cordiè in *Studi francesi*, 35 (1991), 140.

Owen, Robert. *A New View of Society and Other Writings*. London and New York: Penguin Books, 1991. Pp. xxxv + 385.

Palmeri, Frank. *Satire in Narrative: Petronius, Swift, Gibbon, Melville, and Pynchon*. Austin, TX: U. of Texas Press, 1990. Pp. x + 183; bibliography. Cf. *ECCB*, n.s. 16, V:309–10.

Rev. by J. R. Clark in *Choice*, 29 (1991), 274–75.

Chapter 2, "Satiric Materialism in *A Tale of a Tub*," (pp. 39–63) concerns Swift while Chapter 3, "Satire, Epic, and History in *The Decline and Fall of the Roman Empire*," (pp. 64–85) discusses Gibbon.

Patterson, Annabel. *Fables of Power: Aesopian Writing and Political History.* (Post-Contemporary Interventions.) Durham, NC, and London: Duke U. Press, 1991. Pp. vi + 178; bibliography; 8 figures.

Quoting from a fly (p. 1), Duke's Annabel Patterson spins a critical fable that snags Stanley Fish, Fredric Jameson, and the entire Duke critical tackle box in the entanglements of its intra-referential net. Fresh from the Duke Press, this hothouse production began in closed-circuit cybersex: Patterson and her husband's Rockefeller-supported "manuscripts grew side by side on identical laptops and were finished together in congenial collaboration" (p. vi). A "post-contemporary intervention" (pp. ii, 178) into "the deep penetration of the fable into culture" (p. 54), *Fables of Power* swells and implodes on its sheer internality—its pressured enclosure in a world of conflicted theories and critical clientage.

"Intervention" has a military ring. Patterson carpet-bombs Aesop's past. She lauds the oppressed and overlooked, but she limits most of her 158-page text to canonical works. "The Sixteenth Century" (Chapter 2) means "Spenser." Expunging the full range of Aesopians, she patronizes an elite sub-Augustan corps who, while busily rioting for food, clairvoyantly "grasped" her critical concepts (p. 122). Popular and visual fable traditions, whether emblems or medals, cannot attract Patterson's haughty patrician eye. What we find on her foreground is an assortment of magic, often weirdly italicized or capitalized buzzwords: "body," "Self," "Other," "mere" as in "merely ethical," "cultural signifier," "inside/outside dialectic," even "grumpy." In one *piece de resistance*, three big-name critics, a foreign language, and the plus-word "slave" huddle in one dull line (p. 13). From the dark cloud of Patterson's Napalmizing prose precipitate such searing sentences as "Himself, as I have shown, an extremely 'prudent' fabulist in *The Shepheardes Calendar*, he can be accused in this stanza from *The Faerie Queene* of no policy other than social reconciliation" (p. 112).

Patterson's predictable thesis argues that an amorphous gang "in cahoots with the political system" (p. 156) repressed the Aesopian tradition of spunky slaves. Were such a thesis true—Patterson's cache of Aesopian writings disproves it—readers would still battle "conceptual narcissism" (p. 12). Biographical self-citation may be quaintly tolerable: "When I wrote . . . I left out . . . I intuited that . . . I made the opposite mistake . . . I confine myself" (p. 5). But self-reflective phraseology like "the unease of Shakespeare's readers" (p. 118) warrants excision. True, Shakespeare has readers. He also has a theatrical *audience*. Unfortunately, Patterson's cold post-contemporary inn has no room or compassion for *difference* or *history* or *context*. La Fontaine is spanked for excluding certain episodes "which, for me, constitute the essential Aesop—*the philosopher of materialism and the body*" (p. 38; my emphasis). An equally proclamatory "I recuperate it [Aesop's writing] now" (p. 15) depreciates Aesopians' power to speak for themselves.

Fables of Power dishes out several sub-theses. Patterson tries for a post-Hegelian distinction between the fabulist and the idealist Aesops (pp. 6–7). Alas, pesky Socrates perturbs "elitist" (p. 11) Platonism. The search for a theory of fable (pp. 13ff.) runs aground on fabulists' diversity. Patterson's critical mosaic includes five tautological commandments, including "3. writing is authorized by authorship" (p. 15). Sometimes Aesop himself intervenes in the discourse, as "the point of convergence of gross body and ironic wit" (p. 31). Wit soon wears out its welcome in Patterson's humorless world. We learn that tidy Aesop keeps an "ironic distance" from excrement, being "neither its celebrant nor despiser" (p. 26). Accusations of race and gender discrimination abound, but Patterson offers no primary texts to confirm the alleged deracination of "negroid" slave Aesop (an illustration of Aesop's Versailles statue on page 19 reveals no cover-up of his social status). Boasts Patterson, "if one starts, however, with a bias *in favor* of political consciousness, it greatly enhances one's capacity to recognize its presence" (p. 130); *Fables of Power* lacks the instructions for Aesop's assembly.

Despite biases and blunders—John Gay wrote in 1628 (p. 149), Dodsley's 1772 work counts as a "nineteenth-century collection" (pp. 34–35)—Patterson's book could stimulate future research. Meriting further consideration are Patterson's treatments of Aesop's *Life* as a "metafable" (p. 37), of Aesop's renewability (p. 52), of the appropiation of Aesop by Royalists (p. 87), and of fabulists' referentiality (p. 105). The best long passage in the book is the fine juxtaposition of neo-Aesopians Roger L'Estrange and Samuel Croxall (pp. 139–146).

Patterson's posterity should refrain from declaring their opinions "inarguable" (p. 47 and *passim*). They should address wit and the aesthetics of the impromptu (see pp. 55, 94), should deal fully with the popular tradition, should face up to Dryden's enjoyable *Fables* as well as his tense *The Hind and the Panther*, should avoid declaring war on evidence (on page 137 John Locke gets slapped for "contributing to that misperception of the fable against which this entire project protests"), and should not refuse to discuss John Gay's politically inexpedient "crystalline moralism" (p. 149). Patterson deserves praise for reviving Aesop as a topic of critical discussion. Her book, with its extenuated air of breathless enthusiasm over the resuscitation of long-expired theories, could profit from a breeze through musty research libraries. Only genuine critical and bibliographical diversity can liberate the legacy of antiquity's adage-enriched slave.—Kevin L. Cope.

Patterson, Michael. *The First German Theatre: Schiller, Goethe, Kleist and Buchner in Performance*. (Theatre Production Studies.) London and New York: Routledge, 1990. Pp. ix + 207; appendices; bibliography; illustrations.

Rev. by Y. Shafter in *Choice*, 28 (1991), 1322.
"Introduction. German Theatre in the Eighteenth Century" (pp. 1–20), "Schiller at Mannheim: *The Robbers*" (pp. 21–52), "Goethe at Weimar: *Iphigenia on Tauris*" (pp. 53–110), "From the Eighteenth into the Nineteenth Century" (pp. 111–22), and "Kleist in Performance: *The Prince of Homburg*" (pp. 123–39) concern the Eighteenth Century.

Paul, Jean. *Army-Chaplain Schmelzle's Journey to Flaetz and Life of Quintus Fixlein*. Translated from German by Thomas Carlyle. (Studies in German Literature, Linguistics, & Culture, 57.) Camden House, 1991. Pp. xxii + 309.

Includes new sixteen-page introduction.

Paulson, Ronald. *Breaking and Remaking: Aesthetic Practices in England, 1700–1820*. New Brunswick, NJ: Rutgers U. Press, 1989. Pp. xiv + 363.

Rev. by Robert Markley in *The Scriblerian*, 23 (1991), 271–73; (favorably) by Sean Shesgreen in *Notes and Queries*, 236 (1991), 237–38.

Pearson, Jacqueline. *The Prostituted Muse: Images of Women and Women Dramatists 1642–1737*. New York: St. Martin's Press, 1988. Pp. xii + 308; bibliography. Cf. *ECCB*, n.s. 16, V:310; 14, V:237–38.

Rev. (with another work) by Nancy Cotton in *The Scriblerian*, 23 (1991), 264–65.

Perfezou, Laurence. *Les Fausses Confidences. Marivaux*. (L'Oeuvre au clair, 21.) Paris: Bordas, 1991. Pp. 95.

This small, concise tome is not a scholarly, interpretative work per se. Laurence Perfezou's study guide to Marivaux's *Les Fausses Confidences* belongs to a series designed to familiarize the student of French literature with general knowledge of a specific period as well as specific knowledge of a general analytical method.

Perfezou begins by presenting useful if not indispensable points of reference. He situates Marivaux in his century, and *Les Fausses Confidences*, in Marivaux's works. Though Perfezou introduces biographical data, he also acknowledges that such personal footnotes alone are insufficient for profound comprehension of a work. Perferzou continues with a brief discussion of the play's structure and of the unities of idea, character and language that he perceives throughout the piece. He then organizes the three subsequent chapters around three major themes: the character of the valet Dubois; love in conjunction with its obstacles and prejudices; and language. This entire study of the relationship between *forme* and *fond* is punctuated by a short synthesis.

The outline of each chapter is parallel. Perfezou's analysis of a specific passage is followed by an *application pratique,* in which he illustrates his approach, and by *exercices* that allow the student to implement the same instruments of analysis. The final section of the book, accompanied by a *lexique* of pertinent terms, contains sample essay questions, and possible answers, resembling those found on the *baccalaureat* examination.

Certainly the almost intrinsic French proclivity for formal analysis is undisguised. That fact notwithstanding, it would be short-sighted to dismiss Perfezou's effort as inconsequential for American students. Among the attributes of this work are the often slighted means of penetrating the multiple layers of a work to reveal its essential meaning. The typically French approach, therefore, is not a drawback but rather a source of appeal. By reorienting students so that they accord primacy to the author's pen and so that they appreciate the unavoidability of mastering a specifiable analytical method to achieve understanding, Perfezou transcends his own subject matter and demonstrates the bases of the kind of solid writing that educators of every discipline would like to see reborn in their classroom.—Marie Wellington.

Pollack, Rhoda-Gale (ed.). *A Sampler of Plays by Women.* Frankfurt am Main and New York: Peter Lang, 1990. Pp. 399.

Rev. (with reservations) in *The Scriblerian*, 24 (1991), 79–80.

Popp, M. *Die englische Aussprache im 18. Jahrhundert im Lichte englisch-französischer Zeugnisse, I, Das Dictionnarie de la Pronunciation angloise 1756.* (Anglistische Forschungen, 199.) Heidelberg: Carl Winter, 1989. pp. xix + 185.

Rev. by E. G. Stanley in *Notes and Queries*, 236 (1991), 365–66.

Porter, Dennis. *Haunted Journeys: Desire and Transgression in European Travel Writing.* Princeton, NJ: Princeton U. Press, 1991. Pp. xi + 341; frontispiece; illustrations.

This is not a book for travelers—or readers of travel writing—who simply want to enjoy themselves. Addressing a less sanguine audience, Dennis Porter investigates the motives behind the writings of those who travelled with mental attitudes that, in various ways, "haunted" them while they were away from home. Selecting from the vast store of European travel writing, he concentrates on well-known French and English male authors from the mid-eighteenth century to our time, interpreting their individual texts in an intelligent and lively manner. Under the heading of "Romantic Transgressions" (Part Two of the book), Porter characterizes Stendhal, Darwin, and Flaubert, respectively, as a traveler for the travel's sake, a passionate voyager, and a perverse traveler. "Europe and its Discontents" and "Postcolonial Dilemmas" (Part Three and Four) deal particularly with D. H. Lawrence, Gide, Levi-Strauss, and V. S. Naipaul, pointing out the ways in which these authors experienced feelings of flight, anxiety, or displacement during their travels. For the eighteenth century, Porter explores comparable tendencies under the heading "Enlightenment Europe and Its Globe" (Part One), concentrating on some of the period's most prominent travelers: behind Boswell's Grand Tour rhetoric Porter detects the desire to escape from paternal authority, as well as the behavior pattern of a neurotic who puts himself in situations where he could not live up to his own high standards. Diderot's *Journey to Holland* reveals an almost obsessive search for alternatives to the political, social, and cultural conditions of the *ancien regime*, accounting for the book's numerous plagiarisms. The discussion of Bougainville and Cook stresses how much their pursuit of an earthly paradise was motivated by their wish to put the follies and illnesses of European civilization behind them. Observations such as these lead Porter to suggest that various eighteenth-century travelers anticipated Levi-Strauss's critical assessment of the world in the wake of modern European colonialism.

As Porter explains in his comprehensive introduction, an impetus to undertake his research came from Edward

Said's study *Orientalism*, which in turn is indebted to Michel Foucault's writings. Consequently, discourse theory has had a strong impact on Porter's interpretations, as have Roland Barthes's concepts of literary seminology, the principles of psychoanalysis, and gender criticism. Relying on such approaches, Porter is indeed prepared to see the authors he has chosen as "haunted" by their conscious or unconscious desires in their confrontations with foreign cultures. His immense learnedness and his joy in displaying it make his book a rewarding, although not always an easy reading experience.—Peter Boerner.

Potkay, Adam. "Classical Eloquence and Polite Style in the Age of Hume." *Eighteenth-Century Studies,* 25 (1991), 31–56.

Given the classical connections among eloquence, liberty, and virtue, the failure of Hanoverian Britain to produce a sublime orator indicates and indicts its anti-republican nature. But Hume recommended politeness rather than eloquence.

Probyn, Clive. " 'Travelling west-ward': The Lost Letter from Jonathan Swift to Charles Ford." *Studies in Bibliography,* 44 (1991), 265–271; photographic facsimile.

Promis Ojeda, Jose. *The Identity of Hispanoamerica: An Interpretation of Colonial Literature.* Translated by Alita Kelley. Tucson, AZ: U, of Arizona Press, 1991. Pp. 150.

Quintero, Maria Cristina. *Poetry as Play: Gongorismo and the Comedia.* (Purdue University Monographs in Romance Languages, V.) Amsterdam and Philadelphia, PA: J. Benjamins, 1991. Pp. xviii + 260.

Racault, Jean-Michel. *L'Utopie narrative en France et en Angleterre, 1675–1761.* (Studies on Voltaire and the Eighteenth Century, 280.) Oxford: The Voltaire Foundation at the Taylor Institution, 1991. Pp. xii + 830.

In this extensive study, originally published as a doctoral dissertation, Jean-Michel Racault offers his readers a commendable, in-depth study of the theme of utopia in French and English literature between 1675 and 1761. This geographical and chronological delimitation is founded on the 1675 publication of the English version of a "texte fondateur," the *Histoire des Sevarambes* by Veiras and the 1761 publication of *La Nouvelle Héloïse,* in which Rousseau fully integrates into his fictional text the utopian life at Clarens.

Racault divides his work on five major sections, each of which is enhanced by its richness of presentation and the profusion of texts examined. Part I, the Utopian Mode, describes utopian movements, social experimentation, and community practises, such as the evolution of the Quaker movement and religious communities in North America. Racault's references to colonial undertakings include Locke's *Constitutions de la Caroline* and the Jesuit colony in Paraguay.

Part II defines the utopian genre and traces its diffusion, translations and literary transformations. Of special interest here is Racault's treatment of *Robinson Crusoe* which he establishes as a paradigmatic text.

Canonical forms and models of the utopian genre are thoroughly analysed in Part III. Racault examines the "crise du roman," the new romanesque forms, and also travel literature. Here Veiras' *Histoire des Sevarambes* is presented as the incarnation of the utopian narrative in its classical form. There follows a detailed and lengthy analysis of the structure and techniques of this novel which exercised considerable influence on the development of utopian literature, especially in France and England.

Part IV treats human nature and the contradictions of reason. Gabriel de Foigny's *La Terre australe connue*, a utopian work at the end of the classical period and contemporary with Veiras' *Histoire des Sevarambes*, also initiates the major lines of utopian writings to be developed during the Enlightenment. A half century later Swift's *Gulliver's Travels* articulates the same fundamental questions about mankind.

The eighteenth century does clearly renew the utopian genre. In his Part V, Racault presents a thorough analysis of the micro-utopia. One example he chooses, Voltaire's *Eldorado*, illustrates the potential dual nature of the utopian theme: an independent episode of a single element within a text. It is Rousseau's world of Clarens which exemplifies the total integration of the utopia of small societies in the novel itself. In *La Nouvelle Héloïse* virtue does triumph over human weakness, but at the cost of artifice and falsehood. At first sight Clarens suggests a new Eden; in the end, it reveals itself as only an image where opposites and contradictions have been artfully masked.

The novels of two English women, Sarah Scott and Lady Mary Walker, *Millenium Hall* and *Munster Village*, illustrate a double orientation: agriculture and industry or the passage from a pastoral utopia to a model of industrial development. Here pastoral nostalgia is replaced by industrial reality as factories are installed in the countryside by philanthropic industrialists.

Certainly Racault's illuminating and stimulating study of the utopian genre merits the attention of the serious reader. His impressive work is further enhanced by an extensive bibliography and an index of titles and persons cited.—Lois Ann Russell.

Ranger, Paul. *Terror and Pity Reign in Every Breast: Gothic Drama in the London Patent Theatres, 1750–1820*. London: The Society for Theatre Research, 1991. Pp. x + 195; bibliography; illustrations; indices.

This is a good overview of gothic dramatic productions in London—the stock characters in thrilling plots, the (usually) spectacular scenery and technical effects, and the moral lessons for responsive audiences. If that sounds like what we call melodrama, it is, and if Ranger's work is missing anything, it is an explantion of just how melodrama differed from or was related to gothic drama. The term melodrama is barely mentioned (it doesn't even appear in the index), and the implication seems to be that gothic drama was a precursor. The standard ingredients are about the same: fair damsels in distress, wicked villains in pursuit, near disasters and lucky escapes, dank dungeons in old castles, wild natural settings, romantic searches for the sublime in situations fraught with danger, and audiences happy to play the game of make-believe because it was often exciting theater, if not good drama.

Ranger might have explained how all this fit into the development of Romantic melodrama, and he might have made more use of Coleridge as critic, especially his discussion in the *Biographia Literaria* (III, 6) of the willing suspension of disbelief, to explain why theatergoers fell for so much theatrical balderdash. But we can thank Ranger for what he has given us: a careful and often stylishly written, appropriately urbane examination of the gothic spirit; a good study of the chief features that thrilled playgoers when they came to gothic dramatic productions; nice comparisons with the works of novelists, painters, and landscape architects; vivid descriptions of the stage spectacle and acting; and—a nice touch—case studies of three works: Home's *Douglas* (1757), Lewis's *The Castle Spectre* (1797), and Sheridan's *Pizarro* (1799), though the chapter on them needs a clearer focus.

There are many illustrations, some quite splendid, but the relationship of picture to text is not always made clear (see the confusion on p. 128, for example), and in a few cases Ranger cites an illustration that for some reason is not reproduced. The best pictures, alas, are not scenic designs but paintings, like the frontispiece by Pain or de Loutherbourg's *Conway Castle* on pp.118–19; good British stage designs of the period are not abundant. The author's documentation is thorough, though it is odd that Barnett's *The Art of Gesture*, Roach's *The Player's Passion*, and West's *The Image of the Actor* are missing from the bibliography. There are two very helpful indices, one a chronological list of gothic plays and the other thumbnail biographies of people cited in the text.—Edward A. Langhans.

Ray, William. *Story and History: Narrative Authority and Social Identity in the Eighteenth-Century French and English Novel*. Cambridge, MA, and Oxford: Basil Blackwell, 1990. Pp. viii + 362.

Rev. by Geoffrey Bennington in *TLS*, (Mar. 15, 1991), 20; by Barry Roth in *Notes and Queries*, 236 (1991), 392–93; by G. R. Wasserman in *Choice*, 28 (1991), 1304.

Reinhardt, Steven G. *Justice in the Sarladais, 1770–1790.* Baton Rouge, LA, and London: Louisiana State U. Press, 1991. Pp. xxi + 301; bibliography.

Toward the end of the *ancien regime*, an individual in dispute with a neighbor or in violation of the law sought redress of defense through a network of three forms of justice. Popular justice offered both arbitration and measured violence; seigneurial justice or the local seigneur's tribunal handled minor disputes; and royal justice or the courts of the *marechaussee* and the *senechaussee* acted on capital cases and unresolvable disputes. This system, often functioning in parallel, ensured civil peace.

Reinhardt examines this system in the Sarladais which contemporary observers thought an isolated *pays* in the Périgord. Reinhardt chooses it for the "internal unity and stability of [its] judicial and repressive institutions" (p. xiv). His sources are the departmental archives and the secondary literature in criminology, legal anthropology, and popular culture.

The beginning is a digression: an economic description of the Sarladais and its demographic crises with a picture of a *pays* already de-Christianized before the Revolution. This chapter is never clearly tied to the rest of the book. The real book begins with a description of the three forms of justice, followed by an analysis of the dynamics of the judicial processes. He shows that during the last decades of the *ancien regime* the royal courts, once at the periphery of daily affairs, assumed increasing importance in people's lives while the seigneurial courts were reduced to petty matters.

Because of the added caseload, the royal courts did not always welcome this reliance. Through numerous and ignored decrees, the royal courts tried to prod the seigneurial courts into useful litigation. The royal courts were thus hardly instruments of political terror (p. 162). In fact, as the author himself argues, the increased number of cases brought before these courts tended to confirm popular reliance on the king's justice. (The increase, the author cautions, did not mean a crime wave just before the Revolution.)

By contrast, popular and royal justice were often complementary. While serious cases like murder were brought directly to the royal courts, minor infractions and disputes were "accommodated," often over long periods of time, before referral to the royal court. Of the 477 cases heard by the *senechaussee*, 7% contain references to previous extralegal settlements. A harsh sentence was frequently a cumulative verdict against someone who had finally, sometimes after years, crossed a boundary of neighborly tolerance.

Where have the archives led the author? Reinhardt concludes skillfully with remarks that describe the changes that were gradually taking place in the Sarladais. The bourgeois were turning to the royal courts to assert their place in society and to protect their contractual interests, which the seigneurial courts were incompetent to handle. (The bourgeois were chiefly rentiers, legal professionals and tax collectors.) The peasants discovered that they could use the royal courts in civil disputes with seigneurs but not always. The courts discovered they had a dual role to perform—dispense justice and protect property rights—without provoking riots. The *cahiers de doleance* show which way the scales usually tipped. Finally, there were hints that even in the isolated Sarladais new assumptions about society were becoming commonplace. Lawyers defending a servant girl in 1778 used terms like "natural reason" and "liberty common to all citizens." The French Revolution was already in motion, or at least its rhetoric was current. Individuals, once subjects, now asserted rights as "citizens," a shift that Simon Schama illuminates in *Citizens.* The Sarladais was not as isolated as it appeared.—Richard Holbrook.

Rener, Frederick M. *Interpretation: Language and Translation from Cicero to Tytler.* Amsterdam and Atlanta, GA: Rodopi, 1989. Pp. 367.

Rev. by L. G. Kelly in *Historiographia Linguistica,* 18 (1991), 394–98.

Renwick, John (ed.). *Language and Rhetoric of the Revolution.* Edinburgh, Scotland: Edinburgh U. Press, 1990. Pp. x + 106.

Rev. (briefly) by Terry Edwards in *French Studies,* 45 (1991), 467–68.

Richards, Jeffery H. *Theater Enough: American Culture and the Metaphor of the World Stage, 1607–1789.* Durham, NC and London: Duke U. Press, 1991. Pp. xxi + 335; bibliography.

Ringe, Donald A. (Rev. ed.). *Charles Brockden Brown.* (Twayne U.S. Authors Series.) Boston, MA: G. K. Hall, 1991. Pp. xii + 141; frontispiece.

Rivara, Annie. *Les Soeurs de Marianne: Suites, imitations, variations 1731–1761.* (Studies on Voltaire and the Eighteenth Century, 285.) Oxford: The Voltaire Foundation at the Taylor Institution, 1991. Pp. 499.

This densely crafted work compares thirty-five novels published between 1731–1761 based on Pierre Carlet de Marivaux's *La Vie de Marianne* (1731–1742). Marivaux's novel, inherently contradictory according to Rivara, remained unfinished. The realistic representation of aristocratic obstacles to bourgeois social mobility and of Marianne's innate merit as she confronts these obstacles could not be achieved through closure. Marivaux's novel explores the possibility of social mobility for a poor but virtuous female orphan, questioning whether such a heroine can be percieved as a viable subject of serious literature. Constituting a new and complex feminine literary model, Marianne was the inspiration for numerous novels. The variations, imitations and continuations of Marivaux's project reflect a society's moral and political preoccupations as well as the literary destinies of marginal heroines.

Part I of Rivara's work focuses on attempts to continue or finish *La Vie de Marianne*. While these texts lack the complexity and ambiguities of their model, Marie Jeanne Riccoboni's "Continuation de *La Vie de Marrianne*" succeeds in reproducing the tone and multi-layered narration of the original.

Part II traces the theme of the virtuous orphan whose ultimate nobility integrates her into society. The influence of Marivaux's novel is evident in abbé Lambert's *La Nouvelle Marianne* (1740), Mouhy's *La Paysanne parvenue* (1735–1737), and Gaillard de la Bataille's *Jeanette second ou la nouvelle paysanne parvenue* (1744). Madame de Tencin's *Les Malheurs de l'Amour*, Mme de Lambert's *La Femme ermite*, Beliard's *Rezeda* and Gueullette's *Memoires de Mademoiselle de Bontems*, among others, enrich Rivara's discussion of the "Marianne" theme.

Moral, philosophic and stylistic problems posed by Marianne's literary descendants form the basis of part III. Rivara's interesting analysis of *romanesque* spaces such as churches and convents leads to a commentary on the function of *libertinage* as a literary topos, culminating in insights on the relationship between fictitional heroines, education, and the condition of women in eighteenth-century France. The bourgeoisie, in an effort to assert its power, confronted a crumbling aristocratic code of honor which created barriers to bourgeois aspirations. Concurrently, marginalized heroines in novels reflected the ambitions of real-life impoverished women, whose condition had little influence on the *philosophes'* projects for social reform. Marivaux's heroine inscribes the spiritual journey of an autonomous, responsible female subject whose destiny challenges social hierarchies.

Focusing on primary sources rather then theoretical frameworks, Rivara's carefully structured arguments are at times tedious and repetitious. Her readings of the novels, however, are informed by knowledge of the social, political and economic forces interacting with literary production, as well as the feminist philosophy to which she subscribes. Students of Marivaux and the French novel will find many useful insights in this book. Especially impressive is the twenty-two page bibliography.—Felicia Sturzer.

Rodriguez, Pierre, and Michele Weil (eds.). *Actes. Quatrieme Colloque international. Sator. Vers un Thesaurus informatise: Topique des ouvertures narratives avant 1800.* Montpellier: Universite Paul Valery, 1991. Pp. 449.

This volume covers two general topics: the topoi of narrative openings (ouvertures), and the progress of work on the establishment of a data bank for narrative topoi (or topos) of pre-1800 French novels.

Readers wishing to familiarize themselves with the activities of Sator should begin with Henri Coulet's presidential address, "Le topos," which presents a history of the society as well as a discussion of practical and theoretical problems involved in the study of topoi and in the creation of a computer inventory.

Pierre Rodriguez, in an essay entitled "Des Souris, des topoi, et des hommes," gives a clear account of the difficulties encountered by Sator in its work while holding out the possibility of a fruitful collaboration between literary and computer specialists.

To the term narrative opening (ouverture) Sator's members have given various meanings. Eleven of the papers in this book interpret it as paratext: preface, forward, letters of dedication, titles, and section heads. Colette Piau-Gillot, for example, studies the letter of dedication in Madame de Genlis' *Voeux temeraires* (1799), showing a considersble inconsistency between its discourse and that of the text. A reading of the dedication alone, according to Piau-Gillot, would lead to an erroneous interpretation of the novel's discourse. Where, then, does the narrative begin, if the formal topoi are dissociated from the content topoi?

Again, Wim de Vos is able to trace the evolution of Charles Sorel's literary and theoretical thought by analyzing the prefaces of *Francion, Le Berger extravagant*, and *Polyandre*.

On the other hand, 21 other papers in this collection understand narrative opening to apply to the incipit. Three of them study the novel before 1600. The others deal with 17th and 18th century novels. Nicole Boursier studies the renewal of narrative openings and the transition from the novel (Grand roman) to the short story in the work of Madeleine de Scudery.

Bernard Bray, in a toposemantic study of the introductions to five secondary narratives in *La Princesse de Cleves*, shows how topic repetition was used both to awaken the reader's curiosity and to communicate a sense of the ineluctable. Alain Niderst, analysing the opening topoi of forty 17th and 18th century fairy tales, is able to throw new light on C. Perrault's originality. He alone among writers of such tales avoided what Niderst refers to as a "Hellenistic degradation" caused by the stuffing of the tale with complicated ostentation.

Specialists in narratology will be interested in the emphasis given to that field in most of the papers in this book.

While it is true that after four international conferences the Sator group still has not managed to establish a satisfactory definition of topos—will it ever be able to do so?—it has certainly undertaken much noteworthy research. The essays contained in this volume will provoke some useful thought about the novel as a genre while throwing new light on the particular novelists studied.—Marie-France Silver.

Romanciers du XVIIIᵉ siècle. (Littératures Classiques, 15) Paris: Klincksieck, 1991. Pp. 315.

Rev. (briefly) by Catherine Bonfils in *Revue d'histoire littéraire de la France*, 91 (1991), 99.

Romaschko, Sergej A. "Sprachwissenschaft, Aesthetic und naturforschung der Goethe-Zeit: Theorie und Empirie im Ursprung der Vergleichenden Grammatik." *Historiographia Linguistica*, 18 (1991), 301–20.

Schlegel's conception of Sanskrit as "the ideal *Ursprache* of Indo-European" was informed by the "organic" concept of nature.

Rosenmeier, Rosamond. *Anne Bradstreet Revisited.* Boston, MA: G.K. Hall, 1991. Pp. xvi + 174; chronology; frontispiece; selected bibliography.

Over the three and a half centuries since the publication of Anne Bradstreet's *The Tenth Muse*, critical opinion of her poetry has reached some agreement. Much of her early work is now considered derivative, but her later poems are valued for their personal lyricism, reflecting the conflict between her emotions and her Puritan conscience. Rosamond Rosenmeier's study does not challenge current assessments of individual poems or contribute much that is new to our knowledge of New England Puritanism. These were not her goals. Her Twayne volume cetainly supersedes that of Josephine K. Piercy (1965), whose approach was largely determined by English Romanticism. Rosenmeier's introduction to Bradstreet's life and works benefits from recent developments in literary, biblical, historical, and gender studies. Drawing on this scholarship, she examines the concepts of role and identity in the poetry as a reflection of the poet's own experiences.

Rosenmeier sees in Bradstreet a seventeenth-century feminist, a woman who was, in Hélène Cixous's terms, "writing herself." Because Bradstreet drew heavily on Renaissance sources, Rosenmeier turns to these for her own interpretations. Her consideration of biblical studies, especially in the area of the Solominic tradition, in which Wisdom is personified as female, adds to the picture of Bradstreet as feminist. Notable is Rosenmeier's use of sources in the Renaissance sciences, which she employs to demonstrate connections among Bradstreet's seemingly diverse interests. And her discussion of the Renaissance gender debate helps us understand some of the resonance Bradstreet's poetry must have had for her contemporary audience.

An introductory chapter surveys the history of Bradstreet criticism and outlines Rosenmeier's methodology. The remaining three chapters consider Bradstreet's dual roles as "daughter-child," "sister-wife," and "mother-artist." In each, Rosenmeier provides first an overview of a portion of Bradstreet's life and then interpretations of poems in which the speaker, like the author, finds herself fulfilling one of these roles. Rosenmeier's decision to intermix biographical sequences and chronologically unrelated poems can occasion some confusion for the reader. That difficulty aside, her close reading of the primary texts is the main value of her study. She supplies enough of each poem in the form of quotation and paraphrase so that the reader need not have Bradstreet's complete works at hand, although with the less familiar poems, providing the full text would enhance Rosenmeier's readings. The index, notes, and selected annotated bibliography are helpful. The student new to Bradstreet will find this book easy to use, and the more experienced scholar will no doubt find it informative.

Rosenmeier's organizing principles of role and identity allow her to see in Bradstreet's body of poetry more unifying themes than have previously been noted. In helping the reader discern that overall unity, Rosenmeier has contributed to our appreciation of Bradstreet's considerable conscious artistry.—Victoria Thorpe Miller.

Ross, Deborah. *The Excellence of Falsehood: Romance, Realism, and Women's Contribution to the Novel.* Lexington, KY: U. of Kentucky Press, 1991. Pp. xi + 249; bibliography.

The 1980s and early 1990s have seen a number of serious and detailed feminist accounts of works by women that in earlier decades were either dismissed entirely or studied with a kind of arm's-length distaste. Books by Jane Spencer, Janet Todd, and Mary Anne Schofield, for example, have discussed in detail texts previously deemed unreadable, trivial, or solely of interest as precursors to better fiction. Deborah Ross's study of Restoration and eighteenth-century women writers—Behn, Manley, Lennox, Haywood, Burney, Radcliffe, and Austen—makes a significant addition to this re-evaluation of women's fiction. Although it appears in its early stages to suffer from a somewhat tentative sense of the categories it investigates, *The Excellence of Falsehood* develops into a complex and absorbing account of the countervailing pressures of "romance" and "realism" on women authors and their fictions. Ross's book has a tighter focus than Spencer's purposely more encyclopedic and summarizing *The Rise of the Woman Novelist* (1986), and it provides as well a valuable context for the numerous single-author critical and biographical studies of Behn, Burney, and Austen. As she traces the state of female authors pulled in different directions by romance and realism, Ross tries also to counteract a trend in feminist criticism that has, in her view, obscured the value of some of the works she treats: she argues that the prevalent American form of feminist literary analysis associated with Sandra Gilbert and Susan Gubar, which looks for the subversive subtext, has been unproductive and misleading as an approach to these writers. Thus, while Ross grapples well with the problems and dissatisfactions produced by the fictions she treats, she does not judge them in terms of their failure to promote forms of feminism developed in the nineteenth century or later. This judicious approach allows Ross, notably in her analyses of Haywood's *Betsy Thoughtless* and Lennox's *Harriot Stuart*, and in her discussion of Burney, to confront the problems of complicity with and confusion about the double standard in these novels.

Ross begins by placing the novels in the context of the d'Urfe-Scudery tradition of French romance; while her discussion of *Clelie* and *L'Astree* is of interest, the introduction at times falls into a form of speculative psychologizing about romance readers that belies Ross's claims to a historicist approach. At this point the reader may wish that Ross had taken more cognizance of such discussions of women and romance as Janice Radway's work on twentieth-century readers of series romances. A similiarly oversimplified and underhistoricized psychology at times undermines the Behn and Manly chapters, although the Manly chapter in particular raises important questions about autobiography and the woman writer's reputation, questions that have a substantial resonance in the chapter on

Lennox and Haywood. The Behn chapter brings an analysis of the poetry to bear on *Oroonoko*, but gets mired in biographical ironies, as does the Manly chapter.

The problems with these chapters on Behn and Manly, however, become strengths in the chapters on *Betsy Thoughtless* and *Harriot Stuart*, *The Female Quixote*, Burney, and *The Italian*, where the categories of romance and realism are brought into often satisfying and revealing play. For instance, in her discussion of Charlotte Lennox's most famous novel, Ross perceptively observes: "The morality of *The Female Quixote* is contradictory because the novel contains two worlds: one drawn from romance and one from reality. Ironically, the morality propounded by the novel's realist philosophy operates only in the world of romance. The novel asks the reader to wake up, to surrender her dreams like Arabella, but once she has done so, she can hardly expect that her father will reward her with a Glanville" (p. 105). Although one might quarrel with Ross's occasionally flat view of literary "reality," or with her assumptions about "the reader," her formulations here exhibit the considerable strengths—as well as some of the limits—of her method and choice of subject. In *The Excellence of Falsehood* Ross offers illuminating readings of some undervalued texts, and gives a useful context for several more familiar novels.—Tassie Gwilliam.

Roston, Murray. *Changing Perspectives in Literature and the Visual Arts.* Princeton, NJ: Princeton U. Press, 1989. Pp. xv + 453.

Rev. by Vincent Carretta in *The Scriblerian*, 23 (1991), 273–74.

Rousseau, G. S., and Roy Porter (eds.). *Exoticism in the Enlightenment.* Manchester, UK: Manchester U. Press (distributed through New York: St. Martin's Press), 1990. Pp. x + 230; 2 illustrations. Cf. *ECCB*, n.s. 16, V:317–18.

Rev. (favorably) by Michele E. Farrell in *L'Esprit createur*, 31 (1991), 78–79.

Rubin, David Lee (ed.). *Continuum: Problems in French Literature from the Late Renaissance to the Early Enlightenment.* Vol. III: *Poetics of Expositions and Libertinage and the Art of Writing, I.* New York: AMS Press, 1991. Pp. 289.

Rubin, David Lee, and John D. Lyons (eds.). *Continuum: Problems in French Literature from the Late Renaissance to the Early Enlightenment.* Vol I: *Rethinking Classicism: Overviews.* New York: AMS Press, 1989. Pp. ix + 299.

Rev. by Terence Allott in *Modern Language Review*, 86 (1991), 1011–12; by Ian M. Richmond in *Modern Philology*, 88 (1990–91), 442–45.

Rumbold, Valerie. *Women's Place in Pope's World.* Cambridge, and New York: Cambridge U. Press, 1989. Pp. xvii + 315.

Rev. by Katherine M. Rogers in *The Scriblerian*, 23 (1990), 221–23.

Saint-Hyacinthe, Themiseul de. *Le Chef d'oeuvre d'un inconnu.* Paris: Editions du CNRS, 1991. Pp. 196.

Salvaggio, Ruth. *Enlightened Absence: Neoclassical Configurations of the Feminine.* Chicago and Urbana, IL: U. of Illinois Press, 1988. Pp. 169. Cf. *ECCB*, n.s. 16, V:318; 14, V:246–47.

Rev. (with another work) by Anne Williams in *Eighteenth-Century Studies*, 24 (1991), 402–08.

Sbiroli, Salkin (ed.). *Libertine e madri ilibate. Una discussione settentesca su sesso e fecondazione.* Venice: Marsilio, 1989. Pp. 161.

Rev. by Franco Piva in *Studi francesi,* 35 (1991), 140–41.

Schatzberg, Walter, Jonathan K. Johnson, and Ronald A. Waite (eds.). *The Relations of Literature and Science: An Annotated Bibliography of Scholarship.* New York: MLA, 1987. Pp. xix + 458.

Rev. by G. A. Wells in *Modern Language Review,* 86 (1991), 153–54.

Schmidt, J. N. "Von der Restauration zur Vorromantik." Pp. 149–216 of *Englische Literaturgeschichte.* Edited by H. -U. Seeber. Stuttgart: J. B. Metzler, 1991. Pp. x + 461; bibliography.

Schofield, Mary Anne. *Masking and Unmasking the Female Mind: Disguising Romances in Feminine Fiction, 1713–1799.* Newark, DE: U. of Delaware Press; London and Toronto: Associated University Presses, 1990. Pp. 217; bibliography. Cf. *ECCB,* n.s. 16, V:319.

Rev. by Deborah D. Rogers in *Eighteenth-Century Studies,* 24 (1991), 546–48.

Schofield, Mary Anne, and Cecilia Macheski (eds.). *Curtain Calls: British and American Women and the Theater, 1660–1820.* Athens, OH: Ohio U. Press, 1991. Pp. xxiii + 403; frontispiece; 27 illustrations.

In *Curtain Calls,* editors Mary Anne Schofield and Cecilia Macheski continue the work they began with *Fetter'd or Free? British Women Novelists, 1670–1815* (1986). Intent on enlightening readers about literary women long ignored by literary history, they offer here the first critical anthology on women in the Restoration and eighteenth-century theater. Some of the most provocative essays in the collection take direct aim at cultural and critical assumptions that have obscured the achievements of women dramatists in this period. Kathryn M. Kendall and Jessica Munns, for example, question our conception of sexual identity: Kendall, in an intriguing study of erotic female friendships in women's drama, and Munns, in a lively, witty, and wide-ranging examination of the "sexual space" defined by Aphra Behn's career. Linda R. Payne also challenges established opinion, arguing that the plays of Margaret Cavendish are feminist "dreamscapes" rather than the unreadable lunacy they were long assumed to be.

But few essays make such overt bids for re-evaluation; rather, much of the volume prepares for later revision of the canon by introducing us to authors and works deserving further study. Noteworthy in this effort are the comprehensive checklist of "Women Dramatists in England, 1660–1800" by Judith Philips Stanton and a Hume-like survey of "Serouis Plays by Women on the London Stage, 1660–1737" by William J. Burling. Most of the other essays provide a different kind of information; they illuminate the psychological, political, economic, and social conditions in which women of the theater worked. The most interesting and consistently well-written section is that called "Stage Business." Here Maureen E. Mulvihill documents the carefully orchestrated image and career of Katherine Philips, while Deborah C. Payne traces Aphra Behn's complex and shifting attitudes toward patronage. Betty Rizzo identitfies the degrading, but successful "guerilla" tactics employed by Elizabeth Griffith—primarily against the powerful David Garrick. And Ellen Donkin speculates on the anxiety induced in Hannah Cowley and Hannah More by Garrick's posthumous influence.

Clearly, *Curtain Calls* has much to offer. But it also disappoints. Many accomplished and ground-breaking scholars, such as Laura Brown, Catherine Gallanger, and Susan Staves, do not contribute. And despite the balance implied by the subtitle, only three of twenty-two essays discuss American theater, while five essays are devoted exclusively to Behn, the only canonized woman dramatist of the period. Moreover, the organization of the volume, which extends the theater metaphor of the title, is more clever than helpful; one should not have to consult the editors' "Prologue" to understand why the section titled "Closet Drama" includes an essay on one of the most frequently produced plays of the period, *A Bold Stroke for a Wife*. Finally, as in *Fetter'd or Free?*, the proofing is careless: a note number is printed, but no note follows (p. 291); parentheses are not closed (p. 329); and spelling errors abound.

In the editors' "Prologue"—where on a single page "Philips's" twice should be "Philips," a quotation ends without beginning, and "network" is "newwork" (p. xix)—this carelessness is especially disturbing, because it extends beyond typography to matters of substance. As Schofield and Macheski attempt to summarize and relate the essays they have collected, they not only attribute to Frances M. Kavenik a quotation from Munns (p. xxi), they also misrepresent Deborah Payne's outstanding essay by conflating (with the pronoun "this") two perspectives on patronage that the essay carefully distinguishes: one, liminal and taunting, the other, royalist and sanctimonious. Moreover, the editors ignore Payne's emphasis on how eagerly Behn assumed the role of grateful playwright as "necessary camouflage" (p. 116), simply asserting instead that "in the final analysis . . . Behn does not fit this 'royalist/patronal/male dynamic' " (p. xix). One suspects, however, that what "does not fit" are subtle analyses like Payne's into the editors' simple thesis of relentless victimization and patriarchal control.

Fortunately, the collection itself presents a more complex introduction to the lives and careers of women long forgotten or caricatured. In addition to the strong contributions already cited, the volume includes fine essays on Elizabeth Inchbald by Katherine M. Rogers, Mercy Otis Warren by Jean B. Kern, and Sarah Siddons by Pat Rogers. Better books about women and the eighteenth-century theater will be written, but all will be indebted to *Curtain Calls.*—Peggy Thompson.

Schwartz, Richard B. (ed.). *Theory and Tradition in Eighteenth-Century Studies.* Carbondale, IL: Southern Illinois U. Press, 1990. Pp. xii + 193. Cf. *ECCB*, n.s. 16, V:320.

Rev. by Annette Wheeler Cafarelli in *Journal of English and Germanic Philology*, 90 (1991), 568–70; by Brian McCrea in *The Scriblerian*, 24 (1991), 56–58.

Schweitzer, Ivy. *The Work of Self-Representation: Lyric in Colonial New England.* (Gender and American Culture.) Chapel Hill, NC: U. of North Carolina Press, 1991. Pp. xi + 306.

Scodel, Joshua. *The English Poetic Epitaph: Commemoration and Conflict from Jonson to Wordsworth.* Ithaca and London: Cornell U. Press, 1991. Pp. viii + 425; figures.

"This book narrates the rise and fall of the English literary epitaph as a vital literary genre" (p. 6). Indeed it does. Scodel has written a definitive study of the genre that is a model of literary-historical and critical commentary. *Multum in parvo*, the aesthetic of the epitaph, applics to Scodel's own study, which combines close readings of selected epitaphs by Jonson, Donne, Carew, Crashaw, Herrick, Marvell, Cowley, Dryden, Pope, Johnson, Gray, and Wordsworth, with comprehensive discussion of social, religious, and artistic context. Although Scodel is writing about a minor, marginal genre, we finish the book with a deeper understanding of his chosen authors' major works. He reads individual epitaphs with the critical brilliance of Stephen Booth on Shakespeare's sonnets, and an extraordinary ear for echoes of classical, Renaissance, and English sources, combined with an exacting mastery of scholarship. Scodel does not mention Swift's epitaph—*Ubi Saeva Indignatio/Ulterius/Cor Lacerare Nequit*—which made Yeats say that "Swift sleeps under the greatest epitaph in history," but he gives us all we need to evaluate Yeats's enthusiastic judgement.

Part One devotes three chapters to "Ben Jonson and the Epitaphic Tradition," illustrating the conflict between costly monuments and Jonson's humanistic epitaphs. "The Poetics of Brevity" (Chapter 2) demonstrates how radically Jonson's epitaphs undermine traditional hierarchies, offering a reading of "On My First Daughter" (pp. 75–85) that shows how Jonson's modification of a Latin formula enables him to speak in his own voice "in hitherto impersonal poem" (p. 83). "Mourning and Praise" (Chapter 3) contains an equally close contextual reading of Jonson's epitaph "On My First Sonne" (pp. 92–109), a fine analysis of Jonson's "poetics-as-child topos" (p. 105), and echoes of Greek and Latin texts.

Part Two begins with a chapter on Donne's idiosyncratic "poetics of death" (p. 119), comparing Donne's "Epitaph on Himselfe" to Thomas Carew's elegy. "Praising Honest Men" (Chapter 5) analyzes the trope of the *honnete homme* in epitaphs of James Shirley and Richard Crashaw, and the "thwarting . . . of the 'honest' ideal" (p. 161) in comic epitaphs on the lower orders. "Herrick and the Epitaph of Retreat" (Chapter 6) discusses Herrick's strategy of simultaneous assertion and retirement in epitaphs, drawing illuminating comparisons to classical poets like Theocritus and Propertius (pp. 172-73). "The Politics of Nostalgia" (Chapter 7) shows how late seventeenth-century poets like Cotton, Waller, Cowley, Marvell, and Dryden "use the dead to condemn the living" (p. 203).

Part Three begins with two splendid chapters on Pope: the first on Pope's epitaphs upon himself, showing how Pope "attempts to immortalize himself as the definitive poet of retirement-unto-death" (p. 254), including a discussion of the Westminster Abbey anti-epitaph (pp. 264–74), shrewdly commenting on Pope's emulation of Cowley and Prior. "Grafting Fame" (Chapter 9) offers a fascinating analysis of Pope's epitaphs on the Stanton Harcourt lovers killed by lightening, reflecting Pope's "poetic obsession with self-commemoration," and the "epistolary fantasies" (p. 284) of his correspondence with Lady Mary. "Kindred Spirits" (Chapter 10) shows how the cult of sentiment changed eighteenth-century epitaphs and monuments, concentrating on Gray's elegy, and Jonson's "epitaphic poetics . . . [through which] he self-consciously both adapts and resists features of the prevailing epitaphic style" (p. 332). The new sentimental taste prepares Wordworth's move from epitaph to elegy as the epitaph gives way to the obituary, culminating in Yeats's iconoclastic epitaph on himself in " 'Under Ben Bulben': 'Cast a cold eye / On life, on death / Horseman, pass by!' " (p. 410).

This superb book brings us the glad tidings that the scholar-critic is not extinct in eighteenth-century studies, that an exemplary work of literary history can be written in the Age of Theory, combining brilliant critical reading with scholarship that improves on Loeb translations, corrects Sherburn's dating of a Pope letter (p. 301, n. 90), and Helen Gardner on Donne's religious beliefs (p. 80). Scodel displays a discriminating control of secondary sources with the tact to state precisely the extent of his agreement with various critics like Doody, Weinbrot, and others. The book is beautifully organized, and well composed (witness the pictorial conclusion to Chapter 10, making good use of two of seven half-tone illustrations). This book must rank as a model for the revision of a dissertation (*DAI* 47/04A [Yale 1985], p. 1339) into a scholarly book of enduring value, marred only by fondness for one repeated phrase ("to have it both ways"), and a few typos (pp. 73, p. 365 n.; p. 391).—Morris R. Brownell.

Scott, Virginia. *The Commedia dell'Arte in Paris, 1644–1697*. Charlottesville, VA: U. Press of Virginia, 1990. Pp. xii + 459; bibliography; illustrations.

Rev. (favorably) by F. K. Barasch in *Choice*, 28 (1991), 791.

Seelye, John. *Beautiful Machine: Rivers and the Republican Plan, 1755–1825*. New York and Oxford: Oxford U. Press, 1991. Pp. xii + 430; bibliography; illustrations.

Beautiful Machine is the second of John Seelye's projected series on the rivers of America. (The first, *Prophetic Waters*, appeared in 1977.) The "beautiful machine" of the title refers to Robert Fulton's steamboat, which made its inaugural voyage in 1807; the book examines the forces leading to the technological triumph—the system of locks and canals linking the Ohio and Mississippi rivers to the Hudson—that made the steamboat so useful to an expanding American empire.

Before Lewis and Clark proved otherwise, the Missouri River was thought to approach the Pacific as closely as Ohio did the Atlantic. To the eighteenth-century mind, this apparent neoclassical symmetry suggested a landscape laid out according to a divine plan lacking only a system of interconnecting canals to complete it. George Washington, aware of the political and commercial advantages of such a system, favored a plan that would access the Ohio via the Potomac, thereby ensuring the South's participation in future western trade. The Potomac, however, proved unsuitable as a link to the West, just as the Missouri would later prove an impractical route to the Pacific.

Geography dictated instead a series of canals linking the Ohio to the Hudson by way of the Great Lakes—a route that promised to funnel western wealth through New York, bypassing the South entirely. Seelye notes that, long before the slavery issue came to a head, votes concerning the funding of canals already tended to split Congress along what would come to be familiar sectional lines. He reminds us that, when the Erie Canal opened in 1825, the "thunderous salute of guns that signalled . . . the passage of the ceremonial fleet" down the Hudson also signified "the opening of the eastern portals to the West, a geopolitical shift of power" (389) that would determine the career of one of the spectacle's viewers—the young West Point cadet, Robert E. Lee.

The impact of riverine geography on American expansion unifies Seelye's readings of a variety of texts, including the well known writings of Jefferson, Washington, Lewis and Clark, William Bartram and Joel Barlow, as well as those of lesser-known writers such as Jonathon Carver and John Neal. He also analyzes the iconography of such contemporary illustrators as George Catlin, William Rush, Thomas Pownall, and John Hill.

Beautiful Machine is competently, occasionally even eloquently, written. But it makes less use than it might of contemporary literary theory, and there are practically no women in it. Perhaps its most serious omission—one made all the more obvious by the Indian names, the Potowmacs and Monongahelas and Mississippis that pulse through the book like a powerful undercurrent—is the absence of any sustained discussion of native Americans and how they figured in the imperial appropiation of American waters. Early in the book, Seelye notes that "European explorers uniformly tell of meeting with Indians at the river entrances to the continent, wild men who held the knowledge needed by the agents of civilization but who yielded it reluctantly, often refusing to the point of fiercely resisting entry" (5), but he fails to elaborate further. Had he done so, *Beautiful Machine* might have been a better book.—David Mazel.

Seth, Wolfgang. *George Lillos Dramen: der Versuch der "Verbürgerlichung" des englischen Dramas im 18. Jahrhundert*. Essen: Blaue Eule, 1991. Pp. 308.

Sgard, Jean (ed.). *Dictionnaire des Journaux: 1600-1789*. Vol. I & II. Oxford: The Voltaire Foundation at the Taylor Institution, 1991. Pp. xi + 1209; indices.

Jean Sgard's editorship of this monumental work is an outstanding contribution to seventeenth and eighteenth century studies. The *Dictionnaire* has 1267 entries providing information about all French language journals published between 1600 and 1789. If the stated intention of a journal was to appear periodically, it is included even if only one issue was published, as was the case, for example, of many journals issued during the Fronde. Each entry provides information as to title (and changes thereof), the dates and frequency of publication, a description of the journal, the publisher, the editors, its contents (actual and stated) with the main authors studied, the location of the collection consulted, and, finally, any bibliographical data, either historical or contemporary.

The 141 collaborators were not bound by any limitations on the length of their articles. Length was determined by the information available about the journal in question. The Ancien Regime scholar can read comprehensive and valuable articles on the major journals of the time, such as the *Journal des Savants*, the *Memoires de Trevoux*, and the *Mercure de France*, but also learn about hundreds of specialized journals dealing with topics as varied as education, fashion, women's issues, and economics. One can explore the preoccupations of the provincials; the *Affiches* from the different provincial towns reveal specific concerns of the citizenry. The *Affiches d'Angers*, for example, has many articles dealing with local problems, among others the difficulties encountered when cultivating the potato. Yet, on a national level, one can follow the political vagaries of the times and the cultural battles waged by different journals—Fréron's *Année Littéraire*, for example, seduced by the excitement of the intellectual climate of the age, yet fearful of the revolutionary implications. One can use the *Dictionnaire* to follow pre-revolutionary journals and those which started publication prior to 1789 and continued throughout the Revolutionary period. After 1789, as Sgard states, there was a true explosion of the press with 250 journals appearing in that year alone. The editorial decision not to include journals which began publication in 1789 and thereafter is wise given the already comprehensive scope of the *Dictionnaire*.

The postface (by Jean Sgard) outlines a typology of the periodical press studied. He makes a broad distinction between journals dealing with current events and those dealing with culture. In the first category he counts 80 *Gazettes*, 87 *Affiches*, 75 general information journals, and about 200 reviews dealing with politics and history. The cultural press includes 46 *Bibliothèques Savantes*, 140 literary reviews, 40 literary selections, 25 anthologies from the press, 80 *Spectateurs*, and about 260 specialized journals. 200 unclassified titles remain, mainly pre-1680 as 'genre' defintion was not clearly established at that date. The tables appended provide interesting information about the growth and durability of the periodical press. The period of strongest growth appears to have been between 1730 and 1749.

Comprehensive indices are invaluable for the researcher. They list places of publication, the names of printers and publishers, of authors cited, of editors and principal journalists, a chronology of titles and an alphabetical listing of titles. Combined with the *Dictionnaire des journalistes 1600–1789* (P.U.G., 1976) and its five supplements (1980–1987), this 2 volume work is the indispensable source for the history of the periodical press. We are fortunate to have in Jean Sgard, a man of encyclopaedic range and vision, a modern Diderot who has accomplished an awesome task of compilation and editorship with the assistance of some of the finest scholars of the Ancien Regime society of our times. Not only are the scholarly standards impeccable, but the production quality is superb. These two volumes are a vital addition to any serious research library.—Kay S. Wilkins.

Sherbo, Arthur. *The Birth of Shakespeare Studies: Commentators from Rowe (1709) to Boswell-Malone (1821).* (Studies in Literature, 1500–1800.) East Lansing, MI: Colleagues Press, 1986. Pp. xvi + 203. Cf. *ECCB*, n.s. 16, V:322; 14, V:250; 12, V:376–77.

Rev. by Brian Vickers in *Modern Language Review*, 86 (1991), 398–99.

Sheridan, Geraldine. *Nicolas Lenglet Dufresnoy and the Literary Underworld of the Ancien Régime.* (Studies on Voltaire and the Eighteenth Century, 262.) Oxford: The Voltaire Foundation at the Taylor Institution, 1989. Pp. ix + 433. Cf. *ECCB*, n.s. 15, V:247.

Rev. (favorably) by Sean O'Cathasaigh in *Modern Language Review*, 86 (1991), 1024–25; (briefly) by Paolo Alatri in *Studi francesi*, 34 (1991), 527–28.

Shevelow, Kathryn. *Women and Print Culture: The Construction of Feminity in the Early Periodical.* London and New York: Routledge, 1989. Pp. x + 236. Cf. *ECCB*, n.s. 16, V:322; 15, V:248.

Rev. (with other works) by Clare Brant in *Review of English Studies*, 42 (1991), 302–04.

Shields, David S. *Oracles of Empire: Poetry, Politics, and Commerce in British America, 1690–1750.* Chicago, IL, and London: U. of Chicago Press, 1990. Pp. xiv + 295; bibliography; illustrations.

Rev. by D. D. Knight in *Choice*, 28 (1991), 1312; by W. A. Speck in *TLS*, (Mar. 15, 1991), 21.

Sitter, John. *Arguments of Augustan Wit.* (Cambridge Studies on Eighteenth-Century Literature and Thought, 11.) Cambridge and New York: Cambridge U. Press, 1991. Pp. xiii + 188.

An odd book, this: odd in conception and odd in organization. Odd in conception in that readers will probably have difficulty identifying its intended audience. From its title one might reasonably expect that Sitter wants to reinvestigate the history of the late seventeenth and early eighteenth-century arguments over the definition and value of the term *wit*. But, for the most part, he writes as if he assumes his audience to be familiar with those arguments and their context. Instead, for much of the book, including its first chapter, *wit* goes largely unmentioned. On the other hand, "a book that emphasizes the materialism [i.e., the concern with representations of bodies and bodily functions] of Augustan writing" (p. xi) will not surprise many specialist readers with the novelty of its subject, especially since most of Sitter's examples are taken from the works of the Scriblerians.

In his first chapter, Sitter discusses "a mode of presenting character that seems peculiar to the period from roughly the 1670s to the 1740s, a kind of character sketch I will call the character progress" (p. 6). This new

"Hogarthian" character progress "differs from the static character in being a story, in having a plot rather than a list of ingredients" (p. 7). Sitter's argument for the peculiarity of this mode of presentation might be stronger if he did not assume that no visual tradition preceded Hogarth's "memorable examples" (p. 6), and if he had situated his poetic examples in the tradition of narrative verse.

Chapter 2 takes up the topic of *wit*, centering on Locke's definition and evaluation of the term, as well as his role in provoking discussion of the subject. Here Sitter reminds readers, as he does throughout the book, that eighteenth-century literature was predominately *rhetorical*, in the classical sense of that term, which assumes that an author was attempting persuasive communication with an audience about something extratextual. Again, students of the period are not likely to need reminding. At the center of this chapter is Sitter's discussion of the eighteenth-century concepts of *wit* and *judgement* in relation to Roman Jakobson's distinction between *metaphor* and *metonymy*, a discussion that many students of the period may feel unnecessary, given Brian Vickers' convincing estimate in *In Defence of Rhetoric* (1988) of the "effects of Jakobson's dichotomizing reduction of rhetoric [as having been] disastrous" (p. 448). Similarly, in his "Conclusion," Sitter devotes several pages to arguing the irrelevance to eighteenth-century studies of what Paul de Man misunderstands to be the meaning of *rhetoric,* even though Sitter acknowledges in a footnote (p. 162) that Robert Scholes has already pointed out that de Man confuses *rhetoric* and *poetry.* Even earlier, in reviews that appeared in the *ECCB* (1980) and in *Comparative Literature Studies* (1982), Jeffery Barnouw has demonstrated that de Man's formulations depended upon a combination of ignorance and misreading.

Sitter's Chapters 3 and 4 take up the material subject matter of the authors under study. Here and throughout his book, Sitter shows himself to be a perceptive reader of texts, including relatively little-read works of Pope (his poems in response to *Gulliver's Travels*) and Prior (*Alma*, "A Dialogue between Mr. John Locke and Seigneur de Montaigne"). He also draws interesting parallels between works of Berkeley and Swift. Chapter 5 argues "that a reluctance to give much weight to historical particularity leads to neglect or distortion of much Augustan literature and especially of satiric writing" (p. 179). The recent rise of various "historicisms" should make that reluctance less evident. The book has a brief but incomplete index mostly of proper names. —Vincent Carretta.

Sitter, John (ed.). *Eighteenth-Century British Poets, First Series.* (Dictionary of Literary Biography, 95.) Detroit, MI, and London: Gale Research, 1990. Pp. xi + 436; illustrations. Cf. *ECCB*, n.s. 16, V:323–24.

Sitter, John (ed.). *Eighteenth-Century British Poets, Second Series.* (Dictionary of Literary Biography, 109.) Detroit, MI, and London: Gale Research, 1991. Pp. xi + 385; illustrations.

Rev. by Lionel Basney in *South Atlantic Review*, 56 (Nov. 1991), 103–104; by Mark Y. Herring in *American Reference Books Annual*, 22 (1991), 1224.

Smith, Julia J. "Susanna Hopton: A Biographical Account." *Notes and Queries,* 236 (1991), 165–72.

Smith, Margaret M. (comp.). *Index of English Literary Manuscripts, Vol. III, 1700–1800. Part 2, John Gay-Ambrose Philips.* London and New York: Mansell, 1989. n.p.

Rev. by J. D. Fleeman in *Notes and Queries*, 235 (1990), 390–92; by Ian Jack in *Review of English Studies*, 42 (1991), 429–30.

Soriano, Marc. *La Brosse a reluire sous Louis XIV: 'L'Epitre au Roi' de Perrault anotee par Racine et Boileau.* (Biblioteca de Quaderni del Seicento Francese, 6.) Fasano: Schena; Paris: Nizet, 1989. Pp. 99.

Rev. (severely) by Robin Howells in Modern Language Review, 86 (1991), 1023–24.

Spacks, Patricia Meyer. *Desire and Truth: Functions of Plot in Eighteenth-Century English Novels*. Chicago, IL, and London: U. of Chicago Press, 1990. Pp. ix + 262; bibliography. Cf. *ECCB*, n.s. 16, V:326.

Rev. by P. D. McGlynn in *Choice*, 28 (1991), 779; (with another work) by Alexander Pettit in *Modern Language Quarterly*, 52 (1991), 210–15.

Spector, Robert D. *Backgrounds to Restoration and Eighteenth-Century English Literature: An Annotated Bibliographical Guide to Modern Scholarship*. (Bibliographies and Indexes in World Literature, 17). New York: Greenwood, 1989. Pp. xxiv + 553. Cf. *ECCB*, n.s. 16, V:327; 15, V:250.

Rev. (with another work) by Donald C. Mell in *The Scriblerian*, 23 (1991), 286–89.

Stafford, Fiona. *The Sublime Savage: James Macpherson and the Poems of Ossian*. Edinburgh, Scotland: U. Press of Edinburgh, 1989. Pp. 240.

Rev. by David H. Radcliffe in *South Atlantic Review*, 56 (Nov. 1991), 105–108.

Stanitzek, Georg. *Blodickeit: Beschreibungen des Individuums im 18. Jahrhundert*. (Hermaea: Germanistische Forschungen. Neue Folge, Band 60.) Tubingen: Max Niemeyer Verlag, 1989. Pp. x + 322.

Rev. by Hans Graubner in *Journal of English and Germanic Philology*, 90 (1991), 118–20.

Starobinski, Jean. *Le Remède dans le mal: Critique et Légitimation de l'artifice à l'âge des Lumières*. Paris: Gallimard, 1989. Pp. 286. Cf. *ECCB*, n.s. 15, V:250.

Rev. (with reservations) by Angelica Goodden in *Modern Language Review*, 86 (1991), 459–60; by Ruth Plaut Weinreb in *Eighteenth-Century Studies*, 24 (1991), 531–34.

Stevenson, John Allen. *The British Novel, Defoe to Austen: A Critical History*. (Twayne's Critical History of the Novel.) Boston, MA: Twayne, 1990. Pp. xiii + 153. Cf. *ECCB*, n.s.16, V:329–30.

Rev. (favorably) by D. Landry in *Choice*, 28 (1991), 1489.

Stewart, Susan. *Crimes of Writing: Problems in the Containment of Representation*. New York and Oxford: Oxford U. Press, 1991. Pp. x + 353; figures; frontispiece.

Stout, Janis P. *Strategies of Reticence: Silence and Meaning in the Works of Jane Austen, Willa Cather, Katherine Anne Porter and Joan Didion*. Charlottesville,VA: U. Press of Virginia, 1990. Pp. xii + 228; bibliography.

Rev. (favorably) by T. S. Kobler in *Choice*, 28 (1991), 1138.

Struever, Nancy S., and Brian Vickers. *Rhetoric and the Pursuit of Truth: Language Change in the Seventeenth and Eighteenth Centuries*. Los Angeles, CA: U. of California Press, 1985. Pp. vi + 122.

Rev. by B. D. Miller in *Review of English Studies,* 42 (1991), 237–39.

Tearle, John. *Mrs. Piozzi's Tall Young Beau.* Madison, NJ: Fairleigh Dickinson U. Press, 1991. Pp. 252; illustrations.

Temmer, Mark J. *Samuel Johnson and Three Infidels: Rousseau, Voltaire, Diderot.* Athens, GA, and London: U. of Georgia Press, 1988. Pp. xiii + 212; bibliography. Cf. *ECCB,* n.s. 14, VI: 340.

Rev. by Frederick M. Keener in *Diderot Studies,* 24 (1991), 205–07.

Teysseire, Daniel. "A Propos de l'*Encyclopédie méthodique.* Le Quadruple inventaire de la Bibliothèque mazarine." *Recherches sur Diderot et sur l'*Encyclopédie, 11 (1991), 142–49; 6 illustrations.

Thibault, Gabriel-Robert. "L'Harmonie imitative Essai historique et anthropologique." *Dix-huitiéme siécle,* 21 (1991), 357–68.

Thickstun, Margaret Olofson. *Fictions of the Feminine: Puritan Doctrine and the Representations of Women.* Ithaca, NY, and London: Cornell U. Press, 1988. Pp. ix + 176; bibliography. Cf. *ECCB,* n.s. 16, V:332; 14, V:254–55

Rev. by Amy Schrager Lang in *Modern Philology,* 88 (1990–91), 440–42.

Thomas, David (ed.). *Restoration and Georgian England, 1660–1788.* (Theatre in Europe: A Documentary History.) Cambridge, and New York: Cambridge U. Press, 1989. Pp. xxx + 460; bibliography; illustrations; plans; portraits. Cf. *ECCB,* n.s. 16, V:332; 15, V:253.

Rev. by Michael Dobson in *Essays in Criticism,* 41 (1991), 166–72.

Tieck, Ludwig. *Novellas of Ludwig Tieck and E. T. A. Hoffmann.* Translated by Thomas Carlyle, with an introduction by Eitel Timm. Columbia, SC: Camden House, 1991. Pp. xiv + 317.

Tinkler-Villani, Valeria. *Visions of Dante in English Poetry: Translations of the "Comedia" from Jonathan Richardson to William Blake.* (Costerus, 72.) Amsterdam: Rodopi, 1989. Pp. viii + 358; 17 illustrations. Cf. *ECCB,* n.s. 15, V:254.

Rev. by Piero Boitani in *Modern Language Review,* 86 (1991), 979–80.

Todd, Janet. *The Sign of Angellica: Women, Writing, and Fiction, 1660–1800.* London: Virago; New York: Columbia U. Press, 1989. Pp. vii + 328; bibliography. Cf. *ECCB,* n.s. 16, V:332; 15, V:254–55.

Rev. (with other works) by Clare Brant in *Review of English Studie*s, 42 (1991), 302–04.

Trisolini, Giovanna. *Rivoluzioni e scena. La Dura realta (1789–1799).* (Biblioteca di Cultura, 368.) Rome: Bulzoni, 1988. Pp. 606; bibliographies.

Rev. by Stella Gargantini Rabbi in *Studi francesi*, 34 (1991), 523; by Suzanne Jean-Bérard in *Revue d'histoire littéraire de la France*, 91 (1991), 105–06.

Uphaus, Robert W. (ed.). *The Idea of the Novel in the Eighteenth Century.* (Studies in Literature, 1500–1800, 3.) East Lansing, MI: Colleagues Press, 1988. Pp. xii + 144. Cf. *ECCB*, n.s. 15, V:268.

Rev. (with another work) by Kathryn Sutherland in *Review of English Studies*, 42 (1991), 272–73.

Uphaus, Robert W. and Gretchen M. Foster. *The "Other" Eighteenth Century: English Women of Letters, 1660–1800.* East Lansing, MI: Colleagues Press, 1991. Pp. ix + 465; illustrations.

In choosing material for *The "Other" Eighteenth Century,* Robert W. Uphaus and Gretchen M. Foster will not please everybody, but they have selected samples from every genre except fiction about these "other" women writers to help refine the earlier scholarship of Joyce Horner (1930), Bridgit McCarthy (1944), and J. J. S. Tompkins (1961) (the omitted genre of fiction is by now available in the Garland Publishers or Scholarly Facsimile reprints). Despite the plethora of available texts, we have yet to see much theoretical material, which may explain why we welcome each new anthology, such as Roger Lonsdale's *Eighteenth Century Women Poets* (1990), and also look beyond Uphaus and Foster's more varied examples of poems, plays, essays, letters, and criticism to Dale Spender's promised anthology *Living by the Pen* of modern critical essays on ten eighteenth-century women novelists. Gradually we should acquire enough texts and enough criticism to make up our minds on what value we find in these new anthologies.

In their introduction, Uphaus and Foster state that "the purpose of this textbook is to reclaim the tradition of women's writing in England during the period 1660–1800 and to restore this tradition to its rightful place in the canon of eighteenth-century literature." While this suggests new authors discovered and rescued "from an unsettling combination of ignorance and distortion of literary history" (p. 1), actually the writers anthologized are nearly all accessible. Even so, the selection sometimes seems capricious. Why print all seventy-five pages of an Aphra Behn play (*The Lucky Chance*) when her plays are readily available (even though Germaine Greer has announced her intention of bringing out a new, more accurate edition)? On the positive side, reprinting Hannah Cowley's *The Belle's Stratagem* (1780), rather than her sentimental, occasional poetry, seems much more justifiable, since it allows for interesting comparisons with Farquhar's *The Beaux Stratagem* produced nearly seventy-five years earlier (although the Cowley and Behn plays make the anthology top-heavy with drama). The editors have also shown good judgement in printing only a small portion of Mary Wollstonecraft's *Vindication of the Rights of Woman,* including instead a longer selection of her less well known letters from the Scandinavian countries, which furnish a more complete knowledge of her character. The inclusion of Joanna Baillie's little known dramatic criticism is another pleasant surprise, because it contains her theory of passions, and because it reveals her awareness of both Wordsworth and various contemporary women writers, such as Maria Edgeworth and Anna Barbauld. Other welcome texts even less well known include Lady Rachel Russell's moving letters begging for the life of her husband who was imprisoned for high treason by Charles II in 1683. Even after he was beheaded, she continued her effort to clear his name; that she wished to arrange secure marriages for their three children is an obvious motivation, and her letters are a rare bit of social history of the troubled court of the Restoration. Elizabeth Carter's poem "On the Death of Mrs. Rowe" (pp. 214–15) poses a puzzle, however. The editors state in a headnote that the text is based on Carter's *Poems on Several Occasions* (1762), the same source Lonsdale claims for his entirely different version of the poem in *Eighteenth-Century Women Poets;* while Lonsdale's text matches the claimed source, the same cannot be said for the text here.

Uphaus and Foster have produced an anthology of representative, valuable selections. Only occasionally do they surprise readers with new material. Writers like Anne Finch, Katherine Philips, Mary Astell, or Lady Mary Chudleigh have been known to scholars of literature for some time and are likely to appear again in other anthologies, while the best women writers in the late eighteenth century, such as Frances Burney, Charlotte Lennox, Charlotte Smith, and of course Jane Austen, are in no danger of being neglected. That this volume contains so many unique items as well as suggestions on the "Introduction" of themes for further studies should stimulate students to pursue these "other" writings. It is also gratifying, in these days of high publishing costs, to find a final "Appendix" (pp. 453–65) containing reproductions of frontispieces, illustrations, and portraits that give the reader some idea of the dress and furniture of the period.—Jean B. Kern.

Vance, Norman. *Irish Literature: A Social History: Tradition, Identity, and Difference.* Cambridge, MA, and Oxford: Basil Blackwell, 1990. Pp. xv + 315; illustrations; maps. Cf. *ECCB*, n.s. 16, V:333–34.

Rev. by R. J. Thompson in *Choice*, 28 (1991), 1643.

van Tassel, Mary M. "Spear and Petticoats: The Tatler and the Instability of Language." *Journal of English and Germanic Philology*, 90 (1991), 327–41.

The classifications of language can reconcile or steady some of the instabilities of society, but language can be perverted, and Bickerstaff, himself a paradox, has doubts about the nature of language.

Velie, Alan R. (ed.). *American Indian Literature: An Anthology.* London and Norman, OK: U. of Oklahoma Press, 1991. Pp. x + 373; illustrations.

The second edition of Alan Velie's *American Indian Literature: An Anthology* includes the same six genres as his first edition: tales, songs, oratory, memoirs, poetry and fiction. Making room for the post-1980 explosion of native writing, Velie removes three tales and four songs and adds such new voices as Maurice Kenny, Paula Gunn Allen, Linda Hogan, Gerald Vizenor and Nila Northsun. But where Velie's 1979 edition grouped the texts along a contact/conquest continuum—traditional/pre-contact, transitional/early contact, and modern/significantly post-contact—the 1991 edition claims a more artistically-based model. Here he describes two primary literary modes: "traditional (oral) native forms, (tales, songs, and oratory), and "mainstream" of imported forms (memoirs, poetry and fiction).

By shifting away from the historical model, Velie attempts to focus on the survivability of traditional modes. Rather than being lost in the pre-contact past, "traditional" Indian genres "[have] been composed on this continent for thousands of years" (3) and are now seen as building blocks in a cumulative native American artistic repertoire. But where both traditional and mainstream forms are now written primarily in English, traditional forms were originally "composed in tribal languages for a tribal audience" while "mainstream texts are "works . . . in one of the standard American genres—fiction, poetry, biography, history" (ibid.). With this realignment, Velie solves the problem of defining the Indian artist in terms of outside (white) forces. His concurrent insistence that selections be judged as "serious literature" rather than as ethnographic relics, however, leads to a more insidious problem. Failing to define the criteria upon which his literary evaluations are based, Velie omits a number of important texts which reveal his bias towards bifurcating Indian art as either 'true'—timeless and essentially Indian—or westernized, effectively assimilated.

In the "traditional" category, he fails to include examples of contemporary artists crafting traditional forms (such as Peter Blue Cloud's coyote trickster tales), and further suggests that traditional literature is ahistorical or atemporal by presenting these texts as outside of a historical framework. Even more troubling, he excludes all "mainstream" texts written by Indian authors between 1700 and 1900. Marking the 1968 publication of N. Scott Momaday's *House Made of Dawn* as the beginning of "the Renaissance in American Indian literature," Velie dismisses as "pretty pedestrian" (8) all pre-1960s mainstream Indian texts (though he does include selections from white-authored biographies). Even his "traditional" category includes only three early speeches (totaling less than 20 pages) by pre-twentieth-century voices: chiefs Red Jacket (Seneca, 1752), Pontiac (Ottawa, 1763), and Tecumseh (Shawnee, 1811). The personal narratives of Samsom Occom (1768) and William Apess (1837) are absent, as are the writings of such later figures as Sarah Winnemucca Hopkins, John Rollin Ridge, D'Arcy McNickle, and Zitkala-Sa. Despite Velie's assertion that "Indians have always been highly verbal people" (9), what they said before 1950 is apparently not worth hearing. And while it is true that much pre-twentieth century material is indeed 'non-literary' in form, (e.g. speeches, treaty documents, letters), the collection would nonetheless benefit from their inclusion. More than "quaint relics" they demonstrate that, despite both popular stereotype and Velie's model, the seventeenth, eighteenth and nineteenth-century native American was neither silent nor inarticulate. (For a more thorough collection of texts from this period, see Colin G. Calloway's 1994 *The World Turned Upside Down: Indian Voices from Early America.* Boston and New York, Bedford Books of St. Martin's Press.)

   Velie's collection does indeed offer a fine general introduction to a wide variety of written and oral texts crafted by native American artists, and provides insightful introductions to a number of genres, tribes, and individual writers. In each of the six sections, Velie offers general overviews of specific forms as well as information on particular tribal histories, and does a good job of discussing the artistic strategies of contemporary writers. For the general reader interested in an introduction to native American artists and stories, the anthology is a fine beginning. But it must be read with caution. Velie's second edition simply repackages old stereotypes in new boxes: in the place of the conquered Indian it offers the timeless traditional, outside of the historical process, and in the place of the "modernized" or assimilated Indian it presents the Renaissance writer, effectively mastering contemporary, imported forms. Trapped between these are a number of voices that are valuable both intellectually and artistically, and to which we must also give our attention.—Carol Bodeau.

Versini, Laurent. *Le XVIIIe. Littérature Francaise.* (Collection Phares.) Nancy: Presses universitaires de Nancy, 1988. Pp. 151; bibliography. Cf. *ECCB*, n.s. 14, V:257.

Rev. by Edouard Guitton in *Revue d'histoire littéraire de la France*, 91 (1991), 104.

Vest, James M. *The French Face of Ophelia from Belleforest to Baudelaire.* Lanham, MD: University Press of America, 1989. Pp. x + 223. Cf. *ECCB*, n.s. 15, V:269–70.

Rev. by Derek F. Connon in Modern Language Review, 86 (1991), 1025-26.

Wagner, Peter (ed.). *Erotica and the Enlightenment.* (Britannia, 2.) Frankfurt am Main and New York: Peter Lang, 1991. Pp. 368; illustrations.

Wain, John (ed.). *The Oxford Anthology of English Poetry.* I: *Spenser to Crabbe*; II: *Blake to Heaney.* New York and Oxford: Oxford U. Press, 1990. Pp. xxiv + 659; xx + 770.

Rev. by Philip Cox in *Notes and Queries*, 236 (1991), 548–49.

Warner, Michael. *The Letters of the Republic: Publication and the Public Sphere in Eighteenth-Century America.* Cambridge, MA: Harvard U. Press, 1990. Pp. xv + 205; bibliography.

Rev. (favorably) by J. D. Wallace in *Choice*, 28 (1991), 780.

Watson, J. R. (ed.). *Romanticism in English Poetry of the Eighteenth Century: The Poetic Art and Significance of Thomson, Gray, Collins, Goldsmith, Cowper & Crabbe. A Casebook.* (Casebook Series.) Basingstoke, UK, and London: Macmillan, 1989. Pp. 263. Cf. *ECCB*, n.s. 16, V:336.

Rev. by Allan Ingram in *Modern Language Review,* 86 (1991), 395.

Weber, Donald. *Rhetoric and History in Revolutionary New England.* New York and Oxford: Oxford U. Press, 1988. Pp. xii + 207; bibliography; illustrations. Cf. *ECCB*, n.s. 14, V:259.

Rev. (with another work) by Christopher Looby in *Modern Philology*, 88 (1990–91), 446–48.

Wendorf, Richard. *The Elements of Life: Biography and Portrait-Painting in Stuart and Georgian England.* Oxford: Clarendon Press, 1990. Pp. xxiii + 308; frontispiece; plates. Cf. *ECCB*, n.s. 16, V:338–39.

Rev. by Catherine Ezell in *The Scriblerian*, 24 (1991), 85–86.

Wesley, Charles. *The Unpublished Poetry of Charles Wesley, Vol.I.* Edited by Oliver A. Beckerlegge, and S. T. Kimbrough. Nashville,TN: Abingdon, 1988. Pp. 325.

Rev. by Mary McBride in *The Scriblerian*, 24 (1991), 77.

Welsh, Alexander. *Strong Representations: Narrative and Circumstantial Evidence in England.* Baltimore, MD, and London: Johns Hopkins U. Press, 1991. Pp. xiii + 262.

"Strong representations," apparently Alexander Welsh's own coinage, is a phrase offered by him to identify narratives of arguments that represent and depend upon circumstantial evidence in order to make a case, arrive at a conclusion or conviction, or achieve closure. Although not the sole aim of his book, a major purpose of his study for students of the eighteenth century is to demonstrate how the realism associated with the eighteenth-century novel arose concurrently with the English legal system's turning somewhat away from relying upon the evidence of witnesses' direct testimony in criminal trials in favor of presentations based upon circumstantial evidence, buttressed by the maxim "circumstances cannot lie."

Welsh's text itself at times takes on the quality of a well-annotated legal brief as he cites numerous legal histories, case reports, and standard reference works, particularly on the nature and use of evidence, to set up his argument for the increasing importance of strong representations in both the legal and the story-telling worlds of eighteenth-century England. Most interestingly he looks at the reports of two notorious poisoning trials, *R v. Blandy* (1752) and *R v. Donellan* (1781) (poisoning being a crime difficult to detect by eyewitnesses), to abstract a theory of narrative that he can then use to examine the way Fielding and Scott represent the "cases" of Tom Jones and Edward Waverly.

Using his theory of strong representation as a critical or interpretive method works particularly well in his analysis of Tom Jones as a narrative of indictment, trial, defense, and acquittal. Welsh also ingeniously uses his theory to examine the rhetoric of Maurice Morgann's *An Essay on the Dramatic Character of Sir John Falstaff* (1777), in which the author sought to defend Falstaff against charges of cowardice by inviting the reader to examine not the speech and action of Falstaff and others but his circumstances.

From here, Welsh moves on to synopses and discussions of a wide variety of succeeding narratives and literary studies, including A. C. Bradley and Ernest Jones on *Hamlet, In Memoriam, The Moonstone, The Ring and the Book,* and *The Golden Bowl,* in the last of which Welsh perceives narrative realism turning from making a case or creating a defense by strong representations to solely representing experience. In some of these, his arguments become rather complicated, as if he were perhaps trying to accommodate too much evidence into his representations, but Welsh has provided a welcome new narrative theory, not revolutionary, but nicely complementary to several others and has clearly shown how useful it can be in examining the rhetoric of the narrative realism of the last three centuries.—Bryon Gassman.

West, Shearer. *The Image of the Actor: Verbal and Visual Representation in the Age of Garrick and Kemble.* New York: St. Martin's Press, 1991. Pp. xiii + 191; bibliography; 60 illustrations.

The Image of an Actor is a trendy study that attempts to show how artists, book publishers, reviewers, and the general public constructed the visual and verbal portraits of the actors on the English stage from 1747–1817. West's aim is "to expose the subtexts, to reveal not only how actors were perceived, but how these perceptions relate directly to political, social, and aesthetic concerns of the eighteenth century" (p. 5).

West is most successful when dealing with aesthetic issues in eighteenth-century responses to the growing power of the actor-manager. She clearly points out the growing influence of Sir Joshua Reynolds and the Royal Academy on the "Grand Style" of acting embodied by Kemble and Siddons. But, her misreading of Reynolds' prose leads her to confuse theatrically painted scenes and costumes with historical settings and period dress (p. 42). As Kalem Burnim and Ronald Paulson have shown, the stage "pomp" that Reynolds warns his followers against bore little similarity to the apparel used in *Garrick as Kitel*, or *Mrs. Abington as Miss Prue*. West's assertion of influence of Dutch genre painting on the theatrical paintings of Johann Zoffany is amply illustrated, but she fails to relate Zoffany to an English tradition of idealized stage painting, beginning with Hogarth's various versions of *The Beggar's Opera*, a series that should be central to her study, but which she fails to mention.

West lucidly explains the relationship between the various London booksellers and the theater. She notes that illustrations were far more important than text in the marketing of *Bell's British Theatre*, and how by 1795, illustrations were fabricated to sell the volumes. But, in her zeal to discredit Garrick's reputation as a realistic actor, she cites illustrations of Garrick as Periander in Mallet's *Eurydice* and Demetrius in Young's *The Brothers* from the dubious *Bell's British Theatre* (p. 63). Indeed, most of the problems in West's study stem from her general lack of knowledge of the plays and players of the period. She states that Lear was not one of Garrick's stronger roles (p. 29), although in fact he performed it eighty-five times from the beginning to the end of his career. A quick glance at *The London Stage* would have informed her that *Antony and Cleopatra* was indeed performed on the eighteenth-century stage, and a look at any of the editions in print of Dryden's *All for Love* would have shown her that Dryden did not substitute "rhyming couplets for blank verse" (p. 56). West is surely right in her contention that the "codes" of art theory were used in the depiction of the stage by artists, but she never considers that actors may have employed these "codes" on stage. Garrick lent Francis Hutcheson's *An Essay on the Nature and Conduct of the Passions and Affections* (1728) to Henry Gifford for study, and the pose that Mrs. Abington strikes in Reynolds's *Mrs. Abington as the Comic Muse* is one that the actress could have used countless times upon the stage.

West praises Joseph Roach's insightful study of Garrick's acting style, but faults him for "falling back on the cliche of Garrick's realism" (p. 159). But, all she can offer as an alternative is an interpretation of Garrick's art as a "bustling, believable shadow of reality" (p. 68). West's superficial examination of this varied period of English theater does demonstrate the need for much more careful scholarly study.—Jeffery Lawson Laurence Johnson.

Wild, Peter. *Alvar Nunez Cabeza de Vaca.* (Boise State University Western Writers Series, 101.) Boise, ID: Boise State U. Printing and Graphics Services, 1991. Pp. 51; bibliography.

Williamson, Marilyn L. *Raising Their Voices: British Women Writers, 1650–1750.* Detroit, MI: Wayne State U. Press, 1990. Pp. 339; bibliography. Cf. *ECCB*, n.s. 16, V:340.

Rev. by V. M. Vaughan in *Choice*, 28 (1991), 780.

Wilson, Jean. *The Challenge of Belatedness: Goethe, Kleist, Hofmannsthal.* (German Literature, Art & Thought.) Lanham, MD: U. Press of America, 1991. Pp. 254.

Yeazell, Ruth Bernard. *Fictions of Modesty: Women and Courtship in the English Novel.* Chicago, IL, and London: U. of Chicago Press, 1991. Pp. xii + 306.

Although young women posed on the threshold of marriage and adult life are a recognized staple of the English novel, courtship as a literary phenomenon has not often been isolated for specific investigation. In this book, Ruth Yeazell analyzes the "fictions of modesty" that shed new light on six major heroines spanning a full century.

Her first section deals with the representations of courtship and modesty. Philosophers like Mandeville, Hume, and Rousseau debated whether modesty was natural or social. Moralists in the press decried the French Catholic convent and extolled the English Protestant drawing room as the appropriate place to educate young girls for marriage. Conduct books identified the behavior that defined the ideal young woman. How paradoxical her modesty was! To be virtuous a maid should be unaware of what threatened her modesty. Indeed, one writer-male, of course, wanted her to be as insensible as "if she were a post" (p. 56).

Armed with this code of modesty, Yeazell applies it in her second part. Pamela is a most problematic heroine because she seems more artful than modest, too clever to be honest, too aware to be a post. Since, after her wedding, the novel loses its dramatic edge, we realize that Richardson's fictionalization of modesty, however paradoxical it was then and remains today, is essential to *Pamela*'s artistic impact.

Fanny Hill seems to be a poor choice here, but Yeazell succeeds in showing how she too retains a certain modesty. Evelina embodies all the contradictions inherent in the modest blush and lives its double-bind. Burney's heroine is embarrassed whenever she is seen in the "wrong" company of her cousins and grandmother. But that is precisely what accounts for her virtuous success with all the young men. *Mansfield Park* upsets convention. Fanny Price's modesty is aware and informed and thus by definition should not be virtuous. She resists Henry Crawford not as a part of a courtship fiction, but because her heart is sincerely taken by another. Charlotte Brontë locates *Villette* at modesty's breaking point. Lucy Snowe obeys the injunction that a modest girl should never make herself the subject of her own story. But her curious absence or displacement from the center of the fiction seriously weakens the novel even as it accentuates her modesty.

The last novel is in a sense the first because Gaskell's *Wives and Daughters* (1864–66) is the most conservative, the one that respects most faithfully the courtship paradigm of unconscious modesty. Molly's exemplary status is captured by Dr. Gibson's description of "her perfect innocence—ignorance, I should rather say" (p. 195). We have at last found our post.

In a brief third section, Yeazell echoes her opening with a look at science. She compares Darwin's discourse on sexual selection with the courtship plot. She points out that Havelock Ellis thought that the peculiarly feminine habits of reticence indicate not refusal but a promise of fulfillment. By claiming that the timid woman was secretly the most ardent, he reproduces in science the narratives of modesty and courtship that Yeazell finds in the novel.

Delays and deferrals are essential both to the narrative and to courtship: slowing down the rush to marriage allows the time to tell about it. Yeazell plots this "long circuiting" of the modest consciousness which cannot speak its own desire until a man says the word and thus ends her story. —Peter V. Conroy Jr.

Yolton, Jean. "Authorship of A *Lady's Religion* (1697)." *Notes and Queries*, 236 (1991), 177.

William, rather than Edward, Stephens.

Ziff, Larzer. *Writing the New Nation: Prose, Print, and Politics in the Early United States.* New Haven, CT, and London: Yale U. Press, 1991. Pp. xiii + 209.

Zimbardo, Rose A. *A Mirror to Nature: Transformations in Drama and Aesthetics, 1660–1732.* Lexington, KY: U. Press of Kentucky, 1986. Pp. viii + 248. Cf. *ECCB*, n.s. 15, V:274; 14, V:263; 12, V:390–91.

Rev. by John Sitter in *The Scriblerian*, 23 (1991), 265–67.

Individual Authors

Joseph Addison (1672–1719)

Corse, Taylor. "An Echo of Dryden in Addison's Cato." *Notes and Queries*, 236 (1991), 178.

"What dire effects from civil discord flow" is a quotation from "The First Pastoral" of Virgil.

Nablow, Ralph A. *The Addisonian Tradition in France: Passion and Objectivity in Social Observation*. Rutherford, NJ: Fairleigh Dickinson, 1989. Pp. 278.

Rev. by Charles A. Knight in *The Scriblerian*, 24 (1991), 64–65.

Jean le Rond d'Alembert (1717–1783)

Chouillet, Anne-Marie. "Du Nouveau sur l'Encyclopédie: Une Lettre inédite de d'Alembert." *Recherches sur Diderot et sur l'Encyclopédie*, 11 (1991), 18–31; illustration.

Important letter to Mauperuis dated August 4, 1752.

John Aubrey (1626–1697)

Tylden-Wright, David. *John Aubrey: A Life*. London: Harper-Collins Publishers, 1991. Pp. xv + 270; illustrations; maps.

Rev. by Katherine Duncan-Jones in *TLS*, (Dec. 27, 1991), 7.

William Bartram (1739–1823)

Bartram, William. *Le voyage de William Bartram (1773–1776): Découverte du paysage et invention de l'exotisme américain*. Translation and presentation by Yvon Chatelin. Paris: Éditions Karthala et Orstrom, 1991. Pp. 296; illustrations.

As its title page suggests, this handsome, sturdy paperback is both a "traduction" of William Bartram's travels through North and South Carolina, Georgia and Florida (Philadelphia, 1791; London, 1792) and a "presentation" of the life, accomplishments, and reputation of its author. Aiming more at popular than at a scholarly audience, Yvon Chatelin the presenter-translator reproduces some thirty of Bartram's drawings and includes approximately one-half of the original Travels in nine chapters interspersed with five of her own that presents Bartram's "Vie et Oeures" and take up two-fifths of the work. A French reader needing the full translation of Bartram must, therefore, continue to employ—with its obvious deficiencies—the two-volume 1799 Benoist translation.

William Bartram was in his own day a favorite of such people as Coleridge, Wordsworth, and Carlyle, who were attracted by his idealism and humanity, his Quaker pantheism, his first-hand knowledge of American natives, his keen observation of nature reflected both in his writing and his attractive drawings, and his obviously—though modestly presented—talents in botany, orinthology, and geology, talents trained by one of the best field scientists of the eighteenth century, his father John Bartram, who was for years the "King's botanist" in America. And in our day William has been a favorite with both scholars and general readers. So it is not surprising to find him being reintroduced to a France that once knew him reasonably well through Crevecoeur's "Letter" about John and through Chateaubriand's use of William's travels as an inspiration for Atala and Rene and, more particularly, as the prime source for details about the southeast United States used in a journey there which Chateaubriand, writing over thirty-five years after the fact, claimed to have made but did not make.

In fact, Mlle Chatelin at some length suggests that on his trip to America in 1791, the young French aristocrat may have visited with William Bartram at his home in Philadelphia. Such a meeting almost surely did not occur, however, for two reasons. First, Chateaubriand landed at Baltimore July 10, 1771, immediatately took coach to Philadelphia to deliver a letter of introduction to the then-President (even though he claimed to have done so), and then hurried on to Albany and Niagara Falls. Second, William's one book did not appear until some six weeks after Chateaubriand arrived in Philadelphia. Almost surely, then, Chateaubriand at that time had not heard of William and would not know and use his book until the period of 1793 to 1800, when he lived as a refugee in London compiling the great notebook that would lead to Atala, his own Voyage en Amerique, and other works, and where he would have access to the 1792 London edition of William Bartram's Travels.

A touch of wishful thinking will not, however, keep this new volume from being a success at what it aims to do—and that is to introduce French readers to an eighteenth-century American writer who is not only important to their great literary tradition but worthy of even wider recognition in his own country. William Bartram is difficult to translate. Perhaps no one can imitate his style, and perhaps no one would want to. But anyone who comes to William Bartram through Mlle Chatelin's book will discover a very attractive human being and perhaps be led to the original Travels and that pleasantly unique style.—Percy G. Adams.

Pierre Augustin Caron de Beaumarchais (1732–1799)

Dunkeley, John. *Beaumarchais "Le Barbier de Séville."* (Critical Guides to French Texts, 86.) London: Grant & Cutler, 1991. Pp. 92.

Morton, Brian N., and Donald C. Spinelli. *Beaumarchais: A Bibliography.* Ann Arbor, MI: The Olivia and Hill Press, 1988. Pp. xxiii + 374. Cf. *ECCB*, n.s. 15, VI:278.

Rev. by Fernande Bassan in *Revue d'histoire du théâtre*, 42 (1991), 312; by Gunnar von Prosch in *Revue d'histoire littéraire de la France*, 91 (1991), 101–03; (anonymously) in *Studi francesi*, 33 (1989), 349.

Pucci, Suzanne R. "The Currency Exchange in Beaumarchais' *Mariage de Figaro*: From the 'Master Trope' Synecdoche to Fetish." *Eighteenth-Century Studies*, 25 (1991), 57–84.

The "droit de seigneur" has been converted to a financial transaction, with arbitrary value, instability, and disruptive functions for the signifying system.

William Beckford (1760–1844)

Beckford, William. *The Transient Gleam: A Bouquet of Beckford's Poesy.* Edited by Devendra P. Varma. Upton, Cheshire, UK: Aylesford, 1991. Pp. 101.

Aphra Behn (1640–1689)

Behn, Aphra. *The Uncollected Verse of Aphra Behn.* Edited with an Introduction and Notes by Germaine Greer. Essex: Stump Cross Books, 1989. Pp. x + 224. Cf. *ECCB*, n.s. 16, VI:345; 15, VI:279.

Unlike the thorough and authoritative Stump Cross edition of Katherine Philips's poetry, this little volume of Aphra Behn's uncollected verse was frankly a stopgap, to provide scholars with the poems left out of the dated and faded Montague Summers edition of 1915. Now that a new scholarly edition is appearing, the sixteen poems in Greer's editions—which have been at various points mislineated or otherwise have come to grief in the production stage—can be set aside. But Behn's poems were never the most energetic part of the volume, which begins with Germaine Greer's withering inventory of the editorial and personal deficiencies of Montague Summers and ends with sixty pages of detailed and free-spoken notes and commentary.

An account of how Summers felt he should groom his "Bonny Mrs. Behn" for public presentation might have been an illuminating little study in the combined annals of scholarship, sex, and manners. A deeper question, frequently, than what a man is slighting is what he is protecting. How these added poems alter Behn's image is still more worth addressing. Most are long, public, hard-worked, fervidly pro-Stuart, written for money, and Behn's seventeen-hundred-line translation from Cowley's *Of Plants,* which is not about botany but royalist history, shows a new level of ambition and sustained skill. Instead, judging Summers to have been "cavalier" and condescending, Greer royally outdoes him.

Her annotations too can be somewhat electrifying. Rather in the style of John Harold Wilson's *Court Satires of the Restoration,* they relay all the news that is fit to print and then some about the people in the poems, their looks and their backsides, dissipations and subsequent diseases, crimes and manipulations, meanwhile filling in the generally unnewsworthy abandonments and pregnancies that were common in women's lives. Greer knows the Restoration world and she certainly knows about animus, and some of her notes are more pointed than those in Janet Todd's new edition. When a poet is compared to "an Ungrateful Bird" that "Bewrayst thy Nest," for example, he does something rather worse than expose or betray it. When Behn pretends to imagine how she might "glide/With the fair prosperous Gale" under William, or tells some extravagant partisan whopper, Greer reacts sharply. Janet Todd incorporates Greer's learning, builds on or tempers her judgments, and carefully evaluates her theories, so not much has been lost, but still I would recommend Greer's notes to students for her view of a world before sending them to dignified editorial adjudication.—Joanna Lipking.

Craft, Catherine A. "Reworking Male Models: Aphra Behn's *Fair Vow-Breaker*, Eliza Haywood's *Fantomina*, and Charlotte Lennox's *Female Quixote*." *Modern Language Review*, 86 (1991), 821–38.

These "subversive female stories and tales picture heroines who are in control, both of themselves and of the men around them"; "they topple the male stereotypes of women."

Crompton, Virginia, and Janet Todd. "Rebellion's Antidote: A New Attribution to Aphra Behn." *Notes and Queries*, 236 (1991), 175–77.

Duyfhuizen, Bernard. " 'That Which I Dare Not Name': Aphra Behn's 'The Willing Mistress'."
  English Literary History, 58 (1991), 63–82.

The text's production and "unconscious" reveal the problems of female sexuality in a patriarchal culture.

Pearson, Jacqueline. "Gender and Narrative in the Fiction of Aphra Behn." *Review of English
  Studies*, 42 (1991), 40–56; 179–90.

Her female narrators reveal "difficult and painful contradictions," some narrative, some cultural, and some
unconscious or unacknowledged.

Jeremy Bentham (1748–1832)

Crimmins, James E. *Secular Utilitarianism: Social Science and the Critique of Religion in the
  Thought of Jeremy Bentham*. New York: Oxford U. Press; Oxford: Clarendon Press, 1990.
  Pp. xi + 348; bibliography.

Rev. (favorably) by J. R. Breihan in *Choice*, 28 (1991), 1361.

George Berkeley (1685–1753)

Atherton, Margaret. *Berkeley's Revolution in Vision*. Ithaca, NY, and London: Cornell U. Press,
  1990. Pp. xii + 249; figures.

Rev. by Geneviève Brykman in *Revue philosophique de la France et de l'étranger*, (1992), 628–630; by S. Fuller in
Choice, 28 (1991), 1323.

Baxter, Donald L. "Berkeley, Perception, and Identity." *Philosophy and Phenomenological
  Research*, 51 (1991), 85–98.

According to D. L. Baxter, Berkeley wrote, concerning perception, that one never perceives the same thing by sight
and touch. But Berkeley also wrote that we sometimes do perceive the same thing by sight and touch. How is this
contradiction to be explained? Baxter's answer is that in one sentence Berkeley is talking about strict truth; in the
other, he was speaking of common sense and practicality.

Dancy, Jonathan. *Berkeley: An Introduction*. Oxford: Basil Blackwell, 1987. Pp. vii + 165.

Rev. (favorably) by Kenneth P. Winkler in *The Philosophical Review*, 100 (1991), 329–331.

Muellmann, Robert. "The Role of Perceptual Relativity in Berkeley's Philosophy." *Journal of the
  History of Philosophy*, 29 (1991), 397–425.

Undergraduate students often feel quite clear about what Berkeley wrote and taught. But among recent scholars there
are many disagreements. For example, there are debates about how Berkeley meant to use the argument from
perceptual relativity. R. Muellmann is convinced that Berkeley used the argument only negatively, as a sort of ad
homine argument against his philosophical opponents.

Walmsley, Peter. *The Rhetoric of Berkeley's Philosophy*. (Cambridge Studies in Eighteenth-Century English Literature and Thought, 6.) Cambridge and New York: Cambridge U. Press, 1990. Pp. xv + 205; bibliography; portrait.

Rev. (favorably) by G. J. Stack in *Choice*, 28 (1991), 1795.

Jacques-Henri Bernardin de Saint-Pierre (1737–1814)

Robinson, Philip. *Bernardin de Saint-Pierre*: Paul et Virginie. (Critical Guides to French Texts, 51.) London: Grant & Cutler, 1986. Pp. 80; chart; map. Cf. *ECCB*, n.s. 15, VI:281–82; 12, IV:517.

Rev. (briefly) by Renata Carocci in *Studi francesi*, 34 (1991), 532.

William Blake (1757–1827)

Adams, Hazard (ed.). *Critical Essays on William Blake*. (Critical Essays on British Literature.) Boston, MA: G.K. Hall, 1991. Pp. ix + 214; bibliography.

This valuable assemblage of essays on William Blake, and of excerpts from essays or books on him, is divided into two sections, concerned respectively with Blake's reception in his own day and with modern interpretations of him. The former section contains an overview by Deborah Dorfman and comments on Blake by Henry Crabb Robinson and a few other contemporary observers. The second section consists of pieces, written since 1950, by Northrop Frye, David V. Erdman, Jean H. Hagstrum, Thomas R. Frosch, Alicia Shaviro, Robert N. Essick, and the editor, Hazard Adams, who contributes both an afterword essay and a useful introduction. The introduction surveys the history of Blake exegesis and very briefly summarizes the essays included in the present volume.

Some of the pieces included are classics, and all seem at least reasonable choices, except for Shaviro's, perhaps, the mode of which is typified by language like "situates them in their (im)possibility of the non-scene of non-origination" (p. 173). Frye's 1950 essay on Blake's archetypes is vintage Frye, at once vatic, polemical, and almost casual. Erdman's treatment of "Visions of the Daughters of Albion" contains material so central to our understanding of Blake that it is startling to be reminded that someone had to unearth the material for the first time, in 1954. Ostriker's essay, "Desire Gratified and Ungratified," outlining Blake's views of the sexes and sexuality, is as acute and just plain right about Blake as anything of essay length that has been written about him. And it is surely imperative to include Essick, whose book on Blake and language, *William Blake and the Language of Adam* (1989), is a critical and scholarly masterpiece.

The roster of eminent Blakeans represented in the book warrants that no reasonable reader will feel shortchanged, exactly. Nor should anyone envy the editor his difficult assignment, which no two people would carry out in the same way, of representing the cream of Blake interpretation in 200 pages. All this conceded, however, some cavils seem in order. Surely we ought to have something by either the early or the later Harold Bloom, if only because Bloom is Bloom, and something by Nelson Hilton, whose book, *Literal Imagination* (1983), has probably done more than any other recent work to alter the methodology of reading and understanding Blake.

There are a number of other writers on Blake who would seem as worthy of inclusion as most of those actually included. I'll mention a few, not so much to protest what, after all, are editorial judgement calls but rather to expand the field of view (I considered by the editor and omitted only reluctantly). Either something by Hilton or Thomas A. Volger's essay on "Visions of the Daughters of Albion" in the *Critical Paths* (1987) volume or Adams' own essay "Synecdoche and Method," in the same book, would have served better than the Shaviro essay to exemplify good Blake criticism in recent critical veins. In a somewhat more traditional mode, something by Morris Eaves's 1978 prize-winning *PMLA* article, would have been welcome. Any of several parts of Vincent Arthur De Luca's wonderful treatment of Blake and the sublime, *Words of Eternity* (1991), and *Blake and His Bibles* (1990), are of hall-of-fame caliber, though it's likely that these two pieces came out too recently for inclusion in the Adams collection. The Apector essay, for my money, ranks with the included essay by Ostriker as one of the two best article-length studies of Blake. Martin K. Nurmi's small but influential piece on Blake's chimney sweepers (1964) would also be in the running if it were not so narrowly focussed on particular poems and the Adams collection were not oriented toward treatments of more general issues in Blake. (This policy does not consistently govern, though; the included essays by Fox and Paley, for example, concentrate repectively on "Milton" and "Jerusalem".) One also misses Robert F. Gleckner and Leopold Damrosch, Jr.—Brian Wilkie.

Bentley, G. E., Jr. "Blake and Napoleon Rediivivus." *Notes and Queries*, 236 (1991), 293–94.

Reconsiders John Oswald's likeness to Napoleon.

Bentley, G. E., Jr. "Mainaduc, Magic, and Madness: George Cumberland and the Blake Connection." *Notes and Queries*, 236 (1991), 294–96.

Cumberland resisted the occult, but gave Blake access to it.

Bigwood, Carol. "Seeing Blake's Illuminated Texts." *The Journal of Aesthetics and Art Criticism*, 49 (1991), 307–315.

C. Bigwood argues that a proper reading of Blake's texts requires using insights supplied by such modern phenomenologists as Heidegger and Merleau-Ponty.

Billigheimer, Rachel V. *Wheels of Eternity: A Comparative Study of William Blake and William Butler Yeats*. New York: St. Martin's Press, 1990. Pp. ix + 243; bibliography; frontispiece. Cf. *ECCB*, n.s. 16, VI:347–48.

The goal of this comparative study is to show "a deep relationship" between Blake and Yeats "in spite of their very different worlds" (p. 1). Yet what this relationship might be, and the significance of the differences between Blake and Yeats are never argued. Billigheimer focuses on both poets' use of circle symbolism, especially the great cyclical structure of mythic history adumbrated by Yeats in *A Vision* and evoked by Blake through allusions to the eight "Eyes of God" scattered through his late epics. She does not argue for any particular influence or indebtedness or common background between Blake and Yeats. While she correctly criticizes Yeats's occult reading of Blake, she does not examine in detail how this misprision might have functioned. When poetic parallels are noted, they are characteristically qualified by phrases such as "in some sense" (p. 3), "to some degree" (p. 15) or "bears some resemblance" (p. 55). She does not subsequently distinguish in what respects they may be related, or how a broad parallel or a similar motif should be understood. The lack of a detailed comparative analysis may be attributed in part to the conditions of this book's publication. Its two long chapters on Blake are essentially unrevised versions of previously published articles. Several chapter sections on Yeats similarly recycle earlier essays. Each poet is discussed, as a result, largely in isolation from the other, without the occasion to integrate separate strands of argument or to articulate specific points of connection.

The lengthy discussion of Blake's references to the eight "Eyes of God" is perhaps the best and most thorough aspect of this book. The two chapters devoted to this topic adopt the synoptic critical method of S. Foster Damon or Northrop Frye: Billigheimer collates all appearances of the "Eyes of God" motif, notes poetic parallels or historical sources, and on this basis elaborates a structural schematic that is then held to underlie and to unify the comparatively inchoate narrative surface of Blake's poetry. Billigheimer compiles the range of possible analogues previous commentary on this motif had noted, and thereby makes available a densely textured set of allusions and internal repetitions that are a characteristic feature of Blake's poetry. Yet her careful account of the eight "Eyes of God" does not attend to the different dramatic contexts and narrative effects of widely separated passages. She explicates, in effect, some fairly arcane references in Blake's text, but never explains how they function in his poetic narratives.—Stephen L. Carr.

Blake, William. *The Complete Poems of William Blake*. Edited by W. H. Stevenson. (Longman Annotated English Poets.) 2nd ed. London: Longman, 1989. Pp. xxiv + 886. Cf. *ECCB*, n.s. 15, VI:283.

Rev. by David Fuller in *Review of English Studies*, 42 (1991), 612.

Bloom, Harold (ed.). *William Blake: Modern Critical Views*. New York: Chelsea House Publishers, 1985. Pp. 209; bibliography. Cf. *ECCB*, n.s. 13, VI:386.

Rev. by Dean Wentworth Bethea in *South Atlantic Review*, 56 (Jan. 1991), 114–116.

Brewster, Glen E. " 'Out of Nature': Blake and the French Revolution Debate." *South Atlantic Review*, 56 (Nov. 1991), 7–22.

Butlin, Martin. *William Blake, 1757–1827*. 3rd. ed. (Tate Gallery Collections, 5.) London: Tate Gallery, 1990. Pp. 251; illustrations (some colored).

Rev. (favorably) by T. J. McCormick in *Choice*, 28 (1991), 1116.

Clark, Lorraine. *Blake, Kierkegaard, and the Spectre of Dialectic*. Cambridge and New York: Cambridge U. Press, 1991. Pp. xii + 238; bibliography.

See sec. 5 for review.

Cox, Philip. "Blake, Marvell, and Milton: A Possible Source for a Proverb of Hell." *Notes and Queries*, 236 (1991), 292–93.

"Bring out number, weight & measure" echoes Marvell's "On Mr. Milton's 'Paradise Lost'."

Crisman, William C. "Blake's 'The Crystal Cabinet' as a Reworking of Thomson's The Castle of Indolence." *English Language Notes*, 29 (1991), 52–59.

De Luca, Vincent Arthur. *Words of Eternity: Blake and the Poetics of the Sublime*. Princeton, NJ: Princeton U. Press, 1991. Pp. xv + 238; illustrations.

It is the great virtue of this book not only to fill a gap but to show how much greater the gap was than we thought. The sublime in Blake has been discussed at article length, and in Thomas Weiskel's book, but De Luca has now displayed in full detail its pervasive presence as theme, setting, style, structure, and effect on the reader. He qualifies Weiskel's contention that Blake's sublime is radically different from Burke's or Kant's: Blake is drawn to the Burkean complex of obscurity, mystery, vastness, etc., even while relegating it to the "corporeal understanding." The distinctively Blakean sublime (though it was not altogether without precedent) might not have been called sublime at all by most of his contemporaries: it is visionary, perspicuous, ultimately inviting and not forbidding to the imagination. It is embodied not in the mountains, chasms, seas, or thunderstorms, but mainly in language, texts, and works of art, the "textual sublime" and "iconic sublime." In the end the sublime is Blake's *Jerusalem*: it "functions as a sublime object" (p. 133) itself, and its reader is brought by means of its peculiarities and difficulties to a kind of intellectual homecoming at the highest level

De Luca carries to sublime heights the familiar Blake-can-do-no-wrong assumption, according to which those very features that have turned off two centuries of readers are made to seem the lineaments of greatness. Though in his second-to-last paragraph (p. 230) he praises another book as "valuable precisely because it avoids an uncritically adulatory approach to Blake," De Luca finds everything intentional and everything masterly. What still causes most readers to skip is Blake's "magisterial erection of barriers and curbs" (p. 101). His texts have "numerous poetic felicites" (p. 123) but never any infelicities. This self-sealing assumption, however, serves De Luca well, for by persisting in this folly, he approaches Blake's own point of view very closely, I think, and forces issues to conclusions that cast many odd features of Blake in a new light.

De Luca's own style, thankfully, is directed to our corporeal understandings: it is lucid, intelligent, interesting, and entirely free of franglais. De Luca is very helpful on many disparate aspects of the sublime: on the word "astonish," a favorite of Blake's; on the experience of reading Blake; on bards; on what Blake found important in Ossian, Lowth, Burnett, and others; on the sublime side of the syncretist mythographers such as Bryant; and on many difficult Blakean passages. He does not always convince on the passages: he tries to show that the famous "vortex" passage from *Milton* (15.21–35) is "clearly iconic" in that it "enacts the effects attributed to the object it purports to describe" (p. 83), whereas I think the passage, however mysterious, is manifestly a serene account of a pilgrim's "wondrous journey" through a benevolent world. Even where I disagree, however, I find his discussions astute and provocative.

De Luca falls afoul of the intentional fallacy when he enters the vortex of the *Vala / The Four Zoas* manuscript, which he accords the same status as Blake's engraved works. Thus interpolation becomes a structuring principle, which Blake "happily permits" (p. 115) even in *Milton* and *Jerusalem* (one can easily detect different styles, and thus dates, on engraving), but De Luca ignores the fact that Blake did not happily permit the manuscript to be published. De Luca invokes intentions where it suits. Speaking of a new departure in *Vala* where there is also a change in kind of paper, he says "Blake chooses to emphasize rather than conceal this sense of disjunction by using the new paper" (p. 122), but for whom is Blake emphasizing, from whom is he concealing anything in a work he abandoned and would never have published on that paper?

I would have wished, finally, that De Luca would have considered the "revolutionary sublime," about which scholars are writing today. Burke is invoked as a theorist of the sublime, but you would never know he was an M. P. who wrote about the French Revolution. By confining the sublime to art, in the end, De Luca seems to shut his eyes to a large area of Blake's life and passionate concern.—Michael Ferber.

Dörrbecker, D. W. "Blake and his Circle: An Annotated Checklist of Recent Publications." *Blake*, 25 (1991), 4–59.

Downes, Margaret J. "Benediction of Metaphor at Colonus: William Blake and the Vision of the Ancients." *Colby Quarterly,* 27 (1991), 174–83.

Essick, Robert N. *William Blake and the Language of Adam*. Oxford: Clarendon Press, 1989. Pp. x + 272. Cf. *ECCB*, n.s. 16, VI:348; 15, VI:285.

Rev. (favorably) by Brian Wilkie in *Modern Language Review*, 86 (1991), 670–71.

Essick, Robert N. *William Blake's Commercial Book Illustrations: A Cataloque and Study of the Plates Engraved by Blake after Designs by Other Artists*. New York: Oxford U. Press; Oxford: Clarendon Press, 1991. n.p.; bibliography; illustrations.

This spendid book, printed and illustrated with equal splendor by Clarendon, is effectively the completion of a project begun in the 1970s by Essick in collaboration with Roger Easson, the first volume of which was *William Blake: Book Illustration* (1972), under the auspices of the sadly now defunct American Blake Foundation, and the second of which, under the same title, was published in 1979. The final volume was never published, nor was the second volume very widely distributed. While this 1991 book is not a revision in the ordinary sense of the Essick-Easson first volume, it is a major redoing of Volume II and of course the doing of Volume III. On the other hand, it does not repeat the earlier published detailed bibliographical descriptions, which are available *in extenso* in G. E. Bentley, Jr.'s 1977 *Blake Books* and its forthcoming supplement. What Essick does provide here are the illustrations' size, inscriptions, and progressive states, the location of preliminary drawings, and the identification of all documents related to the plates' production. In addition we were accorded analyses of each plate's graphic technique and style, Blake's revision of preliminary designs, motifs that Blake borrows from his earlier work, the succinct, precise, and readable survey of Blake's career as a commercial book engraver.

There are riches aplenty, well worth the price of admission, but Essick also essays with his usual shrewdness and enviable fund of knowledge the ways in which these productions may be related profitably to Blake's other graphic works and his writings. More broadly he argues that on the basis of the progress of the produced plates themselves a kind of system for understanding the entire progress of the production of intaglio copperplate illustrations in the late eighteenth century and early nineteenth centuries—a process that is elaborate and multi-personed, dependent upon a rigorous division of labor, and therefore repeatability. For Essick the high point of Blake's achievement, as well as of his professional standing in this somewhat unBlakean plurality of laborers, is his *Beggar's Opera* engraving of 1788, for by the end of the century lack of employment all but drove Blake out of the profession to Felpham and Hayley's largesse. Back in London in 1803–04 Blake's career in book illustration revived, largely through Flaxman's intervention, but by 1818 his career as a graphic artist was virtually over. Yet, as Essick argues, without that earlier training and years of practice at his craft, his Virgil, Job, and Dante plates probably would have been impossible—at least in their present striking form.

Other goodies are here as well. As always in such matters, Essick has no peer—and, as always, we are in his debt once again.—Robert F. Gleckner.

Ferber, Michael. *The Poetry of William Blake.* (Penguin Critical Studies.) London and New York: Penguin Books, 1991. Pp. xv + 120.

Michael Ferber's *The Poetry of William Blake* is a book designed for Blakean beginners. It contains readings of the *Songs of Innocence and Experience*, *Thel*, *The Visions of the Daughters of Albion*, *America*, and *The Marriage of Heaven and Hell*, but almost no discussion of Blake's other work, though that other work is sometimes mentioned in passing or in support of some interpretive point. Ferber prefers allegorical readings (Thel as a dewdrop, Oothoon as a sigh or a thought), and his are competent if narrow. He picks not quite at random from the *Songs*, and there as elsewhere, he tends more to translate Blake than to enlighten the reader. He says little about Blake's designs, less about Blake's biography, and virtually nothing about Blake's method, or theories of language, or metaphor, or narrative. As such the book is of little help to the reader who seeks a guide to the later work, or who seeks a more composite knowledge of the man, his work, and his times.

This is not to say that Ferber does not make a nice point or two. He twice notes Blake's important pedagogical strategy of "precept and example," though without exploring the implications of that strategy (pp. 60, 144). Discussing "The Human Abstract," and drawing lines from Jerusalem, he remarks neatly that " 'we become what we behold' and confirm our own narrow beliefs by shrinking ourselves until we fit them" (p. 37). After dismissing one derivation of Thel's name by an unnamed "influential Blake scholar," he succinctly sidesteps the derivation question while making an important observation about Blake's method, saying that the "echo of familiar words" in Blake's names, "their air of 'etymologicity,' comes from an assertion of priority, as if they belonged to the first language on earth" (pp. 54–55). Yet having made that point, Ferber finds no occasion to comment on the fact that the appropriation of origins, an assertion of priority at various levels, is one of Blake's most common rhetorical strategies.

The most irritating aspect of the book is Ferber's handling of Blakean criticism. Early in the discussion, after dismissing the arguments of two unnamed critics concerning the "Introduction" to *Songs of Innocence*, Ferber says, "I mention these supposed shadows and ambiguities here because, if some recent critics [again unnamed] are to be believed, Blake is filled with secondary and tertiary counter-meanings that lurk like trapdoors or quicksand underfoot" (p. 5). In response to these critics, Ferber adds, "this book will assume, as most readers and critics have always assumed until recently, that interpretation is possible, that there are principles for eliminating all but one or a small number of readings in nearly all cases" (p. 6). He criticizes the "systematic interpreters of Blake . . . the 'one big poem' school," among whom he does name Northrop Frye, for possibly "lead[ing] us to impose meanings that are not 'there' " (p. 10). Unfortunately for the uninitiated Blake reader, Ferber does not mention that these related issues—"imposed" interpretations, possible "counter-meanings," and the "principles for eliminating" alternatives—constitute the central problem of Blake's work. Throughout the book Ferber quarrels with unnamed critical opponents whose arguments he reduces to a glib phrase or two. If these disagreements are to be raised at all, it would be more fair and require little effort to name the critics involved, and even this small effort would go far toward introducing the beginning Blake reader to the landscape of critical resources.—R. Paul Yoder.

Fitch, Donald. *Blake Set to Music: A Bibliography of Musical Settings of the Poems and Prose of William Blake*. (University of California Publications: Catalogs and Bibliographies, 5.) Berkeley, CA, and Oxford: U. of California Press, 1990. Pp. xxix + 281; frontispiece.

Rev. (favorably) by William S. Brockman in *American Reference Books Annual*, 22 (1991), 1252.

King, James. *William Blake—His Life*. London: Weidenfeld & Nicolson; New York: St. Martin's Press, 1991. Pp. xviii + 263; illustrations.

Rev. by G. A. Cevasco in *Choice*, 29 (1991), 282; (severely) by Grevel Lindop in *TLS*, (Mar, 29, 1991), 5–6.

In her finely detailed judicious account of "The Blake-Cromek Controversy," which appeared in *Blake: An Illustrated Quarterly*, 22 (1988/89), 80–92, Aileen Ward underscores yet again "the need for a critical re-examination of [Blake's] life as a whole. In the process the critic must scrutinize the minutest particulars of fact, weigh conflicting testimony, and keep constantly in mind the ambiguity of interpretation and the fallibilty of memory" (p. 80). Although James King does so scrutinize, weigh, and keep constantly in mind, and although thereby he produces an unexceptionable biography of fact (insofar as that is finally determinable), I cannot muster the sort of enthusiasm the dustjacket quotations from Patricia Meyer Spacks and Charles Ryskamp exhibit. If indeed, as Spacks says, this is a "learned . . . account," it is hardly "imaginative" (her adjective) as King's grasp of Blake's "time" (except for the art world of the day) falls dismally short of Erdman's, Bronowski's, Essick's, and a host of others largely unrepresented in King's bibliography.

Moreover, and more seriously in my judgment, there is little or no "keen sympathy for all of [Blake's] work," as Ryskamp generously asserts. As a broadly reliable source for the student or sometime reader of Blake who wants to know the particulars of his life, it will do; but for the substantial host of Blake aficionados who have read him, with some care, who more or less (or even assiduously try to) keep up with the flood of critical and scholarly work on him, this work has to be a disappointment. Bentley's *Blake Records* and its recent supplement (not to say his decades-long outpouring of the minute particulars of Blake's life) are still the places to turn. Indeed, it is where King turns—according to his notes about 250 times (just about the same number of references as to Erdman's edition of Blake's writings, mostly the prose)—quite literally a tissue of *ibids* that eloquently bespeaks King's writing a kind of discursive version of Bentley with Blake himself speaking in the interstices.

What is woefully absent in those interstices—as well as throughout the book—is any real sense on King's part of what the totality of Blake's life and career as poet-artist was. The few attempts he makes at moving his quotidianism toward *something* like a critical biography are disastrously bland, self-defeatingly brief and hence plot-summary-like, and critically rudimentary. And, finally, the attempt to string all of his factual beads on the thematic thread of (to quote from the dust jacket) Blake's being "a man with deeply divided feelings about sexuality and aware of dark inner forces that threatened to conquer him, but against which he did battle" is but half-hearted at best, at worst simplistically gratuitous.

Finally, the book is replete with gaffes of one sort or another: a few samples will do. "Blake's deeply divided feelings about sexuality have been neglected in previous accounts." Blake was Bunyan's "literary child." Joseph of Arimethea clothing, in Blake's engraving "appears to weigh him down" despite its sparseness. "Institutional charity is praised in 'Holy Thursday'." "'The Little Boy Lost" assures us there will be "a happy ending." Enitharmon, in *Europe*, "is a corrupt person." "Reynolds and Blake acquiesced on many things." "By being a generous friend to

Blake, [Linnell] was able to keep in touch with alienated aspects of himself." The "books and articles which [King] found especially useful in writing his *Life* I would hope are not responsible for such as these, even if, on other scholarly/critical grounds, the "Select Bibliography" is at best an idiosyncratic selection.

In all, then, I for one am more than content to wait, now even more eagerly, for Aileen Ward to give us *her* Blake to rival, and possible outdo, her Keats, not to say shoulder aside King's earnest but only minimally useful effort.—Robert F. Gleckner.

Otto, Peter. *Constructive Vision and Visionary Deconstruction: Loss, Eternity, and the Productions of Time in the Later Poetry of William Blake*. New York and Oxford: Oxford U. Press, 1991. Pp. 260.

The nods to post-structuralism in its title and jacket copy notwithstanding, this discussion of *Milton* and *Jerusalem* belongs to the great synoptic tradition of Blake criticism, following the high priests of Blake's presumptive "symbolic code." Symptomatically, Otto most frequently cites Damon and Erdman as authorities for stabilizing the particulars of the texts, while he barely mentions a single post-structuralist critic, who in fact might argue for a semiotic or rhetorical rather than a hermeneutical approach. In this book we find the portentous assertions of Blake as humanistic emancipatory Christian exhorting us to transform from isolated selves to relational selves in order to enjoy unfettered—and unproblematic—liberty: "It is in this constant casting off of the world of the self that we are able to elaborate a history of freedom" (p. 217), or "to be formed by Jesus is to allow the Spectrous world of the self to be moved by the call of another and so allow one's being to be recast" (p. 221). We also find unquestioned assumptions about the nature of Blake's textual strategies that are obviously opposed to post-structuralism; significantly, and like Damrosch, Otto presumes that the texts compose a unified corpus and elaborate a coherent philosophy commensurate with the liberal humanistic tradition, a philosophy drawn from statements made by diverse characters in diverse rhetorical situations.

Nonetheless, the introduction tries to establish affinities between the traditional hermeneutic approach and the post-structuralist analysis of language. Adducing Derrida's *differance* as a model for Blake's criticism of both phenomenological and totalizing philosophies, Otto makes a point that critics from Adams to Ault have demonstrated: "in Blake's poems—as in Derrida's philosophy—the labyrinth of the fallen world appears as a result of saptial and temporal distancing (*differance*) which occurs *prior to the appearance of the world in which we live*" (my italics, p. 21). However, this suggestive connection—one explored fully in Ault's *Narrative Unbound*—is almost immediately rejected, as Ault redefines *differance* only to eliminate it. It is this rather different understanding of *differance* which forms one of the major points of divergence between Derrida's sceptical philosophy and Blake's visionary art. It is because, in Blake's understanding, the world is not formed in an anonymous, ahistorical movement of *differance*, but in a particular stance taken by Albion towards others, that this stance and therefore the world can be changed" (p. 21). Finally, Otto fails to understand the fundamental post-structuralist notions. To take only one glaring example, he claims that "unlike Derrida, Blake is not concerned simply to show the impossibility . . . of all attempts to close this world within a metaphysics based on a limited set of axioms, but to uncover the relationships in whch this labyrinth itself appears" (pp. 20–21). At the least, Otto manifests his ignorance of the quantity of engaged deconstructive social analysis that elaborates how various relationships are produced and deployed through ideological assertions of ontological priority.

Given, then, that this book—despite its claim to the contrary—seeks to reinstate a traditional approach to Blake's work, what does it offer? A long-awaited and welcome attempt to establish a reading of the later poems that conforms with the traditional trajectory of Blake criticism for the earlier works. Otto takes on the complex and heroic task of providing a sustained discussion of both *Milton* and *Jerusalem*, in order to clarify their narrative structures and philosophical positions. Two chapters on *Milton* compose Part I, "The Moment of Embrace," the remaining five chapters of Part II, "Visionary Construction," concerns *Jerusalem*. If his method of asserting interpretations rather than arguing for them raises questions, if the demonstration of visionary deconstruction never appears, if the methodological assumptions seem at variance with Blake's practice, still Otto's attention to an important Blakean theme—the relational production of subjectivity and society—and his alertness to its subtleties provide what Otto rightly claims is the function of the poems themselves, to serve as "the ground for the movement forward" (p. 217).—Molly Anne Rothenberg.

Raine, Kathleen. *Golgonooza, City of Imagination: Last Studies in William Blake*. Hudson, NY: Lindisfarne Press, 1991. Pp. 182.

Kathleen Raine has been a prominent and influential Blakean since the publication of her massive *Blake and Tradition* in 1968, but as she herself would surely agree, her work is distinctly that of, precisely, a Blakean rather than a Blake critic. As Raine puts it, "Blake has not been my 'subject' but my Master, in the Indian sense of the word" (p. 2). At a time when critics of Romanticism have been establishing a self-consciously critical detachment from the so-called "Romantic Ideology," Raine's reverential posture seems strikingly old-fashioned, but she would not be distressed by such a criticism—the tradition in which she places both Blake and herself is indeed an old one, stretching back to "Plato and the pre-Socratics, Plotinus, and the Neoplatonic succession" (p. 3), and including the esoteric writings of Ficino, Joachim of Flora, Jacob Boehme, Swedenborg, Blake himself, and Carl Jung. For Raine, it makes no sense to seek critical detachment from the "spiritual masters" of a "sacred tradition" (p. 4), and the strength of her own writing results from her passionate commitment, from within the tradition, to Blake's thought and art. She has read widely, deeply, and sympathetically in the esoteric traditions familiar to Blake, and she intelligently and perceptively elucidates his uses of what she calls *the* tradition.

   Nevertheless, the eight essays in this book have little new to offer serious critics of Blake's work—they are all based on lectures delivered from 1981 to 1988, and the lectures themselves were based primarily on Raine's own earlier published works. Further, Blake's somewhat more critical admirers may well be disturbed by Raine's promotion of him as "a prophet of the New Age" (p. 76), especially since she claims that "it is, in essence, the doctrines of Swedenborg that Blake's works embody and to which they lend poetry and eloquence" (p. 76). Despite her reverential attitude toward him, Raine's Swedenborgian New Age Blake ultimately seems less compelling than the Blake who both acknowledged his debts to Swedenborg, and asserted his critical detachment from him in a devilish voice from *The Marriage of Heaven and Hell*: "Now hear a plain fact: Swedenborg has not written one new truth. Now hear another: he has written all the old falsehoods. And now hear the reason: He conversed with Angels who are all religious and conversed not with Devils who all hate religion." It is not fair, I think, to suggest that Raine has conversed too exclusively with the angels of her chosen tradition, and that in making a religious figure of Blake, she has too much neglected his energetically critical, anti-religious impulses. Further, by placing her exclusive emphasis on Blake's relation to other writers and artists, and to what she sees as the universal and timeless truths of the Imagination (which she always capitalizes), Raine seems to remove Blake from the immediacy of his historical moment, to make the struggling artist into an idealized and disembodied spirit, and to reduce the richly ambivalent, often inconsistent and confused body of his works into the too perfect coherence of a canon of sacred truth—she is even able to claim, in her introduction, that having wound the "Golden String" of Blake's thought into a ball, she is now amazed by "the golden simplicity of the sphere that remains" (pp. 1–2) in her hands.—David G. Riede.

Storch, Margaret. *Sons and Adversaries: Women in William Blake and D. H. Lawrence*. Knoxville, TN: U. of Tennessee Press, 1990. Pp. xiii + 226; bibliography; illustrations. Cf. *ECCB*, n.s. 16, VI:351.

Rev. (favorably) by Brenda Maddox in *TLS*, (June 7, 1991), 10.

Theophile de Bordeau (1722–1776)

Rey, Roselyne. "La Théorie de la sécrétion chez Bordeu, modèle de la physiologie et de la pathologie vitalistes." *Dix-huitième siècle*, 21 (1991), 45–58.

James Boswell (1740–1795)

Baruth, Philip E. "The Problem of Biographical Mastering: The Case for Boswell as Subject."
Modern Language Quarterly, 52 (1991), 376–403.

Boswell's various "textual identities" need to be released from the intrusions and "interpretive boundaries" of recent
editors, especially Pottle.

Boswell, James. *Boswell: The Great Biographer, 1789–1795.* Edited by Frank Brady and
Marlies K. Danziger. (The Yale Edition of the Private Papers of James Boswell.) London:
Heinemann; New York: McGraw-Hill, 1989. Pp. xxvii + 371; 10 illustrations. Cf. *ECCB*,
n.s. 16, VI:352–53; 15, VI:290–91.

Boswell, James. *The Journals of James Boswell, 1762–1795.* Edited by John Wain. London
and New Haven, CT: Yale U. Press, 1991. Pp. xxxiii + 412.

Rev. by Paula R. Backscheider in *Journal of English and Germanic Philology*, 90 (1991), 435–37; by Paul Clayton
in *Notes and Queries*, 236 (1991), 115–18.

John Wain's anthology of Boswell's journal is engrossing throughout. How could it not be, when an
experienced and appreciative novelist yokes undisputed highlights from the thirteen volumes of the Yale Boswell in
one volume of less than four hundred pages? The seven "chapters" include a substantial portion of the *London
Journal* ("Louisa," of course); interviews with Rousseau, Voltaire, Paoli, and Hume; John Reid's suspenseful last
days and Boswell's plan to resuscitate him; the perilous voyage in the Hebrides from Skye to Coll and the
predictable conflict between Johnson and Lord Auchinleck; representative Johnsonian dialogue, though not enough;
the "Tacenda" of April 1783; Johnson and Boswell's last meeting; his mesmerizing entanglement with the Earl of
Londsdale; the death of Margaret Boswell; and Boswell's final days. Wain sacrifices Boswell's correspondence with
Zelide, but refers the reader to the Holland journal. Lesser known extracts are frequently imaginative and rewarding.

But as one might expect, the steady, less glamorous bass of Boswell's life is muted or silenced, notably his
activities as advocate, political aspirant, and laird among family, friends, and colleagues, many of them notable, in
Scotland. Except for her letter accepting Boswell's offer of marriage, Margaret Boswell, the mainstay of his life,
figures little. She is not even named—merely "the lady in question" (p. xiv)—when Wain reports Boswell's choice
of a wife in the biographical review in the "Introduction." Nor is Margaret identified in the "Chronology" or in the
"Who's Who" of twenty nine persons in the end matter, where Margaret Caroline Rudd, Boswell's ill-famed mistress
in 1785–1786, gets the most lines. The comparison is instructive. Serious as he is, Wain could not resist a
disproportionate attention to Boswell's feverish heart and sexual adventures.

The cost is Boswell's intellectual development. There is much raging after women in Italy, for example, but
little of Boswell's systematic study of the classical there. His introduction to the Enlightenment at the German
courts is wholly excluded. We are not told that Boswell wrote the sketch of his life for Rousseau in French and that
the English text is a translation by Frederick Pottle. Thus Wain's ambition to fashion a "slender . . . but servicable
thread" of interconnecting information into an "entertaining and sometimes moving story of Boswell's life, told in
his own words" (p. xxviii), is imperfectly realized. The task is daunting, of course, but it is subverted in part by the
lure of a popular audience and success in the marketplace.

Wain is a self-effacing editor. His editorial links are minimal, and what readers cannot grasp in context they are
expected to learn from the front matter, the spare endnotes, or the index. Generally the extracts are self-explanatory
and the "story" hurries one on. But sometimes the "slender thread" snaps and all the apparatus fails. A brief
identifying phrase in link or note and a more precise index, citing at least first names and status or profession, would
have illuminated the text more fully, expanded the enquiring reader's knowledge of the eighteenth century, and yet
enlarged the volume very little. What are the roles of Michael Naismith and Charles Hayt that they are so actively
involved in the Reid case? Just as well not to ask, perhaps. A "writer," we are told in an endnote, is a "minor

lawyer" (p. 336, 2nd n. 6). All the necessary information is available in the Yale Boswell, from which Wain freely acknowledges his volume derives.

I believe that Wain genuinely hopes to spur readers of his high-keyed conflation to read individual volumes of Boswell's journal. To this end, he not only leaps years, several times as many as five, but also deletes and yokes phrases, sentences, paragraphs, and whole sections without notice or elipsis. The seamless volume is therefore misleading: it is not truly *journal*. How could I use it, as I do the *London Journal*, to teach that form? Unacknowledged editing also makes Boswell a uniformly more fluent and engaging writer than even he is. Turning to the unabridged source and the routine, daily notations, the new reader will feel let down in both style and matter. *The Heart of Boswell*, Mark Harris's fine edition of the first six volumes of Boswell's journal (1981), proves that an abridgement can indicate omissions without distracting the reader or disfiguring the page.

Students will respond enthusiastically to Wain's anthology. Would I adopt it as a text, therefore, if it is published in paperback at a reasonable price? Only, I think, together with the assignment of paper in which students compare parallel sections of it with a full-length journal of their choice. The idea excites me as an exercise in scholarship and criticism.—Irma S. Lustig.

Boswell, James. *The Life of Johnson, Abridged Edition.* Edited by John Canning. London: Methuen, 1991. Pp. 366; illustrations.

Clingham, Greg (ed.). *New Light on Boswell: Critical and Historical Essays on the Occasion of the Bicentenary of* The Life of Johnson. Cambridge and New York: Cambridge U. Press, 1991. Pp. xix + 235; illustrations.

David Daiches entitles his introduction to this collection "Boswell's Ambiguity" and begins it "James Boswell is one of the world's most fascinating and puzzling figures in literary history." A century ago there was no ambiguity or puzzlement about Boswell. Macaulay had taught that, although Boswell personally was a disgrace to Scotland, he had miraculously written the world's greatest biography, and that was that.

Some uneasiness about this began to be felt when Boswell's Journals first started to appear in 1928, and increased with the "trade" edition (just completed, in thirteen volumes). Can we assert that the *Life of Johnson* is greater than, say, Richard Ellman's superlative biography of James Joyce when many of the most quoted "sayings" of Johnson are found in a substantially different form in the Journals, or, like "The woman's a whore, and there's an end on't," not found there at all? Conversely, Macaulay's denunciation of Boswell's unedifying day-to-day life has received a good deal of extenuation and forgiveness. The present volume reflects something of these developments. Perhaps it should not have been called New Light, for there is very little new, hard information about Boswell in it, but, if not New Darkness, then perhaps New Puzzlement.

The first of its three sections is called "Boswell and Eighteenth-Century Scottish Culture." This seems somewhat paradoxical, given Boswell's persistent desire, eventually realized, to escape from Scotland. In his "Boswell and the Rhetoric of Friendship," Thomas Crawford studies his letters to three friends (though one of them, Temple, was definitely English). But he makes his point—Boswell could be an excellent letter-writer. Richard B. Sher's "Scottish Divines and Legal Lairds: Boswell's Scots Presbyterian Identity" goes into the intricacies of factions in the Church of Scotland, one subject on which Boswell seems to have been definately ambivalent. Pat Rogers writes on "Boswell and the Scotticism"—the long debate about the desirability of (Lowlands) Scots acquiring a command of standard English pronunciation and diction. I think he makes Boswell a more patriotic Scot than he was: I wish I could remember where he epitomizes his distaste for Scottish culture by quoting a Scots hostess inviting him, "Wull ye no hae some jeel?" ("Won't you have some jelly"). Joan H. Pittock's "Boswell as Critic" which has little to do with Boswell's Scottishness—discusses his few and not very memorable pieces of literary criticism.

The second section is titled "Contexts for The Life of Johnson"—whatever that may mean. Thomas M. Curley has a lively and appreciative discussion of Boswell's Account of Corsica. Gordon Turnbull's learned account of the trial of John Reid, the sheep-stealer, duplicates much of what can be found in W. K. Wimsatt's edition of Boswell for the Defence. Richard B. Schwartz's "Boswell and Hume: The Deathbed Interview" is the most thoughtful essay in the book—a brilliant analysis of Boswell's account, which demonstrates a very inadequate understanding of Hume's position. Susan Manning, in "Philosophical Melancholy: Style and Self in Boswell and Hume," comes to much the same conclusion as Schwartz: Hume understood the subject much better than Boswell did.

The third section, *"The Life of Johnson* Reconsidered," is on the whole a disappointment. John J. Burke, Jr. gives a replay of the quarrel between Johnson and Chesterfield, which I can't see adds very much to what we already know. Marlies K. Danziger on "Authorial Comments on the Life" again seems to add little. I wish she had included comment on Boswell's harsh denunciations of *The False Alarm* and *Taxation No Tyranny* and of Johnson's abolitionist stance on Negro slavery. Paul J. Korshin's "Johnson's Conversations in Boswell's *Life of Johnson*" points out, rightly, that "the reaction" of Johnson's words "is not an accurate one." The U.S. Supreme Court recently ruled, in the libel case of Masson vs. Malcolm, that the right of redacting a subject's words, in a work intended for public consumption, has strict limitations. Miss Malcolm, charged with infraction of those limitations, defended herself by comparing her practice to Boswell's. Donna Heiland's "Remembering the Hero" is summed up in Greg Clingham's essay, "Truth and Artifice"—a broad subject—as Boswell is "metonymically to Johnson as parasite to host." Well, that has been said before. Clingam quotes Ralph Rader as proposing "a distinction between factual and fictional works." Public libraries long ago made that distinction. Perhaps in view of some of the arguments by recent Boswellians, they should move the *Life* from their non-fiction to their fiction section.

I note some errors. "Lyttleton" and "guerilla" are regularly misspelled. Burke's notes draw heavily on a non-existent work he calls *The Early Biographers of Samuel Johnson* (it should read *Biographies*). I strongly object to a misquotation and misinterpretation of Jane Austen by Bruce Redford (as given by Crawford, p. 11) of the famous "(two inches wide) of ivory," rendered here as "one square of ivory." The passage needs to be read in full context (*Letters*, ed. Chapman, No. 134). This is a forty-year-old woman with four acclaimed novels to her credit, writing a brash seventeen-year-old who is trying to write a macho, blood-and-thunder novel, and complains that some chapters of his manuscript are missing. I didn't steal them, his aunt writes; how could I join "your strong, manly, spirited sketches" to my "two inches," etc.? It is a hilarious piece of irony, of which she was always a master. She is not apologizing to the boy for her "limitations"; she has a just sense of the worth of those four great novels, and knows that there is nothing "limited" or "miniaturist" about them.—Donald Greene.

Gilmore, Thomas B. "James Boswell's Drinking." *Eighteenth-Century Studies*, 24 (1991), 337–57.

Robert Boyle (1627–1691)

Boyle, Robert. *The Early Essays and Ethics of Robert Boyle.* Edited and annotated with an introduction by John T. Harwood. Carbondale, IL: Southern Illinois U. Press, 1991. Pp. lxix + 330; frontispiece.

Charles de Brosses (1709–1777)

Brosses, Charles de. *Lettres familières.* Edited by Cagliano de Azevedo, Giuseppina Cafasso, and Letizia Norci. Preface by Giovanni Macchia. (Mémoires et documents sur Rome et sur l'Italie méridionale, Nuova series, 4.) Rome: Centre Jean Bérard, 1991. Pp. xi + 1445.

Charles Brockden Brown (1771–1810)

Brown, Charles Brockden. *Wieland and Memoirs of Carwin the Biloquist.* Edited and with an introducton by Jay Fliegelman. New York: Viking Penguin, 1991. Pp. xlv + 365.

Ringe, Donald A. *Charles Brockden Brown.* Revised edition. (Twayne United States Authors Series; TUSCAS 98.) Boston: Twayne Publishers, 1991. Pp. x + 141; bibliography.

This study, like others in the Twayne series, is primarily oriented toward the general reader rather than the specialist. Nevertheless, Twayne studies have a certain importance and merit the attention of specialists because they influence many readers, acting as frequently-consulted sources of information perceived as "authoritative" and often as a first and only orientation to an author or work. These volumes introduce a writer—in this case Brown (1771–1810), the best known of early American novelists—synthesize recent scholarship, and constitute original studies insofar as they develop an independent perspective and provide commentary on particular works. In scholarly terms, the interest of this new edition, a revision of Ringe's first 1966 version, consists in asking how it responds to the extensive changes twenty-five years have brought to the study of Brown. This question is particularly germane because, as Ringe notes in his "Preface" (ix), Brown studies have "advanced markedly" since the sixties. Indeed, they have developed from a relatively sleepy corner of Americanist literary criticism, rarely frequented by top-level scholars, to an active, sophisticated, interdisciplinary field (the most recent book is by historian Steven Watts) characterized by significant interventions from major commentators (e.g. Davidson, Tompkins, Warner) and by increasingly refined methodological perspectives that reveal a more fascinating and challenging writer and cultural context than the one constructed by earlier criticism.

From this perspective, Ringe's study remains a useful introduction to Brown, especially in its detailed and informative summaries of the novels, and in the welcome new emphasis, in this revised edition, on the multiple generic references (gothic, sentimental, and "Jacobin" fiction, captivity narratives, etc.) that inform their notoriously complex narratives. The study's overall interpretaiton of Brown's career and writing, however, remains sketchy on the crucial 1790s cultural context of Brown's writings and thus never elucidates the specific cultural conflicts and events these writings respond to. The study constitutes a useful introduction, then, but one that has not fully incorporated the important new information and shifts in critical perspective made available by recent scholarship on Brown and the culture of the early republic. The revised bibliography, for example, does a good job of directing readers to significant post-1960s work, from landmark books like Davidson's *Revolution and the Word* and Tompkin's *Sensational Designs* to influential articles by Daniel Cohen and Shirley Samuels. But apart from references to the "Historical Essay" accompanying each novel in the Kent State edition of Brown's works (1977–87), the text of the study does little to take account of recent scholarship and its large-scale shift towards contextualization and various modes of critical historicization. Like the first, 1966 edition, this study's commentary and conclusions are guided by New-Critical textualism and psychologism. Its most significant conceptual sources, cited in Chapter One, "Prelude," are important but extremely dated works from the 1950s, e.g., Richard Volney Chase's *The American Novel and Its Tradition* (1957), Lewis' *The American Adam* (1955), and Warner Berthoff's articles on Brown, which appeared from 1956 to 1958. Most Americanists would concur that theese studies are more notable today for their significance in past critical developments than for their relevance to contemporary research.

This is certainly not to imply that this study is merely "out of style" or that finding important sources or insights in New Criticism renders it *de facto* inadequate. Rather, the difficulty is that, in relying on such dated material for its basic critical orientation, the study remains silent on the extensive differences between "newer" and "older" Brown scholarship, and consequently on the rather different image of Brown's work that emerges in the post-New Critical era. For example, one of the most basic achievements of recent work on Brown, especially post-Davidson and post-Tompkins, is the way it has overcome the narrowly belle-lettristic anachronism of earlier criticism, i.e., the notion that Brown's work is to be evaluated according to supposedly objective standards of literary excellence (New Critical concepts of "unity" of character, situation, etc.), or that Brown is significant primarily insofar as he can be read as prefiguring a later, "canonical" American literature (meaning, in this context, the Masterpiece Theatre scenario of Hawthorne-Melville-James, with all its ethnic, class, and gender implications). Nevertheless, Ringe's revised study registers no change on these central assumptions and maintains that Brown's work is "flawed" but significant primarily because it marks the "starting point of American fiction" and "foreshadows so much of what was to come" (p. 1–3; cf. 10, 69, 84, 114-15).

In fact, recent scholarship has made it clear that the once-common literary-historical claim that Brown marks the "starting point" of American fiction is incorrect both literally and figuratively: literally, because there are numerous significant American novels and other forms of fiction before Brown, and figuratively because the "sentimental" novels of the 1790s, such as Rowson's *Charlotte Temple* and Foster's *The Coquette* have more cultural impact than those of Brown and in certain ways are precedents for Brown's own work, notably *Clara Howard* and *Jane Talbot.* Contemporary criticism examines the formal aspects of Brown's novels not in relation to the purely aesthetic norms of a later period but in terms of their largeer eighteenth-century context (Sensibility, Revolution debates, the multiple generic referents Ringe refers to, etc.) and the specific ideological conflicts Brown addresses. Similarly, it locates Brown's larger significance not in connection to the perceived continuity of a later Canon, but in the way his work represents and comments on multiple aspects of cultural conflict in the late 1790s, for example reactionary political demonology, the replacement of republicanism by liberal capitalism as the legitimating discourse of the social order, and the backlash against the progressive "Wollstonecraftian" feminism of the early 1790s.

Overall, although it remains an informative introduction to the texts of Brown's novels, this study leaves the reader largely uninformed about the crucial contextual aspects of Brown's work and about what most contemporary commentators identify as the source of Brown's lasting significance; that is, the way all his writings (there is much more than the novels) are engaged in complex, intellectually ambitious and serious explorations of some of the major cultural debates and anxieties of American society at the turn of the nineteenth century.—Philip Barnard.

John Bunyan (1620–1688)

Batson, Beatrice. *John Bunyan's* Grace Abounding *and* The Pilgrim's Progress*: An Overview of Literary Studies, 1960–1987.* New York: Garland Publishing, 1988. Pp. xx + 245. Cf. *ECCB*, n.s. 16, VI:353; 15, VI:293; 14, VI:277.

Rev. (with other works) by Nancy Arneson in *Religion & Literature*, 23 (1991), 81–86.

Bunyan, John. *A Defence of the Doctrine of Justification by Faith.* Edited by T. L. Underwood. (The Miscellaneous Works of John Bunyan, 4.) Oxford: Clarendon Press, 1989. Pp. lv + 408.

Rev. by N. H. Keeble in *Notes and Queries*, 236 (1991), 230–31.

Bunyan, John. *Solomon's Temple Spiritualized, The House of the Forest of Lebanon, The Water of Life.* Edited by G. Midgley. (The Miscellaneous Works of John Bunyan, 7.) Oxford: Clarendon Press, 1989. Pp. li + 236.

Rev. (favorably) by N. H. Keeble in *Notes and Queries*, 236 (1991), 109–10.

Collmer, Robert G. (ed.). *Bunyan in Our Time.* Kent, OH, and London: Kent State U. Press, 1989. Pp. viii + 243. Cf. *ECCB*, n.s. 16, VI:354; 15, VI:294.

Rev. (with other works) by Nancy Arneson in *Religion & Literature*, 23 (1991), 81–86; by John R. Knott in *Modern Philology*, 89 (1990–91), 278–80.

Keeble, N. H. (ed.). *John Bunyan: Conventical and Parnassus.* Oxford: Clarendon Press, 1988. Pp. x + 278. Cf. *ECCB*, n.s.15, VI:295; 14, VI:279–80.

Rev. (with other works) by Nancy Arneson in *Religion & Literature*, 23 (1991), 81–86; by Robert G. Collmer in *Journal of English and Germanic Philology*, 90 (1991), 425–27.

Edmund Burke (1729–1797)

Burke, Edmund. *The Writings and Speeches of Edmund Burke: Vol. 8, The French Revolution 1790–1794*. Edited by L. G. Mitchell. Textual Editor William B. Todd. Oxford: Clarendon Press, 1989. Pp. xvi + 552. Cf. *ECCB*, n.s. 16, VI:355; 15, VI:295.

Rev. by John Faulkner in *Eighteenth-Century Studies*, 24 (1991), 537–46.

Ritchie, Daniel (ed.). *Edmund Burke: Appraisals and Applications*. (The Library of Conservative Thought.) New Brunswick, NJ: Transaction Publishers, 1990. Pp. xxvi + 291.

Rev. by E. J. Eisenach in *Choice*, 28 (1991), 1223.

Stanlis, Peter J. *Edmund Burke: The Enlightenment and Revolution*. (The Library of Conservative Thought.) New Brunswick, NJ: Transaction Publishers, 1991. Pp. xxiii + 259.

Rev. by E. J. Eisenach in *Choice*, 29 (1991), 351.

Charles Burney (1726–1814)

Burney, Charles. *The Letters of Dr. Charles Burney*. Vol. I: *1751–1784*. Edited by Alvaro Ribeiro. New York: Oxford U. Press; Oxford: Clarendon Press, 1991. Pp. xxxiv + 501; frontispiece.

Fanny Burney (1752–1840)

Burney, Fanny. *The Early Journals and Letters of Fanny Burney*. Volume I: *1768–1773*. Edited by Lars E. Troide. Oxford: Clarendon Press, 1988. Pp. xlvi + 353. Cf. *ECCB*, n.s. 15, VI:296; 14, VI:283.

Rev. (with another work) by John A. Dussinger in *Modern Language Review*, 86 (1991), 407–08.

Burney, Fanny. *The Early Journals and Letters of Fanny Burney*. Vol. II: *1774–1777*. Edited by Lars E. Troide. Montreal and Toronto: McGill-Queen's U. Press (distributed through Toronto: U. of Toronto Press); Oxford: Clarendon Press, 1990. Pp. xxiii + 311; appendices; frontispiece; illustrations. Cf. *ECCB*, n.s. 16, VI:356.

Rev. (favorably) by D. Landry in *Choice*, 29 (1991), 277.

Burney, Frances. *The Wanderer*. (The World's Classics.) Edited by Robert L. Mack and Peter Sabor. Introduction by Margaret Anne Doody. New York and Oxford: Oxford U. Press, 1991. Pp. 1008.

David, Gail. *Female Heroism in the Pastoral*. (Gender & Genre in Literature, 2.) London and New York: Garland Publishing, 1991. Pp. xxv + 258; bibliography.

Rev. by W. C. Snyder in *Choice*, 29 (1991), 278–79.

Chapter 2, "Female Heroics in Three Places," (pp. 59–111) is divided between *Evelina* and *The Mysteries of Udolpho*.

Doody, Margaret Anne. *Frances Burney: The Life in the Works*. Cambridge and New York: Cambridge U. Press, 1988. Pp. xx + 442. Cf. *ECCB*, n.s. 16, VI:357; 15, VI:297.

Rev. (with another work) by John A. Dussinger in *Modern Language Review*, 86 (1991), 407–08; by Judy Simons in *Review of English Studies*, 42 (1991), 275–276.

Epstein, Julia. *The Iron Pen: Frances Burney and the Politics of Women's Writing*. Madison, WI: U. of Wisconsin Press, 1989. Pp. xii + 276. Cf. *ECCB*, n.s. 16, VI:357; 15, VI:297.

Rev. by Lillian D. Bloom in *Modern Philology*, 88 (1990–91), 329–32.

Kelly, Linda. *Juniper Hall: An English Refuge from the French Revolution*. London: Weidenfeld & Nicolson, 1991. Pp. xv + 135; illustrations; map.

Rev. by Sarah Bradford in *TLS*, (Mar. 29, 1991), 6.

Rogers, Katharine M. *Frances Burney: The World of "Female Difficulties."* London: Harvester Wheatsheaf; Savage, MD: Barnes & Noble, 1990. Pp. 211. Cf. *ECCB*, n.s. 16, VI:357.

Rev. (with another work) by Ian A. Bell in *TLS*, (Mar. 29, 1991), 6.

Robert Burns (1759–1796)

Bold, Alan. *A Burns Companion*. Basingstoke: Macmillan, 1990; New York: St. Martin's Press, 1991. Pp. xiv + 447; appendices; bibliography; illustrations; map.

Rev. (favorably) by H. M. Barber in *Choice*, 28 (1991), 1611–12.

Few students of Burns would disagree with Alan Bold's controlling premise that Burns, the institution, has come to overshadow Burns the poet. This state of affairs was captured years ago by Hugh MacDiarmid: "No wan in fifty kens a wurd Burns wrote / But misapplied is a 'body's property." Burns, Bold argues, is a sort of "nationally symbolic lifeforce" (p. 156), and as such has been made subservient to the needs of whatever group or individual takes him up. Few would disagree, either, with Bold's claim that Burn's "whole life was an astonishing exercise in role-playing, and he was so good at adopting attitudes that he became all things to all men" (p. 154). Burns seems almost to connive at his own appropriation by others when he deliberately makes himself into an object of their desires and calls into question his own central values. Accordingly, one of Bold's main goals in this *Companion*—apart from the essential one of providing sound, factual information—is to untangle this "complex of contradictions" (p. 173), ultimately demythologizing Burns by returning readers to his art itself. For Bold, Burns' "art is more meaningful than his immortal memory" (p. 171).

Bold accomplishes his task very well within the limits of a single *Companion* volume. Like other volumes in this series, it is part handbook and part critical explication. In the handbook portion, Bold is especially good at uncovering the complex currents of thought that underlie Burn's poetry. His politics, for example, are too often simplified into radical republicanism, on the one hand, or craven temporizing, on the other. Bold shows, however, that Burns was not simply one or the other, but someone who had to embrace republicanism in very reactionary times. These critical explications of the poems are intended for those who are relatively new to Burns, and they do not take on difficult issues of interpretation. Nonetheless, Bold sometimes discloses new and surprising material (at least for this reader), as in his contextualizing of such familiar poems as "Scots, wha hae" and "Red, Red Rose."

As a handbook and as a preliminary guide, then, this book is a success. But it also raises and leaves unanswered some important questions. Specifically, don't we need a study of how Burns's "immortal memory" was in fact originated, developed, and perpetuated? Instead of trying to discover the *true* Burns (won't that be different for every investigator), it might be better to see what words, if we are to grasp the full complexity of Burns, we may have to see him for what he wrote "in itself" and for what he represents for those who read (or misread) him. Not many poets have that privileged station, and it is clearly a part of what Burns is. To deny the legitimacy of Burns's role as a "nationally symbolic lifeforce" in which he must be "a 'body's property'" is to engage in yet another simplification of him—all in the name of one formulation of "true" art. Thus, Bold reminds us that there is much work to be done with Burns, not the least of it a study of the many different things that Burns has represented during the last two troubled centuries of Scottish cultural history.—Jeffrey Smitten.

Burns, Robert. *Selected Poetry*. Edited by Angus Calder and William Donnelly. Harmondsworth, UK: Penguin, 1991. Pp. 440.

Fowler, Richard Hindle. *Robert Burns*. London and New York: Routledge, 1988. Pp. xii + 280. Cf. *ECCB*, n.s. 15, VI:298.

Rev. by Thomas Crawford in *Modern Language Review*, 86 (1991), 174.

Jacques Cazotte (1719–1792)

Bottacin, Annalisa. *Jacques Cazotte et la "Querelle des Bouffons."* Este: Libreria Editrice Ziela, 1991. Pp. 116.

Rev. by Rosa Maia Frigo in *Studi francesi*, 36 (1992), 373.

Robert Challe (1659–ca. 1720)

Weil, Michelle. *Robert Challe romancier*. (Histoire de Idees et critique litteraire, 298.) Geneva: Droz, 1991. Pp. 340.

This is a substantive and intelligent study of one of French literary history's most original, and still least known, works, Robert Challe's *Les Illustres Françaises* (1713). Published at the end of the siècle de Louis XIV, this novel (or collection of interrelated stories) is a perfect place to begin a study of the transition that brought French thought and fiction into the Age of the Enlightenment. Michèle Weil writes clearly and forcefully about the narrative traditions that influenced Challe, about the relationship between fiction and philosophy, and about the cognitive value of fiction writing itself. This is not only the story of a book and of a man, but an intelligent introduction to the spirit of a still relatively unstudied period, the first two decades of the 18th century.

Thanks to work done by Frédéric Deloffre especially, among others, we know about as much as we can about Robert Challe, an intellectual adventurer who travelled more than once to the "new" world, and who felt that his life had been, in general, a failure. When he died in 1721, he in effect entered into a penumbra of oblivion that only the careful work of twentieth-century scholars has begun to remove. This is strange indeed, for *Les Illustres Françaises* is a remarkable piece of prose fiction.

Weil begins her study with an analysis of the role of first-person narrator, both as a narration stance and as a cognitive device. She leads us to see that, for Challe (and, it is inferred, for many of his intellectual contemporaries), the terrain between sociability and the authority of the "I" needed to be much worked. Fascinated with the communication that formed the matter of the social web, Challe (and Marivaux, his most comparable contemporary) sought to understand how dialogue was an epistemological concept as much as a social technique.

Knowledge, he felt, was contingent, and his characters show that it is only through knowing the world as interpreted by others that ignorance can be avoided. Received knowledge has its value, but that value is only relative.

Challe was also fascinated with class, with the transformation of the concept of the nobility into a larger, less definable class, but one nevertheless that could have had as its motto *bourgeoise oblige*. It is the story of the appropriation of the best values of the nobility by the bourgeoisie that makes *Les Illustres Françaises* a source of information on class transformations of the early 18th century. Challe succeeds, according to Weil, in creating a world where perceived reality is changed through dialogue which is itself a result of the merging of class values.

Weil uses subtly and unpretentiously the work of such critics as Bakhtin, Genette, and Benveniste to give a rigorous, clear, and persuasive account of the techniques used by Challe in constructing his novel; yet, she does not stop there, going on to give us a compelling aperçu through this technically sophisticated study of the intellectual underpinnings of the period in which the novel was conceived and eagerly published.

A short review cannot even approach doing justice to this rich study. It is a book that teaches us much about the society in which *Les Illusters Françaises* was written and about the ideas that would bear fruit throughout the Enlightenment.—Ronald C. Rosbottom.

Isabelle Agneta de Charrière (1740?–1805)

Charrière, Isabelle de. *Lettres neuchâteloises*. Edited by Isabelle and Jean-Louis Vissière. Preface by Christophe Calame. (700 ans de littérature en Suisse romande.) Paris: La Différence, 1991. Pp. 110.

A scholarly edition of Madame de Charrière's short 1784 novel, this is not, nor does it claim to be. The notes are almost inexistent; the introductions will bring nothing to anyone even vaguely familiar with Madame de Charrière. But it is a pretty little book, much more pleasant to read than the *Oeuvres complètes*. Another volume by the same author is planned in the same series.—Adrienne D. Hytier.

François-Auguste-René de Chateaubriand (1768–1848)

Dubé, Pierre Herbert. *Chateaubriand's* Les Aventures du dernier Ancérage*: Past and Present*. Frankfurt am Main and New York: Peter Lang, 1989. Pp. 119.

Rev. by Anne Sanderson in *Modern Language Review*, 86 (1991), 1029–30.

John Clare (1793–1864)

Clare, John. *The Early Poems of John Clare, 1804–1822*. Edited by M. Grainger, D. Powell, and E. Robinson. 2 vols. Oxford: Clarendon Press, 1989. Pp. xxxiv + 599; xii + 835.

Rev. by Mark Storey in *Notes and Queries*, 236 (1991), 120–22.

John Cleland (1708–1789)

Kibbie, Ann Louise. "Sentimental Properties: *Pamela* and *Memoirs of a Woman of Pleasure*." *English Literary History*, 58 (1991), 561–77.

Both works reflect the tensions of female characters who are subject to the currency of exchange and the constancy of property.

Marie Jean Antoine Nicolas Caritat, marquis de Condorcet (1743–1780)

Condorcet, Marie Jean Antoine Nicolas Caritat, marquis de. *Condorcet: Ecrits sur l'instruction publique*. Vol. I: *Cinq Mémoires sur l'instruction publique*. Edited by Charles Coutel and Catherine Kintzler. (Les Classiques de la République.) Paris: Edilig, 1989. Pp. 296.

Rev. by R. Niklaus in *Modern Language Review*, 86 (1991), 466–67.

Condorcet, Marie Jean Antoine Nicolas Caritat, marquis de. *Ecrits sur l'instruction publique*. Volume II: *Rapport sur l'instruction publique*. Edited by Charles Coutel. Preface by Catherine Kintzler. (Les Classiques de la République.) Paris: Edilig, 1989. Pp. 327.

Rev. by R. Niklaus in *Modern Language Review*, 86 (1991), 729–30.

Pappas, John. "Condorcet, 'le seul' et 'le premier' féministe du 18e siècle?" *Dix-huitième siècle*, (1991), 441–43.

William Congreve (1670–1729)

Erskine-Hill, H., and A. Lindsay (eds.). *William Congreve: The Critical Heritage*. London and New York: Routledge, 1989. Pp. xiv + 494. Cf. *ECCB*, n.s. 15, VI:304–05.

Rev. by Brean S. Hammond in *Notes and Queries*, 236 (1991), 231–32; by Eric S. Rump in *The Scriblerian*, 23 (1991), 259–60.

Peters, Julie Stone. *Congreve, the Drama, and the Printed Word*. Stanford, CA: Stanford U. Press, 1990. Pp. viii + 286; bibliography; illustrations. Cf. *ECCB*, n.s. 16, VI:362–63.

Rev. (with reservations) by J. Douglas Canfield in *Eighteenth-Century Studies*, 25 (1991–92), 227–31; by E. D. Hill in *Choice*, 29 (1991), 100.

Benjamin Constant (1767–1830)

Annales Benjamin Constant, No. 12. *Benjamin Constant: philosophe, historien, romancier, homme d'Etat*. (Actes du Colloque de l'Université du Maryland.) Lausanne: Institute Benjamin Constant, 1991. Pp. 188.

This volume contains ten papers originally presented at a "colloque" on Benjamin Constant at the University of Maryland in October of 1989, together with a meticulous report by Jean-Daniel Candaux of Constant manuscripts sold on the market between 1976 and 1989, a useful bibliography of works about Constant published in the period 1986–1990 by Sylvie Colbois, and one book review. These pieces, especially taken in conjunction with a most interesting account by C. P. Courtney of the work-in-progress on the editing of Constant's correspondence, are sufficient in themselves to invite scholars into this book. Moreover, excellent articles on a variety of Constant's interests—religion, political thought, and literature—will induce them to linger thoughtfully between its covers. Several are especially noteworthy.

Pierre Thompson succeeds in using approaches borrowed for the deconstruction movement without becoming embroiled in some of its excesses in his "Benjamin Constant: L'allégorie du polythéisme." Since Constant was obliged by the oppressive political climate of the Concordat period to veil his critique of Christianity, he used polytheism as an allegory through which to express himself, with confused results, as Thompson convincingly and illuminating demonstrates. The deep influence of classical antiquity on Constant is, for Ephrain Harpaz in "Benjamin Constant entre la République et la Monarchie," and for Biancamaria Fontana in "Publicity and the 'Res publica': the concept of public opinion in Benjamin Constant's writings," a major explanatory force. The former traces the trajectory of Constant's political stances in a troubled period, while the latter pursues an elusive but central concept throughout his work. Kurt Kloocke in "Les Lettres de Benjamin Constant a Juliette Recamier ou la presence de la fiction dans la vie," discovers that the boundaries between life and art are blurred. "L'un conditionne l'autre et vice-versa, de sorte que nous ne saurions dire avec precision si la fiction émane de la vie ou sinous vivons la fiction, si nous lisons un roman vrai ou si les lettres d'amour adressées à Juliette sont un vrai roman" (p. 96). His perceptive reading serves as a smooth transition to those articles about Constant as literary critic and as writer.

Caught between claim and counterclaim regarding Constant's merit as a literary critic, Martine de Rougemont endeavors interestingly if somewhat inconclusively to set up a *Corpus* of critical work and some central questions to be posed. Lieve Spaas' examination of a meta-discourse within *Adolphe* recalls that blurring of boundaries so nicely set out by Kloocke's piece. Finally, Carol A. Mossman finds in an economic model, that of investment and foreclosure, a fascinating metaphor for the study of the interpersonal relations in that novel.

Because of their varied approaches and well-developed theses, these articles will find responsive readers from a number of fields. It is regrettable that five years have passed since they were first presented. However, they are fresh enough to be enjoyed with profit today.—Charlotte Hogsett.

Constant, Benjamin. *Adolphe: anecdote trouvée dans les papiers d'un inconnu.* Edited by C. P. Courtney. (Blackwell French Texts.) Oxford: Basil Blackwell, 1989. Pp. 127.

Rev. by Dennis Wood in *Modern Language Review*, 86 (1991), 1027–28.

Constant, Benjamin. *The Affair of Colonel Juste de Constant and Related Documents (1787–1796).* Published with an introduction by C. P. Courtney. Cambridge: Daemon Press, 1990. Pp. lxviii + 304.

Rev. (favorably) by Dennis Wood in *French Studies,* 45 (1991), 468–69.

Constant, Benjamin. *Benjamin Constant: Political Writings.* Translated and Edited by Biancamaria Fontana. Cambridge and New York: Cambridge U. Press, 1988. Pp. x + 350. Cf. *ECCB*, n.s. 15, VI:305.

Rev. by Nigel Addinall in *Modern Language Review*, 86 (1991), 1028–29.

Constant, Benjamin. *Fragments d'un ouvrage abandonné sur la possibilité d'une constitution républicaine dans un grand pays.* Edited by Henry Grange. Paris: Aubier, 1991. Pp. 506; bibliography.

Abraham Cowley (1618–1667)

Cowley, Abraham. *The Collected Works of Abraham Cowley*, I, *Poetical Blossomes, The Puritans Lecture, The Puritan and the Papist, The Civil War*. Edited by T. O. Calhoun, L. Heyworth, and A. Pritchard. Newark, DE: U. of Delaware Press; London and Toronto: Associated University Presses, 1989. Pp. 447. Cf. *ECCB*, n.s. 16, VI:364; 15, VI:306.

Rev. (favorably) by David Hopkins in *Notes and Queries*, 236 (1991), 385–86.

George Crabbe (1754–1832)

Crabbe, George. *The Complete Poetical Works*. Edited by Norma Dalrymple-Chapneys and Arthur Pollard. 3 vols. Oxford: Clarendon Press, 1988. Pp. l + 820; x + 1010; x + 540. Cf. *ECCB*, n.s. 16, VI:365; 15, VI:307; 14, VI:293.

Rev. by O M Brack, Jr. in *Modern Philology*, 88 (1990–91), 333–36.

Claude Prosper Jolyot de Crébillon (1707–1777)

Crébillon, Claude (Crébillon fils). *La Nuit et le moment*. Theatrical adaptation by Charles George. Presentation by Dominique Triaire. (Espaces Théâtre.) Montpellier: Espaces 34, 1991. Pp. 58.

As noted in Dominique Triaire's excellent introduction, Crébillon's novel is "l'histoire d'une conquête." Two characters are involved: Clitandre, and the object of his siege, Cisalise. What results is a most subtle (and often amusing) exploration of the nature of love.

I think Charles George's dramatic adaptation of this work of an almost forgotten eighteenth-century writer is most skillful and stage-worthy, as well as true to the spirit of the original novel, and that a first-rate production of this adaptation, enhanced by superb acting, would prove to be a most rewarding experience.—William Rothwell.

Richard Cumberland (1732–1811)

Cumberland, Richard. *The Unpublished Plays of Richard Cumberland*. Vol. I. Edited by Richard J. Dircks. New York: AMS Press, 1991. Pp. xlii + 428.

Daniel Defoe (1661–1731)

Backscheider, Paula. *Daniel Defoe: His Life*. Baltimore, MD, and London: Johns Hopkins U. Press, 1989. Pp. xv + 671. Cf. *ECCB*, n.s. 16, VI:367; 15, VI:308–09.

Rev. by Marlies K. Danziger in *Journal of English and Germanic Philology*, 89 (1990), 566–68; by Frank H. Ellis in *Review of English Studies*, 41 (1990), 580–82; by Manuel Schonhorn in *South Atlantic Review*, 56 (Jan. 1991), 110–112; by Michael Seidel in *Modern Philology*, 89 (1990–91), 124–27.

Defoe, Daniel. *Memoirs of a Cavalier*. (The World's Classics.) Edited by James T. Boulton. New Introduction by John Mullan. New York and Oxford: Oxford U. Press, 1991. Pp. 352.

Defoe, Daniel. *A Tour Through the Whole Island of Great Britain.* Abridged and edited by P. N. Furbank and W. R. Owens. Picture research by A. J. Coulson. London and New Haven, CT: Yale U. Press, 1991. Pp. xiii + 417; illustrations (some colored); maps.

Rev. (briefly and favorably) in *TLS,* (Nov. 8, 1991), 32

Dijkstra, Bram. *Defoe and Economics: The Fortunes* Roxana *in the History of Interpretation.* Basingstoke, UK, and London: Macmillan, 1987. Pp. xvi + 247. Cf. *ECCB*, n.s. 16, VI:368; 15, VI:310; 14, VI:296; 13, VI:416.

Rev. by John McVeagh in *The Scriblerian*, 23 (1991), 256–57; (with another work) by John Richetti in *Modern Language Review*, 86 (1991), 396–98.

Flynn, Carol Houlihan. *The Body in Swift and Defoe.* (Cambridge Studies in Eighteenth-Century English Literature and Thought, 5.) Cambridge and New York: Cambridge U. Press, 1990. Pp. viii + 231.

Rev. by Kirk Combe in *Notes and Queries*, 236 (1991), 544–45; by Everett Zimmerman in *The Scriblerian*, 24 (1991), 51–52.

Furbank, P. N., and W. R. Owens. *The Canonization of Daniel Defoe.* London and New Haven, CT: Yale U. Press, 1988. Pp. xii + 210. Cf. *ECCB*, n.s. 16, VI:368; 15, VI:310; 14, VI:296–97.

Rev. by G. A. Starr in *Modern Philology*, 88 (1990–91), 317–20.

Green, Martin. *The* Robinson Crusoe *Story.* University Park, PA: Pennsylvania State U. Press, 1990. Pp. 221. Cf. *ECCB*, n.s. 16, VI:368–69.

Rev. by K. P. Mulcahy in *Choice*, 29 (1991) 85–86.

Lovett, Robert W., with Charles C. Lovett. *Robinson Crusoe: A Bibliographical Checklist of English Language Editions (1719–1979).* (Bibliographies and Indexes in World Literature, 30.) New York: Greenwood Press, 1991. Pp. xix + 303.

Macaree, David. *Daniel Defoe: His Political Writings & Literary Devices.* (Studies in British Literature, 10.) Lewiston, NY: Edwin Mellen Press, 1991. Pp. 192.

Milchert-Wylezich, Margret. "Zur Arbeutsethik des Puritanismus in den Schriften Daniel Defoes." Pp. 21–29 of *Vom Wert der Arbeit: Zur literarischen Konstitution des Wertkomplexes "Arbeit" in der deutschen Literatur (1770–1930).* Edited by Harro Segeberg. Tübingen: Niemeyer, 1991. Pp. 423; illustrations.

Seidel, Michael. Robinson Crusoe*: Island Myths and the Novel.* (Twayne's Master Work Studies, 64.) Boston, MA: Twayne, 1991. Pp. xiv + 134; illustrations.

Rev. by K. P. Mulcahy in *Choice*, 29 (1991), 102.

Statt, Daniel. "Daniel Defoe and Immigration." *Eighteenth-Century Studies*, 24 (1991), 293–313.

Traces the importance of Defoe's ideas and encouragement of immigration throughout his works.

Watt, W. S. "Reply: Defoe's Quotations." *Notes and Queries*, 236 (1991), 349–50.

Latin sources for several quotations from the *Tour Through Great Britain*.

Denis Diderot (1713–1784)

Ages, Arnold. "Diderot's Personal Credo: The Testimony of the Correspondence." *The Romanic Review*, 82 (1991), 25–35.

Organized along three themes: "Existential ennui," "virtue vs. passion," and "equilibrium."

Albertan, Christian. "autographes et documents." *Recherches sur Diderot et sur l'*Encyclopédie, 10 (1991), 174–79.

Albertan, Christian., and Anne-Marie Chouillet. "Autographes et documents." *Recherches sur Diderot et sur l'*Encyclopédie, 11 (1991), 184–202.

List of autographs concerning, directly or indirectly, Diderot.

Anderson, Wilda. *Diderot's Dream*. Baltimore, MD, and London: Johns Hopkins U. Press, 1990. Pp. vii + 259; frontispiece. Cf. *ECCB*, n.s. 16, VI:370.

Rev. by D. A. Collins in *Choice*, 28 (1991), 1140; (favorably) by Diane Fourny in *Rocky Mountain Review of Language and Literature*, 45 (1991), 85–86; by Julie C. Hayes in *Eighteenth-Century Studies*, 24 (1991), 508–12; by Ruth P. Thoman in *The French Review*, 65 (1991), 311–12; (with reservations) by Ann Thomson in *Recherches sur Diderot et sur l'*Encyclopédie, 11 (1991), 157–158.

Becq, Annie (ed.). *L'Encyclopédisme*. Actes du Colloque de Caen (12–16 January, 1987). Paris: Aux Amateur de livres (distributed through Paris: Klincksieck), 1991. Pp. 592.

Rev. by Roselyne Rey in *Recherches sur Diderot et sur l'*Encyclopédie, 12 (1992), 186–189.

Bernard Baertschi. "L'athéisme de Diderot." *Revue philosophique de Louvain*,83 (1991), 421–449.

Diderot observes that the developments of science endanger the proofs of the existence of God that have been proposed since the time of Descartes. He is a witness to and inaugurator of a conception of nature that has remained important up to the present day.

Cernuschi, Alain. "Diderot mis en pièces." *Recherches sur Diderot et sur l'*Encyclopédie, 11 (1991), 173–181; illustrations.

Rev. of a Diderot colloquium in Geneva, April 26 and 27, 1991.

Chouillet, Anne-Marie (ed.). "Trois lettres inédites de Diderot." *Recherches sur Diderot et sur l'*Encyclopédie, 11 (1991), 9–17; illustrations.

Three interesting letters of Diderot (to Maupertuis June 12, 1749; to La Condamine and to Suard?); marred by a number of typos.

Chouillet, Jacques (ed.). *L'Encyclopedie, Diderot, l'esthétique.* Paris: Presses Universitaires de France, 1991. Pp. 336.

Connon, Derek F. *Innovation and Renewal: A Study of the Theatrical Works of Diderot.* (Studies on Voltaire and the Eighteenth Century, 258.) Oxford: The Voltaire Foundation at the Taylor Institution, 1989. Pp. 204. Cf, *ECCB*, n.s. 16, VI:371; 15, VI:313.

Rev. by Agnes G. Raymond in *Modern Language Review*, 86 (1991), 465–66.

Couvreur, Manuel. "Diderot et Philidor: Le Philosophe au chevat d'*Ernelinde*." *Recherches sur Diderot et sur l'*Encyclopédie, 11 (1991), 83–107.

Discusses the part which Diderot did in fact play in the elaboration of the opera *Ernelinde* by Philidor (libretto by Poinsinet).

De La Carrera, Rosalina. *Success in Circuit Lies: Diderot's Communicational Practice.* Stanford, CA: Stanford U. Press, 1991. Pp. xii + 242.

This book is a study of Diderot from the standpoint of communication theory in the manner of Michel Serres and a reading of *La Religieuse* as the exemplary text of the *oeuvre*. The latter novel reveals (through the famous *Préface-Annexe*, in particular) a model of communication that rejects a binary type of discourse in favor of a "ternary" one. The latter "opens out to the reader and draws him in as one of its terms." Through "points of contact" of this kind readers touch the "body" of the text, a physical contact that changes ways of thinking. The model is called a materialistic one. It is maintained in three other texts of the *philosophe* (all of which are discussed in the book). They are: *L'Histoire des Deux Indes, L'Essai sur les règnes de Claude et de Néron,* and *Le Rêve de d'Alembert.*

   Readers of *Success in Circuit Lies* may well raise questions as to how ternary discourse differs from self-reflexive irony; and the value of reducing so imaginatively rich and hilarious an *oeuvre* to dry theories of communication is far from clear. Yet De la Carrera's study is for all of its inevitable problematical areas an intriguing and useful one. The readings offered are clearly written and offer numerous insights of interest (Diderot's role as "metaphistorian" in the *Histoire des Deux Indes*, for example, the status of the *Préface-Annexe* as a "letter that was never sent"). The translation of the latter into English (the first of its kind) is a welcome event.

   What is most attractive about the book, though, is the choice of texts. The range offered is an impressive one including several writings that have yet to receive their due. It is to the author's credit to have recognized their literary interests. It is no less so to have done so against the background of a view of Diderot which is one of the surprises of this decidedly "sciences humaines" reading. It is the ultimate order, even unity, of the *oeuvre* as a whole: "the consistent recurrence of the same mechanism in these different contexts that brings into play an unexpected unity in what at first looks like a disparate corpus."—Stephen Werner.

Delon, Michel, and Wolfgang Drost (cds.). *Le Regaud et l'objet: Diderot critique d'art.* Actes du second colloque des universités d'Orleans et de Siegen. Heidelberg: Carl Winter Universitätsverlag, 1989. Pp. 142; 26 illustrations. Cf. *ECCB*, n.s. 15, VI:314–15

Rev. (briefly) by Gianluigi Goggi in *Studi francesi*, 35 (1991), 148.

Diderot, Denis. *Le Paradoxe sur le comédien*. Edited by Henri Baudin. (Univers de lettres.) Paris: Bordas, 1991. Pp. 125.

This school edition, the newest Diderot title in the Univers des lettres series, presents the 1830 text of the *Paradoxe*. Passages dating from Diderot's review in the *Correspondance littéraire* of *Garrick ou les acteurs anglais,* point of departure of the essay, are clearly indicated by the use of brackets. Any important variants appear in footnotes. Guides for directed study of important developments in the work appear throughout the text. An interesting and comprehensive étude d'ensemble, appropriately titled "Dialogue des vivants et des morts" presents the editor, M. Henri Baudin, in an imaginary conversation with critics of the *Paradoxe*. Here a multiplicity of points of view and of reactions are expressed by actors, directors, critics, philosophers, professors, and littérateurs from the time of Diderot down to the present.—Frederick A. Spear.

Diderot, Denis. *Oeuvres complètes*. Vol. 16: *Salon de 1767*. *Salon de 1769*. Edition critique et annotée par Else Marie Bukdahl, Michel Delon and Annette Lorenceau. Paris: Hermann, 1990. Pp. xii + 697; illustrations.

Rev. by Pierre Retat in *Recherches sur Diderot et sur l'*Encyclopédie, 11 (1991), 152–53.

Diderot, Denis. *Saggi sulla Pittura*. Edited by Massimo Modica. Palermo: Aestetica Edizioni, 1991.

Rev. by Aurelio Principato in *Recherches sur Diderot et sur l'*Encyclopédie, 11 (1991), 153.

Diderot, Denis. *This Is Not a Story and Other Stories*. Translated with an Introduction by P. N. Furbank. Columbia, MO: U. of Missouri Press, 1991. Pp. viii + 166; bibliography.

Dixon, B. Lynne. *Diderot, Philosopher of Energy: The Development of his Concept of Physical Energy 1745–1769*. (Studies on Voltaire and the Eighteenth Century, 255.) Oxford: The Voltaire Foundation at the Taylor Institution, 1988. Pp. xi + 205. Cf. *ECCB*, n.s. 16, VI:372; 15, VI:315; 14, VI:301–02.

Rev. by R. Niklaus in *Modern Language Review*, 86 (1991), 466.

Dulac, Georges (ed.). *Editer Diderot*. (Studies on Voltaire and the Eighteenth Century, 254.) Oxford: The Voltaire Foundation at the Taylor Institution, 1988. Pp. xviii + 555. Cf. *ECCB*, n.s. 16, VI:372; 15, VI:315; 14, VI:302–03.

Rev. by Peter Jimack in *Modern Language Review*, 86 (1991), 723–24.

Dulac, Georges. "Politique, littérature et mystification: Echec à Rulhière. Un Récit inédit de Diderot rapporté par D. Golitsyn." *Dix-huitième siècle*, 21 (1991), 213–222.

Fellows, Otis. *Diderot*. New revised edition. (Twayne's World Authors Series, 425.) Boston, MA: G. K. Hall, 1989. Pp. xviii + 190. Cf. *ECCB*, n.s. 15, VI:316.

Rev. by Derek F. Cannon in *Modern Language Review*, 86 (1991), 724–25; by Lynn Salkin Sbiroli in *Studi francesi*, 34 (1991), 530.

Fellows, Otis, and Diana Guiragossian Carr (eds.). *Diderot Studies XXIV.* Geneva: Droz, 1991. Pp. 246.

Rev. by Lynn Salkin Sbiroli in *Studi francesi*, 34 (1991), 530.
  Includes the following articles:
  Marie-Hélène Chabut, *"Le Supplément au voyage de Bougainville*: Une Poétque du déguisement," pp. 11–23.
  Huguette Cohen, "Diderot et les limites de la littérature dans les *Salons*," pp. 25–45.
  Peter V. Conroy Jr., "Gender Issues in Diderot's *La Reliqieuse*," pp. 47–66.
  Thierry Durand, "Diderot et Heidegger: a Poétique du Bavardage dans *Jacques le fataliste et son maître*," pp. 67–84.
  Béatrice Durand-Sendrail, "Diderot et Heidegger: Archéologie d'une polémique," pp. 85–104.
  Robert Niklaus, "Le *Plan d'une université* de Diderot et le plan d'instruction publique de Condorcet mis en regard," pp. 105–19.
  Elizabeth Potulicki, "Eclairé, clairvoyant (adj. Gramm), un article de l' *Encyclopédie* ou la présence dialogue de Diderot," pp. 121–36.
  Bonnie Arden Robb, "The Making of Denis Diderot: Translation as Apprenticeship," pp. 137–54.
  Frederick A. Spear, "Bibliographie de Diderot, supplément No. 4," pp. 155–73.

Gauthier, Michèle. "Fonds Diderot—Caroillon de Vandeul (suite)." *Recherches sur Diderot et sur l'*Encyclopédie, 11 (1991), 150–51.

Hayes, Jules Candler. *Identity and Ideology: Diderot, Sade and the Serious Genre.* West Lafayette, IN: Purdue U. Press, 1991. Pp. xiv + 186.

See sec. 5 for review.

Ibrahim, Annie. "Sur l'Expression, chez Diderot, autour du *Paradoxe sur le comédien* et des *Pensées sur l'interprétation de la nature." Recherches sur Diderot et sur l'*Encyclopédie, 10 (1991), 91–106.

Jüttner, Siegfried (ed.). *Présence de Didero*t. Internailes Kolloquium zum 2000. Todeshahr von Denis Diderot an der Universität GH Duisbourg vom 3–5 Oktober 1984. Bern and Frankfurt am Main: Peter Lang, 1990. Pp. v + 315. Cf. *ECCB*, n.s. 16, VI:373.

Rev. by Anthony Strugnell in *Recherches sur Diderot et sur l'*Encyclopédie, 11 (1991), 161–63.

Kafker, Frank A. "Les Encyclopédistes et le Paris du dix-huitième siècle." Translated by Bruno Brauntot. *Recherches sur Diderot et sur l'*Encyclopédie, 10 (1991), 113–21.

Kaplan, James M. "L'*Avis aux gens de lettres* de Marmontel: Une Versification du *Neveu de Rameau." Recherches sur Diderot et sur l'*Encyclopédie, 11 (1991), 73–82.

Main idea: Marmontel knew at least parts of Diderot's *Neveu de Rameau* and was inspired by it in his 1779 poem *Vous Avez tort. Avis aux gens de lettres* which is quoted *in extenso*.

Karp, Serguei. "Bibliographie de Diderot en URSS (1980–1990)." *Recherches sur Diderot et sur l'*Encyclopédie, 10 (1991), 139–54.

87 items.

Karp, Sergueï, Sergueï Iskul with the collaboration of Georges Dulac and Nadejda Plavinskaya. "Les Lettres inédites de Grimm à Catherine II." *Recherches sur Diderot et sur l'*Encyclopédie, 10 (1991), 41–53; 2 illustrations.

Includes a long letter of Grimm started October 20 (31) 1984 and dealing mostly with Diderot.

Lepape, Pierre. *Diderot*. Paris: Flammarion, 1991. Pp. 445; illustrations.

A journalist from *Le Monde* in close touch with literary and scholarly circles, Lepape brings a keen sense of artful presentation to a biography of Diderot accessible to the general public and which is in many ways a trove of new facts, documents and interpretations on Diderot that may appeal to academia. The initial trick of starting *in medias res* with Diderot's imprisonment at Vincennes in 1749 gives us a portrait of the writer in midlife in which he does not appear as a hero—he confessed his so-called *forfaits littéraires* and made amends for them—but from such an experience he went out with the symbolic stature of the Socrates of the Parisian Enlightenment.

    Nowhere is the split personality of the French *philosophes* more obvious than in Diderot's biography. His father, a cutler from Langres, wanted his son to succeed him or to become a priest or to marry into money: he disappointed his father's wishes in these three instances and became the craftsman of subversion with his twenty-two year's hackney work on the *Encyclopédie*, an all-but avowed atheist and the husband of a poor old maid. The bourgeois virtues, however, appealed to him throughout his life: he was an exemplary friend, an affectionate son, an attentive though often unfaithful husband, and a father keen on finding—with success—a good match for his only daughter. Among the French eighteenth century big Five (Montesquieu, Voltaire, Rousseau, Buffon and himself), he was the only one in touch with the world of small craftsmen and mechanics to whose class he remained attached to the end. His many contradictions prove that his mind raced ahead of his manners. Diderot's ideas stand between Voltaire's utopia of enlightened despotism and Rousseau's proclamation of popular despotism. All problems set to Diderot are as many obstacles to solve on the way to rational knowledge and contented happiness which he could not in fact fortunately reach, as he was perpetually confronted with new questions and queries.

    As in all conscientious intellectual biographies, the writer's works are analyzed and commented upon and in this respect Lepape's opinions on *Le neveu de Rameau*, *Le Religieuse* and *Jacques le fataliste* are brilliant and convincing. The third stands out as a masterpiece combining the virtues of the Spanish picaresque tradition, of Laurence Sterne's *Tristram Shandy* and of Bertolt Brecht's *Herr Puntila and his Man Matti*. Diderot's pioneer work in art criticism, drama criticism, anthropology with his *Supplément au voyage de Bougainville* (1773) and even biology is shown with due emphasis in every case on his a-systematic trend. A master craftsman and a bourgeois Bohemian, a visionary and a Stoic, Diderot combined the ancient virtues of a Diogenes, a Socrates, or a Seneca with the modern ideal of fighting injustice and ignorance. Lepape's biography throws into strong relief all the aspects of a man who worked in the present and wrote for the future.—Jean Rivière.

Loty, Laurent. "*Jacques le fataliste et son maître*: Une Tragédie érotique." *Recherches sur Diderot et sur l'*Encyclopédie, 11 (1991), 169–71.

Review of dramatic adaptation of Diderot's novel March 5–April 20, 1991.

Malo, Denis. "Diderot et la librairie: L'Impensable propriété." *Recherches sur Diderot et sur l'*Encyclopédie, 10 (1991), 57–90.

Concerning the *Lettre sur le commerce de la librairie* "nous proposons une lecture qui partirait des 'tiraillements' du texte, de ses contradictions, des éléments qui ne sont pas tous, . . . d'ordre politique: une lecture qui, révélant une tension interne à Diderot placerait cette lettre, au—coeur d'une interrogation sur le statut de l'oeuvre de pensée: à la fin du XVIIIe siècle."

Mortier, Roland (ed.). "Didier Diderot lecteur de Denis: Ses Réflexions sur l'*Essai sur le mérite et la vertu.*" *Recherches sur Diderot et sur l'*Encyclopédie, 10 (1991), 21–39; illustrations.

The second half of notes of abbé Diderot on his brother's works will be published in a later issue.

Pellerey, Roberto. "Diderot: Il Teatro de teatro. Un'analisi del *Paradoxe sur le comédien.*" *Studi francesi*, 34 (1991), 403–16.

Pérol, Lucette. "Didier Diderot lecteur de Denis: Ses Réflexions sur *Le Fils naturel.*" *Recherches sur Diderot et sur l'*Encyclopédie, 11 (1991), 33–47.

Comments of Diderot's brother on *Le Fils naturel* and the *Entretiens.* His comments on the *Essai sur le mérite et la vertu* were published by Roland Mortier in vol. 10 (1991) of the same publication.

Rebejkow, Jean-Christophe. "De Quelques problèmes d'interpretation posés par les maximes des *Principes de politique des souverains de Diderot.*" *Recherches sur Diderot et sur l'*Encyclopédie, 11 (1991), 63–72.

For various reasons, the author prefers the *Correspondance littéraire*'s version of the text.

Reeves, Eileen. "Charles Bonnet's *Roman philosophique* and *Jacques le fataliste.*" *French Forum*, 16 (1991), 285–303.

Rey, Roselyne. "Dynamique des formes et interprétation de la nature." *Recherches sur Diderot et sur l'*Encyclopédie, 11 (1991), 49–62.

On the *Pensées sur l'interprétation de la nature.*

Stenger, Gerhardt. "Deux Manuscrits inconnus de Diderot: *Madame de La Carlière* et *Sur les Femmes.*" *Dix-huitième siècle*, 21 (1991), 435–40.

Varloot, Jean. "Vrais ou faux amis. L'Original des *Eleuthéromanes.*" *Recherches sur Diderot et sur l'*Encyclopédie, 10 (1991), 9–20.

On two very different manuscripts of Diderot's poem.

Ventury, Franco. *Giovinezza di Diderot (1713–1753).* (La diagonale, 30.) Palermo: Sellerio, 1988. Pp. 337.

Rev. by Gianluigi Goggi in *Recherches sur Diderot et sur l'*Encyclopédie, 10 (1991), 158–63. Italian version of the well-known work published in French in 1939.

Viard, Georges. "Aubervive et Monsieur de Vandeul." *Recherches sur Diderot et sur l'*Encyclopédie, 10 (1991), 123–36; illustration.

On real estate purchased by Diderot's son-in-law during the Revolution.

Wachs, Morris. "L'Identité de quatre interlocuteurs de la *Satire première*." *French Studies*, 45 (1991), 143–51.

Scholarly comments on the sentence quoted in the title.

John Dryden (1631–1700)

Bywaters, David. *Dryden in Revolutionary England*. Berkeley, CA, and Oxford: U. of California Press, 1991. Pp. xiii + 196; bibliography.

Rev. (favorably) by G. R. Wasserman in *Choice*, 29 (1991), 590.

David Hopkins' *John Dryden* (1986) and James Winn's biography (1987) prompted the recent shift in Dryden scholarship away from the better known political satires of the early 80s toward the less frequently discussed works of the 90s. Taylor Corse (1991) has devoted a book to Dryden's *Aeneid*; Cedric Reverand, one to the *Fables* (1988). This shift has refocussed needed attention on the richness and complexity of Dryden's literary allusiveness as he redefined himself and his audience after losing public office, but, except for Winn's biography, it has tended to emphasize the philosophical Dryden at the expense of the political Dryden. If Dryden's role as public orator became more complicated and uncomfortable after the Revolution, he nevertheless did not retreat from politics. David Bywaters shrewdly demonstrates the artfulness with which Dryden merged his political and poetic selves between 1687 and 1700.

For Bywaters, Dryden's digressive allusiveness is less self-expressive than rhetorical; his political career following his conversion consists of four stages of rhetorical self-definition in which he comes increasingly to replace the authority he lost with his public office with the authority vested in him as a member of a transcendant literary tradition. To the first stage belongs *The Hind and the Panther*, written during the period of political upheaval and uncertainty after Dryden's conversion and before the Revolution. No longer able to speak for or persuade his nation, Dryden speaks against it, recording "in verse the relationship of his principles to the faithlessness and hypocrisy with which he felt himself surrounded and of which he knew himself accused" (p. 22).

Until 1692, Dryden would use the literary past as a norm against which to measure the present. The second stage begins after the Revolution when Dryden, now free from defending James's policies, enshrouds himself in literary detachment while resorting to barely concealed political parallel in *Don Sebastian* and *Amphitryon*. *Don Sebastian*, for instance, provides a vision of endless counterrevolutions, a vision emphasized by its "Dedication" to Philip Sidney, who retired from public life in the revolution preceding the one that ousted Dryden from public office. *Amphitryon*, Bywaters argues, exposes "contemporary politics to ridicule by weaving it carefully into the farcical comedy that Plautus and Moliere had made of the Amphitryon story. *King Arthur* and *Cleomenes* belong to the third stage, which Bywaters presents, suprisingly in the case of *Cleomenes*, as an experiment in conciliation. For Bywaters, *King Arthur*'s cloying nationalism is meant to appeal to the court; its panegyrical praise of qualities the country obviously lacked is offered for the opposition; its emphasis on patience and providence sounds a common Jacobite theme. Bywaters makes a convincing case that *Cleomenes* is not simple Jacobitism. While sympathy for the Spartan hero/James is certainly suggested by his role as a tragic figure, his excessive ambition at the expense of others' peace suggests, particularly when he is compared to Pantheus, a qualified praise of James.

After 1692, Dryden no longer uses the literary past as a norm against which to measure the present; rather he sees in the past patterns that inevitably if lamentably repeat themselves. His Olympian perspective allows him to re-enter politics as a poet responsible both for making political commentary and, given sufficient patronage, immortalizing the nation. Even the thematic incoherence of *Fables*, for instance, displays Dryden's communion with poets of all ages and all kinds" (p. 127). The *Discourse on Satire* and the "Dedication" of the *Aeneid* offer opportunities for discussing the relation between poet and state, a relation Dryden devoted his life to exploring. David Bywaters has articulated that relation forcefully and intelligently.—Anna Battigelli.

Corse, Taylor. "An Echo of Dryden in Addison's *Cato*." *Notes and Queries*, 236 (1991), 178.

"What dire effects from civil discord flow" is a quotation from "The First Pastoral" of Virgil.

Corse, Taylor. *Dryden's* Aeneid*: The English Virgil*. Newark, DE: U. of Delaware Press (distributed through Cranbury, NJ, and London: Associated University Press), 1991. Pp. 151.

Rev. by G. R. Wasserman in *Choice*, 29 (1991), 91.

Much recent discussion of Dryden's translations after 1688 has explored the veiled politics of his prefaces thereto and of the changes he makes in his originals. Taylor Corse adverts to these political readings but prefers to find the value of Dryden's late translations elsewhere. This brief and learned monograph studies about twenty passages and episodes from Dryden's *Aeneid*. Such analysis shows that rhetorical and inter-textual criticism may continue to make this poetry exciting; its value cannot be reduced to the successes of a search for allusions to William III and the king over the water and to Dryden's implied attitudes toward them.

Corse loves Dryden's translations, and he repeatedly defends them from the criticism of the long series of their detractors. Although Corse's norms of value for Dryden's superiority to other translations vary, he most often returns to the idea of organicity. He writes: "despite Dryden's variance from his source, most of his additions grow out of Virgil" (p. 16). Dryden's changes, which at first may seem arbitrary or simply wordy, often retell the themes and concerns of the translated epic as a whole. The thesis of organicity is not overstated; Corse's principle method is exacting, detailed analysis of Virgil's texts and its translations, chiefly Dryden's.

Corse is learned. The slim book gives evidence of his mastery of: the senses of the Latin and the quantities of its syllables; English translations of Virgil, especially after Dryden, his announced field of inquiry; rhetorical terms, which he abundantly and freshly employs; parallel imagery in sixteenth-, seventeenth-, and eighteenth-century verse; recent commentary on both Virgil and Dryden; and the copious notes of Carolus Ruaeus, whose text, *in usum delphini*, Dryden used. Like Corse, readers of Dryden's *Aeneid* will for many years be indebted to the commentary of Volume VI of the California Dryden. In at least six places Corse shows how the notes of Ruaeus are absent from Volume VI, though the editors discuss Ruaeus elsewhere, and also absent from the two previous essays on Dryden and Ruaeus by J.G. Bottkol (1943) and Arvid Losnes (1963). Corse's painstaking research is full and original.

Corse's study may raise at least two problems that he does not choose to explore. Can a theory of imitation and originality be constructed from Dryden's translations, and how would such a theory complement models based on later literature? Also, if organicity validates Dryden's translations, do they in turn validate an organic theory of literature? Does the source of value have theoretical as well as practical relevance? Corse's study lacks any passion for theory, the price one pays, I suppose, for its excellent comparative exegesis.

Corse modestly stresses that his own work only partially fulfills the task of a comprehensive study of Dryden's *Aeneid*; he points out several goals towards which new critical work might advantageously tend. Scholars following Corse's leads might have profited from an index of topical entries as well as proper names, but there is a very good bibliography of relevant secondary works.—Gerard Reedy.

Dryden, John. *The Works of John Dryden*, Vol. XX: *Prose, 1691–1698: De Arte Graphica and Shorter Works*. Edited by George R. Guffey and A. E. Wallace Maurer. Berkeley, CA: U. of California Press, 1989. Pp. xi + 521. Cf. *ECCB*, n.s. 15, VI:321.

Rev. by Robert W. McHenry, Jr. in *The Scriblerian*, 24 (1991), 54–56.

Foster, Gretchen M. *Pope Versus Dryden: A Controversy in Letters to* The Gentleman's Magazine, *1789–1791*. (English Literary Studies Monograph Series, 44.) Victoria: U. of Victoria, 1989. Pp. 156.

Rev. by James A. Winn in *The Scriblerian*, 23 (1991), 258–59; (with reservations) by David Womersley in *Notes and Queries*, 236 (1991), 235–36.

Hammond, Paul. *John Dryden: A Literary Life.* (Literary Lives.) New York: St. Martin's Press, 1991. Pp. x + 184.

On first sighting Paul Hammond's *John Dryden: A Literary Life*, Dryden students will exclaim, "Why another life of Dryden after Winn's?" Although "for reasons of economy, repeated cross-references to Winn's book are not given" (p. 71), Hammond pays generous attention to Winn's biography: Winn is welcome everywhere in this book, not just for his new materials, but for his method, the only one left in a three-century search to get Dryden's motives and merit right. Because new primary evidence is "almost certainly absent," Winn had to "use inference and speculation" (Winn, *John Dryden and His World* [1987], p. xiii). Like Winn, Hammond indicates that he too has only "texts . . . interpretations . . . inferences" (p. x).

Hammond does not use Winn's method to surpass him. Rather, he follows the aim of the series, *Literary Lives*, edited by Richard Dutton: countering a deconstructionist argument that dethrones the author and recognizes the reader and the linguistic text as the source of understanding of writing, for the text "has no other origin than language itself, language which ceaselessly calls into question all origins" (Roland Barthes, "The Death of the Author," from *Image-Music-Text* [1977], p. 146). Hammond accepts the challenge to deny the "death of the author."

Hammond's slender volume belies its intellectual magnitude and cognitive daring. He argues that Dryden the author exists in his literary voice, the result of pressures in what the Series preamble calls "professional, publishing, and social contexts" (p. i). Hammond infers this voice from seven such contexts against a wide-ranging backdrop of twentieth-century Dryden scholarship. Like Winn, when primary material is absent (nearly always), he will infer Dryden the author from meditated and mediated contexts.

Risking distortion, I depict Hammond's method and developing picture of Dryden the author as evident in just one of seven chapter/contexts, Chapter 2, "The New Writer: 1660–67." For context, Hammond brings together Dryden's marriage into a family of complex allegiances, a kingship that passes through Commonwealth rationalizations of human nature and governance, Dryden's praising while questioning and instructing that kingship, his grasping political realities of installing order while epistemologically tantalized about limits of thought, his perception of historical particularity but also of impenetrable fortune. From this context Hammond infers an emergent voice: committed and skeptical. Similarly, Hammond constructs Dryden the author inferentially from six other contexts in the remaining chapters: "The Apprentice: 1652–59"; "The Dramatist: 1663–85"; "The Critic: 1668–84"; "The Political Writer: 1678–85"; "The Religious Writer: 1665–87"; "The Translator: 1680–1700." Out of these seven contexts emerges, for Hammond, Dryden the author characterized by "integrity and . . . freedom," traits issuing from lifelong "commitment and skepticism, belonging and alienation" (p. 170).

Is Hammond right? One realizes that sensitive twentieth-century listeners have heard individual Dryden works, as well as the whole corpus, differently, according to different contexts. In *Religio Laici*, Harth hears "an articulate expression of the Anglican via media" against the seventeenth-century religious spectrum (*Contexts of Dryden's Thought* [1968], p. 224); Reverand, *a via media* right of center against perceived variants and dialectical cancellation (*Dryden's Final Poetic Mode* [1988], pp. 81–82, 97–98); Zwicker, opportunism and hypocrisy disguised as reason and charity against analysis of seventeenth-century use of language as disguise in mortally dangerous times (*Politics and Language in Dryden's Poetry* [1984], pp. 53–54); Winn, "reverent humility" against Dryden's frequenting of coffee houses, his structural concentrations of topic in *Religio Laici*, his book purchases (Winn, pp. 372–79); Hammond, adroitness against Dryden's recently becoming controversial (p. 130).

Without more primary evidence, one must gauge inferences and bases. I find Hammond's mediated scope of Dryden's work and modern scholarship as comprehensive as any current, and his conclusion finely plausible. But the inferential method bars his entry into the Promised Land of Certainty, done in by the inevitable "perhaps," "may seem," even "know nothing" (pp. 16, 21, 22, passim). Once, too, Hammond accepts a long unexamined inference about the timing of *Absalom and Achitophel* (p. 96) destroyed by Harth ("Legends No History: The Case of *Absalom and Achitophel*," *Studies in Eighteenth-Century Culture*, 4 [1975], 13–29). Considering, however, my own last-ditch use of inference atop evidence (*Papers on Language and Literature*, 27 [1991]: 320–37), I will venture with Hammond that a courageous, capacious, unretreating mind and art of John Dryden are responsible for the authorship of literature bearing his signature. Yet, to give Dryden the last word, his life "is not yet sufficiently explicated," maybe because he did not give Aubrey the one he apparently promised (p. ix).—A. E. Wallace Maurer.

Hopkins, David. "Reply: Dryden Epigram." *Notes and Queries*, 236 (1991), 521.

Levasseur, Sherry. "John Dryden's Views of Charles I, Cromwell, and Charles II." *Notes and Queries,* 236 (1991), 173–75.

McHenry, Robert W., Jr. "Betrayal and Love in *All for Love* and *Bérénice*." *Studies in English Literature 1500–1900*, 31 (1991), 445–61.

Rev. by A. E. Wallace Maurer in *Modern Philology*, 88 (1990–91), 314–17.
Develops the implications of "the many verbal and situational parallels" with the Racine play, especially in Act V.

Maria Edgeworth (1767–1849)

Kowaleski-Wallace, Elizabeth. *Their Fathers' Daughters: Hannah More, Maria Edgeworth, and Patriarchal Complicity.* New York and Oxford: Oxford U. Press, 1991. Pp. xiii + 235.

Elizabeth Kowaleski-Wallace takes on a difficult enterprise in this book: she attempts to explain sympathetically in feminist terms the anti-feminist ideology of two conservative writers. Using recent feminist theory, Kowaleski-Wallace "scrutinize[s] selected aspects of the biographies and careers" (p. ix) of More and Edgeworth to argue that both writers "thematize the family" (p. x), reject the maternal model, and embrace the role of the "good" daughter defined and empowered by the father. She maintains that this complicity in the patriarchy allows both writers to escape identification with the physically and morally threatening aspects of womanhood represented by Mother Eve, and to define themselves as rational, self-disciplined, and enlightened.

After the first chapter briefly discusses breast-feeding, family dynamics, and the "new-style patriarchy," the book divides into two sections, each prefaced by an introduction to the pertinent issues. Kowaleski-Wallace argues that More and Edgeworth are seduced into complicity with the father by means of the relations established by a Lockean educational paradigm, whereby the father uses love and reason to control the daughter through "normative values" while ostensibly encouraging her "independence" (p. 20). Nonetheless, both women enjoyed limited power and a form of self-definition through their identification with patriarchal politics. Kowaleski-Wallace sees in More's Evangelicalism and in her association of Milton with her father signs of complicity with patriarchy; she avoids certain kinds of misogyny by "privileging" Milton's Eve, who mediates between nature and culture, over Mother Nature, whose female energy More associates with savagery, irreligion, revolution, and excess. Edgeworth is seen as embracing a domestic ideology parallel to Anglo-Irish political attitudes; she locates danger and shame in maternal inheritance, symbolized by Mother Ireland, and authority in the progressive patriarchy that controls female desire. The final chapter briefly argues that Charlotte Brontë's *Shirley* attempts to define women by rejecting the dismissive patriarchal categories of "Other."

Among many illuminating close readings are analyses of More's letters to Wilberforce in *Mendip Annals*, and of *Belinda* and *Ennui*, anatomizing the implicit criticism of the mother. While the quotations are excellently chosen, and the prose usually precise, if labored, detailed summaries of feminist theory distract the reader from consideration of the literary subjects. A few grammatical problems stem from poor editing, although the index is useful.

As the author admits, this book offers two parallel, rather than symmetrical, discussions. Partly because Kowalski-Wallace elides the distinction between More's fictional and "non-fictional" documents, the section on Edgeworth is the most coherent. One particularly successful point is the identification of More's and Edgeworth's social snobbery and religiosity with a gender-based anxiety about the containment of the female, physical energies.

The method of selection omits large portions of each writer's biography as well as a developed, comparative framework. This organization is problematical: Kowaleski-Wallace has deleted Burney from her study, but a broader context would strengthen her argument, and help to integrate the close readings with the theory. The lack of a conclusion, only a brief comparison of the two writers in the middle of the book, and the relegation of many interesting points to footnotes further weakens an intriguing enterprise studded with provocative insights.—Barbara M. Benedict.

Jonathan Edwards (1703–1758)

Keating, AnnLouise. "The Implications of Edwards' Theory of the Will on Ahab's Pursuit of Moby Dick." *English Language Notes*, 28 (1991), 28–35.

Uses *A Careful and Strict Inquiry into the Prevailing Notions of the Freedom of the Will.*

Morris, William Sparkes. *The Young Jonathan Edwards: A Reconstruction.* (Chicago Studies in the History of American Religion, 14.) Brooklyn, NY: Carlson Publishing, 1991. Pp. xvi + 688; bibliography.

François de la Mothe Fénelon (1651–1715)

Dédéyan, Charles. Télémaque *ou la liverté de l'esprit.* Paris: Nizet, 1991. Pp. 344.

Fénelon's *Télémaque* is not widely read today. Yet several excellent recent studies have been made of its content and significance. In this book, Charles Dédéyan addresses a subject which he first treated in his *Le Télémaque de Fénelon* (Paris: 1958), his Sorbonne lectures. This contribution has strengths and weaknesses.

Dédéyan has a three-fold approach to the work. Initially, he situates it in relation to contemporary educational theory, and particularly in relation to the educational philosophy of Fleury who was Fénelon's collaborator and co-tutor to the young royal princes. The bulk of the study is devoted to an extremely detailed account of the genesis and content of *Télémaque*. Dédéyan rightly emphasizes the importance of Fénelon's religious vocation and desire to educate a Christian king. Moral education is paramount for Fénelon. His own values—his hatred of tyranny and war, his cosmopolitanism, his praise of the simple life and a laissez-faire economy and his encouragement of an agriculturally based society—are all echoed in *Télémaque*.

Dédéyan painstakingly discusses all the significant characters in the work and shows his erudition and familiarity with the classics by carefully analyzing the differences and similarities to Homer's work. His consideration of the poetic qualities of *Télémaque* is less successful. It consists rather of a listing of, for example, word usage, and does not add greatly to our appreciation of Fénelon's style.

The latter part of Dédéyan's work concentrates on reactions to, and criticisms of, Fénelon in the eighteenth, nineteenth and twentieth centuries. The longest chapter deals with nineteenth- century commentators. Although extremely comprehensive, Dédéyan again tends to list allusions to Fénelon from a variety of authors rather than making evaluations of the significance of the comments.

There are a number of appendices including Ramsay's *Discours sur le poème épique* (applied to *Télémaque*), a number of Fénelon's writings for his young pupils, and also his *Examen de conscience sur les devoirs de la royauté*. Dédéyan apparently wished to provide additional primary source material reflecting Fénelon's educational opinions and his religious stance, and even excerpts from some satirical reactions to *Télémaque*.

There is no doubt that Dédéyan is a preeminent Fénelon scholar, who wishes to make known the importance of a work which is little read today. Unfortunately, he has fallen into much the same trap as his author, the trap of tedium. The study should have been more effectively edited and be more evaluative. Listing of references is informative, but little more. There are many typographichal errors, again indicating carless editing. The bibliography is not in alphabetical order, and does not appear to follow any particular ordering principle, chronological, for example. It is unfortunate that Madame du Deffand's evaluation of Fénelon's *Télémaque*—"il est ennuyeux à la mort"—could easily be applied to Dédéyan's *Télémaque*.—Kay S. Wilkins.

Henry Fielding (1707–1754)

Battestin, Martin C., and Ruthe R. Battestin. *Henry Fielding: A Life*. London and New York: Routledge, 1989. Pp. xviii + 738. Cf. *ECCB*, n.s. 16, VI:379; 15, VI:327–28.

Rev. by William J. Burling in *South Atlantic Review*, 56 (Sept. 1991), 117–120; (favorably) by Clive Probyn in *Modern Language Review*, 86 (1991), 401–03.

Burrows, J. F. " 'I Lisp'd in Numbers': Fielding, Richardson, and the Appraisal of Statistical Evidence." *The Scriblerian*, 23 (1991), 234–41.

Replies to comments in *The Scriblerian* 22 (1989), 14 on an article in *Eighteenth-Century Studies*, 21 (1988), 427–53.

Costa, Astrid Masetti Lobo. "Up and Down Stairways: Escher, Bakhtin, and *Joseph Andrews*." *Studies in English Literature 1500–1900*, 31 (1991), 553–68.

The paired hierarchies are interchangeable.

Fielding, Henry. The Covent-Garden Journal *and* A Plan of the Universal Register Office. Edited by Bertrand A. Goldgar. Middletown, CT: Wesleyan, 1988. Pp. 561. Cf. *ECCB*, n.s. 16, VI:379; 15, VI:328–29.

Rev. by Pat Rogers in *The Scriblerian*, 23 (1991), 254.

Fielding, Henry. *New Essays by Henry Fielding: His Contributions to the* Craftsman *(1734–1739) and Other Early Journalism.* Edited by Martin C. Battestin with a Stylometric Analysis by Michael G. Farringdon. Charlottesville, VA: U. Press of Virginia, 1989. Pp. xliv + 604; appendices. Cf. *ECCB*, n.s. 15, VI:329–30.

Rev. (with another work and with reservations) by Ian A. Bell in *TLS,* (Jan. 4, 1991), 6; by Harold Love in *Journal of English and Germanic Philology*, 90 (1991), 432–35; by Simon Varey in *The Scriblerian*, 24 (1991), 61–62.

Fielding, Henry. *The History of Tom Jones, A Foundling*. Introduction by Claude Rawson. New York: Knopf/Random House, 1991. Pp. xxvi + 427.

Hume, Robert D. *Henry Fielding and the London Theatre 1728–1737*. New York: Oxford U. Press; Oxford: Clarendon Press, 1988. Pp. xix + 283. Cf. *ECCB*, n.s. 16, VI:380; 15, VI:331; 14, VI:319–20.

Rev. (favorably) by Calhoun Winton in *Journal of English and Germanic Philology*, 90 (1991), 430–32.

Klein, J. "Romantheorie und Romanstruktur in Henry Fielding's *Joseph Andrews*." *Anglia*, 109 (1991), 377–409.

Mace, Nancy A. "Henry Fielding's Classical Learning." *Modern Philology*, 88 (1990–91), 243–60.

Tabulations of Fielding's library, translations, parodies and citations indicate that he had a strong knowledge of Latin and a pretty good knowledge of Greek, and was more influenced by Horace than Lucian.

McCrea, Brian. *Addison and Steele are Dead: The English Department, Its Canon, and the Professionalization of Literary Criticism.* Cranbury, NJ: The U. of Delaware Press, 1989. Pp. 280.

Reilly, Patrick. Tom Jones: *Adventure and Providence.* (Twayne's Masterwork Studies, 72.) Boston, MA: Twayne, 1991. Pp. xv + 162; bibliography; chronology.

Rev. (favorably) by R. G. Brown in *Choice*, 29 (1991), 100.
 Patrick Reilly devotes the three main chapters of his book to a Christian reading of *Tom Jones*. The chapter entitled "Fighting the Pharisees" claims that "the novel becomes a forum for a debate as to how we should deal with sinners and try to reform sin," and that "Fielding set out to . . . provide a complete taxonomy of the malady [Pharisaism]" (p. 32). By recalling the Pharisee putting himself at the head of the table, we can best understand Fielding's "otherwise misleading opening metaphor" (p. 35) of the novel as feast. Likewise, *Tom Jones* "considered as a total structure, is a complex and elaborate extension" of the parable of the two sons (p. 35), the one who promises to obey his father's will and does not, and the one who refuses at first but then obeys.
 "Judging the Jurors" compares Fielding favorably to Swift. Whereas Swift entraps the reader and condemns him, Fielding acts the benevolent magistrate who guides the reader, as juror, into a correct view of life. But "jury service is not as simple or straightforward as we imagined," and the tests Fielding proposes, after we see him through Mrs. Wilkins, "increase in complexity and difficulty" (p. 76), and lead us to the problem of Allworthy, whom we cannot condemn without avoiding Fielding's judgment on ourselves (p. 81). "*Tom Jones* is a text deliberately . . . crafted to frustrate the Pharisaism of the reader, to show him that he is finally just as gullible . . . as any blundering character within the book" (p. 84). Because fooling the reader is a function of the book's message about love and judgement, the "narrative style, the form created by Fielding for his fable, matches perfectly its moral meaning" (p.88).
 "Christening the Comedy" argues that Fielding's novel affronts "our modern pieties . . . about the nature of the novel" (p. 102), namely that it is based on uncertainty. Rather, "his novel replicates God's providential plan and predicts our eventual destiny: all shall be well" (pp. 103–4). Fielding is "the last complete comedian in European literature" (p. 106) because his comedy is an act of faith: " 'no God, no comedy' is the slogan at the entrance to his fiction" (p. 107). Rather than being a blind Pollyanna or a failed artist, Fielding derives his love of life and his art from his Christian faith, as he instructs us not to be prudent but generous.
 Reilly's book clearly poses a challenge to contemporary criticism, whose tendency is to deconstruct Fielding's orthodoxy. Although, on the whole agreeing with Reilly, this reviewer wishes that he had not found it continually necessary to praise Fielding at the expense of Richardson, whose world is characterized as "shrunken," and "fetid" (pp. 6-7), or "pent-up, claustrophobic, voyeuristic" (p. 105); these are fighting words that touch the taste of women readers and feminist critics. Furthermore, Reilly fails to resolve the persisting opposition in *Tom Jones* between morality and permissiveness. Christ forgives a sexual sinner but tells her to go and sin no more. But Reilly slights the second half of this proposition and separates sexual sins, which are according to him hardly venial, from mortal sins such as hypocrisy. Fraud may be a greater crime than lust, but traditionally both of them will get us into Hell. It was just this opposition between realism and optimism, between God's creation (nature) and Fielding's (art), between the Kingdom of Heaven and its secularization, or between prudence and selflessness. To this end, he might have made better use of Empson's great insight about Fielding's double irony. Reilly is an able defense attorney, but at crucial moments he relies more on assertion than proof.—William Park.

Thomas, Donald. *Henry Fielding.* London: Weidenfeld & Nicolson, 1990; New York: St. Martin's Press, 1991. Pp. x + 436; bibliography; 12 illustrations.

Rev. (with another work) by Ian A. Bell in *TLS,* (Jan. 4, 1991), 6; by Pat Rogers in *New York Times Book Review,* 96 (July 7, 1991), 9–10.

Wanko, Cheryl. "Characterization and the Reader's Quandary in Fielding's *Amelia.*" *Journal of English and Germanic Philology,* 90 (1991), 505–23.

The reader must learn to be a better judge of character than Amelia is.

Sir Robert Filmer (d. 1653)

Filmer, Sir Robert. *Patriarcha and Other Writings.* Edited by Johann P. Sommerville. (Cambridge Texts in the History of Political Thought.) Cambridge and New York: Cambridge U. Press, 1991. Pp. xlvi + 330; bibliography.

Jean Marie Jérome Fleuriot (1749–1807)

Fleuriot, Jean Marie Jérome. *Voyage de Figaro en Espagne.* Edited by Robert Favre. Société française d'Etude du XVIIIe siècle. Saint-Étienne: Publications de l'Université de Saint-Étienne, 1991. Pp. 105.

Bernard le Bovier de Fontenelle (1657–1757)

Bott, François. *L'Entremetteur: Esquisses pour un portrait de Monsieur de Fontenelle.* (Perspectives critiques.) Paris: Universitaires de France, 1991. Pp. 112.

This is a very light sketch on Fontenelle, as the subtitle implies. Bott seems to aspire to emulate the special touch, the insouciance of Fontenelle, but this is not so easy to do because Fontenelle always had something of importance to communicate under that deceptively frothy facade. Bott is enamoured of both the form and content of Fontenelle's oeuvre, opening and closing his book with the metaphor of flight that the galant Fontenelle so skillfully exploited to transport himself and his readers throughout space and time. In Bott's hands, however, it becomes a pedestrian flirtation on an airplane. Again, Fontenelle's penchant for the fair sex was legendary, but he never really allowed himself a serious romantic involvement, nor did he ever lose sight of a fundamental respect for women. Bott has the patronizing habit of referring to the women in his story by their first names—Mme de Tencin is Alexandrine, Mme de Staal-Delaunay is Rose. Such indiscretions Fontenelle would not have allowed himself in print.

Bott actually covers some ground considering the modest dimensions of his book, but too often his preciousness interferes with his message, and it is unfortunate because there are some valuable insights here, especially on the subject of Fontenelle's private philosophy of living, his inimitable brand of discrete and tranquil happiness, his insatiable curiosity. At times Bott even writes quite poetically about Fontenelle's gift for savoring life in a manner that seems to elude our modern age and that we might do well to recapture. But in his determination to maintain the breezy tone throughout, Bott takes liberties with history and literature that obscure the logic of Fontenelle's life work. It only confuses things, for example, to lump him together with La Boétie, Montaigne, Descartes, Pascal and La Rochefoucault, arguing that they all wrote essays and thus had in common a genre that is a "French specialty."

There are also typographical inaccuracies; Fontenelle was not elected to the Académie Francaise in 1791 (when he had already been dead for over thirty years).

It seems so me that only readers with substantial prior knowledge of Fontenelle will be able to follow the convoluted presentation of thoughts in this little book. And such readers will glean little new from it.—Nina Rattner Gelbart.

Fontenelle, Bernard Le Bovier de. *Entretiens sur la pluralité des mondes*. Preface by François Bott. (Poussières.) La Tour d'Aigues, France (distributed through Arles: Harmonia Mundi), 1991. Pp. 130.

It is not clear for whom this edition of the *Entretiens* is intended. Scholarly readers at this late date do not need a text which makes no pretense of supplementing or rectifying the preceding ones; and the general reader will surely need help of a kind which is not to be found here. The two-and-a-half page introduction by François Bott very briefly places the composition of the book in Fontenelle's career, reveals that the true name of the Marquise was Mme de la Mèsangère, pronounces the book a brief masterpiece, and sends it on its way.

The text is entirely without annotation, and one wonders what the general reader will make of sentences like this one: "Ainsi la Terre, toute massive qu'elle est, est aisément portée au milieu de la matière céleste qui est infiniment plus fluide que l'eau et qui remplit tout ce grand espace où nagent les planètes"? Or what that reader will know about "les tourbillons de Descartes . . . dont le nom est si terrible et l'idée si agréable"? Again, the modern reader must bring to the text at least a tincture of Newtonianism, and therefore simple justice to Fontenelle would seem to have required noting somewhere that the *Entretiens* (1686) appeared before, though within a year of the *Principia mathematica* (1687).

The typography and layout of the book are attractive. No typographical errors were noted. The lines are generously spaced and the margins add to the aerated appearance of the text. Spelling and punctuation have been modernized so as to make the reader's task as easy as possible. But who will that reader be?—Donald Schier.

Niderst, Alain. *Fontenelle*. Paris: Plon, 1991. Pp. 439; bibliography.

Niderst, Alain (ed.). *Fontenelle. Actes du colloque tenu à Rouen du 6 au 10 octobre 1987*. Preface by Jean Mesnard. Paris: Presses Universitaires de France, 1989. Pp. 710; plates. Cf. *ECCB*, n.s. 16, VI:381; 15, VI:334–35.

Rev. by Fanny Népote-Desmarres in *Revue d'histoire littéraire de la France*, 91 (1991), 973–75; by Franco Piva in *Studi francesi*, 34 (1991), 525.

Benjamin Franklin (1706–1790)

Cohen, I. Bernard. *Benjamin Franklin's Science*. Cambridge, MA: Harvard U. Press, 1990. Pp. xii + 273; bibliography; illustrations. Cf. *ECCB*, n.s. 16, VI:382.

Rev. by J. W. Dauben in *Choice*, 28 (1991), 800; Rev. in rev. article ("Secrets of Benjamin Franklin") by Edmund S. Morgan in *New York Review of Books*, 38 (Jan. 31, 1991), 41–46; (severely) by Stephen Pumfrey in *TLS*, (Jan. 18, 1991), 22.

Franklin, Benjamin. *The Papers of Benjamin Franklin*. Vol. XXV: *October 1, 1777 through February 28, 1778*. Edited by William B. Willcox (gen. ed.), Douglas M. Arnold, Dorothy W. Bridgwater, Jonathan R. Dull, Claude Anne Lopez, Catherine M. Prelinger (assoc. eds.), and Ellen R. Cohn (asst. ed.). London and New Haven, CT: Yale U. Press, 1986. Pp. lxv + 779; 7 illustrations. Cf. *ECCB*, n.s. 12, VI:447–48.

Rev. in rev. article ("Secrets of Benjamin Franklin") by Edmund S. Morgan in *New York Review of Books*, 38 (Jan. 31, 1991), 41–46.

Franklin, Benjamin. *The Papers of Benjamin Franklin*. Vol. XXVI: *March 1 through June 30, 1778*. Edited by William B. Willcox (gen. ed.), Douglas M. Arnold, Dorothy W. Bridgwater, Jonathan R. Dull, Claude A. Lopez, Catherine M. Prelinger (assoc. eds.), and Ellen R. Cohn (asst. ed.). London and New Haven, CT: Yale U. Press, 1987. Pp. lxxiii + 756; illustrations.

Rev. in rev. article ("Secrets of Benjamin Franklin") by Edmund S. Morgan in *New York Review of Books*, 38 (Jan. 31, 1991), 41–46.

Franklin, Benjamin. *The Papers of Benjamin Franklin*. Vol. XXVII: *July 1 through October 31, 1778*. Edited by Claude A. Lopez (gen. ed.), Douglas M. Arnold, Dorothy W. Bridgwater, Ellen R. Cohn, Jonathan R. Dull, and Catherine M. Prelinger (assoc. eds.). London and New Haven, CT: Yale U. Press, 1988. Pp. lxix + 727; illustrations.

Rev. in rev. article ("Secrets of Benjamin Franklin") by Edmund S. Morgan in *New York Review of Books*, 38 (Jan. 31, 1991), 41–46.

Franklin, Benjamin. *The Papers of Benjamin Franklin*. Vol. XXVIII: *November 1, 1778 through Febrary 28, 1779*. Edited by Barbara B. Oberg (gen. ed.), Dorothy W. Bridgwater, Ellen R. Cohn, Jonathan R. Dull, and Catherine M. Prelinger (assoc. eds.), Marilyn A. Morris (asst. ed.), Claude A. Lopez (consulting ed.). London and New Haven, CT: Yale U. Press, 1990. Pp. lxxi + 708; illustrations.

Rev. in rev. article ("Secrets of Benjamin Franklin") by Edmund S. Morgan in *New York Review of Books*, 38 (Jan. 31, 1991), 41–46.

Franklin, Benjamin. *Writings: Boston and London, 1722–1726, Philadelphia, 1726–1775, Paris, 1776–1785, Philadelphia, 1785–1790, Poor Richard's Almanack, 1733–1758, The Autobiography*. Edited by J. A. Leo Lemay. (The Library of America, 37.) New York: The Library of America (distributed through New York: Viking), 1987. Pp. 1605; bibliography.

Rev. (favorably) in rev. article ("Secrets of Benjamin Franklin") by Edmund S. Morgan in *New York Review of Books*, 38 (Jan. 31, 1991), 41–46.

Lopez, Claude Anne. *Le Sceptre et la foundre: Franklin à Paris, 1776–1785*. (Collection Domaine historique.) Paris: Mercure de la France, 1990. Pp. 335; 8 plates.

Rev. (favorably) in rev. article ("Secrets of Benjamin Franklin") by Edmund S. Morgan in *New York Review of Books*, 38 (Jan. 31, 1991), 41–46.

Seavey, Ormond. *Becoming Benjamin Franklin: The* Autobiography *and the Life*. London and University Park, PA: Pennsylvania State U. Press, 1988. Pp. xiii + 266; portrait. Cf. *ECCB*, n.s. 15, VI:335; 14, VI:322.

Rev. (favorably) in rev. article ("Secrets of Benjamin Franklin") by Edmund S. Morgan in *New York Review of Books*, 38 (Jan. 31, 1991), 41–46; by Gordon O. Taylor in *Modern Language Review*, 86 (1991), 400–01.

Smith, Jeffrey A. *Franklin and Bache: Envisioning the Enlightened Republic*. New York and Oxford: Oxford U. Press, 1990. Pp. 222; bibliography; frontispiece; illustrations. Cf. *ECCB*, n.s. 16, VI:382.

Rev. (with reservations) by M. J. Birkner in *Choice*, 28 (1991), 993.

Wright, Esmond (ed.). *Benjamin Franklin: His Life As He Wrote It*. Cambridge, MA: Harvard U. Press, 1990. Pp. x + 297; illustrations; portraits. Cf. *ECCB*, n.s. 16, VI:383.

Rev. (with reservations) in rev. article ("Secrets of Benjamin Franklin") by Edmund S. Morgan in *New York Review of Books*, 38 (Jan. 31, 1991), 41–46.

John Gay (1685–1732)

Dugaw, Dianne. "Folklore and John Gay's Satire." *Studies in English Literature 1500–1900*, 31 (1991), 515–33.

Folk lore, ballads, and motifs serve as ironic backdrops and "thematic and structural templates," and enliven common people in Gay's work.

Lewis, Peter, and Nigel Wood (eds.). *John Gay and the Scriblerians*. (Critical Studies Series.) London: Vision Press; New York: St. Martin's Press, 1988. Pp. 224. Cf. *ECCB*, n.s. 16, VI:383; 15, VI:336; 14, VI:324–25.

Rev. by Paul Alkon in *Modern Language Review*, 86 (1991), 399–400.

Edward Gibbon (1737–1794)

Craddock, Patricia B. *Edward Gibbon, Luminous Historian, 1772–1794*. Baltimore, MD, and London: Johns Hopkins U. Press, 1989. Pp. xv + 432; bibliography; frontispiece; illustrations. Cf. *ECCB*, n.s. 15, VI:336.

Rev. (with another work) by John Vladimir Price in *Modern Philology*, 88 (1990–91), 324–29.

William Godwin (1756–1836)

Crowder, George. "Godwin." Pp. 39–73 of *Classical Anarchism: The Political Thought of Godwin, Proudhon, Bakunin, and Kropotkin*, by George Crowder. New York and Oxford: Oxford U. Press, 1991.

Godwin, William. *The Collected Novels of William Godwin*. Edited by Pamela Clemit, Maurice Hindle, Mark Philip. 8 vols. London: Pickering & Chatto, 1991.

Johann Wolfgang von Goethe (1749–1832)

Arens, Hans. *Kommentar zu Goethes* Faust *II*. (Beiträge zur neueren Literaturgeschichte, Dritte Folge, Bd. 86.) Heidelberg: Carl Winter Universitätsverlag, 1989. Pp. 1083.

Rev. by John Gearey in *Journal of English and Germanic Philology*, 90 (1991), 604–05.

Boyle, Nicholas. *Goethe: The Poet and the Age*. Vol. I: *The Poetry of Desire (1749–1790)*. New York: Oxford U. Press; Oxford: Clarendon Press, 1991. Pp. xx + 807; bibliography; illustrations; map.

Rev. by Richard Holmes in *New York Review of Books*, 38 (Oct. 24, 1991), 3–5; (favorably) by Christoph Schweitzer in *New York Times Book Review*, 3 (July 28, 1991), 25; (favorably) by Theodore Ziolkowski in *TLS*, (May 10, 1991), 3–4.

Edinger, Edward F. *Goethe's* Faust: *Notes for a Jungian Commentary*. (Studies in Jungian Psychology by Jungian Analysts, 43.) Toronto, Canada: Inner City Books, 1990. Pp. 111; bibliography.

Rev. by W. C. Buchanan in *Choice*, 29 (1991), 450–51.

Fink, Karl J. *Goethe's History of Science*. Cambridge and New York: Cambridge U. Press, 1991. Pp. xii + 242; bibliography; illustrations.

Goethe, Johann Wolfgang von. *Selections from Goethe's Letters to Frau bon Stein, 1776–1789*. Edited and translated by Robert M. Browning. (Studies in German Literature, Linguistics, and Culture, 48.) Columbia, SC: Camden House, 1990. Pp. 307.

Rev. by E. Glass in *Choice*, 28 (1991), 936.

Mandelkkow, Karl Robert. *Goethe in Deutschland*. *Rezeptionsgeschichte eines Klassikers*. Vol. II: *1919–1982*. Munich: Bech, 1989. Pp. 351.

Rev. by H. G. Haile in *Journal of English and Germanic Philology*, 90 (1991), 400–01.

Morgan, Peter. *The Critical Idyll: Traditional Values and the French Revolution in Goethe's* Hermann und Dorothea. (Studies in German Literature, Linguistics, and Culture, 54.) Columbia, SC: Camden House, 1990. Pp. 183.

Rev. (favorably) by Hans-Wilhelm Kelling in *Rocky Mountain Review of Language and Literature*, 45 (1991), 109–10.

Weisinger, Kenneth B. *The Classical Façade: A Non-Classical Reading of Goethe's Classicism*. University Park, PA: Pennsylvania State U. Press, 1988. Pp. viii + 224. Cf. *ECCB*, n.s. 16, VI:388; 15, VI:341.

Rev. (severely) by T. J. Reed in *Modern Language Review*, 86 (1991), 511–14.

Winkelman, John. *Goethe's "Elective Affinities": An Interpretation.* (American University Studies.) Frankfurt am Main and New York: Peter Lang, 1987. Pp. 158.

Rev. by Lesley Sharpe in *Modern Language Review*, 86 (1991), 785–87

Carlo Goldoni (1701–1793)

Goldoni, Carlo. *L'Adulateur.* Paris: L'Arche, 1990. Pp. 160.

Rev. (favorably) by Rose Marie Moudouès in *Revue d'histoire du théâtre*, 43 (1991), 376–77.

Goldoni, Carlo. *Les Cancans.* Translated by Ginette Herr. (Scène ouverte.) Paris: L'Arche, 1991. Pp. 128.

Goldoni, Carlo. *La Locandiera.* (Folio bilingue, 19.) Paris: Gallimard, 1991.

Oliver Goldsmith (1728–1774)

Derry, Stephen. "Jane Austen's Use of *The Vicar of Wakefield* in *Pride and Prejudice.*" *English Language Notes*, 28 (1991), 25–27.

A few slight parallels in wording, plot, character, and nomenclature.

Dixon, Peter. *Oliver Goldsmith Revisited.* (Twayne's English Author Series, 10.) Boston, MA: Twayne, 1991. Pp. xi + 157; bibliography; chronology.

Since 1967 when Clara Kirk's Twayne biography of Goldsmith appeared, there has been a revived interest in the author and his works, much of it fueled by Arthur Friedman's authoritative edition of the collected works. Peter Dixon's *Oliver Goldsmith Revisited*, relying on Friedman and others, offers a readable, reasoned portrait of Goldsmith. Instead of constructing a critical biography by primarily recounting Goldsmith's quaint reactions in social situations (something that has enchanted and perplexed past biographers), Dixon seeks to answer one of the most persistent questions about Goldsmith: what are we to make of the contradictions between his behavior and his writings? Samuel Johnson's well-known observation, cited by Dixon, sums up this paradox: "No man was more foolish when he had not a pen in his hand, or more wise when he had" (p. vii).

Given the Twayne format—biographical sketch, close readings, a chronology, brief bibliography, and index—Dixon presents a competent introduction to Goldsmith. Better, he also offers a convincing reconciliation to the separate elements that made Goldsmith seem, at times, like a genius, and at other times, like an idiot savant incapable of writing as appealingly as he did in multiple genres. For example, what Boswell interpreted as bragging was, in fact, an oblique devotion to justice: "In company Goldsmith was forever attempting to counteract the praise of others' talents, most commonly parading his own. He seems to have had so deep a suspicion that any kind of spoken praise was more than half-way to becoming a treacherous flattery, that he wished to stifle adulation at whatever cost to his own image and reputation" (pp. 27–28).

In addition to describing Goldsmith's character without patronizing him or turning him into a sardonic ironist (the two major dangers when writing about the author), Dixon provides a compilation of recent biographical material and convincing explications of the author's major works. The first chapter details Goldsmith's life in Ireland as a clergyman's son and takes him to the beginnings of his life as a writer in London. In the second chapter, Dixon examines Goldsmith's critical principles. Goldsmith disliked: romances, too many epithets, affectation, obscurity, prolixity, slavishly imitated classical forms, and blank verse (preferring rhyme because it forced discipline). As

Dixon notes, "Goldsmith's own economy of expression signals . . . qualities of personal modesty and respect for his readers" (pp. 23–24). Goldsmith's versatility had a dark side; it meant he was also scattered— "the lure of the miscellaneous was something that Goldsmith found difficult to resist" (p. 34).

Subsequent chapters consider Goldsmith's major works. Dixon often refers to recent critical studies, such as when he sees *The Vicar of Wakefield* as realistic because it frequesntly demolishes romantic notions. But Dixon does not concur with Robert Hopkins, who maintains that Goldsmith is "artfully burlesquing the coventions of pastoral; . . . to see burlesque in these scenes is to weaken the forces of aggression that disrupt them" (p. 82). Dixon takes his final characterization of Goldsmith from the writer's description of his contribution to the dinner in "Retaliation"—is a gooseberry fool: "The dish is wittily chosen, an honest acknowledgment that he was often and widely regarded as foolish in his talk and behavior, but also a just characterization of his writings. A gooseberry fool is a teasing, paradoxical confection, simultaneously sweet and sharp" (p. 141).—Laura B. Kennelly.

Françoise d'Issembourg d'Happoncourt de Graffigny (1695–1758)

Douthwaite, Julia V. "Relocating the Exotic Other in Graffigny's *Lettres d'une Péruvienne.*" *The Romanic Review*, 82 (1991), 456–74.

Groupe d'Etudes du XVIIIe Siècle (Strasbourg). *Vierge du soleil/Fille des Lumières*: La Péruvienne *de Mme de Graffigny et ses* Suites. (Travaux et recherches, 5.) Strasbourg: Presses Universitaires de Strasbourg, 1989. Pp. 189; appendices. Cf. *ECCB*, n.s. 15, VI:342.

Rev. by Ronald C. Rosbottom in *The French Review*, 65 (1991), 125–26.

Thomas Gray (1716–1771)

Clark, S. H. " 'Pendet Homo Incertus': Gray's Response to Locke; Part One: 'Dull in a New Way'." *Eighteenth-Century Studies*, 24 (1991), 273–91.

Gray's steady analysis of his own sensations and inaction, a powerful attribute of Lockean empiricism and the "attrition of the self," inform his letters and his poetry, especially the Eton Ode.

Clark, S. H. " 'Pendet Homo Incertus': Gray's Response to Locke; Part Two: 'De principiis Cogitandi'." *Eighteenth-Century Studies*, 24 (1991), 484–503.

The Latin poems allow for a sufficient, fully Lockean complexity of epistemology.

Jestin, Loftus. *The Answer to the Lyre: Richard Bentley's Illustrations for Thomas Gray's Poems.* Philadelphia, PA: U. of Pennsylvania Press, 1990. Pp. ix + 355.

Rev. (favorably) by Alan T. McKenzie in *The Scriblerian*, 23 (1991), 290–91.

Weinfield, Henry. *The Poet Without a Name: Gray's* Elegy *and the Problem of History.* Carbondale, IL: Southern Illinois U. Press, 1991. Pp. xx + 236; bibliography.

Rev. by D. Garrison in *Choice*, 29 (1991), 286.

Henry Weinfield deserves credit for tackling the central problem with Gray studies head-on: how can Gray be rescued from the somewhat dismal status of a representative or transitional figure, and regarded instead as a writer of importance in his own right. Weinfield's response centers on one text, the "Elegy," a focus justified on the grounds that the poem, despite or perhaps because of its popular reputation, has suffered prolonged critical neglect (his claim on page xv that the poem has "has never really been understood," however, conflicts with his apparent deference to the common reader). Such a concentrated focus has the advantage of allowing for reasonably comprehensive coverage, although more an eighteenth-century reception would have been welcome (Johnson in this instance is highly untypical). One nevertheless regrets the absense of a more extended treatment of the rest of Gray's English poetry and the fine Latin verse. The poem is also segregated from the Graveyard School of the 1740s. While one may appreciate Weinfield's desire to detach Gray from Blair, Hervey, and Young, some explanation is needed of how this particular funeral meditation manages to escape comparably histrionic morbidity.

The "problem of history" of the title does not refer to anything so mundane as cultural context. No attempt is made to establish Gray's views as the Regius Professor of Modern History at Cambridge, or to chart the influence of contemporary historiography on his work. Instead we are offered a mixture of genre and eschatology, based on a supposed dialectic between loss within, and redemption through, history. These in turn are identified with the utopian dimension of the pastoral and the ethic of transformative labor in the georgic: the "Elegy" by combining these modes represents both their culmination and expiry.

The opening chapter launches a salutary polemic against too ready acceptance of belatedness, making some cogent points about over-reliance on the copious annotation on Lonsdale's edition, and on Bloom's insouciant generalizations. The second analyzes the New Critical tradition of reading the "Elegy." More, perhaps, might have been made of its capacity to generate a "situation of infinite regress" (p. 36) with its audacious conjuring of an apparently limitless cast of dramatis personae. The subsequent history of interpretation receives scant attention; despite Weinfield's demurrals, his book represents not so much a release from formalism, as its continuation by other means (although it is perhaps none the worse for that). Chapter 4 offers a somewhat meager generic contextualization, leaping from Gay in 1714 to Goldsmith in 1783, neglecting more immediate precursors such as Hammond and Shenstone. The chapter treating the relation of Milton to Wordsworth reduces Gray to the highly traditional role of intermediary. It is also patently incorrect to assume that Gray's influence was restricted to the "Elegy"; at the very least some consideration of the "Odes" and the journals is required.

The extended close reading of the "Elegy" in Chapter 3 is the heart of the book. Weinfield's initial claims to be phenomenological in orientation, temporal rather than spatial (p. xviii), cannot withstand close scrutiny; but the exegesis offered is attentive, scrupulous, and generally illuminating. The tension between universal and particular in the rhetoric is convincingly mapped onto the opposition between death and death-in-life, the human condition of mortality and the contingencies of social deprivation. Weinfield is also persuasive on the essential secularism of the poem, and the degree to which its pathos derives from an embeddedness within historicity. One might query individual points: more evidence needs to be offered that Gray was a "thoroughgoing Platonist" (p. 48); the psychological resonance of Memory is somewhat cursorily dismissed (p. 69); and the degree of self-reflexivity concerning place in the poem might have been expanded. The adducing of Donne's bell tolling "for thee" (pp. 131–34) to explain the textual crux of lines 93–94 is also notably unconvincing. Nevertheless, such limitations do not detract from the overall quality of the reading, although one may still wonder whether an essay might have been a more appropriate and economical format for its insights.—Steve Clark.

Zionkowski, Linda. "Bridging the Gulf Between: The Poet and the Audience in the Work of Gray." *English Literary History*, 58 (1991), 331–50.

Gray was disgusted by the commodification of texts and disturbed by the widening of the audience for poetry.

Albrecht von Haller (1708–1777)

Rudolphi, Gerhard. "La Méthode hallérienne en physiologie." *Dix-huitième siècle*, 21 (1991), 75–84.

James Harris (1709–1780)

Probyn, Clive T. *The Sociable Humanist: The Life and Works of James Harris, 1709–1780: Provincial and Metropolitan Culture in Eighteenth-Century England.* New York: Oxford U. Press; Oxford: Clarendon Press, 1991. Pp. xv + 371; appendices; bibliography; figures; illustrations.

Rev. by L. G. Mitchell in *Notes and Queries*, 236 (1991), 546–47; by Pat Rogers in *TLS,* (May 24, 1991), 25.

It is a rather rare occurrence these days for a researcher to come across a neglected trove of papers relating to an eighteenth-cenutry English literary figure. Yet that was precisely what happend to Clive Probyn (Monash University). Before his arrival on the scene, the letters and other manuscripts of James "Hermes" Harris (1709-80) lay mostly untouched among the forty-eight volumes of family papers held by Harris's direct descendants, the earls of Malmesbury. Probyn has used these and other sources to good effect. The result is the first full-scale biography of a man who contributed to the fields of philosophy, music, poetry, literary theory, aesthetics, linguistics, and politics.

Probyn takes great pains to portray Harris both as a provincial savant of Salisbury, Wiltshire, and as a literary figure of some national renown. His literary reputation is based primarily on four works. *The Three Treatises* (1744) suggests how the arts can be integrated and ordered hierarchically, with poetry being the highest. It is a work that influenced Joshua Reynolds's much more famous *Discourses on Art*. The book that gave Harris his nickname, *Hermes, or a Philosophical Inquiry Concerning Language and Universal Grammar* (1751), is among the first works in English to carry the discussion of grammar principles beyond those found in Latin. As such, it appears in many twentieth-cenutry histories of linguistic theory. *The Philosophical Arguments* (1775) is an attempt to swim against the materialist tide by using idealist, anti-Lockean principles to fashion a synthesis of the major philosophical theories of the West. Finally, *The Philological Inquiries* (posthumously published in 1781) comprises a discussion of critical theory, an analysis of selected literary topics (including drama, prose style, and editing), and a detailed survey of medieval literature.

As a generous host to prominent Londoners who were visiting Salisbury, and then as a Whig member of Parliament from 1761 to 1780, Harris was able to imbibe metropolitan culture and act as a medium of cultural exchange between London and the West Country. His activities in Salisbury's Society for Lovers of Musick (sic) illustrate this quite clearly. For the Society's annual music festival, he was able to acquire and adapt new works by Handel and many Italian composers; to compose works of his own; and to make these works available for use on the London stage, especially in productions of his friend, David Garrick. This metropolitian-provincial interchange can also be seen in the links Harris forged with some of the leading literary figures of the day, especially Henry and Sarah Fielding.

The Sociable Humanist has many additional virtues. A dozen illustrations provide a visual record of Harris at various stages in his life and of the world in which he moved. There are four appendices of previously unpublished material. The most significant are Harris's biographical sketch of Henry Fielding (pp. 303–13) and his essay "Upon Ridicule" (pp. 313–33). The excellent "Complete Chronology" (pp. 338–53) lists all editions of Harris's printed works down to 1980 and also his major unpublished pieces.

There are only a few weaknesses. While the text is clear and well organized, it is also overloaded with the names, dates, and accomplishments of Harris's relatives, friends, or friends of relatives, and relatives of friends—many more than are needed to locate Harris in the various networks in which he moved. There is, moreover, precious little psychological insight, even of a basic sort that would have helped to bring Harris to life. Something could have been done, for example, with the potential tensions between his "sociability" and his expectations of deference from social inferiors.

In sum, this is a workmanlike biography of a notable provincial man who belongs to the second rank of eighteenth-century writers and public figures. While Probyn's account does not greatly alter standard interpretations of eighteenth-century British culture, it will probably remain the definitive account of Harris's life for a long time to come.—Robert Glen.

Eliza Haywood (1693?–1756)

Blouch, Christine. "Eliza Haywood and the Romance of Obscurity." *Studies in English Literature 1500–1900*, 31 (1991), 535–51.

Provides biographical details and critical considerations in an examination of her marginality.

Craft, Catherine A. "Reworking Male Models: Aphra Behn's *Fair Vow-Breaker*, Eliza Haywood's *Fantomina*, and Charlotte Lennox's *Female Quixote*." *Modern Language Review*, 86 (1991), 821–38.

These "subversive female stories and tales picture heroines who are in control, both of themselves and of the men around them"; "they topple the male stereotypes of women."

Firmager, Gabrielle M. "Eliza Haywood: Some Further Light on her Background." *Notes and Queries*, 236 (1991), 181–83.

Claude-Adrien-Helvétius (1715–1771)

Allan, Peter, Alan Dainard, Marie-Thérèse Inguenaud, Jean Orsoni, and David Smith. *Correspondance générale d'Helvétius*. Vol. III: *1761–1774. Lettres 465–720*. Toronto, Canada: U. of Toronto Press, 1991. Pp. xxii + 483; illustrations.

Thanks to the editors of this third volume of the Helvétius correspondence readers can now appreciate a thoughtful and well annotated reconstruction of the final decade of the writer's life through his letters. The 255 documents found here point up, moreover, just how different Helvétius was from the other more prominent members of the Enlightenment coalition.

Helvétius's letters do not possess the breadth of interest of Voltaire's letters, the brilliant volatility and literary élan of Rousseau's epistolary communications nor the philosophical profundity of some of Diderot's missives. None of the letters by Helvétius approach several of the 10,000 word novellae that Diderot composed in his correspondence. However, in their own quiet way, Helvétius's letters contain a charm which is sui generis.

Part of that charm derives from Helvétius's sheer normalcy. Unlike the three other main *philosophes* mentioned above, Helvétius was happily married to a beautiful woman (a fact attested to by Edward Gibbon, enjoyed financial security and didn't have to worry about state-sponsored persecution. While nature is virtually absent in the letters of Voltaire and Diderot, Helvétius dotes on descriptions of gardens and topiaries (especially in England)—not with Rousseau's botanical manias but with the gentleman's enjoyment of an aesthetic experience.

The success he achieved with his *De l'Esprit* (1758) brought in its wake some controversy but nothing comparable to the scandals which overtook his better known contemporaries. Accordingly, his letters during the period 1761–1771 reflect the ideas of a much admired, happy, highly intelligent observer of the European scene who enjoyed his fame and looked forward to the triumph on progressive ideas. In the advocacy of those ideas in his letters one notes, optimism, quiet persuasion—never abrasive on combative polemics.

While numerous themes abound in this volume, they can be compressed, for the sake of instruction, into two main broad categories. The first, the letters to his wife and several other correspondents describe the social whirl he experienced in France, England and Prussia. Here he provides ample and occasionally amusing commentary on the great and near greats who paid homage to him in Paris, English women, the dangers of illicit assignations and the bizarre spectacle (for Frenchmen) of cock-fights. The sedentary habits of the Prussian court in Potsdam, among other interesting social habits, also attracted his attention.

The second category which might loosely be characterized as the intellectual focus, pivots around Helvétius obiter dicta on subjects as diverse as the uphill battle for liberal ideas, the pursuit of truth (in a note to Arnaud), sexual fertility (in a letter to Pouilly) and Prussia's taxation policies. Because of the relatively small number of letters he wrote, it is difficult, however, in the Helvétius letters (unlike those of Voltaire, Rousseau and Diderot) to abstract a thematic analysis of his ideas.

This volume is enhanced by the inclusion of letters written to Helvétius, about Helvétius by third parties and correspondence among his admirers after his death. The scholarship is meticulous and the editing magisterial.—Arnold Ages.

Johann Gottfried von Herder (1744–1803)

Gaier, Ulrich. *Herders Sprachphilosophie und Erkenntniskritik*. (probemata, 118.) Stuttgart and Bad Cannstatt: Frommann-Holzboog, 1988. Pp. 220.

Rev. by K. F. Hilliard in *Modern Language Review*, 86 (1991), 510–11.

Norton, Robert E. *Herder's Aesthetics and the European Enlightenment*. Ithaca, NY, and London: Cornell U. Press, 1991. Pp. xiii + 257; bibliography.

Thomas Hobbes (1588–1679)

Catalupo, Charles. *A Literary* Leviathan: *Thomas Hobbes's Masterpiece of Language*. Lewisburg, PA: Bucknell U. Press (distributed through Cranbury, NJ, and London: Associated University Presses), 1991. Pp. 279; illustration.

In *A Literary Leviathan*, Charles Cantalupo sets out to provide a commentary on Thomas Hobbes' philosophical masterpiece, one that emphasizes its "literary style and content" and assumes that "a written work considered to be philosophy can be read as a literary work as well" (p. 15). Accordingly, the book is organized in terms of the major sections of the *Leviathan*; after an introduction devoted to general issues, successive chapters deal with the dedicatory epistle and the four major sections of the text: especially of Man, of the Common-Wealth, and of the Kingdoms of Darknesse. The advantage of this approach is that it enables Cantalupo to treat matters that are rarely discussed in more conventional studies of Hobbes—e.g., his anthropology, moral psychology, and theology. The obvious disadvantage is that it prevents him from considering complex issues in detail; readers are not likely to find Cantalupo's passing observations on Hobbes's nominalism, for example, as useful as more systematic treatments of the subject. Indeed, the strength of Cantalupo's study lies in its local perceptions rather than its theoretical investments. The introduction in which he examines the relation between literature and philosophy or between logic and rhetoric is likely to leave one uncertain as to his overall point of view toward these issues or, for that matter, toward Hobbes himself. This may be why *A Literary Leviathan* is best read alongside an open copy of the *Leviathan*. With Hobbes's text in hand, the reader can readily appreciate Cantalupo's acute sensitivity to shifts in style and tone, his attentiveness to nuances of word and phrase. For a reader who wishes to savor a close reading of a favorite passage—e.g., Hobbes's account of life in a pre-political *l'etat d'nature*—Cantalupo's commentary is a good place to turn.—Charles H. Hinnant.

Ewin, R. E. *Virtues and Rights: The Moral Philosophy of Thomas Hobbes*. Boulder, CO: Westview Press, 1991. Pp. ix + 212.

Kraynak, Robert P. *History and Modernity in the Thought of Thomas Hobbes*. Ithaca, NY, and London: Cornell U. Press, 1990. Pp. vii + 224.

Rev. by P. J. Johnson in *Choice*, 28 (1991), 1502.

William Hogarth (1697–1764)

Dabydeen, David. *Hogarth, Walpole and Commercial Britain*. London: Hansib, 1987. Pp. 167.

Rev. (with another work) by Herbert M. Atherton in *The Scriblerian*, 23 (1991), 269–71.

Wagner, P. "Eroticism in Graphic Art: The Case of William Hogarth." *Studies in Eighteenth-Century Culture*, 21 (1991), 53–75.

Wagner, P. "Hogarth's Graphic Palimpsests: Intermedial Adaptation of Popular Literature." *Word and Image*, 7:4 (1991), 329–347.

Paul Henry Thiry d'Holbach, baron d'Holbach (1723–1789)

Lurbe, Pierre. "D'Holbach et le 'Whig Canon'." *Dix-huitième siècle*, 21 (1991), 321–20.

Friedrich Hölderlin (1770–1843)

Del Caro, Adrian. *Hölderlin, The Poetics of Being*. Detroit, MI: Wayne State U. Press, 1991. Pp. 145; bibliography; portrait.

Wilhelm Humboldt, Freiherr von Humboldt (1767–1835)

Manchester, Martin L. *The Philosophical Foundations of Humboldt's Linguistic Doctrines*. (Amsterdam Studies in the Theory and History of Linguistic Science. Series III: Studies in the History of the Language Sciences, 32.) Amsterdam and Philadelphia, PA: Benjamins, 1985 [1986]. Pp. xi + 216.

Rev. by Theodore Bynon in *Modern Language Review*, 86 (1991), 138–40.

David Hume (1711–1776)

Baier, Annette C. *A Progress of Sentiments: Reflections on Hume's* Treatise. Cambridge, MA: Harvard U. Press, 1991. Pp. xi + 333; bibliography; illustrations (some colored).

Rev. (favorably) by H. Storl in *Choice*, 29 (1991), 461.

Danford, John W. *David Hume and the Problem of Reason: Recovering the Human Sciences*. London and New Haven, CT: Yale U. Press, 1990. Pp. xii + 228.

Rev. by M. Andic in *Choice*, 28 (1991), 792.

Deleuze, Gilles. *Empiricism and Subjectivity: An Essay on Hume's Theory of Human Nature*. Translated and with an Introduction by Constantin V. Boundas of *Emirisme et subjectivité: essai sur la nature humaine selon Hume* (Paris, 1953). New York: Columbia U. Press, 1991. Pp. xi + 163; bibliography.

Flage, Daniel E. *David Hume's Theory of Mind*. London and New York: Routledge, 1990. Pp. ix + 197.

Rev. (favorably) by M. Andic in *Choice*, 28 (1991), 793.

Gardies, Jean-Louis. *L'Erreur de Hume*. (Philosophie d'aujourd'hui.) Paris: Presses universitaires de France, 1987. Pp. 135. Cf. *ECCB*, n.s. 13, VI:454.

Rev. by Michel Puech in *Etudes philosophiques*, (1991), 537.
    A clear and demonstrative work that argues that Hume was wrong when he insisted upon a rigorous demarcation between fact and value.

Goodman, Dena. "The Hume-Rousseau Affair: From Private *Querelle* to Public *Procés*." *Eighteenth-Century Studies*, 25 (1991–92), 171–201.

Traces "the process by which a private matter became a public affair, readers became writers, and the reading public played its role as the tribunal of public opinion."

Graefrath, Bernd. "Hume's Metaphysical Cognitivism and the Natural Law Theory." *Journal of Value Inquiry*, 25 (1991), 73–79.

There is much debate today as to how Hume's ethical (or metaethical) theory is to be interpreted. The author of this essay classifies Hume's view as "non-descriptivist cognitivism."

Groarke, Leo, and Graham Solomon. "Some Sources of Hume's Account of Cause." *Journal of the History of Ideas*, 52 (1991), 645–663.

It is well known that Hume had rather skeptical views concerning how much could be known about the cause and effect of relation. Hume himself said much of his thought could by traced to such thinkers as Bayle and Malebranche. But Groarke and Solomon are convinced that his thought had many more ancient sources. This essay is concerned with Hume's debt to the skepticism of Sextus Empiricus.

Klemme, Heiner. "And Time Does Justice to All the World": Ein unveröffentlichter Brief von David Hume an William Strahan. *Journal of the History of Philosophy*, 29 (1991), 657–664.

This short discussion article is written in German, but it is important because it includes a previously unpublished letter by David Hume (in English). The letter is from Hume to his publisher William Strahan. Hume discusses Strahan's opinion that the sale of his works had been saved by the clergy, but expresses his pleasure at the "approbation of so many men of sense and learning."

Murphy, Richard T. "Husserl and Hume: Overcoming Scepticism." *Journal of the British Society for Phenomenology*, 22 (1991), 30–44.

David Hume's philosophy is popular today, and has been used by philosophers in many other schools of thought. In this essay, R. Murphy shows how the phenomenologist Husserl used some of Hume's own insights to overcome excessive skepticism.

Olshewsky, Thomas M. "The Classical Roots and Hume's Skepticism." *Journal of the History of Ideas*, 52 (1991), 269–287.

David Hume was a skeptic, in some senses of the term. It is also agreed (by most scholars) that his skepticism has ancient sources. Olshewsky agrees with Peter Jones that Hume's skepticism was probably derived from Cicero rather than Sextus Empiricus.

Pears, David. *Hume's System: An Examination of the First Book of His* Treatise. New York and Oxford: Oxford U. Press, 1990. Pp. ix + 204.

Rev. by John Cottingham in *TLS*, (Aug. 9, 1991), 27; (with reservations) by F. Wilson in *Choice*, 29 (1991), 119.

Shirley, Edward S. "Hume's Ethics: Acts, Rules, Dispositions, and Utility." *Southwest Philosophy Review*, 7 (1991), 129–139.

Shirley is convinced that Hume's ethical theory was utilitarian. But he thinks Hume emphasized the role of dispositions to avoid some of the problems of both act—and rule—utilitarianism.

Siebert, Donald T. *The Moral Animus of David Hume*. Newark, DE: U. of Delaware Press; London: Associated University Presses, 1990. Pp. 245. Cf. *ECCB*, n.s. 16, VI:394.

Rev. by Hohn A. Vance in *South Atlantic Review*, 56 (Sept. 1991), 112–114.

Snare, Francis. *Morals, Motivation and Convention: Hume's Influential Doctrines*. (Cambridge Studies in Philosophy.) Cambridge and New York: Cambridge U. Press, 1991. Pp. xii + 322; bibliography; figures.

Rev. (with reservations) by F. Wilson in *Choice*, 29 (1991), 609.

Wertz, S. K. "Hume and the Paradox of Taste Again." *Southwest Philosophy Review*, 7 (1991), 141–150.

Are there really standards of taste, rules to be applied to discover when an art work is good or bad? What did Hume think? The answer is not entirely clear. Wertz claims that Hume did think there are rules—otherwise how could he be so sure that Milton was a greater poet than Drummond of Hawthornden? —but that such rules were difficult to discover.

Winkler, Kenneth P. "The New Hume." *The Philosophical Review*, 100 (1991), 541–579.

Histories of philosophy continue to be written, and interpretation of the great philosophers are frequently changed. It has recently been argued that David Hume was less skeptical than he has previously been thought and that he was in fact, a "casual realist." In this paper, Winkler seeks to show that earlier interpretations of Hume have been too easily set aside.

Yandell, Keith E. *Hume's "Inexplicable Mystery": His Views on Religion*. Philadelphia, PA: Temple U. Press, 1990. Pp. xvii + 360; bibliography.

Rev. by M. Andic in *Choice*, 28 (1991), 796.

Thomas Jefferson (1743–1826)

Miller, Charles A. *Jefferson and Nature: An Interpretation.* Baltimore, MD, and London: Johns Hopkins U. Press, 1988. Pp. xii + 300.

Rev. (with other works) by John Allphin Moore, Jr. in *Eighteenth-Century Studies*, 24 (1991), 363–69.

Samuel Johnson (1709–1784)

Bogel, Fredric V. *The Dream of My Brother: An Essay on Johnson's Authority.* (English Literary Studies Monograph Series, 47.) Victoria: U. of Victoria Press, 1990. Pp. 94; appendices. Cf. *ECCB*, n.s. 16, VI:395–96.

Readers already familiar with Fredric Bogel's "Johnson and the Role of Authority" in *The New Eighteenth Century*, edited by Felicity Nussbaum and Laura Brown (1987), will find little that is new here except a few more pages of psychoanalytical biography drawn largely from Walter Jackson Bate and some thirty pages of rhetorical, phenomenological, and deconstructive analysis, a mixed bag of William Wimsatt, Kenneth Burke, William Dowling, Steven Knapp, Roland Barthes, and Paul de Man. Otherwise, this monograph incorporates, usually word for word, the earlier essay, sometimes adding quotations or expanding those already used. Finally, two appendices, "Allegory, Authority, and 'The Vision of Theodore' " (pp. 72–77), and "De Man on Allegory" (pp. 78–81), offer material that could surely have been inserted in the body of the text.

Despite the repetition of work, Bogel's insightful analysis here of the first three *Rambler* essays as a context for understanding Johnson's allegorical style enforces the original thesis about a Conradian doubleness in the moralist's voice, between an authoritative, public stance, on the one hand, and a private self of agonizing doubts and fears, on the other. To call into question the motives behind a powerful, authorial presence may itself appear politically as well as morally subversive to a readership that has clung to a Johnson or an Austen as therapy while coping with the modern and "post-modern" world. But no matter how "speculative," as Bogel's literal-minded detractors will continue to complain, his approach is largely a post-structuralist refinement of Bronson's Johnson Agonistes portrait.

Without having any serious difficulties with Bogel's critical methodology or the practical applications to Johnson's writings, I nevertheless find this monograph disappointingly tentative. The whole problem of a writer's authority—not just Johnson's—and indeed of the reader's need of such an authority could lead to a major book, something akin to Alvin Kernan's *Printing Technology, Letters and Samuel Johnson* (1987). Bogel was apparently unaware that Kernan had also emphasized the famous three-legged arm chair that Johnson habitually used in his Gough Square garret as if to remind himself of the writer's unstable posture toward his public (pp. 314–16). Rather than yet more psychoanalytical/rhetorical interpretations of Johnson's selfhood and textuality, Bogel might have followed Kernan's path and situated the problem of writerly authority in the historical literary marketplace itself. Although taking into account Pat Rogers's work on Grub Street and the popular press, Bogel pays little heed to the formation of both reader and writer in print culture.—John A. Dussinger.

Brooks, Christopher. "Johnson's Insular Mind and the Analogy of Travel: *A Journey to the Western Islands of Scotland.*" *Essays in Literature*, 18 (1991), 21–36.

Imperialism made Johnson's mind more insular, as evidenced by "recurrent imagery of insulation and isolation."

Brownell, Morris R. *Samuel Johnson's Attitude to the Arts.* Oxford: Clarendon Press, 1989. Pp. xviii + 195. Cf. *ECCB*, n.s. 16, VI:396; 15, VI:347.

Rev. (with another work) by Charles A. Knight in *Journal of English and Germanic Philology*, 90 (1991), 243–46; (with another work) by A. F. T. Lurcock in *Notes and Queries*, 236 (1991), 113–15.

Davis, Philip. *In Mind of Johnson: A Study of Johnson's* The Rambler. Athens, GA: U. of Georgia Press, 1989. Pp. viii + 318. Cf. *ECCB*, n.s. 15, VI:348–49.

"Johnson," says Philip Davis in this study, "is one...in his two minds" (p.92), and Davis's book displays even more heterogeneity than its subject. First, it is an argument about Johnson's sensibility, principally in *The Rambler*, and the heart of this argument is that Johnson brings together opposing categories: aggressiveness and sympathy, singularity and commoness, ambition and a demystified view of the hollowness of ambition, a longing for finality and a commitment to process, discoursing like an angel and living like a man, victory and defeat, a reliance on reason and a distrust of reason, the superiority of an observer or "speculatist" and the embeddedness of a "reporter from experience," and more. These categories, moreover, appear not serially but simultaneously, in mutual and often agonistic implication:

For in reading Johnson we can always see something of the personal history of what he has learnt, checked and acquired, in almost archaeological layers within the syntax, and we can recognize what younger primary forces beneath the achievements both challenge them and make them necessary, though difficult, to retain. (p.57) This is an argument with which I have considerable sympathy, and I find it the most interesting and useful aspect of Davis's project. Would it were all he undertook.

But the book is also a counterblast to academic criticism. The self-serving blurb announces that Davis's approach "flies in the face of established critical fashions and preconceptions and ...reveals Johnson in a completely new light." But Davis gives little indication that he has *read_* any modern criticism of Johnson apart from the biographies by Bate and Wain, and his own approach is not "completely new" but remarkably old-fashioned. Avoiding the allegedly idolatrous treatment of literary works by professional critics, Davis simply dusts off that golden calf of an earlier age, the author's personality, and falls to his knees before it. Why?

Because the book is also a self-help text, seeking to recover (and the prose of this sentence is all too typical) "what it might be like to be with Johnson and read Johnson while he was alive and real and strong and weak: (p.6). Davis wants to incorporate Johnson's example into our lives–no crime, certainly. But to establish an ethos of warm sincerity rather than cold professionalism, he has recourse to a lax, verbose, sermonical style (at the turn of the century, this book would have been titled *Johnson: How to Know Him*): he resorts to drifting and indefinite argument, a high proportion of assertion to demonstration and of speculation to assertion, and an inability to conceive himself less than edifying. Perhaps to strengthen this image of unprofessional sincerity, Davis sprinkles his text with little odd, lax moments that attest to his eye's being on the *important* thing: he forgets that in the end of *Rasselas* the prince is not "full circle back in Abissinia" but only resolving to return (p.252); he quotes *The Vanity of Human Wishes* most often from the manuscript version without disclosing why–or that–he is doing so (and he quotes inaccurately); he takes his title from a remark by "Gerald" (presumably, William Gerald) Hamilton; and he seems to understand Hamilton's remark only in the vaguest sense. After Johnson's death, Hamilton had said, "no man can be said to put you in mind of Johnson," that is, to remind you of Johnson. Davis says: "I have written this book in order to try to be truly'in mind of Johnson'" (p.1)–meaning what? To keep Johnson in mind, or to be in his mind? To remember Johnson correctly? To remind readers of Johnson? Like much of this book, the phrase won't hold a sharp outline. But as Davis says later, "I favor blurring" (p.5).

Critical study, anti-professional polemic, lay sermon, the book is also an oblique autobiography focusing on "the second stage of life" ("Acknowledgements"). As becomes clear later (pp.55, 181–82), the problem of the second stage of life is that we lose our earlier energy and purposefulness. Davis's readers will experience the same problem.—Fredric V. Bogel.

Rev. (with another work) by Charles A. Knight in *Journal of English and Germanic Philology*, 90 (1991), 243–46.

Ferrero, Bonnie. "Samuel Johnson and Arthur Murphy: Curious Intersections and Deliberate Divergence." *English Language Notes*, 28 (1991), 18–24.

Considers one or two acts of plagiarism, a misattribution, and the "filtering out" of some anti-semitism in the *Gray's Inn Journal*.

Ferrero, Bonnie. "Johnson, Murphy, and *Macbeth*." *Review of English Studies*, 42 (1991), 228–32.

Much of Murphy's paper in the *Gray's Inn Journal* of 1753 is borrowed from Johnson's *Miscellaneous Observations* of 1745.

Greene, Donald. *The Politics of Samuel Johnson.* 2nd edition. Athens, GA: U. of Georgia Press, 1990. Pp. lxxix + 356. Cf. *ECCB*, n.s. 16, VI:396–97.

Rev. (severely and with another work) by A. F. T. Lurcock in *Notes and Queries*, 236 (1991), 545–46.

Johnson, Samuel. *Rasselas and Other Tales*. Edited by Gwin J. Kolb. (Yale Edition of the Works of Samuel Johnson, 16.) London and New Haven, CT: Yale U. Press, 1990. Pp.lxx + 290; facsimiles.

Rev. (severely) by H. R. Woudhuysen in *TLS*, (Sept. 13, 1991), 24; correspondence from C. C. Thompson in *TLS*, (Nov. 1, 1991), 15.

Maner, Martin. *The Philosophical Biographer: Doubt and Dialectic in Johnson's* Lives of the Poets. Athens, GA: U. of Georgia Press, 1989. Pp. 187. Cf. *ECCB*, n.s. 16, VI:400; 15, VI:352–53.

Rev. (with another work) by Allan Ingram in *Modern Language Review*, 86 (1991), 403–04.

Page, N. *A Dr. Johnson Chronology.* (Macmillan Author Chronologies.) Basingstoke, UK, and London: Macmillan, 1988. Pp. xv + 136. Cf. *ECCB*, n.s. 16, VI:400.

Rev. (severely and with another work) by A. F. T. Lurcock in *Notes and Queries*, 236 (1991), 545–46.

Parke, Catherine N. *Samuel Johnson and Biographical Thinking.* Columbia, MO: U. of Missouri Press, 1991. Pp. xi + 178.

"Biographical thinking" here means a characteristic mode of thought Catherine Parke finds in much of Johnson's writing, something close to his "imagining other people's lives and minds" (p. 2), evident in much of Johnson's work besides the overtly biographical. The study "also and perhaps more largely examines his theory and practice of education" (p. 2), a theory based on the notion that to teach requires imaginative identification with the learner.

Parke wants to explore central questions in Johnson and to connect them to practical and ethical life. She takes a particular interest in convergences she finds between Johnson and twentieth-century thinkers whom she admires—Gregory Bateson, Carl Becker, Sissela Bok, Kenneth Burke, Michael Polyani, Gertrude Stein. There are good ideas about Johnson's prefaces, *Rasselas*, and some aspects of the *Lives*. Readers may accept her general notion of biographical thinking.

This book is, however, so badly flawed that there is real danger most readers will not finish it. The author writes with terrible imprecision about the most formidably precise of writers, and presumably to readers schooled by him. There are astonishing errors and confusions everywhere.

Some are small. "The kind of educational activity most interesting to Johnson cannot . . . be assessed in terms of either memory or mastery, though they may include both" (p. 44); "the intervening time between the publication of each essay . . ." (p. 61), as if one thing could be between another. These slips betray loose logic, and logic is loose at every level. "It is the lexicographer's consciousness about language and his task, less than his experience as such, that distinguishes him from other people" (p. 37)–she means "more than"; "our identities have boundaries to which we give the names *self* and *other*" (p. 58)—no, that's not what the *boundaries* are called; "One fear replaces another yet more encompassing one" (p. 60)—she means "is replaced by." Such errors breed suspicion that other sentences, which might otherwise be taken for suggestive paradoxes, are merely nonsense: "Martin can legitimately be held accountable by his readers for knowing more than he possibly could have known" (p. 122); "One might even say that for him probability thinks us and biography lives us" (p. 162). It is hard to look patiently for sense in "Sanity and gratitude intersect in the realm of history" (p. 147), or in this description of Johnson's compulsive bodily tics: "Together they enact a reaffirming, systematic choreography of reality" (p. 112).

Some words are used with a misunderstanding of their meanings, and contribute disorder in sentences where the meaning is already uncertain: "This incident suggests dramaturgically [*dramatically*, if anything similar makes sense] his belief in thinking as a vital principle" (p. 154), or, in the very next sentence: "His sense of what thinking was withstood the modern temptation to divide life (*soma*) from mind or soul (*psyche*)." *Soma* means not "life" but "body," and the error vitiates an already doubtful effort to call Johnson's thinking *psychosomatic*, for what purpose is not clear.

Finally, these lapses of local clarity are matched in efforts to place ideas in relation to one another, especially Johnson's to those of some modern thinker: "In his typically Johnsonian manner [Kenneth] Burke proposes hypnosis as a figure for the way we learn by analogy" (p. 151). Johnson's ideas are confused with those of another, and are asserted to be the same: "Johnson, like Bok, identifies . . . lying as a fundamental act of violence" (p. 89). Parke's own ideas are represented as his: "a committment to the truth of efficiency, as Johnson distinctly defines that truth to mean being true to time . . ." (p. 148). There is more more of error, vagueness, and incoherence, sadly making real insights in the book almost inaccessible.—Mark Booth.

Parker, G. F. *Johnson's Shakespeare*. Oxford: Clarendon Press, 1989. Pp. xx + 204. Cf. *ECCB*, n.s. 16, VI:400; 15, VI:353–54.

Rev. (favorably) by James Gray in *Modern Philology*, 89 (1990–91), 27–31; by David Hopkins in *Review of English Studies*, 42 (1991), 271–72; (with another work) by Allan Ingram in *Modern Language Review*, 86 (1991), 403–04.

Reddick, Allen. *The Making of Johnson's Dictionary, 1746–1773*. (Cambridge Studies in Publishing and Printing History.) Cambridge and New York: Cambridge U. Press, 1990. Pp. xiii + 249; bibliography; 6 illustrations. Cf. *ECCB*, n.s. 16, VI:401.

Rev. (favorably) by W. B. Carnochan in *TLS*, (Apr. 19, 1991), 9–10.

Tomarken, Edward. *Johnson, Rasselas, and the Choice of Criticism*. Lexington, KY: U. Press of Kentucky, 1990. Pp. 224.

Rev. by John P. Zomchick in *South Atlantic Review*, 56 (Sept. 1991), 124–117.

Tomarken, Edward. *Samuel Johnson on Shakespeare: The Discipline of Criticism*. Athens, GA, and London: U. of Georgia Press, 1991. Pp. xiii + 205.

Despite the attention paid over the years to the preface to Johnson's *Shakespeare*, the hundreds of interpretive, evaluative, and emendatory notes remain largely unread. Walter Raleigh and Arthur Sherbo both tried to lure Johnsonians into spending more time with the notes, but even when scholars did so, it was to gather information on other aspects of Johnson's work. In this book Edward Tomarken declares his intention to study the notes as innovative and important literary criticism in their own right. Despite that declaration, however, Tomarken's interests, like those of his predecessors, turn out to lie elsewhere.

Tomarken dedicates a chapter each to Johnson's notes on one or the other of eight Shakespearean plays. The procedure is to work through a selection of the notes and the "stricture" on a given play, moving towards Johnson's interpretation of it, and setting this in the context of other eighteenth-century commentary. Tomarken then turns to the preface for the theoretical underpinning of the interpretation and, finally, broadens his discussion to explore the relevance of Johnson's insights to issues of concern to modern critics. The method sounds promising, though it proves disappointing in its results.

The Johnson interpretations that Tomarken attempts to reconstruct are in large part unconvincing and are elaborated in ways one can hardly imagine crossing Johnson's mind. It's all rather puzzling until one reaches the closing pages of each chapter, where it becomes clear what has been driving Tomarken's efforts all along. He brings to his work an array of his own intellectual commitments, which he then uses to justify his reconstructed Johnson, chapter by chapter. We never, finally, get Johnson on Shakespeare: instead, we get Tomarken on everything, using Johnson as a stalking horse, if not an excuse.

Tomarken admits this. Not all of his conclusions, he says, are Johnson's, though "they result from my attempt to adapt Johnson's critical procedures to the problems of our day" (p. 6). To this extent, his study is "an imitation of Johnson's Shakespeare commentary," in the eighteenth-century sense of an adaptation of another's work as a vehicle for one's own ideas. But Tomarken underestimates how deeply this approach compromises the usefulness of his book. As a professed "imitation," it is neither quite a study of Johnson's notes nor a straightforward contribution to critical theory and practice.

In his intellectual committments, Tomarken represents a generous, traditional, almost courtly humanism, from which, however, he curiously attempts to distance himself. Like Johnson, Tomarken sees the need for an openly ethical approach to criticism, distinguishing this however from the merely didactic. In discussing Johnson's responses to *Henry IV*, Tomarkin argues that Johnson's concern over Hal's personal ethical sensitivity parallels the concerns of modern ideological critics over Hal's politics. Like Johnson again, Tomarken believes that literature has something to say about life; though, rather than make quite so bold a statement, Tomarkin prefers vague references to the relation between the "literary" and the "extraliterary." In fact, his stress on the relevance of literature to human existence makes it disappointing to see him characterize mimeticism as "an outmoded theory based upon an outmoded ideology" (p. 88). Tomarkin speaks frequently of "the human situation," "the human dilemma," even "man's place in the cosmos," and concludes that the ultimate goal of literary criticism is "to enable us to better endure and understand the human condition" (p. 179). In the light of so boldly a traditional stance, his retreat from mimeticism seems inconsistent, almost ungallant.

Tomarken is at his best a historian of criticism. He demonstrates indefatigable scholarship and the ability to grasp and clarify the main lines of continuity and change in a critical debate. He also provides useful insights on how Johnson's notes do their critical work. Tomarken requires us, for instance, to reassess the relationship between Johnson's notes and the more famous preface, arguing that the latter was actually written to illuminate and support the former. Tomarken also draws attention to what he calls Johnson's "variorum technique," his use of his own notes in conjunction with those of his predecessors to explore multiple sides of an interpretive problem. Finally, and most importantly, Tomarken makes the case that the notes to Johnson's *Shakespeare* represent a significant critical achievement and deserve extensive interpretive study in their own right. The irony is, they still do.—Lance Wilcox.

Wiltshire, John. *Samuel Johnson in the Medical World: The Doctor and the Patient.* Cambridge and New York: Cambridge U. Press, 1991. Pp. x + 293; bibliography; frontispiece.

Rev. by G. Scholtz in *Choice*, 29 (1991), 286.

A frequent ploy in reviewing scholarly books is for the reviewer to chide the writer for not having written the book he would like to have read. What a pleasure it is to report that John Wiltshire's account of Samuel Johnson and the medical aspects of his life is just the sort of exposition and analysis that this reviewer once considered writing and that Wiltshire has done it better and on a broader canvas.

Wiltshire starts with a review of Johnson's own medical history: juvenile scrofula, poor vision in one eye, the famous "tics and gesticulations," gout, asthma, a stroke with transcient aphasia, and finally "dropsy" with death due to arteriosclerotic heart disease with congestive failure. Add to this an account of his recurrent attacks of melancholia, and the patient is clearly revealed. By his own statement, Johnson was a "dabbler in physic," and the reader is given a full account of Johnson's medical readings and how he assimilated his knowledge for purposes of self-medication. Johnson's doctors—Bathurst, Lawrence, Brocklesby, Heberden, and others—are not neglected.

In further chapters Wiltshire sets forth considerable useful information about medicine in eighteenth-cenutry England, its theories, its mode of practice. Judicious use of primary sources and an aptitude for telling vignette combine to make these chapters useful and intelligible to a reader unfamiliar with the period. Wiltshire makes full use of Johnson's own writing, especially the essays in *The Rambler* and *The Idler*, to analyze Johnson's frequent, almost habitual use of medical ideas as metaphors.

A well-shaped chapter deals with the atronomer in *Rasselas* as an example of the man of learning whose actions are limited by a psychiatric disability. Unique in the annals of Johnsonians is a full treatment of Dr. Robert Levet, an unlicensed practitioner who was a valued member of Johnson's peculiar household, and Wiltshire's close reading of Johnson's elegy on Levet is welcome and commendable. The monograph concludes with a chapter on therapeutic friendship, dealing chiefly with Johnson's efforts to steer Boswell into a more sensible way of life and behavior. These were only transiently effective because Boswell was less than candid to his mentor about his compulsive drinking and whoring.

Some minor cavils: occasional paragraphs are devoted to the exposition and dismissal of various psuedo-psychoanalytic theories about Johnson's personality, a waste of time and space because no Johnson scholar relies on them. Also, the exposition of medical ideas about melancholia relies chiefly on the contribution of William Battie; the two Scotsman, William Cullen and Robert Whytt, deserve equal billing for their contributions to mid eighteenth-century ideas on melancholia. But the balance of Wiltshire's book is sound and sensible, a distinguished contribution not only to Johnsoniana but to the wider field of eighteenth-century studies.—William B. Ober. M.D.

Woudhuysen, H. R. (ed.). *Samuel Johnson on Shakespeare*. Harmondsworth, UK: Penguin, 1991. Pp. 288.

Immanuel Kant (1724–1804)

Allison, Henry E. *Kant's Theory of Freedom*. Cambridge and New York: Cambridge U. Press, 1990. Pp. xii + 304; bibliography. Cf. *ECCB*, n.s. 16, VI:403.

Rev. by Martha Klien in *TLS*, (Aug. 9, 1990), 26; by B. S. Llamzon in *Choice*, 28 (1991), 1323; (somewhat critically) by Onora O'Neill in *Mind*, 100 (1991), 373–376.

Aquila, Richard E. *Matter in Mind: A Study of Kant's Transcendental Deduction*. Bloomington, IN: Indiana U. Press, 1989. pp. xiv + 245. Cf. *ECCB*, n.s. 16, VI:403; 15, VI:356.

Rev. favorably by Ralf Meerbote in *Philosophy and Phenomenological Research*, 51 (1991), 929–934; (with another work) by Paul Guyer in *The Philosophical Review*, 100 (1991), 703–710.

Aquila, Richard E. *Representational Mind: A Study of Kant's Theory of Knowledge*. Bloomington, IN: Indiana U. Press, 1983. Pp. xii + 206.

Rev. (with another work) by Paul Guyer in *The Philosophical Review*, 100 (1991), 703–710.

Arendt, Hannah. *Juger, sur la politique de Kant.* Followed with interpretive essays by Ronald Beiner and Myriam Revault d'Allones. Translated by Myriam Revault d'Allones. Paris: Editions du Seuil, Collection Libre Examen, 1991.

Bernet, Rudolf. "Loi et éthique chez Kant et Lacan." *Revue philosophique de Louvain*, 83 (1991), 450–468.

Bowie, Andrew, *Aesthetics and Subjectivity: From Kant to Nietzsche.* Manchester, UK: Manchester U. Press, 1990. Pp. 284.

Rev. by Nicholas Davey in *The British Journal of Aesthetics*, 31 (1991), 370–373.

Crowther, Paul. *The Kantian Sublime: From Morality to Art.* Oxford: Clarendon Press, 1989. Pp. 178.

Rev. favorably by Kenneth F. Rogerson in *The Journal of Aesthetics and Art Criticism*, 49 (1991), 379–381.

Den Ouden, Bernard (ed.). *New Essays on Kant.* Frankfurt am Main and New York: Peter Lang, 1987. Pp. 269.

Rev. favorably by Elizabeth Potter in *The Philosophical Review*, 100 (1991), 341–344.

Derrida, Jacques. "Interpretations at War: Kant, the Jew, the German." *New Literary History*, 22 (1991), 39–95.

Earls, C. Anthony. "The Case of the Unmitigated Blackguard or Saving Kant's Moral Feelings." *Southwest Philosophy Review*, 7 (1991), 119–128.

If we are moral agents only when we act rationally, then it is not clear how Kant can accept any notion of "moral feeling" at all. But Earls thinks that, in the end, it is this "moral feeling" that motivates.

Guyer, Paul. *Kant and the Claims of Knowledge.* Cambridge and New York: Cambridge U. Press, 1987. Pp. xiv + 482. Cf. *ECCB*, n.s. 16, VI:404; 14, VI:343.

Rev. (favorably) by T. H. Irwin in *The Philosophical Review*, 100 (1991), 332–341.

Falkenstein, Lorne. "Kant, Mendelssohn, Lambert and the Subjectivity of Time." *Journal of the History of Philosophy*, 29 (1991), 227–251.

It is usually thought that Kant believed that space and time were "subjective conditions," that our minds "impose" on the data of our senses. That is, we cannot prove that things really exist in space and time, but our minds cannot understand things except in space and time. Falkenstein is concerned that the "imposition" theory is a misunderstanding of Kant. That is, Kant did, Falkenstein believes, defend some such view in his *Inaugural Dissertation* of 1770, but later abandoned the theory.

Galvin, Richard. "Does Kant's Psychology of Morality Need Basic Revision?" *Mind*, 100 (1991), 221–236.

Kant is often criticized as cold and unfeeling because he did not think that desire or inclination (even in the form of love or kindness) should be appropriate motives for moral action. Galvin seeks to show that such criticisms are mistaken.

Hatfield, Gary. *The Natural and the Normative: Theories of Spatial Perception from Kant to Helmholtz.* Cambridge, MA: MIT Press, 1990. Pp. xii + 366; bibliography.

Rev. (favorably) by G. Zoeller in *Choice*, 29 (1991), 524.

Heidegger, Martin. *Kant and the Problem of Metaphysics.* Translated by Richard Taft of *Kant und das Problem der Metaphysik* (4. erw. Aufl., Frankfurt am Main, 1973). 4th edition, enlarged. (Studies in Continental Thought.) Bloomington, IN: Indiana U. Press, 1990. Pp. xix + 197; illustrations.

Rev. (favorably) by N. Lukacher in *Choice*, 28 (1991), 947–48.

Hymers, Michael. "The Role of Kant's Refutation of Idealism." *The Southern Journal of Philosophy*, 29 (1991), 51–67.

Clearly, Hymers claims, Kant's brief "refutation" of idealism in the first edition (1781) of the *Critique of Pure Reason* is part of an argument against skepticism. But the brief argument requires development. Hymers claims the point is that the possiblity of illusion surpasses a background of vertical perception, much as telling a lie requires a context in which the truth is normally told.

Kant, Immanuel. *Qu'est-ce que les Lumières?* Choix Textes, translation, preface and notes by Jean Mondot. (Lire le Dix-huitième Siècle, 2) Saint Etienne: Publications de l'Université de Saint-Étienne, 1991. Pp. 142.

The title of this volume does not quite correspond to its contents. Kant's famous text, *Was ist Aufklärung?* given here in both French and German, is but one among several other texts bearing on or specifically answering that question. There are texts by well-known writers and philosophers such as Kant, Moses Mendelssohn, Herder, and Wieland, and there are others by less well known writers such as Bahrdt, Biester, von Knoblausch zu Hatzbach, Reinnhardt, Riem, Wekhrlinm Weishaupt and Zöllner. A biographical repertory at the close of the texts is most useful on these writers, journalists, pastors, philosophers (but not *philosophes*) who with their texts offer an excellent and varied *aperçu* of German answers to this eminently German question posed in the late 1780s.

The essays in various forms, articles, exhortations, dialogues, treatises, range from masonic-lyrical out-pourings to rather pedantic, rationalistic, scholastic definitions in the form of distinctions, su-divisions, and su-subdivisions. The result is a distinctly different sense or feeling that from any English or French answer one might have gotten had the French or English ever bothered to pose such a question. That the Germans did pose it shows to this reviewer that in Germany philosophers were even more "academic," in today's American usage of the term, than philosophers in Scotland. Indeed this reader could not imagine the question would have been posed elsewhere and reading the texts he could not imagine himself in either London or Paris, Edinburgh or Geneva, Lausanee or Philadelphia. Perhaps Berlin? Perhaps, though note that the answers to the question did not come from any one of the then still relatively small German cities but from various places. Nor did the question arise in some salon or club or Academy but in the pages of the *Berlinische Monatschrift* so that one might say that the *Aufklärung* was rather more restricted in its resonance in Germany than it was in France or Britain. Indeed this journal debate is rather reminiscent of a current on-going debate about the question: *Was ist Post-Modernismus?* If one reads Stanley Rosen's *Hermeneutics as Politics* (Oxford U. Press, 1987), one will see the two questions are not only related but that the last is impossible without the former.

The German essays presented here give one the impression one is no longer in the Enlightenment but already in the age of Romanticism. There is a great deal of attention paid to the freedom of the self, as if reasoning and imagination were the same; there is emphasis on universal Humanity, on the impossiblity of restraining Enlightenment or *Aufklärung* to the State even while one alludes to Frederick's famous words: reason all you want on what you want but obey! Indeed these various discourses are informed with fear of the State and far more anti-clericalism than one might have expected. It is also a discourse limited to the circle of the *Gelehrter*, the educated and those within government who are also educated; a discourse trying to reassure these that the *Aufklärung* is not dangerous and through Riem one is assured that Prussia is the most enlightened State in the world. This did not prevent Riem from being exiled from this enlightened State in 1793 for advocating a foreign policy rapprochement with then revolutionary France. So the writers knew what *Aufklärung* but they also knew they did not yet benefit from it.—R. G. Saisselin.

Kemal, Salim. *Kant and Fine Art: An Essay on Kant and the Philosophy of Fine Art Culture*. Oxford: Clarendon Press, 1986. Pp. x + 348. Cf. *ECCB*, n.s. 13, VI:462–63.

Rev. (favorably) by Oliver Leaman in the *Journal of Speculative Philosophy*, 5 (1991), 26; (favorably) by Robert E. Wood in *The Review of Metaphysics*, 44 (1991), 846–848.

Kitcher, Patricia. *Kant's Transcendental Psychology*. New York and Oxford: Oxford U. Press, 1990. Pp. xiii + 296; bibliography.

Rev. (with another work) by Quassim Cassam in *TLS,* (Aug. 9, 1991), 26; (favorably) by G. Zoeller in *Choice*, 28 (1991), 1652.

Makkreel, Rudolf. *Imagination and Interpretation in Kant: The Hermeneutical Impact of the* Critique of Judgment. Chicago, IL: U. of Chicago Press, 1990. Pp. x + 187; bibliography. Cf. *ECCB*, n.s. 16, VI:405.

Rev. (favorably) by Salim Kemal in *The Journal of Aesthetics and Art Criticism*, 49 (1991), 388–390; (somewhat critically) by Oliver Leaman in *The British Journal of Aesthetics*, 31 (1991), 269–271; (favorably) by G. Zoeller in *Choice*, 28 (1991), 948.

Michalson, Gordon E., Jr. *Fallen Freedom: Kant of Radical Evil and Moral Regeneration*. Cambridge and New York: Cambridge U. Press, 1990. Pp. xii + 172; bibliography.

Rev. by G. Zoeller in *Choice*, 29 (1991), 464.

Mondot, Jean (ed.). *Qu'est-ce que les Lumières?* Société française d'Etude du XVIIIᵉ siècle. Saint-Étienne: Publications de l'Université de Saint-Étienne, 1991. Pp. 142.

Pippin, Robert B. "Idealism and Agency in Kant and Hegel." *The Journal of Philosophy*, 88 (1991), 531–541.

Most modern scholars are aware of Kant's discussions of freedom and how these relate to morality and rationality. R. Pippin compares Kant's treatment with that of Hegel.

Plumer, Gilbert. "Kant's Neglected Argument Against Consequentialism." *The Southern Journal of Philosophy*, 29 (1991), 501–520.

David Hume has an argument that if the world supplied more than any of us could want or need, there would be no reason for justice, perhaps no reason to be morally good at all. On Palmer's reading, Kant claims this argument actually shows that consequentialism is false, since obviously, Kant thought, we ought always to be just.

Powell, C. Thomas. *Kant's Theory of Self-Conciousness*. New York: Oxford U. Press; Oxford: Clarendon Press, 1990. Pp. viii + 268.

Rev. by G. Zoeller in *Choice*, 28 (1991), 1328.

Reed, T. J. "Coming of Age in Prussia and Swabia: Kant, Schiller, and the Duke." *Modern Language Review*, 86 (1991), 613–26.

Discusses Karl Eugen and the Karlsschule as patrons of intellectual freedom.

Rose, Paul Lawrence. *Revolutionary Antisemitism in Germany from Kant to Wagner*. Princeton, NJ: Princeton U. Press, 1990. Pp. xviii + 389.

Rev. by Anthony Quinton in *New York Review of Books*, 38 (Nov. 7, 1991), 38–40.

Schwyzer, Hubert. *The Unity of Understanding: A Study in Kantian Problems*. New York and Oxford: Oxford U. Press, 1990. Pp. 172.

Rev. by B. S. Llamzon in *Choice*, 28 (1991), 949.

Stern, David S. "Autonomy and Political Obligation in Kant." *The Southern Journal of Philosophy*, 29 (1991), 127–147.

Stern takes up the difficult issue of how, in Kant's moral philosophy, political obligations can be binding on autonomous individuals.

Sullivan, Roger J. *Immanuel Kant's Moral Theory*. Cambridge and New York: Cambridge U. Press, 1989. Pp. xvii + 413. Cf. *ECCB*, n.s. 16, VI:407; 15, VI:359.

Rev (somewhat critically) by Stephen Engstrom in *Ethics*, 102, (1991), 167–169.

Volkley, Richard L. *Freedom and the End of Reason: On the Moral Foundation of Kant's Critical Philosophy*. Chicago, IL: U. of Chicago Press, 1989. Pp. xxi + 222.

Rev. briefly by Mark Packer in *Ethics*, 101 (1991), 892.

Waxman, Wayne. *Kant's Model of the Mind: A New Interpretation of Transcendental Idealism*. New York and Oxford : Oxford U. Press, 1991. Pp. x + 306.

Rev. (favorably with another work) by Quassim Cassam in *TLS,* (Aug. 9, 1991), 26.

Yovel, Yirmiyahu (ed.). *Kant's Practical Philosophy Reconsidered*. Dordrecht: Kluwer Academic Publishers, 1989. Pp. x + 262.

Rev. briefly by Richard Veldley in *Ethics*, 101 (1991), 440.

Heinrich von Kleist (1777–1811)

Kleist, Heinrich von. *Amphityron*. Edited by Roland Reuss and Peter Staengle. (Berliner Ausgabe. Sämtliche Werke, I/4.) 2 vols. Basel: Stroemfeld/Roter Stern, 1991. Pp. 145; 65.

Rev. (with other works) by Jeremy Adler in *TLS*, (0ct. 4, 1991), 7–8.
   Commentary volume has title: *Berliner Kleist-Blatter 4*.

Kleist, Heinrich von. *Five Plays*. Translated with an Introduction by Marvin Greenberg. London and New Haven, CT: Yale U. Press, 1988. Pp. liii + 373; illustrations.

Rev. (favorably and with other works) by Jeremy Adler in *TLS*, (Oct. 4, 1991), 7–8; by H. M. Brown in *Modern Language Review*, 86 (1991), 514–17.
   Five plays are "Amphitryon," "The Broken Jug," "Penthesilea," "Prince Frederick of Homburg," and "A Fragment of the Tragedy of Robert Guiscard, Duke of the Normans."

Kleist, Heinrich von. *Michael Kohlaas*. Edited by Roland Reuss with Peter Staengle. (Berliner Ausgabe. Sämtliche Werke, II/l.) 2 vols. Basel: Stromfeld/Roter Stern, 1990. Pp. 301; 124.

Rev. (with other works) by Jeremy Adler in *TLS*, (Oct. 4, 1991), 7–8.
   Commentary volume has title: *Berliner Kleist-Blatter 3*.

Kleist, Heinrich von. *Sämtliche Werke und Briefe*. Vol. II: *Dramen, 1808–1811. Penthesilea, Das Käthchen von Heilbronn, Die Hermannsschlacht, Prinz von Homburg*. Edited by Ilse-Marie Barth and Hinrich C. Seeba, with Hans Rudolf Barth. (Bibliothek deutscher Klassiker, 26.) Frankfurt am Main: Deutscher Klassiker Verlag, 1988. Pp. 1316.

Rev. (with other works) by Jeremy Adler in *TLS*, (Oct. 4, 1991), 7–8.

Kleist, Heinrich von. *Sämtliche Werke und Briefe*. Vol. III: *Erzahlungen, Anekdoten, Gedichten, Schriften*. Edited by Klaus Muller-Salget. (Bibliothek deutscher Klassiker, 51.) Frankfurt am Main: Deutscher Klassiker Verlag, 1989. Pp. 1299.

Rev. (with other works) by Jeremy Adler in *TLS*, (Oct. 4, 1991), 7–8.

Friedrich Gottlieb Klopstock (1724–1803)

Klopstock, Friedrich Gottlieb. *Briefe 1767–1772*. Edited by Klaus Hurlebusch. Band 1: *Text*. (Friedrich Gottlieb Klopstock. Werke und Briefe. Historisch-kritische Ausgabe ... Abteilung Briefe: Vol. 1.) Berlin and New York: Walter de Gruyter, 1989. Pp. (4) + 336 + (1).

Rev. by P. M. Mitchell in *Journal of English and Germanic Philology*, 90 (1991), 121–22.

August Friedrich Ferdinand von Kotzebue (1761–1819)

Mandel, Oscar. *August von Kotzebue: The Comedy, the Man. Including the Good Citizens of Piffelheim.* London: The Pennsylvania State U. Press, 1990. Pp. 132; bibliography.

Rev. (briefly) by Rose Marie Moudouès in *Revue d'histoire du théâtre*, 43 (1991), 378.

Pierre Ambroise François Choderlos de Laclos (1741–1803)

Bougy, Patrice, Elisabeth Coss and Geneviève Dewulf. *La Passion amoureuse: Tristan, Shakespeare, Laclos.* Preface by Laurent Versini. (Prépa-concours.) Nancy: Presses Universitaires de Nancy, 1991. Pp. 304.

Brinsmead, Anne-Marie. *Stategies of Resistance in* Les Liasons dangereuses*: Heroines in Search of "Authority."* Lewiston, NY, and Queenston, Ontario: Edwin Mellen, 1989. Pp. 195.

Rev. by Simon Davies in *Modern Language Review*, 86 (1991), 728–29.

Byrne, Patrick W. Les Liasons dangereuses: *A Study of Motive and Moral.* Glasgow, Scotland: U. of Glasgow French and German Publications, 1989. Pp. 179.

Rev. by Philip Thody in *Modern Language Review*, 86 (1991), 727–28.

Laclos, Pierre Choderlos de. *De L'Education des femmes 1783.* Text presented by Chantal Thomas. (Mémoire du corps.) Grenoble: Jérome Millon, 1991. Pp. 138.

One year after the publication of the *Liaisons dangereuses* (1782), Laclos began composing his "Discours sur la question proposée par l'Académie de Châlons-sur Marne: "Quels seraient les meilleurs moyens de perfectionner l'éducation des femmes;" but he never completed it. Instead he wrote an essay, "Des femmes et de leur éducation," in twelve chapters on such subjects as "La femme naturelle," "De la puberté," "De la vieillesse et de la mort." This new edition prepared by Chantal Thomas reproduces the 1903 edition of the text by Edouard Champion (Paris: Librairie Léon Verrier) minus the notes in that edition by Charles Baudelaire. Most of the discussion in Thomas's introduction centers on the *Liaisons dangereuses*, with emphasis on its strict relation to the essay as Laclos's attempt to correct the public's view of him. In that essay, he resumes the story of a woman's education as developed in Mme de Merteuil. Thomas presents a lengthy analysis of the Merteuil character as a demonstration of Laclos's conviction that a society that has refused to educate women bears fruits of mistrust and dissembling. Thomas further places Laclos's essay in its context of Rousseau's misogynous views and credits Laclos with boldness in acknowledging women's sexuality.

Few notes accompany the new edition of the essay. The reader would have welcomed a more comprehensive annotation of the text. The absence of a bibliography is regrettable, particularly with the current attention to and interest in the education of women in early modern France.—Ruth Plaut Weinreb.

Laclos, Pierre Choderlos de. *Des Pemes et de leur éducation.* Edited by Chantel Thomas. (Mémoire du corps.) Genoble: Jérome Millon, 1991. Pp. 160.

Messière, Philippe. *Les Liason dangereuses, Laclos*. (L'Oeuvre au clair.) Paris: Bordas, 1991. Pp. 95.

This twenty-fourth in an accruing series of monographs on literary chefs d'oeuvre is the fourth (after *Le Mariage de Figaro, Candide,* and *Les Confessions*) to engage the eighteenth-century canon. The classical French pedagogical apparatus brought to bear on Laclos's epistolary novel aims at synthesizing the knowledge and know-how required for successful performance on the *baccalauréat*. Focus moves from the life and times of Laclos through aspects of narrative structure (including a detailed plot summary) or themes of theatricality, reason, stylistic individuation, and perspectivism. Topics covered discursively are distilled as bullets for easy recall, and extended into model and guided commentaries on a dozen of the novel's most celebrated letters. And underlying premise is that every word counts, all the more so when the novel is epistolary, and the stakes are admission to higher education. The final thirty pages walks candidates through a *commentaire composé* on Tourvel's valedictory spasms and a *dissertation* on the essence (imitative or inventive?) of the novel. Extramural readers will both learn from and be struck by discursive practices no less normative and impersonal than those urged by Merteuil on her pupil Cécile. Measured against state-of-the-art Laclos scholarship, this slim volume is inevitably reductive—too categorical, for example, in casting Valmont as a lesser libertine than Nerteuil and in downplaying the irony of Laclos's "affiliation" with Rousseau. The "woman question" is raised, but remains underdeveloped: a rise of epistolarity is plotted exclusively through male-authored texts; Marie Riccoboni's important contemporary critique is too easily dismissed; Laclos' *De l'education des femmes* is understood to prescribe educational reforms as an adequate solution to gender inequalitites; the outrageousness of Merteuil's autobiographical letter is blunted by selective citation; the hysteria of Cécile's morning after is trivialized as characteristic babbling; and the protagonists' downfall is cryptically linked to their having tangled with a "natural" (?) woman, Tourvel. Acknowledgement of all these texts and contexts nonetheless makes for a more sophisticated apprentice-critic's companion than most. Like that of the *Guide Michelin*, its usefulness does not depend on unquestioning adherence to its magisterial methods, conclusions, and perscription.—Susan K. Jackson.

Madame de Lambert (1647–1733)

Marchal, Roger. *Madame de Lambert et son milieu.* (Studies on Voltaire and the Eighteenth Century, 289.) Oxford: The Voltaire Foundation at the Taylor Institution, 1991. Pp. xvii + 798.

Roger Marchal's revision of his doctoral dissertation [defended in 1985 at the Université de Nancy II] is the first exhaustive study of Madame de Lambert and her *milieu*. Social history, thematic and stylistic analysis, and history of ideas are among the most important of the various methods used by the author to offer us a brilliant book on one of the most important women of the period and on one of the most extraordinary interactions of moral, aesthetic and linguistic phenomena of the times.

Divided into three parts, section one is a detailed biography of the life of the Marquise, her works and her salon. Roger Marchal can pride himself on an important series of "firsts" in this section: he is the first to have dated the end of the famous suits. Consequently he is also the first to have placed the opening of her literary salon in 1692 on the rue de Richelieu instead of 1710 as do most other writers about the Marquise. Furthermore, he establishes a very convincing chronology of the composition and of the publication of her works and proves decidedly through a combination of associations, that the "nouvelle" *La Femme hermite*, which was not included in the latest edition of her works (Granderoute, 1990), is indeed one of her works.

The second part of the book, *Le Lambertinage: Une Ethique*, is a study of the major themes which define the moral values of the *grand siècle*. The author reviews the philosophical thought, science, and technical advancement during the last years of the 17th century in order to emphasize the close relationship between the salon of the Marquise and the life of the mind.

Finally, the third part of the book, *Le Lambertinage: Une Nouvelle préciosité*, using the excellent method developed by Frédéric Deloffre in his *Marivaux et le marivaudage, une nouvelle préciosité*, systematically analyzes the milieu and style. This literary-stylistic analysis demonstrates that the salon of the Marquise and her works were at the heart of a second *préciosité*. Roger Marchal underscores the idea that Mme de Lambert played a primary role in the passage from the first to the second préciosité, from a social feminism to a more intellectual feminism. Moreover, he shows that her salon, cradle of the *Encycloepedia*, assured the transition between the classical age and the Enlightenment. He also scrupulously and thoroughly confirms the filiation between the *lambertinage*, or the Marquise's metaphysics of the heart, and *marivaudage*.

This work is a magnificent detailed document on the reciprocal fecundity between a literary milieu and the formation of the minds. It is also a milestone in the study of the evolution of 18th-century thought and taste. By its solidity, its style, and its elegance, Roger Marchal's book is a definitive work of reference for all scholars of the period.—Marie-José Fassiotto.

Julien Offray de La Mettrie (1709–1751)

La Mettrie, Julien Offray de. *Oeuvres philosophiques* (Corpus des oeuvres philosophiques en langue française.) Paris: Fayard, 1987.

Rev. (with another work) by Charles Porset in *Lendemains*, 16 (1991), 157–58.

Gottfried Wilhelm Leibniz (1646–1716)

Brown, Clifford. *Leibniz and Strawson: A New Essay in Descriptive Metaphysics.* Hamden, CT: Philosophia, 1990. Pp. 120; bibliography.

Rev. by F. Wilson in *Choice*, 28 (1991), 792.

Kulstad, Mark. *Leibniz on Appreciation, Consciousness and Reflection.* Munich: Philosophia, 1991. Pp. 182.

Sleigh, R. C. *Leibniz & Arnauld: A Commentary on Their Correspondence.* London and New Haven, CT: Yale U. Press, 1990. Pp. xv + 237.

Rev. (favorably) by C. J. Shields in *Choice*, 28 (1991), 1328–29.

Wilson, Catherine. *Leibniz's Metaphysics. A Historical and Comparative Study* Manchester, UK: Manchester U. Press, 1989.

Rev. by Dominique Berlios in *Etudes philosophiques*, (1991), 273–274.

Jakob Michael Reinhold Lenz (1751–1792)

Lenz, Jakob Michael Reinhold. *Dramen des Sturm und Drang.* Edited by Erich Unglaub. Munich: Piper, 1988. Pp. 456.

Rev. by John Guthrie in *Modern Language Revew*, 86 (1991), 1049–50.

Alain René Lesage (1668–1747)

Cook, Malcolm. *Lesage* Gil Blas. (Critical Guides to French Texts, 72.) London: Grant & Cutler, 1988. Pp. 75. Cf. *ECCB*, n.s. 16, VI:409; 14, VI:348.

Gotthold Ephraim Lessing (1729–1781)

Lessing, Gotthold Ephraim. *Werke und Briefe.* Edited by Wilfried Barner and others. Volume I: *Werke 1743–1750.* Edited by Jürgen Stenzel; Volume VIII: *Werke 1774–1778.* Edited by Arno Schilson. (Bibliothek deutscher Klassiker.) Frankfurt am Main: Deutscher Klassiker Verlag, 1989. Pp. 1459; 1188.

Rev. by H. B. Nisbet in *Modern Language Review*, 86 (1991), 243–44.

Charles Joseph, Prince de Ligne (1735–1814)

Ligne, Charles Joseph Prince de. *Coup d'Fil at Beloeil and a Great Number of European Gardens.* Edited and translated by Basil Guy. Berkeley, CA: U. of California Press, 1991. Pp. xviii + 297; appendices; bibliography; figures; frontispiece; illustrations; maps.

Having already published widely on Prince de Ligne, Professor Basil Guy is giving, in his own English translation, a critical edition of the French last version (1795) published in Dresden, revised by Prince de Ligne of *Coud d'Oeil sur Beloeil*, treatise dedicated to his Gardens and many others in Europe, of which the first rare edition was published in 1781 and the best known in 1786 in Belgium. Born in 1735 in Brussels, a subject of the Hapsburg, Ligne received a French education. Exiled in Vienna and ruined by the French Revolution, he tried to make a living with his pen. As many of his contemporaries, Ligne was preoccupied with the subject of gardens. Having redesigned the gardens of his family estate near Mons in Belgium, with the help of the architect Bélanger, he is said to have advised Marie-Antionette at the Petit-Trianon, and he had visited the most important gardens in Europe before the French Revolution.

A short preface explains the choice of the 1795 edition, the relevance of the subject to present criticism of the eighteenth century, and the fact that not only Beloeil, Ligne's estate, including eighteenth century garderns, still belongs to his descendants, but also that many of the gardens he describes still exist.

In an Introduction of 66 pages Professor Guy gives the main aspects of Ligne's life, interests, and thought in general, and especially in regard with the theory of gardens: "Like his contemporaries, the Prince de Ligne was not slow to seek through garden design, the answers to Philosophical questions about such a concept and perhaps to find those answers in the picturesque rearrangement of nature (p. 48)." It is divided into six parts: "Ligne and the Picturesque," "The Achievement of the Coup d'Oeil," "Remarks on the Translation." Ligne's text of the 1795 edition (198 pages) then follows with an epigraph to Horace, a short preface, and a one page poem to French Abbé Delille who was famous in his time and wrote poetry on gardens where Beloeil was mentioned. The book is divided into four parts. The first part "Coup d'Oeil at Beloeil" (33 paragraphs) and the second part "The Surroundings" (31 paragraphs are devoted to Beloeil, the castle, the park and the land around them). The third part "Coup d'Oeil at the Handsomest Sites and Natural Gardens" (97 paragraphs) deals with gardens Ligne visited in France, Austria, Romania, Switzerland, Provence, and finally Crimea where the prince was given land by Catherine the Great. Part IV (171 paragraphs) is "filled with the aphorisms that have established Ligne's reputation" (Introduction, p. 20), and takes the reader to various parts of England, France, Austria, Poland, etc.

According to Professor Guy, "the prince bridges the classicizing Eighteenth century and the Romantic movement, summing up in his work and his life the transition from one age to the other (Introduction, p. 17).

The appendices contain a comparison between the 1786 and 1795 editions and a complete list of the gardens in the *Coup d'Oeil*, with their location, the dates of creation, the architects, and the present condition. There is an exhaustive bibliography and an index. The text is enhanced by numerous illustrations going back to the eighteenth century and taken from many libraries in Europe and in the United States. The translation is thorough.

Chosen as one of the books that the University of California Press (founded in 1893) is printing to celebrate its centennial, *Coup d'Oeil at Beloeil* is not only an art book but also the excellent work by a consummate scholar of the eighteenth century.—Madeleine Rousseau Raaphorst.

Ligne, Charles Joseph, Prince de. *Lettres et pensées du Prince de Ligne d'après l'édition de Madame de Staël*. Edited by Raymond Trousson. (Collection In-texte.) Paris: Tallandier, 1989. Pp. 387.

Rev. (severely) by Roger Pearson in *French Studies*, 45 (1991), 469–70; by Dennis Wood in *Modern Language Review*, 86 (1991), 726.

George Lillo (1693–1739)

Wallace, David. "Bourgeois Tragedy or Sentimental Melodrama? The Significance of George Lillo's *The London Merchant*." *Eighteenth-Century Studies*, 25 (1991–92), 123–43.

By "establishing a relationship between a socio-economic ethic and a private moralilty, [the play] provides the foundation for a new dramatic form: modern naturalist tragedy."

John Locke (1632–1704)

Ayers, Michael. *Locke*. Vol. I: *Epistemology*. Vol. II: *Ontology*. London and New York: Routledge, 1991. Pp. vi + 341; bibliography; notes.

Rev. (favorably) by F. Wilson in *Choice*, 29 (1991), 1407.

Dunn, John. *La Pensée politique de John Locke. Une Présentation historique de la thèse exposée dans les deux traités du gouvernement*. Translated by Jean-François Baillon. (Leviatan.) Paris: Presses Universitaires de France, 1991. Pp. 288.

Fox, Christopher. *Locke and the Scriblerians: Identity and Conciousness in Early Eighteenth-Century Britain*. Berkeley, CA: U. of California Press, 1988. Pp. x + 174; bibliography. Cf. *ECCB*, n.s. 16, VI:411; 15, VI:364; 14, VI:350–52.

Rev. by Kevin L. Cope in *South Atlantic Review*, 56 (May 1991), 137–140; by Carolyn Williams in *Modern Language Review*, 86 (1991), 669–70.

Hutchison, Ross. *Locke in France: 1688–1734*. (Studies on Voltaire and the Eighteenth Century, 290) Oxford: The Voltaire Foundation at the Taylor Institution, 1991. Pp. ix + 251.

Jamais il me fut peut-être plus sage, plus métodique, un Logicien plus exact que Mr. Locke . . .

This is the judgment which opens the thirteenth of Voltaire's *Lettres philosophiques* and which dominated the French intellectual community for the balance of the 18th century. But how did Locke acquire such a preeminent position among French intellectuals?

The purpose of Hutchison's book is precisely to answer that question. "It is perhaps surprising," he remarks, "that there has been no systematic study of the reception and influence of Locke's ideas; the majority of works on the Enlightenment, in so far as they mention these topics at all, take them very much for granted" (p. 1). Hutchison's project, then, is to supply such a 'systematic study,' to explore in considerable detail the diffusion and impact, 'the reception and influence of Locke's ideas' in France, during the late 17th and early 18th centuries.

Hutchison limits his investigation to the period from the publication of the *Abrégé*—an abriged French version of Locke's *Essay*—in 1688, to the publication of Voltaire's *Lettres philosophiques* in 1734. For, by the latter date, Locke's status was secure. In order to support this claim, Hutchison considers the following topics: "political theory and the natural law tradition, concentrating on the decisive role of the scholar and translator Jean Barbeyrac; the implications of Lockean doctrines for questions about the nature of language and the methods that should be used to teach Latin, examining in particular the work of Du Marsais; more general pedagogical questions and their relation to Locke's theory of ideas, as discussed especially by the Jesuit Buffier; and the whole question of animal souls and thinking matter, set as fully as possible into its contemporary context" (pp. 1,2). In each case Hutchison shows how Locke's ideas were *used* by French intellectuals to further their own critical agendas, thereby transforming the notion of 'reception and influence' from the passive to the active.

Voltaire was likewise interested in using Locke as well as in introducing him to a wider French audience. Hutchison offers a detailed analysis of the thirteenth of Voltaire's *Lettre philsophiques*, which is largely devoted to a presentation of Locke's ideas; but he also shows (in part, by comparing the thirteenth letter with an earlier draft—the 'Lettre sur l'ame') how Voltaire "decisively appropriated Locke for the side of radical and reforming views on central philosophical questions. His focus is almost entirely on three areas, all of which had already been often mentioned in French discussion of Locke, but which Volatire highlights with new clarity . . . [First, Locke's methodology; second, innate ideas; and third, 'thinking matter.'] Locke is the wisest product of an England which Voltaire is concerned to hold up (for the instruction of those who oppose intellectual liberty in France as a model of tolerance, enlightenment, and unfettered pursuit of truth." (p. 222)

As this passage suggests, Hutchison's account of how Locke acquired a reputation for wisdom among French intellectuals is linked, in the end, to Voltaire's campaign for tolerance and intellectual liberty. It is an account, then, of the appropriation of Locke by French polemicists no less than of the 'reception and influence' of his ideas.—Howard R. Cell.

Locke, John. *The Correspondence of John Locke.* Edited by E. S. de Beer. Vol. 8. Oxford: Clarendon Press, 1989. Cf. *ECCB*, n.s.15, VI:364.

Rev. by Michel Malherbe in *Etudes philosophiques,* (1991), 255.

Locke, John. *Locke on Money.* Edited with Ancillary Manuscripts, an Introduction, Critical apparatus, and Notes by Patrick Hyde Kelly. 2 vols. (The Clarendon Works of John Locke.) New York: Oxford U. Press; Oxford: Clarendon Press, 1991. Pp. 664; bibliography; 617–38.

Pitassi, Marie-Cristina. *Le philosophe et l'Ecriture. John Locke exégète de Saint Paul (Cahiers de la Revue de Théologie et de Philosophie 14.)* Lausanne: Lausanne Press, 1990.

Rev. by Hubert Bost in *Etudes thélogiques et religieuses,* (1991), 453–454.

A scrupulous study of Locke's *Paraphrases and Notes on the Epistles of St. Paul and Essay on the Understanding of St. Paul's Epistles* (published 1705–1707). Pitassi corrects the common image of Locke as a Deist.

Yolton, John W. *Locke and French Materialism*. New York: Oxford U. Press; Oxford: Clarendon Press, 1991. Pp. 239; bibliography.

Rev. by Ross Hutchinson in *French Studies*, 46 (1992), 72–73; (favorably) by H. Storl in *Choice*, 29 (1991), 610.

An outgrowth of the Yolton's *Thinking Matter: Materialism in Eighteenth-Century Britain* (1984), this meticulous study confirms the author's authority as an historian of eighteenth-century ideas. While covering the period 1700–1770, it concentrates on mid-century debate as revealed in a vast library of scientific, journalistic and philosophical writing.

The introductory chapter characterizes the book as "an attempt to trace the transmission to France of [Locke's] suggestion [that God could superadd the power of thought to matter], with reactions to it" (3). Although Locke's suggestion is only a "conceptual aside" (209) in his *Essay Concerning Human Understanding*, Yolton examines its "adventures" (3), how it was given a central role in the wider controversy surrounding the mind-body problem. Yolton thus does not propose a comprehensive study of Locke's influence on French thought. However, his limited exercise provides remarkable insights into the whole process of Continental intellectual debate at the time.

Just as the British discussion of Locke's suggestion was taken up on the Continent, so the debate in France was echoed in intellectual entres outside the country. In this sense the book's title is slightly misleading. Periodicals published in Switzerland and Holland are included in Yolton's survey, as are books by authors writing outside France.

The book's introduction describes early diffusion in France of Locke's ideas, even before the publication in 1700 of Coste's translation of the *Essay*. By 1720 Locke was already "an important author" (5). However, the attacks on Locke which intensified during the decade of the 1750s are Yolton's principal concern.

Chapter 1 elucidates the main elements of the mind-body debate. While certain notions are universally accepted (correspondence of perceptions to changes in sense organs, importance of perception in the formulation of ideas), authorities disagreed concerning the link between bodies and ideas. Three hypotheses were presented to explain the correspondence: direct physical influence (the materialist view), occasional causes (divinely-inspired coincidence of sensation and perception), and pre-established harmony (mind programmed by God to represent the pre-ordained patterns). The dogmatic determinism of the latter two hypotheses is set against the radical materialism of the first, with which Locke was associated.

Chapters 2 to 8 examine how these hypotheses were presented, circumscribed and modified in the course of the mind-body debate. Texts by Voltaire, Condillac, d'Argens, Hume, Berkeley, Diderot, La Mettrie and d'Holbach, to name only the most eminent writers, are analyzed in detail, as are other documents by a host of minor contributors (most notably D. R. Boullier). Locke's thought permeated the mind-body debate; his name arose whenever writers addressed the problem.

It may be objected that Yolton has insufficiently stressed the extent to which the philosophical controversy he chronicles is determined by ideological rivalry among its participants. He refers on numerous occasions, especially in the introductory and concluding paragraphs of his central chapters, to the place of this controversy in the wider conflict between representatives of traditional Christian orthodoxy and the younger generation of modern thinkers. However, he underplays the particular inspiration of the latter group, hungry for influence and authority, anxious to recast thought patterns in their own mould, possessed of sparkling erudition and eclectic method. This otherwise exemplary study hesitates to remind readers more forcefully of the deeper motivations of the mind-body debate by linking it to the broader dynamics of the ferocious ideological conflict in which writers were engaged.—Dennis F. Essar.

Gabriel Bonnot de Mably (1709–1785)

Mably, Gabriel Bonnot de. *De l'Etude de l'histoire: a Monseigneur le prince de Parme*. Paris: Fayard, 1988. Pp. 405.

Rev. (with another work) by Charles Porset in *Landemains*, 16 (1991), 157–58.

James Macpherson (1736–1796)

Gaskill, Howard (ed.). *Ossian Revisited*. Edinburgh, Scotland: Edinburgh U. Press, 1991. Pp. ix + 250.

In the *Journey to the Western Islands of Scotland*, Johnson established firmly what he took to be the terms of the debate about the Ossian Poems:

I believe they never existed in any other form than that which we have seen. The editor, or author, never could shew the original; nor can it be shewn by any other; to revenge reasonable incredulity, by refusing evidence, is a degree of insolence, with which the world is not yet acquainted; and stubborn audacity is the last refuge of guilt.

In Johnson's hand, the literary question becomes a moral one, and he insists on the stark absolutes of guilt and innocence, deception and truth. However, in the hands of more recent critics, moral absolutes have given way to historical empathy as they have tried to reconstruct Macpherson's work within his own frame of reference. Among the most recent work, one thinks, for example, of Fiona Stafford's *The Sublime Savage: James Macpherson and the Poems of Ossian* (1988) or of Paul de Gategno's *James Macpherson* (1989) in the Twayne series. Both books survey Macpherson's entire poetic career, and both situate Macpherson within the context of eighteenth-century culture. Howard Gaskill's fine collection of essays follows this path, with its particular concern being the different contexts in which *Ossian* has been or should be read.

Gaskill's own introductory essay focusses on the authenticity dispute, as he asks the inevitable question: "Why then should we persist in taking a Johnsonian view of Macpherson and his poetry?" (p. 15). He makes a strong case for laying the Johnsonian view aside and moving on to the kind of historical empathy that the contributors to the volume demonstrate. Following this lead, the opening pair of essays looks backward and forward from Macpherson's time: Donald E. Meek helpfully discusses the Gaelic ballad tradition in Scotland that underlies *Ossian*, and Fiona Stafford explicates Wordsworth's sometimes puzzling and contradictory responses to the poems. There follows another pair of essays that situate *Ossian* in foreign contexts: Uwe Boker examines the distribution and reception of the poems in Germany, while Paul de Gategno analyzes Jefferson's reading of them. The remaining five essays all concentrate on various British contexts. John Vladimir Price shrewdly assesses the means by which the poems were introduced into the canon of the Scottish Enlightenment, with their appeal to both the old and the new. Steve Rizza provides a close and thorough reading of Hugh Blair's *Critical Dissertation*, working up from the premise that it is a "tightly woven set of arguments" (p. 144). David Raynor deftly explains Hume's changing response to the poems as he moves from early enthusiasm to later skepticism. John Dwyer offers the book's most wide-ranging cultural assessment of *Ossian*, arguing that "the real significance of the Ossianic poems resides less in their cultural and historical roots than in the way in which they reflected the values and spoke to the needs of eighteenth-century men and women" (p. 165). Those values, he maintains, center on sentimental discourse, and *Ossian* powerfully articulates the aesthetic and social ideals of that discourse. The concluding essay by Richard Sher is an authoritative discussion of the dispute occurring in the 1780s between Thomas Percy and Adam Ferguson over the authenticity of the poems' sources. Sher's essay is a fitting conclusion to the collection because it demonstrates vividly the extent to which national prejudice underlies the whole debate over authenticity. Johnson's high moral ground has to be seen in this rather unflattering light.

Ossian Revisited is an attractive and stimulating collection, and it points up the need for further work on two major projects. First, we still do not have an integrated view of Macpherson's total career that would link his work in poetry, history, and politics. To understand the poetry fully, it would be necessary to see how they are related to the other facets of his career—especially if we are going to treat matters of political or cultural ideology in them. Second, we need a systematic comparative study of how the poems were received in various European and American contexts. It is clear from this volume—as well as from previous work—that *Ossian* served widely varying cultural interests. On the one hand, Jefferson could see in the poems support for his revolutionary democratic vision; on the other, the Edinburgh literati could see in them support for a fundamentally aristocratic society. What would be valuable would be to bring these and other readings into relationship with each other. Perhaps by defining the cultural work the poems perform we may not only put the question of authenticity into the background, but also be able to arrive at a fuller appreciation of what the *Ossian* poems actually are.—Jeffrey Smitten.

Bernard Mandeville (1670–1733)

Mandeville, Bernard. *The Fable of the Bees: or, Private Vices, Publick Benefits.* Edited by F. B. Kaye. 2 vols. Indianapolis: Liberty Classics, 1988. Pp. ii + cxlvi + 412; v + 481.

Rev. (with another work) by M. M. Goldsmith in *The Scriblerian*, 23 (1991), 251–54.

Mary de la Rivere Manley (1663–1724)

Rivere Manley, Mary de la. *New Atlantis.* Edited by Rosalind Ballaster. London: Pickering & Chatto, 1991. Pp. xxviii + 305; bibliography; chronology.

This modern edition of Mrs. Mary de la Rivere Manley's *The New Atlantis* will be welcomed by scholars working in several disciplines. It makes easily accessible the major work of the leading woman writer of the first decade of the eighteenth-century, adding another alternative to the usual canonical texts of Defoe, Swift, and Addison. Historians studying the reign of Queen Anne have known about and referred to *The New Atlantis*, but before this edition have had little opportunity to compare it with the work with which it is usually cited, Swift's *Conduct of the Allies*. The impact of Manley's longer allegorical attack on Marleborough, the Junto, and on the Duchess of Marlborough in particular will be much more easily understandable with the text readily available.

Rosalind Ballaster has done a sound job in editing the text for Pickering's Women's Classics Series. She has used the two volume in one edition of 1709, with some modernization in punctuation and "appearance" (p. xxii), presumably mainly the elimination of italics. There is extensive annotation, not only identifying the personae of the story from the several keys to the text published with later editions, but also identifying eighteenth-century and mythological terms. No doubt these latter are prescribed by the editors of the series, for the sake of that mythic general reader who might not know, for example, who Jupiter is (p. 269, n. 4), or what a cabaret or a dernier is (p. 271, nn. 32, 33). Would such a person really pick up *The New Atlantis* for a good read?

In her introduction Ballaster gives a brief account of Manley's life and the circumstances of her writing *The New Atlantis*, including also a chronology of her life, a bibliography of her work, and a bibliography of secondary works. The editor argues that Manley maintained a "feminocentric" view (p. xiii), though she often, especially in *The New Atlantis*, sacrificed her "clear-sighted recognition of women's material and ideological oppression" (p. xix) to the Tory cause. Throughout her commentary, however, Ballaster is more reliable on the literary aspects of Manley's works than on the political context in which she operated and wrote—the introduction, for example, is not particularly satisfactory, nor always accurate, in explaining the complex Parliamentary politics of Anne's reign. The reader who wants to understand the world in which *The New Atlantis* made such a stir would be well-advised to look further afield than Ballaster's account.—Barbara Brandon Schnorrenberg.

Pierre Carlet de Chamblain de Marivaux (1688–1763)

Coulet, Henri, Jean Ehrard and Françoise Rubellin. *Marivaux d'hier, Marivaux d'aujourd'hui.* Paris: Editions du CNRS, 1991. Pp. 232.

Howells, Robin. "Structure and Meaning in the *Incipit* of Marivaux's Comedies." *Modern Language Review*, 86 (1991), 839–51.

The first two scenes in each of the 35 extant comedies prepare for the play that followed it: "The Duo; Distinction and Commonality; Project or Test; Disguise or Trick; Metadiscourse."

Marivaux d'hier, Marivaux d'aujourd'hui. Actes du Colloque de Riom (8–9 octobre 1988) sous la direction de Henri Coulet et Jean Ehrard; Actes du colloque de Lyon (22 avril 1988) sous la direction de Françoise Rubellin. Paris: Edition du Centre National de la Recherche scientifique, 1991. Pp. 232.

More than the tercentenary of his birth, 1988 marks the critical turning point in the posthumous career of Pierre Carlet de Chamblain de Marivaux (1688–1763), in short, the moment when his stature as a dominant French rococo figure (along with Montesquieu and Voltaire) is formally acknowledged. Official consecration came not only via the establishment of a Société Marivaux (whose first annual *Revue Marivaux* will not appear until 1990, however) but also in the form of a commemorative symposium, in fact, two: first in Lyon and later Riom. Both meetings are included in the present volume, but in reverse order since the Riom gathering (October 8–9) chose as its theme "Marivaux and our time"—a double orientation clearly expressed in the title of the collected papers. As for the participants, many of whom attended both celebrations, they represent some of the most visible among today's "Marivaldians" in France (9 in all), Italy (3) and America (1). It will therefore not come as a surprise to learn nearly every contribution is stimulating, instructive and well presented.

The eleven Riom papers on Marivaux in his time range from a depiction of that Auvergnat town in the eighteenth century, while, that is, the young Pierre Carlet was growing up there (J. Ehrard and B. Dompnier), to an examination of the author's political, religious and social ideas (H. Coulet, M. R. Ansalone, B. Didier, M. Gilot), to his presentation of contemporary reality (F. Rubellin, G. Bonaccorso), to reflections on the Marivaldian themes of coquetry (M. Matucci) and disguise (J. d'Hondt), even to a character portrait of Marivaux based on his occasional remarks and those of contemporaries (Wm. Trapnell). The eight Lyon communications divide equally between applied commentary (to wit: Marivaux in America, in Italy today, his improving image in French school manuals over the last 150 years, practical problems in editing his works—by F. Deloffre, M. R. Ansalone, F. Rubellin, H. Coulet respectively) and theoretical remarks on new, still untried ways for interpreting *La Vie de Marianne* (B. Dider), the role of Marivaux's three journals in preparing his two great, unfinished novels (M. Matucci) and, finally, two general considerations on our author's theater (C. Bonfils, M. Gilot). In point of fact, the latter two papers and J. d'Hondt's on disguise are the only ones to pay serious attention to Marivaux's work for the stage. To the extent the others raise literary questions (and most of the articles do) they stress the journalistic creations or the novels, the youthful ones as well as the *Marianne* plus *Le Payson parvenu*, in a more limited way. Thus, the present volume cannot pretend to "cover" the ever-growing field of Marivaux studies, a claim it would never think of making. But what the volume has undertaken it has accomplished for the most part with insight, originality, and infectious enthusiasm.—Philip Koch.

Perfezou, Laurent. *Les Fausses Confidences. Marivaux.* (L'Oeuvre au clair, 21.) Paris: Bordas, 1991. Pp. 95.

See sec. 5 for review.

Trapnell, William H. *Eavesdropping in Marivaux.* (Histoires des idées et critique littéraire, 254.) Geneva: Droz, 1987. Pp. 120; bibliography. Cf. *ECCB*, n.s. 16, VI:416; 15, VI:369; 14, VI:357; 13, VI:476–77.

Rev. (favorably) by Ronald Rosbottom in *Diderot Studies,* 24 (1991), 228–29.

Jean François Marmontel (1725–1799)

Revaz, Françiose. "Rhétorique du récit. Un Débat narratologique toujours actuel: Marmontel contre Le Bossu." *Etudes de lettres,* (October–December 1991), 113–31.

Studies the points of view of Pére Le bossu (in *Traité du poème épique*, 1675) and Marmontel (in *Elements de littérature*, 1787) concerning epic poetry.

Andrew Marvell (1621–1678)

Chambers, A. B. *Andrew Marvell and Edmund Waller: Seventeenth–Century Praise and Restoration Satire.* University Park, PA: Pennsylvania State U. Press, 1991. Pp. viii + 208; bibliography.

Rev. in *PMLA,* 105 (1990), 1408.

Kermode, Frank, and Keith Walker (eds.). *Andrew Marvell.* (The Oxford Authors.) New York and Oxford: Oxford U. Press, 1990. Pp. xvi + 362; bibliography.

Rev. by A. A. Labriola in *Choice*, 29 (1991), 283.

Kermode, Frank, and Keith Walker (eds.). *Andrew Marvell.* (The Oxford Authors.) Oxford: Oxford U. Press, 1991. Pp. 400.

Rev. in *PMLA,* 105 (1990), 1416.

Molière (1622–1673)

Knutson, Harold C. *The Triumph of Wit: Molière and Restoration Comedy.* Columbus, OH: Ohio State U. Press, 1988. Pp. xii + 192; bibliography; 24 illustrations; 5 plates. Cf. *ECCB*, n.s. 15, VI:372; 14, VI:357.

Rev. by Christopher Smith in *Modern Language Review*, 86 (1991), 453–54.

Lodge, Anthony. "Molière's Peasants and the Norms of Spoken French." *Neuphilologische Mitteillungen*, 92 (1991), 485–99.

Lady Mary Wortley Montagu (1689–1762)

Horwarth, Peter. "Name and Location of Lady Mary Wortley Montagu's 'Rascian Town.' " *Notes and Queries*, 236 (1991), 189.

Lew, Joseph W. "Lady Mary's Portable Seraglio." *Eighteenth-Century Studies*, 24 (1991), 432–50.

Her letters to women critique both Ottoman and British culture.

Charles Louis de Secondat, Baron de Montesquieu (1689–1755)

Carrithers, David W. "Not So Virtuous Republics: Montesquieu, Venice, and the Theory of Aristocratic Republicanism." *Journal of the History of Ideas*, 52, (1991), 245–268.

The author's claim is that a larger area of Montesquieu's thought has been neglected by scholars, i.e. the part in which Montesquieu described hereditary aristocracies. He often saw such governments leading to despotism.

Ehrard, Jean. "Esthétique et philosophie des lumières: La 'Chaine' de *L'Esprit des lois.*" *Landemains*, 16 (1991), 64–72.

Sophisticated article which aims to prove that, despite what critics have said, there is a *chaine* in *L'Esprit des lois*.

Gargett, Graham. "Jacob Vernet editeur de Montesquieu: La Première edition de *L'Esprit des lois.*" *Revue dhistoire littéraire de la France*, 91 (1991), 890–900.

Throws new (and unfavorable) light on the personality of the Genevan protestant minister.

Rosso, Corrado. *La réception de Montesquieu, ou Les silences de la harpe éolienne.* Pisa: Editirice Liberia Goliada, 1989.

Rev. (tepidly) by W. H. Barber in *French Studies*, 45 (1991), 463–64; by Paulette Carrive in *Etudes philosophiques*, (1991), 558–560.

Shackleton, Robert. *Essays on Montesquieu and on the Enlightenment.* Edited by David Gilson and Martin Smith. Oxford: The Voltaire Foundation at the Taylor Institution, 1988. Pp. vii + 498. Cf. *ECCB*, n.s. 16, VI:422; 14, VI:361.

Rev. (with another work) by Sheila Mason in *Modern Language Review*, 86 (1991), 209–10.

André Morellet (1727–1819)

Morellet, André. *Lettres d'André Morellet.* Publiées et annotées par Dorothy Medlin, Jean-Claude David and Paul Leclerc. Vol. I: *1759–1785, Lettres 1–262.* Oxford: The Voltaire Foundation at the Taylor Institution, 1991. Pp. xlvi + 624; appendices; illustrations.

The Voltaire Foundation has made available to Englightenment scholars a whole series of critical editions of important French-language correspondence: it has published the Besterman, Leigh and Smith editions of the letters of Voltaire, Rousseau and Helvétius, is pursuing the Dainard edition of those of Mme de Graffigny, and has announced a forthcoming edition of the Bayle correspondence. This catalogue has now been enriched by the first of three volumes to be devoted to the letters of the abbé André Morellet (1727–1819), and with it the debt of gratitude owed by 18th-century specialists continues to grow. They will already be familiar with the rigor of the critical apparatus, which need not therefore be described in detail here.

A man of letters of secondary importance, as his editors concede, Morellet is nevertheless a significant figure in the second half of the French Enlightenment. Cosmopolitan approach and catholic in taste, he was in close touch not only with the Encyclopedists in France, but also with the English-speaking world (Hume, Garrick and Franklin). He played an active role in many major controversies of his age; the inquisition, music, economics, censorship, inoculation, and penal reform all attracted his attention. These letters reveal a *philosophe*, of modest means, conscientiously and shrewdly furthering his career. We see him gathering information, exchanging manuscripts with kindred spirits, and cultivating useful relationships with men of influence.

The letters of this first volume bring us from the first surviving letters (in 1760, the abbé finds himself in the Bastille) up to his election to the French Academy in 1785. Many letters are in the municipal library in Lyon, but the editors have been diligent in tracking down others in private hands and in over seventy institutions in Europe and the USA. Only letters *by* Morellet are reproduced; letters addressed *to* him, when available, are referred to in the notes. In fact, they are seldom available. There are gaps in the Morellet letters as well; on the average about ten letters per year have survived. In this first volume, two of his correspondents between them account for virtually one half of the letters: Turgot, Morellet's classmate at the Sorbonne, and William Petty, 2nd earl of Shelburne and later marquis of Landsdowne, English statesman and patron of literature and the fine arts. We must therefore not expect insights into the day to day activities of the abbé, nor a comprehensive account of his many and varied activities. The surviving correspondence is usefully complemented by the author's *Mémoires*, relevant passages of which are referred to by the editors.

It is thus the formidable task of the annotators to give some coherence to what could have been frustratingly incomplete, disjointed and one-sided. They acquit themselves splendidly, providing the reader with authoritative information over an impressive range of issues.—Neal Johnson.

Etienne-Gabriel Morelly (fl. 1760)

Labib, Abdelaziz. "La *Basiliade*: Une Utopie orientale?" *Dix-huitième siècle*, 21 (1991), 307–20.

Arthur Murphy (1721–1805)

Ferrero, Bonnie. "Johnson, Murphy, and *Macbeth*." *Review of English Studies*, 42 (1991), 228–32.

Much of Murphy's paper in the *Gray's Inn Journal* of 1753 is borrowed from Johnson's *Miscellaneous Observations* of 1745.

Johann Karl August Musäus (1735–1787)

Musäus, Johann Karl August. *Stories by Musäus & Fouqué*. Translated from German by Thomas Carlyle. (Studies in German Literature, Linguistics & Culture, 61.) Introduction by U. Scheck. (German Romance, 1.) Columbia, SC: Camden House, 1991. Pp. 337.

Sir Isaac Newton (1642–1727)

Belcher, Zev. *Newton's Physics and the Conceptual Structure of the Scientific Revolution*. (Boston Studies in the Philosophy of Science, 127.) Boston, MA, and Dordrecht: Kluwer Academic Publishers, 1991. Pp. xviii + 588; bibliography; illustrations.

Roger North (1653–1734)

Chan, Mary. "Roger North's *Life* of Francis North." *Review of English Studies*, 42 (1991), 191–211.

A careful account of various versions of the manuscripts and of Montagu North's treatment of them.

Thomas Paine (1737–1809)

Paine, Thomas. *Les Droits de l'homme*. Introduction and translation by Bernard Vincent. Nancy: Presses Universitaires de Nancy, 1991. Pp. x + 287.

Paine's *Rights of Man* made up the essentials of the debate between Burke and himself as the controversy over the French Revolution raged across the English Channel. The first French translation by François Coulès was published as early as May 1791, hardly three months after the London February 1791 edition. A second complete edition was issued in 1792 in Paris and in 1793 in Rennes: it included the second part. For two centuries, no new translation into French appeared and Claude Mouchard's publication of *Les Droits de l'homme* (Paris: Belin, 1987) was in the François Coulès version. Bernard Vincent's contribution is therefore welcome for two reasons. First, any important work of art or of reflexion needs periodic new translations more fitted to the atmosphere of the time and in the case of the present version, many errors, approximations or awkward phrases were corrected by Vincent. Second, the 18-page introduction is a useful summary of the main arguments exchanged between Burke and Paine, their validity, the extent of the author's good faith and the impact and veracity of their conclusions. It also sums up the problem of the relations between the French and English governments from the storming of the Bastille to Louis XVI's execution in January 1793 and enlightens the problems of the stormy relations between the Jacobin minority in Britain and the powers that were. The reactions of public opinion burning the effigy of the author together with his book, the king's attorney charging Paine with trying to uproot the people's love for their constitution, the heavy prison sentences against H. D. Symonds, a London publisher and the printer Fische Palmer are in keeping with Paine's perpetual banishment from his native country by court order. Bernard Vincent's many works on the subject contribute much to popularizing Paine and the 1991 creation of a French Association. Thomas Paine is a harbinger of a new lasting interest for Paine in French historiography.—Jean Rivière.

Thomas Parnell (1679–1718)

Parnell, Thomas. *Collected Poems of Thomas Parnell*. Edited by F. P. Lock and Claude Rawson. London and Toronto: Associated University Presses; Newark, DE: U. of Delaware Press, 1989. Pp. 717. Cf. *ECCB*, n.s. 16, VI:423; 15, VI:379.

Rev. (favorably) by J. D. Fleeman in *Notes and Queries*, 236 (1991), 388–389; by Ann Cline Kelly in *Journal of English and Germanic Philology*, 90 (1991), 570–72.

Blaise Pascal (1623–1662)

Norman, Buford. *Portraits of Thought: Knowledge, Methods, and Styles in Pascal*. Columbus, OH: Ohio State U. Press, 1989. Pp. xx + 236.

Rev. by Richard Parish in *Modern Language Review*, 86 (1991), 454–55.

Thomas Percy (1729–1811)

Davis, Bertram H. *Thomas Percy: A Scholar-Cleric in the Age of Johnson*. Philadelphia, PA: U. of Pennsylvania Press (distributed through London: American U. Publishers Group), 1989. Pp. xi + 361; frontispiece; illustrations. Cf. *ECCB*, n.s. 16, VI:424; 15, VI:380.

Rev. by W. E. K. Anderson in *Notes and Queries*, 236 (1991), 235; (with another work) by Allan Ingram in *Modern Language Review*, 86 (1991), 404–06; (favorably) by J. T. Scanlan in *Religion & Literature*, 23 (1991), 93–96.

Hester Thrale Piozzi (1741–1821)

Piozzi, Hester Lynch. *The Piozzi Letters: Correspondence of Hester Lynch Piozzi, 1784–1821 (formerly Mrs. Thrale)*. Vol. I: *1784–1791*. Edited by Edward A. Bloom and Lillian D. Bloom. London and Toronto: Associated University Presses; Newark, DE: U. of Delaware Press, 1989. Pp. 417; illustrations; portraits. Cf. *ECCB*, n.s. 16, VI:425; 15, VI:381.

Rev. by Allan Ingram in *Modern Language Review*, 86 (1991), 406–07; (with reservations and another work) by A. F. T. Lurcock in *Notes and Queries*, 236 (1991), 113–15; by Claude Rawson in *Journal of English and Germanic Philology*, 90 (1991), 437–39.

Piozzi, Hester Lynch. *The Piozzi Letters: Correspondence of Hester Lynch Piozzi, 1784–1821 (formerly Mrs. Thrale)*. Vol. II: *1792–1821*. Edited by Edward A. Bloom and Lillian D. Bloom. Newark, DE: U. of Delaware Press (distributed through Cranbury, NJ, and London: Associated University Presses), 1991. Pp. 592; illustrations.

Rev. (favorably) by N. Fruman in *Choice*, 29 (1991), 448; (favorably) by Pat Rogers in *TLS*, (Sept. 27, 1991), 6.

It may be Hester Lynch Piozzi's fate to exist in a more or less permanent state of rediscovery. In reading about Johnson, we encounter Piozzi's *Anecdotes* and the Johnson/Mrs. Thrale correspondence, but there our reading stops. Piozzi's other works, such as *Retrospection* or *British Synonymy*, seem destined to retain readers only among specialists, despite calls by William McCarthy and Margaret Anne Doody to take Piozzi, the professional author, more seriously. If, however, Piozzi ever does move into the foreground of eighteenth-century studies, it may be because of the fine and welcome edition of her letters by Edward A. and Lillian D. Bloom.

The Blooms have gathered, edited, and annotated over half of Piozzi's 2,000 extant letters, starting at 1784, the year of Johnson's death. The letters in Volume II are those of Hester Piozzi in her fifties. The Streatham period is now many years in the past, as we see when Piozzi has trouble remembering who Bennet Langton was, exactly. She lives now mostly at Brynbella, her Welsh estate, patching up uneasy alliances with her estranged daughters and fulminating over the outrages of the French Revolution. The kindly, fretful, valetudinarian Gabriel Piozzi looks out around the margins of the letters, smiling bravely through his gout. And, from her sidelined position, Hester Piozzi gives the impression of one who has lived long, and been appalled, or at best grimly amused, by most of it.

For a variety of reasons, the letter may be the form best suited to Piozzi's talent and temperament. She is an acute observer, intellectually tough and independent, and has a flair for elegant, evocative comic English prose. "I have been blamed and hooted many a Time when I have not deserved it—but the Blamers and Hooters come by the worst at last, and the hunted Duck oyls her Feathers after all quietly by the Side of her old Canal" (p. 344). "I like the Sight of London looking like an Anthill suddenly stirred with a stick" (p. 480). "Truth is always cold from being naked perhaps" (p. 532). She is, furthermore, incapable of the urbane detachment of a Walpole; she fills her quiet, rural, aristocratic life with a remarkable amount of Sturm und Drang, and then turns a sardonic eye on herself for doing so. Reading through the letters, in fact, gives one the impression of discovering the raw material of an unusually contentious, convoluted, and downright cranky Jane Austen novel.

Despite the richness of the Blooms' collection, this is not a complete set of Piozzi's letters. Besides those already easily attainable in print and those the editors could not get permission to publish, the Blooms refrain from printing some of the correspondence because they find the letters inconsequential or redundant. It would be preferable to have all the available letters before us and make such judgments for ourselves. At the very least, we would like to know where the sequence of letters is incomplete and what the unpublished letters concern.

The major achievement of the editors, besides gathering Piozzi's impossibly scattered correspondence in the first place, is their annotation. The footnotes provide the historical, political, and social context of each letter for great thoroughness. The editors also serve us well by frequently quoting at length from the letter Piozzi is answering or by printing it in full. We thus, for instance, get to read the letter Cecilia Thrale wrote her mother immediately after eloping to Scotland—a social and literary performance entirely worthy of Lydia Bennet (pp. 264–65). The Blooms deserve our thanks for making these intelligent and entertaining letters readily available.—Lance E. Wilcox.

Tearle, John. *Mrs. Piozzi's Tall Young Beau, William Augustus Conway.* Rutherford, NJ: Fairleigh Dickinson U. Press (distributed through Cranbury, NJ, and London: Associated University Presses), 1991. Pp. 252; illustrations.

Hester Lynch Thrale Piozzi had more than a fair share of detractors in her day for not tending to Samuel Johnson after the death of her first husband and her marriage to an Italian singing master. Nor did the frank *Anecdotes of the Late Samuel Johnson, D.D.* enhance her reputation among the literati, especially those in Johnson's circle. In 1843 an anonymous editor added more fuel to the anti-Piozzi fire by publishing *Love Letters of Mrs. Piozzi, written when she was eighty, to (Wm) Augustus Conway,* the man in question, an actor and the natural son of the Marquis of Hertford who attracted Hester Piozzi's patronage. Much debated, the authenticity and significance of these rather one-sided letters are the subjects of this book.

According to documentation in diaries and other (autograph) letters located by author John Tearle, Hester Piozzi wrote these letters when she was Conway's theatrical patron. She was approaching eighty years and he was almost thirty, a "tall young Beau." Fanned by the existence of seven apparent "love letters," rumors were rife about a liaison between the unlikely pair, who quickly became "the gossip of the Green Room and the Pump Room." According to the tally of her letters to Conway that Hester Thrale kept in her pocket diaries, it seems that very few of the seventy-five letters that she probably wrote to him have survived.

Tearle supplies a full record of Hester Piozzi's correspondence on the subject of her unabashed feelings for Conway: "This moment and not before—Wednesday, June 9th [1819]—blows Sir James Fellowes hither—And now, says he is Conway? He is your favorite! Ay replied I" (p. 93). We even learn of her concern when Conway suffers a "vile sore throat," and at one point, again in 1819, Piozzi is so affected by being with Conway that she chokes.

A major controversial point in the correspondence is Hester Piozzi's alleged proposal to Conway. Teasing out the scant evidence, Tearle concludes that "the revelations . . . are not contradicted by other circumstantial evidence" (p. 185). And there is decent evidence that Conway felt himself overwhelmed by Hester Piozzi's insistent attention (p. 89).

Although the principle weight of evidence is epistolary, slightly less quotation from the letters and more analysis by Tearle (who writes with a lively style) might have freed up the prose. At times the reader feels weighed down by the unrelenting weight of constant quotation from the letters. However, for a synopsis of contemporary chit-chat, of news about drama circles in the provinces, especially around Bath, and for information about Hester Piozzi's exacting cultural agenda, her engaged dramatic commentary, her complex relationship with Penelope Pennington, and her intrepidly arduous itinerary in the last years of her life, this book offers a fascinating cultural read.—Moira Ferguson.

Alexander Pope (1688–1744)

Corse, Taylor. " 'Another Yet the Same': Joseph Hall and *The Dunciad.*" *Notes and Queries*, 236 (1991), 183–84.

Damrosch, Leopold, Jr. *The Imaginative World of Alexander Pope.* Berkeley, CA: U. of California Press, 1987. Pp. x + 310; 3 illustrations. Cf. *ECCB*, n.s. 16, VI:425; 15, VI:382; 14, VI:367; 13, VI:488–90.

Rev. by William Bowman Piper in *The Scriblerian*, 24 (1991), 47–48.

Foster, Gretchen M. *Pope Versus Dryden: A Controversy in Letters to* The Gentleman's Magazine, *1789–1791*. (English Literary Studies Monograph Series, 44.) Victoria, Canada: U. of Victoria Press, 1989. Pp. 156. Cf. *ECCB*, n.s. 15, VI:382–83.

Rev. by James A. Winn in *The Scriblerian*, 23 (1991), 258–59; (with reservations) by David Womersley in *Notes and Queries*, 236 (1991), 235–36.

Fox, Christopher. "Pope, Perhaps, and Sextus: Skeptical Modes in *Moral Essay I*." *English Language Notes*, 29, 2 (1991), 37–48.

Traces the skepticism and the argument of Montaigne and Sextus.

Foxon, David. *Pope and the Early Eighteenth-Century Book Trade*. (Lyell Lectures in Bibliography, 1975–1976.) Revised and edited by James McLaverty. New York: Oxford U. Press; Oxford: Clarendon Press, 1990. Pp. xvii + 270; illustrations.

Rev. (favorably) by Pat Rogers in *TLS,* (Apr. 26, 1991), 5–6.

Without ever once mentioning either Roland Barthes, Michel Foucault, or Pierre Macherey, David Foxon (with the expert aid of his former student James McLaverty) has written a magesterial work on authorship and textual production. Although coming out in print for the first time fifteen years after their original appearance as lectures, Foxon's pages show no signs of being dated. The author and his collaborator have thoroughly revised and edited the original material to incorporate research done in the period between delivery and publication. And much of the intervening research by others was influenced by Foxon's unpublished Lyell Lectures. As students of Pope and bibliography know, Foxon's lectures have been available in typescript to scholars since 1976, left on deposit at several research libraries. But now we have them updated and beautifully illustrated.

Foxon's account of Pope's role in the development of the book trade is too richly detailed to be easily summarized. From the beginning of his career, Pope was one of the innovators of the developing commercial press, many of whose producers and distributors, Foxon reminds us, were women.

In the first half of his publishing career, up to the *Dunciad* of 1728, Pope dealt with established booksellers and printers, Tonson or Lintot, Watts or Bowyer, and for the first five years he depended on selling his copyrights in order to gain an income from his writing. For his Homer, starting with the *Iliad* from 1715 to 1720, he turned to publication by subscription, and thereby made his fortune; but even in the very earliest years his dealings with the trade show him taking an innovatory role. (p. 12)

Among the innovations Pope embraced were the English adoption of the continental Elzevier style of typography and the Maittaire practice of publishing classical authors in octavo format; the use in "an English book of verse in octavo . . . [of] the engraved headpieces, tailpiece, and initial letter that had previously been reserved for the pompous folio" (p. 43); and authorial supervision of illustrations and printing. Later in his career, as his control of the printing of his texts became even greater, Pope abandoned such typographical conventions as catchwords and routine capitalization of all nouns. Since his early fame outpaced the sale of his works, when Pope published his first collected *Works* of 1717, he chose to do so with the octavo format (as well as in folio) with a title at the time associated with classical ancient and modern authors. His elevation of his own literary status was supported by the appearance in the *Works* of engraved illustrations, which he also included in his translation of Homer. Because we know that his contract with Lintot for the *Iliad* gave Pope control over the design of the book, Pope must be given credit for the choices of paper, typography, and for the replacement of facing-page decorations with illustrative headpieces that often suggest interpretive commentary on the accompanying text. Foxon confesses to being tempted (rightly, I think) "by the proposition that Pope himself had a hand in designing the plates" (p. 80). We know that Pope later designed a frontispiece for the *Essay on Man*.

What may be the most significant conclusion Foxon draws from his research on Pope and the book trade serves as a challenge to the current dominant bibliographical theory of copy-text:

In the light of Pope's continual revision of accidentals, and the changes in typography that he pioneered, any idea of following the accidentals of a first edition copy-text (as some of the *Twickenham* editors did) is clearly wrong; in some cases even the punctuation is grossly unsatisfactory. Commonly accepted textual principles do not work in this situation: Greg's assumption that compositors "will normally follow their own habits or inclination," may be true of the Elizabethan printing house, but not of Pope's. Moreover, in the case of Pope the accidentals of his manuscripts, such as textual critics have thought it their duty to try and recover, are quite clearly not those which he wished to be printed, as we see by the changes he made in proof and later editions. (pp. 225–226)

McLaverty has chosen well-reproduced figures to illustrate the formats, revisions, and typography of Pope's texts over the course of his publishing career. Seventeen tables list publishers, formats, contents, and dates of Pope's works, as well as the costs and profits involved in their production. Appendices deal with "Pope and Copyright" and "Gay and Capitals and Italics." Anyone interested in Pope, the eighteenth-century book trade, or the theory and practice of textual bibliography will find Foxon and McLaverty's work indispensable.—Vincent Carretta.

Furbank, P. N., and W. R. Owens. "Dangerous Relations." *The Scriblerian*, 23 (1991), 242–44.

Reply to J. F. Burrows' reply in *The Scriblerian*, 23 (1991), 234–41.

Pope, Alexander. *Alexander Pope: Selected Poetry and Prose.* (Routledge English Texts.) Edited with an Introduction by Robin Sowerby. London and New York: Routledge, 1988. Pp. vii + 306; bibliography. Cf. *ECCB*, n.s. 14, VI:371.

Rev. by Thomas J. Regan in *The Scriblerian*, 23 (1991), 257–58.

Pope, Alexander. *Pope's* Dunciad *of 1728: A History and Facsimile.* Edited by David L. Vander Meulen. Charlottesville, VA, and London: U. of Virginia Press, 1991. Pp. xvii + 174; appendices; illustrations.

Readers of Pope will be grateful to the Bibliographical Society of the University of Virginia and the New York Public Library for *Pope's* Dunciad *of 1728: A History and Facsimile*, an important complement to previous studies, which advantageously brings together between two covers relevant biographical, bibliographical, and textual information—much of it new. Most immediately, this book provides readers with a photo-facsimile of the Berg Collection's copy of the large paper, octavo issue of the first edition. This photo-facsimile was required, given Pope's concern with typography, demonstrated by Foxon. The first impression duodecimo might have been chosen, were it not for the need to reproduce annotations by Jonathan Richardson, Jr., in the Berg copy, but an appendix provides the fifteen variant readings between the first and second impressions.

Richardson, like his father a friend of Pope, recorded variants from a collation of the edition with a prepublication manuscript, dating from 1726–27, which Richardson or perhaps Pope called the "First Broglio MS." At Pope's request Richardson transcribed variants of this and two other copies that Pope provided him. In a copy of the 1736 *Dunciad*, also in the Berg Collection, Richardson recorded variants once found in a "Second" Broglio MS (like the first Broglio MS, no longer extant); in a copy of the 1728 octavo of *The Dunciad* now at the Huntington he inserted four dozen markings, here transcribed, which according to Vander Meulen record changes in subsequent editions. Richardson's gleanings from the two Broglio MSS, partly reprinted in notes to the Elwin-Courthope edition, were not made available until Mack transcribed them in *The Last and Greatest Art* (1984).

The photo-facsimile, in its original size, provides much clearer access to these readings, allowing scholars to avoid errors in Mack's transcription and to assess Mack's interpretations. In an hour's comparison of Mack's transcription against the photo-facsimile, I discovered a dozen errors in accidentals, frequent underlinings and apostrophes not recorded (as on p. 13), and several omissions, like the reference to Horace on page 11, and "weekly" on page 28 (omitted from Mack pp. 103 and 115). The first might be missing since Mack supposed it (being in pencil) was not in Pope's hand, but it is worthwhile having a photocopy of all Richardson's marginalia. Also, lines bracketed with "inf." beside them on page 4 are mistakenly noted by Mack as ll. 69–72 (they are ll. 77–78 of the

Twickenham Edition; Mack, p. 102). Only photo-duplication can capture the complexity of extensive annotations on many pages (e.g., p. 16). Mack's treatment of *The Dunciad*, however, remains essential for studying this photo-facsimile; for instance, it explains the placement of extensive variants recorded apart from their location in the text, as on the verso of the half-title and the final page (p. vii) of the preface. Vander Meulen more fully explains Richardson's handling of variants and his notational system, calling attention through his choice of examples to MSS not recorded in *The Last and Greatest Art*.

Vander Meulen never criticizes Mack's transcription, but one wishes that he had at least commented generally on Mack's arguments regarding the chronology of variant readings and the second Broglio MS. One significant disagreement between Mack and Vander Meulen involves the dating of the second Broglio MS, Mack placing it before the *The Dunciad Variorum*, 1729. Vander Meulen, however, argues that "not only the first but the Second Broglio predated the 1728 publication" (p. 51). If he is correct, and certainly he answers previously articulated arguments for a post-1728 dating, then this study ought also to include a photo-facsimile of the 1736 octavo with the Second Broglio variants.

Vander Meulen's introduction succinctly and conveniently draws together much of what is known about the composition, publication, and revision of *The Dunciad*, the physical characteristics of the first edition, the provenance of its annotated copies, and the nature of Richardson's annotations. There is a just survey of Swift's encouragement and suggestions and of the impetus added by attacks on Pope. Vander Meulen's command of the bibliography allows him to offer new insights into the keys of *The Dunciad* (pp. 20–22) and into a Dublin and also a second (probably Scottish) edition of 1728. For example, he is able to note that the six known copies of a second key to *The Dunciad* are all found attached to the "gold chains" edition (so named for a variant at l. 76). The section of the edition makes more conveniently available Vander Meulen's important analytical work on the running titles, variants, and paper of the first edition. He does not alter here his earlier placement of the five impressions of the first edition into chronological sequence—in fact, scholars will still need to consult the 1982 article in *Studies in Bibliography*. However, the first appendix offers a historical collation of the variant readings in the five impressions of the first edition, noting what resetting occurred in the second through fifth impressions. Also, the textual relations of the Dublin and "gold chains" editions to the *editio princeps* are discussed. Although variant readings in these two editions are not recorded, to indicate how contemporary Dubliners read the work and suggest some of Pope's targets, Vander Meulen has provided an appendix with variants involving personal names inserted into the 1728 Dublin reprint. Finally, the introduction and third appendix provide unpublished information about alterations in Pope's frontispieces.

This is unquestionably fine scholarship, often extraordinarily scrupulous, perhaps sometimes excessively so. Vander Meulen's continuing work on a forthcoming bibliography of Pope allows him to assure us that the Berg copy differs from twenty other copies of the issue that he has examined only with respect to a broken comma! Vander Meulen has gone far beyond his strict intention of placing the Richardson copy "in the wider context of its impression and edition."—James E. May.

Rosslyn, Felicity. *Alexander Pope: A Literary Life*. (Macmillan Literary Lives.) Basingstoke and London: Macmillan, 1990. Pp. xiii + 176; portrait. Cf. *ECCB*, n.s. 16, VI:429.

Rev. (favorably) by Peter Dixon in *Notes and Queries*, 236 (1991), 232–33; by Richard Striner in *The Scriblerian*, 24 (1991), 49–51.

Rumbold, Valerie. *Women's Place in Pope's World*. Cambridge, and New York: Cambridge U. Press, 1989. Pp. xvii + 315. Cf. *ECCB*, n.s. 15, VI:384–86.

Rev. by Katherine M. Rogers in *The Scriblerian*, 23 (1990), 221–23.

Salmon, F. E. "Alexander Pope and Circe's Sacred Dome." *Review of English Studies*, 42 (1991), 523–31.

An early sketch for the gardens at Marble Hill.

Williams, Carolyn D. "Otho: Emperor or Artefact?" *The Scriblerian*, 23 (1991), 293–94.

One of the twelve Caesars, mentioned in *Dunciad* IV and *To Mr. Addison*.

Williams, Carolyn D. "Pope and Granville: Fictions of Friendship." *Notes and Queries*, 236 (1991), 184–86.

Discusses and dates "A Letter with a Character of Mr. Wycherly."

Jean Potocki (1761–1816)

Triaire, Dominique. *Potocki*. Arles: Actes Sud, 1991. Pp. 267.

Rev. (favorably) by Jean Decottignies in *Revue des sciences humaines*, 226 (1992), 217–19.

Antoine François Prévost (1697–1763)

Gilroy, James P. *Prévost's Mentors: The Master-Pupil Relationship in the Major Novels of the Abbé Prévost*. (Scripta Humanistica, 58.) Potomac, MD: Scripta Humanistica, 1989. Pp. 113. Cf. *ECCB*, n.s. 15, VI:388–89.

Rev. by R. A. Francis in *Modern Language Review*, 86 (1991), 1025.

Lazzaro-Weis, Carol M. *Confused Epiphanies: L'abbé Prévost and the Romance Tradition*. (American University Studies: Series II, Romance Languages and Literature, 161.) Frankfurt am Main and New York: Peter Lang, 1991. Pp. vi + 190; bibliography.

Pailloux, Sophie. *Manon Lescaut, l'abbé Prévost.* (L'Oeuvre au clair, 28.) Paris: Bordas, 1991. Pp. 93.

Prévost, Antoine Francois Abbé. *Histoire d'une Grecque moderne.* Edited by Jean Sgard. Genoble, France: Presses Universitaires de Grenoble, 1989. Pp. 207. Cf. *ECCB*, n.s. 15, VI:388.

Rev. by Franco Piva in *Studi francesi*, 34 (1991), 528.

Richard Price (1723–1791)

Price, Richard. *The Correspondence of Richard Price: Volume II: March 1778–February 1786.* Edited by D. O. Thomas. Cardiff: U. of Wales Press; Durham, NC: Duke U. Press, 1991. Pp. xxv + 348.

Guillaume Raynal (1713–1796)

Lüsebrink, Hans-Jürgen, and Mandred Tietz (eds.). *Lectures de Raynal: L'Histoire des deux Indes en Europe et en Amérique au XVIIIe Siècle* (Studies on Voltaire and the Eighteenth Century, 286.) Oxford: The Voltaire Foundation at the Taylor Institution, 1991. viii + 399.

Rev. by Sylviane Albertan-Coppola in *Recherches sur Diderot et sur l'Encyclopédie*, 12 (1992), 193–94.

Thomas Reid (1710–1796)

Lehrer, Keith. *Thomas Reid.* (The Arguments of the Philosophers.) London and New York: Routledge, 1989. Pp. xii + 311. Cf. *ECCB*, n.s. 16, VI:432.

Rev. (somewhat critically) by P. B. Wood in *Mind*, 100 (1991), 155–57.

Rowe, William L. *Thomas Reid on Freedom and Mortality.* Ithaca, NY, and London: Cornell U. Press, 1991. Pp. x + 189.

Nicolas-Edme Restif de la Bretonne (1734–1806)

Coward, David. *The Philosophy of Restif de la Bretonne.* (Studies on Voltaire and the Eighteenth Century, 283.) Oxford: The Voltaire Foundation at the Taylor Institution, 1991. Pp. x + 878.

Restif de la Bretonne, a self-proclaimed "people's philosopher," wished to be remembered as a thinker and architect of a new society, but as David Coward argues in this new study, Restif's real value as a writer lies not in his ideas but in the energy of his imagination. Calling Restif "one of the more personally and intellectually eccentric figures in an age which did not lack eccentrics," a "frustrated idealist with a dark, compulsive side, and the need to justify himself in his writing," Coward also makes the case that Restif is a "dealer in human truth."

Dismissed by his own century as an oddball and pornographer, and neglected, misunderstood, or extravagantly praised by subsequent critics, Restif produced a corpus of some 207 volumes (as recently reissued by Slatkine), which, both by its size (more than 60,000 pages) and uneven quality, continues to be a challenge to readers. Coward's study runs to just under 900 pages, and would appear to be something of a challenge, but counterbalancing length, is the clarity of its prose and the evenness of his judgments. He has written a work that is a model of descriptive, analytical literary criticism.

Refusing to make excessive claims for his subject whom he designates as a second-class writer and an undisciplined and frequently inadequate abstract thinker, Coward, nonetheless, does take him seriously as a writer. He suggests that Restif's writing has a real modernity to it, since the pen becomes for him the means both of delivering himself from his demons and of creating a better society in which to live. Hence, Coward suggests, much of Restif de La Bretonne's writing should be read as fulfilling a therapeutic purpose, with the utopias he created providing a kind of tidiness that did not exist in his own life.

Dividing his work into four parts—the formative years, reform of society, theory, and utopia—Coward presents a complete and judicious picture of the man and his thinking and writing. Using frequent excerpts from Restif's writing, he meticulously documents his discussions, and is always careful to recount the facts without making moralistic judgments on his subject. In addition, he offers many helpful critical evaluations of the critical work done by other scholars on Restif, plus giving indications of opportunities for further research. Additional scholarly apparatus includes a 9 page bibliography and a 25 page index.

While few readers may have the time to test Coward's claim that Restif's works reveal in their entirety a unifying vision, and others may not be wholly convinced that Restif's social philosophy merits so many pages of the repetitive, banal, and disgusting, nearly everyone should agree that Coward has done a first-rate job in presenting this paradoxical and unstable, but often fascinating, thinker.—Suellen Diaconoff.

Restif de la Bretonne, Nicolas-Edme. *Le Drame de la vie contenant un homme tout entier; pièce en 13 actes des ombres et en 10 pièces régulières.* Preface by Jean Goldzink. (Le Spectateur francais.) Paris: Imprimerie Nationale, 1991. Pp. 514.

This is the first edition of *Le Drame de la vie* since its publication in 1793. Réstif de la Bretonne intended it as a dramatic complement to his autobiographical *Monsieur Nicolas* and claimed it as a unique attempt to put a man's life "en drame avec une vérité qui le fait agir au lieu de parler" (*Avis*, 31).

The *Drame* certainly represents a challenge for the modern reader, or indeed for the reader of any era. It consists of ten conventional plays corresponding to the major phases of Réstif's emotional life, each spanning about a four year period. Each play is centered on a woman, for example, Madame Parangon, the idealized version of the wife of Réstif's employer, the master printer Fournier whom he loved, or Zéphire, the prostitute with the heart of gold, and many others. The *Drame* also includes six acts of *Ombres chinoises* portraying transitional events in Réstif's life between and before the plays, one act of marionettes, and five *Scènes détachées* amplifying further events. The scope is enormous.

Following Diderot's precepts about the purpose of theatre, Réstif tried to create a "théâtre à usage personal." He wanted to show life in all its miniscule detail and attempted, as Goldzink notes, to give the freedom of subjectivity full range in his encyclopedic theatre. Hence current events are of little interest—the Revolution, for example, is discussed only in the last few pages of Act V of the *Scènes détachées*. Réstif tries to make his drab life exciting by making the imaginary a mode of the real.

There are many problems with his endeavour. Technically, staging the *Drame* is impossible. One modern attempt was a reading over a period of fifteen evenings. The vast number of actors—two hundred and fifty in the last five acts of the *Scènes détachées* compounds the problem. The plays are static. There is no true understanding or development of the hero's character. The fragmentation is further heightened by the constant changes in name of the hero. The vast array of characters, most of whom are one-dimensional and interchangeable, makes the plays almost unreadable. Those who do resist find a failed experiment in what is almost magic realism. We learn about the fantasy life of a man who believes he is loved by hundreds of women. Throughout the plays his constant discovery is of his illegitimate children, all girls. The numerous suggestions of incest reflect, as Pierre Testud has argued, that the man's search for tranquillity implies his need to be both father and lover.

I cannot recommend *Le Drame de la vie* for its literary qualities. For the specialist, the work represents further insight into Réstif's personal obsessions, and perhaps serves as an object lesson in the incompatibility of narcissism and successful theatre. This is a handsome edition, with modernized orthography and punctuation, and makes a highly esoteric work available to a wider specialized public.—Kay S. Wilkins.

Restif de la Bretonne, Nicolas Edme. *Monsieur Nicolas.* Edited by Pierre Testud. Vol. I: *Première à cinquième époque.* Vol. II: *Sixième époque.* Paris: Gallimard, 1990. Pp. 1,594; 1,852.

Rev. (favorably) by Vivienne Mylne in *French Studies*, 45 (1991), 465.

Williams, D. Anthony. "Une Chanson de Réstif et sa récriture par Flaubert." *Revue d'histoire littéraire de la France*, 91 (1991), 239–42.

The blindman's song in *Madame Bovary* was found by Flaubert in Restif, but he modified the text.

Sir Joshua Reynolds (1723–1792)

Watson, George. "Joshua Reynolds's Copy of Richardson." *Review of English Studies*, 42 (1991), 425–28.

An Essay on the Theory of Painting (1715), with one annotation.

Samuel Richardson (1689–1761)

Beebee, Thomas O. Clarissa *on the Continent: Translation and Seduction.* University Park, PA: Pennsylvania State U. Press, 1990. Pp. xi + 228.

Rev. (favorably) by R. G. Brown in *Choice*, 28 (1991), 928.

Burrows, J. F. " 'I Lisp'd in Numbers': Fielding, Richardson, and the Appraisal of Statistical Evidence." *The Scriblerian*, 23 (1991), 234–41.

Replies to comments in *The Scriblerian*, 22 (1989), 14 on an article in *Eighteenth-Century Studies*, 21 (1988), 427–53.

Doody, Margaret Anne, and Peter Sabor (eds.). *Samuel Richardson: Tercentenary Essays.* Cambridge and New York: Cambridge U. Press, 1989. Pp. xviii + 306; chronology; illustrations. Cf. *ECCB*, n.s. 16, VI:433; 15, VI:392–93.

Rev. by Jeffrey Smitten in *Review of English Studies*, 42 (1991), 269–70.

Kibbie, Ann Louise. "Sentimental Properties: *Pamela* and *Memoirs of a Woman of Pleasure.*" *English Literary History*, 58 (1991), 561–77.

Both works reflect the tensions of female characters who are subject to the currency of exchange and the constancy of property.

Lehmann, Christine. *Das Modell Clarissa: Liebe, Verführung, Sexualität un Tod der Romanheldinnen des 18. Und 19. Jahrhunderts.* Stuttgart: J. B. Metzler, 1991. Pp. 217.

Mebold, Adrian. *Rhetorik und Moral in Samuel Richardson's* Clarissa*: ein systemtheoretischer Versuch.* Bern and New York: Peter Lang, 1991. Pp. xvi + 424.

Ostovich, Helen M. " 'Our Views Must Now by Different': Imprisonment and Friendship in *Clarissa.*" *Modern Language Quarterly*, 52 (1991), 153–69.

Clarissa's personality has been damaged by confinement in ways corroborated by recent psychological studies and experiments on prisoners and hostages. Other unconfined characters in the book are unable to comprehend her.

Jean-Jacques Rousseau (1712–1778)

Beaudry, Catherine A. *The Role of the Reader in Rousseau's* Confessions. (The Age of Revolution and Romanticism: Interdisciplinary Studies, 2.) Bern and New York: Peter Lang, 1991. Pp. viii + 176; bibliography.

Although much has already been written about Rousseau's monumental autobiography, the richness and complexity of its multiple levels of meaning are far from having been exhausted. Fresh attempts at shedding new light on authorial intentions and textual implications are therefore both justifiable and welcome. Beaudry's project is an attempt to account for what has already been done on the role of the reader in Rousseau as well as to advance our understanding of various textual strategies Rousseau employs to counter or to mold the reactions of the anticipated readers of his work. Beaudry's principal aim is to show that Rousseau feels increasingly alienated from his contemporaries; he tends to address himself more and more to posterity and neglect or even reject the readers of his time.

The approach chosen by Catherine Beaudry is a promising one, especially in light of the theoretical work on the role of the reader that has been carried out over the last two or three decades. Her essay is nevertheless flawed in two important regards. First, the theoretical framework for the discussion of such notions as author, narrator, narratee, and reader is never fully developed and suffers from a number of inconsistencies. While such theorists as Wolfgang Iser, Gerald Prince, and Mikhail Bakhtin are invoked sporadically, their theories, as well as the relevance of these theories to the subject at hand, are mentioned only in passing, if at all. Beaudry explains, for example, that the continuing popularity of the *Confessions* is due to the relationship Rousseau was successful in establishing with his reader: "with the readers of posterity there is no doubt of Rousseau's success in maintaining contact with his audience" (8). Yet we are also told that the inscribed audience, sympathetic to Rousseau, was one that knew "all the customs of Paris and the calumnies being spread about him" (76). The reader thus turns out to be a curious composite of the author's wishful projections and of actual persons—the readers of posterity who become the incarnation of the inscribed reader.

The second flaw is one for which the publisher is as much to blame as the author. The book, having evidently been written in a hurry by someone who is not at home in the English language, has the overall appearance of a very rough draft. The constant misspellings, ambiguous and dangling modifiers, awkward, illogical, and incoherent constructions—all serve to devalue an otherwise defensible argument. The best parts of the book are those providing close readings of Rousseau's text. They show that Beaudry can be a careful and sensitive reader. It is unfortunate that the same care could not have gone into the preparation of the manuscript before it went to press.—Karlis Racevskis.

Behbahani, Nouchine. *Paysages rêvés, Paysages vécus dans* "La Nouvelle Héloïse" *de Jean-Jacques Rousseau*. (Studies on Voltaire and the Eighteenth Century, 271.) Oxford: The Voltaire Foundation at the Taylor Institution, 1989. Pp. 180; bibliography. Cf. *ECCB*, n.s. 16, VI:437; 15, VI:396.

Rev. by Robin Howells in *Modern Language Review*, 86 (1991), 722–23; (favorably) by Timothy Scanlan in *The French Review*, 64 (1991), 689–91.

Besse, Guy. *Jean-Jacques Rousseau, l'apprentissage de l'humanité*. (Collection Terrains.) Paris: Editions Sociales, 1988. Pp. 444; bibliography. Cf. *ECCB*, n.s. 14, VI:380–81.

Rev. by Vincent J. Errante in *Diderot Studies, 24* (1991), 194–96.

Burgio, Alberto. *Eguaglianza interesse unanimità. La Politica di Rousseau.* Naples: Bibliopolis, 1989. Pp. 447. Cf. *ECCB*, n.s. 15, VI:397.

Rev. by Lelia Pezzillo in *Studi francesi*, 34 (1991), 529–30.

Cell, Howard R., and James I. MacAdam. *Rousseau's Response to Hobbes.* (American University Studies, series 5: Philosophy, 37.) Bern and New York: Peter Lang, 1988. Pp. xii + 271. Cf. *ECCB*, n.s. 16, VI:437.

Rev. (favorably) by Robert Yennah in *Revue d'histoire littéraire de la France*, 91 (1991), 99–100.

Cranston, Maurice William. *The Noble Savage: Jean-Jacques Rousseau, 1754–1762.* Chicago: U. of Chicago Press; London: Allen Lane/Penguin Press; New York: Viking Penguin, 1991. Pp. xiv + 399; bibliography; illustrations.

Rev. (favorably) by D. A. Collins in *Choice*, 29 (1991), 599; (favorably) by Norman Hampson in *TLS,* (Mar. 1, 1991), 10; by Malcolm Jack in *Eighteenth-Century Studies*, 25 (1991–92), 235–37; by John Sturrock in *New York Times Book Review* 3 (July 28, 1991), 12.

This second of a three-volume biography follows his *Jean-Jacques: The Early Life and Work of Jean-Jacques Rousseau, 1712–1754.* New York: W. W. Norton, 1983. Pp. 382; bibliography; 8 plates. Cf. *ECCB*, n.s. 11, VI:639; 10, VI:697; 9, VI:692.

The Noble Savage is the second volume of what now promises to be a three-volume biography of Rousseau by Maurice Cranston. This volume covers the prolific middle years of Rousseau's life, when he lived in relative seclusion and produced *Emile, Julie,* and *The Social Contract.* This second volume has already been glowingly reviewed by one critic who is pleased to discover that "we cannot help coming to like Jean-Jacques," or at least Jean-Jacques as Cranston describes him. But a more complex and ambiguous Rousseau seems always to hover around the edges of Cranston's depiction of him. For example, in Cranston's account of "The Year of *Julie*," Rousseau simply "fell in love" with Mme d'Houdetot, and created in himself a "model of the Romantic hero" who compensates for disadvantages of wealth and appearance with "a soul" that "knows better how to love." Her attraction to Rousseau, on the other hand, is said to be based simply on his "literary celebrity," since "as such he enjoyed in eighteenth-century France an undoubted sex appeal." Such psychological speculation can easily cut both ways; some readers might imagine Rousseau exploiting his celebrity for sexual purposes, or even using Sophie d'Houdetot to stimulate an intensity of desire in himself which was only consummated in his work.

Cranston's explanations of Rousseau's political writings will, similarly, satisfy the already converted. But those readers, from Crocker to Derrida, who have criticized Rousseau in terms ranging from the political to the metaphysical are unlikely to be persuaded that the seeming paradox in the formula that social man "shall be forced to be free" is resolved by Cranston's judgment that "it would be wrong to put too much weight on these words." While Cranston acknowledges that the pedagogical methods of Emile's tutor are sometimes "sadistic," he sees nothing Orwellian in reporting that Rousseau viewed prisons as "a device for helping the individual in his struggle against his own passions."

Those who would view Rousseau as sympathetically as Cranston does will undoubtedly feel that pressing too hard on such points leads one into the anachronistic fallacy of viewing Rousseau through the prism of what Cranston called, in reference to other biographers of Rousseau, a "contemporary deterministic culture." But reading Rousseau as something other than a straightforward idealist is not a modern invention. In 1839, Mary Shelley suggested that Rousseau's theory of the "natural man" as solitary, indolent and irresponsible to his offspring was a rationalization of his guilt over abandoning his own children, but she still concluded her essay on Rousseau with the judgement that "no author is more eloquent in paradox, and no man more sublime in inculcating virtue." The admission of Rousseau's capacity for paradox should be no impediment to an appreciation of his genius, but the insistence on "liking Jean-Jacques" can interfere with the perception of the profound ambivalence of his life and his work.—James O'Rourke.

Etudes Jean-Jacques Rousseau. La Nouvelle Héloïse *aujourd'hui.* Reims: Editions a l'Ecart, 1991. Pp. 258; illustrations.

Contains the following articles:
  Laurent Versini, "*La Nouvelle Héloïse* aujourd'hui," pp. 1–4.
  Henri Coulet, "Rousseau et Gellert: De la Comtesse suédoise à *La Nouvelle Héloïse*," pp. 5–16.
  Jean Roussel, "Les Confessions de *La Nouvelle Héloïse*," pp. 17–28.
  Claude Labrosse, "Puissance de la fiction, pouvoirs de l'instant," pp. 29–44.
  Michel Delon, "*La Nouvelle Héloïse* et le théâtre," pp. 45–64.
  Laurence Viglieno, " '*Julie* ou la nouvelle Eurydice': Mort et renaissance dans *La Nouvelle Héloïse*," pp. 65–76.
  Isabelle Brouard-Arends, "*Les Solitaires* et *La Nouvelle Héloïse* ou l'ambiguïté féminine chez Jean-Jacques Rousseau," pp. 77–84.
  Christian Destain, "Julie, Saint-Preux et Wolmar: De la Faute à l'amour divin," pp. 85–98.
  Tanguy l'Aminot, "*Julie* libertine," pp. 99–126.
  Jacques Domenech, "*La Nouvelle Héloïse* parangon des romans épistolaires antiphilosophiques," pp. 127–44.
  Philippe Koeppel, "Stendhal et *La Nouvelle Héloïse*," pp. 145–61.
  Li Ping-oue, "*La Nouvelle Héloïse* en Chine," pp. 163–65.

Fauconnier, Gilbert. *Index-Concordance de* Julie *ou* La Nouvelle Héloise*: tome I.* (Etudes Rousseauistes et Index des oeuvres de J.-J. Rousseau.) Geneva and Paris: Editions Slatkine, 1991. Pp. 553.

Fauconnier, Gilbert. *Index-Concordance de* Julie *ou* La Nouvelle Héloise*: tome II.* (Etudes Rousseauistes et Index des oeuvres de J.-J. Rousseau.) Geneva and Paris: Editions Slatkine, 1991. Pp. 700.

The Fauconnier *Index-Concordance de* Julie *ou* La Nouvelle Héloise adds another volume to the database of works by Rousseau which have been produced at the University of Nice. The compilation is based on an electronic version of Rousseau's novels at the Institut de la Langue Française in Nancy, but updated according to the canonical Pléiade edition, which includes Rousseau's notes and appendices. Following conventions previously established, and summarized in a two-page Forward, the *Index* contains, in addition to the *Héloïse*, the two prefaces (original and *Entretien sur les romans*), *Les amours de milord Edouard Bomston*, and *Sufets d'estampes*. Over 300,000 words (*formes*) have been processed.

Volume 1 contains an Index which gives the number of occurances of 'content' words and their address in the Pléiade edition, followed by a Dictionary which shows the location high-frequency 'function' of words. Thus, the user can easily locate a target word by page (in the Pléiade edition) and/or by Book. Volume 1 also contains lists of 'significant' vocabulary: 691 words with occurances higher than expected; 665 words used less than expected. Volume 1 presents an alphabetized Concordance in KWIC (Key-Word-In-Context) form. Punctuation signs and high frequency grammatical words have been excluded because their presence would have extended the concordance to 'unreasonable' lengths (e.g., the preposition *de* = 16, 536 occurences). Thus, users of the *Index-Concordance* will be able to locate content words of particular interest in several textual environments.

As for the statistically significant vocabulary in the *Héloïse*, based on Brunet's method of factor analysis, the 1356 words which obtain a so-called z-score (*écart réduit*) of plus or minus 2 identify deviations which exceed normal probabilities (i.e., the null hypothesis is rejected; the verbal behavior is not the result of chance, but 'deliberate'. To obtain the profile of words used more or less than expected in the Rousseau corpus 11, other Rousseau texts at the I. L. F. totaling some one million words have been processed: *Réveries, Dialogues, Consider . . . Polognne, Lettre à d'Alembert,* two *Discours,* and *Le Devin du village.* Beginning with *tu, je, te, me, ton, ami, mon, vous, toi, ta, votre, ma, lettre, tes, mylord, coeur, cousin, elle, ha . . .,* the signifiers with the largest positive z-scores highlight *grosso modo* communicative and affective relationships (deictics, names).

The 20 words with the largest negative z-scores—*avoir, avec, il, les, loi, au, des, donc, par, homme, gouvernement, ce, peuple, voiler, public, on, citoyen, ils, corps, auteur*—encompass socio-political relationships and institutions. While both the z-positive and z-negative groups seemingly reconfirm the *Héloïse* as a novel of *sensibilité*, would-be users of the Fauconnier lists as well as the other volumes in the Rousseau database should not be deterred from using the vocabulary in other configurations such as collocations, thematic-clusters, and focal levels. The *Index-Concordance* and its cohorts can be viewed, then, not as a *terminus ad quem*, but as an invitation to explore further the yet uncharted seas of Enlightenment lexicology.—Richard L. Frautschi.

Fidler, David P., and Stanley Hoffmann (eds.). *Rousseau on International Relations.* Oxford: Clarendon Press, 1991. Pp. lxxx + 214; bibliography.

Over the last few years, different aspects of Rousseau's political thought have attracted the attention of scholars, the exception being his writings on international relations. Although C. J. Carter did study the subject in 1987, the most recent translation of the *Abstract* and *Judgement of Saint-Pierre's Project for Perpetual Peace*, that of E. N. Nuttall, dates from 1927.

S. Hoffmann and D. P. Fidler's recently published anthology of translated texts is thus most welcome. The introduction underlines Rousseau's profound pessimism regarding the possibility of peaceful coexistence among nations. Whereas the general will is the foundation of political life and of the existence of the state, the law of nature alone governs international relations. In Rousseau's eyes, the Abbé-Pierre's project of federation was fundamentally utopian and likely to aggravate the very imbalance it claimed to correct, for though it is in the true interest of monarchs to govern peacefully, there will always be those among them who choose to pursue more selfish ends. Thus, if even one country rules by the law of the strongest, all others will have to follow suit, and just princes will be obliged to behave like tyrants in order to ensure the survival of their state. In the absence of a miracle solution, Rousseau advises the weakest states to reduce their dependence on the outside world, to cultivate a defensive patriotism whose dissuasive force would keep any possible conquerors at a distance.

The editors attempt to situate Rousseau with regard to Hobbes and Kant. Hobbes believed violence to be innate in humans whereas Rousseau attributed it to life in society. The latter also rejected Hobbes' opinion that the very existence of states softened the disagreements between peoples. Rousseau also repudiates the three suppositions upon which Kant's optimism rests: 1st that a constitutional government, by allowing citizens to control the exercise of power, would reduce the danger of conflict; 2nd that the improvement of armaments will make men more afraid of war; 3rd that the development of commercial ties between nations will also favour peace.

In additon to the two texts inspired by the Abbé Saint-Pierre (fragments entitled *The State of War* and *Fragments on War*), the anthology includes lengthy excerpts of the *Discours on Political Economy*, six chapters (two given in full of the first version of the *Social Contract*, the most significant parts of the *Constitutional Project for Corsica* and a few chapters of the *Considerations on the Government of Poland*). The texts chosen form a coherent whole which presents Rousseau's political thought from a new and unusual angle.

The translation is both elegant and precise. One is even tempted to say that, in some ways, it is more harmonious and more regular than the original, particularly in those texts that have retained something of the improvided feel of a first draft. In the "Foreword" of the *Constitutional Project for Corsica* we read: ". . . a government without laws cannot be a good government. *I do not say that the Corsican people is in that condition*; on the contrary, no people impresses me as being so fortunately disposed by nature to receive a good administration" (p. 139). The underlined sentence was added by the translators. The passage no doubt gains thereby in clarity, but by becoming more explicit, perhaps it loses something of its expressiveness.

The texts are followed by a bibliography on the theme of international relations in Rousseau's work and an analytical index referring to key words and to their commentary in both the introduction and the excerpts.—Jean Terrase / Jane Everett (trans.).

Gautier, Roger. "Les Idées sociales et politiques dans le théâtre de Jean-Jacques Rousseau." *Revue d'histoire du théâtre*, 43 (1991), 305–11.

Goodman, Dena. "The Hume-Rousseau Affair: From Private *Querelle* to Public *Procés*." *Eighteenth-Century Studies*, 25 (1991–92), 171–201.

Traces "the process by which a private matter became a public affair, readers became writers, and the reading public played its role as the tribunal of public opinion."

Heckle, Patrizia Longo. *The Statue of Glaucus: Rousseau's Modern Quest for Authenticity.* (American University Studies, Series X:33.) Bern and New York: Peter Lang, 1991. Pp. xiv + 178; bibliography.

This is a tightly-knit account of Rousseau's overall project, the leading thread of which is the problem of self-knowledge and of the unity of the self. In relation to the dominant ethics of autonomy, Heckle sees in this quest for an ethics of authenticity the originality of Rousseau's work. Beyond the values of freedom, equality, and justice through the emancipation of social relations, the attention given by Rousseau to the gap between being and appearance makes him introduce the need for psychological changes and for a transformation of man himself which requires a new beginning of history. Many of the important issues of the *Discourses*, the *Social Contract, Emile,* and the autobiographical writings are carefully explained and synthesized in this context. Surprisingly, however, very little attention is given to such figures as the Savoyard Vicar and Wolmar, and to the significance of their religious experience, and some of Rousseau's major discussions concerning authenticity, notably in *La Nouvelle Héloïse* and the *Letter to d'Alembert*, are overlooked.

The theme is dealt with mainly in three central chapters, each one approaching the problem of identity from a different angle: truth, moral psychology, and political theory. These chapters are bracketed by some solid, albeit familiar, material on Rousseau's relation to the Enlightenment and on how his theoretical critique of modern society emerges from his personal experience of it. While concentrating on the classic problems of Rousseau's position on original sin and of his basic distrust in man's capacity to tolerate freedom, the chapter on morality provides a useful clarification of Rousseau's admiration for the military virtue of Sparta. Similarly, the chapter on politics contains, among other things, a clear treatment of the status of religion in Rousseau's project, as well as of his anti-modernist views on political economy. Heckle convincingly shows that the self is, for Rousseau, the ulitmate constituent of the moral world order, and that in so thinking he discovers what Hegel was to call "the moral view of the world." But the best chapter is certainly the one dealing with the epistemological basis for this moral and political quest. It includes some good analyses of language, style and music, and it ends with a discussion of the tricky "Fourth Promenade" in the *Rêveries* on the relation between truth, fiction and moral utility. Again, some reference to the *Letter to d'Alembert* would have been pertinent here to paint a more complete picture of Rousseau's position, but this chapter is nonetheless a fine piece on this intricate issue.

The book owes some of its appeal to many brief but useful historical references which underpin its interpretation throughout, for example to Pascal, to Hegel, and to some of Plato's major themes (including the statue of Glaucus, of course, which Rousseau borrows from *The Republic* and adapts to his purpose). On the down side, however, it must be said that this book lacks polish. There are too many typographical errors for such a short work, especially in names and titles (for instance: Fontanelle, Réaumur, McIntyre's *After Utopia*). Furthermore, some of the footnote references are incomplete, and some of Heckle's translations of Rousseau's text seemed to me rather awkward. Notwithstanding this, such an "existential" approach of Rousseau's thought is clearly fruitful and has produced some of the best commentaries written on him, like those by Brugelin and Starobinski. Although its limited scope and relative unoriginality make of Heckle's essay only a minor contribution to this tradition, her book does offer a good, dense introduction to Rousseau.—Philip Knee.

Jones, James F. *Rousseau's "Dialogues": An Interpretive Essay.* Geneva: Droz, 1991. Pp. 211.

Rev. (severely) by Philip Robinson in *French Studies*, 46 (1992), 331–32; (favorably) by Timothy Scanlan in *The French Review*, 66 (1992), 136–37.

Many writers have treated Rousseau's *Dialogues*. Jones' bibliography lists twenty-seven references and does not claim to be exhaustive. His effort at interpretation indicates he leans heavily on an approach used by M. M. Bakhtin, known through translations: "regrettably, Russian is beyond my expertise" (14).

The first chapter sketches the history of the text from its first appearance to the present and is designed to place it within the "autobiographical renaissance that has characterized so much of our post-structural intellectual history" (14). The second chapter studies the form of the dialogues and why Rousseau used this method of presentation. In the third chapter, perhaps the most interesting, Jones traces the devices of the argumentation and stresses affirmative/negative oppositions: "Rousseau chooses as the basis for his procedure the litotes from classical rhetoric categorized by Quintillian and those who came after him as the establishment of a fact by the denial of its opposite. The argument advanced in the *Dialogues* will be to disprove methodically the worst that has been said about Rousseau the author (incarnate in the character 'Jean-Jacques') so that the truth about him will become manifestly evident" (106). The fourth and final chapter, "A Sense of Non-Ending(s)," insists on the ambiguities of the work's conclusion (the *Dialogues* do stop, but the central question is left unresolved), perhaps not too surprising a revelation in a century in which the dialogues of so many other authors are characterized by heuristic rather than maieutic procedures. The reasons for this lack of closure are to be seen (1) in the nature of Rousseau's text (perhaps all autobiographical writings?), in which the truth is "always immanent, always yet to be revealed" (166); (2) in the fact that the text has taken on a life of its own, so that Rousseau is not "as much the director of the conversation" as one "directed" by it (167); (3) in the failure of reason, which means that, like the Frenchman, we must accept 'Jean-Jacques' in a religious act of conversion, for the essence of Rousseau must be defined "by the word beyond language" (172).

Jones finds Rousseau's main contribution to modern autobiography, that of "the fragmentary split recognized and accepted as such from the outset of the quest" for self-discovery, and on this basis detects a clear departure from the Descartes of the "Cognito" (180–181), but without sufficient evidence in my opinion, since there is no discussion of *Les Passions de l'âme*, and one senses the need also for distinctions to be made between Rousseau's view of the self and those of Saint-Augustine, Montaigne, and Pascal. As for the non-endings, this feature is held to be present in *Emile* and the *Nouvelle Héloïse*, and that may be true, but again the conclusion is reached without adequate discussion (six pages, 172–178).

Jones has given the reader a valuable discussion of the *Dialogues*, with arguments supported by an abundance of citations.—Merle L. Perkins.

Kavanagh, Thomas M. *Writing the Truth: Authority and Desire in Rousseau.* Berkeley, CA: U. of California Press, 1987. Pp. xii + 227; bibliography. Cf. *ECCB*, n.s. 15, VI:402; 13, VI:505–06.

Rev. by Patrick Coleman in *Diderot Studies, 24* (1991), 181–83.

Leigh, R. A. (ed.). *Correspondance complète de Jean-Jacques Rousseau.* Vol. 50: *Table chronologique des lettres et autre documents; Table alphabétiques des correspondants; Table chronologique des lettres citées dans les notes; Table alphabétiques des lettres citées dans les notes; Liste des appendices.* Etablies par Janet Laming. Oxford: The Voltaire Foundation at the Taylor Institution, 1991. Pp. 618.

Leigh, R. A. *Unsolved Problems in the Bibliography of J. J. Rousseau.* Edited by J. T. A. Leigh. (The Sanders Lectures in Bibliography.) Cambridge and New York: Cambridge U. Press, 1990. Pp. xi + 155; illustrations. Cf. *ECCB*, n.s. 16, VI:438.

Rev. (favorably and with another work) by Jean-Daniel Candaux in *TLS,* (Aug. 9, 1991), 28.

Markovits, Francine. "Rousseau et l'éthique de Clarens: Une Economie des relations humaines." *Stanford French Review*, 15 (1991), 323–48.

McEachern, Jo-Ann E. *Bibliography of the Writings of Jean-Jacques Rousseau to 1800.* Vol. 2: *Emile, ou de l'education.* Oxford: The Voltaire Foundation at the Taylor Institution, 1989. Pp. ix + 473; appendices; bibliography; facsimiles; illustrations.

Rev. by Jean H. Bloch in *Modern Language Review*, 86 (1991), 463–65; (favorably) by Peter Jimack in *French Studies*, 45 (1991), 81; (favorably) by Vivienne Mylne in *Notes and Queries*, 236 (1991), 118.

Melzer, Arthur M. *The Natural Goodness of Man: On the System of Rousseau's Thought.* Chicago, IL: U. of Chicago Press, 1990. Pp. xi + 308. Cf. *ECCB*, n.s. 16, VI:439–40.

Rev. (favorably and with another work) by Maurice William Cranston in *TLS*, (Feb. 15, 1991), 6.

Messiére, Evelyne. *Les Confessions, Rousseau.* (L'Oeuvre au clair, 22.) Paris: Bordas, 1991. Pp. 95.

Jean-Jacques Rousseau believed that societies that existed after his death could be judged by how they honored his memory. What would he have thought of a book published today to help students pass their *épreuve de francais* for the *Baccalauréat*? Honor comes in many forms, and the fact that the *Confessions* is among the two dozen French literary works to be acknowledged as indispensable to one's education might have gratified, if not satisfied Rousseau's ambition.

A work devoted to preparing large numbers of students for a standardized test requires fidelity to conventional wisdom rather than daring breaks with orthodoxy. Fortunately conventional wisdom about the *Confessions* has been established by scholars as distinguished as Philippe Lejeune and Jean Starobinski. Evelyne Messiere has used their insights and, occasionally, built on them. She emphasizes the literary character of the autobiography as a sort of novel or myth, rather than any claim it may have to factual truth. Following Lejeune, she distinguishes this genre by means of the *pacte autobiographique* between author and reader. The most valuable part of the book consists of the perceptive treatment of Rousseau's use of language, with several examples of close textual analysis and model lessons for imitation by students. These features would make this book useful for American instructors who teach the *Confessions* in a course oriented toward a close reading of texts or toward teaching the complexities of French composition.—Christopher Kelly.

Noble, Richard. *Language, Subjectivity, and Freedom in Rousseau's Moral Philosophy.* (Political Theory and Political Philosophy.) London and New York: Garland, 1991. Pp. 249; bibliography.

Noble's title accurately describes his book's main topics. Examining Rousseau's *Essai sur l'origine des langues*, *Discours sur l'inégalité (Second Discourse)*, and *Émile*, Noble aims to elucidate Rousseau's view of freedom by exploring his understanding of human subjectivity in the context of his philosophical anthropology, where language figures significantly. Primarily expository, with critical comments on both Rousseau and some interpreters, Noble's book treats a complex nexus of concepts with clarity and intelligence.

Noble focuses on Rousseau's antinomy of nature and culture. So sharply does Rousseau distinguish natural man—innocent, independent, and good—from his civilized, dependent, and corrupt descendants that linking nature and culture historically poses severe difficulties. Both the antinomy and its overcoming force attention onto the origins and growth of language, because asocial natural man cannot have language, but civilized man clearly does. So Rousseau's speculative history includes an intricate conceptualization of subjectivity: he combines a quasi-Cartesian view that human beings have (not rationality but) free will and *perfectibilité*, with a Lockean or empiricist view of individuals as constituted in and through their experience. Rousseau thus sees natural man as both good and capable of development, including linguistic development, when new experiences and environments stimulate novel responses.

Resolving the problem of language, Rousseau's theory of subjectivity also is intimately related to freedom: both anthropologically (because man in the state of nature can be asocial and so naturally free) and as a prescription for contemporary, civilized human beings (because our *perfectibilité* allows envisioning a moral freedom [in *Émile*] wherein we both recover our natural passions and engage in rational self-legislation [p. 125]).

In the first half of his book, Noble presents the 18th-century dilemmas surrounding language cogently and emphasizes the double roots of Rousseau's idea of subjectivity. He also discusses *perfectibilité* amply; he proposes that the "golden age" of the *Discours* is an extended stage of man's natural being; and, through a kind of genealogy of language, he suggests that mankind's language in that age was a more authentic language of passions than the civilized language of needs and reason, which easily allows manipulation and deceit. The second half of the book, by contrast, seems truncated and lacks closure. Compelling reasons to discuss only the *Émile* are lacking. Two potentially devastating criticisms are left hanging: Rousseau insists that Émile have no feelings for his tutor, which seems implausible and impinges on Rousseau's attempt to link the poles of the nature-culture antinomy (pp. 199–203); and Rousseau's discussion of compassion and pity seems incapable of bearing the moral weight he gives it (pp. 214–25).

One in a series of "previously unavailable British theses and studies," Noble's book differs from many dissertations: it is clear, inquires about significant questions, and does not get bogged down in secondary sources or minor interpretive disputes. Although he summarizes his major points too frequently and allows too many typos, Noble's lucid presentation of important issues performs a valuable service.—Peter G. Stillman.

Roger, Philippe. "Rousseau selon Sade ou Jean-Jacques travesti." *Dix-huitiéme siécle*, 21 (1991), 383–405.

Rousseau, G. S. (ed.). *The Languages of Psyche: Mind and Body in Enlightenment Thought.* (Clark Library Lectures, 1985–1986.) Berkeley, CA, and Oxford: U. of California Press, 1990. Pp. xix + 480; bibliography; 27 plates.

It is difficult to imagine, in or with whatever part of the mind or body one brings to such a task, a more promising topic, or an editor better able to assemble a cohort of experts to do it justice. But more has already been written on this "problem"—as this collection insists on regarding it—than most minds would be able to cope with in several lifetimes. This collection may well convince readers to leave the topic to those who already have the dozens of requisite texts well in mind and the hundreds of essential citations well entered on their disk drives. It would take the most diligent reader several weeks to assemble, and several months to read, only the eleven weighty sources cited in the five footnotes on pages 21–22.

G. S. Rousseau's "Introduction" provides an able survey of several hundred secondary sources, mentioning all the right names (Broad, Gay, Hunter and Macalpine, Langer, MacIntyre, Porter, Rorty, Searle, Spacks) and a goodly number of less inevitable, but no less essential ones (Camporesi, Goldstein, Lamerton, Maudsley, Mayr). The most noticeable absence is Schiebinger. The spirit of Michel Foucault, who was to have provided a theoretical framework illuminating "the semiotics and signposts of mind and body during the Enlightenment" (p. xii), hovers over the entire collection, while the efforts and publications of the industrious editor are acknowledged in the footnotes on page after page.

In spite of the phrase before the colon in the book's title, the contributors are not always attentive to the language of the works they study—still, in my opinion, the best access to the mind of the writer and the age in which he wrote. Smollett's medical Latin, Bentham's nomenclature, Sade's several vocabularies, and Jewish and Adamic language, are all mentioned, but only Sade's language is well dealt with. Thomas Willis's prose is much more vigorous and intriguing than this book suggests, while Hume's style and content are made to sound as bland as Locke's.

While this book was by no means produced in haste (the lectures were given in 1985–86), it abounds in lapses: "to put it crudly," "the more idealistic doctrinces," "the transdendental voluntarism," and "Pardoxically again"—all from the "Introduction." One might also wish that the illustrations had been extended to include at least one of Wren's very fine drawings for Willis's *Cerebri anatome* and a reproduction of Fragonard's erotic swing.

The swing is mentioned in Carol Houlihan Flynn's chapter on writers who disturbed the mind as deliberately and ingeniously as doctors disturbed the body—an analogy she tries to pass off as an explanation. Most of the chapters reflect their origins as lectures in their clarity of organization and lucidity of utterance, but the chapter by Antonie Luyendijk-Elshout is beset with disorders and confusions that the editor should have taken in hand. Roy Porter's cognitive map (actually more of a time line) is ingeniously drawn from curious and instructive texts, especially Schimmelpenninck, Tylor, and Gautier. Philippa Foot's chapter on Locke, Hume, and Moral Theory is lucid in disentangling arguments and careful in its classifications, but insufficiently attentive to cause. Robert G. Frank, Jr., on the other hand, is very attentive to the biographical causes, social and scientific circumstances, and resulting intellectual achievements of the acute Thomas Willis, who was deflected into medical circles from the clergy by the Civil War. The intersections of the mind and body were not, however, a problem for Willis, to whom they offered numerous intellectual challenges, and even more career opportunities. Simon Schaffer's chapter on Priestley's pneumatics and Bentham's panopticon is constructed as rigorously and lucidly as the panopticon itself. Although the Enlightenment was excessively concerned with sound minds, the essays in this collection focus disproportionately on the less sound minds and bodies of patients, as dealt with by Willis, Cheyne, Bentham, and Pinel. This anthology also concentrates on writers like Swift, Smollett, Sade, and Sterne—writers who testify, in their works and their lives, to the mind/body problem, but it seems perverse to look primarily to them for illumination. The mind and the body may both be more interesting when they are working badly, but they are not necessarily more instructive then. It says much about the achievements and limitations of this collection that its best chapter is on pain and truth in Sade. Some attention to more humane figures, Arbuthnot, say, or Addison, or Fielding, might have shown how intelligently, indeed, therapeutically, writers of the eighteenth century could carry the body into the mind, in the face of efforts of the materialists and the stooges of sensibility to force all such transactions the other way.—Alan T. McKenzie.

Rousseau, Jean-Jacques. *Correspondance complète.* Edited by R. A. Leigh. Vol. 47: *1792–1794.* Vol. 48: *1794–1795.* Oxford: The Voltaire Foundation at the Taylor Institution, 1988. Pp. xviv + 321; xxv + 285. Cf. *ECCB*, n.s. 16, VI:442; 15, VI:403.

Rev. by Jean Bloch in *French Studies*, 45 (1991), 210–11.

Rousseau, Jean-Jacques. *Rousseau, Judge of Jean-Jacques, Dialogues.* Edited by Christopher Kelly, and Roger D Masters. Translated by Judith R. Bush, Christopher Kelly, and Roger D. Masters. (The Collected Writings of Rousseau, 1.) Hanover, NH: U. Press of New England for Dartmouth College, 1990. Pp. xxxi + 277; illustrations.

Rev. (with another work) by Maurice William Cranston in *TLS,* (Feb. 15, 1991), 6.

Simon-Ingram, Julia. "Alienation, Individuation, and Enlightenment in Rousseau's Social Theory." *Eighteenth-Century Studies*, 24 (1991), 315–35.

The *Discours sur l'inégalité* anticipates some of the oppressions and alienation of the bourgeois individual delineated by Horkheimer and Adorno.

Trouille, Mary. "The Failings of Rousseau's Ideals of Domesticity and Sensibility." *Eighteenth-Century Studies*, 24 (1991), 451–83.

In his correspondence with Henriette.

Trousson, Raymond. *Jean-Jacques Rousseau. Le Deuil éclatant du bonheur.* Vol. II (Figures de proue.) Paris: Tallandier, 1989. Pp. 550. Cf. *ECCB*, n.s. 15, VI:404–05.

Rev. by Jeannette Geffriaud Rosso in *Studi francesi*, 34 (1991), 528–29; by Judith Still in *Modern Language Review*, 86 (1991), 462–63; (favorably) by D. Williams in *French Studies*, 45 (1991), 209–10.

Viroli, Maurizio. *Jean-Jacques Rousseau and the "Well-Ordered Society."* Translated by Derek Hanson. Cambridge and New York: Cambridge U. Press, 1988. Pp. viii + 247; bibliography. Cf. *ECCB*, n.s. 16, VI:444; 15, VI:405; 14, VI:385.

Rev. by Aubrey Rosenberg in *The French Review*, 64 (1991), 847–48.

Wyss, André. *La Langue de Rousseau. Formes et emplois.* Geneva: Slatkine, 1989. Pp. 335. Cf. *ECCB*, n.s. 15, VI:405–06.

Rev. (briefly) by Maria G. Pittaluga in *Studi francesi*, 35 (1991), 149.

Mary White Rowlandson (ca. 1635–ca.1678)

Breitweiser, Mitchell Robert. *American Puritanism and the Defense o' Mourning: Religion, Grief, and Ethnology in Mary White Rowlandson's Captivity Narrative.* (Wisconsin Project on American Writers.) Madison, WI: U. of Wisconsin Press, 1991. Pp. vii + 223; bibliography.

Rev. by B. R. Burg in *Choice*, 28 (1991), 1551.

Donatien Alphonse François, Marquis de Sade (1740–1814)

Airaksinen, Timo. *Of Glamor, Sex and de Sade.* Wakefield, NH: Longwood Academic, 1991. Pp. 220.

One does not require that an academic book be glamorous, but with such a title, the reader may be forgiven some inflated expectations. The title, however, is somewhat misleading: the author clearly states in his introduction that his project is purely philosophical. He intends "to provide a philosophical theory both of Sade and of the wicked will," and he wants "to understand wickedness as such" (xii). To do so, he starts by defining "perversity," using, for some reason which is not clear, Edgar Allan Poe's essay "The Imp of the Perverse." Sade's perversity is therefore called throughout the essay a "Poe-perversity," and characterized as follows: "The perverse person does what he should not, just because he should not do it" (p. 18). The Freudian definition of perversity is rejected because it is sexually loaded, whereas Airaksinen wants to use "perversity" in a wider sense, as "wickedness."

This essay, which does not really renew critical approaches of Sade, will not bring much to eighteenth-century specialists: it is concerned with Sade only insofar as Sade is "wicked." Airaksinen seems to have some difficulty in conceiving, analyzing and understanding "wickedness": his main argument is that there can be no crime without values and laws, and that evil, or wickedness, logically entails the existence of virtue or goodness. Airaksinen grounds his study of wickedness more on an empirical psychology than on a truly philosophical analysis, and does not seem to be familiar with the pertinent texts of Bataille, Klossowski, Blanchot, Barthes and Bennington, who have thoroughly analyzed this argument and the philosophy of evil in Sade's novels. He quotes Barthes one time in the essay (p. 174), but misuses his idea by saying that Sade distorts the laws of grammar, while Barthes had shown that the Sadean crime was grammatically structured.

The reader will discover here and there interesting insights about pleasure understood as transcendence, the parody of the social contract, the libertines' rage and hatred, the falsification of phallocracy (the libertines being dependent of their story-tellers, who are female), the theatrical aspect of Sade's work, and the text itself as Sade's best instrument of torture against his readers: Airaksinen suggests for example that the text which discusses evil, through its repetitions and painful descriptions, is in itself and on purpose an evil thing. However, Airaksinen's aim is ultimately moral: he intends to reveal the primacy of the Good, the importance of love, and Sade's unfortunate mistake, which causes his heroes to be unhappy by any standards. As the author carefully states, "it is not easy to criticize a writer who wants to be wicked" (p. 119).—Catherine Cusset.

Debauve, Jean-Louis. "Sur les Oeuvres politiques du citoyen Sade." *Lendemains*, 16 (1991), 54–56.

Delon, Michel. "Portrait de l'artiste en assassin. Note sur Sade et Michel-Ange." *Lendemains*, 16 (1991), 57–60.

Didier, Béatrice, and Jacques Neefs (eds.). *La Fin de l'ancien régime: Sade, Rétif, Beaumarchais, Laclos. Manuscrits de la Révolution I.* Saint-Denis: Presses Universitaires de Vincennes, 1991. Pp. 203.

See sec. 5 for review.

Frappier-Mazur, Lucienne. *Sade et l'écriture de l'orgie.* (Le Texte à l'oeuvre.) Paris: Nathan, 1991. Pp. 254.

Rev. (favorably) by Jean Decottignies in *Revue des sciences humaines*, 226 (1992), 216–17.

Hayes, Jules Candler. *Identity and Ideology: Diderot, Sade and the Serious Genre.* West Lafayette, IN: Purdue U. Press, 1991. Pp. xiv + 186.

See sec. 5 for review.

Jean, Raymond. " 'L'Enfer sur papier bible'. " *Lendemains*, 16 (1991), 61–63.

On the fact that Pléiade editions will include works of Sade in the near future.

Keenan, Thomas. "Freedom, the Law of another Fable." *Yale French Studies*, 79 (1991), 231–51.

Klossowski, Pierre. *Sade My Neighbor.* Translated by Alphonso Lingis. Evanston, IL: Northwestern U. Press, 1991. Pp. xv + 144; appendices.

This volume presents a translation of the 1967 edition (Editions du Seuil) where Klossowski prefaced his *Sade mon prochain (Sade my Neighbor)* with *Le Philosophe scélérat (The Philosopher-Villain)*, a study that did not appear in the first edition (Editions du Seuil, 1947). The translation here is admirably well done.—Robert E. Taylor.

Laborde, Alice M. *La Bibliothèque du marquis de Sade au château de La Coste.* Geneva: Slatkine, 1991. Pp. 153.

This volume consists of a twelve-page introduction followed by a transcription of the 1776 catalogue of Sade's library at La Coste castle—ff. 196–205 bis of ms. 6185 now at the Bibliothèque Municipale d'Anignon. Several factors, mostly the presence of half-a-page in Sade's hand on the verso of the last folio (here reproduced), enable Alice Laborde to prepose the second half of 1776 for the completion of the list. The introduction seems to imply that the manuscript was discovered in 1989 (p. 11), but does not specify by whom or where. Laborde mentions that the inventory repeats and amplifies the still unpublished list of 1769, and that a comparative study of the two lists is being prepared (p. 12), but does not say whether by herself or by someone else. (I raise the question because, according to M. Delon's review of H. -U. Seifert's *Sade: Leser und Autor* [1983] in *Revue d'Histoire littéraire de la France* [1985–5], A. Bouër, H. Coulet, and J. Deprun have been working on a critical edition of this 1769 list.)

Although a joint publication of the two catalogues would have been preferable, the present one provides a valuable overview of the books that were at Sade's disposal between 1763, when his father gave him permission to reside at La Coste (p. 10), and 1777, when he started his longest stretch in prison and his life as a writer. As pointed out by A. Laborde, the titles testify to Sade's early interest—and possibly that of his ancestors—in ancient and modern history, foreign countries, the sciences and philosophy, and to a strong leaning toward relativism and free-thinking. The catalogue includes not only major and lesser works by 18th-century *philosophes*, essayists and novelists, but also earlier words written in the aftermath of 16th-century religious turmoils and the religious quarrels of the 17th century. Despite some overlapping, it also notably differs from the list compiled by Seifert, which was based on other catalogues and on quotations made by Sade in his novels and correspondence. Laborde's comments include, whenever possible, the dates of publication, as well as the date of condemnation and the penalties incurred by some of the authors. A strange conflation, probably the result of some muddle in the layout, occurs under entries 116 and 117: Gaspard de Coligny dies in 1572 during the Saint-Bartholomew massacre only to be resurrected at the time of the Fronde (1649–53) by the side of the Grand Condé. Overall, the presentation suffers from some carelessness, such as the three separate bibliographical sections which entail unnecessary repetitions of names (Seifert, Deprun, etc.). Most of the introduction does not seem to be addressed to a scholarly audience, and one wonders whether the general public would think of perusing a long list of titles. Yet it should: if the ruins of La Coste can make anybody dream, so might this concrete evocation of Sade's library, with its many "tablettes" and "rayons," its small desk and its large desk, and its *petit* and *grand recueils nécessaires*.—Lucienne Frappier-Mazur.

Laborde, Alice M. (ed.). *Correspondance du Marquis de Sade et de ses proches enrichies de documents et Commentaires.* Geneva: Slatkine, 1991.

Vol. I: *Généalogie et patrimonie du Marquis de Sade.* Pp. 346.
Vol. II: *Lettres des princes reçues par mon père: 1729–1752.* Pp. 373.
Vol. III: *Le Marquis de Sade et son père: 1752–1767.* Pp. 376.
Vol. IV: *L'affaire Kailair: 1767–1771.* Pp. 216.

One must commend Professor Laborde for revealing many letters and documents not hitherto published. Some throw much light on the darker underside of Sade's father; others reveal a more understanding and compassionate mother-in-law than her past portraits. But many of the documents—perhaps detailed building costs at Mazan in 1759 (III:68–), some long lists of "buildings and grounds" expenses (III:278–296), a 17th-century marriage contract (I:167–), or early wills (I:116–)—have little to do with Sade himself.

Her genealogy in vol. I was largely (often word for word) done before her by Lely (correctly spelled *without* an accent) and sometimes when she abbreviates his text she leaves her own unclear: she writes, for example, of the consequences of a mission by Jean de Sade in 1411 (I:48), but her reader does not know what the mission was, for she omitted Lely's three-line explanation of it (See his *Oeuvres complètes du marquis de Sade*, Paris, Au Cercle du Livre Précieux, 1966, (I:18). Professor Laborde does give the genealogy of a few distant branches of the family perhaps thought unimportant by Lely. Her real contribution in this volume is an excellent inconography, some forty-two pages, inserted between pp. 100 and 101.

Professor Laborde's most original contribution is in her second volume wherein she presents a quantity of previously unpublished documents to, by, or concerning Sade's father, the diplomat. This volume is in many respects an enrichment of her own *Le Mariage du marquis de Sade*, 1988, as she herself points out (II:23–24). One learns of his extravagance (II:125–) and his specious justification for it (II:129), of his little regard for his wife

(II:143–), of his professional cunning and dishonesty (II:264–). But much of the material has far more to do with the Electorate at Cologne than with the Marquis de Sade, newborn and scarcely mentioned.

In vol. III Professor Laborde continues to exploit some new materials where Sade's father is concerned, often in the form of complaints of no money and his inability to raise his son properly (III:25–), or of pessimistic judgments concerning his son (III:49–, 93, 108). In a letter not cited by Lely and in Professor Laborde's notes, one learns that the father borrowed heavily from the soon-to-be parents-in-law, assuring them that his son would repay them, and then passing on to his son a title of lieutenant general with all its income for three previous years without telling him that all that income had already been drawn and spent (III:135–138). This volume presents Madame de Montreuil in a good light and offers many of her letters that were only summarized by Lely or not mentioned by him at all (III:165, 169, for example).

Vol. IV, largely devoted to the Keller Affair, offers a remarkable letter by Madame de Montreuil (IV:127–135), many complete documents that Lely only described, but does not add greatly to the revelations of Lely and Heine.

Throughout the volumes, but most particularly in vol. II, the footnotes pose a problem. References in the text to footnotes are not numbered but are indicated only by an asterisk, and once a name has been given an asterisk that asterisk appears attached to it throughout the volume even though the explanatory note appears but once, and not always at the first asterisk! This would lead to total confusion and not just annoyance were it not for an index of proper names at the end of vol. II, but, alas, there are errors there, too: *Laon* (not a proper entry anyway) among the C's (II:364), and no entries in some cases.

Worst of all, the volumes are badly put together. Typographical errors abound in all four volumes (I:57, 64, 65, 177; II:95, 149, 183; III:42, 57, 113, 122, 131, 235; IV:107, 111, 114, 116, 148, 165, 166, 204, 207). More shocking are mechanical errors perhaps connected with a word processor: The last two lines of I:57 are repeated at the top of p. 58; an incomplete sentence at the top of I:67 has no beginning on p. 66; the words at the top of II:293 have no connection with the words at the bottom of p. 292; the last line of text on III:209 is repeated at the top of p. 210; a letter may be described as to paper and ink with footnotes following but the text itself does not appear (III:216–217); a detail in a letter may be followed by an asterisk, and the top of the next page where a footnote ought to appear may be left blank (III:266–267); all but the first two words of the three lines at the bottom of IV:54 are repeated at the top of p. 55; an essential word can be left out of the text (IV:111); in some cases one can only wonder what has been omitted (II:66–67) or what has been garbled (II:119). Words can be misspelled in the editorial commentary itself, *locace* for *loquace*, for example (IV:116). A document appearing in one volume (III:59–60) can be completely reprinted in another (IV:198) and not add much to either one! Professor Laborde's rich findings deserved a better presentation.—Robert E. Taylor.

Laborde, Alice M. *Le Mariage du Marquis de Sade.* Paris and Geneva: Slatkine, 1988. Pp. 218; bibliography. Cf. *ECCB*, n.s. 16, VI:445; 15, VI:407; 14, VI:386.

Rev. (very severely) by Colette Michael in *The French Review*, 64 (1991), 690–91.

Laborde, Alice M. "Notre dette envers Sade." *Lendemains*, 16 (1991), 47–50.

Justification of Sade.

Lambergeon, Solange. *Un Amour de Sade, la Provence.* Le Pontet: Alain Barthélemy, 1991. Pp. 224.

Le Brun, Annie. "Sade, citations et incitation." *Lendemains,* 16 (1991), 51–53.

Lever, Maurice. *Donatien Alphonse François, Marquis de Sade*. Paris: Fayard, 1991. Pp. 912; appendices; bibliography.

Of all the renowned figures of world literature, Sade is neither the most famous nor the most-widely read, but he is the one from whose name some of the most frequently used nouns and adjectives were coined: sadism, sadist, sadistic etc. Maurice Lever's book is all the more welcome in that it tries to throw new light on the character and turns neither into a downright condemnation of Sade or into an apology or a hagiography. New materials were collected from family sources thanks to the recognition by Sade's descendants of the genius of their ancestor: the first appendix provides us with a complete genealogy of Sade from the thirteenth century to the present. Lever also takes advantage of three previous ground-breaking studies: Maurice Heine *Le Marquis de Sade* (Paris, 1950), Gilbert Lély *Vie du Marquis de Sade avec un examen de ses ouvrages* (Paris, 1952–57 and 1989) and Roland Barthes *Sade, Fourier, Loyola* (Paris, 1971). As far as Sade's life is concerned, Lever's study is definitive in many respects. None better than Lever has described Sade as a member of the privileged class: his "sadism" toward women is to a large extent a function of the latter's social position; his complete disregard for his mother is quite in line with an aristocrat's pride in his *lignée*; his protector, the comte de Charolais, was some sort of a monster who used to shoot at tilers working on roofs and killed his eight-month-old natural child by forcing him to drink a draught of brandy. A good part of Sade's childhood was spent with his uncle abbé de Sade whose amorous behaviour reminds us of the most prurient passages of the pornographic literature of the time. An atheist in the tradition of the seventeenth-century *esprits forts*, Sade was also a warring Chérubin "seeking the bubble reputation even in the cannon's mouth." His eroticism relied both on an aristocratic contempt for his fellow men and women and on some sort of spiritual or disciplinary exercise of a perverted will power.

Quite rightly Lever thinks that Sade's behavior during the French Revolution was dictated by his desire to save his life rather than by a liking for the theatricals of the *section des piques*. A sense of theatricals is, however, at the core of Sade's genius: his "wild parties" (Arcueil, Marseilles) were organized with a sense of stage direction that goes down to the minutest detail, and his twelve year stay at the Charenton asylum was allayed only by his staging plays with his inmates. Did not society, both the ancien régime and the Napoleonic bourgeois system, prove more sadistic than Sade in keeping him more than twenty years in confinement? Lever's study reads as the best insight into Sade's ambivalence: the schemer, performer, and dreamer of the wildest sexual fantasies preached in favor of verisimilitude in his works, loved his wife according to his own lights, and did not take revenge on his mother-in-law during the revolutionary years. Eroticism, lived or imagined, has one of its literary sources in Sade, and he stands poles apart from Choderlos de Laclos' intellectual sense of seduction and from Restif de la Bretonne who pandered to the sentimental and sensational. Lever shows us how Sade was a philosopher in keeping with the ideal of his age who gave radical answers to the problems of nature, evil, God, and society. Sade applied to the realm of sexual life the method of experimental rationalism. Lever's book is the best introduction to a literary work that reads as the *Summa Theologica* of a rake's progress.—Jean Rivière.

Lever, Maurice. "Quatre lettres inédites d'Ange Goudar au Marquis de Sade." *Dix-huitiéme siécle*, 21 (1991), 223–32.

Pérez, Concepción. *Estudio temático-estructural del universo narratio de Sade*. Madrid: Universidad Complutense de Madrid, 1988. Pp. 971.

Rev. by Carmen Camero in *Studi francesi*, 35 (1991), 151.

Pfister, Michael, and Stefon Zweifel. "Sadomasochistische Spiele mit dem Sprachleib-Bemerkungen zu Sades Sprache aus übersetzerischer Sicht." *Lendemains*, 16 (1991), 64–68.

Sade, Donatien Alphonse François de. *Oeuvres*. Vol I. Édition by Michel Delon. (Bibliothèque de la Pléiade, 371.) Paris: Gallimard, 1990. Pp. lxxxv + 1363. Cf. *ECCB*, n.s. 16, VI:446.

Rev. by David Coward in *TLS,* (Feb. 15, 1991), 5; by Ernest Sturm in *The French Review*, 65 (1991), 312–13; Correspondence from Claude Rawso in *TLS,* (Mar. 29, 1991), 13.

Seifert, Hans-Ulrich. "Allons saute marquis." *Lendemains*, 16 (1991), 45–46.

In German.

Themiseul de Saint-Hyacinthe (1684–1746)

Saint-Hyacinthe, Themiseul de. *Le chef-d'oeuvre d'un Inconnu*. Preface et annote par Henri Duranton (Editions du CNRS.) Paris: Publications de l'Universite de Saint-Étienne, 1991. Pp. 197.

Themiseul de Saint-Hyacinthe (1684–1746), having graduated at eighteen from the renowned Oratorian College of Troyes, injudiciously opted for a military career, only to find himself a prisoner of war for three years in Holland during which time, however, he was given freedom to enjoy the privileges of Dutch intellectual life. As a result, eventual repatriation led to the discovery that his proper place was back with fellow literary refugees of his exile. Once domiciled in Holland, he helped, in 1713, to launch the *Journal litteraire*, thus finally determining his career.

In 1714, aged thirty, he published, anonymously, the only one of his many writings destined to retain lasting attention, *Le chef-d'oeuvre d'un inconnu*, frequently republished, most recently once in the nineteenth century, and now, in 1991. The title refers to a poem (or *chanson*) in five stanzas of eight brief lines, which the author, when questioned, claimed to have heard sung so often that he learned it by heart, without learning anything about its origin. Of the said poem, the book affords a commentary on each stanza, line and word, by a Doctor Chrisostome Matanasius, portrayed on the cover of the first edition, and on the cover of the present one, as a pompous-looking pedant.

The book's initial object, never quite lost sight of, is to poke gentle ridicule at nit-picking scholars who revel in lengthy explanations of the obvious. Yet Doctor Matanasius gradually unfolds a wealth of reference, in such an interesting, amusing and at times charming way, that the reader intermittently encounters, behind the pretentious *poseur*, the truly erudite and congenial author. It is as if Saint-Hyacinthe so yearns to reveal his own vast repertoire of information that he transforms Doctor Matanasius into himself.

How does this affect the poem? Its commentary continues, enriched from edition to edition by a mixture of heterogenous phenomena, such as the quarrel of the ancients and the moderns, Jansenist dissensions, contemporary authors, writers of the Middle Ages and the sixteenth century (with few exceptions, then neglected or forgotten), anti-Catholic polemic, mimicry of Holy Scripture, and so on, the whole constituting a medley of Saint-Hyacinthe's literary preoccupations and of his observations on social thought and behavior during the first half of the eighteenth century.

Exemplary in rendering the present edition a definitive one, Henri Duranton, of the University of Saint-Etienne, does so by liberating the original text from extraneous material which had accumulated in successive earlier editions, and by providing indispensable notes and a pithy preface, at the close of which he writes: "Derrière la fantasie sans pretention, derrière l'oeuvre de circonstance, se dissimule une pensée qui n'est pas sans audace sur le plan intellectuel et esthetique." This reproduction of a unique work is amply justified by its impeccable presentation.—Robert Finch.

Friedrich von Schiller (1759–1805)

Benn, Sheila Margaret. *Pre-romantic attitudes to landscape in the writings of Friedrich Schiller.* (Quellen und Forschungen zur Sprach-und Kulturgeschichte der germanischen Völker. Neue Folge, 99 [223]) New York: Walter de Gruyter, 1991. Pp. xii + 242.

Drescher, H. W. "Account of *The Robbers*: Text und Verfasserschaft einer zeitgenössischen Besprechung von 1792." *Interdisziplinarität: Deutsche Sprache und Literatur im Spannungsfeld der Kulturen. Festschrift für Gerhart Mayer zum 65. Geburtstag.* Edited by M. Forster and K. Schilling. Frankfurt am Main and New York: Peter Lang, 1991. Pp. 514.

Martin, Graham C. "Historical Fact versus Literary Fiction: Members of the House of Liechtenstein Occurring in Schiller's *Wallenstein* and Grillparzer's *König Ottokar.*" *Modern Language Review*, 86 (1991), 348.

Reed, T. J. "Coming of Age in Prussia and Swabia: Kant, Schiller, and the Duke." *Modern Language Review*, 86 (1991), 613–26.

Discusses Karl Eugen and the Karlsschule as patrons of intellectual freedom.

Reed, T. J. *Schiller.* (Past Masters.) New York and Oxford: Oxford U. Press, 1991. Pp. vii +120; bibliography.

Sharpe, Lesley. *Friedrich Schiller: Drama, Thought and Politics.* (Cambridge Studies in German.) Cambridge and New York: Cambridge U. Press, 1991. Pp. xiv + 390; bibliography.

Friedrich Ernst Daniel Schleirmacher (1768–1834)

Thouard, Denis. "L'esprit et la lettre. Rhétorique et herméutique dans les *Discours sur la religion* de Schleiermacher." *Etudes philosophiques*, (1991), 501–523.

An explanation of the *Discourses* (1799) and their divergent points of view in terms of Schleirmacher's theory and practice of dialectic and rhetoric.

Thomas Shadwell (1642?–1692)

Dopheide, Theodor. *'Satyr the true medicine': die Komödien Thomas Shadwells.* Frankfurt am Main and New York: Peter Lang, 1991. Pp. 275.

Shadwell, Thomas. *Thomas Shadwell's* The Lancashire-Witches, and Teague o Divelly the Irish Priest: *A Critical Old-Spelling Edition.* Edited by Judith Bailey Slagle. London and New York: Garland Publishers, 1991. Pp. viii + 313; bibliography.

Thomas Shadwell's *The Lancashire-Witches, and Tegue o Divelly the Irish Priest*, first performed in 1681, presents a paradoxical, even self-contradictory view of the supernatural. The play ridicules its bumpkins and opportunists for their belief in witches. As Bellfort, one of the play's several rational skeptics, remarks, "I shall not fly from my Belief that everything is done by Natural Causes, because I cannot presently assign those Causes" (IV.460–62; p.

152). Yet the play also presents its witches as genuine, even having the Devil appear to them on stage and present them with powers over the law of nature:

The Sky no more shall its known laws obey, / Night shall retreat while you prolong the day.

(III. 669-70; p. 127)

In three spectacular scenes, the witches fly about the stage, worshipping the devil, initiating a novice, animating matter, and plaguing the country folk with their tricks.

Twentieth-century critics have seen the witch plot as an allegory of the Popish Plot controversy of 1679, or as merely a way for Shadwell to introduce exciting special effects. The fact that the play was heavily censored by the Master of Revels underlines its topicality, but the parts most censored were the religious discussions between the intolerant, upstart Anglican chaplain Smerk and the crudely drawn, unscrupulous Irish Catholic priest, Teague o Divelly.

The Lancashire-Witches has not been edited since Montague Summers' five-volume edition of Shadwell's *Complete Works* in 1927. Although the 1968 Ayer reprint of Summers' edition, which is still in print, is an elegant presentation of the play, Judith Slagle's new, critical, old-spelling edition is more scholarly and thorough, having as it does the advantage of more than sixty year's development of the theory of textual scholarship. Slagle's edition is based on a careful examination of all early editions, including twelve copies of the first 1682 quarto to correct many silent corrections, particularly using the second 1682 quarto to correct the first. Slagle prints a full table of textual variations, including a collation of the four quarto editions (two of 1682 and one each of 1693 and 1694) and a list of press variants in the first quarto. Although general readers will notice little difference between the Summers and Slagle texts, for scholars, Slagle's edition will clearly become the standard one.

Slagle includes a useful, brief discussion of Shadwell's life, placing this play in the context of its author's career and making a modest claim for his significance: "While Thomas Shadwell may not be revered today as a 'great' playwright, he must certainly be considered a good one" (p. 5). Her claim that Shadwell "introduced the character of the country gentleman in *Witches*" (p. 5) is hard to sustain in light of Howard and Buckingham's *The Country Gentleman* of 1669.

Slagle discusses the performance history of the play, including casting, costumes, and stage machinery. She examines Shadwell's sources, including the real-life trials of accused witches in Lancashire in 1612, the 1634 play by Thomas Heywood and Richard Broome, and two plays by Shadwell's acknowledged master, Ben Jonson. Finally, she provides 172 pages of explanatory notes on the text. Her discussion of possible critical approaches to the play does not resolve the apparent contradiction between its skeptical materialism and its farcically triumphant supernaturalism. Perhaps that contradiction cannot be resolved. But whatever hypothesis future critics advance, they will be indebted to Slagle. Her authoritative edition, thoroughly annotated, provides a valuable service to scholarship, for which Judith Slagle and Garland Press deserve our gratitude.—John H. O'Neill.

Frances Sheridan (1724–1766)

Mikhail, E. H. (ed.). *Sheridan: Interviews and Recollections.* (Interviews and Recollections Series.) Basingstoke, UK, and London: Macmillan, 1989. Pp. xviii + 152; bibliography; chronology. Cf. *ECCB*, n.s. 15, VI:409.

Rev. (with reservations) by Brean S. Hammond in *Notes and Queries*, 236 (1991), 236–37.

Richard Brinsley Sheridan (1751–1816)

van Ostade, Ingrid Tieken-Boon. "Social Ambition Reflected in the Language of Betsy and Richard Brinsley Sheridan." *Neuphilologische Mitteillungen*, 92 (1991), 237–46.

Christopher Smart (1722–1771)

Guest, Harriet. *A Form of Sound Words: The Religious Poetry of Christopher Smart.* Oxford: Clarendon Press, 1989. Pp. xiv + 294. Cf. *ECCB*, n.s. 16, VI:448; 15, VI:410–11.

Rev. by Betty Rizzo in *Eighteenth-Century Studies*, 24 (1991), 359–63; by Karina Williamson in *Review of English Studies*, 42 (1991), 273–75; by David Womersley in *Notes and Queries*, 235 (1990), 234–35.

Smart, Christopher. *The Annotated Letters of Christopher Smart.* Edited by Robert Mahoney and Betty Rizzo. Carbondale, IL: Southern Illinois U. Press, 1991. Pp. xxxvii + 185; appendices; frontispiece; plates.

In this small, handsome volume, Betty Rizzo and Robert Mahoney confront yet again problems that have long plagued Christopher Smart Scholarship, focusing this time on the poet's letters. The edition contains the first complete printing of just thirty-three that Smart wrote from 1743–1771. Of those, only fifteen are taken from the actual letters themselves. A nine-page appendix explains in detail about the history of five or six other letters that had been published at one time but are no longer extant. Another four have been noted by the editors "in various book catalogs . . ., the texts of which are at present lost to us" (p. xv). Still five other lost letters "are discussed here because it is at least known that [Smart] wrote them" (p. xv). Added to the small collection are four published letters of dedication by Smart. While the editors assume that the poet, like others of his day, "wrote thousands of letters" (p. xv), so few have surfaced that one wonders again about Smart's reputation from his own day to the present.

In recent years, Smart and his work have enjoyed a modest resurgence of interest among literary critics, sparked by some biographical studies in the 1960s, textual editions in the 1970s and 1980s, and Mahoney and Rizzo's extensive bibliography in 1984. However, in his own day, and for more than a century after his death, Smart suffered from an assessment that depended upon his confinement for madness. Whether one looks at his nephew's collection of Smart's poems (1791) that omitted the magnificent *Song to David*, or at Robert Browning's *Parleyings* (1887) that accorded Smart a moment of poetic genius arising from madness, or at Benjamin Brittain's musical adaptation of *Rejoice in the Lamb*, Smart's affecting lines written in confinement, one finds the results incomplete and slanted.

Rizzo and Mahoney's collection of letters underscore the fate of Smart and his reputation. They note in the introduction that "his wife, daughters, mother, sisters, brother-in-law, and nephew and biographer all destroyed such letters" (pp. xv–xvi) because they believed Smart was insane. Most of the letters in the collection, of necessity then, are not as revealing as one might hope, for they were not preserved by friends or family who knew or honored him. They are instead business letters that for the most part survived in files of men such as Dodsley, raising the hope in the editors that more of Smart's letters may some day surface in catalogues. So if one expects to read Smart's letters to his family or bits and pieces of his poetry, one will be disappointed. What one encounters are brief requests from the poet with occasional responses of note, all accompanied with extensive and informative introductory material by the editors. While we may regret that we learn too little about the poet, we do learn about his relationship with some significant figures of his day. For example, Smart's letter to Pope offering to translate the *Essay on Man* into Latin (pp. 8–9) is preceded by a long introduction (pp. 1–8) and followed by Pope's courteous response (pp. 9–10).

The work is a contribution to the steady flow of information and material on Smart that we have come to expect in the twentieth century. We look forward to more in the future.—Sophia B. Blades.

Adam Smith (1723–1790)

Pack, Spencer J. *Capitalism as a Moral System: Adam Smith's Critique of the Free Market Economy.* Aldershot, UK: E. Elgar (distributed through Brookfield, VT: Ashgate), 1991. Pp. viii + 199; bibliography.

Werhane, Patricia H. *Adam Smith and His Legacy for Modern Capitalism.* New York and Oxford: Oxford U. Press, 1991. Pp. ix + 219; bibliography.

West, Edwin G. *Adam Smith and the Modern Economics: From Market Behaviour to Public Choice.* Aldershot, UK, and Brookfield, VT: E. Elgar, 1990. Pp. vii + 212; illustrations.

Rev. by F. Petrella, Jr. in *Choice*, 28 (1991), 829.

Tobias Smollett (1721–1771)

Adamson, William Robert. *Cadences of Unreason: A Study of Pride and Madness in the Novels of Tobias Smollett.* Frankfurt am Main and New York: Peter Lang, 1990. Pp. 226.

Rev. (severely) by Melvyn New in *The Scriblerian*, 24 (1991), 65–66.

Costopoulos-Almon, Olga. "A Note on Smollett's *Atom.*" *Notes and Queries,* 236 (1991), 191–92.

"The name of Peter Gore of Croton is a pun of paregoric and croton oil."

Smollett, Tobias. *The Adventures of Ferdinand Count Fathom.* Edited by Jerry C. Beasley. (The Works of Tobias Smollett, 1.) Athens, GA: U. of Georgia Press, 1988. Pp. xlii + 480.

Rev. (with another work) by Kathryn Sutherland in *Review of English Studies*, 42 (1991), 272–73.

Smollett, Tobias. *The Expedition of Humphry Clinker.* Introduction and Notes by Thomas R. Preston. Text edited by O M Brack, Jr. (The Works of Tobias Smollett.) Athens, GA, and London: U. of Georgia Press, 1990. Pp. lx + 500; illustrations; map.

Rev. (favorably) by R. G. Brown in *Choice*, 28 (1991), 1783.

Smollett, Tobias. *The History and Adventures of an Atom.* Notes and Introduction by Robert Adams Day. Edited by O M Brack, Jr. Athens, GA: U. of Georgia Press, 1989. Pp. lxxxv + 360.

Rev. by Deborah D. Rogers in *The Scriblerian*, 23 (1991), 254–56.

Anne Louise Germaine Necker de Staël (1766–1817)

Durand-Sendrail, Béatrice. "Madame de Staël et la condition post-révolutionnaire." *The Romantic Review,* 82 (1991), 36–48.

Goldberger, Avriel, Madelyn Gutwirth, and Karyna Szmurlo (eds.). *Germaine de Stäel: Crossing the Borders*. New Brunswick, NJ: Rutgers U. Press, 1991. Pp. xii + 248.

Laurence Sterne (1713–1768)

Bandry, Anne, and Geoffrey Day (eds.). *The Clockmakers Outcry Against the Author of* The Life and Opinions of Tristram Shandy. Winchester, UK: Winchester College Printing Society, 1989.

Rev. in the "Commentary" article, "The Super-foetations of a Rantipole Brain," by Jem McCue in *TLS*, (May 17, 1991), 12.
   200 copies reprinted as *The Shandean; or, An Annual Volume Devoted to Laurence Sterne and His Works*, 1

Gager, Valerie. "Charles Dickens and Yorick: Shakespeare or Sterne." *Notes and Queries*, 236 (1991), 313–15.

Lamb, Jonathan. *Sterne's Fiction and the Double Principle*. (Cambridge Studies in Eighteenth-Century English Literature and Thought, 3.) Cambridge and New York: Cambridge U. Press, 1989. Pp. xii + 161; plates. Cf. *ECCB*, n.s. 16, VI:452; 15, VI:415.

Rev. by Melvyn New in *The Scriblerian*, 23 (1991), 228–31; by Barry Roth in *Notes and Queries*, 236 (1991), 112–13.

New, Melvyn. " 'Scholia' to the Florida *Tristram Shandy* Annotations." *The Scriblerian*, 23 (1991), 296–97.

The Shandean: or, An Annual Volume Devoted to Laurence and His Work. Vol 3. Amsterdam, Netherlands: The Laurence Sterne Trust, 1991.

Volume 3 (November 1991) includes the following items:
   Judith Hawley, " 'Hints and Documents': I: A Bibliography for Tristram Shandy," pp. 9–36.
   Jacques Berthoud, "The Beggar in *A Sentimental Journey*," pp. 37–48.
   Melvyn New, "Swift as Ogre, Richardson as Dolt: Rescuing Sterne from the Eighteenth
Century," pp. 49–60.
   Michael J. O'Shea, "Laurence Sterne's Display of Heraldry," pp. 61–69.
   Diana Patterson, "Tristram's Marbeling and Marblers," pp. 70–97.
   Kenneth Monkman, "Sterne's Farewell to Politics," pp. 98–125.
   Anne Bandry, "The Publication of the Spurious Volumes of *Tristram Shandy*," pp. 126–37.
   Peter Jan De Voogd, "Henry William Bunbury, Illustrator of *Tristram Shandy*," pp. 138–43.
   Madeleine Descargues, "Ignatio Sancho's *Letters*," pp. 145–66.
   Kenneth Monkman, (ed., with notes), "A Letter by Lydia, and a Letter by Elizabeth."
pp.167–82.

Shipley, J. B. "Tristram's Dearly Beloved: Or, His Jenny's an ***." *English Language Notes*, 29, 1 (1991), 45–51.

Links Jenny's name to a bird, a machine, and an ass.

Sterne, Lawrence. *Tristram Shandy*. Introduction by Peter Conrad. New York: Knopf/Random House, 1991. Pp. 750.

Jonathan Swift (1667–1745)

Cronin, Mark. "Rudyard Kipling's Houyhnhnms." *The Scriblerian*, 23 (1991), 294–96.

Cunningham, John. "Perversions of the Eucharist in *Gulliver's Travels*." *Christianity and Literature*, 40 (1991), 345–64.

Frequent figures of the corrupted sacrament impart a Christian significance to the narrative and indicate Swift's concern with the Fall.

Eilon, Daniel. *Factions' Fictions: Ideological Closure in Swift's Satire*. Newark, DE: U. of Deleware Press (distributed through London and Cranbury, NJ: Associated University Presses), 1991. Pp. 212; bibliography.

In his compelling study of "faction" in Swift's satire, Daniel Eilon carefully argues that Swift's work reveals a preoccupation with ideological closure, "the enclosed environment cultivated within cliques, political parties, aristocracies, professions, and religions" (p. 15), and that this preoccupation gives his "politics, ethics, notions of language, and satiric theory . . . analogous structures" (p. 161). The common term on which Eilon's various analogies depend is arbitrary power (or the abuse of power). Factions must create the illusion (the "fiction") that their narrow priorities and arbitrary authority are legitimate and privileged.

Eilon focuses on the Biblical example of Babel as the trope for Swift's fears for his own culture. The story of "rampant pluralism" provides a paradigm for the history of the seventeeth century and its fragmentation into political party, religious dissension, and philosophical relativism. Examples from early works (*A Tale of a Tub*, *Contests and Dissensions in Athens and Rome*) and late (sermons, *Gulliver's Travels*) demonstrate how the shadow of Babel falls over Swift's attacks on personal ambition. What intrigues Swift the satirist is Babel's paradoxical function as simultaneously the origin of faction and language.

In five chapters, Eilon's argument deftly synthesizes examples from Swift's writing with their historical occasions and with contemporary political theory. In a manner comparable to David Noke's *Jonathan Swift: A Hypocrite Reversed* (1985), the range of references to Swift's actual political activities places the satiric fictions firmly in a historical context. Correspondence, sermons, pamphlets, even marginal notations all seem to illuminate Swift's concern with faction. On issues such as consent, contract, and natural law in politics and religion, Eilon's analysis reveals a Swift who moderates between Tory and Whig, conservative and radical. Swift's respect for the past (which includes the tradition of kingship) is balanced against a conviction that only the people as a whole can legitimize political authority.

Ultimately, Eilon attempts to translate political theory into literary practice, to show Swift's obsession with faction as essential to his strategies as a satirist. His powerful ironic negations are explained: "Swift's punitive desire to ablate and veto is based on his perception of the virtuous as an embattled minority, swamped with the multifariousness of the wicked" (p. 136). Even when there is no wicked in evidence, virtue can appear swamped, as revealed in his comments to Stella about Lady Ashburnham: "I hate Life, when I think it exposed to such Accidents, and to see so many thousand wretches burthening the earth while such as her dye, makes me think God did never intend Life for a Blessing" (quoted on p. 136).

Eilon traces changes in Swift's satiric practice as he grows older and more disillusioned about the powers of the virtuous minority in the face of the tyranny of the many: "The final years of Swift's satiric career see him retreating from the reformative undertakings of earlier days into a humor that is private" (p. 155). Eilon claims that the late satire, "in its absurd demands on readers, . . . is self-destructive." Perhaps this turning inward is the inevitable result of the satirist sharing some traits with his target; while criticizing arbitrary power, Swift himself enjoyed the arbitrary wielding of power in irony. Eilon continues: "While it bears the image of the inward unexamined assumption of the ideologies that it parodies, Swiftian satire is the diametric opposite of naive suggestability" (p. 163).

This well-written study contextualizes Swift's ironic practice and shows how it appropriates but transcends the power of faction.—Melinda Alliker Rabb.

Flynn, Carol Houlihan. *The Body in Swift and Defoe.* (Cambridge Studies in Eighteenth-Century English Literature and Thought, 5.) Cambridge and New York: Cambridge U. Press, 1990. Pp. viii + 231.

Rev. by Kirk Combe in *Notes and Queries*, 236 (1991), 544–45; by Everett Zimmerman in *The Scriblerian*, 24 (1991), 51–52.

Forster, Jean-Paul. *Jonathan Swift: The Fictions of the Satirist.* (European University Studies. Ser. XIV: Anglo-Saxon Language and Literature, 220.) Berne and New York: Peter Lang, 1991. Pp. 248.

Rev. (favorably) by R. G. Brown in Choice, 29 (1991), 591–92.

Gray, Jonathan, J. B. Guerinot, and J. K. Welcher. "Re Egg Breakers, Eggcups, and Gulliver." *The Scriblerian*, 24 (1991), 58–61.

The eggs are soft-boiled and eaten from the shell.

Gugler, Mary Beth. "Mercury and the 'Pains of Love' in Jonathan Swift's 'A Beautiful Young Nymph Going to Bed'. " *English Language Notes*, 29 (1991), 31–36.

Corinna is suffering from mercury poisoning.

Hunting, Robert. *Jonathan Swift.* Rev. ed. Boston: Twayne, 1989. Pp. 152.

Rev. in *The Scriblerian*, 24 (1991), 70–71.

McMinn, Joseph. *Johnathan Swift: A Literary Life.* (Literary Lives.) Basingstoke, UK: Macmillan; New York: St. Martin's Press, 1991. Pp. xi + 172.

Rev. (with reservations) by J. Wilkinson in *Choice*, 29 (1991), 446.

Jonathan Swift: A Literary Life is the eighth volume in The Literary Lives series (the others so far in the Restoration and the eighteenth century are Felicity Rosslyn's *Alexander Pope* and Paul Hammond's *John Dryden*), which attempts to "follow the outline of the writers' working lives, not in the spirit of traditional biography," but rather in relationship to the "professional, publishing and social contexts which shaped their writing," and to give both "students and general readers alike . . . a more informed historical reading of their works" (p. ii). Following this critical strategy, McMinn attempts to provide "an account of Swift's formation and development as a writer," to steer a middle course between literary criticism and biographical history, and to exclude "textual interpretation and comprehensive bibliographical detail whenever such factors do not bear on Swift's practice as poet, pamphleteer and correspondent" (p. ix).

McMinn's book is in the tradition of Ricardo Quintana's *Swift: An Introduction* (Oxford, 1955) and Robert Hunting's *Jonathan Swift* (Twayne, 1967; revised G.K. Hall, 1989) in providing brief introductions to the author's life and work that are probably more helpful to the student and the teacher whose specialty is not the eighteenth century. Unlike Quintana and Hunting, however, McMinn provides neither a chronology nor a selected bibliography, both of which would be very helpful to the audience at which the book and the series are aimed.

In seven chapters McMinn analyzes Swift's career from his childhood in Dublin to his death seventy-three years later. Chapter 1, "Secretary and Apprentice," covers the youthful years, the Moor Park interlude, *A Tale of a Tub* and *The Battle of the Books*. Chapter 2, "Pox on the Dissenters and Independents," is concerned with the years between 1704 and 1709. Chapter 3, "A Pact with Power," deals with his political career and writings down to 1714. Chapter 4, "A Deceptive Retirement," discusses the period between 1714 and 1722. Chapter 5, "Literary Triumph in Ireland and England," analyzes *The Drapier's Letters* and *Gulliver's Travels*. Chapter 6, "I Have stretched out my Hand, and no Man regarded," focuses on the years down to 1732, and Chapter 7, "A Poetic Valediction," takes up the last years and works.

McMinn succeeds in giving the reader a clear sense of how Swift's involvement with the political and religious affairs of his day, as well as how his reaction to the intellectual climate of his era, impinged upon his writing. One may occasionally have reservations about one of McMinn's interpretations or emphases, but his interweaving of biography and criticism is both deft and engaging.—Robert C. Steensma.

Mueller, Judith C. "The Ethics of Reading in Swift's *Abstract* on Freethinking." *Studies in English Literature 1500–1900*, 31 (1991), 483–98.

The pamphlet insists that readers assess the "radical voices" in texts on the basis of their own integrity rather than church authority.

Nash, Richard. "Entrapment and Ironic Mode in *Tale of a Tub*." *Eighteenth-Century Studies*, 24 (1991), 415–31.

The reader must be wary of credulity and curiosity, and of allegory and irony.

Noçon, Peter. "Swift Translated: The Case of the Former GDR." *Swift Studies*, 6 (1991), 114–18.

Passman, Dirk Friedrich. *Full of Improbable Lies:* Gulliver's Travels *und die Reiseliteratur vor 1726*. (Aspekte der englischen Geistes und Kulturgeschichte, 10.) Frankfurt am Main and New York: Peter Lang, 1987. Pp. 505; appendices; bibliography.

Rev. by Bernfried Nugel in *The Scriblerian*, 23 (1991), 260–61.

Patey, Douglas Lane. "Swift's Satire on 'Science' and the Structure of *Gulliver's Travels*." *English Language Notes*, 58 (1991), 809–39.

The "new science" of Swift's day claimed to explain too much, and tried to introduce argumentative certainty into the realm of prudence, where only probability and "imitation" were valid.

Probyn, Clive. " 'Travelling west-ward': The Lost Letter from Jonathan Swift to Charles Ford." *Studies in Bibliography*, 44 (1991), 265–271; photographic facsimile.

Regan, Thomas J. " 'Allum Flower' in Swift's *The Lady's Dressing Room*." *The Scriblerian*, 23 (1991), 292–93.

Rielly, Edward J. (ed.). *Approaches to Teaching Swift's* Gulliver's Travels. (Approaches to Teaching World Literature, 18.) New York: MLA, 1988. Pp. ix + 148; bibliography. Cf. *ECCB*, n.s. 16, VI:456–57.

Rev. by James Woolley in *The Scriblerian*, 24 (1991), 66–68.

Rodino, Richard H. " 'Splendide Mendaz': Authors, Characters, and Readers in *Gulliver's Travels.*" *PMLA*, 106 (1991), 1054–70.

Considers the connections between language and power, the instabilities in Gulliver's character and stories, the "texts" that he "reads," the shifts in the reader's role, Swift's disguises, titles, and captions, and the responses to these various schools and modes of criticism.

Smith, Frederick N. (ed.). *The Genres of* Gulliver's Travels. Newark, DE: U. of Delaware Press, 1990. Pp. 265.

Rev. by Leon Guilhamet in *Eighteenth-Century Studies*, 24 (1991), 378–81; by Richard H. Rodino in *The Scriblerian*, 23 (1991), 218–21.

Swift, Jonathan. *Gulliver's Travels.* Introduction by Pat Rogers. New York: Knopf/Random House, 1991. Pp. xli + 318.

Wawers, Elke. *Swift zwischen Tradition und Fortschritt. Studie zum ideengeschichtlichen Kontext von* The Battle of the Books *und* A Tale of a Tub. Frankfurt am Main and New York: Peter Lang, 1989. Pp. 257.

Rev. by Jorg W. Rademacher in *The Scriblerian*, 23 (1991), 256.

Worth, Chris. "Swift's 'Flying Island': Buttons and Bomb Vessels." *Review of English Studies*, 42 (1991), 343–60.

The island has Scriblerian origins, resembles a button, not a sphere, and may have application to Button's Whiggish coffee house.

Zollner, Klaus. *As you can see in the text—:Which Passages Do Literary Scholars Quote and Interpet in* Gulliver's Travels? Frankfurt am Main and New York: Peter Lang, 1989. Pp. 343.

Rev. by Gene Washington in *The Scriblerian*, 24 (1991), 68–70.

Edward Taylor (1642–1729)

Gatta, John. *Gracious Laughter: The Meditative Wit of Edward Taylor.* Columbia, MO: U. of Missouri Press, 1989. Pp. xvii + 228; bibliography; frontispiece. Cf. *ECCB*, n.s. 15, VI:421.

Rev. (with other works) by Darlene Harbour Unrue in *Religion & Literature*, 23 (1991), 87–90.

Lewis Theobald (1688–1744)

Seary, Peter. *Lewis Theobald and the Editing of Shakespeare*. Oxford: Clarendon Press; New York: Oxford U. Press, 1990. Pp. xvi + 248; appendices. Cf. *ECCB*, n.s. 16, VI:458–59.

Rev. by Arthur Sherbo in *The Scriblerian*, 24 (1991), 80; (with another work) by Marcus Walsh in *Essays in Criticism*, 42 (1992), 243–51.

James Thomson (1700–1748)

Crisman, William C. "Blake's 'The Crystal Cabinet' as a Reworking of Thomson's *The Castle of Indolence*." *English Language Notes*, 29 (1991), 52–59.

Sambrook, James. *James Thomson, 1700–1748: A Life*. New York: Oxford U. Press; Oxford: Clarendon Press, 1991. Pp. 332; bibliography; illustrations.

John Vanbrugh (1664–1726)

McCormick, Frank. *Sir John Vanbrugh: The Playwright as Architect*. University Park, PA: Pennsylvania State U. Press, 1991. Pp. ix + 196; illustrations.

As its title suggests, this book is primarily concerned with exploring the possible interrelationships between Vanbrugh's two complementary careers, which McCormick attempts to do by reading all of Vanbrugh's works in the light of his biography. After opening with a cursory review of that biography, McCormick presents a helpful account of the plays, examining their implicit social commentary and emphasizing Vanbrugh's habit of avoiding traditional resolutions, thereby posing intriguing moral questions. This is the book's strongest section; however, when McCormick leaves his prefatory surveys to pursue his central arguments, things begin to go awry.

Basically, McCormick argues that Vanbrugh's theatrical experience influenced his stage-set-like architectural designs; that his childhood in the walled, medieval city of Chester, and his incarceration in the Chateau Vincennes and the Bastille, contributed to his affection for medieval architectural structures; and that his early career as a soldier is accountable for the "vocabulary of siege" he employed both in his plays and in his citadel-like building complexes. Though one might think that four years imprisonment would scarcely inculcate an affection for fortress-like architecture, McCormick's observations otherwise seem at first plausible. Vanbrugh was fond of medieval touches, and his buildings were theatrical—but then again, most baroque architecture is theatrical, and some of it is even mock-medieval. Therein lies McCormick's central problem: he consistently fails to distinguish between what was uniquely Vanbrugh, and what was commonplace. For instance, while it is true that the main block/flanking blocks arrangement Vanbrugh used for Castle Howard (1700–26), Blenheim (1705–16), and Seaton Delaval (1718–29) resembles the standard Restoration stage with backdrop and side wings, it is also the same basic block arrangement Le Vau used for the College des Quatre Nations (1662), Roger Pratt for Clarendon House (1664–67), and Wren for both Chelsea Hospital (1682–92) and Winchester Palace (1683–85), Talman for Kiveton (1694–1704), Wren and Hawksmoor for Greenwich (1696 onwards). Another Vanbrugh architectural characteristic borrowed from the stage, according to McCormick, is the proscenium arch, which we find in Blenheim's Great Hall (1716). But Wren's Pembroke Chapel at Cambridge (1663–65), his Painted Hall at Greenwich (1708–12), and Hawksmoor's St. Anne's Limehouse (1714–30), St. George Bloomsbury (1716–31), and Long Library at Blenheim (1722–25), all feature proscenium arches (in passing, McCormick erroneously attributes Hawksmoor's Long Library to Vanbrugh). True, the block arrangement and proscenium arch are theatrical features, but they were also architectural formulae produced by people whose inspiration was not the theater, but each other. It seems likely that Vanbrugh picked up these stock devices from baroque architecture.

The point about Vanbrugh receiving his "medieval" inspiration from his experiences in Chester and in French prisons is similarly troublesome. McCormick treats Vanbrugh's nostalgia for the medieval as if it were a unique trait, forgetting Wren's mock-medieval St. Mary Aldermary (1681–82), complete with fan vaulting and Gothic tower (1701–2), his Gothic steeple for St. Dunstan-in-the-East (1697–99), Hawksmoor's northern quadrangle of All Souls, Oxford (1716–35) with its crocketed pinnacles, buttresses, and its two Gothic-flavored towers, and his Western Towers of Westminster Abbey (1733–45). Vanbrugh was only one of several baroque architects employing a medieval vocabulary, and we need not look narrowly toward just Chester or France for sources of this inspiration. All Vanbrugh had to do to see medieval, either in genuine or recent form, was to look around him.

The weakest part of this book, however, is its treatment of Blenheim, in which McCormick's tendency to see the particular and ignore the general seems to have gotten the better of his common sense. Not content to observe the many motifs imparting a general military ambience to Blenheim—the cannonball, pike, lance, cuirass, shield, banner, and drum ornamentation scattered about the grounds—McCormick contends that the estate evokes the battle of Blenheim quite specifically. Where Marlborough and his troops crossed the Nebel River, Vanbrugh puts a Grand Bridge across the Glyme; and where Marlborough's army gathered for the impending battle, Vanbrugh places his main block, which "has something of the air of an army massing for attack." Furthermore, the original designs show a polygonal, fortification-like garden appended to the South front, so that "what Belenheim's entrance front [facing North] threatened with all its immense projecting wings to take by force, its garden front gave the appearance of consolidating behind a mass of fortification work garrisoned by legions of arboreal soldiers" (p. 116). The problems here are abundant. First, evidently both the stones and shrubbery represent soldiers, which shouldn't be too surprising, since elsewhere stones can represent both soldiers and fortifications. Second, one notices that the charging army seems to have a garrison at its rear, which does not happen when armies attack from field positions—perhaps the pseudo-garrison is the target town of Blenheim, in which case the army is charging the wrong way. Also, the block is "moving" away from the main entrance, apparently attacking the sheep one usually finds on the hill across the river; and since the southern portico of Blenheim's main block is crowned by a bust of Louis XIV, it raises the question of what Louis is doing in the middle of the English army rather than across the river with his sheep.

If there are fruitful connections between the plays, the architecture, and the biography, and one suspects there must be, McCormick hasn't yet found them.—Cedric D. Reverand II.

Luc de Clapiers, Marquis de Vauvenargues (1715–1747)

Boucherie, Jean-Luc. "Vauvencargues: De l'Inquiétude vécue à l'expérience de savoir." *Dix-huitième siècle*, 21 (1991), 369–81.

Giambattista Vico (1668–1743)

Verene, Donald Phillip. *The New Art of Autobiography: An Essay on the* Life of Giambattista Vico Written by Himself. New York: Oxford U. Press; Oxford: Clarendon Press, 1991. Pp. xi + 263; bibliography; illustrations.

François-Marie Arouet de Voltaire (1694–1778)

Alatri, Paolo. *Introduzione a Voltaire.* (Gli Scrittori, 12.) Rome: Laterza, 1989. Pp. 178. Cf. *ECCB*, n.s.16, VI:460; 15, VI:424.

Rev. (briefly) by Franco Piva in *Studi francesi*, 34 (1991), 527.

Albina, Larissa L. " 'De l'homme': Marat lu par Voltaire." *Revue d'histoire littéraire de la France*, 91 (1991), 932–36.

On Voltaire's reactions to Marat's 1775–76 work.

Bombelles, Marc de. *Journal de voyage en Grande-Bretagne et en Irelande en 1784.* Edited by Jacques Gury. (Studies on Voltaire and the Eighteenth Century, 269.) Oxford: The Voltaire Foundation at the Taylor Institution, 1989. Pp. x + 370.

Rev. by J. Lough in *Modern Language Review*, 86 (1991), 725–26.

Desnè, Roland, and Anna Mandich. "Une Lettre oubliée de Voltaire sur le Messie. Entre Polier de Bottens et l'*Encyclopedie.*" *Dix-huitième siècle*, 21 (1991), 201–12.

Gargett, Graham. "Jacob Vernet's *Lettre À Monsieur Le Premier Syndic*: A Reply to Voltaire and the *Dialogues Chrétiens.*" *Modern Language Review*, 86 (1991), 35–48.

Lafarge, Francisco. *Voltaire en Espagne 1734–1835.* (Studies on Voltaire and the Eighteenth Century, 261.) Oxford: The Voltaire Foundation at the Taylor Institution, 1989. Pp. vii + 251; appendices; bibliography. Cf. *ECCB*, n.s. 15, VI:428.

Rev. (briefly) by Paolo Alatri in *Studi francesi*, 34 (1991), 527.

Mason, Haydn T. (ed.). *Studies on Voltaire and the Eighteenth Century.* Vol. 256. Oxford: The Voltaire Foundation at the Taylor Institution, 1988. Pp. 333.

Rev. By D. J. Adams in *French Studies*, 45 (1991), 80; by Paolo Alatri in *Studi francesi*, 34 (1990), 140–41; by D. Williams in *Modern Language Review*, 86 (1991), 456–58.

Mason, Haydn. T. (ed.). *Studies on Voltaire and the Eighteenth Century.* Vol. 260. Oxford: The Voltaire Foundation at the Taylor Institution, 1989. Pp. v + 512. Cf. *ECCB*, n.s. 16, VI:463.

Rev. by D. Williams in *Modern Language Review*, 86 (1991), 719–20.

Mason, Haydn. T. (ed.). *Studies on Voltaire and the Eighteenth Century.* Vol. 266. Oxford: The Voltaire Foundation at the Taylor Institution, 1989. Pp. v + 512.

Rev. by Vivienne Mylne in *Modern Language Review*, 86 (1991), 721–22.

Mason, Haydn. T. (ed.). *Studies on Voltaire and the Eighteenth Century.* Vol. 284. Oxford: The Voltaire Foundation at the Taylor Institution, 1991. Pp. vi + 399.

Nineteen separate pieces ranging in length from notes to a monograph defy individual review. Suffice it to say that the quality is for the most part high, and that students of the various authors and issues covered will find profit and stimulation from this volume, whose contents will no doubt already have appeared in Klapp's *Bibliographie* by the time this review sees the light of day (*mea culpa!*). As usual, it is a pleasure to note *SVEC*'s loyal commitment to solid scholarly work *sine metaphysica*.

All the more regrettable it is, then, that the 70-page mongraph on the *Nouvelle Héloïse* chosen to head the collection should display serious scholarly weaknesses. It is hard to read with confidence beyond the statement on p. 6 that Saint-Preux's relationship with Julie "reste uniquement platonique." How carefully can the author have read

Part I, letters LIII, LIV, LV, LVII (especially the penultimate paragraph), LVIII (first paragraph), LXIII (the postscriptum), LXV (first paragraph), and Letter IV (penultimate paragraph) of Part II? The text clearly establishes that, at Julie's invitation, the two lovers spend a night of clandestine ecstasy together, and that Julie later suffers a miscarriage following the physical abuse inflicted by her father. Some Platonic relationship! Other minor signs of carelessness: Henri Coulet's name is spelled correctly and incorrectly, seemingly at random, and two grammatical errors introduced (p. 53) into a single sentence quoted from François Bluche's *La Vie quotidienne de la noblesse française au 18e*. Far more serious than these lapses is, however, the fact that in substance the study presents nothing new for any alert member of the special reading public who would be reading Rousseau's novel anyway. *SVEC* is not to be commended on its editorial board's work in this instance. Still, in all fairness to the author and *SVEC*, half-baked publications will continue to plague our discipline as long as American universities continue to reward faculty on the basis of title-count.—Robert J. Ellrich.

Mason, Haydn. T. (ed.). *Studies on Voltaire and the Eighteenth Century: Lectures de Raynal*. Vol. 286. Oxford: The Voltaire Foundation at the Taylor Institution, 1991. Pp. viii + 399.

Mervaud, Christiane, and René Pomeau. *De la Cour au jardin. 1750–1759*. Oxford: The Voltaire Foundation at the Taylor Institution, Oxford, 1991. Pp. vii + 416.

Rev. by D. J. Adams in *French Studies*, 45 (1991), 80; by Paolo Altri in *Studi francesi*, 34 (1990), 140–41.

The fine qualities of this study of Voltaire, the third in a projected five-volume collaborative biography of the literary symbol of the French Enlightenment, make it safe to affirm that its system of joint authorship has succeeded marvelously well. Not only does this volume in particular embody the final word on the major problems in the events of Voltaire's life, but its literary style conforms to the highest standards of contemporary literary biography. The life history of a major intellectual figure in a national literature, with the dimensions of the present collaborative enterprise, must concern itself with at least three elements—narration of the major events in the subject's life, delineation of the historical and intellectual milieu, and portrayal of the documentary sources on which the narrative is based. Biographies intended for mass consumption concentrate on the first area almost to the exclusion of the other two; whereas mainstream academic works stress either the narrative or the intellectual side and reduce the documentary structure to a subordinate, almost invisible, adjunct. The present volume fits neither pattern, for some chapters seem in varying degrees to be more concerned with tracing antecedent scholarship and pointing out its errors than with explicating Voltaire's writings. In an academic atmosphere such as that now generally prevailing in which theory reigns supremely over fact, this may not be a bad thing. Unfortunately the scholarly rigor of this volume causes the narrative to lose some of the dramatic and emotional intensity that it might otherwise possess.

From the narrative perspective, the most successful chapters of the book are those dealing with Voltaire's ordeal at Frankfurt, when he was held prisoner by blundering municipal sychophants under the impression they were carrying out the orders of Frederick II. In a lively recounting of this "rocambolesque" episode, the arch-villain Freytag is reinterpreted as a downright scoundrel, not merely a dull-witted buffoon. This episode, taking place in the first half of the book, represents the dramatic climax of the narrative, which then trails off in various directions in the remaining pages. On the intellectual side, the authors justifiably focus on the *Essai sur les moeurs*, but undermine their efforts at interpretation by dwelling on versions, rewritings, and competing editions. The most valuable sections on historical background deal with the military campaign of Frederick II and the ravages of the Lisbon earthquake. The organization of the book, along with its title, points to *Candide* as a determining force in Voltaire's life. The authors modestly recognize the impossibility of analyzing the esthetic qualities that have authoritatively placed the work within the context of Voltaire's literary production up to its date of composition. They argue that *Candide* represents a change of direction in his intellectual career consisting of a relentless attack on religious superstition in contrast to the view of some other critics that opposition to religious fanaticism had been a prevailing motivation ever since the "Epitre à Uranie" and even the *Lettres philosophique* in Voltaire's early years.—A. Owen Aldridge.

Mervaud, Christiane. *Volatire en toutes lettres*. Paris: Bordas, 1991. Pp. 165; appendices; illustrations.

In the framework of the series *En toutes lettres*, Christiane Mervaud, professor at the University of Rouen and author of a well-received study entitled *Voltaire et Frédéric II. Une dramaturgie des Lumières* (SVEC 234 [1985]), accepts a daunting challenge: to encompass all of Voltaire in a short book, obviously an impossible task, on the face of it. All the more remarkable, then, is her success, not only in covering the ground, but in doing so in a lively style, allusive yet jargon-free, that does not suffer even by its juxtaposition with that of the Master himself, whose prose is exhibited in numerous, though relatively brief, quotations.

In the book's first secion, "La Vie de Voltaire" (pp. 7–31), Professor Mervaud takes us through the main events of Voltaire's life at a rapid pace, indeed somewhat breathlessly at times, though this is understandable in view of her subject's longevity and her (no doubt editorially imposed) limitations of space. Yet she manages, in what could have been but a sketchy overview of a life, to provide enough colorful detail to suggest its multi-dimensionality.

The second main division of the book (pp. 33–60) is called "Voltaire dans son temps." Professor Mervaud here undertakes to "place" Voltaire in his world, and to show how he became, in the minds of many of his contemporaries, the center of that world, a figure of immense prestige. We see Voltaire, by way of Professor Mervaud's skillful choice of excerpts from his letters as well as from his public writings, not only as a witness of his age, but as a militant and as a leader in the intellectual and social struggles of his time.

The last principal section (pp. 61–165) is entitled "L'Oeuvre." Here Professor Mervaud, in an impressive display of her gift for expressing *multum in parvo*, treats Voltaire's writings under six headings: the poetic and dramatic works, the *romans et contes*, the historical writings, the *sommes philosophiques et critiques* (including the *Lettres philosophiques* as well as the alphabetical works), the polemical writings, and Voltaire's correspondence. Having drawn extensively upon the correspondence in connection with her previous book, Professor Mervaud is in an excellent position to suggest, as she does, various approaches to further scholarly study of it, not only by the advanced graduate students who would be an appropriate audience for the book under review, but also by experienced scholars. Both groups, indeed, have reason to be grateful for the publication of *Voltaire en toutes lettres*.

A final note: The appendices consist of an index of proper names, a chronological table covering Voltaire's life and works by year, with parallel developments in other domains, and three pages of bibliography, in which works in English are not slighted. This little book has been well proof-read: I found only five errors (p. 16: *Nemnon* for *Memnon*; p. 20: *dissenssions* for *dissensions*; p. 25: *dissout* for *dissous*; p. 38: *n'y prendre* for *m'y prendre*; p. 50: *ces* for *ses*.)—Arnold Miller.

Mougenot, Michel. Candide *de Voltaire*. (Parvours de lecture.) Paris: Bertrand-Lacoste, 1991. Pp. 128.

This small book is a guide for an interactive reading of *Candide*. It provides succinctly a wealth of background information on the significance of the text and focuses the reader's attention on additional investigations leading to greater appreciation and enjoyment of the work. Each chapter directs the reader to a particular aspect of the tale, analyzes it briefly, and offers definitions, examples, and interpretative hypotheses. Every chapter also includes under the subtitle of "Prolongements" a list of suggestions for further individual research. Chapter III, for example, entitled "Ironie et humour" starts out by giving examples of each drawn from the text, and follows with a general definition of the concept of irony as well as an analysis of its relation to *Candide*. It then turns to specific advice to the reader on what to look for when identifying irony in any text and finally applies the analysis to a number of specific examples in *Candide*. Humor receives the same treatment. The chapter ends with a list of interesting activities intended to reinforce understanding of the topic under scrutiny and to expand the text. The other chapters focus on the literary techniques used in the tale, on reality, utopia, and on satire.

The book includes a chapter on the quarrel between Voltaire and Rousseau, and thirty pages of excerpts from Voltaire's works are alluded to in the discussion on *Candide*. These are grouped under the overarching title of "Documents complémentaires" and consist of brief segments of Rousseau's *Discours sur l'origine de l'inéalité*, of

Voltaire's *Dictionnaire philosophique, Lettres philosophiques, Essai sur les moeurs*, and the integral text of *Sacramentado*.

Given its size limitations, this volume is quite impressive. It is very well organized, and it presents the latest interpretations of the tale as well as valuable suggestions for further study.—Renee Waldinger.

Vaillot, René. *Avec Madame du Châtelet. 1734–1749.* (Voltiare en son temps, sous la direction de René Pomeau, 2.) Oxford: The Voltaire Foundation at the Taylor Institution, 1988. Pp. vi + 432; bibliography. Cf. *ECCB*, n.s. 15, VI:430; 14, VI:406–07.

Rev. by Franco Piva in *Studi francesi*, 35 (1991) 95–96.

Voltaire, François-Marie Arouet de. *Candide.* New York: Dover, 1991. Pp. 94.

Unabridged re-publication of an anonymous English version (no date given).

Voltaire, François-Marie Arouet de. *The Complete Works of Voltaire.* Vol. VIII: 1731–1732. Oxford: The Voltaire Foundation at the Taylor Institution, 1988. Pp. xxi + 569; bibliography; illustrations; indices. Cf. *ECCB*, n.s. 16, VI:465; 14, VI:407.

Rev. by D. W. Howarth in *French Studies*, 45 (1991), 77–79.

Voltaire, François-Marie Arout de. *The Complete Works of Voltaire/Oeuvres complétes de Voltaire.* Edited by William Barber, Ulla Kölving, and others. Vol. 33: *Oeuvres alphabétiques.* Edited by Jacqueline Marchland, Roland Mortier, and John Renwick. Oxford: The Voltaire Foundation at the Taylor Institution, 1987. Pp. xxxi + 343; appendices; bibliography; xv + 518; bibliography. Cf. *ECCB*, n.s. 15, VI:430; 13, VI:536–7.

Rev. by Franco Piva in *Studi francesi*, 35 (1991), 145.

Voltaire, François-Marie Arouet de. *Corpus des notes marginales de Voltaire.* Edited by S. Manévitch and T. Voronova. 4 vols. Berlin: Akademie, 1979–1988. Pp. iv + 671; 20 plates; iv + 727; 22 plates: iv + 733.

Rev. by D. Williams in *Modern Language Review*, 86 (1991), 460–61.

Voltaire, François-Marie Arouet de. *Corpus des notes marginales de Voltaire.* Volume IV: *G–K.* Berlin: Akademie-Verlag (distributed through Oxford: The Voltaire Foundation at the Taylor Institution), 1988. Pp. 733; appendices; illustrations. Cf. *ECCB*, n.s. 16, VI: 466; 14, VI:408.

Rev. (favorably) by Christiane Mervaud in *Revue d'histoire littéraire de la France*, 91 (1991), 251–52.

Edmund Waller (1606–1687)

Chambers, A. B. *Andrew Marvell and Edmund Waller: Seventeenth-Century Praise and Restoration Satire.* London and University Park, PA: Pennsylvania State U. Press, 1991. Pp. viii + 208; bibliography.

Hammond, Paul. "Echoes of Waller in Marvell's *Horatian Ode*." *Notes and Queries*, 236 (1991), 172–73.

Horace Walpole (1717–1797)

Dabydeen, David. *Hogarth, Walpole and Commercial Britain*. London: Hansib, 1987. Pp. 167.

Rev. (with another work) by Herbert M. Atherton in *The Scriblerian*, 23 (1991), 269–71.

John Wesley (1703–1791)

Wesley, John. *The Works of John Wesley: Volume 20, Journals and Diaries III: (1743–1754)*. Edited by W. Reginald Ward and Richard P. Heitzenrater. (The Bicentennial Edition of the Works of John Wesley.) Nashville, TN: Abingdon Press, 1991. Pp. xii + 496; illustrations.

Christoph Martin Wieland (1733–1813)

Wieland, Christoph Martin. *Musarion and Other Rococo Tales*. Translated by Thomas C. Starnes. (Studies in German Literature, Linguistics, and Culture, 59.) Columbia, SC: Camden House, 1991. Pp. 176; bibliography.

Anne Finch, Countess of Winchilsea (1661–1720)

D'Alessandro, Jean M. Ellis. *When in the Shade . . . : Imaginal Equivalents in Anne the Countess of Winchilsea's Poetry*. Florence: Del Bianco Editore, 1989.

Rev. (severely) by Carol Barash in *The Scriblerian*, 24 (1991), 76–77.

Winchilsea, Anne Finch, Countess of. *The Wellesley Manuscript Poems of Anne Countess of Winchilsea*. Edited by Jean M. Ellis D'Alessandro. Florence, 1988. Pp. 181.

Rev. by Ruth Salvaggio in *The Scriblerian*, 23 (1991), 250–51.

Mary Wollstonecraft (1759–1797)

Lorch, Jennifer. *Mary Wollstonecraft: The Making of a Radical Feminist*. (Berg Women's Series.) Munich and New York: Peter Berg (distributed through New York: St. Martin's Press), 1990. Pp. x + 127; bibliography; chronology; frontispiece. Cf. *ECCB*, n.s. 16, VI:471.

Rev. by Catherine N. Parke in *Eighteenth-Century Studies*, 25 (1991–92), 260–63.

Moskal, Jeanne. "The Picturesque and the Affectionate in Wollstonecraft's *Letters from Norway*." *Modern Language Quarterly*, 52 (1991), 263–94.

The "affectionate tie between the traveling mother and daughter forms the conceptual center of Wollstonecraft's revision of the gendered aesthetic conventions of the picturesque and its concomitant terms, the beautiful and the sublime."

Todd, Janet (ed.). *Mary Wollstonecraft's* Mary *and* Maria; *Mary Shelley's* Matilda. London: Pickering and Chatto, 1991. Pp. xxix + 217; bibliography.

Janet Todd's new mother-daughter edition offers readers the chance to do intensive comparative analysis of Mary Wollstonecraft's first and last, and Mary Shelley's second, novels. Wollstonecraft's novels already exist in readily available, highly reliable paperback editions, but Shelley's *Matilda* has not been accessible as an independent publication. The list price of this book (£24.95) makes it an unlikely addition to most private libraries, but college libraries should stock it: its modernized spelling, clear, readable text, and brief, yet basically informative introduction (twenty pages for two biographies and three analyses) will appeal to undergraduates. Its brief bibliography and lack of an editorial apparatus, however, will minimize its usefulness to scholars and graduate teachers.

Todd expresses the hope in paragraph two of her "Introduction" that *Mary*, *Maria*, and *Matilda* will "gain psychological and allusive resonance through association with each other"; and her biographically sensitive discussion of common thematic threads (specifically, deviant sexuality and suicide) demonstrates how the edition should work for her readers. However, the "Introduction" does not answer one key question that inevitably comes to mind: What were the criteria for selecting these three particular fictions? If the intent was to establish the most suggestive *maternal* context for *Matilda*, then Wollstonecraft's "Cave of Fancy" should have been included. A fragment of considerable importance to an understanding of Wollstonecraft's belief system and at the moment only available in larger collections, it probably gave Shelley the original idea for *Matilda*. If, on the other hand, the intent of selection was to establish the best *family* context for Shelley's novel, why were excerpts from Godwin and Percy Shelley not included?

The question of context for any of Shelley's books is a difficult one ranging far beyond family confines; she was an omnivorous reader, as the many source studies of her first novel, *Frankenstein*, amply illustrate. *Mary* and *Maria*, then, may not shed sufficient light on Shelley's *Matilda*, a novel very firmly embedded in, if a critique of, the Romantic movement. Moreover, *Matilda* and *Mary* may cast Wollstonecraft's *Maria* in the wrong light: *Maria*'s recursive attention to the least savory realities of women's existence in the eighteenth century—marriage for money, lack of legal recourses, wife-selling, wife-beating, wife-imprisonment, prostitution, kidnapping, adultery, gambling, alcoholism, and suicide—and its activist messages are lost, rather than illuminated, in this context. *Matilda* and *Mary* have most in common, yet even they are separated by the considerable gulf of the French Revolution. Wollstonecraft struggles in both her novels to demythologize masculine-feminine relationships; Shelley's impulse is to remythologize what her mother had demystified.

The bibliography contains only sixteen items: seven biographies (but without mentioning Ralph Wardle's of Wollstonecraft, Anne K. Mellor's of Shelley, and William St. Clair's of the Godwins and the Shelleys); six editions; and three critical studies, two of those by Todd. It serves primarily as a reminder that major bibliographical work remains to be done for Wollstonecraft and that an update of Shelley's bibliography is overdue.—Syndy McMillen Conger.

Wollstonecraft, Mary. *A Wollstonecraft Anthology*. Edited by Janet Todd. New York: Columbia U. Press, 1990. Pp. 269.

Rev. (briefly) by Mary A. Favret in *English Language Notes*, 28, 4 (1991) 82–83.

Edward Young (1683–1765)

May, James E. *The Henry Pettit, Edward Young Collection at the University of Colorado at Boulder Libraries*. Boulder: Department of Special Collections, U. of Colorado at Boulder Libraries, 1989. Pp. 86.

Rev. by Stephen N. Brown in *The Scriblerian*, 24 (1991), 86–87.

Young, Edward. *Night Thoughts*. Edited by Stephen Cornford. Cambridge and New York: Cambridge U. Press, 1989. Pp. x + 368. Cf. *ECCB*, n.s. 15, VI:434–37.

Rev. by Harriet Guest in *Review of English Studies*; by James King in *Modern Language Review*, 86 (1991), 173.

INDEX

The index records names of authors, editors, and reviewers in the entries of the Bibliography, and also names mentioned significantly in the reviews and comments. It omits names used only to designate a period or to fix chronological limits, addresses of individual letters, names merely designating association, and passing mention in comments.